THE CAMBRIDGE HISTORY OF
SOCIALISM

This volume describes the various movements and thinkers who wanted social change without state intervention. It covers cases in Europe, the Americas, Africa, and Asia. The first part discusses early egalitarian experiments and ideologies in Asia, Europe, and the Islamic world, and then moves on to early socialist thinkers in Britain, France, and Germany. The second part deals with the rise of the two main currents in socialist movements after 1848: anarchism in its multiple varieties and Marxism. It also pays attention to organizational forms, including the International Working Men's Association (later called the First International); and it then follows the further development of anarchism and its 'proletarian' sibling, revolutionary syndicalism – its rise and decline from the 1870s until the 1940s on different continents. The volume concludes with critical essays on anarchist transnationalism and the recent revival of anarchism and syndicalism in several parts of the world.

MARCEL VAN DER LINDEN is Senior Fellow at the International Institute of Social History and Emeritus Professor of Social Movement History at the University of Amsterdam. He was elected President of the International Social History Association three times, and has (co-)authored and (co-)edited more than fifty books on socialist and labour history.

THE CAMBRIDGE HISTORY OF
SOCIALISM

Divided into two volumes, *The Cambridge History of Socialism* offers an up-to-date critical survey of the socialist movements and political practices that have arisen thus far throughout the world. A much-needed corrective of the current state of the study of socialism from a historical perspective, the volumes use a wider geographical and temporal focus to track the changes and trends in global socialisms and to move beyond the European trajectory. Together they cover anarchism, syndicalism, social democracy, labour, the New Left, and alternative socialist movements in the Global South in one encompassing reconstruction. Featuring fifty-five essays by experts across the field, the volumes will serve as examples of the rich variety of socialist histories and, together, endeavour to reveal the major contours of its development.

VOLUME I

EDITED BY MARCEL VAN DER LINDEN

VOLUME II

EDITED BY MARCEL VAN DER LINDEN

THE CAMBRIDGE
HISTORY OF
SOCIALISM

⋆

VOLUME I

⋆

Edited by

MARCEL VAN DER LINDEN

International Institute of Social History

CAMBRIDGE
UNIVERSITY PRESS

CAMBRIDGE
UNIVERSITY PRESS

University Printing House, Cambridge CB2 8BS, United Kingdom

One Liberty Plaza, 20th Floor, New York, NY 10006, USA

477 Williamstown Road, Port Melbourne, VIC 3207, Australia

314–321, 3rd Floor, Plot 3, Splendor Forum, Jasola District Centre,
New Delhi –110025, India

103 Penang Road, #05–06/07, Visioncrest Commercial, Singapore 238467

Cambridge University Press is part of the University of Cambridge.

It furthers the University's mission by disseminating knowledge in the pursuit of
education, learning, and research at the highest international levels of excellence.

www.cambridge.org
Information on this title: www.cambridge.org/9781108481342
DOI: 10.1017/9781108611022

© Cambridge University Press 2023

First published 2023

Printed in the United Kingdom by TJ Books Limited, Padstow Cornwall

A catalogue record for this publication is available from the British Library.

Two-Volume Set ISBN 978-1-108-61133-6 Hardback
Volume I ISBN 978-1-108-48134-2 Hardback
Volume II ISBN 978-1-108-48135-9 Hardback

Contents

v

Contents

PART II

NEGATING STATE POWER

THE NORTH ATLANTIC REGION

AFRICA, ASIA, LATIN AMERICA

Contents

Figures

Maps

XI

Tables

Contributors to Volume I

ASMA AFSARUDDIN is Professor of Islamic Studies and former chair of the Department of Middle Eastern Languages and Cultures at Indiana University in Bloomington, USA. Her books include *Hermeneutics and Honor: Negotiating Female 'Public' Space in Islamic/ate Societies* (Cambridge, MA, 1999); *Excellence and Precedence: Medieval Islamic Discourse on Legitimate Leadership* (Leiden, 2002); *The First Muslims: History and Memory* (Oxford, 2008); *Striving in the Path of God: Jihad and Martyrdom in Islamic Thought* (Oxford, 2013); and *Contemporary Issues in Islam* (Edinburgh, 2015).

CONSTANCE BANTMAN is Senior Lecturer in French at the University of Surrey, UK. She has edited, with Dave Berry, *New Perspectives on Anarchism, Labour and Syndicalism: The Individual, the National and the Transnational* (Newcastle upon Tyne, 2010); and, with Bert Altena, *Reassessing the Transnational Turn: Scales of Analysis in Anarchist and Syndicalist Studies* (Oakland, CA, 2017).

CLAUDIO BATALHA is Professor in the Department of History, State University of Campinas (UNICAMP), Brazil. He is the editor of *Dicionário do movimento operário. Rio de Janeiro do século XIX aos anos 1920, militantes e organizações* (São Paulo, 2009); and co-editor of *Culturas de classe. Identidade e diversidade na formação do operariado* (Campinas, 2004) and *Organizar e proteger. Trabalhadores, associações e mutualismo no Brasil (séculos XIX e XX)* (Campinas, 2014).

JONATHAN BEECHER is Professor Emeritus of History at the University of California Santa Cruz, USA. His books include *Charles Fourier: The Visionary and His World* (Berkeley, 1986); *Victor Considerant and the Rise and Fall of French Romantic Socialism* (Berkeley, 2001; French translation, 2011); and *Writers and Revolution: Intellectuals and the French Revolution of 1848* (Cambridge, 2021).

FABRICE BENSIMON is Professor of British History at the Sorbonne Université, Paris, France. His books include *Les Sentiers de l'ouvrier. Le Paris des artisans britanniques (autobiographies, 1815–1850)* (Paris, 2017) and *Tramping Artisans: British Migrant Workers in Industrialising Europe (1815–1870)* (Oxford, 2022). He has edited, with Quentin Deluermoz and Jeanne Moisand, *'Arise Ye Wretched of the Earth': The First International in a Global Perspective* (Leiden and Boston, 2018).

GREGORY CLAEYS is Professor Emeritus of History at Royal Holloway, University of London, UK. His books include *Machinery, Money and the Millennium: From Moral Economy to Socialism, 1815–1860* (Princeton, 1987); *Citizens and Saints: Politics and Anti-Politics in Early British Socialism* (Cambridge, 1989); and *Searching for Utopia: The History of an Idea* (London, 2011). He is the editor of *The Selected Works of Robert Owen* (London, 1993) and *The Owenite Socialist Movement: Pamphlets and Correspondence*, 10 vols. (London, 2005).

FELIPE CORRÊA is Professor of Social Sciences and Research at Mackenzie Presbyterian University, Brazil, and co-founder of the Institute for Anarchist Theory and History (ITHA-IATH). His books include *Bandeira Negra. Rediscutindo o anarquismo* (Curitiba, 2015); *Liberdade ou morte. Teoria e prática de Mikhail Bakunin* (São Paulo, 2019); and *Hacia un pueblo fuerte. Anarquismo, organización y poder popular* (Madrid, 2020).

TOURAJ DARYAEE is the Maseeh Chair in Persian Studies and Culture and the director of the Dr Samuel M. Jordan Center for Persian Studies at the University of California Irvine, USA. His books include *Sasanian Persia: The Rise and Fall of an Empire* (London, 2009) and *From Oxus to Euphrates: The World of Late Antique Iran* (Irvine, CA, 2016). He is the editor of *The Oxford History of Iran* (New York, 2012).

GEOFFROY DE LAFORCADE is Professor of Latin American and Caribbean History at Norfolk State University, Virginia, USA. He is the co-editor of *In Defiance of Boundaries: Anarchism in Latin American History* (Gainesville, 2015) and *Migration, Diaspora, Exile: Narratives of Affiliation and Escape* (Lanham, MD, 2020).

WOLFGANG ECKHARDT is a researcher in anarchism and social history living in Berlin, Germany. His publications include the German-language *Bakunin. Ausgewählte Schriften* series, of which six volumes have been published so far under his editorship (1995–2011), as well as *The First Socialist Schism: Bakunin vs Marx in the International Working Men's Association* (Oakland, CA, 2016) and *La Primera Internacional y la Alianza en España. Colección de documentos inéditos o raros* (Madrid, 2017).

GEORGE ESENWEIN is Associate Professor of History at the University of Florida, Gainesville, USA. His books include *Anarchist Ideology and the Spanish Working-Class Movement, 1868–1898* (Berkeley, 1989); *Spain at War: The Spanish Civil War in Context, 1931–1939*, co-authored with Adrian Shubert (London, 1995); and *The Spanish Civil War: A Modern Tragedy* (London, 2005). He was an associate editor and contributor to the six-volume *New Dictionary of the History of Ideas* (New York, 2004), and the editor-in-chief and contributor to the digital online reference series *The College Researcher* (Farmington Hills, MI, 2016).

THOMAS A. FUDGE is Professor of Medieval History at the University of New England, Armidale, Australia. His publications include *The Magnificent Ride: The First Reformation in Hussite Bohemia* (Aldershot, 1998); *Jan Hus: Religious Reform and Social Revolution in Bohemia* (London and New York, 2010); *Medieval Religion and Its Anxieties* (New York, 2016); *Jerome of Prague and the Foundations of the Hussite Movement* (New York, 2016); and *Origins of the Hussite Uprising* (London, 2020).

DAVID GOODWAY is a historian who worked for the School of Continuing Education, University of Leeds, UK, until his retirement. He was then Helen Cam Visiting Fellow in History, Girton College, Cambridge, UK. His books include *London Chartism, 1838–1848* (Cambridge, 1982); *Talking Anarchy*, with Colin Ward (Nottingham, 2003); and *Anarchist*

Seeds beneath the Snow: Left–Libertarian Thought and British Writers from William Morris to Colin Ward (Liverpool, 2006). He has also edited volumes by George Julian Harney, Herbert Read, Alex Comfort, 'Maurice Brinton', Nicolas Walter, and G. D. H. Cole, as well as the correspondence between John Cowper Powys and Emma Goldman.

JOHN MASON HART is Moores Professor of History Emeritus at the University of Houston, USA. His books include *Anarchism and the Mexican Working Class, 1860–1931* (Austin, TX, 1976); *Revolutionary Mexico: The Coming and Process of the Mexican Revolution* (Berkeley, 1987); *Border Crossings: Mexican and Mexican-American Workers* (Wilmington, DE, 1998); and *Empire and Revolution: The Americans in Mexico since the Civil War* (Berkeley, 2002).

JEREMY JENNINGS is Professor of Political Theory at King's College London, UK. His books include *Georges Sorel: The Character and Development of His Thought* (London, 1985); *Syndicalism in France: A Study of Ideas* (London, 1990); and *Revolution and Republic: A History of Political Thought in France since the Eighteenth Century* (Oxford, 2011). Among his edited volumes is *Critical Concepts: Socialism*, 4 vols. (London, 2003).

CHRISTOPHER H. JOHNSON is Professor of History at Wayne State University, Detroit, USA. His books include *Utopian Communism in France: Cabet and the Icarians, 1839–1851* (Ithaca, 1974); *Maurice Sugar: Law, Labor, and the Left in Detroit, 1912–1950* (Detroit, 1988); *Life and Death of Industrial Languedoc, 1700–1920* (New York, 1995); and *Becoming Bourgeois: Love, Kinship, and Power in Provincial France, 1670–1880* (Ithaca, 2015).

RUTH KINNA is Professor of Political Theory at Loughborough University, UK. She is the author of *Kropotkin: Reviewing the Classical Anarchist Tradition* (Edinburgh, 2016) and *The Government of No One: The Theory and Practice of Anarchism* (London, 2019). Her edited volumes include *Anarchism, 1914–1918: Internationalism, Anti-Militarism and War* (Manchester, 2017), with Matthew S. Adams; *Bloomsbury Companion to Anarchism* (London and New York, 2014); and the *Routledge Handbook of Radical Politics* (New York, 2019), with Uri Gordon.

CARL LEVY is Professor of Politics at Goldsmiths, University of London, UK. He is the author of *Gramsci and the Anarchists* (Oxford, 1999); the editor of *Socialism and the Intelligentsia: 1880–1914* (London, 1987) and *Colin Ward: Life, Times and Thought* (London, 2013); and the co-editor of *The Anarchist Imagination: Anarchism Encounters the Humanities and the Social Sciences* (London, 2019) and *The Palgrave Handbook of Anarchism* (Cham, 2019).

MARCEL VAN DER LINDEN is Senior Fellow and former Research Director of the International Institute of Social History, and Emeritus Professor of Social Movement History at the University of Amsterdam, Netherlands. His books include *Transnational Labour History: Explorations* (Aldershot, 2003); *Western Marxism and the Soviet Union: A Survey of Critical Theories and Debates since 1917* (Leiden and Boston, 2007); *Workers of the World: Essays toward a Global Labor History* (Leiden and Boston, 2008); and *The Worldwide Web of Work: A History in the Making* (forthcoming).

GOTELIND MÜLLER-SAINI is Professor of Chinese Studies, University of Heidelberg, Germany. Her books include *China, Kropotkin und der Anarchismus. Eine Kulturbewegung im China des frühen 20. Jahrhunderts unter dem Einfluß des Westens und japanischer Vorbilder* (Wiesbaden, 2001) and *Documentary, World History, and National Power in the PRC: Global*

Rise in Chinese Eyes (London and New York, 2013). She has edited *Designing History in East Asian Textbooks: Identity Politics and Transnational Aspirations* (London and New York, 2011) and co-edited *Chinese Perceptions of Russia and the West: Changes, Continuities and Contingencies during the Twentieth Century* (Heidelberg and Berlin, 2020).

BERTEL NYGAARD is Associate Professor at the Institut for Kultur og Samfund, Aarhus University, Denmark. His books include *Guldalderens moderne politik. Om krisediagnose, utopi og handling hos Johan Ludvig Heiberg* (Aarhus, 2011); *Revolution. Masser af modstand* (Aarhus, 2012); *Det røde spøgelse. Kommunismen og 1840'ernes danske politiske kultur* (Copenhagen, 2014); and *Kærlighedens samfund. Romantiske utopier i 1800-tallets Danmark* (Aarhus, 2016).

LUCIA PRADELLA is Senior Lecturer in International Political Economy, King's College London, UK. She is the author of *L'attualità del Capitale. Accumulazione e impoverimento nel capitalismo globale* (Padua, 2010) and *Globalisation and the Critique of Political Economy: New Insights from Marx's Writings* (Abingdon and New York, 2015); and co-editor of *Polarizing Development: Alternatives to Neoliberalism and the Crisis* (London, 2015) and the *Routledge Handbook of Marxism and Post-Marxism* (New York, 2021).

ALEX PRICHARD is Associate Professor of International Relations in the Department of Politics, University of Exeter, UK. He is the author of *Justice, Order and Anarchy: The International Political Theory of Pierre-Joseph Proudhon* (Abingdon, 2013) and has edited and introduced the first translation of Proudhon's *War and Peace* (Oakland, CA, 2022). He has also edited three collections on the intersections between anarchisms and Marxisms: *Libertarian Socialism: Politics in Black and Red* (New York, 2012); 'Left-Wing Convergence', *Capital & Class* 40, 1 (2016); and 'Pluriversality, Convergence and Hybridity in the Global Left', *Globalizations* 17, 5 (2020).

LUCIEN VAN DER WALT is Professor of Economic and Industrial Sociology, and Director of the Neil Aggett Labour Studies Unit (NALSU), at Rhodes University, South Africa. His books include *Anarchism and Syndicalism in the Colonial and Postcolonial World, 1870–1940: The Praxis of National Liberation, Internationalism, and Social Revolution* (Leiden and Boston, 2010), with Steven Hirsch; *Negro e vermelho. Anarquismo, sindicalismo revolucionário e pessoas de cor na África Meridional nas décadas de 1880 a 1920* (São Paulo, 2014); and *Politics at a Distance from the State: Radical and African Perspectives* (London and New York, 2018), with Kirk Helliker.

ALEXANDER VARIAS teaches intellectual and cultural history at Villanova University, USA, in the Department of History and the Augustine and Culture Seminar Program. He is the author of *Paris and the Anarchists: Aesthetes and Subversives during the Fin de Siecle* (New York, 1996) and, with Lorraine Coons, of *Tourist Third Cabin: Steamship Travel in the Interwar Years* (New York, 2003).

RUDOLF G. WAGNER was Senior Professor at the Department of Chinese Studies at the University of Heidelberg, Germany. His books include *Reenacting the Heavenly Vision: The Role of Religion in the Taiping Rebellion* (Berkeley, 1982); *Inside a Service Trade: Studies in Contemporary Chinese Prose* (Cambridge, MA, 2002); and *A Chinese Reading of the Daodejing: Wang Bi's Commentary on the Laozi with Critical Text and Translation* (Albany, 2003). He is the editor of *Chinese Encyclopaedias of New Global Knowledge, 1870–1930: Changing Ways of Thought* (New York, 2013).

KENYON ZIMMER is Associate Professor of History at the University of Texas at Arlington, USA. He is the author of *Immigrants against the State: Yiddish and Italian Anarchism in America* (Urbana, IL, 2015) and co-editor of *Wobblies of the World: A Global History of the IWW* (London, 2017).

Abbreviations

AAW	Anarchists Against the Wall
ABC	Anarchist Black Cross
ACAT	Asociación Continental Americana de Trabajadores
ADAV	Allgemeiner Deutscher Arbeiter-Verein
AL	Alternativa Libertaria (Italy)
AL	Alternative Libertaire (France)
AL	Awareness League (Nigeria)
AL	Awareness League (South Africa)
ALA	Alianza Libertaria Argentina
AMA	Agrupación de Mujeres Antifascistas
AMZ	Alianza Magonista Zapatista
ANC	African National Congress
ANL	Aliança Nacional Libertadora
APF	Anti-Privatisation Forum
APO	African Peoples Organisation
APOC	Anarchist People of Color
ARM	Anarchist Revolutionary Movement
ASN	Anarchist Studies Network
BASF	Bangladesh Anarcho-Syndicalist Federation
BO	Bloco Operário
BOC	Bloco Operário e Camponês
BR	Brigate Rosse
BSAC	British South Africa Company
CAB	Coordenação Anarquista Brasileira
CABV	Communistischer Arbeiter-Bildungs-Verein
CCMA	Comitè Central de Milícies Antifeixistes de Catalunya
CCOO	Comisiones Obreras
CCP	Chinese Communist Party

CF	Confederación Ferroviaria
CGL	Confederazione Generale del Lavoro
CGT	Confederação Geral do Trabalho (Portugal)
CGT	Confederación General de Trabajadores (Mexico)
CGT	Confederación General del Trabajo (Argentina)
CGT	Confederación General del Trabajo (Spain)
CGT	Confédération Générale du Travail (France)
CGT-SR	Confédération Générale du Travail – Syndicaliste Révolutionnaire
CGTU	Confédération Générale du Travail Unitaire
CIA	Central Intelligence Agency
CIO	Congress of Industrial Organizations
CIPO-RFM	Consejo Indígena Popular de Oaxaca 'Ricardo Flores Magón'
CIRA	Centre International de Recherches sur l'Anarchisme
CLN	Comitato di Liberazione Nazionale
CLNAI	Comitato di Liberazione Nazionale Alta Italia
CNT	Confederación Nacional del Trabajo
COA	Confederación Obrera Argentina
COB	Confederação Operária Brasileira
COBAS	Confederazione dei Comitati di Base
CORA	Confederación Obrera Regional Argentina
COSATU	Congress of South African Trade Unions
CPSA	Communist Party of South Africa
CROM	Confederación Regional de Obreros Mexicanos
CRRA	Comité Regional de Relaciones Anarquistas
CTM	Confederación de Trabajadores de México
CUB	Comitati Unitari di Base
DAF	Devrimci Anarşist Faaliyet
DFS	Dirección Federal de Seguridad
ELAOPA	Encontro Latino Americano de Organizações Populares e Autónomas
ETA	Euskadi Ta Askatasuna
EZLN	Ejército Zapatista de Liberación Nacional
FACA	Federación Anarco-Comunista Argentina
FAF	Fédération Anarchiste Française
FAGI	Federazione Anarchica Giovanile Italiana
FAI	Federación Anarquista Ibérica
FAI	Federazione Anarchica Italiana

FASR	Federación de Agrupaciones Sindicalistas Revolucionarias
FAU	Federación Anarquista Uruguaya
FAU	Freie Arbeiterinnen- und Arbeiter-Union
FdCA	Federazione dei Comunisti Anarchici
FEL	Frente de Estudiantes Libertarios
FIJL	Federación Ibérica de Juventudes Libertarias
FIOM	Federazione Impiegati Operai Metallurgici
FLA	Argentine Libertarian Federation
FOA	Federación Obrera Argentina
FOF	Federación Obrera Ferrocarrilera
FOLS	Federação Operária Local de Santos
FOLS	Federación Obrera Local Salteña
FOM	Federación Obrera Maritima
FOPBA	Federación Obrera Provincial de Buenos Aires
FORA	Federación Obrera Regional Argentina
FORJ	Federação Operária do Rio de Janeiro
FOSATU	Federation of South African Trade Unions
FOSP	Federação Operária de São Paulo
FOT	Federación Obrera del Trabano
FRE	Federación Regional Española
FRELIMO	Frente de Libertação de Moçambique
FTRE	Federación de Trabajadores de la Región Española
FTRJ	Federação dos Trabalhadores do Rio de Janeiro
GAAP	Gruppi Anarchici di Azione Proletaria
GC	General Council
GGAF	Gruppi Giovanili Anarchici Federati
GIA	Gruppi di Iniziativa Anarchica
GMD	Guomindang
IAS	Institute of Anarchist Studies
IATH	Institute for Anarchist Theory and History
ICL-CIT	International Confederation of Labour
ICU	Industrial and Commercial Workers Union
IFA	International of Anarchist Federations
IISH	International Institute of Social History
ILGWU	International Ladies' Garment Workers' Union
ILP	Independent Labour Party
IMF	International Monetary Fund
IRA	Irish Republican Army
IRPGF	International Revolutionary People's Guerrilla Forces

ISL	International Socialist League
ITHA-IATH	Institute for Anarchist Theory and History
IWA-AIT	International Workers Association
IWMA	International Working Men's Association
IWPA	International Working People's Association
IWW	Industrial Workers of the World
LCI	Liga Comunista Internacionalista
LPM	Landless People's Movement
MDC	Movement for Democratic Change
MGRK	Meclîsa Gel a Rojavayê Kurdistanê
MK	uMkhonto weSizwe
MLE	Movimiento Libertario Español
MMD	Movement for Multi-Party Democracy
MPLA	Movimento Popular de Libertação de Angola
NAASN	North American Anarchist Studies Network
NAS	Nationaal Arbeids Secretariaat
NRZ	*Neue Rheinische Zeitung*
NURHAS	National Union of Railway and Harbour Servants
OBU	One Big Union
ORIT	Organización Regional Interamericana de Trabajadores
PCI	Partito Comunista Italiano
PGA	Peoples' Global Network
PLM	Partido Liberal Mexicano
POI	Partito Operaio Italiano
POUM	Partido Obrero de Unificación Marxista
PPAS	Persaudaraan Pekerja Anarko Sindikalis
PPR	Persaudaraan Pekerja Regional
PRC	People's Republic of China
PSI	Partito Socialista Italiano
PSUC	Partit Socialista Unificat de Catalunya
PUDEMO	People's United Democratic Movement
PYD	Partiya Yekîtiya Demokrat
RAF	Rote Armee Fraktion
RAG	Revolutionary Anarcha-Feminist Group
RBF	Red and Black Forum
RICU	Reformed Industrial and Commercial Workers Union
RRAEA	Rhodesia Railways African Employees Association
RRWU	Rhodesia Railway Workers' Union
SAC	Sveriges Arbetares Centralorganisation

SACP	South African Communist Party
SAIF	South African Industrial Federation
SANNC	South African Native Congress
SATU	South African Typographers' Union
SDAP	Sozialdemokratische Arbeiterpartei Deutschlands
SDF	Social Democratic Federation
SDS	Students for a Democratic Society
SFTU	Swaziland Federation of Trade Unions
SLP	Socialist Labor Party (USA)
SLP	Socialist Labour Party (UK)
SPD	Sozialdemokratische Partei Deutschlands
SWAYOCO	Swaziland Youth Congress
TQILA	The Queer Insurrection and Liberation Army
UAI	Unione Anarchica Italiana
UCAA	Unión Comunista Anarquista Argentina
UCL	Union Communiste Libertaire
UDC	Unió de Dones de Catalunya
UGT	Union General de Trabajadores (Argentina)
UGT	Unión General de Trabajadores (Spain)
URW	Union of Russian Workers of the United States and Canada
USA	Unión Sindical Argentina
USI	Unione Sindacale Italiana
USO	Union Sindical Obrera
WB	World Bank
WMA	Working Men's Association
WSF	Workers Solidarity Federation
WSM	Workers Solidarity Movement
ZACF	Zabalaza Anarchist Communist Federation
ZAG	Zabalaza Action Group
ZANU	Zimbabwe African National Union
ZAPU	Zimbabwe African People's Union

Introduction to Volume I

MARCEL VAN DER LINDEN

'Socialism' means different things to different people. The concept denotes a just society in which no individual lacks the basic necessities of life and in which prosperity and knowledge are shared fairly. But opinions on what form such a society should take have always varied widely. Should it be governed centrally? Should it be a federation of small communities? A meritocracy? A democracy? 'Socialism' was, and is, a house with many rooms, and as a political movement it has left a deep mark on the past two centuries. These two volumes attempt to provide a – necessarily incomplete – overview of the non-communist aspect of this tradition; the communist aspect is the subject of a separate publication project.[1]

Egalitarianism

Socialism has its intellectual roots in the French Revolution's pursuit of liberty, equality, and fraternity. There have been myriad debates about how to define these three basic values, about their mutual coherence and relative significance. Does equality encompass only rights, or also outcomes? Is liberty – or freedom – only negative (freedom *from* – restraint or coercion), or can it be positive (freedom *to* – that is, self-determination)? Does fraternity embody the unity of a group or class based on shared interests, objectives, standards, or beliefs? And which of the three core values is the most fundamental? Is liberty conditional on equality, as many socialist French republicans believed in the 1840s? Or is liberty a precondition for equality, as many anarchists argued, because true 'equality' means not 'the forced equality of the convict camp' but

---

1 S. Pons et al. (eds.), *The Cambridge History of Communism*, 3 vols. (Cambridge: Cambridge University Press, 2017).

the ability to live in different ways?[2] And how do liberty and equality relate to fraternity, or to solidarity, a value that appears to have more to do with communities and moral obligations than with individuals, rights, and contracts?

Despite the close relationship among those three core values, it is probably the pursuit of equality that has most distinguished socialism from other movements. Liberals too fought for freedom, and conservative Christians aspired to solidarity, but it was the socialists in particular whose aim was equality, and especially social equality. Eric Hobsbawm rightly noted that:

> Unlike the word 'communist', which always signified a programme, the word 'socialist' was primarily analytical and critical. It was used to describe those who held a particular view of human nature (e.g. the fundamental importance of 'sociability' or the 'social instincts' in it), which implied a particular view of human society, or those who believed in the possibility or necessity of a particular mode of social action, notably in public affairs (e.g. intervention in the operations of the free market). It was soon realised that such views were likely to be developed by or to attract those who favoured equality, such as the disciples of Rousseau, and to lead to interference with property rights.[3]

Supporters and opponents alike regarded socialism primarily as the embodiment of the pursuit of equality – with its opponents in particular often suggesting that socialism would amount to equality without either freedom or solidarity.[4]

The pursuit of social equality has an ancient pedigree that predates socialism as such. In fact there have existed few human societies without a degree of social inequality,[5] and when the first states and social classes emerged with the neolithic revolution structural inequality became a long-term phenomenon.

---

2 C. Coste, '"Si je crois à la liberté c'est que je crois à l'égalité". Philosophie pour une république sociale et pratique de l'égalité autour de 1848', *Revue européenne des sciences sociales* 56, 2 (2018), pp. 209–39; A. Berkman, *What Is Anarchism?* (Edinburgh: AK Press, 2003), p. 164.

3 E. J. Hobsbawm, *How to Change the World: Marx and Marxism 1840–2011* (London: Little, Brown, 2011), p. 24.

4 For example, when, in the late nineteenth century, the German orientalist T. Nöldeke rediscovered the Mazdak Persian egalitarian movement of the fifth and early sixth centuries (described in Chapter 1 in this volume), he wanted to show that such a 'socialist' experiment was necessarily doomed to fail. See T. Nöldeke, 'Orientalischer Socialismus', *Deutsche Rundschau* 18 (1879), pp. 284–91.

5 The gendered division of labour in hunter–gatherer societies does not seem to imply inequality and hierarchy, since 'these societies deliberately level differences'. See Karen L. Endicott, 'Gender Relations in Hunter–Gatherer Societies', in R. B. Lee and R. Daly (eds.), *The Cambridge Encyclopedia of Hunters and Gatherers* (Cambridge: Cambridge University Press, 2004), p. 411.

Since then, the world has witnessed egalitarian revolts over and over again, with subservient groups rebelling against the privileges of the higher echelons. As early as the fourth century BCE, the Athenian philosopher Plato had his teacher Socrates say that, in every city, there are two communities, 'warring with each other, one of the poor, the other of the rich'.[6] There are many examples of egalitarian conflict, but one will suffice here: the rebellion in the province of Jiangxi in eastern China in 1644–5 at the end of the Ming dynasty. One account reported as follows on the rebellious serfs:

> They sharpened their hoes into swords, and took to themselves the title of 'Levelling Kings', declaring that they were levelling the distinction between masters and serfs, titled and mean, rich and poor. The tenants seized hold of their masters' best clothes. They broke into the homes of important families and shared their mansions with them. They opened the granaries and distributed the contents. They tied the masters to pillars and flogged them with whips and with lashes of bamboo. Whenever they held a drinking bout they would order the masters to kneel and pour out the wine for them. They would slap them across the cheeks and say: 'We are all of us equally men. What right had you to call us serfs? From now on it is going to be the other way around!'[7]

But egalitarian sentiments circulated in non-violent form too. Mikhail Bakhtin and others have pointed out that carnivals or carnivalesque behaviour were associated with the transcendence or inversion of social hierarchies, when for a few days peasants and other subalterns could ridicule their rulers with impunity and display eccentric and sacrilegious behaviour.[8] A somewhat less public expression of the same idea was the many variants of an egalitarian parable narrated by radical propagandists in the nineteenth-century Russian Empire. Essentially, it took the following form: the speaker placed a grain of wheat or a hazelnut on the table and asked his listeners, 'What does this mean?' Of course, no one had any idea, so the speaker explained that it was the tsar. Adding more grains or hazelnuts, he explained that these were the governors and other officials, the army officers, the landlords, and the nobility. Finally, he poured a handful of grain or hazelnuts on top of them: 'Look, these are all of us! Can you tell me now who was the tsar, the governor, or the landlord?'[9]

---

6 *The Republic of Plato*, trans. A. Bloom, 2nd edn (New York: Basic Books, 1991), p. 100 (§ 423a).

7 M. Elvin, *The Pattern of the Chinese Past* (London: Eyre Methuen, 1973), pp. 245–6.

8 M. Bakhtin, *Rabelais and His World*, trans. H. Iswolsky (Bloomington: Indiana University Press, 1984). One might debate the extent to which such inversions ultimately strengthen power relations or not.

9 R. Rosdolsky, 'A revolutionary parable on the equality of men', *Archiv für Sozialgeschichte* 3 (1963), p. 291.

Incidentally, most egalitarian movements aimed at achieving equality only among men. Characteristic in this regard was the fairly major uprising that took place in 1416 in part of the Ottoman Empire, with Sheikh Bedreddin as its influential spokesman. He apparently decreed that, 'with the exception of women, everything must be shared in common – provisions, clothing, yokes of beasts, and fields. "I shall have access to your house as though it were mine and you shall have access to my house as though it were yours, with the exception of the female members."'[10] And when in 1791, during the French Revolution, Olympe de Gouges demanded that women be given the same rights as men, she became only the second woman, after Marie Antoinette, to be sent to the guillotine.[11]

The Invention of 'Socialism'

The French Revolution also spawned other thinkers who developed egalitarianism into a radical political programme. The most important was probably journalist and agitator François-Noël (Gracchus) Babeuf. His Conspiracy of the Equals included a number of supporters, such as Sylvain Maréchal and Filippo Buonarroti. Unlike the older egalitarians, they were not obsessed solely with the fair distribution of property and goods, but also developed coherent ideas about an alternative society based on the abolition of private property and the introduction of universal democracy – for men at least. Their manifesto stated:

> Long enough, and too long, have less than a million of individuals disposed of what belongs to more than twenty millions of men like themselves – of men in every respect their equals. Let there be at length an end to this enormous scandal, which posterity will scarcely credit. Away for ever with the revolting distinctions of rich and poor, of great and little, of masters and servants, of *governors* and *governed*. Let there be no longer any other differences in mankind than those of age and sex. Since all have the same wants, and the same faculties, let all have accordingly the same education – the same nourishment.[12]

---

10 Doukas, *Decline and Fall of Byzantium to the Ottoman Turks: An Annotated Translation of 'Historia Turco-Byzantina' by H. J. Magoulias* (Detroit: Wayne State University Press, 1975), p. 120. For the context, see S. Salgırlı, 'The rebellion of 1416: recontextualizing an Ottoman social movement', *Journal of the Economic and Social History of the Orient* 55 (2012), pp. 32–73.

11 S. Mousset, *Women's Rights and the French Revolution: A Biography of Olympe de Gouges*, trans. J. Poirel (New Brunswick and London: Transaction Publishers, 2007); M. Faucheux, *Olympe de Gouges* (Paris: Gallimard, 2018).

12 'Manifesto of the Equals' (1796), in *Buonarroti's History of Babeuf's Conspiracy for Equality* ..., trans. Bronterre (London: Hetherington, 1836), p. 316. See also

When Babeuf attempted to organize a coup, he was arrested and in 1797 guillotined.

Less well known than the Babouvists' manifesto is a pamphlet on *The Rights of Nature* published in that same year by the British radical orator and writer John Thelwall. Inspired by the French Revolution, Thelwall found it intolerable that power should lie with the richest 10 per cent in the country – some of them amounting to no more than 'caterpillars and locusts, the blights and mildews of social industry!' – while the remaining 90 per cent were victims of 'political annihilation'. To remedy this, he proposed a more equitable distribution of wealth, a reduction in working hours, and better education:

> *every* man, and *every* woman, and *every* child, ought to obtain something more, in the general distribution of the fruits of labour, than food, and rags, and a wretched hammock with a poor rug to cover it: and that without working twelve or fourteen hours a day, six days out of seven, from six to sixty. – They have a claim, a sacred and inviolable claim, growing out of that fundamental maxim, upon which all property can be supported, to some comforts and enjoyments, in addition to the necessaries of life; and to some tolerable leisure for such discussion, and some 'means of such information', as may lead to an understanding of their *rights*; without which they can never understand their *duties*.[13]

From the 1820s, ideas like those of Babeuf and Thelwall were sometimes referred to as 'socialism'. Although the word had occasionally surfaced before, it was probably first used in a serious sense in 1827 in *The Cooperative Magazine*, a periodical published by the social reformer Robert Owen and his supporters.[14] In a notice about the Co-operative Benevolent Fund Association – an organization founded six months earlier in Brighton with 170 members and a capital of five pounds – it is noted: 'The chief

---

R. B. Rose, *Gracchus Babeuf: The First Revolutionary Communist* (Stanford: Stanford University Press, 1978); I. Birchall, *The Spectre of Babeuf*, 2nd edn (Chicago: Haymarket, 2016).

13 J. Thelwall, *The Rights of Nature Against the Usurpations of Establishments* . . . (London and Norwich: H. D. Symonds and J. March, 1796), pp. 15–19. E. P. Thompson has argued that Thelwall 'took Jacobinism to the borders of Socialism; he also took it to the borders of revolutionism'. See Thompson, *The Making of the English Working Class* (London: Gollancz, 1963), p. 160.

14 Franco Venturi has pointed out that the word 'socialism' had already been used in Ferdinando Facchinei's *Note ed osservazioni sul libro intitolato Dei Delitti e Delle Pene* (1765); it referred to followers of Jean-Jacques Rousseau, who assumed that people were free and equal on the basis of the *contrat social*. This notion of '*socialismo*' therefore has a meaning different from the English word 'socialism'. See F. Venturi, 'Socialista e socialismo nell'Italia del settecento', *Rivista storica italiana* 75, 1 (May 1963), pp. 129–40.

question . . . between the modern (or Mill and Malthus) Political Economists, and the Communionists or Socialists, is, whether it is more beneficial that this capital [of the fund] should be individual or in common?'[15]

It took several years before the term passed into common usage. In 1833 *The Crisis* magazine wrote about 'The Socialist who preaches of community of goods, abolition of crime, of punishment, of magistrates, and of marriage . . . '[16] This development was crowned in 1837 when in an editorial the Owenist magazine *The New Moral World* argued that the 'Congress of all classes and all nations' should no longer call itself Owenite, but 'socialist': 'We, the disciples of the New Moral World, advocate principles, and aim at establishing a Community-System founded upon these principles . . . are not we socialists as well as this new society?'[17] Perhaps the first to reflect extensively on the term was the French philosopher and political economist Pierre Leroux, who had already written an article on it in 1833.[18] But Robert Owen himself also published his thoughts in his *What Is Socialism?* in 1841.[19]

The word 'socialism' gradually spread from Britain and France to gain currency elsewhere, first in other parts of Europe, and from there all over the world.[20] Although a number of protagonists tended to agnosticism or

15 'Cooperation', *The Cooperative Magazine* (London), November 1827, p. 509, editorial note.
16 'Weekly Proceedings', *The Crisis, and National Co-operative Trades' Union and Equitable Labour Exchange Gazette* (London) 2, No. 35–6 (31 August 1833), p. 276.
17 'Our Name', *The New Moral World and Manual of Science* 3, 21 (No. 125), 18 March 1837, p. 161.
18 P. Leroux, 'Philosophie sociale', *Revue encyclopédique* 60 (October–December 1833), pp. 94–116, reprinted as 'De l'individualisme et du socialisme', in P. Leroux, *Oeuvres 1825–1850* (Geneva: Slatkine Reprints, 1978), pp. 365–80.
19 *What Is Socialism? And What Would Be Its Practical Effects upon Society? A Correct Report of the Public Discussion between Robert Owen and Mr John Brindley, held in Bristol . . .* (London: Home Colonization Society, 1841).
20 See, for example, K. Grünberg, 'Der Ursprung der Worte "Sozialismus" und "Sozialist"', *Archiv für die Geschichte des Sozialismus und der Arbeiterbewegung* 2 (1912), pp. 372–9; G. Deville, 'Origine des mots "socialisme" et "socialiste" et de certains autres', *La Révolution Française. Revue d'histoire moderne et contemporaine* 54 (January–June 1908), pp. 385–401; E. Czóbel, 'Zur Verbreitung der Worte "Sozialist" und "Sozialismus" in Deutschland und in Ungarn', *Archiv für die Geschichte des Sozialismus und der Arbeiterbewegung* 3 (1913), pp. 481–5; R. de Mattei, 'La prima apparizione in Italia dei termini "socialismo" e "socialisti"', *Storia e politica internazionale* 20, 4 (1941), pp. 3–9; A. E. Bestor, Jnr, 'The evolution of the socialist vocabulary', *Journal of the History of Ideas* 9, 3 (1948), pp. 259–302; J. Gans, 'L'origine du mot "socialiste" et ses emplois les plus anciens', *Revue d'histoire économique et sociale* 35, 1 (1957), pp. 79–83; H. Müller, *Ursprung und Geschichte des Wortes 'Sozialismus' und seiner Verwandten* (Hanover: J. H. W. Dietz Nachf., 1967); W. Schieder, 'Sozialismus', in O. Brunner, W. Conze, and R. Koselleck (eds.), *Geschichtliche Grundbegriffe. Historisches Lexikon zur politisch-sozialen Sprache in Deutschland*, vol. v (Stuttgart: Klett-Cotta, 1984), pp. 923–96; G. Spini, 'Sulle origine dei termini "socialista" e "socialismo"', *Rivista storica italiana* 105, 3 (1993), pp. 679–97.

atheism, the new body of thought immediately found support among believers of different persuasions. Because 'socialism' was a previously unknown concept in any language, the English neologism was usually adopted literally: *socialisme* in French, *Sozialismus* in German, *socialismo* in Spanish, *sotsializm* in Russian, *sosyalizm* in Turkish, *sosialisme* in Bahasa Indonesia. In some language areas, however, a completely new term was invented. For example, *shakai-shugi* – formed by the elements *shakai* ('society') and *shugi* ('doctrine') – was introduced in Japan in the 1880s, and this subsequently found its way into Chinese as *shehuizhuyi* ('socialism').[21] In Arabic, *ishtirakiyyah* became fashionable from the second half of the nineteenth century.[22]

The Discovery of Class Struggle

That the concept of 'socialism' originated in Britain had, of course, everything to do with the enormous social and economic upheaval that had been going on there since the late eighteenth century. That upheaval is commonly referred to as the Industrial Revolution, a designation meaningful insofar as a rapidly growing number of workers produced textiles for the market, in cottages, manufactories, and some industrial works – although steam- or water-powered factories did not predominate until the mid-nineteenth century. Men, women, and children all worked, and the formation of proletarian concentrations was conducive to rebellious sentiment. Towards the end of the eighteenth century, John Millar, a leading intellectual of the Scottish Enlightenment, observed the consequences of economic growth:

> As the advancement of commerce and manufactures in Britain has produced a state of property highly favourable to liberty, so it has contributed to collect and arrange the inhabitants in a manner which enables them, with great facility, to combine in asserting their privileges . . . Villages are enlarged into towns; and these are often swelled into populous cities. In all those places of resort, there arise large bands of labourers or artificers, who by following the same employment, and by constant intercourse, are enabled, with great rapidity, to communicate all their sentiments and passions. Among these there spring up leaders, who give a tone and direction to their companions . . . In this situation, a great proportion of the people are easily aroused by every popular discontent, and can unite with no less facility in

21 W. Lippert, 'Marxism and the Development of the Chinese Political Lexicon', in C. Neder, H. Roetz, and I.-S. Schilling (eds.), *China in seinen biographischen Dimensionen / China and Her Biographical Dimensions* (Wiesbaden: Harrassowitz, 2001), pp. 374–5.
22 M. M. Wahba, 'The meaning of ishtirakiyah: Arab perceptions of socialism in the nineteenth century', *Alif: Journal of Comparative Poetics* 10 (1990), pp. 42–55.

demanding a redress of grievances. The least ground of complaint, in a town, becomes the occasion of a riot; and the flames of sedition spreading from one city to another, are blown up into a general insurrection.[23]

Some reformers tried to counteract the alienation and immiseration of the growing working class by setting up new forms of business and alternative communities. They included Robert Owen (1771–1858), the Welsh textile entrepreneur mentioned earlier, and the French philosophers Claude-Henri de Saint-Simon (1760–1825), Charles Fourier (1772–1837), and Etienne Cabet (1788–1856). Striving to overcome social inequality and poverty 'from above' through alternative societies, they are sometimes referred to as utopian socialists or utopian communists. They established their self-created, often quite authoritarian,[24] communities not only in western Europe but also in sparsely populated parts of North America.

Nevertheless, social tensions grew, not only in Britain, but also increasingly in continental Europe and North America. Labour protests had been a feature of Europe since the fourteenth century, but they became more intense and more visible in the early decades of the nineteenth century – especially in the three politically most important countries in western Europe. Between 1831 and 1834 an uprising by silk workers in Lyon triggered a general strike unique for that era, as well as two very bloody confrontations with the authorities.[25] In England the popular Chartist movement for political reform had an enormous impact from 1838.[26] And in 1844 the rebellion of

23 J. Millar, 'The Advancement of Manufactures, Commerce, and the Arts, since the Reign of William III; and the Tendency of this Advancement to Diffuse a Spirit of Liberty and Independence' (c. 1800), in W. C. Lehmann (ed.), *John Millar of Glasgow, 1735–1801* (Cambridge: Cambridge University Press, 1960), pp. 337–9.
24 A contemporary observer criticized, for example, Robert Owen's New Lanark community and its treatment of workers as 'human machines': 'Owen in reality deceives himself. He is part-owner and sole Director of a large establishment, differing more in accidents than in essence from a plantation: the persons under him happen to be white, and are at liberty by law to quit his service, but while they remain in it they are as much under his absolute management as so many negro-slaves.' See R. Southey, *Journal of a Tour in Scotland in 1819*, with an Introduction and Notes by C. H. Herford (London: John Murray, 1929), pp. 263–4. Against this background the attempt of a Mississippi planter to transplant Owen's practices to a slave plantation becomes understandable. See M. Hayek et al., 'Ending the denial of slavery in management history: paternalistic leadership of Joseph Emory Davis', *Journal of Management History* 16, 3 (2010), pp. 367–79.
25 F. Rude, *Les Révoltes des canuts (1831–1834)* (Paris: Maspero, 1982); M. Moissonnier, *La Révolte des canuts, Lyon, novembre 1831* (Paris: Ed. sociales Messidor, 1958). The best monograph in English is R. J. Bezucha, *The Lyon Uprising of 1834: Social and Political Conflict in the Early July Monarchy* (Cambridge, MA: Harvard University Press, 1974).
26 The literature on the Chartists is vast. See, for example, D. Thompson, *The Chartists: Popular Politics in the Industrial Revolution* (London: Temple Smith, 1984), or M. Chase, *Chartism: A New History* (Manchester: Manchester University Press, 2007).

weavers in Peterswaldau and Langenbielau (Silesia) showed that in Germany too the working class were starting to awaken.[27] In addition, in the United States, the first local workingmen's parties were established in Philadelphia and New York during the crisis years of 1827–33.[28]

German intellectuals were generally the first to attempt to draw theoretical conclusions from such developments. They could have recourse to the notions of class and class struggles, which dated back to the eighteenth-century debates. During the decades preceding the revolution of 1789 French social analysts such as François Quesnay and Anne Robert Jacques Turgot had begun to distinguish two or three social classes. In Britain, David Hume, Adam Ferguson, and others developed similar distinctions almost at the same time. A possible explanation for this discovery of social classes is the growth of nation-states, combined with expanding trading circuits, and the concomitant increase in income inequality. Moreover, the rise of manufactures and factories made it increasingly difficult for journeymen and other skilled workers to become independent entrepreneurs themselves.

Reflecting on these trends, in 1842 the social scientist Lorenz von Stein published a study of the socialism and communism of contemporary France in which he argued that the growing industrial society either made workers obstinate and malicious or transformed them into dull instruments and servile subordinates. He considered personal and hereditary property to be the root cause of this decline of the working classes, since it resulted in the dominant power of some and the unfreedom of others. However, a proletarian revolution was not inexorable. Stein proposed a reformist political strategy in which the state guides the redistribution of economic resources so as to prevent class polarization.[29]

In late 1843 or early 1844 Karl Marx characterized the proletariat as 'a class with *radical chains*, a class *in* civil society which is not a class *of* civil society, an estate which is the dissolution of all estates, a sphere which has a universal character by its universal suffering and claims no *particular right* because no

---

27 L. Kroneberg and R. Schlösser, *Weber-Revolte 1844. Der schlesische Weberaufstand im Spiegel der zeitgenössischen Publizistik und Literatur* (Cologne: C. W. Leske, 1979); C. von Hodenberg, *Aufstand der Weber. Die Revolte von 1844 und ihr Aufstieg zum Mythos* (Bonn: Dietz, 1997).

28 H. L. Sumner, 'Citizenship (1827–1833)', in J. R. Commons et al., *History of Labour in the United States*, 2 vols. (New York: Macmillan, 1918), vol. I, pp. 169–332; B. Laurie, *Working People of Philadelphia, 1800–1850* (Philadelphia: Temple University Press, 1980); S. Wilentz, *Chants Democratic: New York City and the Rise of the American Working Class, 1788–1850* (New York: Oxford University Press, 1984), Part III.

29 L. von Stein, *Der Socialismus und Communismus des heutigen Frankreichs. Ein Beitrag zur Zeitgeschichte* (Leipzig: Wigand, 1842).

particular wrong, but *wrong generally*, is perpetrated against it'. The proletariat was the 'all-round antithesis' to existing society, which is 'the *complete loss* of man and hence can win itself only through the *complete re-winning* of man'.[30] Shortly after, in 1845, Friedrich Engels published *The Condition of the Working Class in England: From Personal Observation and Authentic Sources*. Basing himself on Manchester's textile industry, Engels suggested how 'industry has been concentrated into fewer hands', and therefore how the working population had become centralized, as 'Big industrial establishments need many hands massed together in one building. They have to live together and the labour force of even a relatively small factory would populate a village.'[31] In a fragment from 1845–6, Marx and Engels asserted that the abolition of bourgeois society would require a social revolution.[32]

For quite some time it remained unclear who exactly were workers and who were proletarians, for they were not usually seen as separate 'classes'. Some regarded wage labourers as *part* of the proletariat. According to Adolphe Granier de Cassagnac, writing in the 1830s, the proletariat formed 'the lowest rank, the deepest stratum of society', which consisted of four groups, 'workers, beggars, thieves, and public women':

> The worker is a proletarian, because he works in order to live and earns a wage; the beggar is a proletarian, who does not want to work or cannot work, and begs in order to live; the thief is a proletarian, who does not want to work or beg, and, in order to make a living, steals; the prostitute is a proletarian, who neither wants to work, nor beg, nor steal, and, in order to live, sells her body.[33]

According to others, wage labourers were part of the 'producing classes', also termed 'working men'. In 1859 Emile Levasseur defined the 'working classes' as 'All those who earned their living in and from industry, from simple apprentices to great merchants'.[34]

---

30 K. Marx, 'A Contribution to the Critique of Hegel's *Philosophy of Right*' (1843), in *Marx Engels Collected Works* (London: Lawrence & Wishart, 2010) (hereafter *MECW*), vol. III, p. 186; translation corrected.

31 [F.] Engels, *The Condition of the Working Class in England*, trans. and ed. W. O. Henderson and W. H. Chaloner (Oxford: Basil Blackwell, 1958), pp. 27–8; *MECW*, vol. IV, p. 325.

32 K. Marx and F. Engels, 'The German ideology' (1845–6), in *MECW*, vol. V, p. 88. See also M. Hess, 'Consequences of a Revolution of the Proletariat' (1847), in M. Hess, *The Holy History of Mankind and Other Writings*, ed. S. Avineri (Cambridge: Cambridge University Press, 2004), pp. 128–35.

33 A. Granier de Cassagnac, *Histoire des classes ouvrières et des classes bourgeoises* (Paris: Desrez, 1838), p. 30.

34 E. Levasseur, *Histoire des classes ouvrières en France depuis la conquête de Jules César jusqu'à la Révolution*, 2 vols. (Paris: Guillaumin, 1859), vol. I, p. iii.

The 'workers' of whom Stein, Marx, and Engels wrote were not wage-earners in the modern sense of the word. Most of the weavers who rebelled in Lyon and Silesia were self-employed (often female) cottagers; in the Chartist movement, artisanal workers such as shoemakers and mechanics were particularly strongly represented.

In the context of resurgent social struggles, modern forms of internationalism also developed. Britain's dominant position on the world market played a significant role. As the most important economic and political global power, Britain experienced relatively little xenophobia in the mid-nineteenth century. On the contrary, in fact: free migration was actively supported. In a sense, London was the capital of the world. And if one can say that the workers of the capitals on this earth consider themselves to be 'heir to the scepter of the kings who have reared the city', the London workers may be expected to embody a certain hegemonic impulse on a world scale.[35] One can imagine how the social and political conditions in London made it possible for a kind of subculture to arise in which working men of various nationalities communicated with each other and how they developed a deeply rooted awareness of international relations and the necessity of international solidarity.

One of the first expressions of workers' internationalism was a document endorsed by William Lovett's Working Men's Association (WMA) on 1 November 1836. In this document, an *Address to the Belgian Working Classes*, the WMA expressed its conviction 'that our interests – nay, the interests of working men in all countries of the world – are identified'. The Belgian 'brethren' were advised 'to form, if possible, a union with countries around you', because 'a federation of the working classes of Belgium, Holland and the Provinces of the Rhine would form an admirable democracy'.[36]

Soon afterwards, organizations were founded that not only promoted internationalist thinking, but were also composed on an international

---

35 V. Kiernan, 'Victorian London: unending purgatory', *New Left Review* No. 76 (November–December 1972), p. 81.

36 The address is in A. Lehning, *From Buonarroti to Bakunin: Studies in International Socialism* (Leiden: Brill, 1970), pp. 210–14. Lehning also gives the corresponding 'Réponse des ouvriers belges à l'adresse des ouvriers anglais' (pp. 214–18). A few months later, in the spring of 1837, the WMA organized a meeting of more than 2,000 supporters of the rebel 'Patriotes' in Lower Canada: 'If the mother country will not render *justice* to her colonies in return of their allegiance ... she must not be disappointed to find her offspring deserting her for her unnatural absurdities and monstrous cruelty.' The full text, followed by the reply of the Central and Permanent Committee of the County of Montreal, can be found in Working Men's Association, *An Address to the People of Canada: With Their Reply to the Working Men's Association* (London: Cleave, Watson, Hetherington, 1837).

footing. They included the Communistischer Arbeiter-Bildungs-Verein (1840–1917; Communist Workers' Educational Association, CABV), and the Fraternal Democrats (1845–53). All these organizations were multi-national and comparatively small, with at most a few hundred members. They were especially active in London, although not exclusively so. And their membership consisted of highly skilled workers and artisans.[37]

1848 and Afterwards

The CABV also served as a recruiting ground for a secret international organization, the League of Justice, founded in Paris in 1836 at the instigation of the revolutionary–socialist apprentice tailor Wilhelm Weitling (1808–71). It became the Communist League in 1847, after Marx, Engels, and their friend Wilhelm Wolff (1809–64) joined. Based on the debates in the league, Marx and Engels subsequently wrote the *Communist Manifesto*, which was published in February 1848. Its opening sentence became famous: 'A spectre is haunting Europe – the spectre of Communism.'

That was rhetoric, of course – the League had perhaps 500 members – but at the same time the *Manifesto* sketched the main outline of a radical alternative analysis of social development. Starting from the idea that the history of 'all hitherto existing society is the history of class struggles', it described how 'modern bourgeois society' revolutionized all continents – putting an end to 'all feudal patriarchal relations'. But as bourgeois society grew, so did the extent and power of its counterpart, the proletariat: 'a class of labourers, who live only so long as they find work, and find work only so long as their labour increases capital'. Thus the bourgeoisie produces 'its own grave-diggers'. The communists are that part of the proletariat that clearly understands 'the line of march, the conditions, and the ultimate general results of the proletarian movement'. Communists do not invent principles; they 'merely express, in general terms, actual relations springing from an existing class struggle, from a historical movement going on under our very eyes'.[38]

The *Manifesto* appeared at almost the same time as the overthrow of Louis Philippe in France and the establishment of the Second Republic, events that

---

37 A. Brandenburg, 'Der Kommunistische Arbeiterbildungsverein in London. Ein Beitrag zu den Anfängen der deutschen Arbeiterbildungsbewegung (1840–1847)', *International Review of Social History* 24, 3 (1979), pp. 341–70; C. Lattek, *Revolutionary Refugees: German Socialism in Britain, 1840–1860* (London and New York: Routledge, 2006).
38 *Manifesto of the Communist Party* (1848), in *MECW*, vol. VI, pp. 483, 484, 485, 486, 490, 496, 497, 498.

gave birth to a distinctive form of working-class socialism. As Samuel Hayat notes:

> During the weeks that followed the February Revolution, hundreds of news-papers and clubs were created, and the most popular of them were often centred on a socialist figure such as Etienne Cabet or François-Vincent Raspail. For the first time in history, socialists were able to talk publicly to a large audience. More importantly, their ideas started to be discussed in mainstream newspapers: the moderate republican *Le National* became involved in heated debates with Proudhon on the creation of economic value, while the popular comical newspaper *Le Charivari* became filled with caricatures of socialist leaders.[39]

An intellectual like Louis Blanc received broad support when he advocated post-capitalist industrial relations, arguing that, 'No matter what we do, the nineteenth century will always be known as the century of *socialism*.'[40] Such views also found support in other European countries in which revolutionary conditions arose, including Italy and the Habsburg Empire. In Germany, the Arbeiterverbrüderung (Workers' Fraternization) emerged as the first prole-tarian movement of any significance. These developments embodied the breakthrough of socialism as a social movement.

However, the emerging shoots of this nascent movement were soon nipped off. The Revolutions of 1848–9 ended in defeat, to be followed by a period of less intense political protest that continued into the 1860s. During this period, capital accumulation flourished throughout the North Atlantic region, while conservative and reactionary forces prevailed; it was only in Asia that major rebellions occurred. In British India, in 1857–9, the Sepoy Mutiny – regarded later by some as the First War of Independence – broke out. Socialists in Europe and North America who followed these events saw a clear link with their own aspirations. Marx, for example, noted that 'The profound hypocrisy and inherent barbarism of bourgeois civilization lies unveiled before our eyes, turning from its home, where it assumes respect-able forms, to the colonies, where it goes naked.'[41] In a similar way the Taiping Rebellion (1850–64) also had an influence, but the scale of events in China far surpassed that of the Sepoy Mutiny. The Taiping Rebellion was a major revolt that went on for about fifteen years and in which perhaps as

---

39 S. Hayat, 'Working-Class Socialism in 1848 in France', in D. Moggach and G. S. Jones (eds.), *The 1848 Revolutions and European Political Thought* (Cambridge: Cambridge University Press, 2018), p. 128.
40 L. Blanc, *Le Socialisme. Droit au travail, réponse à M. Thiers* (Paris: Michel Levy Frères, 1848), p. 85.
41 K. Marx, 'The future results of British rule in India' (1853), in *MECW*, vol. XII, p. 221.

MARCEL VAN DER LINDEN

many as 20 million people died. 'The revolutionary sparks in Europe of 1848 were a sideshow by comparison.'[42] Moreover, the rebels, led by Hong Xiuquan (1814–64), developed an alternative, authoritarian, and egalitarian model of society inspired by a radical interpretation of the Bible.

The Changing Role of States and Markets

In the second half of the nineteenth century, the roles of state and market changed in the North Atlantic region, but also elsewhere. In large parts of Europe and North America, the capitalist economy – with its dynamism and its inevitable periodic crises – began to penetrate to the fringes of society; first in Britain, of course, but soon elsewhere as well. Urban economies flourished, and rural areas were integrated into commerce. This development continued very unevenly, and a persistent division between industrial and rural areas remained. In the 1840s, Britain's labour markets began to be integrated.[43] In the United States, this process took at least forty years longer.[44]

Parallel with this development, but also part of it, major transformations took place in the role of the state between 1850 and 1880. The United States was reconstituted after the Civil War of 1860–5, serfdom was abolished in Russia in 1861, in Austria-Hungary the Dual Monarchy was established in 1867, while Japan saw the Meiji restored in 1868, Italy and Germany were each unified in 1870–1, and so on. Competitive pressures between states were probably the main cause of this kind of change, although domestic issues also played a role.[45] Relatively comprehensive tax systems emerged – at varying rates in different countries – and non-military state expenditure grew. States 'began to monitor industrial conflict and working conditions, install and regulate national systems of education, organize aid to the poor and disabled, build and maintain communication lines, [and] impose tariffs for the benefit of home industries'.[46] Somewhat paralleling this process,

---

42 R. Boer, 'Marxism, religion and the Taiping revolution', *Historical Materialism* 24, 2 (2016), p. 8.
43 H. Southall, 'Towards a geography of unionization: the spatial organization and distribution of early British trade unions', *Transactions of the Institute of British Geographers* 13, 4 (1988), pp. 466–83.
44 J. R. Commons, 'Introduction', in Commons et al. (eds.), *History of Labour in the United States*, vol. I, p. 8.
45 C. S. Maier, 'Leviathan 2.0: Inventing Modern Statehood', in E. S. Rosenberg (ed.), *A World Connecting: 1870–1945* (Cambridge, MA, and London: Harvard University Press, 2012), pp. 93–4.
46 C. Tilly, *Coercion, Capital, and European States, AD 990–1990* (Cambridge, MA, and Oxford: Blackwell, 1990), p. 115.

systems of surveillance were devised to block the emergence of forms of protest and resistance that might threaten states and their clients. As Eric Hobsbawm wrote:

> In the course of the nineteenth century these interventions became so universal and so routine in 'modern' states that a family would have to live in some very inaccessible place if some member or other were not to come into regular contact with the national state and its agenda: through the postman, the policeman or gendarme, and eventually through the schoolteacher.[47]

It was not only the influence of states that grew as a result, for so too did their size. Previously, the apparatus of the state had been very small (in 1848, the British Home Office had a total of just twenty-two permanent officials, excluding doorkeepers and the like),[48] but now this state apparatus began to be transformed into a bureaucracy, and the number of administrative staff increased sharply. Naturally, these innovations led to an explosive growth in government spending. Around 1890, the economist Adolph Wagner formulated his 'law', which posited that the share of public expenditure rises in parallel with national income. There were three reasons for this, he claimed: the replacement of private activities by public activities; the increase in expenditure on culture, education, and welfare; and the nationalization of natural resources.[49]

These developments necessitated a fundamental reorientation between the emerging labour movements and the socialists who felt closely allied with them. Previously – roughly until the Revolutions of 1848–9 – they had seldom regarded the state as a solution to social and economic problems. On the rare occasions that states did penetrate everyday lives, their main purpose was to *take* (taxes, conscripted soldiers) and almost never to *give*. In these circumstances workers hoping to halt deteriorating conditions or even to improve their fates did not think initially, and probably not at all, of the state. Groups of workers therefore primarily devised alternatives that did not envisage a significant role for the state. In the North Atlantic region, trade unions, journeymen's associations, and the like were transnational

---

47 E. J. Hobsbawm, *Nations and Nationalism since 1780: Programme, Myth, Reality*, 2nd edn (Cambridge: Cambridge University Press, 1992), pp. 80–1.

48 J. Saville, *1848: The British State and the Chartist Movement* (Cambridge: Cambridge University Press, 1987), p. 18.

49 A. H. Wagner, *Finanzwissenschaft*, 3 vols. (Leipzig: C. F. Winter, 1889–92). Wagner's Law has frequently been confirmed by historical research. An attempt at further explanation can be found in J. O'Connor, *The Fiscal Crisis of the State* (New Brunswick: Transaction, 2002), pp. 150–74.

avant la lettre and in many cases co-ordinated operations across national borders. Alternative concepts were based on autonomous co-operatives and on liberal experiments. For 'pre-advanced' populations, the concept of social revolution often exuded a broad appeal as well, as the state tended to be regarded as a hostile military and tax-collecting apparatus that had to be eliminated.

There was a broad *communis opinio* that social justice should be based primarily on autonomous management and that the state could at best merely facilitate this type of activity. The most far-reaching call for state intervention at this time can probably be found in the 'Demands of the Communist Party in Germany' of 1848, which insisted, *inter alia*, that 'Princely and other feudal estates, together with mines, pits, and so forth, shall become the property of the state'; that 'A state bank ... shall replace all private banks'; and that 'All the means of transport, railways, canals, steamships, roads, the posts etc. ... shall become the property of the state and shall be placed free at the disposal of the impecunious classes.'[50] The state should therefore abolish class privileges and take on important infrastructure tasks, but it should not take control of agriculture, industry, or politics. As Otto Kirchheimer said: 'The fight for liberty and equality and the determination of the individual's position were to take place within society with the state coming in only as a regulatory afterthought.'[51]

Economic developments and the increasing interference of states provoked two reactions from socially motivated labour and opposition intellectuals: either they believed that recent developments should be opposed, or they advocated that the new situation be put to strategic advantage. This created a schism within the socialist movement.[52] The contradictions became clear in the International Working Men's Association (IWMA), which later became known as the First International. Founded in London in 1864, the IWMA embodied on the one hand the continuity of the earlier London-based organizations and, on the other, represented a break with the past. The continuity consisted of its explicit ideological internationalism, but the break with the past was revealed in its organization: the new

50 'Demands of the Communist Party in Germany' (1848), in *MECW*, vol. VII, pp. 3–4.
51 O. Kirchheimer, 'Confining conditions and revolutionary breakthroughs', *American Political Science Review* 59, 4 (1965), p. 972.
52 P. Weber, *Sozialismus als Kulturbewegung. Frühsozialistische Arbeiterbewegung und das Entstehen zweier feindlicher Brüder Marxismus und Anarchismus* (Düsseldorf: Droste, 1989).

association had chapters in various nation-states on the continent, in the United States, and even in Latin America. Moreover, it did not limit its activities to education and propaganda; instead it stressed the practical promotion of workers' solidarity. With regard to the latter aspect, it emphasized two activities: financial support of allied organizations and the restriction of international labour mobility.

Within the IWMA, contradictions soon arose between the 'authoritarians' and the 'anti-authoritarians'. The 'authoritarians' sought to streamline the organization and advocated participation in elections, while the 'anti-authoritarians' accused the 'authoritarians' of wanting to subject the International – which until then had been broad-minded and realistic – to a single doctrine, with uniform tactics and authoritarian leadership. Initially, neither current was very distinctive, but among the 'authoritarians' Karl Marx (1818–83) and Friedrich Engels (1820–95) played an important role, while among the 'anti-authoritarians' the supporters of the 'mutualist' Pierre-Joseph Proudhon (1809–65) were influential, followed slightly later by the 'collectivist' Mikhail Bakunin (1814–76) and his supporters.[53] However, there were many who at first were unable to choose between the two camps – or who alternated between them.

The end was already in sight for the IWMA by 1872, when the 'anti-authoritarian' wing became independent. The 'authoritarian' wing managed to prolong its existence into 1876, while the 'anti-authoritarian' wing was disbanded the following year. Trade union consolidation was probably an underlying reason for their demise. The IWMA was founded as an attempt at cross-national solidarity at the local, sub-national level – for example, between London and Paris – at a time when there was no consolidated national trade union confederation. However, the need for such 'sub-national internationalism' was obviated once strong national organizations emerged, with Britain again leading the way with the establishment of the Trades' Union Confederation in 1868. In the decades that followed, most other countries in the North Atlantic region saw similar consolidation. Other factors, too, fuelled the IWMA's collapse, such as the defeat of the Paris Commune in 1871 and, from c. 1873, economic decline.[54]

---

53 On the often extremely heated controversies, in which neither violent language nor antisemitism was eschewed, see W. Eckhardt, *The First Socialist Schism: Bakunin vs Marx in the International Working Men's Association*, trans. R. M. Homsi, J. Cohn, C. Lawless, N. McNab, and B. Moreel (Oakland, CA: PM Press, 2016).

54 F. Bensimon, Q. Deluermoz, and J. Moisand (eds.), *'Arise Ye Wretched of the Earth': The First International in a Global Perspective* (Leiden and Boston: Brill, 2018).

Negating or Transforming State Power?

It was from this 'authoritarian' tendency that social democratic parties emerged. Their aim was to mobilize their supporters to gain influence within and upon legislative and other administrative bodies in order to further the goals of socialism. (These currents are discussed in detail in Volume II.) The 'anti-authoritarian' current gave rise to the anarchism discussed in the present volume – a movement that rejects state intervention and endeavours to create a new, free society through a movement based on federal autonomy. With a period when the state was not needed still fresh in everyone's memory, the anarchists advocated building an alternative society that could dispense with the state from the outset. They drew on earlier ideas, such as those of William Godwin (1756–1836), Ramón de la Sagra (1798–1871), Johann Caspar Schmidt ('Max Stirner', 1806–56), and radicals from the Revolutions of 1848, such as Anselme Bellegarrigue (1813–69?), Ernest Coeurderoy (1825–62), and Joseph Déjacque (1821–64). However, the most influential sources of inspiration were Proudhon and Bakunin, followed later by Peter Kropotkin (1842–1921).

The term 'anarchism' derives from the Ancient Greek *an-archia*. Homer and Herodotus used it to describe 'leaderless' or 'captain-less' troops who behaved in a disorderly and riotous fashion. It was probably not until the early nineteenth century that the word became part of everyday language, when it was used pejoratively to describe destructive rioters. However, in the course of the nineteenth century, for many people the resistance to the state which characterized 'anarchy' changed from being a negative to a positive characteristic – for the reasons outlined above.[55] The origins of this development lay in the French Revolution, but it really only took hold in the period after the Revolutions of 1848. Characteristic of anarchism, in all its many forms, was that it aimed to be more than just an anti-political movement. Its ultimate aim was a reorganization of the whole of human life, a new way of living.

Classical anarchism flourished between roughly 1860 and 1940, reaching its heyday globally in the decades just before the First World War.[56] From

---

55 P. C. Ludz, 'Anarchie, Anarchismus, Anarchist', in O. Brunner et al. (eds.), *Geschichtliche Grundbegriffe. Historisches Lexikon zur politisch-sozialen Sprache in Deutschland*, vol. 1 (Stuttgart: Klett-Cotta, 1974), pp. 49–109.
56 Important overviews for countries not dealt with in the present collection include: P. Avrich, *The Russian Anarchists* (Princeton: Princeton University Press, 1967); P. A. Aršinov, *Le mouvement makhnoviste* (Paris: Bélibaste, 1969); U. Linse, *Organisierter Anarchismus im deutschen Kaiserreich von 1871* (Berlin: Duncker &

Europe, it spread first to the former settler colonies in the Americas in particular: in North America, but perhaps more so in large parts of South and Central America (Argentina, Brazil, Chile, Cuba, and so on). In Africa, anarchist influence was more limited owing to the slow pace of industrialization and proletarianization, but, as Steven Hirsch and Lucien van der Walt have remarked: 'as in the Latin American case, the movement emerged in the areas most closely linked to global processes of capital accumulation and imperial penetration: southern Africa, and the Mediterranean perimeter of North Africa'.[57]

In East Asia, anarchism probably found its first supporters during the Russo-Japanese War of 1904–5, when the pacifist Kōtoku Shūsui read Kropotkin's *Fields, Factories and Workshops* while in prison. Kōtoku approached anarchism 'in terms not of working-class politics but of the self-sacrificing devotion of the high-minded liberals of lower Samurai origins'.[58] In 1911 he was executed for treason. Meanwhile others, such as Ōsugi Sakae, had taken up anarchist ideas, although their influence seems to have remained limited.[59] From Japan, anarchist ideas spread to Korea, at that time a Japanese colony, and to China, where, from 1918 or 1919 until the early 1930s, the movement gained a degree of influence among

---

Humblot, 1969); M. Palij, *The Anarchism of Nestor Makhno, 1918–1921: An Aspect of the Ukrainian Revolution* (Seattle: University of Washington Press, 1976); G. Botz, *Im Schatten der Arbeiterbewegung. Zur Geschichte des Anarchismus in Österreich und Deutschland* (Vienna: Europaverlag, 1977); M. Enckell, *La fédération jurassienne. Les origines de l'anarchisme en Suisse* (Saint-Imier: Canevas, 1991); S. Mbah and I. E. Igariwey, *African Anarchism: The History of a Movement* (Tucson: Sharpe, 1997); B. Anderson, *Under Three Flags: Anarchism and the Anti-Colonial Imagination* (London and New York: Verso, 2005); S. Hirsch and L. van der Walt (eds.), *Anarchism and Syndicalism in the Colonial and Postcolonial World, 1870–1940* (Leiden and Boston: Brill, 2010); I. Khuri-Makdisi, *The Eastern Mediterranean and the Making of Global Radicalism, 1860–1914* (Berkeley: University of California Press, 2013); A. Corlu, 'Anarchists and Anarchism in the Ottoman Empire, 1850–1917', in S. Karahasanoğlu and D. C. Demir (eds.), *History from Below: A Tribute in Memory of Donald Quataert* (Istanbul: Istanbul Bilgi University Press, 2016), pp. 553–83; H. Döhring, *Organisierter Anarchismus in Deutschland 1919 bis 1933* (Bodenburg: Edition AV, 2018).

57 L. van der Walt and S. J. Hirsch, 'Rethinking Anarchism and Syndicalism: The Colonial and Postcolonial Experience, 1870–1940', in Hirsch and van der Walt (eds.), *Anarchism and Syndicalism*, p. xliii.

58 Ch. Tsuzuki, 'Anarchism in Japan', *Government and Opposition* 5, 4 (1970), pp. 501–22, at 502.

59 F. G. Notehelfer, *Kōtoku Shūsui: Portrait of a Japanese Radical* (Cambridge: Cambridge University Press, 1971); *A Short History of the Anarchist Movement in Japan* (Tokyo: Idea Publishing House, 1979); T. A. Stanley, *Ōsugi Sakae, Anarchist in Taishō Japan: The Creativity of the Ego* (Cambridge, MA: Council on East Asian Studies, Harvard University, 1982); I. L. Plotkin, *Anarchism in Japan: A Study of the Great Treason Affair, 1910–1911* (Lewiston, NY: Mellen, 1990); *The Autobiography of Ōsugi Sakae* (Berkeley: University of California Press, 1992); J. Crump, *Hatta Shūzō and Pure Anarchism in Interwar Japan* (New York: St Martin's Press, 1993).

intellectuals and the labour movement.[60] For a time, in his youth, even Mao Zedong felt attracted to anarchism.[61]

From the very beginning, anarchism was an international movement. Militant exiles, tramping artisans, and labour migrants disseminated anarchist ideas across much of the world. Even in the absence of international anarchist organizations, or even if they were weak, there was still a 'Black International' in that sense.[62]

Revolutionary Syndicalism

Towards the end of the nineteenth century, part of the trade union movement became gripped by anarchist ideas and developed into revolutionary-syndicalist organizations. Other terms used in this context include 'anarcho-syndicalism', 'revolutionary industrialism', and 'one big unionism'. Syndicalism was an international movement. To syndicalists, the working class constituted the force that would bring about change, the economic terrain its natural battlefield, direct action its natural weapon, with self-directed labour associations the natural agencies for uniting, marshalling, and applying the collective, revolutionary power of the workers.

Syndicalist movements were active in quite a few countries, from Argentina and Canada to Egypt, Korea, and Uruguay.[63] The significant life span of syndicalism, viewed globally, was between 1900 and 1940 (Table I.1).

60 On Korea, see Ha Ki-Rak, *A History of the Korean Anarchist Movement* (Taegu: Anarchist Publishing Committee, 1986); and D. Hwang, *Anarchism in Korea: Independence, Transnationalism, and the Question of National Development, 1919–1984* (Albany: State University of New York Press, 2016). On China, see J.-J. Gandini, *Aux sources de la révolution chinoise: les anarchistes. Contribution historique de 1902 à 1927* (Lyon: Atelier de Création Libertaire, 1986); A. Dirlik, *Anarchism in the Chinese Revolution* (Berkeley: University of California Press, 1991); and Ming Kou Chan, *Schools into Fields and Factories: Anarchists, the Guomindang, and the National Labor University in Shanghai, 1927–1932* (Durham, NC: Duke University Press, 1991); G. Müller, *China, Kropotkin und der Anarchismus. Eine Kulturbewegung im China des frühen 20. Jahrhunderts unter dem Einfluß des Westens und japanischer Vorbilder* (Wiesbaden: Harrassowitz, 2001).
61 S. R. Schram (ed.), *Mao's Road to Power: Revolutionary Writings 1912–1949*, vol. 1, *The Pre-Marxist Period, 1912–1920* (White Plains, NY: M. E. Sharpe, 1992), p. 380.
62 Over the years, non-anarchists have sometimes developed anti-authoritarian ideas that had consequences compatible with anarchism, even though they were not regarded as anarchists by either anarchists or themselves. Examples include the theoreticians of council communism Anton Pannekoek (1873–1960), Otto Rühle (1874–1943), and Paul Mattick (1904–81), and the advocate of the 'autonomous society' Cornelius Castoriadis (1922–97).
63 M. van der Linden and W. Thorpe (eds.), *Revolutionary Syndicalism: An International Perspective* (Aldershot: Scolar Press, 1990); D. Berry and C. Bantman (eds.), *New Perspectives on Anarchism, Labour and Syndicalism: The Individual, the National and the Transnational* (Cambridge: Cambridge Scholars, 2010); Hirsch and van der Walt (eds.), *Anarchism and Syndicalism*.

Table I.1 The rise and fall of some syndicalist organizations

Movement/country	Year founded	Period of max-imum influence[1]	Later development
Nationaal Arbeids Secretariaat (National Labour Secretariat; NAS, Netherlands)	1893	c. 1920	Dissolved by Nazi occupation, 1940
Confédération Générale du Travail (General Confederation of Labour; CGT, France)	1902[2]	c. 1909–10	By 1914 no longer syndicalist
Industrial Workers of the World (IWW, USA)	1905	1916–17	Marginalized
Sveriges Arbetares Centralorganisation (Swedish Workers' Central Organization; SAC, Sweden)	1910	1924–34	Marginalized; since 1954 co-operation with the state
'Labour unrest' (Great Britain)	1910	1910–14	Mostly not institutionalized
Industrial Workers of the World (IWW, South Africa)	1910	1911–13	Repressed; defunct in 1914
Confederación Nacional del Trabajo (National Confederation of Labour; CNT, Spain)	1910	1936–7	Suppressed by Franco regime, 1939; marginalized and split
Unione Sindacale Italiana (Italian Syndical Union; USI, Italy)	1912	c. 1920	Suppressed by Mussolini regime, 1926
Casa del Obrero Mundial (House of Global Labour; Mexico)	1913	1914–16	Suppressed and marginalized, 1916
Federación Obrera Regional Argentina (Argentine Regional Workers' Federation; FORA-IX, Argentina)	1915	1915–20	Absorbed by Union Sindical Argentina, 1922
One Big Union (OBU, Canada)	1919	1919–20	Marginalized; absorbed by All-Canadian Congress of Labour, 1956
Confederação Geral do Trabalho (General Confederation of Labour; CGT, Portugal)	1919	1919–20	Suppressed by Salazar regime, 1927

Table I.1 (cont.)

Movement/country	Year founded	Period of maximum influence[1]	Later development
Arbeiterunionen (workers' unions; Germany)[3]	1920–1	1922–4	Marginalized; destroyed by Nazi regime, 1933

1 Despite the often indifferent administration of syndicalist unions and the fact that many workers regarded themselves as members without paying dues, I have usually used the number of members (as the firmest measure available) as determining the period of maximum influence.
2 In 1902 the CGT (actually founded in 1895) merged with the Bourses du Travail (labour exchanges).
3 A forerunner, the Freie Vereinigung deutscher Gewerkschaften (Free Association of German Unions), founded in 1897, became syndicalist before 1914.

It was at its most vigorous just before and after the First World War – with Spain in the 1930s being the most important exception proving the rule. Over the course of time, three more or less consecutive 'models' became crystallized, which to a certain extent functioned as nuclei for international syndicalist 'families': the French Confédération Générale du Travail (General Confederation of Labour, CGT), the American Industrial Workers of the World (IWW), and the Spanish Confederación Nacional del Trabajo (National Confederation of Labour, CNT). Factors likely to have played a role in this were international migration, maritime labour (sailors, dockers), and cross-border activities.

For all their regional and national variations, syndicalist organizations shared a number of characteristics. First, their supporters expressed attitudes of class warfare and professed revolutionary objectives. Syndicalists saw class interests as ultimately irreconcilable, and class conflict as therefore inescapable. Consequently, while their labour associations aimed at winning short-term improvements for workers within the existing system, they also espoused the long-term goal of overthrowing capitalism and instituting a collectivized system of worker-managed productive property. Secondly, syndicalists believed that the most effective means to achieve both short- and long-term goals was the collective, direct action of workers, mobilized primarily against the employers on the front lines of the class struggle, but more generally against the entire socio-political system buttressing the capitalist economy. Thirdly, syndicalists insisted that direct action required organizing workers at the point of production, in their capacity as workers. They therefore regarded trade unions as the crucial vehicle of struggle, for both immediate and long-term goals.

Despite the shared attributes of the syndicalist movement, they also varied widely. Some associations, such as the German Allgemeine Arbeiterunion Einheitsorganisation (General Workers' Union), were radically decentralist. Others, such as the IWW in the United States, mostly endorsed centralization. Many syndicalists opposed the political parties that claimed to speak for the workers, but some were prepared to accept parties if they rejected electoral and parliamentary politics. Syndicalist organizations nearly everywhere fervently supported communist internationalism in its infancy, after 1917. But when it became clear that the Communist International insisted upon parliamentarism and the subordination of revolutionary unions to communist parties, supporters went their separate ways: many broke with Moscow, while others discarded their syndicalist views and definitively embraced communism.

Anarchism and syndicalism reached their historic apogee during the Spanish Civil War of 1936–9, when, mainly at syndicalists' instigation, in Catalonia, Aragon, and elsewhere nearly 2 million employees seized control of businesses. But anarchism came under violent attack on two fronts: by Joseph Stalin's Communist International, which tried to suppress all those elements in the Spanish struggle that did not accede to its hegemony, and by the right-wing radical nationalists of General Francisco Franco. Franco's victory in 1939 marked the end, for the time being, of this last major social anarchist/syndicalist experiment.

There were several reasons why the influence of syndicalism began to ebb around 1940, with state repression playing the decisive role – in a number of cases, not only in Spain, but also in the Soviet Union, Italy, Germany, and elsewhere. But repression cannot explain the enduring absence of syndicalist movements in these countries. Why, for instance, were the heirs of the CNT incapable of recovering lost ground after the fall of the Franco dictatorship in the 1970s? More basic underlying causes are apparently at work here. It is likely that the rise of 'Fordist' patterns of production and consumption, and the rise of welfare states, left those movements not already destroyed by state repression with only three options, each of which would ultimately mean their demise. A movement could: (i) hold on to its principles, in which case it would inevitably become marginalized; (ii) change course fundamentally and adapt to the new conditions, in which case it would have to abandon its syndicalist principles; or (iii) if these two alternatives were unpalatable, disband, or, what amounts to the same thing, merge into a non-syndicalist trade union organization. The IWW, which still survives, opted for the first alternative. The French CGT opted for the second. Other movements opted sooner or later for the third.

The Return of Libertarian Politics

State-negating currents have returned since the 1960s, but in a different form. The first wave, in response to the growing influence of the state and major industry, opposed this so-called progress and yearned for an agricultural and artisanal idyll. Supported socially mainly by artisans, workers, and peasants, it aspired primarily to political, social, and economic equality, but often with a masculine undertone. With the euphoric sense of progress coming to an end in recent decades, the 'romantic shortcomings' of anarchism seem to be turning into an advantage for some, while many find that the pursuit of a more humane and ecologically responsible society operating on a smaller scale is wholly or partly in keeping with the old anarchist project. The second wave, still ongoing, is more strongly culturally inspired and attracts followers mainly from among highly educated young people increasingly open to discussions about gender and ethnicity.

There are two remarkable aspects to the renewed engagement of anarchists. The first is that the social movements through which this engagement is expressed are generally not purely anarchist; the anarchist elements are in fact part of a wider libertarian political culture. The Mexican Zapatistas, the Brazilian Sem Terra movement of landless peasants, the opponents of capitalist 'globalization', and the militants of the Occupy movement: none of these were ever anarchist in the strict sense, but all prioritized direct action and emphasized 'exposing, delegitimizing and dismantling mechanisms of rule while winning ever-larger spaces of autonomy from it'.[64]

The second aspect is that the new anarchists draw a great deal of inspiration from societies on the periphery of the world system. They sympathize on the one hand with traditional societies in South America, South-East Asia, and elsewhere that consciously hold back processes of state formation,[65] and

---

64 D. Graeber, 'The new anarchists', *New Left Review* 13 (January–February 2002), p. 68.
65 One of the first authors to explore this was the anthropologist Pierre Clastres, especially in his *La Société contre l'état. Recherches d'anthropologie politique* (Paris: Editions de Minuit, 1974); it is available in English as *Society against the State: Essays in Political Anthropology*, trans. R. Hurley in collaboration with A. Stein (New York: Urizen Books, 1977). Later, the historian Willem van Schendel and the anthropologist James C. Scott drew our attention to large stateless zones in upland South-East Asia: W. van Schendel, 'Geographies of knowing, geographies of ignorance: jumping scale in Southeast Asia', *Environment and Planning D: Society and Space* 20, 6 (2002), pp. 647–

on the other with Rojava in north-western Syria, where, during the Syrian war, from July 2012, three 'autonomous democratic zones' – Cizîrê, Efrîn, and Kobanê – were created in a territory of some 18,000 square kilometres that was home to just under a million people. Formally inspired by the ideas of the North American 'libertarian municipalist' Murray Bookchin (1921–2006), the Kurdish Partiya Yekîtiya Demokrat (Democratic Union Party, PYD) introduced a four-tiered council system in these zones:

> At the base, there is the commune, consisting of a village or 30 to 150 households in an urban neighbourhood. These communes consist of commissions from five to ten persons each that are formed around certain topics such as defence, women, and economy. Delegates of 7 to 30 communes then form a council of a village community or a city district, which, in turn, by analogy to the communes, consists of various commissions. Several of these councils of city districts or village communities then elect city or regional councils, which, again, consist of several commissions. And finally, the city and regional councils elect the People's Council of West Kurdistan (Meclîsa Gel a Rojavayê Kurdistanê, MGRK). All these levels follow the principle of co-chairmanship, that is, all councils are always jointly led by a male and a female. Moreover, in addition there are also autonomous women's councils.[66]

This structure *resembles* the direct democracy pursued by social anarchists, but is in fact completely dominated by the PYD and its front organizations. While there does indeed appear to be a high level of democracy at village level, it clearly decreases in the higher echelons. Of course, it might be argued in its defence that the Rojava experiment is distorted by being carried out in the middle of a war zone, but it remains a historically unique combination of council democracy and a one-party system. Whatever its shortcomings, in the eyes of many anarchists Rojava demonstrates the feasibility of direct democracy.

Both tendencies seem to suggest a rather broad sympathy for autonomous structures, probably especially among young people, of which minority anarchism is an important expression.

The Cambridge History of Socialism

The time seems ripe for a critical survey of socialist movements and political practices thus far. *The Cambridge History of Socialism* (hereafter *CHS*) is

---

68; and J. C. Scott, *The Art of Not Being Governed: An Anarchist History of Upland Southeast Asia* (New Haven and London: Yale University Press, 2009).

66 T. Schmidinger, *Rojava: Revolution, War and the Future of Syria's Kurds*, trans. M. Schiffmann (London: Pluto Press, 2018), p. 134.

intended to contribute to such an overview. (The 'other half' of the field is, as I have said, covered by *The Cambridge History of Communism.*) Much has already been written on the history of socialism. Countless historical accounts, in the form of both national case studies and international surveys, have been authored on each and every trajectory.[67] In spite of their real achievements, these works generally suffer from at least one of four weaknesses: they focus almost exclusively on Europe and its settler colonies; they focus only on a subset of cases; they neglect the social movement aspect; and/or they neglect the gender aspect. Nor are the histories of state-negating and state-transforming socialisms usually seen holistically – unlike in the past, when memories of the 'schism' were still vivid.[68]

The *CHS* presented here tries to overcome these shortcomings. It integrates anarchism, syndicalism, social democracy, labour, the New Left, and alternative trajectories in the Global South in one encompassing reconstruction. It attempts to cover the whole world, inasmuch as this is possible given our current level of historical knowledge and the space available to us. And it pays serious attention to the gendered nature of all movements. A collection such as this cannot hope to be comprehensive: obviously important cases are omitted. The studies included serve as examples of the rich variety of socialist history and, together, endeavour to reveal some major contours of its development.

The first volume is devoted to the early history of proto-socialisms and to those movements that negated state power by building alternative grassroots structures without state involvement, by attempting to destroy state power, or by a combination of both strategies. The second volume reconstructs the trajectory of state-transforming movements, including social democracy, labour, left-socialist parties, and most alternative socialisms in the Global

---

67 The standard general narrative accounts of anarchist history are: M. Nettlau, *Geschichte der Anarchie*, 5 vols. (Vaduz: Topos, 1984); J. Joll, *The Anarchists* (London: Eyre & Spottiswoode, 1964); G. Woodcock, *Anarchism: A History of Libertarian Ideas and Movements* (Cleveland, OH: World Publishing, 1962; several reprints); and P. Marshall, *Demanding the Impossible: A History of Anarchism* (London: HarperCollins, 1992). The standard general narrative accounts of social democracy and left socialism include G. D. H. Cole's classic *A History of Socialist Thought*, 5 vols. (London: Macmillan, 1953–60); J. Braunthal, *Geschichte der Internationale*, 3 vols. (Hanover: Dietz Nachf., 1961–71); J. Droz (ed.), *Histoire générale du socialisme*, 4 vols. (Paris: Presses Universitaires de France, 1972–8); H. W. Laidler, *History of Socialism* (New York: Thomas Y. Crowell, 1968); and D. Sassoon's *One Hundred Years of Socialism* (London: I. B. Tauris, 1996).
68 See for example H. P. G. Quack, *De Socialisten. Personen en stelsels*, 4 vols. (Amsterdam: P. N. van Kampen, 1875–97; later expanded, several reprints); L. Winterer, *Le socialisme contemporain. Histoire du socialisme et de l'anarchisme* (Paris: Lecoffre, 1894; several reprints). An exception confirming this rule is Cole's *History of Socialist Thought*.

South. It also offers transversal essays in which the whole experience of the various socialisms is reconsidered from a number of different angles.

The present volume, Volume I, begins with a reconstruction of some egalitarian experiments and ideologies in Asia, Europe, and the Islamic world. Touraj Daryaee discusses Mazdakism, a religious movement in Sassanian Persia of c. 500 CE that assumed God had originally made all means of subsistence available to everyone on the basis of equality. A minority had then misappropriated most of them, creating the necessity for a radical redistribution of social wealth. Many of the lower classes were drawn to this teaching, and at one point even King Kawād I (498–531) supported the revolt for a time in the hope of weakening the power of the great noble houses. The movement was able to effect important social reforms (especially the redistribution of land), but was violently suppressed after Kawād's death.

In her chapter on Islam, Asma Afsaruddin argues that egalitarianism was a feature of the early period. Several verses in the Qur'an establish that Muslim, Jewish, and Christian communities are all just as praiseworthy as each other when they subscribe equally to values of justice, moderation, and righteousness; other verses posit the complete spiritual and ontological equality of men and women. However, a diachronic analysis shows how later exegeses of these verses progressively subverted their egalitarian thrust. Muslim scholars constructed and permitted inequality based particularly on gender and religion. In contemporary Muslim-majority societies, however, egalitarianism is returning as a 'powerful, emotive topic'.

Thomas A. Fudge points to the widespread urge to revive primitive Christianity (as expressed in the Acts of the Apostles) in late medieval and early modern Europe. He illustrates this by reference to the Hussites (Bohemia, 1420s–50s), the Anabaptists at Münster (1520s–30s), the Hutterites in Moravia (1520s–1620s), the Polish Brethren (1560s–1650s), and the Diggers in England (1649–50). However, the theological idealism of these attempts to form egalitarian communities could not withstand socio-economic reality, ideological contradictions, corrupt leaders, and violent repression.

An impressive successor to the radical Christian tradition described by Fudge emerged onto the world stage in nineteenth-century southern China, when the weakness of the ruling Qing dynasty enabled a radical movement of millions of believers to lay temporary foundations for the evangelically inspired Heavenly Kingdom of Great Peace. Rudolf Wagner describes the theological background and the programme to change land-holding structures. This revolt – which has come to be known as the Taiping Rebellion

(1850–64) – was eventually quelled after a protracted war that claimed millions of lives.

The next part discusses early socialist thinkers in western Europe and North America, the concern of many of whom was to devise plans and projects to establish a better society in the present. Initially, it was members of the elite who defended a top-down approach, but gradually the emphasis shifted to 'plebeian' militancy. An early pioneer was the positivist Claude-Henri de Saint-Simon, discussed by Jeremy Jennings, who believed that the future society should be meritocratic and socially just. There would no longer be any role for parasitic aristocrats, soldiers, and priests. Power would instead be held by *les industriels*, entrepreneurs, bankers, and other productive workers. In his final years, Saint-Simon believed that the revolution could best be accomplished by a new Christian church, with its own clergy and dogma. Throughout the nineteenth century, there were influential individuals who, for a time at least, drew entirely or partially on Saint-Simon (Barthélemy Enfantin, Auguste Comte, Pierre Leroux, Emile Durkheim, and many others).

Another utopia was designed by Charles Fourier. Jonathan Beecher describes Fourier's ideal of a non-repressive society where work is pleasure and everyone can follow their passions. The ideal world would be a global federation of largely self-sufficient, democratic, and sexually free communities (*phalanges*). Fourier attracted few followers during his life, but after his death support for Fourierism grew, partly because it was joined by disappointed supporters of Saint-Simon. The movement founded several communities, especially in the United States. Although usually short-lived, Fourierism continued to exert an influence on emergent socialist movements for decades.

More practical than Saint-Simon and Fourier was Robert Owen. In his paternalistically run textile factory in New Lanark, Scotland, he introduced shorter working hours, healthier working conditions, and a range of social benefits – without affecting profits. Gregory Claeys describes Owen's development, the various social experiments he set up, including those in North America, and the main organization of the 1830s and 1840s he established, the Association of All Classes of All Nations. Claeys shows that elements of Owen's ideology, and political and economic theory, were influential throughout the nineteenth century, including within the social democratic Fabian Society.

Etienne Cabet also managed to attract a considerable following with his ideas, as Christopher H. Johnson shows. In the 1840s he launched the Icarian movement, based on the vision expounded in his novel *Voyage en Icarie* (*Travels in Icaria*, 1839). Cabet advocated collective ownership of the means of production and distribution and, like Fourier, wanted to radically democratize and ameliorate industrial relations. While some of the movement's members had emigrated to the United States (Texas, Illinois, Iowa) a little earlier, his ideas met with massive support during the Revolution of 1848. In practice, Cabet's plans proved difficult to achieve, yet, Johnson argues, three elements of it gained lasting impact: the pursuit of worker self-determination; the necessity of working-class power; and the importance of an appealing design for an alternative society.

As Bertel Nygaard shows in his chapter, the ideas of Fourier, Owen, and Cabet inspired the young Wilhelm Weitling, a German tailor who settled in Paris in the 1830s and joined an expatriate organization called the League of Justice. Weitling's first book was entitled *Die Menschheit, wie sie ist und wie sie sein sollte* (*Humanity as It Is and as It Should Be*, 1838) and came to be regarded as the league's programme. It advocated a free and equal society, without money and private property, which could be the outcome only of an autonomous process of proletarian learning. In later publications too, Weitling argued that only workers were truly capable of formulating workers' views. In doing so, he initiated a new phase in the development of socialism.

The pursuit of the self-emancipation of the oppressed and exploited is central to the last section of the first part. In 1864 the International Working Men's Association was founded in London. Its provisional general rules stated that 'the emancipation of the working classes must be conquered by the working classes themselves'. Fabrice Bensimon describes the brief but intense history of this organization, which united collectivists, mutualists, trade unionists, Lassalleans, and others. Within a few years, divisions emerged between 'centralists' and 'autonomists', with the supporters of Karl Marx and Mikhail Bakunin particularly opposed to one another. The conflict resulted in a split in 1872, one that also implied a definitive schism between those socialists advocating that state power should be ignored or immediately destroyed, and those advocating its transformation.

The most significant advocates of state transformation were undoubtedly Karl Marx and Friedrich Engels. Lucia Pradella traces the relationship between their political and theoretical activities in a period that spans the early 1840s to the consolidation of German social democracy in the 1890s. She situates their writings and activities in the context of the developing workers' movements in Europe and the United States, and of the consolidation of imperialism. She considers not just the 'social issue' but also their evolving assessment of the peasant, colonial, and women's questions.

Initially, the opponents of Marx and Engels were inspired chiefly by Pierre-Joseph Proudhon and, somewhat later, by Mikhail Bakunin. Proudhon was the first to enunciate an ambitious state-negating anti-capitalist theory. Alex Prichard describes the evolution of Proudhon's thinking; if laws were to be replaced by voluntary agreements and mutually accepted obligations between communities and individuals, capitalism could be replaced by mutualism. Prichard shows that these radical ideas of Proudhon were completely permeated by a profound sexism and antisemitism.

Like Proudhon, Bakunin also developed a social revolutionary and anti-statist approach, but with different emphases. He avoided sexism (though not always antisemitism), as Wolfgang Eckhardt shows. Like Marx, Bakunin placed his hopes on the social struggle, but unlike Marx he regarded not only the working class as revolutionary subject, but also poor peasants and the 'lumpenproletariat'. Bakunin strived for a revolutionary emancipatory community to combat the creation of a central power and a centralized economy because, he argued, they embodied the immediate danger of a 'Red bureaucracy'. Land and raw materials were to become fully democratized collective property, so that everyone could dispose of the fruits of their labour, at least as long as they were not employers. Bakunin's ideas were widely adopted, especially in the Iberian peninsula, France, and Italy.

The third influential early anarchist, after Proudhon and Bakunin, was Peter Kropotkin. Ruth Kinna shows how he represented a new generation that tried to integrate scientific insights from biology, ecology, and geography into state-negating thinking. Kropotkin advocated a communist, decentralized federal economy, with increased production at the local level. To achieve this, agriculture and industry had to be unified, human needs reassessed, and energy needs reduced. Kropotkin criticized the first globalization ('internationalism') and opposed colonialism and nationalism, but was in favour of an Allied victory during the First World War because a German victory would entail the end of freedoms that were better guaranteed in France and Great Britain than they were in Germany.

The second part deals with state-negating movements. It follows the development of anarchism and its 'proletarian' sibling, revolutionary syndicalism – their rise and decline from the 1870s to the 1940s on different continents. The first section starts with a number of case studies from the North Atlantic region, beginning with southern Europe. Alexander Varias describes how from the 1880s France's anarchist movement became concentrated in Paris, where it held a small, if vocal, position within the larger dynamics of movements such as socialism and republicanism. Artists and critics were attracted to it but so too were workers, though not in large numbers. That changed from the 1890s when a revolutionary-syndicalist movement developed, crystallized by the important Confédération Générale du Travail. The First World War and the rise of communism put an end to this revival of anarchism and syndicalism. For a long time the movement remained marginal, but May 1968 saw its resurgence, embedded in a broader libertarian culture.

In Spain, anarchism and syndicalism reached their historical apogee. George Esenwein points out that the movement had already started during the IWMA, partly under the influence of Bakunin. However, a mass movement – which continued to encompass conflicting ideological currents – emerged only with the rise of anarcho-syndicalism, which rapidly gained many supporters during the First World War and became extremely large by 1919. State repression under dictator Miguel Primo de Rivera forced the movement underground. The establishment of the Second Republic in 1931 saw the re-emergence of anarcho-syndicalism onto the public stage. In 1936 a spontaneous popular revolution broke out, coinciding with the onset of civil war. Driven by their desire to defend the revolution, many anarchists became politicized, and some even joined the republican government. In 1939 the battle was decided in favour of the Francoists, and the anarchists and syndicalists were driven underground or forced into exile. It was only after 1975 that the movement saw a limited revival.

Italy was the third European country in which anarchism and syndicalism were of importance. Carl Levy presents an overview, beginning in the aftermath of the *Risorgimento* in the 1860s. He discusses the evolution of anarchism during the First International and its transformation in the 1880s and 1890s, discussing the personalities, political culture, institutions, and doctrines of anarchism and syndicalism. Both currents retained a clear influence until the rise of communism and the fascist regime (1922–1943/5) and later played a role in the anti-fascist and resistance movements. From the late 1960s, anarchism saw something of a comeback. Levy emphasizes the importance of women in the movement.

In the United Kingdom, neither anarchism nor syndicalism ever managed to gain an influence comparable to what they had in southern Europe, as David Goodway shows. With liberalism the dominant force in the UK, anarchism never became a significant movement, except among Jewish workers in the East End of London. Women were always readily accepted, and indeed prominent. Relatively separately from anarchist circles, a significant, more or less syndicalist, 'labour unrest' evolved in the period 1910–14 and persisted until after the First World War. In the intellectual field, important libertarian contributions were made by, among others, the designer and utopian thinker William Morris (1834–96), the guild socialist G. D. H. Cole (1889–1959), and in more recent years the mutualist theoretician Colin Ward (1924–2010).

For a time, anarchism and later syndicalism both gained wide followings in the United States, in part owing to the influence of European immigrants. According to Kenyon Zimmer, anarchism existed sporadically before the Civil War, but it was not until the 1880s that a large-scale movement emerged. This first wave ended with the Haymarket massacre of 1886 and the harsh repression that followed. In the early 1900s, influenced by syndicalism, interest in revolutionary unions grew; the founding of the Industrial Workers of the World in 1905 led to what Zimmer calls 'the apex of US anarchism'. During the First World War, harsh repression followed once again. After the October Revolution in Russia, many in the American movement joined the communists, and the movement became a more or less spent force, though it saw a modest revival from the 1960s.

The second section considers developments in the Global South. As in the United States, European migrants played a crucial role in Latin America as intermediaries. According to John Mason Hart, in Mexico the radical-democratic ideology fitted well with the co-operative culture that had existed in villages since pre-Columbian times. The first major movements of urban and rural workers emerged, inspired by the Paris Commune of 1871, but were quickly suppressed. After the turn of the century, Mexico saw a major revival stimulated by cross-border connections with Mexican workers and the IWW in the United States; this revival was a contributing factor to the revolution of 1910–20 but subsequently fell victim to repression once again. A new turning point took place with the Tlatelolco massacre in Mexico City in 1968. It was not only intellectuals and workers who radicalized; so too did poor peasants, in Chiapas province for instance, where the Zapatista movement became an important force after 1994.

In his chapter on Argentina, Geoffroy de Laforcade too emphasizes the role of European migrants, but argues that the movement that emerged from the 1880s soon assumed a direction all its own. Motivated by anarcho-communist ideas, a powerful syndicalist workers' movement emerged, reaching its apogee around 1919–20 and probably constituting the second-largest such movement in the world, after the Spanish one. The 1930 military coup and the rise of corporatist trade unions seriously weakened anarchism and syndicalism, though both remain visible minorities today.

In Brazil, Claudio Batalha argues, anarchist ideas had been circulating on a small scale since the 1890s, partly due to the role of Italian immigrants, but it was not until the early years of the twentieth century that a breakthrough occurred with the emergence of militant unions that soon adopted a syndicalist strategy. As in Argentina, the influence of anarcho-communism was considerable. After peaking in 1917–20, the movement was weakened by a combination of repression and communist competition – a downturn exacerbated by the right-wing populist *coup d'état* that brought Getulio Vargas to power in 1930. The movement never fully recovered.

Lucien van der Walt describes other international connections. Anarchist and syndicalist movements emerged in the economically fast-growing South Africa of the 1880s. Under Anglo-US influence, they were at first marginal but grew later. Predominant in the South African labour movement was a racist species of 'White Labourism' that combined social democratic demands with support for segregation. However, there was a breakthrough after 1915, when a powerful multi-racial syndicalism surfaced. A few years later, this movement played a role in the establishment of the Communist Party, in which it continued to have a noticeable influence for years and managed to retain a following in the 1920s among both black and white workers. In the 1930s the anarchist and syndicalist current largely ebbed away as an organized force, but has since the 1990s seen a revival, although on a smaller scale.

In China, as Gotelind Müller shows, anarchism was introduced not by immigrants but actually the reverse, for it was brought back by Chinese nationals who came into contact with it abroad. In 1907 they formed distinct anarchist groups in Tokyo and Paris that were much concerned from the beginning with gender, new lifestyles, and matters of language, advocating, for example, the adoption of Esperanto. After the fall of the Qing dynasty in 1911–12, anarchism and syndicalism were able to take root in China itself, their influence peaking during the May Fourth movement of 1919. During the 1920s contradictions among anarchist-syndicalists, Guomindang, and the Communist Party increased, with the Shanghai massacre of 1927 as a dramatic nadir. The outbreak of the Sino-Japanese War in 1937 brought a permanent end to the movement.

These various case studies prove that anarchist and syndicalist movements were not 'national' phenomena. They should always be seen in a transnational context, and have experienced a modest revival in many places over the past few decades. The chapters in the final section of this volume explore these aspects. Constance Bantman draws attention to what she calls 'the transnational turn in the historiography of anarchism' – a recent development that provides insight into the (mostly informal) international and inter-continental circulation of individuals and groups, printed matter, financial resources, and ideas. Bantman explores the complexities of such exchanges, which led not only to 'transfer' but also to interaction and mutual learning. At the same time, this transnationalism was constantly thwarted by language problems, nationalist sentiment, censorship, and police surveillance. Bantman also considers the role women have often played, despite male dominance – a role frequently rendered invisible.

Felipe Corrêa closes this volume with a wide-ranging chapter in which he points to the importance of developments in Africa, Asia, and Latin America. Corrêa presents a preliminary typology of six major currents in contemporary anarchism and syndicalism, ranging from trade union organizations to insurrectionaries. Most such movements are active transnationally or have formed international associations, and, while the impact of many of them is marginal, a number are of greater significance. At the same time, it is difficult to build sustainable organizations and the movement is struggling with unresolved practical and theoretical dilemmas.

Acknowledgements

Five years ago, Michael Watson and Bethany Thomas invited me to co-ordinate this project on behalf of Cambridge University Press. I thank them for their faith in me, and I thank the six anonymous reviewers who provided constructive comments on my proposal, along with the Cambridge Syndicates who approved it. In the work that followed I was fortunate to be able to rely on the efficient support of the Press's Elizabeth Hanlon, as well as Victoria Phillips, Emily Sharp, Karen Anderson, Lyn Flight, and Lisa Carter.

Scholars from six continents agreed to write chapters. With admirable patience they endured my exhortations, my critical remarks, and my no doubt tiresome requests to shorten, expand, or revise their work. I can only hope they are pleased with the result. I would like to extend a particular word of thanks to Professor Catherine Vance Yeh who, after the sad death of her husband Rudolf Wagner, agreed to complete his text.

In preparing this volume I benefited from the institutional support of my colleagues Aad Blok, Karin Hofmeester, Leo Lucassen, and Jacqueline Rutte. I received valuable advice from a number of experts: Gilbert Achcar, Touraj Atabaki, Rossana Barragán, Gregor Benton, Alina-Sandra Cucu, Leon Fink,

Terry Irving, Philippe Kellermann, Marta Kirejczyk, Jaap Kloosterman, Jürgen Kocka, Reinhart Kössler, Anja Kruke, David Mayer, Christine Moll-Murata, Alice Mul, Gotelind Müller-Saini, Bryan Palmer, Herman Pieterson, Lucas Poy, Dilip Simeon, Heinz Sünker, Göran Therborn, Reiner Tosstorff, Raquel Varela, and Susan Zimmermann. The fine translation of the introductory chapters is by Chris Gordon.

PART I

★

BEGINNINGS

EGALITARIANISM

Mazdak and Late Antique 'Socialism'

TOURAJ DARYAEE

During the reign of Kawād I (AD 498–531), king of Ērānšahr (Realm of the Iranians), a Zoroastrian priest by the name of Mazdak, son of Bāmdād, appears in some sources whose rulings about property and ownership have been deemed proto-socialist. According to sources in Middle Persian of the late Sasanian Empire (AD 224–651), Mazdak promoted the sharing of women and property. Mazdak's socialist message called for the creation of an egalitarian system of the distribution of wealth during a time of famine and political turmoil. The lower classes appear to have favoured Mazdak's beliefs, and he claimed his rulings were based on his interpretation of the Zoroastrian holy text, the *Avesta*. The reason for Mazdak's ruling was to provide aid to the hungry and the naked, but, more importantly, he also wanted to make substantial social and economic changes in an otherwise stratified Iranian society.[1] With Mazdak and the backing of the king, a social and economic revolution took place in the Sasanian Empire, which empowered the state at the cost of the nobility, and enabled the kings of Iran to rule for another two centuries.

If we take Mazdak as a historical personage,[2] it appears that he enjoyed the support of a major segment of the population: those who were destitute (a condition mainly caused by a recent famine and economic hardship). Mazdak specifically had the support of those who were simply the poor (*driyōš* / Eng. Derwish). Mazdak and his followers were able to instigate a social revolution that broke the power of the great noble houses (*wuzurgān*), stripping away their wealth and property and, in some cases, abducting female members of the aristocratic houses. The redistribution of wealth, land, and women was made

---

1 T. Daryaee, *Sasanian Persia: The Rise and Fall of an Empire* (London: I. B. Tauris, 2013), pp. 86–8. Unless otherwise noted, all non-English terms are from Middle Persian.

2 H. Gaube, 'Mazdak: historical reality or invention?', *Studia Iranica* 11 (1982), pp. 111–22, has suggested that he did not exist. However, even if Mazdak did not exist, the movement named after him did, and it brought changes to Iranian society.

possible through Mazdak's interpretation (*zand*) of the *Avesta*. There is no doubt that Kawād I supported the movement, or at least allowed it to take hold throughout the Sasanian Empire. The consequences of the Mazdakite movement for Iranian society and that of modern Iran and Iraq were long-lasting. It created fundamental changes in Iranian societal structure, and furthered egalitarian and anti-state movements in the early Islamic world until the tenth century A D.[3] The Mazdakite movement became a focal point both for Soviet social historians of antiquity[4] and for twentieth-century leftists and revolutionaries in Iran.

In late antiquity (A D 200–700), the ideal Zoroastrian social order, according to the *Avesta*,[5] was imposed on Iranian society by the Sasanians and the nobility. The classes (*pēšag*) of the social order included the priests (*āsrōnān*), the warriors (*artēštārān*), husbandmen (*wāstaryōšān*), farmers (*dahīgān*), and artisans (*hutuxšān*).[6] This meant that a large segment of the population who were not attached to any of these classes were left out, mainly the landless peasants, the poor, and what we may call the underclass. In Middle Persian literature, the poor are divided into two groups: those who sometimes merit help, collectively known as the *driyōšān*; and those termed the insolent and rowdy poor, known as the *škōhān*.[7] While Sasanian wisdom literature in Middle Persian, specifically the *Dēnkard* V I (Acts of Religion), provides much encouragement in helping the mendicant poor as an act of piety,[8] at the same time there were severe punishments meted out in order to keep the insolent poor and the underclass in check. For example, stealing or being insolent to those of the upper classes or the state resulted in branding (*drōš*),[9] beating, or amputation of hands,[10] and imprisonment. In extreme cases, people became 'deserving of death' (*margarzān*).[11]

---

3 The two important studies that cover the entire Mazdak episode and its consequence are E. Yarshater, 'Mazdakism', in E. Yarshater (ed.), *The Cambridge History of Iran*, vol. III, Part 2 (Cambridge: Cambridge University Press, 1983), pp. 991–1024; and A. Gariboldi, *Il regno di Xusraw dall'anima immortale. Riforme economiche e rivolte sociali nell'Iran sasanide del VI secolo* (Bologna: Mimesis, 2009).

4 P. Ognibene and A. Gariboldi, *Conflitti sociali e movimenti politico-religiosi nell'Iran tardo antico. Contributi della storiografia sovietica nel periodo 1920–1950* (Bologna: Mimesis, 2004).

5 E. Benveniste, 'Les classes sociales dans la tradition avestique', *Journal Asiatique* 221 (1932), pp. 117–34; E. Benveniste, 'Traditions indo-iraniennes sur les classes sociales', *Journal Asiatique* 230 (1938), pp. 529–49.

6 Daryaee, *Sasanian Persia*, pp. 42–8.   7 Ibid., p. 57.

8 *The Wisdom of the Sasanian Sages (Dēnkard VI) by Aturpāt-i Ēmētān*, trans. S. Shaked (Boulder: Westview Press, 1979).

9 Daryaee, *Sasanian Persia*, p. 57.

10 H. Chacha, *Gajastak Abālish* (Bombay: Fort Printing Press, 1936), p. 42.

11 Those guilty of capital offences became 'deserving of the death penalty'. See A. Perikhanian, *Book of a Thousand Judgements [Farraxvmart i Vahraman]: A Sasanian Law Book* (Costa Mesa, CA: Mazda Publishers, 1997), p. 372.

From the third to the fifth century AD, the political and economic structure of the Sasanian Empire was such that those of the noble houses who owned vast land-holdings supported the King of Kings of Ērānšahr by providing payments, in terms of either cash or commodities and men, to the state during times of war and peace. No doubt this system was part of an earlier order that had existed under the preceding dynasty, namely that of the Arsacid/Parthian Empire (247 BC–AD 224). Even the number of these noble houses, namely seven, is a vestige of an older tradition in Iranian history. During the time of Darius I (522–490 BC), the 'Seven πρῶτοι [First]' were noble families who had banded together.[12] The names of these noble houses of old who held large landed estates are recorded as Surēn, Kāren, Zig, Mehrān, Spahbad, Spandiād, and Nahābad.[13] However, in time, through the emergence of the bureaucratic class (*dabīrān*) as well as other administrative changes, the Sasanian world moved towards a centralized empire, as opposed to that of its Arsacid predecessor.[14]

Furthermore, the great noble houses directly controlled the revenues from their estates, which did not allow the state to collect its dues properly. One of the ways in which, from the very beginning, the Sasanians attempted to bring important economic regions under their control was to establish royal cities.[15] These cities are known in Middle Persian as *dastgerd*, which means 'built by hand' (Gr. κτίσμα).[16] They numbered in the dozens, with the names of the Sasanian kings attached to them, and had both economic and military purposes.[17] These cities were part of early plans to control the economy, as well as other efforts towards centralization, by the Sasanian Empire. The early list of cities established by the first two kings of the Sasanian Empire, their incursions into Syria, Anatolia, and later the Caucasus, and the resettlement of

---

12 P. Briant, *From Cyrus to Alexander: A History of the Persian Empire* (Winona Lake, IN: Eisenbrauns, 2002), pp. 128–9.

13 A. Christensen, *L'Iran sous les Sassanides* (Copenhagen and Paris: Levin & Munksgaard and P. Geuthner, 1944), pp. 103–4; A. S. Shahbazi, 'Haft', in E. Yarshater (ed.), *Encyclopaedia Iranica*, vol. XI, Part 5 (2002), pp. 511–15.

14 R. N. Frye, 'Feudalism in Sasanian and Early Islamic Iran', in *Jahiliyya and Islamic Studies in Honour of M. J. Kister* (Jerusalem Studies in Arabic and Islam 10) (Jerusalem: Magnes Press, 1987), p. 18.

15 R. Gyselen, 'Economy. IV. In the Sasanian Period', in Yarshater (ed.), *Encyclopaedia Iranica*, vol. VIII, Part 1 (1997), pp. 104–7.

16 P. Gignoux, 'Dastgerd', in Yarshater (ed.), *Encyclopaedia Iranica*, vol. VII, Part 1 (1994), pp. 105–6; W. Skalmowski, 'On Middle Iranian DSTKRT(Y)', in W. Skalmowski and A. van Tongerloo (eds.), *Medioiranica: Proceedings of the International Colloquium Organized by the Katholieke Universiteit Leuven from the 21st to the 23rd of May 1990* (Leuven: Peeters, 1993), p. 159.

17 Most of the cities are mentioned in R. Gyselen, *La Géographie administrative de l'empire sassanide. Les témoignages épigraphiques en moyen-perse* (Bures-sur-Yvette: Groupe pour l'étude de la civilisation du Moyen-Orient, 2019).

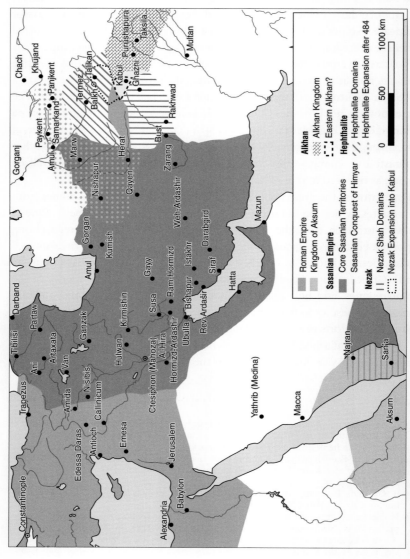

Map 1.1 The Sasanian Empire and its neighbours c. 550 CE. Redrawn based on a map by Khodadad Rezakhani.

skilled labourers in these cities, many of whom were Christian and under the direct control of the crown, were signs of the Sasanian Empire's goals and aspirations. However, the noble houses resisted the state's complete control over their affairs. This fact is significant, as agriculture was the most important means of wealth for the Sasanian state. Records show that small land-holders were allowed to have subsistence living from their own labour and to have one wife, while obeying the nobility in all aspects of life.[18]

In the fifth century AD, the Sasanians faced a new threat that would change many of the political, social, and economic realities of the empire. Kawād I came to power as a result of his father's death in a battle near Balkh in AD 484. From the fourth century, there had been a steady movement of people from central and inner Asia towards the Iranian plateau. In the fifth century, the Hephthalites had encroached onto Sasanian territory. King Pērōz had an army prepared to face them, but he was killed in battle, and many of his retinue, along with his son Kawād, were captured. As a result, the Hephthalites not only annexed an important part of the eastern territories of the Sasanian Empire and captured its royal mint, but they also exacted a heavy tribute from the Sasanians.[19] The income that had previously come from the Silk Road trade in the East also withered away. In a sense this Eastern defeat, coupled with the existing social and climatic situation, caused severe pressures on the empire. From then onwards, the Hephthalites were also able to influence imperial policy, suggesting that the Sasanian Empire was on its knees and at its weakest since its establishment in the third century AD.

The events of the next decade are somewhat unclear and full of controversy, as Kawād I came to the throne and was then deposed, and was then brought back to the throne. For some unknown reason, Kawād I was removed from his first and brief short reign (AD 488–96), and Walāxš was placed on the throne by the nobility.[20] It is quite possible that Kawād I was removed because he had the support of the Hephthalites. However, a certain noble named Sukhrā, along with a group of other nobles, was responsible for bringing him back to power.[21] It is during the second period of Kawād I's rule (AD 498–531) that Mazdak, with his views and policies,

18 M. Shaki, 'Class System III. In the Parthian and Sasanian periods', in Yarshater (ed.), *Encyclopaedia Iranica*, vol. V, Part 6 (1992), pp. 652–8.

19 K. Rezakhani, *Reorienting the Sasanians: Eastern Iran in Late Antiquity* (Edinburgh: Edinburgh University Press, 2017), p. 128.

20 T. Daryaee, 'Coins of Hukay: Sasanian Ideology and Political Competition in the Fifth Century CE', in T. Daryaee and M. Compareti (eds.), *Studi sulla Persia sasanide e suoi rapporti con le civiltà attigue* (Bologna: Casa Editrice Persiani, 2019), p. 25.

21 Rezakhani, *Reorienting the Sasanians*, pp. 132–3.

became important.[22] In order to understand the reasons for the reforms, which have been deemed socialistic, we need to understand the gravity of the situation in the Iranian plateau during the late fifth to early sixth centuries. While the rigidity of class structure in Sasanian society has already been discussed, less is known about the environment's effects on the Sasanians. Thankfully, there is now more robust research. Historians, as well as Middle Persian encyclopedic texts (*Mojmal*), have recorded that there was a period of drought followed by famine during the time that Mazdak appeared: 'There was much famine and Mazdak b. Bāmdād, was the Chief Mowbed, and he brought the religion of Mazdak.'[23] Thus, the famine must have been caused by a drought, which the Zoroastrian encyclopedic texts mention took place during the time of Kawād I's father, Pērōz (*Bundahišn* 33.22): 'During the rule of Pērōz, son of Yazdgerd there was no rain [*wārān nē būd*] for seven years, and harm and serious difficulty came to people.'[24] These observations by primary sources are supported by a recent study of soil samples and related scientific data, which indicate that, of the eight episodes of high aeolian input that coincided with dry or drought conditions, one occurred during the middle of the Sasanian period.[25] This fact, combined with the loss of trade on what has come to be called the Silk Road, which was now in the hands of the Hephthalites, along with the monetary shortage due to the large indemnity paid, brought the survival of the empire into question. As has been discussed, from this moment there was a significant shift towards the west by the Sasanians, who invested heavily in Mesopotamia, and deported the population from Syria in order to resettle them in the western part of the empire, perhaps to offset the losses in the east.[26] However, this was not sufficient to save the Sasanians from the quagmire in which they found themselves. A more substantial change was needed to make sure that the Sasanian Empire survived, but in a stronger and more resilient fashion.

It is in this light that we must view the gravity of Kawād I's situation as the ruler of an empire in dire straits in the fifth century A D. Mazdak, as a Zoroastrian priest whose dictums could legitimize a total restructuring of the Sasanian

---

22 P. Crone, 'Kavād's heresy and Mazdak's revolt', *Iran* 29 (1991), pp. 21–42.

23 M. Bahār, *Mojmal at-Tawārīkh wa'l-Qisas* (Tehran: n.p., 1939), p. 73.

24 T. Daryaee, 'Historiography in Late Antique Iran', in A. Ansari (ed.), *Perceptions of Iran: History, Myths and Nationalism from Medieval Persia to the Islamic Republic* (London: I. B. Tauris, 2014), p. 72.

25 A. Sharifi et al., 'Abrupt climate variability since the last deglaciation based on a high-resolution, multi-proxy peat record from NW Iran: the hand that rocked the cradle of civilization?', *Quaternary Science Reviews* 123 (2015), pp. 225–7.

26 Rezakhani, *Reorienting the Sasanians*, p. 231.

Fig. 1.1   Silver coin of Kawād I, who ruled during the time of Mazdak. (Private collection.)

Empire, aided the king's actions. Mazdak, son of Bāmdād, is generally claimed by Zoroastrian Middle Persian sources to have been an arch-heretic whose inter-pretation of sacred scripture brought havoc to Ērānšahr. His followers came to be known as *zandīg*s who, according to hostile sources, were trying to remedy the ills of the time by reinterpreting the sacred teachings. The *zandīg*s would change the social and religious history of the Near East in the following centuries, and survived in various forms and sects in the Islamic period.[27] Still, their immediate effect on the Sasanian Empire was important and decisive in many ways. The new pro-Mazdakite and anti-Roman policy of Kawād I succeeded, with the backing of the Hephthalites, against some of the aristocracy and the anti-Hephthalite faction.[28] The questions are: how did the Mazdakites relate to society, and how did they interact with the state?

The Poor and the Underclass

In all of this havoc, the poor, whose number must have been large, were most affected, and they played a role in the uprising. In the fourth century AD,

27 For the successive movements inspired by the Mazdakites in the Islamic period, see P. Crone, *The Nativist Prophets of Early Islamic Iran: Rural Revolt and Local Zoroastrianism* (Cambridge: Cambridge University Press, 2012).

28 J. Wiesehöfer, 'Kawād, Khusro and the Mazdakites: A New Proposal', in P. Gignoux et al. (eds.), *Trésors d'Orient. Mélanges offerts à Rika Gyselen* (Paris: Cahiers de Studia Iranica, 2009), p. 401.

Ammianus Marcellinus provides an interesting reference in regard to the slaves and the poor of Sasanian society, in which the upper class had powers such as 'claiming the power of life and death over slaves and commoners'.[29] The term *'plebeii obscuri'*, used by Ammianus in this regard, has been suggested by Jairus Banaji to stand for the *driyōšān*. For Banaji, the *driyōšān* stand for the mass of commoners who were to become a kind of social group, from which the Mazdakites drew their ranks.[30]

In the Zoroastrian text *Dēnkard* VI, there are a number of passages which appear to be portraying a tension existing between the poor (*driyōš*) and the wealthy or the rich (*tawānīg*). For example (*Dēnkard* VI.147): 'They held this too: If the poor (*driyōšān*) set right this one thing, the contempt of wealthy people of high standing (*tawānīgān*), in a century not one of them will go to hell.'[31] From such passages, one gets the sense that due to certain events the *driyōšān*'s contempt for the wealthy or upper class (*tar-menišnīh ī andar mehān tawānīgān*) was further manifested. Hence the dichotomy of *driyōš–tawānīg* (poor–wealthy), which is apparent not only in the *Dēnkard* VI but also in other Middle Persian texts, which exhibit social or class conflict in one form or another. Outside the moralistic text of the *Dēnkard* VI, in the genre of Middle Persian apocalyptic literature, the dichotomy of poor–wealthy manifests itself more forcefully and outside the niceties of respect for the poor. Historians studying these texts have usually paid attention to historical events and characters, such as Alexander the Great's conquest and the Arab Muslim conquest, and the early Islamic movements of the *Siyāh-Jāmagān* and *Sorkh-Jāmagān* (Bābak Khorramdēn movement). It is these events that call for the evoking of the end of times and the chaos and commotion that are involved with it. This end of time, or eschaton, is imagined as a time of disorder, and the *Jāmāsp-Nāmag* states (*Jāmāsp Nāmag* 16.7): 'In this time, the spiritual ones [*tawāngarān*] consider the poor [*driyōš*] to be fortunate, but truly the poor are not fortunate.'[32] As Bruce Lincoln has perceptively observed regarding the social and cosmic confusion of the apocalyptic age, the place of the lower social classes – that is, the poor (*driyōš*) – is only then considered as fortunate

29 Ammianus Marcellinus, *History*, vol. I, books 14–19, trans. J. C. Rolfe (Loeb Classical Library 300) (Cambridge, MA: Harvard University Press, 1950), pp. 392–3.
30 J. Banaji, 'Late Antique Aristocracies: The Case of Iran', in J. Banaji, *Exploring the Economy of Late Antiquity: Selected Essays* (Cambridge: Cambridge University Press, 2016), pp. 170–1.
31 *The Wisdom of the Sasanian Sages*, p. 61.
32 B. Lincoln, 'The earth becomes flat: a study of apocalyptic imagery', *Comparative Studies in Society and History* 25, 1 (1983), pp. 145–6; D. Agostini, *Ayādgār ī Jāmāspīg. Un texte eschatologique zoroastrien* (Rome: Biblica et Orientalia, 2013), p. 76.

(*farrox dārēnd*).[33] In terms of social confusion in Sasanian Iran, of course, one can only first be reminded of the Mazdakite revolt. While most scholars dealing with these texts have paid attention to the theme of national liberation, the apocalyptic texts partly describe social revolution and class struggle as well. Thus, the theme of these Middle Persian texts revolves not only around the issue of the conquered and the conquerors, but also around that of class antagonisms.[34] In regard to King Kawād I and Mazdak, an important Persian text (*Mojmal*) states:

> During the time of Qobād [Kawād], Mazdak was made manifest . . . and said: 'In wealth and women, whatever there is, it must be distributed equally, and no one is superior to another, and a people became his followers, and the poor [*darwišān*] and the illiterate [*johal*] were very much agreeable with this religion . . . till Nowšīrwān brought Hormizd Āfrīd and Mehr Ādūr Parsī and several other mowbeds from Pārs [and] invalidated [that religion] with proof.[35]

This is one of the few places where the *driyōšān* are mentioned as such: in Islamic tradition other terminology is usually used. For example, in another unique passage on Mazdak, he is mentioned as having achieved the support of the poor specifically.[36] In the Middle Persian commentary on the *Avesta* from the Sasanian period (3.41 A–B), one reads:

> For, the Mazdayasnian (Zoroastrian) religion, O Spitama Zarthushtra (Zoroaster), throws away the (judicial) sentence for the man who (has done) the confession (of faith) [the (judicial) sentence to which he has to be given]; (the Mazdayasnian religion) throws away the punishment [they know that stealing is not allowed, but they consider that 'when I steal from the rich (*tawānīgān*) and give it to the poor (*driyōšān*), it will be a good deed for me'].[37]

This Robin Hood attitude in the Sasanian period may be connected first and foremost with the Mazdakites, who are generally accused of taking from the rich. Here in the legal parlance of the *Avesta*, the gloss by the Sasanian Zoroastrian priests demonstrates tension because of wealth disparity between the wealthy and the poor.

---

33 Lincoln, 'The earth becomes flat', p. 147.   34 Ibid., p. 152.

35 Bahār, *Mojmal ut-Tawārīkh*, p. 75.

36 M. Shaki, 'The social doctrine of Mazdak in the light of Middle Persian evidence', *Archiv Orientální* 46, 4 (1978), p. 305

37 M. Moazami, *Wrestling with the Demons of the Pahlavi Widēwdād: Transcription, Translation, and Commentary* (Leiden and Boston: Brill, 2014), p. 93.

Khosrow I: The 'Great' Reformer

After the death of Kawād I, two of his sons, namely Kawūs from the north, backed by the Mazdakites,[38] and Khosrow, supported by the Hephthalites, came to blows. Khosrow was victorious in this battle, while Mazdak and his followers were defeated. With the coming of Khosrow Anušīrwān (AD 531–79), severe measures were taken to put down the Mazdakites. The great Persian epic, the *Shahnāmeh* (*Book of Kings*) by Ferdowsī, gives a vivid description of Mazdak, his career, and his ultimate fate after a debate between the Zoroastrian priests and him at court. 'Justice' was meted out to Mazdak in the following manner:

> Then Cosroe [Khosrow] had a high gallows set up from which dangled a braided noose, and he had the unfortunate heretic hung alive, with his head downwards, and he killed him with a shower of arrows. If you have a healthy intellect, do not follow in Mazdak's footsteps! And so the nobles became secure in their possessions, and women, and children, and their rich treasures.[39]

The theme of chaos brought by Mazdak and the reordering of the society by Khosrow I as the epitome of the just king is a hallmark of Iranian history. By the time of Khosrow I's reign, there had been a decade or two of what can be termed social revolution, and in some ways a levelling of Sasanian society had taken place. The state had allowed the sacking of the granaries, mostly those belonging to the well-to-do, while women had been taken from the noble houses and married off to those of lower classes. This also meant the breaking of the backs of the seven great noble houses, as well as the lesser nobility (*āzādān*). The accusation by the anti-Mazdakites of the alleged sharing of women by the Mazdakites needs some attention. The issue of women at this time had more to do with a reproductive inequality caused by the Zoroastrian legal tradition, which allowed a man to have multiple wives and concubines, depending on his wealth and status. While statistics are lacking, we do know that the wealthiest King of Kings may have had up to 15,000 wives and concubines,[40] while the poor and downtrodden would have been without a wife. Hence, it was only the nobility and priests who could afford and, according to Zoroastrian law, engage in polygamy.[41] One should also note that

38 Gariboldi, *Il regno di Xusraw*, pp. 112–13.
39 A. Bausani, *Religion in Iran: From Zoroaster to Baha'ullah*, trans. J. M. Marchesi (New York: Bibliotheca Persica Press, 2000), p. 100.
40 W. Scheidel, 'Sex and Empire: A Darwinian Perspective', in I. Morris and W. Scheidel (eds.), *The Dynamics of Ancient Empires: State Power from Assyria to Byzantium* (Oxford: Oxford University Press, 2010), p. 278.
41 Perikhanian, *Book of a Thousand Judgements*, pt 2, p. 1.

women slaves (*bandag*) who were non-Iranian (*an-ēr*), while having legal status, were the property of their owners, who were obviously well-to-do. According to Zoroastrian law, the dowry or security for a wife amounted to 2,000 *drahms* (silver coins weighing 4.15 grams), or more than 8 kilograms of silver. There were also temporary marriages which carried their own dowries, and therefore were out of the reach of the poor.[42]

Hence, Mazdak's ruling was an attempt to remedy this inequality in marriage by introducing a new interpretation of Zoroastrian law.[43] While there was a redistribution of women at the time of Kawād I, it appears that Khosrow I re-established the old order and attempted to set boundaries for marriage and class. One can suggest that it is for this reason that, in Zoroastrian law, the legal term *xwarāyēn* – women who have left the house without sanction of the *pater familias* – is mentioned in many law cases, as are men who are classified as adulterers or *sine manu mariti* (*gādār*).[44] That is, this late Sasanian legal classification is a result of Mazdak and Mazdakite actions regarding women. This fact becomes more apparent when we read that, within the offence of adultery, a distinction is made between habitual offence, which is those who commit adultery on a regular basis, and those who committed adultery just once, or more probably were forced into it. In the legal rulings of the late Sasanian period, the latter offenders, that is the women, do not lose their status, while the former do.[45] This interpretation of the law probably allowed for women abducted by the Mazdakites to return to their homes and not lose their status. This was a new way of remedying Mazdak's legal ruling, which had caused the sharing of women.

Re-establishing Economic Order and Foundations for the Poor

It appears that with Kawād I and his son, Khosrow I, there was a move towards monetization of the economy, where taxes were measured by the new type of coinage, with mint marks and exact administrative location. This monetization appears to have taken place both to facilitate transactions in the marketplace (*wāzār*) and to tax the new smaller land-owners, who had

---

42 M. Shaki, 'Family Law in Zoroastrianism', in Yarshater (ed.), *Encyclopaedia Iranica*, vol. IX, Part 2 (1999), pp. 184–96.

43 Crone, 'Kavād's heresy and Mazdak's revolt', p. 25; Scheidel, 'Sex and Empire', p. 280.

44 Perikhanian, *Book of a Thousand Judgements*, sections 24, 8, 9; 33, 1; 83, 8; A13, 5; A14, 3.

45 Ibid., sections 24, 7–10.

replaced the large land-owners.[46] The money taken from the Mazdakites was redistributed to the people, and some care was given to the poor. It is only in this social context that the creation of the office of the 'Protector of the Poor and the Judge [*driyōšān jaddagōw ud dādwar*]' makes sense. This office and its seal were created in the following manner, according to the Sasanian law book *Book of a Thousand Judgements* (*Mādayān ī Hazār Dādestān* 93, 4–9):

> The official seal [*muhr*] of mowbeds and finance officials was first introduced at the order of Kawād son of Pērōz, and the official seals of judges under Khusrow son of Kawād. When the seal of the mowbed of Pārs was cut, the mowbed was inscribed [on its legend] as being not according to [his] mowbed, but was inscribed according to the title of 'Protector of the Driyōšān'.[47]

So far fifteen toponyms[48] have been found, mainly in the western part of the empire. The sudden manifestation of this office during the rule of Kawād I, and then more robustly under Khosrow I, no doubt was a result of the Mazdakite revolt.[49] In a sense, the state began to take control of the affairs of the poor through an organized system.[50] The holder of this office most likely acted as a sort of carrot-and-stick officer, who could aid (*ayyār*) the *driyōš* by acting legally in their defence, but could also exact judgement in their case.[51] Either way, there appears to have been a system of control or maintenance that was placed on the *driyōšān* after the Mazdakite revolt. One can suggest, at least for now, that the praise of the *driyōšān* in the Middle Persian Andarz literature is specifically the result of the post-Mazdakite revolt, and the reason for which the mendicant poor were placed on a spiritual pedestal. However, as the apocalyptic text of the *Jāmāsp Nāmag* suggests, the disruption of class order and the power of the *driyōšān* over the upper classes can only be seen as part of a society in turmoil.

46 R. Göbl, 'Aufbau der Münzprägung', in F. Altheim and R. Stiehl (eds.), *Ein asiatischer Staat. Feudalismus unter den Sasaniden und ihren Nachbarn* (Wiesbaden: Harrassowitz, 1954), pp. 117–18.
47 Perikhanian, *Book of a Thousand Judgements*, pp. 214–15.
48 Gyselen, *Géographie administrative*, p. 266.
49 W. Sundermann, 'Neue Erkenntnisse über die mazdakitische Soziallehre', *Das Altertum* 34, 3 (1988), pp. 183–8.
50 W. Sundermann, 'Commendatio pauperum. Eine Angabe der sassanidischen politisch-didaktischen Literatur zur gesellschaftlichen Struktur Irans', *Altorientalische Forschungen* 167, 4 (1976), pp. 167–8.
51 J. de Menasce, 'Le protecteur des pauvres dans l'Iran Sassanide', in *Mélanges Henri Massé* (Tehran: n.p., 1963), pp. 282–7.

The Effects of the Mazdakite Revolt

It seems that Mazdak's dictums in the form of commentaries on Zoroastrian law (zand) allowed the masses and the downtrodden to revolt, and King Kawād I allowed this uprising to go on so that he would be able to weaken the great noble houses and the existing order, which hindered reform. Once the noble houses were enfeebled and the Zoroastrian religious hierarchy had become powerless in their stance against Mazdak, the king was able to make major changes and restructure the Sasanian Empire. For this chapter, the most important aspect of the revolt was the redistribution of land to what has been called the landed gentry or small land-holders (dehqāns), who managed local affairs and collected taxes from the peasants on behalf of the state. In turn, the dehqāns were to continue cultivating land as an important part of their duty, while having more wealth than a simple peasant.[52] Their status is mentioned in many Zoroastrian texts as standing beside the nobility, while promoting the traditional culture of the empire. The association of the dehqāns with both Kawād I and Khosrow I in the fifth and sixth centuries is pervasive in Perso-Arabic sources. From the time of King Wahrām Gūr to Kawād I and to Khosrow I, all either are said to have mothers from dehqān lineage, or have sayings about the care of the dehqāns.[53] The dehqāns then became a stabilizing source for the state, and they cared for the existing culture and tradition of Sasanian Iran. Ferdowsī, the famous writer, was indeed a dehqān who recognized the end of the existing order at hand and put into rhyme the history of Iran's past for posterity.

The Modern Study of Mazdak as a Socialist

It is was with Theodor Nöldeke's translation in 1879 of Tabarī's history that substantial attention was given to Mazdak. Nöldeke was the first to discuss Mazdak's movement in relation to socialism.[54] In 1906 Edward G. Browne, in another influential work on the literary history of Iran, mentioned Mazdakism in passing as a community when speaking of the famous Iranian statesman and bureaucrat Nizām ul-Mulk (1018–92) during the Seljuk period.[55] No doubt

---

52 A. Tafazzolī, *Sasanian Society* (New York: Bibliotheca Persica Press, 2000), p. 40.
53 Ibid., pp. 41–3.
54 T. Nöldeke, *Geschichte der Perser und Araber zur Zeit der Sasaniden aus der arabischen Chronik des Tabari. Übersetzt und mit ausführlichen Erläuterungen und Ergänzungen Versehn* (Leiden: E. J. Brill, 1879), p. 459.
55 E. G. Browne, *A Literary History of Persia*, vol. I (London: Psychology Press, 1906; reprint 1988), p. 214.

Nizām ul-Mulk, who probably had access to a book on Mazdak (*Mazdak-nāmag*),[56] provided lessons from history for the ruler of his time, teaching how to deal with heresies and adversaries of the Seljuk state.[57] This was followed by a small work by the Iranist Otto G. von Wesendonk, who was one of the first scholars to see the Mazdakite movement as a revolution from above, rather than a mass revolt.[58] But among Persian circles in Iran Mazdak was also a figure of interest because of two works. The first, perhaps the first academic study of Mazdak, titled 'Bolshevism in Ancient Iran', was written by Mohammad-Ali Jamalzadeh in 1920.[59] Obviously, the Bolshevik Revolution in Russia in 1917 had made its impact on Iran and Iranians, although Jamalzadeh was writing in Berlin, a place equally impacted by Vladimir Lenin and Russia.

However, it was Arthur Christensen's short book on the reign of Kawād I (1925) that popularized the notion that Mazdak, the Zoroastrian priest of the late fifth to early sixth centuries, had been a 'communist'.[60] The book was translated from French into Persian in the late 1920s, but with the coup of Mohammad Reza Shah in 1921 and his coronation in 1925, the anti-leftist sentiment of the government did not even allow the book to have its title printed in Persian and, although it has been continuously republished in Iran ever since, the term 'communism' has been deleted from its title.[61] One may suggest that Christensen himself, belonging to a middle-class family in Denmark and working as a teacher and journalist, was keenly interested in class politics and so became an early scholar of Iran in order to research such issues.[62]

The peasant revolt of antiquity had left its mark on European orientalists, as they were also seeing similar revolts in their own time.[63] Thus the interest in Mazdak became intense, especially after the Russian Revolution. The famous Russian orientalist Vasilii Barthold had written his first piece in St

56 Important details are provided on Mazdak which could only have come from the now lost text of Mazdak-nāmag. See Nizām ul-Mulk, *Siyar al-mulūk*, ed. M. Este'lamī (Tehran: Negār Publishers, 2011), pp. 257–73.

57 S. J. Tabatabai, *The History of Iranian Political Thought* (Tehran: Mēnu-ye Kherad Publisher, 2015), p. 172.

58 O. G. von Wesendonk, 'Die Mazdakiten. Eine kommunistisch-religiöse Bewegung im Sassanidenreich', *Der Neue Orient* 6 (1919), pp. 35–41.

59 M.-A. Jamalzadeh, 'Bolševism dar Irān-e qadim', *Kāveh* 38 (1920), pp. 5–10.

60 A. Christensen, *Le règne du roi Kawadh I et le communisme mazdakite* (Copenhagen: Host & Son, 1925).

61 A. Birshak, 'Preface', in *The Reign of Qobad and the Appearance of Mazdak* (Tehran: Tahūrī, 1995), pp. 7–8.

62 J. Asmussen, 'Christensen, Arthur Emanuel', in Yarshater (ed.), *Encyclopaedia Iranica*, vol. v, Part 5 (1991), pp. 521–3.

63 H. Yilmaz, *National Identities in Soviet Historiography: The Rise of Nations under Stalin* (London and New York: Routledge, 2015), p. 39.

Petersburg on social movements in Iran,[64] and would make an important contribution on Mazdak for the *Great Soviet Encyclopedia*.[65] Three other scholars from the communist sphere must be mentioned, as they had a significant impact on the historiography of Mazdak as an alleged socialist. The first is Nina Viktorovna Pigulevskaia, whose several works contributed to the study of late antique Iranian society and economy,[66] and more specifically that of Mazdak.[67] Ilia Pavlovich Petrushevskii also contributed significantly to the social history of Iran, Mazdak, and early Islam.[68] Otakar Klíma was a Czech scholar who wrote two major books on Mazdak, presenting him not just as a revolutionary who brought social change, but also as the subject of *damnatio memoriae* in the Sasanian historiographical tradition.[69] The works of these three authors were also translated into Persian, which engendered a political movement during the Pahlavi regime (1925–79) based around Mazdak and his name. In the minds of the intellectuals of the time, Mazdak appeared as a socialist whose aspirations for Iran in late antiquity had been the same as those of the contemporary left. Even in Algeria, Mazdak was considered a revolutionary.[70] Hence, Mazdak became known as a socialist or communist among the Iranian intelligentsia, and his stories could be used

---

64 All of the works of Soviet bloc scholarship on Mazdak that follow have been gathered by Ognibene and Gariboldi, *Conflitti sociali e movimenti politico-religiosi*; and V. Barthold, 'K istorii krestianskikh dvzhenii v Persii' [On the History of Peasant Movements in Persia], in *Iz dalekogo i blizkogo proshlogo. Sbornik etiudokh iz vseobshchei istorii v chest 50-letiia nauchnoi zhizni* [In the Distant and Near Past: Collection of Sketches from World History in Honour of the Fiftieth Anniversary of Scientific Life] (Petrograd and Moscow: N. I. Kareea Moskava, 1923), pp. 54–62.

65 V. Barthold, 'K voprosu o feodalizme v Irane' [On the Issue of Feudalism in Iran], *Novyi Vostok* [New East] 28 (1930), pp. 108–16.

66 N. V. Pigulevskaia, 'K voprosu o podatnoi reforme Chosroia Anushirvana' [On the Issue of Khosroy Anushirvan's Tax Reform], *Vestnik Drevnei Istorii* [Herald of Ancient History] 1 (1937), pp. 143–54.

67 N. V. Pigulevskaia, 'Mazdakitskoe dvizhenie' [The Mazdakite Movement], *Izvestiia Akademii Nauk SSSR, seriia istorii i filosofii* [News of the USSR Academy of Sciences, History and Philosophy Series] 4 (1944), pp. 171–81; N. V. Pigulevskaia, 'Ideia ravenstva v uchenii mazdakitov' [The Idea of Equality in Mazdakite Teachings], in *Iz istorii sotsial'no-politicheskikh idei. Sbornik statei k semidesiatiletiiu akademika V* [From the History of Socio-Political Ideas: A Collection of Articles Dedicated to the Seventieth Anniversary of Academician V] (Moscow: Volgina, 1955), pp. 97–101.

68 I. P. Petrushevskii, 'K istorii mazdakitov v epokhu gospodstva islama' [From the History of the Mazdakites in the Era of Islamic Domination], *Narody Afriki i Azii* [The Peoples of Africa and Asia] 5 (1970), pp. 71–81.

69 O. Klíma, *Mazdak. Geschichte einer sozialen Bewegung im sassanidischen Persien* (Prague: Československá Akademie Věd, 1957), and more importantly his *Beiträge zur Geschichte des Mazdakismus* (Prague: Československá Akademie Věd, 1977).

70 D. Ide, 'Who's Afraid of Mazdak? Prophetic Egalitarianism, Islamism, and Socialism', *Hampton Institute* (2016), www.hamptonthink.org/read/whos-afraid-of-mazdak-prophetic-egalitarianism-islamism-and-socialism.

for their own struggle. It is interesting that the debates around social movements and peasants' rights in Iran in the 1960s coincided with Mohammad Reza Shah's White Revolution, which was an attempt to break the power of the large land-owners and redistribute land to the landless *dehghāns*, a term which by now meant not a member of the landed gentry but a landless peasant. The White Revolution from the top was meant to annul any chances of a Red Revolution from below[71] – the king himself could break the power of the land-owning elite in Iran. Needless to say, the endeavour was a failure, and the landless peasants and the poor poured into shanty towns around the major cities. In 1979 they staged another revolution, around another religious cleric.

Conclusion

How should we contextualize Mazdak and his beliefs? What really happened in late antique Iran?[72] Was Mazdak a revolutionary priest who started a social movement under the guise of a religious interpretation of the *Avesta*, or did the king use this priest to force through reforms in the name of Zoroastrianism?[73] Was Mazdak a powerful confidant, what is known in Middle Persian as a counsellor (*andarzgar*), who manipulated King Kawād I so that the poor and downtrodden could have their way? Or was it simply a religious–scholastic reinterpretation of laws relating to marriage and property that brought a proto-socialist movement to the fore, which then stayed alive in various religious movements during the Islamic period?[74]

No doubt any movement in late antiquity tended to take place against a religious background.[75] Hence, Mazdak should be seen as someone whose religious power allowed for his dictums to be taken seriously by the masses, as well as by the king. Otherwise, the Mazdakite movement would not have gathered such force, nor would it have had a lasting effect on Iranian and Near Eastern society. The question is whether his ideas were inspired by

71 E. Abrahamian, *A History of Modern Iran* (Cambridge: Cambridge University Press, 2018), p. 134.
72 All the possible answers have been posited by the excellent chapter by G. Gnoli, 'Nuovi studi sul Mazdakismo', in Accademia Nazionale dei Lincei (ed.), *La Persia e Bisanzio. Atti dei convegni Lincei 201* (Rome: Accademia Nazionale dei Lincei, 2004), pp. 439–56.
73 Daryaee, *Sasanian Persia*, p. 29.
74 G. H. Sadighi, *Les mouvements religieux iraniens au IIe et au IIIe siècle de l'hégire* (Paris: Les Presses Modernes, 1938); Crone, 'Kavād's heresy and Mazdak's revolt'.
75 Z. Rubin, 'Mass Movements in Late Antiquity', in I. Malkin and Z. Rubinsohn (eds.), *Leaders and Masses in the Roman World: Studies in Honor of Zvi Yavetz* (Mnemosyne supplement 139) (Leiden and Boston: Brill, 1995), pp. 187–91.

gnostic and earlier religious ideas of a man by the same name,[76] or was this Mazdak's new interpretation (zand) of Zoroastrian law? All of these are real possibilities. However, after a century of scholarship, because of the nature of primary sources on the Sasanian period, specifically their being a product of post-Sasanian periods, it is still difficult to sift fact from fiction and come to a decisive conclusion. Since most sources are mainly compilations from a later period, they tend to present a confusing timeline and details.

But what can be said with some certainty is that, in the aftermath of the Mazdakite movement, there were robust economic and military reforms, which in turn allowed for some social reform. These reforms in turn reduced the societal pressures that had brought danger to the well-being of the Sasanian state. The reforms brought new societal allies for the Sasanian Empire, not simply the nobility who at one time considered themselves the upper crust of Ērānšahr, but also smaller land-owners (dehqāns) and tribal groups who entered the military and brought new modes of state solidarity. The reforms also brought a more equitable form of taxation[77] and, most importantly for the Sasanian Empire, a firm grasp on its territory as a centralized state of late antiquity. Mazdak may have become a story of the past, but his influence allowed for major changes, and the man in the flesh became a case study for statecraft in Medieval Persian Fürstenspiegel.

Further Reading

de Blois, François, 'A New Look at Mazdak', in Teresa Bernheimer and Adam Silverstein (eds.), Late Antiquity: Eastern Perspectives (Exeter: E. J. W. Gibb Memorial Trust, 2012), pp. 13–24.

Crone, Patricia, 'Zoroastrian communism', Comparative Studies in Society and History 36, 3 (July 1994), pp. 447–62.

Daryaee, Touraj, Sasanian Persia: The Rise and Fall of an Empire (London: I. B. Tauris, 2013).

Shaki, Mansour, 'The social doctrine of Mazdak in the light of Middle Persian evidence', Archív Orientální 46, 4 (1978), pp. 289–306.

Yarshater, Ehsan, 'Mazdakism', in The Cambridge History of Iran, vol. III, The Seleucid, Parthian and Sasanian Periods, Part 2 (Cambridge: Cambridge University Press, 1983), pp. 991–1024.

---

76 F. de Blois, 'Mazdak the Ancient and Mazdak the Last: further remarks on the history and religious typology of Mazdakism', Studia Iranica 53 (2015), pp. 141–53.

77 Gariboldi, Il regno di Xusraw, pp. 34–5.

2

Egalitarianism in Islamic Thought and Praxis

ASMA AFSARUDDIN

Egalitarianism is a high ideal within Islamic thought. Apart from monotheism, the proclamation of the equality of all human beings in the eyes of God is understood to be one of the most distinctive features of Islam, which strikingly sets it apart from pre-Islamic (Jāhilī) Arab society. Extant sources inform us that Arabs in the pre-Islamic period recognized many cleavages in their society based on tribal membership, kinship, and gender. The pagan inhabitants of Mecca, where Islam began, took great exception to the idea of egalitarianism, in addition to monotheism, espoused by Muḥammad ibn ʿAbd Allāh, the prophet of Islam. Such an idea ran counter to the values that undergirded pre-Islamic society.

To assess the revolutionary nature of the egalitarianism that informed early Islam, we need to turn our attention first to its central text, the Qurʾān, divinely revealed in Arabic to the Prophet Muḥammad, as Muslims believe, in the seventh century of the Common Era.[1] A number of verses in this sacred text refer to the equality of all human beings in the eyes of God, transcending notions of tribal belonging, blood relationships, race, ethnicity, and gender.

In addition to the Qurʾān, the concept of egalitarianism can be exhumed from the *ḥadīth* literature, which contains the sayings of Muḥammad that are not regarded as part of the divine revelations recorded in the Qurʾān. The biographical literature (*sīra*) that documents the life of the Prophet can also be fruitfully mined to retrieve accounts of historical events and references to specific documents that assert the importance of egalitarianism as a socio-organizational principle.

Next, historical chronicles and legal texts delineate for us how egalitarianism was practised on the ground in the early centuries but, also, as time went on, how this principle became progressively compromised in specific

---

1 In this chapter, all dates refer to the Common Era, and all non-English terms are from Arabic unless otherwise noted.

historical and political circumstances. In the legal domain in particular, early egalitarian practices were subjected to scrutiny by certain jurists who would find them to be inimical to their more exclusivist concerns.

And, finally, when we move into the modern period, we find that egalitarianism re-emerges as a powerful, emotive topic in many Muslim-majority societies. In this period, modernist reform-minded Muslim scholars began to return to the Qur'ān in order to launch critiques against discrimination based particularly on gender and religious affiliation, and to argue that such forms of discrimination were antithetical to the egalitarian and pluralist ethos of the Qur'ān. This final section will focus briefly on these modernist critiques and reveal how egalitarianism remains a dynamic and contested concept in the Muslim-majority world to this day.

The Qur'ān and Its Exegesis

Our focus on egalitarianism within the Qur'ān begins with a discussion of Qur'ān 17:70 that refers to the intrinsic dignity/honour (karāma) of 'the children of Adam'. The verse states: 'And We have certainly honoured the children of Adam and carried them on land and sea and provided for them of the good things and clearly preferred them over much of what We have created.'[2]

One of the earliest Muslim scholars who comments on this verse is the eighth-century exegete Muqātil ibn Sulaymān (d. 767), whose life straddled the late Umayyad and early Abbasid periods.[3] Muqātil explains that in this verse the divine author states that he had preferred humans over other beings, except for the angels (who are understood to be perfectly formed, unlike humans). This divine preference for humans over all other earthly beings is reflected in their unique physique and their ability to travel freely on land in order to seek the bounties of God.[4] The celebrated late ninth-century exegete Muḥammad ibn Jarīr al-Ṭabarī (d. 923) similarly emphasizes the unique nature of human beings and the unique privileges they have been granted on earth vis-à-vis other earthly creatures.[5] Fakhr al-Dīn al-Rāzī (d. 1210) in the late twelfth century emphasizes that humans are superior to

---

2 Translations of the Qur'ān are mine.
3 The Umayyad period lasted from 661 to 750 and the Abbasid period from 750 to 1258.
4 Muqātil b. Sulaymān, Tafsīr [Commentary], ed. 'Abd Allāh Maḥmūd Shiḥāta (Beirut: Mu'assasat al-ta'rīkh al-'arabī, 2002), vol. II, pp. 541–2.
5 Muḥammad b. Jarīr al-Ṭabarī, Tafsīr al-Ṭabarī [Commentary of al-Ṭabarī] (Beirut: Dār al-kutub al-'ilmiyya, 1997), vol. VIII, p. 115.

animals on account of their intellectual abilities, which allow them to comprehend reality as it is. This intellectual or rational ability allows them to gain knowledge of God and represents a sacred essence within all human beings that sets them apart from plants and animals. By virtue of their intellect, only humans are able to acquire true knowledge and noble virtues.[6]

It is evident from this cursory sampling of exegeses of Qur'ān 17:70 that pre-modern Qur'ān commentators in general recognized that all human beings enjoyed physical, moral, and intellectual superiority over all other creatures by virtue of being human. This observation did not, however, prompt them to reflect on the further consequences of this ontological superiority for humans themselves – in other words, they did not go on to assert that this meant that women were equal to men and that non-Muslims were equal to Muslims in all respects *in this world*. In all fairness, such a conceptualization of egalitarianism could not have been part of the medieval imaginary – while all human beings were understood to be created equal, their fundamental equality was understood to be circumscribed by differential physical, moral, spiritual, and intellectual endowments. In other words, they were equal but different. This is a point that becomes evident in my discussion below.

Taqwá and Earthly Human Difference

While all humans are ontologically equal, the Qur'ān also recognizes differences among human beings mainly on the basis of personal piety and righteousness, called taqwá in Arabic. Taqwá, according to the prominent modern scholar of Islam Fazlur Rahman, can also be translated as 'God-consciousness', referring to the believer's constant awareness of God and the desire to please him through faith and righteous actions.[7] Several verses in the Qur'ān emphasize the importance of this concept. The Qur'ān states in several places that one cannot be a true believer unless one possesses taqwá (Qur'ān 5:57, 5:88, 49:13, and others). In other words, it is not enough to simply make a public proclamation of faith and carry out basic religious duties without this inner God-consciousness. Taqwá in fact became the building block for the supra-national Muslim community called umma in

---

6 F. al-Dīn al-Rāzī, *al-Tafsīr al-kabīr* [The Large Commentary] (Beirut: Dār iḥyā' at-turāth al-'arabī, 1999), vol. VII, pp. 372–5.

7 F. Rahman, *Major Themes in the Qur'an*, 2nd edn (Minneapolis: Bibliotheca Islamica, 1989), p. 28.

Arabic and replaces the pre-Islamic notion of tribal solidarity (*aṣabiyya*) as the basis of social belonging.[8]

One should realize that this notion of communal membership based on the principle of personal piety was highly revolutionary in seventh-century Arabia and subversive of many of its cherished values at the time. Pre-Islamic Arabian society was organized on the basis of tribal affiliation. The concepts of *nasab* ('lineal descent' or 'kinship') and *ḥasab* ('inherited merit') determined the individual's status in such a tribal society. *Ḥasab* in particular referred not to the individual's personal accomplishments but to the sum total of achievements attributed to one's tribal ancestors. The individual member of the tribe was regarded as serving as a repository of these collective accomplishments.[9] Membership in a larger, more illustrious tribe therefore granted the individual higher status in society; those belonging to less powerful tribes had a correspondingly lower standing in society. The concepts of *nasab* and *ḥasab* clearly ran counter to the Qur'ānic emphasis on personal piety and deeds, on the sole basis of which the individual accrues merit (*al-faḍl*). However, these concepts would survive well into the Islamic period; Islamic ideals of egalitarianism and pre-Islamic notions of hierarchical privilege would continue to remain at loggerheads for most of Islamic history.

Physical differences among human beings on the basis of skin colour, race, ethnicity, and gender have no bearing on the ontological equality of humans in the Qur'ān. Instead, such physical differences are meant to be embraced as part of the divine design that adds to the richness of human life. Within the earthly community of human beings who are created religiously equal before the Divine Being, linguistic, ethnic, and cultural differences are to be understood as positive signs of God's benevolence within the Qur'ān. 'And of His signs', the Qur'ān says, 'is the creation of the heavens and the earth and the diversity of your tongues and colours. Surely there are signs in this for the learned' (30:22).

In another significant verse (Qur'ān 49:13), God addresses humans, 'O humankind, surely We have created you from a male and a female, and made you peoples and tribes that you may know one another [*li-taʿārafū*]. The most noble in the sight of God is the most pious among you.' According to this verse, variegated identities stemming from ethnic and tribal affiliations

---

8 F. Rahman, 'Some key ethical concepts of the Qur'ān', *Journal of Religious Ethics* 11 (1983), pp. 177–85.
9 R. P. Mottahedeh, *Loyalty and Leadership in an Early Islamic Society* (Princeton: Princeton University Press, 1980), pp. 98–104.

should prompt humans to learn about one another out of a healthy respect for and curiosity about difference. In the ideal conception, such knowledge should be the basis for affirming the common humanity of diverse peoples, and not to generate conflict. The verse further reminds the reader that individuals find esteem before God only on the basis of piety.

Our ninth-century exegete al-Ṭabarī extrapolates from this verse a command to people to get to know one another so that they may discover their bonds of kinship. He warns that knowledge of such kinship is not meant to induce any sense of superiority but rather 'to bring you closer to God, for indeed only the most pious among you is the most honourable'.[10] Al-Ṭabarī, like many other pre-modern exegetes, was able to discern the egalitarianism embedded in this verse but unable to transcend the parochialism of his time, which restricted knowledge of others to one's extended family and place of residence. Some modern Muslim exegetes of the Qur'ān read into this verse a more sweeping command for humans to proactively get to know one another, regardless of their nationality, race, and so forth – a perspective that can only be imagined in our twenty-first-century globalizing world.[11]

Egalitarianism in the Ḥadīth Literature

There are a number of ḥadīths – reports containing the sayings of the Prophet – which assert the equality of all human beings. Such sayings often directly contradicted the sentiments current among pre-Islamic Arabs by emphasizing that there is no superiority inherent in being an Arab, in speaking the Arabic language, or in belonging to a powerful tribe like the Quraysh, to which Muḥammad himself belonged. One such notable report states:

> O people! Arabic is not a father or grandfather but rather a spoken tongue. Whoever speaks in it is an Arab except that [all of] you are the children of Adam and Adam is of dust. By God, an Abyssinian enslaved man who obeys God is better than a Qurayshi chieftain who disobeys God. Indeed the most honourable among you is the most righteous among you.[12]

This ḥadīth hits hard at the conceit of the pre-Islamic Arabs that they were superior to non-Arabs by virtue of birth and ethnicity and reminds the reader

---

10 Al-Ṭabarī, Tafsīr, vol. XI, p. 398.

11 See my own discussion of this in A. Afsaruddin, 'Celebrating pluralism and dialogue: Qur'anic perspectives', Journal of Ecumenical Studies 42 (2007), pp. 389–406.

12 Al-Qummī, Tafsīr [Commentary] (Beirut: Dār al-surūr, 1991), vol. II, p. 94.

instead of the theological conception of the common humble origins of human beings from dust. Most subversively, the last part of the ḥadīth contains a sharp reprimand to the pagan Meccans, in particular, who recognized leadership as being based on kinship and tribal affiliation. The ḥadīth affirms instead that a leader who belongs to the prestigious tribe of Quraysh has no automatic advantage over anyone else; any superior qualification that one may have for public office is based squarely on the righteousness and personal integrity of the individual concerned, even if he (or she) were from a lowly social status and an enslaved person. The last sentence echoes the content of Qur'ān 49:13 which similarly stresses the link between righteous conduct and honour.

Another well-known saying of the Prophet that unambiguously asserts the equality of all human beings, regardless of their race, tribal affiliation, and social status, dates from the last year of his life (632 CE). In this year, on his return trip from the pilgrimage to the Kaaba, Muḥammad gave a farewell address that has justly become famous. A significant segment of this sermon states:

> O humankind! Your Lord is one, your parents [Adam and Eve] are one; there is no superiority of an Arab over a non-Arab, or of a non-Arab over an Arab, and no superiority of a white person over a black person or of a black person over a white person, except on the basis of personal piety and God-consciousness [*taqwá*].[13]

This portion of the sermon is frequently quoted in Islamic sources to establish the normativity of the principle of egalitarianism, which ideally recognizes no distinction between Arab and non-Arab or among humans based on skin colour.

These sayings of Muḥammad must be regarded as genuinely archaic since they reflect the radically egalitarian élan of the Qur'ān from the seventh century. But as time went by, and we arrive at the Umayyad period (661–750), the egalitarianism of the time of Muḥammad and his four righteous successors (see further below) began to be progressively compromised, although never fully eliminated. We find traces of these changes in the historical and literary sources of the later period, which document that this early emphasis on egalitarianism began to erode in subsequent centuries. This erosion is to be attributed primarily to the external influences seeping in from more hierarchical societies like the Persian and Byzantine ones by the Abbasid period. During and after the translation movement that began in Baghdad

---

13 Ibn Hishām, *al-Sīra al-Nabawiyya* [Biography of the Prophet], ed. Suhayl Zakkār (Beirut: Dār al-fikr, 1992), vol. II, pp. 1023–4.

under the Abbasid caliphs in the ninth century, ancient Greek thought, especially that of Plato and Aristotle, became available to learned Muslim elites.[14] Persian literary works, particularly from the Mirror for Princes genre, when translated into Arabic, became very popular in administrative circles and highly influential in the way they affected political thought and notions of social belonging.[15] In a nutshell, both these foreign sources of cultural influence introduced hierarchization of society, especially along occupational lines. In order of descending importance, four main occupations based on (1) rulership, (2) craftsmanship, (3) commerce, and (4) agriculture came to be recognized. The cumulative effects of these progressive societal transformations resulted in the creation of a learned Muslim elite, who, like their counterparts in other pre-industrial societies, shared many of the principles underlying the Platonic view: these principles include the importance of contributing one's talents and labour to the larger community, the significance of heredity, a conservative social attitude, the association of intellectual and moral qualities with certain professions, and the ideal of social harmony based on a division of labour.[16]

From the Abbasid period on, these hierarchical ideas took deep root within Muslim societies and fundamentally undermined the egalitarianism that was a striking feature of the early Muslim community.

Historical Documents, Institutions, and Movements

An examination of early historical documents, institutions, and socio-political movements often reveals the centrality of the principle of egalitarianism in the formative period of Islam and its contestation in many quarters. The most prominent of these documents, institutions, and movements are described here.

The Constitution of Medina

The earliest political document we have testifying to the application of the principle of egalitarianism is what is commonly called in English the 'Constitution of Medina' (in Arabic Ṣaḥīfat al-Madīna). This term refers to

14 D. Gutas, *Greek Thought, Arabic Culture: The Graeco-Arabic Translation Movement in Baghdad and Early 'Abbasid Society (2nd–4th/5th–10th c.)* (New York: Routledge, 1998), pp. 107–41.

15 The Mirror for Princes was an Islamic literary genre that offered pragmatic advice and guidance to rulers on how to govern effectively. This genre can be compared to the European *Fürstenspiegel* that similarly offered advice to rulers.

16 L. Marlow, *Hierarchy and Egalitarianism in Islamic Thought* (Cambridge: Cambridge University Press, 1997), p. 176.

the document drawn up by Muḥammad after his famous migration to Medina from Mecca in 622 CE, an epochal event known in Islamic history as the *hijra*. This document is particularly noteworthy because of its unique focus – certainly by pre-modern standards – on the equal status of all members of Medinan society at that time, regardless of tribal, ethnic, and religious affiliation. These members included the *Muhājirūn* (migrant Muslims from Mecca), the *Anṣār* (lit. 'helpers'; namely, the Medinan Muslims), and the various Jewish tribes of Medina. All these groups together were understood in the Constitution to constitute a 'single community' (*umma wāhida*).[17] In recent times, there has been renewed attention paid to this highly important document by a number of modern Muslims as an early testament to the pluralist connotations of the concept of *umma*, or the transnational, global Muslim community – a point to which I shall return.

The Office of the Caliph

After the Prophet's death, four men successively became the ruler of the Muslim polity based in Medina and ruled between 632 and 661. These men – Abū Bakr, 'Umar, Uthmān, and 'Alī – are collectively known as the 'Rightly Guided Caliphs' (in Arabic, *al-Khulafā' al-Rāshidūn*) in broad recognition of their moral excellence, their record of service to Islam, and their upholding of key Islamic ideals and practices, especially egalitarianism and consultative governance (*shūrá*).[18]

Abū Bakr, the first caliph, was not regarded as the obvious candidate to assume leadership of the Muslim community after the Prophet's death. According to the majority of Muslims, the Prophet had left no specific instructions for the selection of his successor nor did he so designate any specific Companion, a term used for a close associate of Muḥammad. This has become the axiomatic position of the Sunnīs (*Ahl al-sunna*; broadly glossed as 'people who adhere to the custom of the Prophet'), who today comprise about 85 per cent of the world's approximately 1.8 billion Muslims. The rest of the Muslims belong to the Shī'a (short for *shī'at 'Alī*, 'the partisans of 'Alī'), who came to subscribe to the position that Muḥammad had designated 'Alī ibn Abī Ṭālib (d. 661 CE), his cousin and son-in-law, to be his immediate successor. This difference of view over the issue of succession

---

17 The articles of this document have been preserved in Ibn Hishām, *Sīra*, vol. I, pp. 351–4. For the full text of the Constitution in English translation, see M. Watt, *Muhammad at Medina* (Oxford: Oxford University Press, 1956), pp. 221–5.

18 For an account of their collective reign, see A. Afsaruddin, *The First Muslims: History and Memory* (Oxford: Oneworld Publications, 2008), pp. 19–58.

became the primary distinction between the two principal branches of Islam. The initial political disagreement would in the course of time also acquire theological overtones.

It is part of received wisdom to maintain that 'Alī's earliest supporters pressed his claim to the caliphate by emphasizing his blood kinship with the Prophet and his prior designation as Muḥammad's successor. However, a careful scrutiny of early sources reveals that, contrary to what became the standard position of the Shī'a in the later period, the early supporters of 'Alī, in tandem with the early supporters of Abū Bakr, stressed the greater moral excellence of 'Alī to establish his superior qualifications for the office of the caliph. An emphasis on kinship at this early stage would, after all, have flown in the face of the Qur'ānic espousal of individual merit and piety in establishing a person's moral and social standing and would have been rightly perceived as a throwback to pre-Islamic values. 'To humans belong only what they themselves strive for', declares the Qur'ān (53:39).[19]

Significantly, some early Shī'ī traditions preserve for us the tension between the religious egalitarianism advocated by the Qur'ān and the notion of inherited merit (hasab) on account of kinship with the Prophet. One early report from the eighth Shī'ī imam (religious leader) 'Alī al-Riḍà (d. 818) states that the Prophet counselled his associates, 'Come to me with your individual works and not with your kinships or collective [tribal] accomplishments', in exegesis of the Qur'ānic verse (23:101), 'When the trumpet is blown, there will be no kinships and you will not ask one another.'[20]

The proto-Shī'a appear to have adhered to such Qur'ān-based egalitarian views through the early Umayyad period. Kinship became the cornerstone of Shī'ī doctrine starting sometime in the late seventh century, since the Umayyads had based their own political legitimacy on kinship to the Prophet. In order to establish the legitimacy of their political and religious authority, the supporters of 'Alī would similarly forcefully highlight their kinship to the Prophet. Eventually this claim would become incorporated into fundamental Shī'ī doctrine, standing in sharp contrast to the egalitarianism that continued to be espoused, at least in principle, by Sunnī political thinkers.[21]

19 A. Afsaruddin, *Excellence and Precedence: Medieval Islamic Discourse on Legitimate Leadership* (Leiden: Brill, 2002), pp. 146–83.
20 Muḥammad Bāqir al-Majlisī, *Biḥār al-anwār* [Seas of Lights] (Tehran: al-Islāmiyya, 1956–83), vol. VII, pp. 241–2.
21 Afsaruddin, *Excellence and Precedence*, pp. 146–96.

Khārijism

Egalitarianism was a prime concern of other groups from the first four centuries of Islam in particular. An early faction called the Khārijites came into being after the death of the Prophet during the caliphate of ʿAlī b. Abī Ṭālib and made egalitarianism its clarion call. They notably espoused the position that any Muslim from any tribe could become the caliph (in Arabic *khalīfa*, the title for the leader of the community). This position was in sharp contrast to what became the classical Islamic view that only men who descended from Muḥammad's tribe of Quraysh could legitimately become the caliph. The radical egalitarianism of the Khārijites led them to believe that property should be held communally; one faction among them also held that women could become caliphs.[22] Some of the poetry written by some Khārijites survives to this day and conveys to us the tenor of their strongly held beliefs. For example, the Khārijite poet ʿAmr ibn Dhukayna warned the Umayyad caliph ʿUmar ibn ʿAbd al-ʿAzīz (d. 682) against emphasizing kinship over personal piety since that was fundamentally against Islamic tenets.[23]

The Abbasid Uprising

The Abbasid revolt against the Umayyads affords us another opportunity to assess the importance of the concept of egalitarianism in the self- and communal identities of pre-modern Muslims. According to our historical sources, the Umayyad dynasty (r. 661–750) was notorious for reverting to the pre-Islamic values of tribalism and instigating a specific policy of showing favouritism towards Arabs over non-Arabs, even when these non-Arabs were Muslims. A sense of collective grievance against such discriminatory policies led to the Abbasid revolution, which ended the Umayyad dynasty in 750 CE and ushered in a more cosmopolitan society in which non-Arabs, particularly Persians (referred to as *mawālī* in Arabic, meaning 'clients' of Arab tribes), enjoyed greater rights.

---

22 They acquire their Arabic name *al-Khawārij* ('those who go out') because they seceded from ʿAlī's army during the battle of Ṣiffīn in 628, which was fought against Muʿāwiya, the governor of Syria at the time. Despite their egalitarianism, the Khārijites were extremely intolerant of other Muslims who did not subscribe to some of their controversial positions.

23 See J. Bellamy, 'The Impact of Islam on Early Arabic Poetry', in A. T. Welch and P. Cachia (eds.), *Islam: Past Influence and Present Challenge* (Albany: State University of New York Press, 1977), pp. 141–67.

The Shu'ūbiyya

Emboldened by the Abbasid victory, certain Persian Muslims would subsequently initiate a cultural movement known as the Shu'ūbiyya ('the populist movement') in which they pushed back against Arabization. Using Islamic arguments, they asserted their equality with Arab Muslims, while simultaneously stressing the superiority of their ancient civilization over that of the Arabs.[24] The Shu'ūbiyya movement essentially disappeared after the twelfth century, as non-Arabs became increasingly assimilated into the predominant Arab culture in the Islamic heartlands, while Arabs became Persianized in Iran. The appearance of the Shu'ūbiyya in the ninth century, however, provides valuable testimony to the emotive appeal of the Islamic ideal of egalitarianism that could be invoked in different places and times to resist social inequalities and political injustices, real and perceived.

Economic Equity and Related Issues

As is well known, one of the five pillars of Islam is zakāt, an obligatory alms or poor tax that must be paid by adult Muslims who meet a certain economic threshold. This poor tax was assessed at 2.5 per cent of an adult Muslim's surplus wealth. In the early history of Islam, this tax was paid directly to the government in Medina and, afterwards, as Islamic realms expanded, to state officials in the various provinces. The amount can also be disbursed privately as alms to the poor and destitute in general (particularly widows, orphans, and travellers in distress), to ransom prisoners of war, or to aid impoverished students and others in need of financial support. A number of Qur'ānic verses exhort Muslims to give both the required zakāt and voluntary alms (known as ṣadaqa), as do many ḥadīths, to help the poor and the unfortunate; such religious texts promise that prodigious acts of charity wipe out sins and earn heavenly reward for the giver. The Qur'ān forbids the hoarding of money and speaks harshly of those who refuse to share their wealth with the less fortunate (Qur'ān 9:34; 57:20).

The Qur'ān's concern for the equitable distribution of wealth does not translate, however, into any explicit prohibition against private ownership of property. It encourages humans to travel and engage in trade and commerce to earn their livelihood (Qur'ān 2:164; 4:29; 30:46). Certain ethical business

---

24 R. P. Mottahedeh, 'The Shu'ubiyah controversy and the social history of early Islamic Iran', *International Journal of Middle East Studies* 7 (1976), pp. 161–82; Marlow, *Hierarchy*, pp. 104–8.

practices are instituted, however, to regulate trade and commerce; the Qur'ān forbids using false weights in measuring goods and cheating people of their belongings (Qur'ān 26:181–3), and warns against charging exorbitant rates on loans or usury (*riba*; Qur'ān 2:275–81; 30:39; 4:161). A *ḥadīth* prohibits fixing prices, which has been interpreted as supporting free markets. Proceeding from these ethical principles and stipulations, Islamic law came to forbid the earning of excessive profit from commercial pursuits and to prohibit 'uncertainty' and 'deception' (*gharar*) in contracts of sale by insisting that all conditions be clearly laid out in such transactions. The office of the market inspector (*muḥtasib*) was created in the first century of Islam to allow for the oversight of business transactions and to ensure that such regulations were enforced in the marketplace.

In support of free markets, the fourteenth-century social historian and theorist Ibn Khaldun (d. 1406) noted that the forces of supply and demand determine the prices of goods.[25] Rather anomalously, the mystic–revolutionary Sheikh Bedreddin of the Ottoman period called for the communal ownership of property as part of his social reform agenda; such ideas did not gain traction after his death in 1420. In the twentieth century, the Iranian revolutionary thinker Ali Shariati (d. 1977), influenced by Marxist ideas, also wanted to dissolve private ownership of property, which he considered to be against Islamic principles of economic equity and non-exploitation of the common people. Other twentieth-century Muslim thinkers and revolutionaries, such as Abu al-Ala al-Mawdudi (d. 1979) and Sayyid Qutb (d. 1966), stressed that 'Islamic economics' (*al-iqtiṣād al-islāmī*) charts a middle course between capitalism and socialism in its advocacy of free markets, equitable distribution of wealth, and proscription against unprincipled profiteering and therefore offers a superior alternative to both of these flawed financial systems. They also stressed the traditional Islamic ban against *riba*, which was interpreted by them to refer to extortionate usurious practices, as well as simple interest paid on loans and bank accounts. While the former is universally understood to be proscribed, there is no consensus among Muslim scholars today on whether the latter should be included under *riba*. Conservative Muslim economists eschew all forms of interest as instances of *riba* and have helped to create 'Islamic banking' systems that charge no interest on loans as well as 'Islamic investment companies' that avoid investing in prohibited substances, such as alcohol and drugs.

---

25 Ibn Khaldun, *The Muqaddimah*, trans. Franz Rosenthal (London: Routledge and Kegan Paul, 1967), vol. II, pp. 276–8.

Slavery and Its Challenge to Egalitarianism

The existence of slavery (*riqq*) in the pre-modern Islamic world represents a major challenge to the narrative on egalitarianism. The Qur'ān recognizes the existence of enslaved persons in the seventh century and strongly urges righteous believers to manumit them as an act of charity (Qur'ān 9:60). Enslaved persons who embraced Islam were considered to be the spiritual equals of free-born Muslims, famously exemplified by the enslaved Ethiopian Bilāl ibn Rabāḥ, who was appointed the first muezzin (public caller to prayer) in Islam by Muḥammad after his manumission. In contrast to chattel slavery in the Americas and Europe, slavery was largely not a racialized institution in the Islamic world. People who were taken captive and enslaved, mostly during wars, could be from Slavic, Turkish, African, Indian, and other ethnic backgrounds. Under Islamic law, enslaved persons had a measure of legal autonomy – for example, they could not be forcibly converted to Islam nor married off against their will. Free men are instructed by the Qur'ān (24:33) not to force their enslaved females into unwanted sexual relations. If an enslaved female gave birth to a child by her master, the child was born free and had the same legal rights as the child of a free-born wife. The master could no longer sell the mother and, upon his death, she was set free. If the master was from an elite background, the child born of an enslaved mother inherited his high social status and could aspire to high political positions. An influential dynasty of rulers – the Turkic Mamluks who ruled between 1250 and 1493 – were of slave origin, as their name indicates (*mamlūk* in Arabic means 'owned').

Since the Qur'ān had not banned slavery outright, it remained a legal, even morally acceptable, practice among Muslims in the pre-modern period. This perception began to change in the early modern period, when pro-abolition sentiment among Muslims began to surface, as such sentiments gained ground elsewhere in the world. The ownership of one human being by another as property was increasingly understood to be a morally reprehensible practice that could no longer be tolerated. The Qur'ān's and the Prophet's exhortation to manumit enslaved persons as a meritorious act of expiation for wrong-doing was cited as creating an urgent moral imperative to end slavery once and for all and thereby fulfil the sharī'ah's overall objective of ensuring justice for all. One of the earliest calls for the abolition of slavery was issued by the Imamate of Futa Toro in West Africa around 1787. Subsequently, the abolitionist movement gained momentum throughout the nineteenth century and led to the eventual outlawing of slavery in all Islamic lands by the second half of the twentieth century.[26]

Egalitarianism and Religious Minorities

Another area where the principle of egalitarianism faced a major challenge was in the area of Muslim–non-Muslim relations. Muslim jurists by the tenth century – when the major legal schools had been formed – came to recognize and enforce certain socio-legal differences between Muslim and non-Muslim inhabitants in Islamic realms. Some of their legal rulings may be understood to countermand several passages in the Qur'ān in which righteous Jews and Christians are deemed to be equal to righteous Muslims. The Qur'ān promises such righteous Jews and Christians (frequently referred to as 'People of the Book', meaning those who have a revealed scripture) their reward in the next world on a par with righteous Muslims (Qur'ān 2:62; 5:69). Furthermore, the Qur'ān recognizes righteous Jews and Christians as constituting moderate and upright communities (Qur'ān 5:66; 3:113–15), equivalent to the moderate or just Muslim community described in Qur'ān 2:143. In these verses, the Qur'ān indicates that, on the basis of a shared standard of righteousness, various religious communities can achieve spiritual and social parity in Muslim societies.[27]

However, this is not how many Muslim exegetes have interpreted these verses over time. A diachronic survey of key exegetical works from the pre-modern and modern periods reveals that a number of influential exegetes resorted to certain reading strategies by the third century of Islam (ninth century of the Common Era) that allowed them to undermine the ecumenical potential of these verses, chief among which was the invocation of the principle of supersessionism. Muslim supersessionists, who eventually formed the predominant school of thought, subscribed to the superiority of Islam over other revealed, mainly monotheistic religions (though not necessarily denying their validity).

---

26 For a recent comprehensive historical account of slavery in Islamic lands, see J. A. C. Brown, *Slavery and Islam* (London: Oneworld Academic, 2019).

27 See further A. Afsaruddin, 'The hermeneutics of inter-faith relations: retrieving moderation and pluralism as universal principles in Qur'anic exegeses', *Journal of Religious Ethics* 37 (2009), pp. 331–54; and A. Afsaruddin, 'The "Upright Community": Interpreting the Righteousness and Salvation of the People of the Book in the Qur'ān', in J. Meri (ed.), *Jewish–Muslim Relations in Past and Present: A Kaleidoscopic View* (Leiden and Boston: Brill, 2017), pp. 48–69.

This happened despite the fact that no explicit principle of supersession may be adduced from the Qur'ān, which instead refers to itself as confirming prior revelations. The first part of Qur'ān 5:48 states: 'And to you [O Muḥammad] we have sent down the Book [the Qur'ān] in truth confirming the Books [that is, prior revelations] which have come before it and as a protector over them.' However, most exegetes privileged a different verse – Qur'ān 3:85 – over Qur'ān 5:48, which states, 'Whoever desires another religion than Islam, it shall not be accepted of him; in the next world he shall be among the losers.' Here, 'Islam' may be understood as a verbal noun that refers to the submission of all righteous believers to God, a usage attested in the Qur'ān itself. This understanding would allow for an egalitarian relationship to be maintained at least among the followers of the monotheistic Abrahamic religions. Exegetes who subscribed to supersessionism, however, understood 'Islam' in a narrow, confessional sense so that Muslims would be considered superior to practitioners of other faiths.[28]

How to explain such interpretive proclivities? Specific historical developments and demographic shifts occurring between the eighth and thirteenth centuries clearly account for significant attitudinal changes on the part of many Muslim scholars towards the non-Muslims who lived in their midst. These included fraught relations with the Byzantines during the Umayyad period and continuing through the Abbasid period, the growing influence of religious minorities in the urban areas of the Islamic world from after the eighth century, and the onset of the Crusades, followed by the Spanish Reconquista and the Mongol attacks from the twelfth century onward, all of which left their mark on how Muslims envisioned their relations with non-Muslims in these specific historical contexts. The egalitarian spirit of roughly the first two centuries of Islam would be progressively compromised by these conflictual circumstances as well as by internally changing self-perceptions of Muslims vis-à-vis religious minorities.

Legal works supplement exegetical works as important sources for tracing changing views on the social and legal status of non-Muslims in the Muslim polity. These shifting views come into the sharpest focus on the issue of the division of spoils among non-Muslim participants in battles. When early and late legal treatises are compared, we find that a variety of practices, both egalitarian and non-egalitarian in their approach, existed among Muslims in the pre-modern period. When the early jurist al-Fazārī (d. c. 802) discussed

28 For this important discussion, see A. Sachedina, *The Islamic Roots of Democratic Pluralism* (Oxford: Oxford University Press, 2001), pp. 31–5.

the topic of the division of war spoils in his legal treatise, he documented that early authorities, such as Ibn Shihāb al-Din al-Zuhrī (d. 742), affirmed that the Prophet gave Jews and Christians who took part in battles with him two shares of the spoils, equal to what he gave Muslims.[29]

References to such egalitarian practices continue to be replicated in later legal works, so that they constituted a normative precedent for later generations, since it was Muḥammad himself who had instituted such practices. However, they were not to the liking of many of the later jurists. In the eleventh century, the well-known jurist al-Māwardī (d. 1058) asserted in his legal treatise that non-Muslims (along with women and enslaved persons) should be given only a small compensation rather than a full share for their presence on the battlefield, for (in his view) only the free, adult Muslim male would be entitled to a full portion.[30]

In pre-modern societies, Jews and Christians were generally granted a legal status within the Muslim polity as *ahl al-dhimma* ('protected people'). In juridical and administrative usage, the term *ahl al-dhimma* overlapped with the Qur'ānic *ahl al-kitāb* (People of the Book), and was often shortened to *dhimmi*. In return for the payment of a kind of poll-tax (*jizya*) levied on able-bodied, financially solvent Jewish and Christian men who did not wish to serve in the state army, their communities were granted protection for their lives and property and the right to practise their religion. If non-Muslim males enlisted in the army, they were exempt from the poll tax. Over time, this status was extended to Zoroastrians, Hindus, and Buddhists as well. Increasingly after the ninth century, however, as earlier tolerant attitudes towards non-Muslims sometimes hardened, often in times of crises, payment of the *jizya* began to be conceptualized by a number of influential jurists as a marker of inferior socio-legal status for the non-Muslim.[31]

Through specific legal and hermeneutical stratagems, the tolerance promised in the Qur'ān was therefore gradually whittled down by certain jurists and scholars to 'toleration' of non-Muslims, who continued to enjoy the legal protection of Muslim authorities but whose beliefs and ways of life began to be considered distinctly inferior to those of Muslims. Such perspectives would not be seriously challenged until the modern period.

---

29 Al-Fazārī, *Kitāb al-Siyar* [The Book of the Law of Nations], ed. F. Ḥammāda (Beirut: Mu'assasat al-risāla, 1987), p. 188.

30 For a fuller discussion, see A. Afsaruddin, 'Jihad, gender, and religious minorities in the *siyar* literature: the diachronic view', *Studia Islamica* 114 (2019), pp. 1–26.

31 For these changing attitudes, see A. Afsaruddin, *Striving in the Path of God: Jihad and Martyrdom in Islamic Thought* (Oxford: Oxford University Press, 2013), pp. 75–9.

Egalitarianism and Gender

In any discussion of gender egalitarianism in the Islamic milieu, it is appropriate to start with a reference to Qur'ān 33:35, which states:

> Those who have surrendered to God among males and females; those who believe among males and females; those who are sincere among males and females; those who are truthful among males and females; those who are patient among males and females; those who fear God among males and females; those who give in charity among males and females; those who fast among males and females; those who remember God often among males and females – God has prepared for them forgiveness and great reward.

In this passage, the Qur'ān specifically uses language deliberately inclusive of women and establishes the religious and spiritual equality of women and men.

The Qur'ān also asserts the ontological equality of men and women in a key verse – Qur'ān 4:1 – which addresses humanity in the following manner:

> O humankind! Be mindful of your duty to your Lord Who created you from a single soul [nafs wāḥida] and from it created its mate, and from them both He spread abroad a multitude of men and women.

Simultaneous creation from 'a single soul', as described in this verse, negates the possibility of the male being granted an ontologically superior status by virtue of having been created first, from whose body is then derived the woman's.[32] In this verse, the Qur'ān thus undermines the notion of an unequal, hierarchical relationship between men and women. Furthermore, in its accounts of the creation of the first human beings, the Qur'ān either (1) blames Adam exclusively for the Fall or (2) blames Adam and his wife equally for giving in to the blandishments of Satan (Qur'ān 2:30–9; 7:11–27; 15:26–43; 20:115–24; and 38:71–85). The Qur'ān therefore does not assign any kind of ontological moral failing to the woman companion of Adam (called Eve in the commentary literature) and thus by extension to womankind in general.[33]

Elsewhere the Qur'ān describes women as enjoying moral agency equal to that of men and being their partners in 'commanding what is good and forbidding what is wrong' (Qur'ān 9:71), a fundamental ethical imperative

---

32 To be compared to Genesis 2:22, where the woman is described as having been created from the rib of Adam and made subservient to him. Interestingly, this biblical account was later imported into Qur'ān commentaries to subvert the egalitarianism of Qur'ān 4:1.

33 For an insightful analysis of these verses, see B. Stowasser, *Women in the Qur'ān: Traditions and Interpretation* (Oxford: Oxford University Press, 1994), pp. 25–38.

Fig. 2.1 Muslim pilgrims from all over the world circumambulate the Kaaba, Islam's holiest shrine, together, regardless of race, gender, ethnicity, or class. (Photo by Ahmad al-Rubaye/AFP via Getty Images.)

within Islam. The Qur'ān confers specific legal rights on women, some of which were quite revolutionary in their consequences at the time. For example, Muslim women acquired the right to inherit property from their relatives and to hold property in their own names even after marriage. Their consent was required for a legitimate marriage, and they could seek divorce under specific conditions. The Qur'ān (2:187; 30:21) describes marriage as a conjugal union characterized by love, mercy, and sexual fulfilment for both parties. The Qur'ān does not require wives *qua* wives to obey their husbands *qua* husbands, although there are statements attributed to Muḥammad of dubious reliability that mandate such obedience.[34]

On specific marital and domestic matters, the Qur'ān, however, assigns duties and rights differentially between men and women. Men are required to financially maintain their families (Qur'ān 4:34) and women are entrusted with nursing their children (Qur'ān 2:233). Husbands can discipline errant wives who do not fulfil their marital obligations (Qur'ān 4:34); wives can also

---

34 See K. M. Abou El Fadl, *And God Knows the Soldiers: The Authoritative and the Authoritarian in Islamic Discourses* (Lanham, MD: University Press of America, 2001), pp. 62–82.

seek redress against errant husbands but are not advised to chastise them (Qur'ān 4:128). According to Islamic law, women have to make a special petition to dissolve their marriages whereas men can divorce with greater ease.

With regard to property and legal rights, women in general inherit half the amount of wealth and property that men do; the one exception is in the case of parents, where the mother and the father inherit equally from a deceased child. There is also a verse that calls for two female witnesses to replace one male witness specifically in the case of loan transactions (Qur'ān 2:228). Despite the identification of this specific circumstance, a general assumption was made by many jurists that a woman's legal testimony is worth only half of that of a man. In actual practice, however, male jurists often gave equal weight to a woman's testimony, especially in matters where she would be assumed to have equal or greater expertise, such as pregnancy and child-bearing issues.

Outside the domestic sphere, women in early Islamic society sometimes played prominent public roles. In religious scholarship in particular, women frequently played noteworthy roles as teachers and transmitters of the ḥadīths.[35] Since the basis for religious and moral leadership in the Islamic milieu was grounded in the possession of knowledge rather than in any process of ordination, gifted women scholars sometimes achieved exceptional recognition in the cloistered academic world.[36] During Muḥammad's time, some women participated in battle, whether as combatants or non-combatants, and received shares equal to that of men, as previously noted. As occurred in the case of non-Muslims, this egalitarian practice was discouraged and even abrogated by later jurists.

The gradual diminution in the socio-legal rights of women by the ninth century is a consequence of significant cultural and political shifts that affected juridical interpretations of the religious law. As indicated above, outside cultural influences from Byzantine and Persian societies became quite strong in the Abbasid period. Such societies, which were hierarchical in nature, automatically favoured men who occupied prestigious and lucrative positions in society and, therefore, placed women, who did not have access to such positions, at a serious disadvantage. Hierarchical societies are

35 See A. Sayeed, *Women and the Transmission of Religious Knowledge in Islam* (Cambridge: Cambridge University Press, 2013).
36 A. Afsaruddin, 'Knowledge, Piety, and Religious Leadership in the Late Middle Ages: Reinstating Women in the Master Narrative', in S. Guenther (ed.), *Knowledge and Education in Classical Islam* (Leiden and Boston: Brill, 2020), pp. 941–59.

also typically patriarchal; this, by design, places women under the control of their fathers, brothers, and husbands. Islamic societies were not immune to such changes, which began to be reflected in *fiqh*, the Arabic name for Islamic jurisprudence.[37]

Thus, we find that Muslim jurists from the tenth century on began to reconceptualize the family as the site of male dominance over females, extending that dominance to non-domestic spheres as well. Some scholars also began to consider women to be ontologically inferior to men, invoking Qur'ān 4:34 in particular to make this case, even though the verse refers to the differentiated roles of men and women solely within the context of the family. These non-egalitarian interpretations proceeded from the juridical assumption that, although women were the religious and spiritual equals of men, they were also different by virtue of their biology, which entailed a hierarchy of differentiated roles, not just within the family but in the larger society as well.

Understanding Egalitarianism in the Modern Period

Egalitarianism has re-emerged as a powerful, emotive topic in many Muslim-majority societies today. As became evident above, despite the Qur'ān's assertion of the intrinsic dignity and equality of human beings, Muslim scholars went on to construct and sanction inequality based particularly on gender and religion. Since the nineteenth century, reform-minded Muslim scholars have been arguing against discrimination based on gender and religion as being antithetical to the egalitarian ethos of the Qur'ān.

On the topic of gender, starting in the twentieth century, Muslim feminists (including both female and male scholars) have typically argued that scriptural exegesis undertaken almost exclusively by male scholars in the pre-modern period has all but occluded the gender egalitarianism of the Qur'ān and undermined the impact of its gender-inclusive language. This has led to the creation of a moral and religious paradigm that privileges the male over the female and accords to the former 'guardianship' over the latter. When the Qur'ān is read holistically and cross-referentially, however, different interpretive possibilities come to the fore, they argue, so that the full import of individual verses becomes apparent within the larger Qur'ānic context. Thus, when Qur'ān 4:34 is read along with Qur'ān 4:1, 33:35, and 9:71, the

---

37 Although erroneously conflated with what is called in English 'shariah law', Islamic law is actually a reference to *fiqh* or jurisprudence, which is the result of human juridical interpretations of religious and non-religious sources.

proclamation of women's ontological equality to men and the affirmation of their independent moral agency in the last three verses can be understood to trump the particularist understanding of feminine limitation indicated in the first verse, which can be attributed to historical contingency.[38] Thus, men who were understood to be the sole financial providers within the pre-modern family and assumed to be the 'guardian' of their wives can be displaced from such a position in the modern world where women can assume equal or even superior roles as financial providers. Contingent functional roles, which primarily have to do with economic opportunities rather than with ontological qualities, cannot be understood to set up absolute gendered hierarchies, since they can and do change with time.

It is furthermore argued that, since possession of knowledge is the main criterion for holding positions of religious, moral, and political authority within the Islamic milieu, such positions should be equally accessible to women in the modern world who are increasingly acquiring the requisite scholarly and professional expertise that qualifies them for such positions. Qur'ān 2:228, which refers to two female witnesses to replace one male witness in the case of loan transactions, can be understood to have been superseded in modern times, since women are now regarded as just as competent as men in financial matters.

In a similar vein, the historically unequal status of religious minorities in Muslim-majority societies is being revisited in the contemporary period. Once again, reformists tend to argue that such legally mandated inequalities can be circumvented by appealing directly to Qur'ānic directives and to early historical precedents that were egalitarian in nature. Thus, some modern Muslim scholars will point to the previously mentioned Constitution of Medina as establishing a blueprint for a just Muslim polity that treats all its members equally, regardless of their religion and ethnicity. This model of pre-modern egalitarian 'citizenship' is understood to be broadly compatible with modern liberal notions of political belonging and available for replication *mutatis mutandis* in modern Muslim-majority societies.[39]

Furthermore, reformist Muslims will typically argue that the *dhimmī* system, which was humane and tolerant for its time, is a human legal construct that has become obsolete in the modern period. This is in fact

---

38 For an excellent discussion of this kind of holistic reading, see A. Barlas, *'Believing Women' in Islam: Unreading Patriarchal Interpretations of the Qur'an* (Austin: University of Texas Press, 2019).

39 For example, A. Bulac, 'The Medina Document', in C. Kurzman (ed.), *Liberal Islam: A Sourcebook* (Oxford: Oxford University Press, 1998), pp. 169–84.

what the influential Egyptian reformer Muḥammad ʿAbduh (d. 1905) affirmed in the late nineteenth century. For ʿAbduh, the Islamic nature of a given nation-state is established not through a consciously cultivated Islamic identity and Islamicizing rhetoric but through the enactment of recognized Islamic ethical principles, primary among which are justice and mercy. Just Muslim nation-states should treat all their citizens, including non-Muslims and the non-religious, equally without exception, he asserted.[40]

There has also been renewed attention focused on Qurʾān 17:70 as a verse that mandates equality for all human beings without exception. The modern Mauritanian Muslim scholar Abdullah bin Bayyah has stressed the importance of this verse by commenting that ʿThe dignity of humanity precedes the dignity of faith and is subordinate to it.ʾ[41] Such views are embraced by Muslims of a liberal bent in the contemporary period.

For many modern Muslims, therefore, the twenty-first century presents unique opportunities for reimagining relations between men and women and between different religions and cultures on a firmly egalitarian basis. Scriptural hermeneutics and a more critical engagement with past theological and legal discourses will remain vital dimensions of this process of reconceptualization for the foreseeable future.

Further Reading

Abou El Fadl, *Reasoning with God: Reclaiming Shariʿah in the Modern Age* (Lanham, MD: Rowman & Littlefield, 2017).

Esposito, John, *Islam: The Straight Path* (Oxford: Oxford University Press, 2016).

Fadel, Mohammad, ʿTwo women, one man: knowledge, power and gender in medieval Sunni legal thoughtʾ, *International Journal of Middle East Studies* 29 (1997), pp. 185–204.

Hodgson, Marshall, *The Venture of Islam: Conscience and History in a World Civilization*, 3 vols. (Chicago: University of Chicago Press, 1974).

Izutsu, Toshihiko, *Ethico-Religious Concepts in the Qurʾān* (Montreal: McGill University Press, 1966).

Khalil, Mohammad Hassan, *Islam and the Fate of Others: The Salvation Question* (Oxford: Oxford University Press, 2012).

Kurzman, Charles (ed.), *Modernist Islam: A Sourcebook* (Oxford: Oxford University Press, 2002).

---

40 Muḥammad ʿAbduh, *Tafsīr al-qurʾān al-ḥakīm* [Commentary on the Wise Qurʾān], ed. Ibrāhīm Shams al-Dīn (Beirut: Dār al-kutub al-ʿilmiyya, 1999), vol. X, p. 61.
41 Cited in R. S. Kazemi, *Common Ground between Islam and Buddhism: Spiritual and Ethical Affinities* (Louisville, KY: Fons Vitae, 2010), p. 133.

Lapidus, Ira, *A History of Islamic Societies*, 3rd edn (Cambridge: Cambridge University Press, 2014).

Lings, Martin, *Muhammad: His Life Based on Earliest Sources* (Cambridge: Islamic Texts Society, 1991).

Nasr, Seyyed Hossein, et al., *The Study Qur'ān: A New Translation and Commentary* (New York: HarperOne, 2015).

3

Egalitarianism in Europe: Hussites, Anabaptists, Racovians, Hutterites, and Diggers

THOMAS A. FUDGE

Introduction

There were a number of religiously inspired European experiments in communal living, social egalitarianism, and the apostolic sharing of goods, especially between the fifteenth and seventeenth centuries. This chapter offers an analysis of concepts of egalitarianism as implemented around 1420 by the Hussites at Tábor in the Kingdom of Bohemia. There was a variation of this experiment by the next generation of Hussites in the late 1450s but it was spread much farther afield. Of equal value and interest are two related but quite different attempts to establish a form of social egalitarianism by sixteenth-century Anabaptists. The two began roughly simultaneously at Münster in north-western Germany and the other among the Hutterites in Moravia. The latter lasted significantly longer. Anabaptist efforts diverged around debates concerning the legitimacy of the sword, with the former taking up arms to defend their way of life while the latter were thorough-going pacifists. Hussites and Anabaptists are the best examples of pre-modern European egalitarianism. Two later manifestations of religiously inspired egalitarianism are also examined briefly, first the Polish Brethren at Raków in Poland and then the English Diggers (or the 'True Levellers').

Critical to this inquiry is an investigation aimed at determining to what extent these efforts at egalitarianism were motivated by eschatological apocalypticism, or chiliasm.[1] This concerns the doctrine of last things, the violent consummation of history, and the realization of the kingdom of God on earth. Commensurate with those doctrines latent within Christian history is the identification that the challenge to social order was not simply religious in

---

1 N. Cohn, *The Pursuit of the Millennium: Revolutionary Millenarians and Mystical Anarchists of the Middle Ages*, revised edn (New York: Oxford University Press, 2004).

nature but also included legal, social, economic, and political alternatives, all of which were rooted in religious beliefs that ultimately threatened and subverted the established medieval order. Assessing the nature of egalitarian principles in these fledging communities also requires a careful consideration of gender as a verifiable factor.

Ideologically, each of these expressions of egalitarianism arose from early Christian ideas codified in the Acts of the Apostles, where the historic foundational principles are located. Chapter 2:44–5 records that true believers stayed together and shared everything in common. Chapter 4:32 notes that none of the believers claimed private ownership of any possessions, but held everything in common. The community of goods, based on the New Testament, was, controversially, taken literally to mean that all things were held jointly but this generally did not include the communal or sexual sharing of women. We find at least two contentious exceptions to that general rule, briefly in Hussite Bohemia and more publicly in the sixteenth century in Anabaptist Münster.

These indications of early egalitarian experiments were shaped by a recurring yet vivid expectation of eschatological transformation. At the end of the Middle Ages, we find a widespread urge to revive primitive Christianity, and this can be related to specific eschatological commitments and convictions within a developing apocalyptic mood that conceived of the imminent consummation of the world and history itself. Apocalypticism is a concept implying that history possesses inherent meaning. That meaning can be grasped by means of eschatology or the last things, encompassing particular goals or the culmination of a process, in this case history itself. Two models can be found within Christianity. The first is specifically historical, relating to last events wherein time and history culminate. The second is meta-historical (otherworldly) and provides a means for solving cosmic mysteries. These systems of thought promoted and sustained action that illuminated meaning in the final stages of the struggle between good and evil. One Christian response to evil was social egalitarianism and the communal sharing of goods.

Another theme that cannot be excluded from a consideration of late medieval and early modern experiments with social egalitarianism is the ongoing debates over the legitimacy or illegitimacy of the sword. This was a frequent factor that determined the nature of these communities and the form of egalitarian identity that emerged. Competing ideas about the use of force, whether offensive or defensive, appear prominently in the communities that endeavoured to practise egalitarianism, and the doctrine of the sword often distinguished one experiment from the other. This matter is not inconsequential.[2]

Hussites

After the Prague priest and theologian Jan Hus was burned alive in 1415, revolution convulsed Bohemia. Detractors called the revolutionaries 'Hussites'. They self-identified as 'those who favoured Jan Hus and advocated the communion of the chalice'. The capital city, Prague, became the 'New Jerusalem' but that apocalyptic image later shifted. A particular (radical) Christian idea formed that found established social structures incompatible with a Christian worldview. Embracing early Christian ideals and motivated by eschatological anxiety, an intentionally world-denying community was established in 1419 predicated upon a keen desire for religious and social reform and committed to egalitarian principles. The Táborite community and its satellites represented political, religious, and social revolution.

The establishment of the experiment proceeded under the principle that personal belongings and private property were forbidden. Thousands congregated at the hilltop community from across the Czech lands. Those who came sold their property, placing the proceeds into the hands of the leaders who established community chests, and everything was shared equally by all those committed to the ideal. We find these chests operating in several locations in south Bohemia. These could be as rudimentary as barrels and tubs set up in town squares with nominated administrators tasked with overseeing and addressing the needs of the community. A new social order emerged.[3] The communities featured common goods and elimination of social divisions and hierarchies, so no lords and servants; fees for rent or services were outlawed, existing legal codes were ignored, debtors walked away from previous obligations with impunity, and all people were brothers and sisters having refused to conform with established social divisions and hierarchies.

This bold initiative threatened the nature of social stability and political arrangements as observed by medieval communities, and, since existing social structures were regarded as divinely ordained, the innovations were

2 J. M. Stayer, *Anabaptists and the Sword* (Lawrence, KS: Coronado Press, 1972).
3 Thomas A. Fudge, '"Neither mine nor thine": communist experiments in Hussite Bohemia', *Canadian Journal of History* 33 (April 1998), pp. 25–47; H. Kaminsky, *A History of the Hussite Revolution* (Berkeley: University of California Press, 1967).

palpable. For example, the three social estates that formed the medieval world experienced immediate intellectual and theoretical challenge by Peter Chelčický, who wrote a searing Czech-language critique 'On the Triple Division of Society'.[4] Others within the Hussite orbit, especially at Tábor, shared his point of view, and this general ethos may have contributed to the rise of the communal sharing of goods or 'communism' and of more widespread efforts at egalitarianism in the late medieval world. This moment is an indisputable milestone in the formation of a new egalitarian community. That new community was one of eschatological expectation, apocalyptic anxiety, hope, fear, and violence. It produced both a vision and a practice of religious reform. Utraquism, the shared reception of the eucharist *sub utraque specie* around a common table, was introduced, featuring a common meal (bread and wine) for all Christians, each of whom was considered equal regardless of social station. As the central symbol of the Hussite movement, the eucharist also functions as a ritual of eschatologically shared social integration of the entire Táborite community. Some Hussites understood these egalitarian experiments as functioning as real communities in history but eschatologically significant as a stage in the history of salvation. Hussite egalitarianism was fundamentally religious and socially visible.

It would be a mistake to assume that only peasants or disadvantaged people were attracted to the egalitarian communities established by the Hussites. In some cases the enthusiasm was so striking that entire villages became ghost towns practically overnight, as the residents abandoned their homes and journeyed to Tábor. Naturally, many peasants responded but we find also burghers, village magistrates, potters, priests, carpenters, town councillors, cobblers, blacksmiths, barbers, and cooks active in Táborite affairs.[5] Whether all of these supported all of the radical principles cannot be precisely determined. Nevertheless, we can find clear evidence of a desire for a more just social order.[6] Hussite ideologues suggested the way forward included seizing towns, fishponds, pastures, forests, and other natural resources that were under the control of governments, lords, and social power-brokers.

What about women? There is plenty of evidence for a female presence among the Hussites. But Hussite women cannot be studied apart from their male counterparts for the simple reason that most medieval records

---

4 H. Kaminsky (trans.), 'Treatises on Christianity and the social order', *Studies in Medieval and Renaisssance History* 1 (1964), pp. 137–67.

5 Fudge, '"Neither mine nor thine"', pp. 30–1.

6 Kaminsky, *History of the Hussite Revolution*, pp. 329–60.

(including those from the Hussite period) have been written by men. It is essential to distinguish women as historical subjects in their own right from women as objects represented by men. Medieval women were greatly restricted in terms of being able to express ideas, thoughts, feelings, and attitudes. In consequence, we know little about Hussite women. From a gender perspective, the Hussite revolution promised more than it delivered. In theory, men and women were equal theologically, but in society this was not achieved. We find leading Hussite thinkers expressing general negativity about women. Females were considered the shame of all humanity. All evil, including heresy in the church, was thought to have female origins. Congregations of women were responsible for the worst delusions spreading throughout the kingdom. This is the bias radical Hussitism sought to overcome. We hear rumours and catch glimpses in various sources of women preaching, participating in the liturgy, and exercising spiritual leadership. There are inquisitorial reports suggesting that women heard confession, claimed sacerdotal powers of absolution, and may even have occasionally consecrated the sacrament. There was sufficient gossip along these lines to cause the Council of Constance to pass a resolution forbidding women to preach, and this is prior to the foundation of the rural communities that included egalitarian commitments.[7]

Considered on balance, the argument for female equality among some Hussite groups is little more than a historically conditioned cliché. Like all clichés, such assumptions avoid profound analysis. Politicizing history is always costly to scholarship because it assumes or takes for granted what in fact must be proven. We know almost nothing about how women responded to the Hussite egalitarian agenda. The surviving references reveal but also conceal. It is very difficult to reconstruct the lives of these women. What can be found in the sources are shadowy images, usually anonymous, and these glimpses generally provide no access to the thought world of women. Thus it may be argued that no medieval society offered equality to women. But none offered this to men either. The world of the Middle Ages did not regard all people as equal.[8] Drawing attention to the alleged uniqueness of Hussite women in contrast with the rest of medieval Europe may be little more than drawing distinctions without differences.

7 J. Klassen, *Warring Maidens, Captive Wives, and Hussite Queens: Women and Men at War and Peace in Fifteenth-Century Bohemia* (New York: Columbia University Press, 1999).
8 C. Klapisch-Zuber (ed.), *A History of Women in the West*, vol. II, *Silences of the Middle Ages* (Cambridge, MA: Harvard University Press, 1992).

A faction within the Hussite movement did introduce a more radical understanding of egalitarian communalism. The so-called Adamites or Pikarts advanced the principle to its logical limit and introduced the communal sharing of women. The point was not kept secret: the enthusiasts declared that everything should be held in common, including women. The future pope Pius II, Aeneas Sylvius, summarized this practice in his 1458 *History of Bohemia*, noting they held women in common and carnal relations were common. Community elders permitted couples who burned with strong desire to seek fulfilment. One woman named Maria is known to history but is represented as a naked nymphomaniac roaming Bohemian forests. This aspect of communal sharing was rejected outright by the vast majority of the Hussites, and when the Pikarts refused to conform they were exterminated.[9]

The Czech experiments with egalitarianism were short-lived. The communal chests were not bottomless. Early Táborite society bought fully into the expectation of an end-of-world mentality, and, when the prophecies around this expectation failed to materialize, disenchantment set in. By late 1420, the fledging community could no longer sustain itself economically; the egalitarian principles were set aside, and the leaders reverted to taxation and sought to collect those obligations from community members. Hussite egalitarianism arose on an unstable foundation of shared goods. The eschatological motivation that spurred the Hussites to form egalitarian communities also doomed those experiments. Ideologically, these Hussites were convinced from their reading of scripture that the world had to end, the return of Christ was a logical and imminent event, the abolition of evil would occur, the sinful wicked would be annihilated, and the law of God would prevail. Fanatical idealism prevailed. So convinced were the Hussites of the rectitude of their thinking that they destroyed all booty captured, including money, fortified treasuries, and all goods belonging to the enemies of God. A steadfast belief in the consummation of history prevented the Táborites from taking the step from consumption communism to production communism. The latter idea seemed incongruous with their eschatological convictions. This factor, which limited the exploration of egalitarianism, indicates theology and religious practices were more determinative than were social and economic considerations. Once the apocalyptic-eschatological-chiliastic ideology faded, Hussites reversed policy and used guerrilla warfare not only to harass their enemies but also as a means of

---

9 Fudge, "'Neither mine nor thine'", pp. 36–7.

maintaining the community chests. By that time, the heart of their egalitarian ideology had been abandoned and medieval feudal structures reintroduced. Archaeological evidence indicates housing at Tábor was unequal: some dwellings were larger and better situated, although too much may be made of such evidence. After all, it cannot be determined with precision who lived in such households or the nature of life therein, and obviously not all dwellings could be centrally located.

By the 1450s, the early spirit of Hussite radicalism devoted to the ethos of the early church emerged once again. Understanding the gospel as a paradigm of equality and adherence to the law of God, a community came into being in north-east Bohemia. We find some replication of the earlier experiment: social divisions abolished, participation in state government discouraged, accumulation of personal wealth prohibited, engagement in trade frowned upon, and commitment to egalitarian ideals fostered. The thought of Peter Chelčický appears to have been a seminal motivation.[10] Community members were obliged to renounce private property, wealth, and rank and embrace the principles of shared goods, pacifism, and essential separation from the world. By 1464 these ideas were formally ratified and the concept of egalitarianism was deemed obligatory and consistent with the principles of early Christianity; this period came to be privileged by all Hussites and Anabaptists. The Unity of Brethren, as they were known, avoided dissolving the traditional family unit and did not adopt notions around the communal sharing of women. This renewed version of early Hussitism spread through Bohemia, Moravia, and Poland, and there were a number of thriving communities.[11] Like the Táborites before them, the Unity did not pursue a fully fledged form of communal existence. Private ownership of property slowly emerged within the communities of the Unity, and in due course personal property was forbidden only to clergy. As time progressed, even the initial obligatory communal sharing of goods was relaxed. As a result of frugality and attention to detailed industry, the Unity became well off, and their popularity led to revised and more lenient standards for community membership. By 1490, an official edict allowed that members might even hold public office. There was resistance to these liberalizing tendencies, which precipitated a schism within the ranks. A rump

---

10 Kaminsky, 'Treatises on Christianity and the social order', pp. 104–79; M. Wagner, *Petr Chelčický: A Radical Separatist in Hussite Bohemia* (Scottsdale, AZ: Herald Press, 1983), pp. 85–147.

11 P. Brock, *The Political and Social Doctrines of the Unity of Czech Brethren in the Fifteenth and Early Sixteenth Centuries* (The Hague: Mouton, 1957), pp. 251–4.

movement clung to the ideals of egalitarianism but the majority no longer considered such commitments essential to the gospel or to authentic Christianity. By the mid-sixteenth century, even the stalwart holdouts for the more radical social agenda had relented, and the ideals became fossilized.[12]

It is doubtful an argument for full inclusion of gender egalitarianism can be sustained. Hussite Bohemia is representative. At Tábor, neither communism nor egalitarianism was truly successful. The former was enforced for a time while the communities of the Unity deemed it optional. The Táborites strove to achieve a semblance of social democracy and equality for women. The Unity do not seem to have even made the effort, and those communities remained patriarchal. Both boys and girls received a rudimentary education at Tábor but definite leadership was accorded to women only among the libertine sect of the Adamites. The question of female egalitarianism remains little more than an ideal. The Pikarts believed in and practised the communal sharing of women, but those who resisted these opportunities were dealt with harshly, and we read of unwilling females being executed. Moreover, we find no evidence that women were permitted to practise the communal sharing of men. The thought was too appalling for these open-minded medievals. The question of same-sex experimentation fell outside the boundaries of religious freedom and social acceptance even in the more broadthinking communities of heresy and social dissent. Arguments for gender equality in Hussite Bohemia are tenuous not because they are necessarily incorrect but because that posture undermines creative research (which has yet to be fully undertaken) by asserting a conclusion in advance.

The failure of the Hussite dalliance with social egalitarian experiments must be attributed to a decline in commitment to religious principles and an increasingly greater concern with social and economic realities. Bohemia was not anomalous in terms of late medieval fluctuating economies. When there is economic tranquillity, there is scope for idealism. The Hussites had to cope with unemployment, rising costs, poverty, inflation, static wages, cultural upheaval including foreign invasion, crusades, internecine warfare, political instability, currency devaluation, exorbitant taxation, and a host of social anxieties. Naturally, there were true believers but there were also those with less salutary motives who decided to throw in their lot with the communities in rural Bohemia and Moravia. Even some of the leaders seemed unwilling to

---

12 Ibid., pp. 241–73; J. K. Zeman, *The Anabaptists and the Czech Brethren in Moravia 1526–1628: A Study of Origins and Contacts* (The Hague: Mouton, 1969).

embrace completely the radical implications of their own agendas. Power always has the tendency to corrupt, and despite egalitarian claims there were those in Hussite communities who seemed to enjoy that equality a bit more than others. The same can be said for similar communities in the German, Swiss, and Dutch territories, in Poland, in Transylvania, and elsewhere. Beyond this, we find evidence of dictatorial leadership, cultural isolation, intolerance, and unbearable strictures both in ideology and in practice. These pressures proved too great to sustain and internecine conflict and external pressures undermined the early ideals and contrived to erode meaningful commitment to societies based upon policies and principles of egalitarianism.

Anabaptists

There are several terms used to designate these Protestants of the sixteenth and seventeenth centuries. The traditional designation has been Anabaptists, although the term is inadequate, implying that adherents of these movements practised adult or believers' baptism and that this rite lies at the core of their religious doctrine and practice. The claim is arguable. Roland Bainton suggested these groups might be designated the 'left wing of the Reformation'.[13] That term never took hold in early modern European historiography. More recently, George Williams has suggested the conglomeration of such movements might simply be called the 'Radical Reformation'. The last suggestion is best but the former has been used for its recognized value.[14]

It is possible to identify a number of common elements of the Anabaptists or the radical reformers. In distinction to Luther and Calvin, the Anabaptists were much preoccupied with ethical concerns. Theologically understood, there was a clear emphasis on soteriological synergism, or a joint effort involving both humans and God. Like the Hussites before them, Anabaptists strove to return to the ideals and principles of primitive Christianity. Biblical literalism was often evident. Some were New Testament literalists and endeavoured to restore the gospel pattern by reviving the discipline of Matthew 18, the religious communism of Acts, non-resistance, the no swearing of oaths

13 Roland H. Bainton, 'The left wing of the Reformation', *Journal of Religion* 21, 2 (1941), pp. 124–34.
14 H. S. Bender, *The Anabaptist Vision* (Scottsdale, AZ: Herald Press, 1944); M. G. Baylor (ed. and trans.), *The Radical Reformation* (Cambridge: Cambridge University Press, 1991). The definitive overview is G. H. Williams, *The Radical Reformation*, 3rd edn (Kirksville, MO: Truman State University Press, 2000).

found in the Sermon on the Mount, and the rituals of foot-washing and baptism by immersion for adults only. Old Testament literalists revived polygamy. As with the Hussites, we find considerable eschatological apocalypticism, along with the separation of church and state. The programme of the radical Anabaptists was threefold: freedom of conscience, the separation of church and state, and voluntarism in religion. With few exceptions, the Anabaptists taught that coercion in matters of faith was inherently wrong. To put someone to death for their religious beliefs was reprehensible. Secular power and spiritual power should be kept quite separate.

To underscore the diversity of the Radical Reformation in terms of religiously inspired egalitarianism, we look at two different types of communities. The Kingdom of Münster was the result of years of grievance, along with alleged church and governmental abuses. There were popular uprisings in 1525, 1527, and 1529, all of which marked stages along the road to the great experiment.[15] Leading influences at Münster included former Lutheran pastor Bernd Rothmann, the cloth merchant Bernd Knipperdolling, and the radical lay preacher Melchior Hoffman, the last of whom emphasized apocalypticism and an apolitical approach. In 1534 the Dutch baker Jan Matthijs moved to Münster and began to preach the end of the world. He legitimated the sword. He did not brook dissent, and a blacksmith who challenged him was killed on the spot. This outburst of violence signals a drift away from Hoffman's apolitical philosophy to a crusading mentality. The radical leaders taught that Münster was a divinely chosen city of refuge. Letters summoned true believers to come, and thousands responded. The goods of the wealthy were seized, a utopian communism began, the money economy was abolished, and letters of indebtedness and records of debts were destroyed. Iconoclasm led to the destruction of feudal records of land title. Religious houses were converted into settlements for the steady stream of refugees arriving in the 'New Jerusalem'.

Political authorities took fright. A rumour circulated that the local bishop was gathering forces to destroy the radicals. It was predicted the world would end before Easter 1534. The apocalyptic bubble burst when Easter passed uneventfully. In an act of desperation, Jan Matthijs rode out to meet the besieging forces and his own death on Easter Day. The control of Münster then fell to Jan of Leiden, who had been there since 1533. He proclaimed himself king and claimed that God had made him king over

---

15 R. Po-Chia Hsia, *Society and Religion in Münster, 1535–1618* (New Haven: Yale University Press, 1984).

the whole world; the Münsterites became convinced that King Jan would kill all other rulers. In consequence, he abolished the council and declared the holy city of Münster would thereafter be governed by a holy constitution.

Polygamy began to be practised, and Jan enjoyed the company of at least sixteen wives. This was a serious threat to the social order and attracted severe criticism. Rothmann decreed that egalitarianism did not extend to women and mandated that every woman or girl had to be ruled by a man. Some objected to polygamy and were summarily put to death. Other women continued to object and were imprisoned or threatened with the sword. One woman was charged by her husband for refusing the marital duty several times and for blaspheming. She was executed. Jan of Leiden personally beheaded one of his own wives in the marketplace for disobedience. She had criticized him. The sword at Münster was two-edged: it pointed outward at the sinful world but it was also an instrument of internal terror. A long siege lasted several months under the direction of the bishop. Inside the city, radicals continued to share everything and copulate voraciously, maintaining the belief that the end of the world was near and that they alone would be spared and protected by God. But the bishop's forces remained at the gates, food supplies dwindled, and divine deliverance failed to materialize. Other radical communities condemned the Münsterites and denounced their experiment. For example, Moravian Hutterites rebuked their ideological cousins at Münster for having been seduced by demonic forces that were manifestly contrary to the gospel of Christ.[16] After a prolonged siege that caused great harm and deprivation within the beleaguered city, Münster fell to the bishop's forces, and most of the inhabitants who had survived the siege and onslaught were slaughtered. The bloodshed of 1534–5 taught the magistrates the valuable lesson that nascent democracy and religious fanaticism often went hand in hand. In the aftermath of the Münster debacle, European authorities exercised greater care in controlling parish affairs under the supervision of a properly constituted city council.

At Münster, there were clear proclamations of economic equality but, equally, we find unimpeachable evidence suggesting that reality did not match rhetoric. In the 1530s one searches in vain for evidence of, intentional policy for, or thoughtful strategy for applying egalitarianism across the community of Münster. At both Hussite Tábor and Anabaptist Münster,

---

16 W. O. Packull, *Hutterite Beginnings: Communitarian Experiments during the Reformation* (Baltimore: Johns Hopkins University Press, 1995).

along with a commitment to apostolic principles, we find privilege, exploitation, greed, and uneven applications of ideological idealism.

There were other dimensions to the Radical Reformation and quite different attempts to develop a community of goods and egalitarian principles. Hutterite communities in Moravia took up the theme of apostolic sharing, common goods, and communal life.[17] These experiments were somewhat different from those in Bohemia and at Münster and lasted infinitely longer. Around 1526, like in Münster, Moravian Anabaptists began pooling resources to help refugees. By 1528 these people split over disagreements with respect to the use of the sword. Some followed the theologian Balthasar Hubmaier and went the way of using the power of the magistrate to curb persecution and retain a measure of protection. Others, influenced by the Anabaptist leader Hans Hut, stressed the need for a true community of goods above the basic willingness to support persons in need. In 1527, Hubmaier and Hut were seized by the authorities, and by 1528 both had been put to death. The followers of Hut continued the radical emphases and formed separate communities; they began practising communist principles.

A number of Hutterite communities sprang up in Moravia in 1528 and 1529 under the leadership of the eventual martyr Jakob Hutter. They survived Habsburg persecution in 1535–6 and the fallout from the Münster debacle in 1536. One of the key features of the community was the *Haushabe* or *Bruderhof*.[18] The structure of this feature was in place by 1538. The components of the *Haushabe* or *Bruderhof* reflected foundational ideology. The community consisted of an assembly of large houses in which members lived in common. The emphasis shifted from single-family units to a larger community identity. Houses were quite large, perhaps seventy feet long and three storeys high. Ground floors were reserved for common work, communal meals, and religious worship. The upper two storeys had small rooms for married couples and their children. Perhaps as many as forty such houses might constitute a single *Bruderhof*. The houses were sometimes arranged around a square or garden used by all members of the community. Larger communities might have three or four dozen buildings. In terms of education, small children were removed from their families after they were weaned and placed in a junior school under a school mother until the age of six.

---

17 B. Scribner, 'Practical utopia: pre-modern communism and the Reformation', *Comparative Studies in Society and History* 36 (1994), pp. 743–74; R. Stayer, *The German Peasants' War and Anabaptist Community of Goods* (Montreal and Kingston: McGill-Queens University Press, 1991).

18 Scribner, 'Practical utopia', pp. 760–5.

Fig. 3.1 Hutterite *Bruderhof*, woodcut, 1589. (Source: Title page of Christoph Erhard, *Gründliche kurtz verfaste Historia. Von Münsterischen Widertauffern: vnd wie die Hutterischen Brüder so auch billich Widertauffer genent werden, im Löblichen Marggraffthumb Märhern, deren vber die sibentzehen tausent sein sollen, gedachten Münsterischen in vilen ähnlich, gleichformig vnd mit zustimmet sein* (Munich: Adam Berg, 1589)).

Thereafter, they transferred to a senior school until they reached the age of twelve, at which point they began to learn a trade. Women cared for the smaller children while older children in general were placed in groups of up to 300. They were housed in a separate school where they slept two to a bed under the supervision of a nurse. Marriage was arranged by the elders of the community rather than by the biological family. Marriage arrangements were unique. On a previously nominated day, all of the young men and women of suitable age for matrimony were assembled and introduced to each other. Each female was given the opportunity to choose a partner from two or three men presented to her. The final decision in these matters was part choice and part prodding by the elders. The ideal of female agency may well have broken down because often it was the men of the community who essentially made the final choice.

By 1547 there were more than 2,000 people living in about 25 *Haushaben*. By 1591, and despite persecution, there were about 70 communities of 400–600 persons each, or about 28,000 people living among the Hutterites. Renewed persecution reduced these communities to about two dozen by 1622. As a result of the Thirty Years' War, Hutterites were expelled from Moravia, marking the end of their experiment, at least on a large scale. We find them in Hungary, Transylvania, Wallachia, Ukraine, and beyond. Like the Bohemian Unity of Brethren, the Hutterites accumulated large sums of money and were sufficiently affluent that in 1592 both the governor of Moravia and Emperor Rudolf II separately approached them seeking financial loans. Remaining true to their principles of avoiding secular power, the Hutterites turned both requests down. Hutterite workers were preferred labourers since they were thought to be more reliable. They proved popular with local farmers because they would deal directly with them and offered better prices when selling grain.

Like the early Táborites, the Hutterites claimed the practice of common goods marked out the true believers and was a crucial indication of the true follower of Christ and practitioner of the gospel. Just as in Bohemia and at Münster, the idea of communal goods posed a serious threat to the stability of hierarchical society and called into question the nature of the medieval social structure. Opposition shadowed Hutterite activities, and the *Bruderhof* existed at the centre of broader ideological conflict. Naturally, the reasons for joining these communities in the sixteenth century were just as many and varied as explanations accounting for the rush to Tábor a century earlier. Religious conviction and eschatological expectations surely caused some to join, while economic motivation and social affinity induced others to forsake their former lives and support egalitarian ideals at a Moravian *Haushabe*. These are doubtless the most common incentives. But there is evidence for altogether unedifying reasons that included men who had abandoned wives, men and women who had run off together, outlaws seeking to evade capture, or those who for various and sundry reasons simply wished to disappear. Where better to avoid the scrutiny of the world than in a secluded Hutterite *Bruderhof* in rural Moravia? In sum, there were idealists and there were those who saw an opportunity to fulfil personal desires.

Eschatological communism strove to become social philosophy but not always successfully. Wilhelm Reublin alleged that in the Hutterite commune at Slavkov (Austerlitz) great inequity abounded. Reublin charged that some communal members ate peas and cabbage in separate chambers while in more elegant dining rooms some of the leaders and their families enjoyed roasted meat, fish, poultry, and good wine. Reublin suggests this type of inequity went on even though small children in the community suffered malnourishment. If Reublin is to be believed, the better-off at Slavkov had access to separate living quarters and dressed and ate better than the rest, while some children were inadequately cared for. As a result and in consequence, tensions arose that threatened the stability of the community. Stung by the biting critique, the Hutterites expelled Reublin from Slavkov.[19]

Despite what must have been irregularities and occasional slippage from agreed-upon ideals and principles, these communities enjoyed a long, if troubled, history. The historical significance of these radical Anabaptists in their quest for social egalitarianism and shared common goods is linked to three key principles. The first is the concept of the voluntary church. The second is an insistence upon the separation of church and state. The third revolves around a doctrine of religious liberty. From the time of Constantinian Christianity to the end of the Middle Ages, these principles had been essentially inactive. For the Moravian radicals these convictions were lionized as a way of life. These ideals became practices as a mandatory ethical and moral stance. The quest for equality was regarded as a witness of their faith and an example to humankind. The commitment to the principles of equality was believed to lie at the core of the Christian gospel. Despite persecution, the Moravian Hutterites defended these values without regard to cost or consequence.[20]

The nature and function of the *Haushabe* or *Bruderhof* represent specifically a Hutterite feature of life and religious faith. These communities were prominent in Moravia throughout the sixteenth century but did not escape censure and condemnation. As early as 1527, the Habsburg Ferdinand I passed a law aimed at Anabaptists wherein doctrines of social egalitarianism were criminalized.[21] Like the early popularity of the communities of Tábor, the outlawing of communal egalitarian practices did not dent enthusiasm for them. For example, at Zollikon on Lake Zurich, almost the entire population turned Anabaptist. Egalitarian principles were put into practice. Doors to houses were left unlocked, all things were held in common, and a community of goods became an active social policy.[22] We find extravagant suggestions that some Swiss Anabaptists held everything in common including women.

---

19 Scribner, 'Practical utopia', p. 760.
20 D. F. Durnbaugh (ed.), *Every Need Supplied: Mutual Aid and Christian Community in the Free Churches, 1525–1675* (Philadelphia: Temple University Press, 1974); L. Zuck (ed.), *Christianity and Revolution: Radical Christian Testimonies 1520–1650* (Philadelphia: Temple University Press, 1975).
21 Packull, *Hutterite Beginnings*, p. 190.
22 Stayer, *German Peasants' War and Anabaptist Community of Goods*, pp. 95–6.

Compelling evidence is scanty. In different ways, Münster and Hutterite Anabaptists reflect efforts at putting into practice religiously inspired egalitarian principles and communities.

Polish Brethren

Currents of thought consonant with core values espoused by Hussites and Anabaptists are also evident in Poland. At Raków in 1569, a 'New Jerusalem' was proposed wherein eschatological convictions produced a commune that ignored social distinctions around rank and estate. Like the Táborites, these dissenters eschewed state authority and the prevailing legal system. Believing their commune to be a manifestation of the kingdom of God, the people at Raków inaugurated equality, pacifism, and a community of goods.[23] In consequence of a commitment to these principles, by the 1570s we find a concerted effort to replicate the practices of the apostolic church.[24]

Poland received anti-Trinitarians, Lutherans, Mennonites, Quakers, Huguenots, Calvinists, Hussites, and others who had been denied religious freedom in their own land. From the middle of the sixteenth century onwards, Poland became known as an asylum and refuge of heretics.[25] In 1567, the town of Raków obtained a royal charter. This agreement guaranteed freedom from payments, rents, or taxes for the next twenty years, to a large extent provided exemption for self-rule, and guaranteed liberty of conscience for all religious confessions. The Racovians built small wooden houses and cottages, they worked the land to the extent of supporting themselves, laboured at manual trades, ignored social hierarchy, and held all things in common. They settled in the town, sold their estates to help the poor, and eschewed the world, the state, war, public offices, and prevailing legal systems. The community at Raków was marked by communal life, debate, meditation, a decision to withdraw from society, and eschatological expectation. Fundamentally, these ideals came together principally not as a result of social discontent, or common suffering, or even an inclination to revolt, but

23 G. H. Williams (ed. and trans.), *The Polish Brethren: Documentation of the History and Thought of Unitarianism in the Polish–Lithuanian Commonwealth and in the Diaspora, 1601–1685*, 2 vols. (Missoula, MT: Scholars Press, 1980); G. H. Williams (ed.), *Stanislas Lubieniecki: History of the Polish Reformation and Nine Related Documents* (Minneapolis: Fortress Press, 1995).

24 S. Kot, 'Polish Brethren and the problem of communism in the sixteenth century', *Transactions of the Unitarian Historical Society in London* 11 (1956), pp. 38–54.

25 J. Tazbir, *A State without Stakes: Polish Religious Toleration in the Sixteenth and Seventeenth Centuries*, trans. A. T. Jordan (New York: Kościuszko Foundation, 1973).

chiefly as a result of conscience. They wished to practise the Christian faith as they understood it. They were not deprived of their possessions but they resigned property and freedom voluntarily. These people discussed notions of abolishing serfdom, common property, pacifism, and the right to exercise civic office. Fundamental ideas of the Polish defenders of egalitarianism included a belief that the state was not a Christian organization and therefore that true Christians should not enter its service. Conversely, the church should be absolutely pacifist, the use of the sword considered un-Christian, and no form of war, even defensive, could be reconciled with the duties of a Christian.

On the strength of religious debates, the community quickly moved from theory to practice. Jan Niemojewski, a respected and prosperous judge from Kujawy, sold his lands in 1566, donned rags and a wooden sword, and appeared in Lublin prophesying doom. Heronim Filipowski, one of the pillars of the Małopolska gentry, abandoned his villages and joined the radical community at Raków. Jan Ożarowski, who controlled a prosperous royal town near Lublin, became obsessed with the fear that by owning property he was in wilful violation of the gospel. He returned the village post-haste to the astonished king. Jan Przykowski liberated his peasants from serfdom in 1572 with the solemn declaration that God recognized people as neither lords nor peasants. The burghers Grzegorz Paweł, Marcin Czechowic, and Piotr of Goniadz went to great lengths to defend the principles of egalitarianism, pacifism, and resistance to state authority in a determined quest to establish and enforce justice.

Despite these initiatives, social radicalism in Poland very quickly lost force. This may be attributed to a number of factors. The religious fervour did not favour transformation into a broad programme of social action. The basis for communal identity and egalitarianism did not arise from economic misery or social inequity. In consequence, there was no viable plan for economic reconstruction, and ultimately, like the Táborites, the principle of common goods was abandoned. The obligation of manual labour that was practised among Dutch and German sectarians failed at Raków because so many in the Polish community were of the gentry and could not easily adapt. A radical spiritualist trend opposing all forms of church hierarchy and organization prevailed, and this had fatal consequences for the development of the community. In the end, radicalism and egalitarianism became humanitarianism.

Moravian Hutterite representatives visited Raków in 1569 but an attempt to reach union failed. The Polish Brethren rejected social radicalism. They definitely stood for private property against the communism of the Moravians. There is some question as to whether or not the community at Raków actually established a real community of goods. Eschewing the more strident sectarian approach of the Moravian Hutterites, the Polish 'New Jerusalem' developed into a busy town of tradespeople and artisans. The stubborn held out resolutely, but many reintegrated back into society. Whatever community of goods existed was eventually abandoned. Raków was finally overwhelmed by the advancing tide of religious intolerance.[26]

Diggers

Many of the egalitarian themes identified in continental Europe can also be located in England. On a cold winter morning, 30 January 1649, Charles Stuart stepped out onto a scaffolding in Whitehall and into history. Within moments of his appearance before the gathered crowd, King Charles I was decollated. The seventeenth century was a time of transition in England. The last vestiges of medievalism were swept away, and modern England began to dawn. The early part of the century featured inflation wherein the price of wheat rose by six times and the general price of goods by four to five times. Industrial expansion was prodigious. For example, coal production went from 200,000 tonnes per year to 1,500,000 tonnes. Iron production increased by five times, and ship-building became a major enterprise. The medieval idea of the divine right of kings was challenged. James I had proclaimed monarchs as divine lieutenants on earth, claiming that even God referred to them as gods. With challenges to this idea of kingship were also significant shifts in the institutions of authority. The Reformation had demolished papal authority in England through its elevation of the divine right of kings and the authority of the Bible. In time, the former fell away and the latter was rendered argumentative on the grounds of interpretation. Emphasis came to be placed increasingly on individual conscience and the advances of the Enlightenment. Still, the business of religion remained a useful rallying call. The abolition of the Star Chamber (a court associated with royal interests and noted for arbitrary and summary procedure) and the High Commission (the supreme ecclesiastical court), the breakdown of censorship, and the impotence of the government allowed religious sects to emerge from

---

26 O. P. Grell and B. Scribner (eds.), *Tolerance and Intolerance in the European Reformation* (New York: Cambridge University Press, 1996).

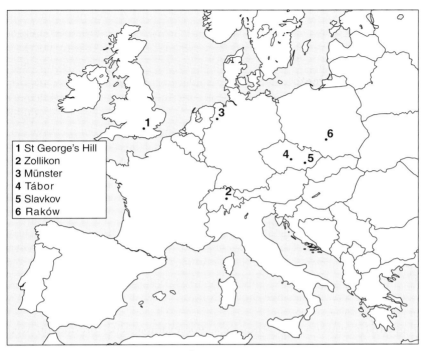

1 St George's Hill
2 Zollikon
3 Münster
4 Tábor
5 Slavkov
6 Raków

Map 3.1   European egalitarian experiments, 1420s–1650s.

underground. Several important groups surfaced in seventeenth-century England in the bellicose context of social upheaval.

The Diggers (also known as the 'True Levellers') were a communist movement that in 1649–50 began to cultivate common land to farm for the poor on St George's Hill near London. They advocated common land-holdings, the abolition of trade, social equality, universal suffrage, education for all, and millennialism. A prominent leader, Gerrard Winstanley, announced that true freedom had to do with the use of the land. The activities of the Diggers were in response to the ravages of the English Civil War, including general economic decline, poverty, food shortages, and the plague.[27] However, like the Hussites, Anabaptists, and Racovians, they were also motivated by the communalism of the early Christians. Winstanley believed that spiritual transformation formed the bedrock of

27 A. Hessayon, 'Early modern communism: the Diggers and community of goods', *Journal for the Study of Radicalism* 3, 2 (2009), pp. 1–49.

common possessions but he excluded the communal sharing of women that had controversially characterized the Pikart and Münster initiatives. Digger ideology was theological. The Levellers also appealed to the hardships of the poor. In the late 1640s a move was made to destroy existing official church structures completely. Prelates were slated for expulsion and replacement by the government according to God's word. Iconoclasm followed, and some priests had their vestments torn from their backs. The main leader was John Lilburne. When brought before the Star Chamber he refused to answer or gave evasive answers, refused to pay the clerk's fee, and was also the first to refuse to take an oath in that court. He was flogged through the streets of London while shouting 'hallelujah'. On 22 January 1648, an anonymous group of London tradesmen, in support of the Leveller cause, issued a summary support statement, under a revealing title: '*The Mournfull Cryes of many thousand Poore Tradesmen, who are ready to famish through decay of Trade. Or, the warning Teares of the Oppressed*'. Social and economic considerations motivated the Diggers, but their religious orientation was the original and fundamental propulsion, and it should be recognized that they had much in common with groups like the Hutterites.

Conclusion

Religiously inspired communal egalitarianism did not appear at tornado speed out of nowhere. Historical and theological precedents are ancient.[28] Late medieval and early modern efforts to establish egalitarian communities foundered on the intellectual disconnect between socio-economic principles and theological idealism. Hussites abolished feudalism and traditional forms of income and likewise set aside the traditional ways and means of production. When their eschatological expectations were thwarted and the consummation of history delayed, such societies experienced irresolvable crises, and it quickly became evident that no community could last long while observing such ideological incongruence. The capacity of the common chests dwindled across the satellite communities in the Hussite constellation. Without raiding the coffers of their neighbours, the Táborites faced ruin. In the absence of industry, trade, or means of stimulating production in order to restock the community chests, the idea of communist egalitarianism was doomed. Radical theology could and did continue, but social ideas around

---

28 I. Forrest, 'Medieval history and anarchist studies', *Anarchist Studies* 28, 1 (Spring 2021), pp. 33–59.

a common sharing of goods and principles of equality soon vanished from the ideology of mature Hussitism.

Apostolic utopian communism was attempted across Europe between 1419 and the 1650s from Poland to England, and Münster to Moravia, although the main period falls between the 1420s and the 1540s. In some cases, this apostolic utopianism failed because the experiment was only a form of consumption communism rather than intentional production communism (Hussite Bohemia). This can be accounted for by taking into consideration the incompatibility of particular religious commitments that embraced the expectation of the Parousia (Second Coming). This undermined egalitarian communalism in the sense that a community could hardly be committed to the imminent end of the world and at the same time be contributing to its furtherance. Other failures can be attributed to a serious gap between theory and practice and corrupt leadership (Münster). Hutterites avoided both snares by extending equality across the board and developing a robust programme aimed at sustaining the community. The short-lived coterie of Racovians and Diggers followed variegated trajectories.

Historical periodization introduces false categories and problematically creates unwarranted challenges. But the idea of *Alteuropa* or an 'Old European Age' spanning the twelfth to the eighteenth centuries is the time during which all these experiments occurred. The harvest of the Renaissance eventually eroded the authority of scripture or at least allowed viable alternatives to emerge, and additionally blunted the sharp edge of eschatological excitement. It can be argued that only when people ceased to take an eschatological worldview seriously were the Middle Ages truly at an end. This does not mean to suggest that apocalyptic-eschatological-chiliastic ideologies vanished nor yet to imply that the Bible lost its force.[29] On the contrary. The latter continued to be used as a vital instrument promoting as well as hindering concepts of social egalitarianism. The use of the sword persisted but continued to function as an ameliorating factor in the formation of communities of faith and often became the decisive subject when determining religious identities and mapping out the geography of toleration. The examples discussed in this chapter indicate that egalitarianism is an old and global phenomenon. What remains incontrovertible is that Táborites, Unity of Brethren, Anabaptist Münsterites, and Moravian Hutterites were determined to fulfil the biblical mandate of being in the world but not of it. Their

---

29 E. Werner, 'Popular ideologies in late medieval Europe: Taborite chiliasm and its antecedents', *Comparative Studies in Society and History* 2 (1959–60), pp. 344–63.

efforts to achieve a more just and equal society provided options and opportunities that enriched their lives, their faith, and their world.[30]

Further Reading

Elmen, Paul, 'The theological basis of Digger communism', *Church History* 23, 3 (1954), pp. 207–18.

Fudge, Thomas A., '"Neither mine nor thine": communist experiments in Hussite Bohemia', *Canadian Journal of History* 33 (April 1998), pp. 25–47.

Hessayon, Ariel, 'Early modern communism: the Diggers and community of goods', *Journal for the Study of Radicalism* 3, 2 (2009), pp. 1–49.

Hsia, R. Po-Chia, *Society and Religion in Münster, 1535–1618* (New Haven: Yale University Press, 1984).

Kaminsky, Howard, *A History of the Hussite Revolution* (Berkeley: University of California Press, 1967).

Kot, Stanislaw, 'Polish Brethren and the problem of communism in the sixteenth century', *Transactions of the Unitarian Historical Society in London* 11 (1956), pp. 38–54.

Luszczynska, Magdalena, 'The Polish Brethren versus the Hutterites: a sacred community?', *Journal of Early Modern Christianity* 4, 1 (2014), pp. 21–46.

Packull, Werner O., *Hutterite Beginnings: Communitarian Experiments during the Reformation* (Baltimore: Johns Hopkins University Press, 1995).

Scribner, Bob, 'Practical utopia: pre-modern communism and the Reformation', *Comparative Studies in Society and History* 36 (1994), pp. 743–74.

Stayer, James M., *The German Peasants' War and Anabaptist Community of Goods* (Montreal and Kingston: McGill-Queens University Press, 1991).

30 Kaminsky, *History of the Hussite Revolution*, p. 494.

4

The Taiping Land Programme: Creating a Moral Environment

RUDOLF G. WAGNER

Introduction

The Heavenly Kingdom of Great Peace sprang from a Chinese Christian evangelical movement with close affinities, but no institutional ties, to evangelical Protestantism in the United States, Great Britain, and the European continent. It originated with a vision of its later leader Hong Xiuquan in 1837, in which he was taken up to heaven and was ordered by an 'old man' to drive out of the heavens the demons who had taken possession of them. After he had accomplished this feat, the 'old man', who originally had created the world, ordered him to descend back down to earth and do the same, that is, drive out the demons, who had not only established control there, but had done so with the connivance of many members of the Confucian elite. With this mandate and the blueprint of his heavenly vision as his guide for future action, Hong Xiuquan – who understood from the fact that the 'old man's' son had called him 'younger brother' that he himself was God's second son – managed to convert a group of mostly Hakka settlers from the vicinity of Canton. He eventually identified the Manchu, the people from north China who ruled all of China under the Qing dynasty, as the 'demons' of the vision and moved to drive them out of China proper. With supreme self-confidence and a rapidly growing army of followers, he marched through half of China and in 1853 established Nanjing as the 'New Jerusalem' of his Heavenly Kingdom. After having ruled much of southern China for the next decade, the Heavenly Kingdom, bereft of further guidance from its leader's vision, was defeated in 1864 after what was probably – with about 30 million dead – the most costly civil war of the nineteenth century.[1]

---

1 For a general description of the Taiping rebellion, see Jen Yu-wen, *The Taiping Revolutionary Movement* (New Haven: Yale University Press, 1973). For an analysis of the role of religion in this movement, see R. G. Wagner, *Reenacting the Heavenly Vision: The Role of Religion in the Taiping Rebellion*, China Research Monograph 25 (Berkeley:

The Taiping policies and the civil war drove many people of wealth and education to the International Settlement in Shanghai, and led to the explosive growth of this settlement, which ended up becoming the engine of China's modernization.

The Taipings were already seen as a 'revolutionary' specimen by Western contemporaries. Hearing of the first rumours of something abroad in southern China, Karl Marx and Friedrich Engels, aided by the total absence of any specific information, provided an instant, complete, and breathless analysis of the Taiping movement in 1850:

> The slowly but steadily growing over-population in this country had long made social conditions there particularly oppressive for the great majority of the nation. Then came the English and extorted free trade for themselves in five ports. Thousands of English and American ships sailed to China and before long the country was glutted with inexpensive British and American industrial manufactures. Chinese industry, dependent on manual labour, succumbed to competition from the machine. The imperturbable Middle Kingdom was aroused by a social crisis. The taxes no longer came in ... the population sank *en masse* into pauperism, erupted in revolts ... The country reached the brink of ruin and is already threatened with a mighty revolution. But worse was to come. Among the rebellious plebs individuals appeared who pointed to the poverty of some and to the wealth of others, and who demanded, and are still demanding, a different distribution of property, and even the complete abolition of private property. When [the missionary R. W.] Herr Gützlaff came among civilised people and Europeans again after an absence of twenty years, he heard talk of socialism and asked what this might be. When it had been explained to him he cried out in horror: 'Shall I then nowhere escape this pernicious doctrine? For some time now many of the mob have been preaching exactly the same thing in China!'

Marx and Engels envisaged the glorious moment 'When our European reactionaries, on their presently impending flight through Asia, finally come to the Great Wall of China ... who knows if they may not read the

Institute of East Asian Studies, 1982). For a study on the death and destruction caused by the Taiping war, see S. Platt, *Autumn in the Heavenly Kingdom: China, the West, and the Epic Story of the Taiping Civil War* (New York: Alfred A. Knopf, 2012). This study challenges standard accounts that blame the Taipings alone, not both sides, for the huge carnage. For a study on how the official master narrative of the Qing court failed to account for its inability to contain the Taipings, for the callousness of many of its officials, and for the ubiquitous massacres, rapes, and pillaging of the Hunan and Anhui armies who were fighting for the Qing, see T. Meyer-Fong, *What Remains: Coming to Terms with Civil War in Nineteenth-Century China* (Stanford: Stanford University Press, 2013).

following inscription upon them: RÉPUBLIQUE CHINOISE: LIBERTÉ, ÉGALITÉ, FRATERNITÉ.'[2]

Other Western contemporaries would speak of the Taiping 'revolution-ists' or some other term with the same content but a different evaluation such as 'patriots', 'a new sect of Christians', 'Mohammedans', 'propagators of the most frightful communism', 'Taeping madmen', 'rebel army', 'Mormonites', and 'Puritan fanatics'; some went so far as to define them as part not of China's deliverance but of judgement for its idolatry.[3] Their history, how-ever, did not end there. In China, the Taipings were adopted by early modern Western-style revolutionaries such as Sun Yat-sen (1866–1925) as their nation-alist predecessors[4] and they were later incorporated into the pedigree of the Chinese communist revolution.[5] Ever since, Chinese Marxist historians have dubbed them a 'revolutionary' movement,[6] a description echoed in many Western publications.

There is strong historical and documentary evidence for the Taipings' attempt to overthrow the Manchu government. However, the Taipings' 'revolutionary' credentials come from their being defined as being politically nationalistic and anti-feudal, socially against the landlords, and internation-ally against the big powers. The lack of evidence to support any of these claims has not led to an abandonment of the Taipings' 'revolutionary' character by many scholars from the People's Republic of China (PRC). History, they would argue, is moving behind the backs of its actors. They do not know, and even cannot know, what they are doing, bereft as they are of historical materialism and the conditions for the rise of this theory – an industrial working class. The pressure thus exerted on the historical record has proved too great for some eager souls to resist the temptation to proceed

2 K. Marx and F. Engels, 'Review (January–February 1850)', in *Marx Engels Collected Works* (London: Lawrence & Wishart, 2010), vol. x, pp. 266–7.

3 For an analysis of the images, analogies, and explanatory models used by Westerners for the Taiping movement, see R. G. Wagner, 'Understanding Taiping Christian China: Analogy, Interest, and Policy', in K. Koschorke (ed.), *'Christen und Gewürze'. Konfrontation und Interaktion kolonialer und indigener Christentumsvarianten* (Göttingen: Vandenhoeck & Ruprecht, 1998), pp. 132–57.

4 *Guofu nianpu* [Chronicle of the Founding Father] (Taipei: Zhongguo Guomindang Zhongyang weiyuanhui dangshi shiliao bianzuan weiyuanhui, 1969), vol. i, p. 18; H. Schiffrin, *Sun Yat-sen: Reluctant Revolutionary* (Boston: Little Brown, 1980), p. 23.

5 In the Commemorative Stele for the Revolution on Tian'anmen in Beijing depictions of the Taipings can be seen at the bottom level.

6 Its official name in PRC dictionaries and handbooks is 'Taiping Tianguo Revolution [*Taiping tianguo geming*]'. See, for example, *Cihai* [Dictionary of Terms] (Beijing: Zhonghua shuju, 1965), p. 1192. For a summary of the historiography of this movement, see Teng Ssu-yu, *Historiography of the Taiping Rebellion* (Cambridge, MA: Harvard University Press, 1962), pp. 64, 83.

to data enrichment. To prove the Taipings' opposition to big landlords, it was claimed during the early 1950s that folk songs still sung in the Guangxi area where the rebellion had started in 1848 showed the peasants cursing the big landlords and glorifying the Taipings who helped to get rid of them.[7] The content and language of these folk songs tie in all too well with supposed popular feeling during the land reform drive of the early 1950s, making their claim for authenticity credible.

To prove the nationalistic opposition of the Taipings to 'foreign' Manchu rule, it had to be shown that they were co-operating in a united front with all who were anti-Manchu. The evident candidates for these united front partners were secret societies such as the Small Sword Society, Xiaodao hui, in Shanghai. As no documentary evidence was forthcoming, around 1962 a senior Taiping scholar in Nanjing proceeded to produce (on original period paper) an 'authentic' correspondence between the Taipings and secret society leaders discussing their co-operation.[8] Evidence for the anti-imperialist character of the Taipings was their ban on opium, and their struggle against Charles George Gordon's Ever Victorious Army of foreign mercenaries.

In this context, there were lively if somewhat abstract discussions during the 1950s about the 'revolutionary character of the Taiping revolution', with an editorial by the *People's Daily* determining that the cause of the Taipings' demise was the absence of a proletarian leadership.[9] Other studies, however, discovered a strong 'proletarian' base for the rebellion among the inland water transport labourers who had lost their jobs when the hub of China's overseas trade shifted from Canton to Shanghai after the Opium War (1839–42).[10]

---

7 Rewi Alley has translated some of these 'authentic' pieces in his *Poems of Revolt* (Beijing: New World Press, 1962), pp. 3–34, starting with 'From Yangtang marched in/our Taiping armies; then were/the granaries of landlords/broken open, the good white rice/divided amongst our poor; ever/the Loyal Prince fights/for all poor tenant farmers.' Luo Ergang's sunny description of the Taiping land system in 1950, *Taiping tianguo dili xiangguo. Tianchao tianmu zhidu kao* [The Ideal State of the Taiping Heavenly Kingdom: A Study of the Heavenly Dynasty's Land System] (Shanghai: Shangwu yinshuguan, 1950), is another retroactive description of the Taipings as forerunners of the communist land reform of the early 1950s.

8 Oral communication from E. Perry during the conference 'Religion and Rural Revolt', April 1982, University of British Columbia, Vancouver. To my knowledge, no research has been published on these fakes, but they have been silently withdrawn.

9 Fan Wenlan, 'Jinian Taiping tianguo qiyi 105 zhounian' [Commemoration of the 105th Anniversary of the Taiping Heavenly Kingdom Uprising], *Renmin ribao* [People's Daily] 11 January 1956. This authoritative statement has become part of the handbook definitions as quoted in n. 6.

10 This story found its way into J. Chesneaux, F. Davis, and Nguyen Nguyet Ho (eds.), *Mouvements populaires et sociétés secrètes en Chine aux XIXe et XXe siècles* (Paris: Maspero, 1970).

Eventually, the Taipings also provided historical models for 'traitors' within the ranks of the revolution such as Peng Dehuai, the PRC minister of defence who had been deposed in 1959,[11] as well as the struggle between the two lines of Confucianism and 'legalism' in history that was at the centre of a Cultural Revolution campaign in 1974.[12]

The past forty years have seen substantial change in Taiping research but it still fits the pattern. In the context of a greater official leeway for addressing issues of religion and a reconsideration of relations with the West, some Chinese scholars have begun paying more attention to the religious aspects of the Taipings and even to their relations with the West, without, however, challenging the overall paradigm.[13] At the same time, the return to private farming in the PRC since the early 1980s has led to a marked decline in official interest in the 'revolutionary' Taiping land policies.

Needless to say, the declining worldwide attraction of revolutionary pursuits since the early 1980s, and especially after the meltdown of socialism in the Soviet orbit, has created a scholarly climate that further eroded the consensus in the traditional perception of the Taipings. At the same time, the resurgence and virulence of today's fundamentalist beliefs, along with their manifest practical impact on national and international politics in industrialized as well as Third World nations, have certainly encouraged studies of religious beliefs and their social consequences which do not subscribe to a worldview that the material base determines the superstructure.

---

11 Li Xiucheng, one of the Taiping leaders captured by Qing government forces, wrote a deposition before his execution in which he was critical of many aspects of the Taiping kingdom. This 'capitulation' to the enemy by a top revolutionary leader was denounced in an indirect attack against plans to rehabilitate Peng Dehuai in 1963. See Qi Benyu, 'Ping Li Xiucheng zishu' [Commentary on Li Xiucheng's autobiographical narrative], *Lishi yanjiu* [Historical Studies] 4 (1963), pp. 27–42, and the summary of this article in *Renmin ribao,* 22 August 1963.

12 Huang Yan, 'Hong Xiuquan he Taiping tianguo fan Kong yundong' [Hong Xiuquan and the Taiping Heavenly Kingdom's anti-Confucian movement], *Xuexi yu pipan* [Study and Critique] 2 (1974), pp. 25–8.

13 Xia Chuntao, *Taiping Tianguo zongjiao* [The Religion of the Taiping Heavenly Kingdom] (Nanjing: Nanjing daxue chubanshe, 1992). Xia's work represents the first PRC effort to address the importance of religion in the Taiping enterprise and critically evaluate claims that Taiping religion was just a disguise to fool the masses. However, it maintains the overall paradigm established by PRC scholarship: Wang Qingcheng, *Taiping tianguo de wenxian he lishi* [Documents and History of the Taiping Heavenly Kingdom] (Beijing: Shehuikexueyuan chubanshe, 1993), chs. 6 and 7.

The Theological Background of Taiping Policies

It is thus quite unclear whether the Taipings qualify for the title of 'revolutionaries' in the modern sense of people aspiring to use collective violence to reset the power relationship between their country or camp and outside powers, and to fundamentally change the internal power relations that are seen as being based on unequal property distribution. Still, whether 'revolutionary' or not, the Taipings were able to attract large numbers to their cause, nearly succeeded in overthrowing the Manchu dynasty, drafted a programme outlining a new land system, and ruled considerable parts of southern China long enough to establish some sort of a social and administrative system. In 1858, their new prime minister, Hong Rengan, came out with a master plan for the Taiping Heavenly Kingdom, which had been agreed upon by the entire leadership. The Taipings might have been blind to the deep currents of history moving behind their backs, but they certainly thought they knew what they were supposed to do, and did their best to communicate their plans to a wide audience through an elaborate propaganda system.[14] This means that those who followed them by and large also knew what the Taipings were about, and joined them because of this programme – if they did not join for lack of an alternative. Rather than taking them as but another example illustrating, and perhaps enriching, the familiar preset categories of revolutionary movements, I therefore propose to take their own political and social statements seriously. After having gone through the evidence, I will return to the question of the relationship of the Taiping Heavenly Kingdom of Great Peace with these categories.

In the view of the Taiping leaders, there was a hierarchy of texts with different levels of authority on which to draw in the formulation of religious doctrine and policies. This hierarchy had originally been established by the 'old man' (God) himself when the Taiping leader Hong Xiuquan was in heaven during his vision in 1837.[15] Such a textual hierarchy was familiar to the Taipings from traditional Chinese political and religious culture as well from the evangelical missionaries with whom they were in constant contact. The Chinese tradition provided this hierarchy with its textual gradations between, at the top, the classics in the Confucian world, Sutras in the Buddhist world, and texts associated with Laozi in the Taoist world. The second layers were

---

14 See R. G. Wagner, 'Operating in the Chinese Public Sphere: Theology and Technique of Taiping Propaganda', in Huang Chun-chieh and E. Zürcher (eds.), *Norms and the State in China* (Leiden: Brill, 1993), pp. 104–38.
15 Cf. Wagner, *Reenacting the Heavenly Vision*, pp. 27–31.

made up of commentaries on these texts, to be followed by independent writings, *lun* or *śāstra*, that purported to elaborate on the classical lore. The status of a text would hinge on the status of the author. The Confucian classics were all associated by tradition with Confucius himself as the last of the sages and the editor; the Buddhist Sutras purported to be records of the Buddha's own words; and the Laozi was seen as the embodiment of the Way itself speaking out in a text called *Laozi*. In similar manner, the evangelical hierarchy began with the word of God in the Testaments, and descended, through commentarial and homiletic material of the respective sect or grouping, to the Sunday sermon in the local church.

The Taipings did not feel free to develop their worldview and policies according to their own lights, and saw themselves in a largely passive position depending on guidance and support from God. Hong Xiuquan had not clamoured for some divine revelation; it had been imposed on him in a moment of great personal distress. Once in heaven, he had not demanded to return to earth to wipe out the demons there, but was sent down against his repeated pleas to be allowed to remain. His Heavenly Father even had to fly into a rage to get him moving. Once back on earth, Hong constantly hankered after his heavenly palace and continued to see himself as dependent on direct divine guidance in a grand millennial plan of which he knew neither the rules nor the odds.

At the top in the Taiping textual hierarchy were emanations from God, Jesus, and Hong Xiuquan himself as Jesus' younger brother. These texts were seen as given to the Taipings, not created by them. They were the Hebrew and Christian testaments as well as the Taiping testament with the record of Hong's experience in heaven, and the statements made by God and Jesus through their mediums Yang Xiuqing and Xiao Chaogui respectively.[16] The term 'text' is used here for a complex body of communicated meaning. These 'texts' might be visions or interventions through mediums. As a rule they would be fixed as real texts for purposes of preservation, exegesis, and propagation. Within this top group, texts that were a direct revelation to the Taipings from God and Jesus had the highest ranking. They were in turn

16 As well as the familiar Taiping sources accessible in translation through F. Michael, *The Taiping Rebellion: History and Documents* (Seattle: University of Washington Press, 1971), vols. II and III, two series of heavenly interventions published in official Taiping documents have been discovered and published; see Wang Qingcheng (ed.), *Tianfu tianxiong shengzhi* [Holy Directives of the Heavenly Father and the Holy Directives by the Holy Elder Brother] (Liaoning: Liaoning renmin chubanshe, 1993). Jonathan Spence was the first to explore these newly discovered records; see J. Spence, *God's Chinese Son: The Taiping Heavenly Kingdom of Hong Xiuquan* (New York: W. W. Norton, 1996).

used as the authentic source for the development of a complete and authentic worldview by the heavenly installed Taiping leaders.

In the second layer were partially authenticated texts. Their authority depended on direct heavenly statements or on their association with texts at the top. As God had maintained that the Confucian classics contained much that was acceptable, their teachings had to be critically cleansed of all demonic pollution, but some of them could be used.[17] A text put together by Liang Afa, the first and most trusted evangelical convert in Canton, *Quanshi liangyan* (*Good Words to Admonish the Age*), contained the biblical excerpts from which Hong got his first interpretation of his vision.[18] John Bunyan's *The Pilgrim's Progress* commanded the highest authority among evangelical missionaries after the Bible, and Hong had probably studied its Chinese translation in Canton with the American missionary Issachar Jacox Roberts, an evangelical Southern Baptist who went to China to convert the 'heathen' before the millennium.[19]

In the third layer were Taiping edicts and documents. Written by the Taipings themselves, these texts were deductions from the base texts and provided the specifics of their religious, military, political, and social systems. Below them came a fourth layer, administrative documents, which translated the general line of the edicts into specific action.

Our investigation will thus proceed in two steps; we will study the texts for the development of Taiping beliefs at the top of the textual hierarchy to depict the premises of their eventual social organization, and then turn to their own edicts and texts, with which they set up this organization.

The authorities Hong met in heaven did not show much interest in the social and political structure of the country after the establishment of the Heavenly Kingdom. Hong's vision in heaven defined China's main problem both in symbolical action and explicitly: China had forgotten the one God whom it had originally worshipped. It has been visibly defiled by the pollution of Satan, and internally corrupted through the influence of Confucius and his followers to the point that the country now worshipped Satan. Hong was to drive out this Satan and his underlings from the earth, bring back to the worship of God those who had been deluded by Satan, and prompt them

---

17 The Taiping leadership spent much time in the later years of the movement coming out with 'cleansed' editions of the classics, including military treatises; see Wagner, 'Operating in the Chinese Public Sphere', pp. 132–41.

18 Liang Afa, *Quanshi liangyan* (Guangzhou: n.p., 1832).

19 The first full translation of this text came out only in 1853. But we know that the text was used in catechism teaching much earlier by China missionaries in Canton and Hong Kong.

to keep the Ten Commandments. China's problem is thus defined in moral and religious, rather than political, economic, or social, terms. The position of the villain is occupied by Satan and his underlings, whom the Taipings later identified with the Manchu, the northern people who had used the opportunity of the collapse of the Ming dynasty to take control of the entire Chinese empire. Satan and his underlings are never accused of being the rich or the almighty bureaucrats, not to mention agents of the Western powers. When Hong's nephew Hong Rengan detailed his uncle's background for a Swedish missionary, he confirmed this focus in his summary of *Good Words to Admonish the Age*, the book that had provided Hong with the key to understand his vision: it 'taught people to believe faithfully in God and Jesus Christ, to obey the Ten Commandments, and never to worship demons'. Hong's own record of his vision, the *Taiping tianri* (*Taiping Heavenly Chronicle*; 1848, printed 1862), also agrees.[20]

The annotations to the Testaments made by Hong Xiuquan do not deal with those passages especially in the Gospels where the religious prospects of the rich and the poor are compared, but with the coded prophecies of Hong's own coming in the Testaments. The Taiping works also never refer to the doctrine of social gospel.[21]

The Taipings wrote down the utterances of the two human mediums speaking for God and Jesus respectively. Some of these writings, especially for the period before 1852, survive, showing an intervention by God or Jesus as often as once every ten days.[22] They address very specific matters such as how a certain Taiping leader dared to cohabit with his wife; who will accompany a Taiping leader to a certain village; or whether a certain Taiping follower still had enough to eat for his family after having donated so much to the common coffers. There is not one incident where they intervene to set a political or social agenda. Evidently, these matters rank low in their priorities. We know very little about the heavenly interventions

---

20 The Swedish missionary Theodore Hamberg interviewed Hong Xiuquan's cousin Hong Rengan about his famous relative before Hong Rengan himself joined the Taipings. Hamberg's book *The Visions of Hung-Siu-Tshuen and the Origin of the Kwang-si Insurrection* (1854; repr. New York: Praeger, 1969) is based on this interview. The *Taiping tianri* is included in Xiang Da (ed.), *Taiping tianguo* [The Taiping Heavenly Kingdom] (Shanghai: Shenzhou guoguang she, 1952), where the passage alluded to is on p. 639.

21 The Taiping Bible with Hong's annotations is preserved in the British Museum.

22 The records newly discovered in 1993 show the interventions, through mediums, by the Heavenly Father and the Heavenly Elder Brother into the early management of the Taiping Kingdom; see Spence, *God's Chinese Son*, pp. 107–40.

of the last decade of the kingdom, but the existing edicts and writs do not refer to such authentication, and we might conclude that the focus of attention of both God and Jesus remained about the same.

Their most authoritative sources allowed the Taipings to determine the moral state of their countryfolk, the commandments they should follow, and the identity as well as the character of their opponent: Satan, whom they identified with the Manchu.[23] The vision also told them that only by violent means would they be able to extract their deluded countryfolk from Satan's grip, but it did not offer the blueprint for a social and political agenda. Big landlords, exorbitant taxes, the institution of the emperor, and encroachment by foreign powers were not included in the themes.

From these documents, however, Hong discovered China's history as a history of salvation. There was a time when 'both sovereign and subjects' in China had served God, namely before the Qin dynasty; at that time China, like other and later Christian nations, had walked on the true path. It was God 'the father', wrote Hong, who had 'placed the Heavenly Kingdom in China. China is the original home of the Heavenly Kingdom.' The evidence is that God encoded his own name into that of China: the *hua* in *yehuohua*, the phonetic rendering for Jehovah, is the same character as the *hua* in a common term for China, *Zhonghua*.[24] This view that China had a 'natural' and 'original' knowledge of the one God had long been supported by the evangelical missionaries, who on this point agreed with the late Ming Jesuits. In the meantime, however, as God told Hong in heaven, 'human beings [in China] had in large numbers no original heart any more'. Although they enjoyed God's creation, 'for large numbers of them their original heart has been obscured and they have not the slightest inclination to honor and fear Me'.[25] God ordered Hong to 'study the histories', and from these Hong supplemented the missing details about China's gradual forgetting of God that ended with God's defilement and even a change of his name.[26] Satan had taken over. The best evidence for this was the common belief that the records of the living were kept in hell, where Yanluo, the Buddhist Dragon King,

23 In Richard Bohr's study, 'The Taipings in Chinese Sectarian Perspective', he argues that the particular Christian elements found resonance within popular Chinese 'folk religious sects' in their beliefs and rituals. See Richard Bohr, 'The Taipings in Chinese Sectarian Perspective', in Kwang-Ching Liu and R. Shek (eds.), *Heterodoxy in Late Imperial China* (Honolulu: University of Hawaii Press, 2004), pp. 393–430.
24 Hong Xiuquan, *Tianwang zhaozhi* [The Heavenly King's Decree], in Xiang Da (ed.), *Taiping tianguo*, p. 678. See also Michael, *The Taiping Rebellion*, p. 940.
25 *Taiping tianri*, p. 633; Michael, *The Taiping Rebellion*, p. 54.
26 Hong Xiuquan, *Sanzijing* [The Three Character Classic] (1853), in Xiang Da (ed.), *Taiping tianguo*, p. 226; Michael, *The Taiping Rebellion*, p. 156.

whose Chinese name had been used to translate 'Satan' from Revelations, made the judgements. Control over God's creation had in fact landed in the hands of Satan.[27]

The specific expression of this loss of the 'original heart' was that people ceased to be 'human beings'. The term *ren*, human being, is here used in the sense of a 'true human being' or, in the parlance of other Taiping tracts, a 'hero'. 'Alas, there are no human beings in China', cried Yang Xiuqing in a tract in 1852; all had been deluded by Satan's underlings.[28] The Taipings did not appeal to the populace as a morally pure, suppressed but upright class, to join in a common enterprise to overthrow the oppressors and to establish a Kingdom of Great Peace. They called on them as a deluded, despicable crowd of slaves. They should confess and repent their sins, and submit to the rigid discipline of the Ten Commandments and Taiping orders in the hope of gaining access to the Heavenly Kingdom on earth and then in heaven under the guidance of the one God's second son, Hong Xiuquan, who had been sent down to earth for this very purpose.

The loss of the 'original heart' was further specified. Hong wrote in 1845 or 1846 in a tract of which we have the version published in 1852:

> Recall the times of Tang and Yu and of the Three Dynasties; in that world, those who had and those who had not were mutually compassionate, and in calamity they aided one another . . . [The sage emperors] Yao and Shun made no distinction between this land and that land. Yu and Ji made no distinctions between this people and that people . . . Tang and Wu made no distinction between this country and that country. Confucius and Mengzi . . . made no distinction between this state and that state. This was because all these Illustrious Ones saw that the mortal earth, when spoken of in its parts, comprises the ten thousand kingdoms, but [that these, in turn], when spoken of collectively, constitute one family . . . China, which is near us, is governed and regulated by the great God; foreign nations, which are far away, are also [governed] thus.[29]

The main problem of China in this vision of things is not an unequal distribution of wealth or the encroachment of foreign powers, but that the Chinese are ruled by *si*, petty concerns that were private or local. These take the form of caring only for one's personal wellbeing and prosperity and not

---

27 *Taiping tianri*, p. 633; Michael, *The Taiping Rebellion*, p. 54.
28 Yang Xiuqing and Xiao Zhaogui, *Banxing zhaoshu* [Issuing the Edict] (1852), in Xiang Da (ed.), *Taiping tianguo*, p. 161; Michael, *The Taiping Rebellion*, p. 145.
29 *Taiping zhaoshu. Yuandao xingshi xun* [A Taiping Edict: Instructions on the Original Way to Awaken the World] (1852), in Xiang Da (ed.),*Taiping tianguo*, p. 91; Michael, *The Taiping Rebellion*, p. 35.

for that of others, of caring only for one's own clan, village, province or state and not for others. They were oblivious of the fact that

> Shangdi, the Heavenly Father, is shared by each human being, all under heaven are one family, and in the world all are brothers . . . Speaking about the souls of human beings, whence are they born? Whence do they spring? They are all born from and have sprung from the breath of the one August Shangdi.[30]

Driven by these petty concerns, 'original settlers' and 'guest settlers', Hakka and Punti, would fight each other, villages would go to war against each other, and the Chinese would battle foreigners who also believed in God. From the juxtaposition of these different social, economic, clan, village, and state-to-state relations it is clear that the notion of *si* is by no means primarily economic, but refers to petty personal interests in a much broader sense.

The general drift of this argumentation is anything but a populist appeal for support. These texts are cursing not only the 'demonic' Manchu, but also the Chinese and their Confucian elite for their abandoning the true God, and for letting themselves be deluded by Satan to follow their narrowest interests. The Taipings here started a tradition that continued well into the twentieth century when even fiercely nationalistic politicians such as Liang Qichao (1873–1929) or Chen Duxiu (1879–1942) would harangue their own country-folk's narrow focus on their own immediate interests in no uncertain terms as the root cause of China's disaster.

The two core terms, *gong* and *liang*, used by Hong to describe *ren*, the true human being, highlight this point. *Gong* is the direct antonym of *si*, and might be translated as public-spiritedness, while *liang* means broad-mindedness. Hong begins his 'Exhortation on the Origin of Virtue for the Awakening of the Age', from which the previous quotations were also taken, with the following words:

> When formerly blessings were great, this was due to broad-mindedness being great, and he whose broad-mindedness was great was a great human being. And when blessings are small, this is due to broad-mindedness being small, and he whose broad-mindedness is small is a petty man.
>
> That is why Mount Tai does not reject [even small] clods of earth, and thus is able to achieve its greatness. The rivers and seas do not disdain [even] the smallest trickle, and thus are able to complete their depth. And [if] a king

---

30 *Taiping zhaoshu. Yuandao jiushi ge* [A Taiping Edict: A Song on the Origin Way and Salvation], in Xiang Da (ed.),*Taiping tianguo*, p. 87. See also pp. 92–3; Michael, *The Taiping Rebellion*, pp. 25, 37.

does not disregard the common people, [he] is able to complete his power [in a later edition: God-on-high broadly creates the multitudes of people, and thus is able to make his power great]. These [the greatness of Mount Tai, the depth of the waters and the greatness of God's power] are all brought about by broad-mindedness.[31]

This broad-mindedness, *liang*, is thus a heavenly virtue, even of God himself, but, as the beginning phrases said, the great and real human being will also have them. Hong continues:

> But this is quite different from times as they are today, and awkward to say. The ways of the present world are perverse and wicked, the hearts of men are evil and shallow, their loves as well as their hates all arise from selfishness. Thus it happens that those from this state hate those from that state; there are even cases within one country where this province, this prefecture, or this district hates that province, that prefecture, or that district ... The ways of the world and the hearts of men having come to this, how could they do otherwise than oppress one another, seize one another, fight one another, and kill one another, and thus perish altogether. [The cause of this] is nothing else but that their horizon is small, and therefore their broad-mindedness is small.[32]

Hong rails against his readers for failing to be real human beings. They can acquire the proper broad-mindedness only if they do two things: first, open their horizons with *liang* to a world perspective where all human beings (with the exception of the demons) are one family of God's children and where thus a commonweal of all of them exists in which they, secondly, can exert their public-spiritedness. To epitomize his point, he stresses that the one and only God, who for most of his audience was identified as the God worshipped by the Westerners, actually was the God worshipped by rulers and commoners in the pre-imperial ideal times of China, and quotes the works of Chinese sages from antiquity side by side with those of 'Western sages'.

The Taipings arose at a time described in the prevailing master narrative as the beginning of imperialist impositions on China with the Opium War. Legitimized as a defence of 'free trade', the narrative goes, these impositions were in fact designed to facilitate the import of opium into China from India by British and other Western traders. With their starting point in south China, the Taipings were close to the Opium War conflagration in terms of space. Their campaign against what Marx would have called a Chinese

---

31 *Taiping zhaoshu. Yuandao xingshi xun* (1852), pp. 91–109; Michael, *The Taiping Rebellion*, p. 35.
32 Michael, *The Taiping Rebellion*, p. 35.

'idiotism' (obsessive concern with oneself and one's immediate environment and ignorance about the rest) included an attack on the denigration of other peoples. The slave/human being dichotomy also applied. The people of 'Christian' Western nations qualified as human beings while the other peoples had to be saved by being re-educated by benign colonizers, among them Taiping Christian China. In this manner, Taiping China would be in the same league as its 'overseas brethren and sisters', from the British Isles, the United States, and so forth. This was another radical and bold move without populist coating that foreshadows notions of 'proletarian internationalism' and the 'brotherhood of socialist states' half a century later, with the dividing line not being the capitalists, colonialists, and imperialists on one side, and the hard-working poor on the other, but faith in the one God as the key link and qualifying criterion.[33] The unfounded post-colonialist assumption that, perhaps unwittingly, the Taipings had been brainwashed by their missionary contacts into actually wishing to defend Western interests does not hold. In a consistent display of their theological and political independence, they maintained that Hong's path to heaven went directly from China unmediated by a missionary figure, eagerly embraced what the missionaries introduced as 'useful knowledge' and its associated institutions such as newspapers, railways, and hospitals, and imposed the death penalty on those caught consuming opium while at the same time cheerfully maintaining that the Westerners were brothers and sisters and would eventually come around to recognize Hong as God's second son.

This attack on *si* focused on a deep-seated contradiction in the structure of Chinese values. On the level of normative values, *si* had an exceedingly bad name, while there was also a consensus among the defenders of these normative values that in their practice people and even part of the elite were driven not by public-mindedness, *gong*, but by *si*. The pressure from this normative value was still visible many years after the Taipings' demise. It took decades of discussions in Shanghai, the town that profited most from the flight of the wealthy and the bright from the Taipings, to develop a credible concept that would justify the pursuit of profit, *li*, the epitome of *si*, by its most prominent citizens, the businesspeople, as something which under certain circumstances could be of public benefit until eventually a term for 'profit with public benefits', *gongli*, was created. The Taiping attack on *si* thus took up a previously existing conflict between normative values and the values seen

33 See R. G. Wagner, 'God's Country in the Family of Nations: The Logic of Modernism in the Taiping Doctrine of International Relations', in J. Bak and G. Benecke (eds.), *Religion and Rural Revolt* (Manchester: Manchester University Press, 1984), pp. 354–72.

as dominating practical action, and created the discursive framework in which the grand debates – no longer on the Heavenly Kingdom, but on the nation's fate altogether – were to be articulated in the decades to come:

> The Taiping followers, these petty people, accordingly, were not a reliable crowd. The first virtue they had to acquire was obedience to the thundering Shangdi and his second son, who will 'with the iron rod' force them out of their evil ways and onto the road of becoming real human beings. In the bluntest statement of the kind in a Taiping official publication we read that Jesus said in December 1851 through his medium Xiao Zhaogui: 'Someone who has become a human being does not act on his/her own.'[34]

This true human being is not defined by gender or economic and political status but by realizing the value of broad-mindedness in actions in obedience to the one God and his Commandments. Even though Hong felt prompted to

德天

Fig. 4.1   Hong Xiuquan (1814–64), leader of the Taiping rebellion. (CPA Media Pte Ltd/ Alamy.)

34 *Tianming zhaoshu* [The Mandate of Heaven Edict] (1852), in Xiang Da (ed.), *Taiping tianguo*, p. 62; Michael, *The Taiping Rebellion*, p. 102.

see himself as God's second son sent to earth to drive out the demons and save the world from Satan's delusions, the Taiping documents do not demand obedience to Hong as an individual but only to the policies dictated by his father and older brother. The Taiping land programme and their social programme as a whole must be understood in this context.

The Taiping Land Programme

The political and social institutions of the Taipings were developed out of a religious and moral impulse. They were to create a social and political climate in which people would not fall into the trappings of *si* and *xiao*, pettiness. Even economic institutions are thus moral in their intent.

In the absence of specific directives from either God or Jesus concerning the economic institutions of the Heavenly Kingdom, the Taipings proceeded in a dogmatically sober and sound manner. These institutions must be those that were in place when China still walked, as God himself had declared, on the road of Christian nations, that is, before the Qin dynasty. In the formative early writings from which I have quoted, a number of core statements and terms occur which are taken from the depictions of the ideal state contained primarily in the *Book of Rites* (*Liji*) and the *Ritual of Zhou* (*Zhouli*), both of which ranked among the classics in the Confucian textual hierarchy under the Qing government.

The depictions of the ideal state in these texts are as moral as those by Hong Xiuquan. The 'Liyun' ('The Conveyance of Rites') chapter of the *Book of Rites* has Confucius sigh about the deterioration of the present times, saying:

> It has not been given to me to see the Great Way being practised and to associate with the heroes of the three dynasties [of Chinese antiquity], but [my] purpose is set on this [emulating these times and heroes].
>
> When the Great Way was being practised, all-under-Heaven was public-spirited, one selected the worthy and the capable, the words were sincere and what they cultivated was in harmony. Therefore, men did not only treat their [own] parents as their parents [but those of others as well], they did not only treat their [own] children as their children [but those of others as well], they took care that the old people were secured until their death, that the able-bodied had employment, and that the young had the means to grow up. They showed kindness and compassion to widows, orphans, and childless men as well as those disabled by disease so that all had a livelihood, the males had their proper work, and the females their homes. As to goods, they disliked abandoning them on the ground, but did not necessarily store them for themselves; as to their strength, they disliked it not being exerted,

but did not necessarily exert it for their own [benefit]. Therefore, [selfish] schemings were closed and did not flourish, robbers, filchers, and rebellious villains did not show themselves. As a consequence. the outer doors [of the houses] were not locked. This was called Great Community, *datong*.[35]

Confucius then goes, much like Hong, into a lengthy diatribe against the society of his day in its moral decay. For Confucius, the instrument to restore this original society is the imposition of behavioural rules, 'ritual'. The Taipings followed this advice by establishing their own rules of conduct regulating religious life, public behaviour, and administrative communications in their realm. In the process, they incorporated many of those features of imperial Confucianism that they considered healthy. The basic motive determining the particulars of the social structure is a didactic one. The heavenly ordained administrators of the Heavenly Kingdom had to protect their subjects from their spontaneous and constantly recurring evil urges by establishing a social environment inimical to such urges, and a state system enforcing what was best for the populace.

Jian Yuwen has stressed the importance of religious factors in the development of the Taiping land system, and has documented some of them.[36] He does not address, however, what I would consider the ultimately religious and moral purpose of the entire system.

Chapters 9 and 10 of the *Ritual of Zhou* outline a system of unified ritual, moral, social, legal, and economic control in the countryside under the grand and small Situ of the Offices of Earth (responsible for the taxation and division of land). The land there is said to be 'equalized' according to the varying levels of soil quality, and the population is enrolled into a tight quasi-military organization controlling all aspects of their lives. Again, the argumentative environment is wholly moral, with the highest value being the stability of the state.[37]

During imperial times, the pressure from the 'equal field system' model supposedly prevalent in antiquity, a physiocratic ideology that saw agriculture as the basis of the economy, and social tensions arising from increased population pressure and accumulation of land by landlords and officials with legal as well as illegal tax exemptions led to repeated efforts to equalize land

35 *Liji*, chapter 'Liyun', in *Mémoires sur les bienséances et les cérémonies*, trans. S. Couvreur (Paris: Cathasia, 1930), vol. I.2, pp. 497–8 (author's translation).
36 Jian Yuwen, *Taiping tianguo dianzhi tongkao* [A Comprehensive Study of the Taiping Heavenly Kingdom's Law Codes] (Hong Kong: Renshi mengjin shuwu, 1958), pp. 1567–2054.
37 *Zhouli*, ed. Shisan jing zhushu (Beijing: Zhonghua, 1980); cf. *Le Tcheou-li ou les rites des Tcheou*, trans. J.-B. Biot (Paris: Imprimerie nationale, 1851), vol. I, pp. 192–4.

holdings, tax burdens, and property rights. These efforts were particularly prevalent in dynasties that set out to emulate antiquity, among them the Taiping Heavenly Kingdom of Great Peace. Theoretically, the state was the ultimate owner of the land and thus could intervene to change land-holding structures. Earlier dynasties had tried to achieve more equally distributed land holdings by encouraging landless peasants to settle on virgin lands or distributing land from areas devastated by war or rebellion, but they all ended up with ever increasing concentration of land in fewer hands, together with increasing numbers of landless tenants and an ensuing rise in social tensions.[38] The Taiping land policies followed a similar track of agrarian reform, unhampered by the need to accommodate elite interests, because most elite members had fled the territory under their control. They radicalized these established policies of many new dynasties to establish an economic environment that promised to be beneficial to their subjects' moral betterment.

For many other aspects of their administration, they also opted for a merger of Chinese and Western elements. Like every new dynasty, they reset the calendar, but emulated the Christian linear calendar (rather than one marked by reign names as under the Qing or programmatic slogans as in previous dynasties) by starting their own with the first year of the Heavenly Kingdom of Great Peace. Their publications used a simplified language with some new words invented and others shunned as taboo, drawing on court-sponsored writings designed to spread imperial Confucianism in the countryside through vernacular texts and on missionary writings in Chinese that tried to reach audiences with low literacy levels. Following Chinese tradition, they opted for a monarchical system with some indication that the throne could be inherited but their system was ideologically anchored in there being only one God and the Taiping Heavenly Kingdom of Great Peace being set up on his direct orders and upon his authority.

The core document of the Taipings on land policy is the *Tianchao tianmu zhidu (Field System of the Heavenly Dynasty)* from 1853, issued shortly after the establishment of the New Jerusalem in Nanjing.[39] It was never put into practice on any greater scale[40] but certainly is of importance as an expression

38 While clan or monastery ownership of land was common, no pre-modern efforts are known to manage land collectively (outside military settlements in border regions).
39 *Tianchao tianmu zhidu*, in Xiang Da (ed.), *Taiping tianguo*, pp. 319–25.
40 Luo Ergang has suggested that this system was enacted at least around Nanjing: Luo Ergang, *Taiping tianguo dili xiangguo. Tianchao tianmu zhidu kao* [The Ideal State of the Taiping Heavenly Kingdom: A Study of the Heavenly Dynasty's Field System] (Shanghai: Shangwu yinshuguan, 1950). There is documentary evidence that, at least

of Taiping thinking. The document establishes in each Taiping army two persons who are in charge of land division. Land is to be classed into nine grades of quality; the quality is determined by grain productivity (other agricultural products such as tea, silk, vegetables, and fruit are not considered). Land is to be allocated by sheer individual numbers, with women receiving, stunningly, an equal share.

The Taiping leadership mostly came from Hakka ('guest people') backgrounds in Guangdong province in China's south. According to lore, the Hakka, who kept their own dialect, had migrated south when non-Han Chinese peoples occupied China's north. As latecomers, they could not get the fertile lands in the valleys, which were in the hands of the Punti ('locals'). Growing crops on the hillsides was unforgiving work with little economic benefit. As the Hakka families were generally rather poor, their women were required to help till the land. This was made possible by their women not having their feet bound. While we do not have a Taiping document banning foot-binding, the distribution of land to women created a substantial incentive for non-Hakka women to discontinue this practice while also cutting links to a beauty ideal adopted by the Confucian elite since the Tang dynasty. The idea of women being entitled to land ownership might go back to relevant laws in some states of the United States since 1809, but the notion that they should get an equal share of land to that of men is derived from the radical Taiping notion of the 'human being'. We also see this in place in another, even more challenging, domain, the military. The Taipings had several military units composed of women and led by women officers. There was no Western model for this, and there is no record of Hakka women taking part in the frequent feuds with Punti in southern China or joining the militias formed for the purpose. Again, their role as soldiers is derived from a radical Taiping reading of the 'human being'. At least during time of war, the Taipings imposed a rigid separation of men and women, including married couples. It was part of a code of rigidly enforced discipline that might have been instrumental in largely preventing the rape and plunder associated with Chinese armies at the time and signalling to the populace that this was a different kind of army.[41] They banned prostitution.

---

for the time being, the Taipings continued to levy regular taxes, handed out deeds of land, and permitted the sale of land. For a most detailed analysis of both the normative rules and the actual practice, see Jian, *Taiping tianguo dianzhi tongkao*, pp. 491–554.

41 According to the PRC historiography about the war with Japan and the Civil War, this was one of the key differences between the Chinese communist armies and their opponents. It helped in developing local support.

Land, however, did not become fully private property. All the world had been created by God, and thus he was considered the owner of the entire land, to be administered by the Taiping leadership. In principle, scholars agree, land would have been treated as Taiping state property. The nation's fields and the harvests are to be considered as a whole. 'All the fields in the empire shall be cultivated by all the people alike', the text says, and continues in an indirect quotation from the *Zhouli*:

> if the land is deficient in one place, then the people must be removed to another, and if the land is deficient in another, then the people must be removed to [the first] place. *All the fields throughout the empire, whether of abundant or deficient harvest, shall be taken as a whole:* If this place is deficient, then the harvest of that abundant place must be removed to relieve it, and if that place is deficient, then the harvest of this abundant place must be removed in order to relieve the deficient place. *Thus all the people in the empire may together enjoy the abundant happiness of the Heavenly Father, Supreme Lord and Great God. There being fields, let all cultivate them; there being food, let all eat; there being clothes, let all be dressed; there being money, let all use it so that nowhere does inequality exist, and no man is not well fed and clothed.*[42]

In order to set up this system, the officials must get hold of the harvest. The text continues:

> At the time of harvest, every sergeant shall direct the corporals to see to it that of the twenty-five families under his charge every individual has a sufficient supply of food, and aside from the new grain each may receive, the remainder must be deposited in the public granary. Of wheat, pulse, hemp, flax, cloth, silk, fowls, dogs etc., and money, the same is true; *for the whole empire is the universal family of our Heavenly Father, the Supreme Lord and Great God.* When all the people in the empire will not take anything as their own but submit all things to the Supreme Lord, then the Lord will make use of them, and in the universal family of the empire, every place will be equal and every individual well fed. This is the intent of our Heavenly Father, the Supreme Lord and Great God, in specially commanding the True Sovereign of Taiping to save the world.[43]

The reserves would be delivered to a public granary to be established for each group of twenty-five families. There were no provisions for collective labour. This system in fact eliminated the local leaders from positions of power, and established the Taiping officials as the men in full control of the

---

42 *Tianchao tianmu zhidu*, p. 321. The translation follows *North China Herald*, 16 September 1854 (emphasis added).
43 *Tianchao tianmu zhidu*, p. 322 (emphasis added).

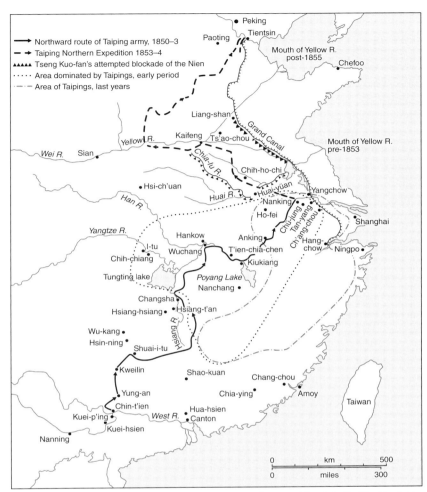

Map 4.1 The Taiping rebellion, 1850–1864. Source: John K. Fairbank (ed.), *The Cambridge History of China*, vol. x, *Late Ch'ing, 1800–1911*, Part 1 (Cambridge: Cambridge University Press, 1978).

allocation of 'necessary' means of survival, and of the entire surplus. Various emoluments and punishments were introduced as incentives to produce more and to deter slackness in work. The system was a part of a broader system of rural control. The boys were to go to church every day to be instructed by the officials; everyone else was to go together on the Sabbath, with men and women sitting separately, as in revivalist churches. In cases of litigation, the local Taiping officials were the sole mediators, and a full chain of command linked them to higher levels up to the court in Nanjing. The system also included military recruitment, and recruitment for official positions. The Taipings ran an authoritarian theocracy.

From this description, it becomes clear that the system is designed to eliminate whatever there might be in terms of *si*, of direct and petty interest, be it in the material or the spiritual realms. The commonality of all-under-Heaven is envisaged not only as the establishment of the equality of men and women, high and low, rich and poor, but also as that between different regions and different parts of the world. It is established not through an appeal to the better urges of mankind, but by administrative order reinforced by massive penal sanctions. What might in one language be described as a life in the hands of God free of the narrow pettiness of *si* and full of public-spiritedness, broad-mindedness, and solidarity may be described in another as the ultimate and benevolent transformation of the rural population into slaves both in the physical and in the spiritual realms.

The system was never fully put into practice.[44] This might have a variety of reasons, among them the inability to come up with the personnel able to staff such a vast bureaucracy, and the continuing warfare, quite apart from the many technical weaknesses of the system that lacked a number of provisions without which it could not become operational, such as the question of land rotation, or the problems arising with people's motivation to produce beyond what they themselves might need for some anonymous state coffer or other region. The Taipings in fact left things as they were: farmers kept their property and were required to pay taxes and, in areas where new land could be distributed because parts of the original population had fled, they handed out land deeds in the traditional manner. There is no language or policy directed against big land-owners or in favour of poor peasants.

The social status associated with being a peasant was most clearly expressed in the fact that it was one of the lighter criminal punishments for Taiping officials to be degraded to the status of a peasant. A sizeable part of those who joined the Taiping cause did so under the assumption that they would never again be farmers, but would become officials of the new dynasty. Statements by both God and Jesus reinforced this expectation. Those who survived the ordeals of Taiping enforcement of the Ten

---

44 This might be seen as a boon rather than a bane for the analysis of the Taipings because their policy statements had not undergone any tempering from the actual experience of implementation.

Commandments and other regulations as well as the gruesome battles were the Human Beings, the Heroes, who would join in ruling the rest of the population with Moses' 'iron rod' to help them never again to deviate from God's stern orders. Obedience to God's orders was the way to life.

Conclusion

Economy and class play no important role in the Taiping land programme. The programme is part of a state structure designed to provide an environment in which the children of God will have neither the urge nor the chance to deviate from God's stern commands. Elaine Pagels has described the development of the Christian state doctrine since Augustine's time;[45] in this doctrine the state plays the role with regard to the populace in which reason and will play within a human being with regard to the evil passions. This power structure finds a counterpart in certain trends in Chinese imperial thinking about the state with which the Taipings linked up. It is the idea of the state being more reasonable than its citizens, and thus able to set up a ritual and economic environment protecting the citizens against their own irrational urges. The traditional Chinese state drew legitimacy for this role from the association of its officials with Confucian morality, ritual, and learning, but not from their being seen as the engineers of effective policies. The Taipings, on the other hand, were justified in their role by a direct mandate from God, and by themselves submitting to the same rigours as their subjects. There is no record of Taiping leaders personally amassing large land holdings or other fortunes.

The state system later envisaged by the new Taiping prime minister Hong Rengan easily incorporated many of the features he had seen and heard about in the British crown colony of Hong Kong.[46] Again, the state described by him, which does not explicitly refer to the land programme, primarily establishes a moral environment conducive to Christian behaviour. With this as the main motive, Hong Rengan was able to suggest a new set of institutions to which the Taiping leadership was able to agree. The differences are merely superficial because the religious purpose of the two blueprints is similar.

I would suggest, however, that this might be an occasion to reconsider the question of whether the self-depiction of communism with its strong

45 E. Pagels, *Adam, Eve, and the Serpent* (New York: Vintage Books, 1988).
46 So Kwan-wai, E. P. Boardman, and Ch'iu P'ing, 'Hung Jen-Kan, Taiping prime minister, 1859–1864', *Harvard Journal of Asiatic Studies* 20, 1–2 (June 1957), pp. 262–94.

materialist and economist emphasis is accurate and credible. In view of the modern Chinese communist experience, I would instead suggest that, if the Taipings do not qualify as the communists' precursors in the latter's terms, the communists might qualify as the Taipings' successors in the Taipings' terms, which has been often suggested to be true for Western communists in their relationship to the Christian tradition. The communist denunciation of the spontaneous tendency, especially of farmers and of businesspeople, to follow their very *si* urges for private profit and security, and to disregard their neighbour's, their nation's, and the socialist camp's precarious fate in the process has led to mass killings (land reform), mass starvation (the Great Leap Forward), and mass persecution and re-education (the Cultural Revolution) on a scale matched by the Taipings only in terms of the high register in which the necessity of these developments was articulated, and the sheer numbers of victims involved. It was a foreigner, himself something like a minister of foreign affairs for the Taipings in their capital Nanjing, who came out with the sternest definition of the alternatives open to an enterprise like the Taipings. On 23 May 1861, Issachar Jacox Roberts, the Southern Baptist missionary who had taught the Taiping leader Hong Xiuquan for a while in Canton, wrote from Nanjing to the *Overland China Mail* in a statement that might reflect the attitude of the Taiping leadership as much as that of many of the most fervent believers in the glory of the Heavenly Kingdom to come:

> A revolution, and especially civil war, is and must always be unpleasant to the common people. But do not editors admit, as well as missionaries, that there is a higher power that rules the nations and if so the one who wrote this article before me [in which the Taipings were criticized] must admit that God has not been an idle spectator of the Teen Wang [Heavenly King, that is, Hong Xiuquan] movement, that it has not all happened so; for He has said 'the nation and kingdom that will not serve me shall perish'. Has not China been tested long enough, and proved by the practice for thousands of years that 'they will not serve' Christ, the Lord? Did not the Canaanites when they had titled up [given name to] their iniquity, perish by Joshua as these are now perishing and more so? And what a hue and cry the editors of that day might have raised against Joshua, about the cruelty of his course, his injury to commerce and a thousand other faults. And how do we know but what the appointment is from the same high authority in this case? It is claimed to be, and the above test seems to favor the idea. *And in fact would it not be better in the highest sense of the word for half the nation to be exterminated, than to go on as they have been doing, if the other half would thereby learn righteousness?*[47]

47 I. J. Roberts, 'Letter', dated Nanking 23 May 1861, *Overland China Mail* 239, 12 July 1861 (emphasis added).

Further Reading

Jen Yu-wen [Jian Yuwen], *The Taiping Revolutionary Movement* (New Haven: Yale University Press, 1973).

Meyer-Fong, Tobie, *What Remains: Coming to Terms with Civil War in Nineteenth-Century China* (Stanford: Stanford University Press, 2013).

Michael, Franz H., *The Taiping Rebellion: History and Documents* (Seattle: University of Washington Press, 1971), 3 vols.

Platt, Stephen R., *Autumn in the Heavenly Kingdom: China, the West, and the Epic Story of the Taiping Civil War* (New York: Alfred A. Knopf, 2012).

Spence, Jonathan, *God's Chinese Son: The Taiping Heavenly Kingdom of Hong Xiuquan* (New York: W. W. Norton, 1996).

Wagner, Rudolf G., *Reenacting the Heavenly Vision: The Role of Religion in the Taiping Rebellion*, China Research Monograph 25 (Berkeley: Institute of East Asian Studies, 1982).

EARLY SOCIALISMS

5

Saint-Simon and Saint-Simonism

JEREMY JENNINGS

Marx and Engels on the Utopian Socialists

Saint-Simon occupies a surprisingly central place in the narrative of what has become the socialist tradition. He does so primarily because he and his contemporaries Charles Fourier and Robert Owen were singled out by Karl Marx and Friedrich Engels in the *Communist Manifesto* as representatives of 'critical-utopian socialism and communism'.[1] In a magnificently polemical tour de force in which Marx and Engels sought to demolish the pretensions of all forms of socialism other than their own – doing so quite brilliantly, as their characterization of 'petty-bourgeois socialism' as a 'pusillanimous hangover' illustrates – Saint-Simon and his fellow utopians were summarily dismissed as purveyors of 'the best possible plan for the best possible society'.[2]

The substance of the charge was that the systems of Saint-Simon et al. were products of the first, but 'undeveloped', period of struggle between the proletariat and the bourgeoisie, with the result that, although their founders saw 'the active elements of dissolution in prevailing society', they could not attribute any historical autonomy to the proletariat. As Marx and Engels explained, 'Since the development of class conflict proceeds in step with the development of industry, they discover few material conditions for the emancipation of the proletariat, and they search for a social science based on social laws in order to create these conditions.' As Marx and Engels brilliantly summarized, 'In place of activity in society they have to introduce their personally invented forms of action, in place of historical conditions for emancipation they have to introduce fantastic ones, in place of the gradually

---

1 For a brief summary of the place of utopianism within the socialist tradition, see G. Claeys, *Searching for Utopia: The History of an Idea* (London: Thames and Hudson, 2011), pp. 140–9.
2 Terrell Carver (ed.), *Marx: Later Political Writings* (Cambridge: Cambridge University Press, 1996), p. 27.

developed organisation of the proletariat into a class they have to introduce a specially contrived organisation of society.' From this point of view, Marx and Engels continued, the proletariat existed only as 'the most suffering class' and the ambition of the utopians was 'to improve the circumstances of all members of society, even the best placed'. All political, and especially revolutionary, action was rejected, with the goal of the utopians to be reached by peaceful means and the power of example. As Marx and Engels concluded, 'to the extent that the class struggle develops and takes shape, this fantastic transcendence of the class struggle, this fantastic attack on the class struggle, loses all practical worth, all theoretical justification'.[3] Was there, we might ask, any substance to these damning remarks?

Claude-Henri de Rouvray, Comte de Saint-Simon

No account of Saint-Simon's thought would be complete without at least a cursory glance at his somewhat unusual life. He was born in 1760 into one of the most distinguished of France's aristocratic families, which, although not very rich, owned a château and extensive estates in the northern province of Picardy. In 1778 he joined the French army and later fought, with some distinction, alongside the American troops under George Washington's command at the Battle of Yorktown against the British. From the outset, he supported the Revolution of 1789, during which he relinquished his title and changed his name to plain Citizen Bonhomme in a ceremony of republican baptism. Support for the revolution did not prevent Saint-Simon from seeking to make a fortune out of property speculation, for which he was arrested in 1793. He was released only after the fall of Robespierre in July 1794 and the end of the Reign of Terror. Under the Directory (1795–9), he expanded his commercial activities and lived in some splendour in Paris, where he hosted a *salon* attended by many of France's leading mathematicians and scientists. He married in 1801; divorced in 1802; was declared bankrupt in 1804; lived off his former butler until 1810; had a nervous breakdown and was hospitalized in 1813; and then spent the remaining years of his life living off a pension provided by his family. Having attempted to commit suicide in 1823 by firing seven bullets into his head, Saint-Simon died in 1825. As Theodore Zeldin remarked a good few years ago: 'Saint-Simon was not only a genius who sometimes resembled a madman; he

---

3 Ibid., pp. 27–9.

actually spent a period in a sanatorium for mental diseases and received treatment from the celebrated Dr Pinel.'[4]

Saint-Simon's publications first began to appear in 1802 with his *Letters from an Inhabitant of Geneva to His Contemporaries*. This was followed by a veritable stream of articles, pamphlets, essays, periodical publications, and manifestos of one sort or another. Most were devoted to science and the reorganization of society, with each piece usually outlining some half-baked scheme or project. Copies would be sent to eminent individuals (including the emperor Napoleon and, later, Louis XVIII). We know for a fact that many remained unread. Saint-Simon's most famous work, *The New Christianity*, was published in the year of his death.

Such profusion has given rise to a distinct set of intellectual problems when dealing with Saint-Simon's thought. One (which will not be dwelt on here) is the extent to which Saint-Simon, rather than Auguste Comte, can be regarded as the founder of positivism and sociology. A second (illustrated by the comments of Marx and Engels) is what Frank E. Manuel called the 'appearance problem'. As Manuel wrote: 'Becoming a precursor, he ceased to be a man.'[5] In brief, Saint-Simon has frequently been seen as a forerunner of later intellectual developments and movements. So, if in his day he was largely seen as a liberal, he has since been seen as a harbinger not only of socialism but also of anarchism, totalitarianism, Christian radicalism, technocratic government, the European Union, and much more. It is testimony to the fecundity of Saint-Simon's ideas that they have been subject to such varied interpretation, but it does add to the problem of deciding where, if at all, he sits within the tradition of socialist thought. As we will see, the same might be said of his devoted (and talented) group of admirers who did so much to perpetuate his memory in the later decades of the nineteenth century.

How then might we summarize the core ideas developed by Saint-Simon? Like many a writer of his day Saint-Simon situated his reflections on contemporary society within an analysis of the broad sweep of history. He therefore divided the history of the Western world into three distinct epochs: the Greek and Roman; the Christian and medieval; and the scientific or 'positive'. At their height, each of these so-called organic epochs was characterized by a prevailing form of explanation, a dominant moral and intellectual system that served to bind society together, and a set of political and social

---

4 T. Zeldin, *Politics and Anger* (Oxford: Oxford University Press, 1979), p. 69.
5 F. E. Manuel, *The New World of Henri Saint-Simon* (Cambridge, MA: Harvard University Press, 1956), p. 4.

institutions in conformity with existing ideas and circumstances. However, if the movement from one epoch to another represented a movement to a superior stage, it meant that society had to pass through a 'critical' or transitional period in which one moral and intellectual system was replaced by another. It was precisely at such a 'critical' moment, Saint-Simon believed, that European civilization then found itself. The Christian and medieval worldview was on the point of collapse, and with that came the disintegration of its social and political institutions.

Saint-Simon highlighted two factors to explain this development. The first was the rise of science from the early Middle Ages onwards. The heroes here were Francis Bacon, René Descartes, Isaac Newton, and John Locke, all of whom had played a major role in undermining the monotheistic explanation of the universe and had brought about a scientific revolution. The second event was the emergence of industry and of the industrial class. This was to be a recurring theme in Saint-Simon's writings but the point here was that, with the rise of *les industriels*, the aristocratic, military, and religious classes that had dominated medieval society had lost their *raison d'être*, and this was so for the simple reason that they no longer had a useful function to perform. This idea was most famously (and controversially) expressed by Saint-Simon in what is known as his 'political parable', published in 1819. Let us imagine, Saint-Simon conjectured, that all of a sudden France were to lose its princes, its aristocrats, its great officers of the Crown, its chief magistrates, its marshals, all its cardinals, archbishops, bishops, and vicars-general, its ministerial employees, its judges, and 'the ten thousand richest property owners who live in the style of nobles'. This accident, Saint-Simon wrote, would no doubt distress the French 'because they are good, and could not regard with indifference the sudden disappearance of such a large number of their fellow countrymen' but this loss would 'only grieve them from a purely sentimental point of view'. This was so because, in terms of the actual functioning of society, this expensive bunch of hangers-on and idlers would not be missed. Indeed, a hindrance to the prosperity of society would have been removed. Let us also imagine, Saint-Simon wrote, that France were to lose its 'three thousand best scientists, artists and artisans' – Saint-Simon's long list includes mathematicians, chemists, painters, architects, doctors, carpenters, and many more – and the nation would immediately become 'a lifeless corpse' and would remain so for at least a generation. It was these people, and not the castes of old, who were 'the most useful to their country, bringing it the most glory and doing most to promote civilization and prosperity'.[6]

6 Taylor (ed.), *Henri Saint-Simon*, pp. 194–6.

However, French (and, more broadly, European) society remained in a situation of crisis precisely because the process of transition from the Christian to the 'positive' epoch had yet to be completed. So, if Bacon and others had revealed 'the most essential faults' of the old, theistic worldview and had 'constructed the first scaffolding for the erection of the new system', their later followers, the *philosophes* of the Enlightenment, had not finished the task, formulating only what Saint-Simon described as a 'general anti-theology'.[7] In other words, if the Encyclopedists and their allies had succeeded in destroying the intellectual foundations of the theological system, they had not been able to construct a new scientific or 'positive' system to replace the 'celestial' worldview they had destroyed. As Saint-Simon famously commented: 'The philosophy of the last century was revolutionary; that of the nineteenth century must be constructive.'[8]

This failure had had important consequences. According to Saint-Simon, the first major political expression of the shift from the theological epoch to the scientific epoch had been the English Civil War, but its greatest manifestation had been the French Revolution of 1789. To France, Saint-Simon wrote, had been reserved 'the glory of ending the great European Revolution'. 'When the French Revolution broke out', Saint-Simon wrote, 'it was no longer a matter of modifying the feudal and theological system which had lost almost all its force. It was a question of organizing the industrial and scientific system summoned by the level of civilization to replace it.'[9] But this had not happened. 'Apart from the fearful atrocities to which the application of the principle of equality led through the inevitable results of putting power in the hands of the ignorant', Saint-Simon wrote in 1802, the revolution 'ended by producing a form of government that was entirely impracticable'.[10] Saint-Simon, like many a French citizen of his and later generations, was therefore left with the task of explaining how this had occurred and how a repetition of the 'madness' and the 'horrors' of the French Revolution could be avoided.

His answer to the first part of this conundrum was that, out of timidity, the newly emerging industrial class had left the leadership of the revolution to lawyers and 'metaphysicians' and their 'abstract' ideas (for example, the

---

7 Ibid., p. 170.
8 F. M. H. Markham (ed.), *Henri Comte de Saint-Simon: Selected Writings* (Oxford: Blackwell, 1952), p. 29.
9 K. Taylor (ed.), *Henri de Saint-Simon 1760–1825: Selected Writings on Science, Industry and Social Organisation* (London: Croom Helm, 1975), p. 228.
10 Markham (ed.), *Henri Comte de Saint-Simon*, p. 8.

rights of man), with 'deplorable' practical consequences. Their role, Saint-Simon argued, should only have been 'modificatory and transitory, and in no way organizational', but by extending what should have been their 'passing existence' they became 'a complete hindrance' to the transformation of the spiritual and temporal spheres. From this failure of leadership and an accompanying failure to apply the new scientific and 'positive' methodology to politics flowed all the revolution's 'misfortunes' and 'strange wanderings' and its final reconstitution of the medieval and theological order in the form of a bourgeois king, the emperor Napoleon.[11]

Unsurprisingly, Saint-Simon believed this state of moral and political disorder had continued to exist under the restored monarchy of Louis XVIII. Here Saint-Simon's 'political parable' merits being quoted at length. 'Society today', Saint-Simon wrote,

> is really a world upside down: because the nation has accepted the fundamental principle that the poor should be generous to the rich, and that consequently the less fortunate should deprive themselves each day of a part of their necessities in order to increase the needless wealth of the great property owners; because the most guilty men, the worst thieves, those who oppress the whole citizen body, and who take from them three millions each year, are entrusted with the punishment of minor offences against society; because ignorance, superstition, idleness, and extravagant pleasure are the prerogative of society's leaders, while those who are able, thrifty, and hard-working are employed only as subordinates and instruments; because, in short, in every kind of occupation, incapable men are in charge of capable men. From the standpoint of morality it is the most immoral men who are called upon to make citizens virtuous. And in terms of distributive justice it is the guiltiest men who are appointed to punish the faults of minor offenders.[12]

For writing these words, Saint-Simon was arrested and imprisoned in January 1820.

How then could this period of crisis be ended? This was a question that Saint-Simon addressed for more than twenty years, providing a series of answers that revolved around a set of common themes. First, the intellectual and moral confusion of the age could be brought to a close only when the sciences had been unified and given a systematic 'positive' foundation. Required was an overarching theory and this Saint-Simon believed, somewhat improbably, was to be found in Newton's theory of 'universal gravitation'. This, he announced in his *Introduction to the Scientific Studies of the*

---

11 Taylor (ed.), *Henri Saint-Simon*, p. 228.　12 Ibid., p. 196.

Nineteenth Century of 1807–8, provided 'a single immutable law' from which it was possible to deduce the explanation of all phenomena. Crucially, this argument entailed the claim that the methods of experimental sciences such as astronomy, chemistry, and physics could be extended to cover the study of the progress of the human mind. Based largely upon what he saw as the advances in physiological theory associated with writers such as Pierre Jean Georges Cabanis and Xavier Bichat, Saint-Simon believed unhesitatingly therefore in the possibility of 'a science of man'. The 'social' sciences would pass beyond the 'conjectural' phase and thereby transform politics, morals, philosophy, and religion. As Saint-Simon wrote: 'The moralist who is not a physiologist has to show how virtue is rewarded in another life, because of his inability to treat moral questions with precision.'[13] Rather worryingly, this faith in a science of man also led Saint-Simon to conclude that, once politics had become a positive science, all political problems would be reduced to those of hygiene. He further envisaged that there would come a time in the nineteenth century when all knowledge would be brought together in an *Encyclopaedia of Positive Ideas*.[14]

But more than this was required to bring an end to the present disorder and confusion. Saint-Simon also believed that it was necessary for us to move from a 'celestial' to a 'terrestrial' morality. Again, this was an argument that appeared throughout his writings, taking a variety of different forms, but the key idea was that morality had to be refashioned in accordance with positive knowledge. This morality was 'terrestrial' not only because it was to be based 'on purely human principles' but also because it gave priority to the achievement of our happiness here on earth. In place, therefore, of the Christian maxim that you should do unto others as you would have others do unto you – a maxim, Saint-Simon believed, that was only indirectly binding and that imposed no obligations on the individual towards him- or herself – was to be the principle that 'man must work'. 'The happiest man', Saint-Simon observed, 'is the worker. The happiest family is the one whose members all employ their time usefully. The happiest nation is the one with the fewest idlers.' Of course, not all work – that of the *rentier*, for example – was to be prized. 'Those engaged in science', Saint-Simon wrote, 'are the most moral and also the happiest because their work is useful to the whole of humanity.'[15]

It followed that the propagation of this new morality could not be left in the hands of the Catholic clergy. 'It is obvious', Saint-Simon wrote in his *Memoir on the Science of Man*, 'that when the new scientific system has been

13 Ibid., p. 113.   14 Ibid., p. 190.   15 Ibid., p. 103.

constructed, a reorganization of the religious, political, ethical and educational system will take place, and consequently the reorganization of the Church.'[16] A new 'spiritual power' had to be brought into existence to provide moral guidance to the nation, and this would largely be composed of a new elite of the enlightened, the *savants* or scientists and artists. Moreover, given that, in Saint-Simon's opinion, most of France's recent political troubles were 'caused chiefly by the people's ignorance of their own interests and the falsity of their ideas', all children were to receive teaching in 'the principles which must serve as the basis of social organization'. This teaching would be codified in the form of a national catechism and, as Saint-Simon made clear, 'nothing will be taught in the schools contrary to the principles established in the national catechism'. Moreover, only those who had sat and passed an examination on the national catechism were to be allowed to exercise the rights of citizenship.[17]

If then spiritual power was to be in the hands of the *savants*, Saint-Simon likewise recommended that temporal power should be in the hands of those he described as *les industriels* or producers. Who were the members of this new grouping? The answer, in short, was 'those who worked to produce'. It therefore included farmers ('all those who cultivate the land, as well as those who direct agricultural work'), all artisans, manufacturers, merchants, those Saint-Simon described as 'entrepreneurs of land and sea transport', all 'positive' scientists, artists who 'contribute to the prosperity of our manufacturing', lawyers of 'a liberal outlook' who defend the producers, the 'small number' of priests who taught 'the obligation to employ one's time and means in useful work', and, finally, 'all citizens … who sincerely employ their talents and their means to free producers from the unjust supremacy exercised over them by idle consumers'. In contrast, what Saint-Simon described as 'the anti-national party' was said to comprise 'those who consume but do not produce; those whose work is neither useful to society nor of assistance to the producers; all those who profess political principles whose application hinders production and tends to deprive *les industriels* of the highest degree of social importance'. Included in this group were nobles and land-owners 'who did nothing', priests who saw morality in terms of blind obedience to the pope, judges who upheld arbitrary rule, and the military who supported it.[18] 'These men', Saint-Simon declared in 1817, 'use force to live off the work of the rest, either off what they are given or what

16 Markham (ed.), *Henri Comte de Saint-Simon*, p. 25.
17 Taylor (ed.), *Henri Saint-Simon*, p. 232. 18 Ibid., pp. 187–90.

they can take. In short, they are idlers, that is, thieves.' For good measure
Saint-Simon added that they were also parasites.[19]

Moreover, Saint-Simon was in no doubt as to the superior moral and
political claims of *les industriels* over their rivals. Echoing the rhetorical device
famously used by the Abbé Sieyès in his pamphlet of 1789, *What Is the Third
Estate?*, to justify the political demands of the Third Estate to lead and
represent the French nation, Saint-Simon asked the similarly rhetorical
question of what position the industrial class should occupy. His answer
was that it should occupy the first place in society because it was the most
important class. And it was the most important class because it was the most
useful class, the most moral class, and the most capable class. Without the
industrial class, no other class could exist.

Saint-Simon's understanding of the appropriate relationship between the
new spiritual and temporal powers changed over time, and it was arguably
never clear as to which one he believed should have supremacy over the
other. However, from his earliest writings onwards, he believed that 'for the
sake of the general good, domination should be proportionate to
enlightenment'.[20] This was a principle that he was to rework many times,
giving rise to a series of improbable schemes designed to transfer power to
those he believed most capable and most worthy of securing the proper
administration of public affairs. These ranged from a Council of Newton
whose members would be the 'twenty-one elect of humanity' to a larger
Parliament of Improvement comprising 'forty-five men of genius'. What all
of these proposals had in common – apart from a fascination with the role of
the genius in politics – was that they revolved around the idea of the existence
of an elite of one description or another who would govern in everybody
else's interest. And this itself tells us something of great importance: the
industrial society of the future envisaged by Saint-Simon would not be
democratic; it would not be egalitarian; it would not be classless; but it
would be relatively homogeneous and efficiently organized.

Furthermore, Saint-Simon did not believe that the transition from
a theological to an industrial society would be limited to France alone. It
would be a truly international phenomenon, and one that, in the first
instance, would embrace the whole of western Europe. Writing in the
immediate aftermath of the Napoleonic wars and as Europe's diplomats
deliberated at the Congress of Vienna, Saint-Simon believed that renewed co-
operation between Britain and France provided the starting point for what he

19 Ibid., p. 158.   20 Ibid., p. 76.

did not hesitate to describe as the reorganization of European society. Of crucial importance was Saint-Simon's insight that the interests of industry and of *les industriels* were the same everywhere and therefore that they transcended national borders. Once again Saint-Simon set out a set of institutional arrangements which, he imagined, would in this case guarantee the peace and stability of Europe. Envisaged was a European confederation with, at its heart, a two-chamber European parliament 'set above all national governments and invested with powers of settling their disputes'.[21] With typical thoroughness, Saint-Simon even considered the sort of person who should sit in these chambers: they must, Saint-Simon wrote, possess the broadness of views and sentiments that were the hallmarks of 'European patriotism'. What else would this European parliament be doing? Its job, Saint-Simon specified, was to control public education and to draw up a code of morals that was to be taught throughout Europe. One of the goals of this education was to teach people that the European confederation was the best way of making society as happy as it could be. The parliament would also have the job of suppressing 'all religions whose principles were contrary to the great moral code'. Given that the new industrial order would eventually spread beyond the confines of Europe, Saint-Simon also envisaged an international dimension to its activities. 'To people the globe with the European race, which is superior to every other human race; to make it accessible and habitable like Europe: there', Saint-Simon wrote, 'is an enterprise by which the European parliament should continually keep Europe active.'[22] As Saint-Simon observed: 'the golden age of the human race is not behind us: it lies before us'.[23]

Finally, it followed from the above that the nature of government would also need to change. Industry, Saint-Simon argued, advances and prospers to the extent that it is not impeded by government. 'Industry', he wrote in 1817, 'needs to be governed as little as possible, and this can only be done if it is governed as cheaply as possible.'[24] Therefore, governments were to have no more than a small amount of power and money at their disposal. All funds would be provided by voluntary contributions, and subscribers would be able to supervise how their money was used. The task of preserving law and order was to be performed by the citizens themselves. In sum, 'governments will no longer command men' but 'should restrict themselves to protecting industry against every kind of impediment and trouble'.[25] It was this idea that was

---

21 Ibid., p. 135.   22 Markham (ed.), *Henri Comte de Saint-Simon*, p. 49.
23 Taylor (ed.), *Henri Saint-Simon*, p. 136.   24 Ibid., p. 159.   25 Ibid., pp. 165–7.

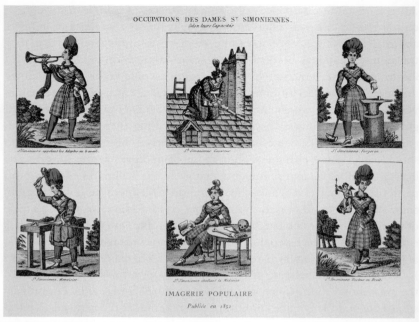

Fig. 5.1 'Occupations of Saint-Simonian Women'. Illustration from *Les Saint-Simoniens*, by Henry-René D'Allemagne, 1830. (Photo by Universal History Archive/Universal Images Group via Getty Images.)

given its famous formulation by Saint-Simon's then secretary and collabor-ator, Auguste Comte, in his *Plan of the Scientific Work Necessary for the Reorganization of Society*, first published in 1824. 'The government of things', Comte wrote, 'replaces that of men.' To this Comte added that 'this law excludes, with the same efficiency, theological arbitrariness, or the divine right of kings, and metaphysical arbitrariness, or the sovereignty of the people'.[26]

Engels on Saint-Simon

More than three decades later, after the publication of the *Communist Manifesto*, Engels was to develop the ideas set out there at greater length in what has since become one of his most famous (and also most controversial) texts: *Socialism: Utopian and Scientific*. Again, the polemical purpose was to

26 See H. S. Jones (ed.), *Comte: Early Political Writings* (Cambridge: Cambridge University Press, 1998), p. 108.

differentiate the scientific socialism of Marx – one, according to Engels, built upon 'two great discoveries, the materialistic conception of history and the revelation of the secret of capitalistic production through surplus value' – from a form of socialism that saw itself as 'the expression of absolute truth, reason and justice' and as something that had 'only to be discovered to conquer all the world by virtue of its own power'. 'The socialism of earlier days', Engels concluded, 'certainly criticised the existing mode of production and its consequences but it could not explain them and, therefore, could not get the mastery of them. It could only simply reject them as bad.'[27]

However, what is intriguing in Engels' argument, and what he adds to the analysis provided in the *Communist Manifesto*, is his account of the historical origins of utopian, and specifically Saint-Simonian, socialism. Not unimportantly, Engels also saw where the strengths and attractions of Saint-Simon's ideas were to be found. In brief, Engels argued that, in its 'theoretical form', modern socialism had its origins as 'a more logical extension of the principles laid down by the great French philosophers of the eighteenth century'. For these philosophers, reason was to be the measure of all things, and everything was to be subject to the most rigorous criticism. Henceforth, superstition and injustice were to be replaced by eternal truth and eternal right in what was 'a kingdom of reason'. Yet, Engels continued, 'we know today that the kingdom of reason was nothing more than the idealised kingdom of the bourgeoisie'. The 'splendid promises of the philosophers', he went on, turned out to be 'bitterly disappointing caricatures'.

There were many aspects to this disappointment. Bourgeois vices had proliferated, trade had become nothing less than cheating, oppression by the sword had been replaced by corruption, but at its heart lay the fact that the antagonism between rich and poor had not been dissolved into general prosperity. Rather, 'the development of industry upon a capitalistic basis made poverty and misery of the working masses conditions of existence of society'. All that was now lacking, Engels concluded, were men able to formulate this disappointment. They duly arrived, he wrote, at the beginning of the nineteenth century in the form of the utopian socialists.

The first among these was Saint-Simon. Here again Engels put in place an important qualification to his comments. 'To the crude conditions of capitalistic production and the crude class conditions', Engels wrote, 'corresponded crude theories.' So, as in the *Communist Manifesto*, the charge was that the

---

27 All quotations in this section are from F. Engels, 'Socialism: Utopian and Scientific', in *Marx Engels Collected Works*, vol. XXIV (London: Lawrence & Wishart, 2010), pp. 281–325.

utopians attempted to find solutions to social problems 'out of the human brain' and to impose these solutions upon society. Foredoomed as utopian, Engels wrote, the more completely these ideas were worked out in detail, 'the more they could not avoid drifting off into pure fantasies'.

Yet Engels was also quick to perceive correctly that Saint-Simon was 'a son of the great French Revolution'. For Engels the Revolution of 1789 represented the conquest of political power by the propertied bourgeoisie but he saw, again correctly, that for Saint-Simon 'the antagonism between the third estate and the privileged classes took the form of an antagonism between "the workers" and the "idlers"' and, moreover, that for Saint-Simon the idlers were not merely 'the old privileged classes' but included 'all who, without taking part in production or distribution, lived on their incomes'. Furthermore, according to Engels, Saint-Simon saw that the revolution had proven that the idlers had lost any claim to intellectual supremacy and political leadership, as similarly the experience of the Reign of Terror had shown this to be true of the non-possessing classes.

Where then did Saint-Simon envisage that leadership would come from? As Engels observed, this was to be achieved through a 'new religious bond' uniting industry and science, uniting, in Engels' words, 'the working bourgeois' and the 'scholar'. Engels was understandably sceptical about Saint-Simon's hope that 'these bourgeois' could be transformed into 'a class of public officials' – as he pointed out, 'they were still to hold, vis-à-vis the workers, a commanding and economically privileged position' – but several things in Saint-Simon's broader argument impressed Engels. The first was that what interested Saint-Simon most was 'the lot of the class that is the most numerous and poorest'. The second was that, from his earliest writings onwards, Saint-Simon advanced the proposition that 'all men should work'. Next was Saint-Simon's recognition that the French Revolution was 'a class war, and not simply one between nobility and bourgeoisie but between nobility, bourgeoisie and the non-possessors'. To have perceived this in 1802, Engels wrote, was 'a most pregnant discovery'. Fourthly, here too was an awareness of 'the complete absorption of politics and economics', a view which disclosed an understanding that 'economic conditions are the basis of political institutions'. From this followed Saint-Simon's idea – 'already very plainly expressed', according to Engels – that in the future 'political rule over men' will be converted into 'an administration of things and a direction of processes of production'. Finally, Engels argued, Saint-Simon showed 'the same superiority over his contemporaries' when in 1814 and again in 1815 he argued for an alliance of England, France, and Germany 'as the only guarantee for the prosperous development and peace of Europe'. To have argued thus in the wake of the Battle of Waterloo, Engels wrote, 'required as much courage as historical foresight'.

Given the demolition job that Marx and Engels had performed upon Saint-Simon and his fellow utopians in the *Communist Manifesto*, Engels' conclusion might therefore be surprising. 'In Saint-Simon', he wrote, 'we find a comprehensive breadth of view, by virtue of which almost all the ideas of later socialists that are not strictly economic are found in him in embryo.'

The Invention of Saint-Simonism

From what we have seen so far, there were certain themes which stood out in Saint-Simon's writings. A scientific or positive epoch would emerge out of the ruins of an earlier Christian or medieval epoch. This new society would have *les industriels* (variously described) as its leaders and would be bound together by a 'terrestrial morality' propagated by a new spiritual power (*les savants*). To this in his final years Saint-Simon added a specifically religious dimension, openly recasting his ideas in the form of a New Christianity. Why he did this is not entirely clear, but by 1825 Saint-Simon had reached the conclusion that his goal of the reorganization of society would be more easily attained through the medium of an organized church, replete with its own clergy and dogmas. Moreover, Saint-Simon was not alone in clothing his project for social amelioration in religious garb. Indeed, it was something of a commonplace. To take but one example, Etienne Cabet did not hesitate to equate communism with the doctrines of a 'true Christianity'.[28]

In brief, Saint-Simon's stated ambition was to purify the Christian religion by divesting it of all the heresies he associated with Catholicism and Protestantism and thereby to return it to the original and single principle first formulated by the early church. When thus regenerated, Saint-Simon believed, Christianity would pronounce as 'impious every doctrine that had for its object to teach men any other means of obtaining life eternal than that of working with all their might to ameliorate the condition of their fellows'. It followed that the 'sublime principle' of the new religion was that 'Men should treat one another as brothers.' According to this principle, Saint-Simon wrote, 'they must organize society to the advantage of the greatest number, and must direct all their work and all their activity towards the aim of improving as quickly as possible the moral and physical condition of the

28 E. Cabet, *Le vrai christianisme suivant Jésus Christ* (Paris: Bureau du Populaire, 1846).

most numerous class'.[29] As Saint-Simon reminded his readers, Jesus Christ had promised eternal life to those who tended to the poor. As such, the New Christianity amounted to a doctrine of fraternity expressed through a very earthly preoccupation with the moral and physical wellbeing of the poor and needy.

Two other elements of the New Christianity merit mention. The first is that Saint-Simon imagined that it would become 'the universal and only religion'. Once the 'true doctrine of Christianity' had been expounded, 'the differences between religious opinions will come to an end'. 'The Asians and the Africans', Saint-Simon wrote, 'will be converted.' The second is that the new religion would not accept 'the first Christian doctrine' that acknowledged that the state and the church should have distinct spheres of authority. As Saint-Simon explained: 'The new Christian organization . . . will direct all institutions, whatever their nature.'[30] Society would be freed from the 'yoke of Caesar' and 'the empire of physical force'.[31]

Saint-Simon's death in May 1825 meant that he was not able to fulfil his promise to set out the doctrines and rituals of the new church in detail. For this we should probably be grateful. However, this, and much more, was a task willingly taken on by a small but loyal group of young followers. These included Olinde Rodrigues, Prosper Enfantin, and Saint-Amand Bazard, all of whom were subsequently to achieve prominence (and, in Enfantin's case, notoriety) in what was to become the Saint-Simonian movement. Their first initiative was the publication of a weekly journal, *Le Producteur* (*The Producer*), in October of that year. Its subtitle, *A Journal of Industry, the Sciences and the Fine Arts*, gave a clear indication of the intention to develop and spread the ideas of the master. At this point, discussion of the new religion was put to one side, emphasis being placed on the project of creating a society organized around industry and the need for leadership by a competent scientific and technical elite. Several articles attacked the free market theories of Jean-Baptiste Say, recommending the association of producers as an alternative. However, an important theme emerged: 'the new philosophy', it was argued, recognized that the principal goal of the human race was 'to exploit and to modify external nature to its greatest advantage'.[32] From this was to develop a near obsession with systems of communication and transport.

Lack of money brought about the closure of *Le Producteur* at the end of 1826. Undeterred, the Saint-Simonians set about conveying their message

29 Taylor (ed.), *Henri Saint-Simon*, p. 289.   30 Ibid., p. 291.
31 *Oeuvres de Claude-Henri de Saint-Simon* (Paris: Anthropos, 1966), vol. III, pp. 187–8.
32 *Le Producteur* I, 1825, p. 5.

through public lectures and then the publication of *Exposition of the Doctrine of Saint-Simon*. Here the ideas of Saint-Simon were taken in a new direction. Now the goal towards which the Saint-Simonians envisaged society to be moving was that of 'universal association' and with that would come the reign of peace, a decrease in the exploitation of one person by another, and a continuous improvement in the intellectual, physical, and moral condition of the human race. However, this argument was given a radical edge through a recognition that this condition was not that of 'the class of proletarians'. 'Reduced to a state of destitution', the text read, 'can the worker have the time to develop his intellectual faculties and his moral sentiments?' A quick glance was enough to show that the worker was treated like the slave of earlier times. 'Physical misery leads to his degradation; degradation leads to abasement, and a vicious circle which at every point inspires disgust and horror.' The root cause of these iniquities was the institution of private property and its hereditary possession. In virtue of both, it was argued, 'men are born with the privilege of doing nothing, of living at the expense of someone else'. Both therefore had to reformed. So too, all privileges deriving from birth were to be abolished. The distributive principle following from this was succinctly summarized: 'to each according to his capacity, to each capacity according to its works'.[33]

Two other developments are worthy of note, considering what was to come. The later parts of the text returned to the theme of a new Saint-Simonian religion. The text also introduced an idea that had not been present in Saint-Simon's writings: the emancipation of women. And so it came to pass that, on Christmas Day 1829, the Saint-Simonian movement was formally transformed into a church with Enfantin and Bazard elected as the church's 'Supreme Fathers'. With this came not only an attempt to formulate the doctrines of this new religion – these came to include the concept of an androgynous God – but also rituals (including baptisms and marriages), colourful regalia and costumes, and an intricate hierarchy of apostles, priests, missionaries, and disciples. Members of the movement were invited to live a communal life in *maisons de famille*. As with many a sect, there soon came schisms and excommunications, with Enfantin successfully seeing off all his rivals to become sole leader of the Saint-Simonian family. For good measure, he then declared himself to be the 'Father of Humanity'. Now the improvement of the condition of the poorest and most numerous class was embraced as 'the will of God'.

33 *Doctrine de Saint-Simon: Exposition* (Paris: L'Organisateur, 1831), pp. 176–7, 179–80, 38.

However, controversy was never far away, and things came to a head with Enfantin's increasingly radical proclamations on the emancipation of women, without which, he believed, the Saint-Simonian society of the future could not be realized. Moreover, according to Enfantin, the equality of the sexes required a new sexual morality. This, Enfantin stated, would include what he described as 'the rehabilitation of the flesh'. Critics within the movement immediately charged Enfantin with encouraging immorality and promiscuity, and it is hard to dismiss the feeling that these were the ideas of a sexual predator. If, for example, Olinde Rodrigues was prepared to accept the legitimacy of divorce, he could not accept Enfantin's view that children should not know the name of their father. With debate and disagreement intensifying, the French state intervened, arresting Enfantin and one of his supporters, Michel Chevalier, on charges of the corruption of morals. With their imprisonment in December 1832, those of the movement who remained set off in search of the female Messiah, a journey which took them first to Constantinople and then to Egypt, where most perished from disease.[34]

The Socialist Legacy?

Enfantin formally announced the dissolution of the Saint-Simonian church on 15 December 1832, but this did not mean that the influence of the movement was at an end. Far from it. Some, like Chevalier, turned the Saint-Simonian fascination with transport into a passion for railway building and free trade. A later Saint-Simonian enterprise was the building of the Suez Canal. Saint-Simonians were also to play a central role in formulating policies designed to achieve French colonization of Algeria.[35] As is well known, Comte went on to develop a full-blown positivist philosophy, but less well known is the fact that some of his followers, most notably Fabien Magnin, established a Circle of Proletarian Positivists in 1863. Not only did the organization affiliate to the First International in 1870 but later advocates of le positivisme ouvrier were to play an important, if rarely recognized, role in the French trade union movement. Although often scarred by their experiences, Saint-Simonian women took some of the first steps towards the creation of an autonomous women's movement in France.

---

34 C. Goldberg Moses, *French Feminism in the Nineteenth Century* (Albany: State University of New York Press, 1984), pp. 41–88.
35 See O. Abi-Mershed, *Apostles of Modernity: Saint-Simonians and the Civilizing Mission in Algeria* (Stanford: Stanford University Press, 2010).

Just as importantly, over the next two decades many prominent former members of the movement were to develop Saint-Simonian ideas in a socialist direction. These included Cabet, Pierre Leroux (famous for coining the word 'plutocracy'), Philippe Buchez (co-author of a forty-volume history of the French Revolution), the political economist and collectivist Constantin Pecqueur, and Louis Blanc (architect of the national workshops during the February Revolution of 1848). It is also recorded that the anarchist Pierre-Joseph Proudhon claimed to have been influenced by Saint-Simon. If some, for example Leroux, continued to feel the need to phrase Saint-Simon's ideas in religious terms, all drew upon his core vision of a society organized by and for the producers.

As we have already seen, Engels was also prepared to acknowledge that there was much in Saint-Simon's writings from which socialists could learn. Moreover, he can be forgiven for believing that the celebrated dictum suggesting that the government of men would be replaced by the government of things was coined by Saint-Simon, as Saint-Simon did just about all he could to hide Comte's authorship, publishing Comte's essay as the third *cahier* or issue of his own *Catechism of the Industrialists*. However, it was as Saint-Simon's phrase that this sentence entered the world of socialist thought. More importantly, it was misunderstood by Engels. As the quotation from Comte above indicates, for him 'the government of things' meant primarily an end to arbitrary government. For Engels, by contrast, the 'administration of things' flowed from a revolution in the mode of production that would render the state obsolete. With class domination at an end, and the state therefore abolished, the only task remaining would be to administer and organize production, something Engels assumed the proletariat would be capable of doing.

This argument was largely accepted by later socialist thinkers. For example, when Vladimir Lenin addressed this issue in his *The State and Revolution* of 1917, he did so principally to denounce his rivals within the socialist movement who understood the idea of the 'withering away of the state' to mean that violent revolution could be avoided. Engels, Lenin insisted, believed that the state had to be abolished. Accordingly, when Nikolai Bukharin and Evgenii Preobrazhenskii published their *ABC of Communism* in 1920, they used the celebrated phrase much as Engels had intended: namely, to indicate that, with the revolution, a state had been established in which the whole working population would participate in the administration of the productive process. It was only with the proclamation of the doctrine of socialism in one country by Comrade Joseph Stalin that the whole idea was abandoned as being inapplicable to a country surrounded by capitalist enemies.[36]

It is therefore interesting to note that it was at the very moment that Marxist socialism began to attain a position of intellectual hegemony within the French left during the 1890s that writers in France sought to confirm Saint-Simon's position as a pioneer of socialism. One example of this is to be found in Emile Durkheim's *Socialism and Saint-Simon*, first given as a set of lectures in Bordeaux from November 1895 to May 1896.[37] From Saint-Simon, Durkheim believed, could be derived the economic principle of socialism; namely, that 'economic life should be subjected to collective and organized control'. From this followed the central tenet of socialist morality that 'the only goal that this collective administration can pursue will be to make the production of wealth as fruitful as possible, so that everyone can receive the most – particularly those whom fate has disinherited the most'. On this account of socialism, the emancipation of the workers was something of an afterthought.[38]

However, this appeal to Saint-Simon was most evident in Georges Weill's *A Socialist Precursor: Saint-Simon and His Work*.[39] It was a mistake, Weill argued, to oppose the utopian socialism of Saint-Simon to the 'scientific socialism of the German economist'. Both believed themselves to be engaged in a scientific inquiry, but both were equally utopian. Worse still, both opened the door to a new form of tyranny, a 'scientific tyranny' in Saint-Simon's case and a 'collectivist despotism' in the case of Marx. Nonetheless, Weill knew which of the two he preferred. Saint-Simon, he concluded, had seen that the only way to solve the problems facing society was to bring about moral and economic reform at the same time, to replace individualism by fraternity and association, a fear of God by philanthropy. The society he dreamed of would not only provide the workers with bread but also enable them to become completely human. And this would be achieved peacefully. 'The social question, according to Lassalle', Weill continued, 'is a question of the "stomach"; Saint-Simon affirms that it is a moral question: there is to be found the great difference between French socialism and German socialism.' The question therefore was which one would preside over the forthcoming social transformation? 'Will it', Weill asked, 'be the violent spirit of Marxism

---

36 See B. Kafka, 'The Administrations of Things: A Genealogy', http://west86th .bgc.bard.edu/articles/the-administration-of-things-a-genealogy/.
37 E. Durkheim, *Socialism and Saint-Simon* (London: Routledge & Kegan Paul, 1959).
38 Ibid., p. 194.
39 Georges Weill, *Un précurseur du socialisme. Saint-Simon et son oeuvre* (Paris: Perrin, 1894).

or the peaceful and generous spirit of Saint-Simonism?'[40] We know the answer.

Further Reading

Carlisle, Robert E., *The Proffered Crown: Saint-Simonianism and the Doctrine of Hope* (Baltimore: Johns Hopkins University Press, 1987).

Grange, Juliette (ed.), *Oeuvres de Henri Saint-Simon* (Paris: Presses Universitaires de France, 2012), 4 vols.

Ionescu, Ghita (ed.), *The Political Thought of Saint-Simon* (London: Oxford University Press, 1976).

Manuel, Frank E., *The New World of Henri Saint-Simon* (Cambridge, MA: Harvard University Press, 1956).

Markham, F. M. H. (ed.), *Henri Comte de Saint-Simon: Selected Writings* (Oxford: Blackwell, 1952).

Oeuvres de Saint-Simon et d'Enfantin (Paris: Dentu, 1865–78), 47 vols.

Taylor, Keith (ed.), *Henri Saint-Simon 1760–1825: Selected Writings on Science, Industry and Social Organisation* (London: Croom Helm, 1975).

40 Ibid., pp. 231–44.

6

Robert Owen and Owenism

GREGORY CLAEYS

Since Karl Marx and Friedrich Engels' derogatory description of Robert Owen and his followers as 'utopian socialists' in the *Communist Manifesto*, they have traditionally been classed among those who denied that proletarian revolution was the chief means of achieving socialism, and whimsically imagined instead that mere spinning 'duodecimo editions of the New Jerusalem' would suffice to persuade the bourgeoisie to abolish capitalism. The Owenites were certainly 'utopians' in the sense of aiming at an ideal or model society where behaviour has substantially improved and 'enhanced sociability' exists.[1] But it is unhelpful to adopt Marx's usage. Here Owen and Owenism are described as 'early' or 'communitarian' socialists and, while any survey of the movement must necessarily touch on its relationship to Marx and Marxism, this chapter offers a schematic overview of Owenism, rather than dwelling on its relative failings. The concentration here is on Owenite conceptions of community, social and economic thought, secularism, and feminism and the family.

Origins

Robert Owen was born on 14 May 1771 in Newtown, Montgomeryshire, Wales. His father was a saddler and ironmonger and the local postmaster. Precocious, and soon the schoolmaster's assistant, he deserted his religious beliefs aged ten, in the belief that 'there must be something fundamentally wrong in all religions, as they had been taught up to that period'. Soon he became apprenticed to a Lincolnshire cloth manufacturer. He moved to London, then in 1788 to Manchester, where, borrowing £100 from his brother William, he commenced cotton-spinning. Aged twenty, in April 1792, he

---

1 See Gregory Claeys, 'News from somewhere: enhanced sociability and the composite definition of utopia and dystopia', *History* 98 (2013), pp. 145–73.

became manager of one of the largest mills in the city, Peter Drinkwater's establishment of 500 employees, where the Bolton and Watt engine was first applied to cotton-spinning in Manchester. He spent six weeks studying the factory and made many improvements to the production process. Though shy, sensitive, prone to blushing, and speaking 'a kind of Welsh English', he was soon hobnobbing with local worthies in the Manchester Literary and Philosophical Society, where he read several papers. Two in particular, 'On the Origin of Opinions with a View to the Improvement of the Social Virtues' and 'Thoughts on the Connection Between Universal Happiness and Practical Mechanics', now lost, indicate his interest in avoiding the degradation facing many among the new industrial workforce, with whom, he later wrote, he had 'successfully commenced' a new approach.[2]

Owen's main opportunity to experiment with these ideas came after he married Caroline Dale, the daughter of a leading, philanthropically minded Scottish cotton-spinner, David Dale, who owned the New Lanark mills (now lovingly restored), on the banks of the Clyde south of Glasgow, built in 1784. Here Owen became manager on the auspicious date of 1 January 1800. Soon he was producing the finest-quality cotton thread available, and after Dale died in 1806 he enjoyed some 40 per cent of the profits of 15 per cent per annum, which totalled some £192,000 from 1814 to 1825.[3] Owen saw the opportunity both to 'reform' the recalcitrant workforce, notable for its idleness and pilfering, and to make conditions better both in the workplace and in the surrounding mill village. He improved the housing, policed cleanliness, bulk-bought goods for the company store to lower prices, raised the working age, and reduced hours of labour from eleven and three quarter-hours to ten and three quarter-hours per day in 1816. There were plans for a public kitchen and dining rooms. One-sixtieth of wages were set aside for sickness and dotage. But those who had illegitimate children were fined, 'neighbourhood divisions' were formed to police the village, and 'bug-hunters' visited each house for weekly inspections, though at first they were resisted. In the factory a 'silent monitor' painted in different colours hung over workplaces to indicate performance. In 1806 Owen won over the workforce by paying wages when a cotton famine made work impossible. When his partners resisted further improvements, he bought them out in 1810, and again in 1813. By 1816, when the Institute for the Formation of

---

2 *Selected Works of Robert Owen*, 4 vols. (London: Pickering and Chatto, 1993), vol. IV, pp. 54, 82, 109.

3 O. Siméon, *Robert Owen's Experiment at New Lanark: From Paternalism to Socialism* (London: Palgrave Macmillan, 2017), p. 122.

Fig. 6.1   Robert Owen, date unknown. (Photo by Time Life Pictures/Mansell/The LIFE Picture Collection via Getty Images.)

Character opened, he had seemingly squared the capitalist circle: his workers were extremely productive, and yet were better off than the vast majority of the burgeoning industrial population. Visitors – as many as seventy a day – poured in to witness the results, and took particular interest in the school, where corporal punishment, threats, and harsh language were forbidden, and music, dancing, and military drill were integrated into the curriculum.

Just why Owen embarked on this experiment, which was not 'socialist', since profits were divided not with the workers but with his partners, who included Jeremy Bentham, remains unclear. Attempting to persuade fellow manufacturers and other philanthropists of the advantages of extending his system more widely in frequent visits to London, he was constantly rebuffed. He met with encouragement, however, from a leading philosopher of the 1790s, William Godwin, whom he met some fifty times after January 1813. Godwin's *Enquiry Concerning Political Justice* (1793) promoted philosophical necessitarianism, or the formation of character by the environment, chiefly aimed at Christian ideas of original sin, as well as a duty to allocate property justly. (Owen was mocked by William Hazlitt for merely repeating Godwinian principles.)

Owen's central principle, already in formation in his Manchester years, was that 'The character of man is formed for him, and not by him', with the result that 'any character might be formed by applying the proper means'. He drew from it the conclusion that punishment for bad behaviour was never justified, and applied this principle in the New Lanark education system. It was outlined in his first major publication, *A New View of Society; or, Essays on the Principle of the Formation of the Human Character* (1813–16), in which he was assisted by the radical tailor Francis Place, who 'found him a man of kind manners and good intentions, of an imperturbable temper, and an enthusiastic desire to promote the happiness of mankind'.[4] Without being 'socialist' in any way, this presented a potpourri of reform measures, including a system of national education, restricting 'gin shops and pot houses', the state lottery, and gambling, and disestablishing the Church of England. The possibility of a Quaker influence here cannot be discounted, as Owen spoke highly of them on various occasions, notably admiring their 'brotherly love – equality – simplicity in language, dress, and all personal externals – kindness and forbearance to all – desire for peace – and patience, under suffering, without resistance', and their refusal to lie.[5] (But Owen never renounced military training as such.) The communistical American sect of Shaking Quakers also met with his approval. Unfortunately Owen never clarified how it might be possible to break from the 'circumstances' of character-formation. He equally described his own personality as formed 'for' him, but never explained why his outlook came to vary so dramatically from others of a similar background and class outlook.

It was not until 1816–17 that Owen began to propound what would by the mid-1820s be termed 'socialism'. A shortened version of what he called his 'social system', this was juxtaposed to the 'principle of individual interest', 'that man can provide better for himself, and more advantageously for the public, when left to his own individual exertions, opposed to and in competition with his fellows, than when aided by any social arrangement which shall unite his interests individually and generally with society'.[6] It is worth briefly commenting on the meaning of 'social' in this context, as it is crucial to

---

4 *Selected Works of Robert Owen*, vol. IV, p. 62; G. Wallas, *The Life of Francis Place* (London: George Allen & Unwin, 1898), p. 63.
5 R. Owen, *The New Existence of Man upon the Earth* (London: E. Wilson, 1854), pt 5, p. 13.
6 *Selected Works of Robert Owen*, vol. I, p. 308.

understanding the tradition as a whole. Britain in the late 1790s and early 1800s had witnessed a number of proposals for land nationalization (Thomas Spence) and for extensive taxation of landed estates (Thomas Paine), and a growing attempt to confront commercial and industrial wealth (the radical lecturer John Thelwall; the London doctor Charles Hall, author of *The Effects of Civilization on the People in European States*, 1805). Some millenarians and utopian republicans, like the Godwinian Thomas Northmore and 'Walking' John Stewart, writing in the tradition of Thomas More, had also suggested community of goods, or communism, as a solution to society's woes.[7] Later the Tory poet Robert Southey, who visited New Lanark in 1819, portrayed Owen as a new More in *Sir Thomas More; or, Colloquies on the Progress and Prospects of Society* (2 vols., 1829).

Owen's opposition to private property as such marked a break from most contemporary reformers. He believed it produced 'vanity, pride, luxury, and tyranny, on the one hand; and poverty and degradation, on the other'. Hence resulted 'insincerity, deceptions and hatred; traffic, robbery, murder; and a system of law, or artificial justice, covering the grossest injustice'.[8] He also condemned the new factories as deeply harmful to their employees. His *Observations on the Effects of the Manufacturing System* (1815) insisted that it bred 'a new character in its inhabitants ... formed upon a principle quite unfavourable to individual or general happiness', and that machinery should thus be adopted 'only in aid of, and not in competition with, human labour'.[9] The 'spirit of competition', 'buying cheap and selling dear', was now condemned. In 1816 Owen urged that the new manufacturing process be 'gradually diminished', and that Britain aim at greater self-sufficiency in food.[10] David Ricardo accused him of being entirely hostile to machinery – just another Luddite – but this was not the case. Those who assumed that Owen proposed a glorified form of benevolent pauper management were now disabused of the idea. His 'Plan' was to abolish poverty and to remoralize humanity.

Owen emerged to national prominence in 1817 when he commenced a propaganda war, advertising the 'Plan' in the daily papers and buying thousands of copies for free distribution, at one point delaying the London

---

7 See Gregory Claeys, '"The only man of nature that ever appeared in the world": "Walking" John Stewart and the trajectories of social radicalism, 1790–1822', *Journal of British Studies* 53 (2014), pp. 1–24, and generally Gregory Claeys (ed.), *Utopias of the British Enlightenment* (Cambridge: Cambridge University Press, 1994), introduction.

8 R. Owen, *Lectures on an Entire New State of Society* (London: J. Brooks, 1830), p. 43.

9 *Selected Works of Robert Owen*, vol. I, pp. 112–13, 154.   10 Ibid., vol. I, p. 126.

mail coaches to the provinces for twenty minutes. In two widely attended public lectures in London in August 1817, Owen attracted reformers of all stripes. His audience was 'thunderstruck' when he denounced teachers of religion for having made man 'a weak, imbecile animal; a furious bigot and fanatic; or a miserable hypocrite'.[11] But there were also loud cheers from working-class secularists. The main purpose of the occasion was to popularize the 'Plan' to rehouse the industrial working classes, and especially the newly unemployed, who were pressing on the existing poor relief system, in rural communities of some 500–1,500 people. These 'villages of union' would be self-subsistent, alternate between farming and industrial labour, and share their produce and property in common. Early engravings of the ideal community often showed manufactories at work, with steam engines spitting smoke into the sky, but at a short remove from fields under cultivation and communal living quarters. Eventually these communities were to replace all existing cities and towns, with the new 'social ethos' being enforced under the 'eye of the community'. (Unfortunately, communitarian zeal never had the success which sectarian religious settlements enjoyed.) This was the moment when British socialism proper was born.

The reasons Owen took this step are, again, unclear. His new theory was first carefully outlined in the *Report to the County of Lanark* (1820), which indicated a receptiveness to Adam Smith's critique, via Adam Ferguson, of the effects of a narrow division of labour on the workforce, which would later become Marx's starting point in the 1844 'Economic and Philosophic Manuscripts'. Owen also championed a labour theory of value which would be central to socialist economic thinking thereafter, as expressed in the principle 'no man has a just right to the labour of any other man, *without giving equal labour or value in exchange for it*'.[12] Here too Owen clearly stated his adherence to 'the principle of *united labour, expenditure, and property, and equal privileges*'.[13] He drew on some earlier models in this period, and reprinted the Quaker John Bellers' plans for a 'College of Industry' (1696), which he claimed as a key inspiration, in 1818. He also proposed wider interim economic reforms, such as a ten-hour labour day.

The term 'socialism' emerged to describe Owen's views in the mid-1820s. It remained synonymous with the little-used 'communism' until the latter term came to designate other sects commending community of goods in the

---

11 Ibid., vol. I, p. 207.
12 R. Owen, *Lectures on the Marriages of the Priesthood of the Old Immoral World*, 4th edn (Leeds: J. Hobson, 1840), p. 30 (*Selected Works of Robert Owen*, vol. II, p. 280).
13 *Selected Works of Robert Owen*, vol. I, p. 305.

mid-1840s, notably by John Goodwyn Barmby and the Icarians. Socialism was broadly to be understood as a search for 'community' from the outset, and in part expressed a nostalgia for village and country life rapidly being left behind by millions across this period. The later development of this theme by sociologists such as Ferdinand Tönnies indicates residual interest in it at least through the 1970s. A sophisticated approach to the concept requires the analysis of such notions as trust, friendship, sociability, and solidarity, and their associations variously with the workplace, the family, and the village or small town. On the left, by the mid-twentieth century, Marx's concept of alienation was the focus of much of this debate.

The social component in Owen's understanding of socialism consisted primarily in the submission of the individual to community life for the good of the whole, with the aim being 'to merge all individualism in the social'.[14] Side by side with this, however, we also encounter anarchical facets in his schemes, some of which may be traceable to Godwin. Owen's later proposal that in the future each might become 'his own priest, lawyer, physician and soldier, in order that each may be the most independent of others that social arrangements can be made to admit' exemplifies this trend.[15]

Owen and Owenism 1820–1858

The new 'Plan' met with resistance from working-class radicals such as William Cobbett, who feared a state paternalist workhouse scheme, and distrusted Owen for refusing to support franchise extension. Owen's attack on organized religion at the 1817 meetings also cost him the support of some philanthropists. Others, however, rallied to the cause. Initially the most active was a Scottish printer, George Mudie (b. 1788), who established the first Owenite periodical, *The Economist* (1821–2), and who indefatigably developed Owen's ideas over many decades. Mudie helped form a small urban community in Spa Fields, London, which included the young Henry Hetherington, later a 'moral force' Chartist leader. He then joined the first Owenite community proper, on 290 acres at Orbiston, south of Glasgow, where 300 members resided from 1825 to 1827. Here, among other issues, the question as to whether distribution should be equal or proportionate to labour proved divisive. In late 1826, more than 200 dined together, proportionately consuming considerably less than the 77 who cared for

---

14 *New Moral World* 13, 8 (17 August 1844), p. 57.
15 *Spirit of the Age* no. 16 (16 November 1848), p. 244.

themselves.[16] Nicknamed 'Babylon', it failed after more than £9,000 had been invested. Mudie lost all his savings.

Owen sought patronage from all quarters in these years, and befriended the duke of Kent, father to the future queen Victoria, who chaired a number of meetings (and borrowed money from Owen) before dying suddenly in 1820. In 1822 Owen then formed another organization, the British and Foreign Philanthropic Society, to raise funds for a community. He travelled to Ireland in 1822–3 in search of support, carrying with him a large model consisting of cubes which represented the relative size of the different classes, thus demonstrating the waste of labour (about a fifth) under the current unproductive system. In 1825, he bought a ready-made community from a German sect, the Rappites, set on 20,000 acres on the banks of the Wabash River in Indiana territory, which he renamed New Harmony. He spent about four-fifths of his New Lanark fortune on its development (1825–8). His publicity was faultless; he addressed the United States president, Supreme Court, and House of Representatives in 1825, and met with large and enthusiastic audiences in many cities. Unfortunately, his newspaper advertisements soliciting members attracted fewer farmers and more adventurers than was desirable among the nine hundred who eventually joined. Owen was forced to conclude that 'experience proved that the attempt was premature to unite a number of strangers not previously educated for the purpose, who should carry on extensive operations for their common interest, and live together as a common family'.[17] His stated goal of 'complete equality' was never attained, and there were accusations of favouritism and special privileges for the more well-to-do.

A number of distinguished intellectuals, such as William Maclure, joined, however. But these soon began disagreeing with Owen, and among themselves. By 1827 the community split into four groups, and then ten. Other Owen-inspired experiments were commenced at Nashoba in Tennessee, where Fanny Wright in 1825 enrolled ex-slaves in a daring extension of the new principles, though the backlash against Wright resulted in Nashoba's former slave residents being expelled to Haiti in 1830. During the 1840s other communities were founded, notably at Yellow Springs, Ohio. None achieved the stature of New Harmony.

---

16 A. Cullen, *Adventures in Socialism: New Lanark Establishment and Orbiston Community* (Glasgow: J. Smith and Son, 1910), p. 293.
17 *New Harmony Gazette*, 23 October 1828, cited in E. Royle, *Robert Owen and the Commencement of the Millennium: A Study of the Harmony Community* (Manchester: Manchester University Press, 1998), p. 32.

In Britain, more than the United States, Owen's principles also extended beyond communitarianism. His proclamation of a future system of equality was understood to encompass women by the 1820s. Owenite feminism grew initially out of Owen's very liberal views on marriage, and occasional hints that community life might entertain more flexible approaches to the family, which he regarded as bastions of personal loyalty and thus rivals to community identity.[18] (Extensions of this principle can be found in many subsequent forms of communism.) Owen certainly supported equal rights for women, and occasionally likened marriage to prostitution, although he never commended a community of wives. He also hoped that birth control would be practised widely in the community, having been named as an opponent in later editions of T. R. Malthus's *Essay on Population*, which insisted that all utopian schemes would run aground through overpopulation. He likely travelled to Paris to learn about new methods of birth control, and may have helped introduce the vaginal sponge to Britain. These themes were further seeded by the influence of Saint-Simonian feminism in Britain in the late 1820s. Besides Owen, their chief propagator within the movement was William Thompson (1775–1833), author with Anna Wheeler of the *Appeal of One Half the Human Race* (1824), the most important feminist text published in Britain between Mary Wollstonecraft's *Vindication of the Rights of Woman* (1792) and John Stuart Mill's *The Subjection of Women* (1869).

The appeal of Owenism from the 1820s can also be linked to religious movements in this period. J. F. C. Harrison notes that Owen early on adopted the language of millenarianism to address the apocalyptic implications of both capitalist crisis and a dramatic change of behaviour in the shift to the 'new moral world', where crime, misery, and poverty would vanish.[19] The social consequences of the widespread disruption that followed the end of the Napoleonic wars and rapid mechanization certainly fuelled this mentality. Owen himself was a deist who moved in Unitarian circles in Manchester. His constant attacks on the established church attracted Nonconformists, and the packaging of Owenism as a 'New Religion' of charity and benevolence declaiming against the widespread spirit of money-getting and selfishness which dominated the age all easily appealed to Christians. Yet, for those who regarded these issues as essentially a distraction, there also emerged in the

18 The main texts here are R. Owen, *Lectures on the Marriages of the Priesthood of the Old Immoral World* (Leeds, 1835) (*Selected Works of Robert Owen*, vol. II, pp. 259–324), and *The Marriage System of the New Moral World* (Leeds: J. Hobson, 1838).
19 J. F. C. Harrison, *Robert Owen and the Owenites* (London: Routledge & Kegan Paul, 1969), p. 92.

same period a non-sectarian 'economic socialism', which insisted that 'Socialism, in a few words, is a system which secures in the best manner the most efficacious production, with the just distribution of wealth. It has nothing to do with religious opinions. It may be carried out by religionists or anti-religionists – by Christians or Heathens.'[20]

The Varieties of Owenism, 1825–1835

The socialist idea originally involved a wedding of utopian republican views of property with secularist and necessitarian theories of education. An opposition to extreme specialization of function and a labour theory of value were loosely derived from Scottish Enlightenment economists. As opposed to the traditional radical explanation of poverty as emanating from state corruption and heavy taxation, Owenism focused on the wage relationship, and the 'unequal exchange' between labourers and capitalists. Wages in future would reflect the much larger share of the workers' real contribution to the product.

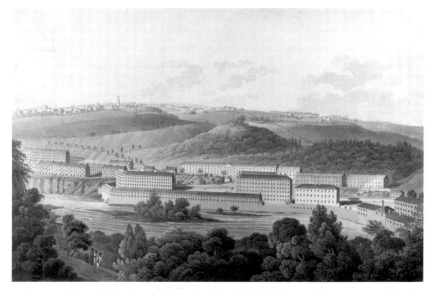

Fig. 6.2   Owen's New Lanark Mills, Scotland. (PHOTOS.com/Getty Images Plus.)

---

20 Quoted in G. Claeys, *Machinery, Money and the Millennium: From Moral Economy to Socialism, 1815–1860* (Princeton: Princeton University Press, 1987), p. 152.

Unproductive labour would be drastically reduced. Needs would be prioritized, and fashion and luxury curtailed. By the late 1820s, Owen also predicted frequent crises in capitalism – the first occurred in 1825 – and insisted that the process of the centralization of wealth would eventually destroy smaller producers and concentrate wealth in the hands of a few great capitalists. His theory of crisis here clearly antedates that of Marx, and again qualifies the 'utopian' label often applied to Owen. The United States would become the paradigmatic example of socialist argument. A notional workingman's paradise, its growing poverty and inequality would seemingly prove the socialist case against capitalism more than any other instance in the nineteenth century.

There was originally no 'politics' attached to the scheme as such; Owen presumed that, as at New Lanark, his paternalist guidance would be accepted by his followers without contradiction. Given his stress on 'harmony', Owen opposed elections in principle as divisive. By 1817 he had settled on a gerontocratic ideal by which each community might 'ultimately be governed by a committee of its own members, from forty to fifty years of age, or should this number be too numerous, it may be composed of all from forty-five to fifty-five years of age'. By the mid-1830s, in his key mature work, *The Book of the New Moral World* (seven parts, 1836–44), this was elaborated into a system of organization in which the entire population would progress through stages based on age. Since all would eventually become governors, Owen thought this would function as a substitute for democracy based on elections and voting. In the future there would be eight age groups, or 'classes', ages 1–5 attending school; 5–10 assisting with domestic labour; 10–15 learning work skills; 15–20 being workers; 20–5 supervising these; 25–30 preserving and distributing wealth; 30–40 running the community; and 40–60 conducting 'foreign affairs'. This scheme, Owen proclaimed, would unite 'in the same individual the producer, and the possessor of wealth, the communicator and the recipient of knowledge, the governor and the governed, to destroy the invidious distinctions that have split up the one great family of man into sections and classes'.[21] There is, however, no reason to presume that more politically minded Owenites, who probably comprised a majority of adherents in the early 1840s, at the peak of the movement, adopted Owen's anti-political views.

During the middle and later 1820s, indeed, all these assumptions came into question as Owenism began to percolate into the wider population. Two writers in particular offered the most impressive accounts of socialist thinking

21 *New Moral World* 13, 48 (24 May 1845), p. 388.

in this period: John Gray (1799–1883) and William Thompson. Gray's *A Lecture on Human Happiness* (1825) presented a pithy account of the benefits of social equality. But by the time of *The Social System* (1831) he had moved further from Owen to emphasize establishing a just means of exchange between workers while minimizing middlemen, and retaining competition without the need for communities. (But a national elected council would supervise all necessary production.) Thompson's *An Inquiry into the Principles of Wealth Most Conducive to Human Happiness* (1824) superadded Benthamite utilitarian principles, an idea of 'voluntary exchange', and an ideal of federative republican government onto Owen's original scheme; it is a moot point as to how far he too can be termed an 'Owenite'. Both writers indeed soon broke with Owen, Gray over the issue of luxury, which he came to view as no obstacle to equality; and Thompson over Owen's paternalistic style, which he rejected in favour of greater democracy. Thompson, however, remained a communitarian and planned a settlement at Cork in 1830. Gray, who had visited Orbiston for two days and found its organization chaotic, soon offered proposals for economic planning on a national scale. Against the autarchic vision popularized by Owen from the outset, Mudie denied that the market could balance supply and demand, and pioneered a vision of socialism based on unlimited production in order to satisfy 'almost unbounded wants'. Here the aim was to ensure that

> there are not too few articles of prime necessity produced for the satisfaction of the wants of the people; that the labourers (including their employers) do not make too many articles of secondary utility, while they neglect to produce sufficient of the necessaries of life, that there is no waste of power, in the production of really useless things or in the excessive produc-tion of commodities, valuable in themselves, but the great superabundance of which is of no value whatsoever; – that the labour and the labourers are properly adjusted, not only so that there shall be no disproportion of products, but that there shall be the due proportion of labourers in each branch, and that one-half of the labourers are not overworked, while the other half are forced to consume their days in idleness and misery.[22]

Several other Owen-inspired attempts at community, notably one pro-jected by the London Co-operative Society in 1826, did not come to fruition. Friction between Thompson and Owen came to a head at the first Co-operative Congress in 1831, when the former's plans for a small-scale com-munity were met by Owen's threat that all marriages would have to be

22 Quoted in Claeys, *Machinery, Money and the Millennium*, p. 75.

dissolved in it. Meanwhile a thriving non-Owenite co-operative movement emerged in the late 1820s, with some 300 societies active by 1830. In 1832–3 'labour exchanges' were founded in London and Birmingham, where small producers such as shoemakers, carpenters, cabinet-makers, and other artisans exchanged goods based on the cost of labour, at a uniform sixpence per hour, and raw materials, using 'labour notes' as the medium of exchange. But the notes were not widely transferable, and there were problems pricing food in particular. For a brief time Owen assisted, as 'Grand Master of the Order', the first national trades union, the Grand National Consolidated Trades Union (1833–4), which amassed as many as a million members. Its main aim was the eight-hour workday, which Owen termed 'the first step necessary to put society into a rational state'.[23] Other short-lived communal experiments occurred at Ralahine in Ireland between 1831 and 1833, and at Manea Fen, Cambridgeshire (1838–41).

The Heyday of Owenism, 1835–1845

After New Harmony, Owen made a vain attempt to gain a large land grant from the Mexican government, and then turned to found a new 'home colony' in Britain, this time acquiring land at Queenwood, Hampshire. Here work commenced on 1 October 1839, thereafter called the first day of the first month of the first year of the 'New Era'. (The words 'Commencement of the Millennium' were etched into the foundation stone of the main building.) To raise funds he formed in 1835 the first large-scale socialist branch-based organization, the Association of All Classes of All Nations, eventually renamed the Universal Community Society of Rational Religionists, or Rational Society for short. Through much of its existence this was controlled by Owen through a Central Board of leading followers. It was initially highly successful, boasting some 15 branches by 1837, with 1,500 members, and 62 by 1840, chiefly in the industrial midlands. These hosted at least 50,000 and perhaps as many as 100,000 visitors weekly. They channelled funds to Queenwood, also called Harmony, on which some £30,000 was expended, though of some 3,300 members in 1839 only 783 were contributing to the community fund.[24]

23 *Rights of Industry: Catechism of the Society for Promoting National Regeneration* (Manchester, 1833), p. 3; British Library Add. MS. 46344 f. 3. The Society's programme is printed in the *Pioneer* no. 14 (7 December 1833), p. 109.
24 R. G. Garnett, *Co-operation and the Owenite Socialist Communities in Britain, 1825–1845* (Manchester: Manchester University Press, 1974), p. 172.

This was because large sums, at least £22,000 in 1839–40, also went towards constructing meeting rooms, called 'Halls of Science', which were eventually capable of holding some 22,000. The first of these, the Salford Social Institution, opened in January 1836 with a capacity of 600, with all members electing a board of governors. (Owen later introduced an 'elective paternal system' by which branch presidents chose most of their assistants.) Rochdale opened a 'social institution' in 1838, and Sheffield followed in 1840. The branches assisted in a massive propaganda campaign to acquaint the public with socialist principles, with at least half a million tracts, newspapers, and placards distributed annually.

At one of the largest Halls of Science, in Manchester, constructed at a cost of £6,000, and opened in 1840, 3,000 could be accommodated. Here in late 1842 a newly arrived German cotton merchant's son, Friedrich Engels, received his first lesson in political economy from the local Owenite 'Missionary', John Watts. The latter's *The Facts and Fictions of Political Economists* (1842) thus forms the starting point for Marxist political economy. Engels indeed flirted with communitarianism briefly in this period, before converting with Marx to the nationally and centrally organized system of statist socialism trumpeted in the *Manifesto*, which owes more to Thomas Carlyle than to Owen. Owenite economic thought should not, however, be categorized in terms of 'Ricardian socialism'. It owed more to Adam Smith in the first instance, and is even termed 'Smithian socialism' by Noel Thompson.[25] It was in any case always critical of 'moral economy' assumptions like those implied by the chief Chartist economic slogan, 'a fair day's wages for a fair day's work'. Collectively, these views were immensely influential by the end of the 1830s, with the *Westminster Review* even claiming in 1839 – the year the prime minister, Lord Melbourne, presented Owen to the young Queen Victoria – that Owen's hostility to competition was seemingly 'the actual creed of a great proportion of the working classes'.[26]

For rank-and-file Owenites, branch life was as important as the prospect of relocating to a community on the land. The branches presented a viable 'alternative' culture which aimed to create a 'rational' character type that was indebted to the Dissenting tradition, and especially Quakerism.[27] In some locations, branches functioned as radical counterparts to Mechanics'

---

25 Noel Thompson, *The People's Science: The Popular Political Economy of Exploitation and Crisis, 1816–1834* (Cambridge: Cambridge University Press, 1984), p. 105.
26 *Westminster Review* 32 (1839), p. 498.
27 See E. Yeo, 'Robert Owen and Radical Culture', in S. Pollard and J. Salt (eds.), *Robert Owen: Prophet of the Poor* (London: Macmillan, 1971), pp. 84–114.

Institutes. Most members appear to have been relatively well-off artisans. Their activities can thus also be understood in part in light of the wider search for 'respectability' in Victorian working-class culture, and as providing a conscious alternative to the public house, blood sports, and other 'rougher' amusements. As part of the activities of Branch A1 in the capital, which had 755 members in 1841, a 'London Socialist and Philosophical Society' was established, and that year a 'London Socialist Museum' was mooted.

Owenism's status in the late 1830s and early 1840s as a quasi-sect is undoubted. In this period Owen, the society's 'Social Father', frequently described his ideals as a 'Rational Religion', and continued to use the language of the millennium which had featured so prominently in his 1817 addresses. Besides hosting regular Sunday lectures, scientific demonstrations, dances, 'Social Soirées' of various types, music, and drama, the Halls of Sciences conducted services at which 'Social Hymns' were sung and a 'Social Bible' was used. Many branch members came from the ranks of Nonconformists, including Baptists and Methodists. Marriages also occurred, one being performed by Owen at the John Street Institution off Tottenham Court Road in early 1842. An Owenite christening came with the naming of Primo Communis Flitcroft, the first child born at Queenwood, to a Bolton bricklayer and his wife.[28] Many Owenites regarded their ethos as analogous to 'primitive Christianity'; as the Birmingham Unitarian and Owenite William Hawkes Smith put it, 'Socialism might be almost called pre-eminently practical Christianity, for it not only says to all, "do as you would be done by" ... but its economics bring in their aid.'[29] To the Liverpool socialist John Finch, a founder of the 'Genuine Primitive Christian (commonly called Infidel) Teetotal Society', Owenism was defined as the religion of Christ, which after the Unitarian fashion meant love to God 'but by love to man'.[30] He asked Owen to make him the first bishop of the new moral world. Others in Owen's inner coterie, like William Galpin, were similarly fanatical millenarians. Lecturers were sometimes addressed as 'Reverend', and eighteen, moving between branches divided into six districts, were formally termed 'Social Missionaries'. Conversion to Owenism could also be analogous to Christian sectarianism; when the Orbistonian founder Abram Combe became an Owenite, he renounced the use of animal foods

---

28 *New Moral World* 10, 29 (15 January 1842), p. 231.
29 Gregory Claeys (ed.), *The Owenite Socialist Movement: Pamphlets and Correspondence*, 10 vols. (London: Routledge, 2005), vol. v, p. 267.
30 John Finch, *The Millennium: The Wisdom of Jesus, and the Foolery of Sectarianism* (Liverpool, 1837), p. 8.

and fermented liquors, and, as his obituary put it, 'the theatre became to him an object of dislike, on account of the low motives and false axioms which abounded in dramatic pieces, and which he now felt to be offensive to his moral sentiments'.[31] The ethos of branch and community activities varied from the more puritanical to the more libertine, however, and at least one Social Missionary raised eyebrows by evidently practising the new liberal views of marriage and sexual relations.

Many branch events aimed to offer 'foretastes of the pleasures of community'. On the occasion of an Owenite steamship expedition, for instance, the principle of communal distribution was taught by having each family bring its own food, which was then 'united in a common stock'.[32] The ethos of the branches was not, however, generally 'class-conscious' in the Marxian sense; Social Festivals indeed rather aimed to 'cultivate kindly feeling and social fellowship among all classes', in the spirit of the Rational Society's original title.[33] Yet Owenism's economic ideals were also conveyed in these public spaces; a banner on the wall at a Salford Social Festival read 'Labour, mental and physical, the only source of wealth'. Annual congresses of the branches were also widely publicized, and produced some lively debates, and abundant opposition to Owen's overly paternalist management from dissidents such as Charles Southwell, who was imprisoned for blasphemy in 1841. Plenty of Owenite works also stressed the division of society into rich and poor, idle and productive, property-owners and labourers, and concluded, with John Francis Bray, that 'Slavery in nature, if not in name, has ever been, is now, and ever will be, the portion of the working classes, in every country where inequality of property exists in connection with the gradation of classes.'[34]

Owenism produced an extremely extensive pamphlet literature and a large number of periodicals, the bibliography of which runs to more than 100 printed pages.[35] The Rational Society's newspaper, *The New Moral World*, ran from 1834 to 1845, and achieved a peak circulation of 40,000 per week. It remains the key source for studying branch life. Among the more intellectually impressive works by later Owenites are John Francis Bray's *Labour's*

---

31 Quoted in Gregory Claeys, '"From Polite Manners" to "Rational Character": The Critique of Culture in Owenite Socialism, 1800–1850', in H. Diedrichs, F. van Holthoon, and L. Heerma van Voss (eds.), *Working Class and Popular Culture in Britain and Holland* (Amsterdam: Stichting Beheer IISG, 1988), p. 26.
32 *New Moral World* 2, no. 91 (23 July 1836), p. 309; no. 85 (11 June 1836), p. 261.
33 Ibid. 1, no. 3 (15 November 1834), p. 23.
34 J. F. Bray, *Labour's Wrongs and Labour's Remedy or, The Age of Might and the Age of Right* (Leeds: n.p., 1839), p. 21.
35 Harrison, *Robert Owen and the Owenites*, pp. 261–370.

Wrongs and Labour's Remedy (1839); the Coventry ribbon-manufacturer Charles Bray's *The Philosophy of Necessity,* which appeared in two editions (1841, 1863); and William Hawkes Smith's *The Errors of the Social System* (1834) and *Letters on Social Science* (1839). Owenism also produced some literary utopianism, notably in the writings of the Christian socialist John Minter Morgan, whose *The Revolt of the Bees* (1826) and *Hampden in the Nineteenth Century* (2 vols., 1834) give a good sense of how some intellectuals understood the new movement; in several pamphlets by Samuel Bower, *The Peopling of Utopia* and *A Sequel to the Peopling of Utopia* (Bradford, 1838); and in John Francis Bray's *A Voyage to Utopia* (1842).[36]

Owen's relationship with the Chartist movement from 1835 to 1845 remained fraught with ambiguity. Most of his followers seem to have subscribed to democratic principles, with the Liverpool Owen loyalist John Finch declaring himself a 'Radical Reformer' in 1838. Owen riled some of his followers by continuing to insist that 'the middle class is the *only* efficient *directing* class in society, and will, of necessity, remain so, until our system shall create a *new* class of very superior *directors,* as well as *operators'.*[37] Some Owenites recognized that traditional radical explanations for poverty had now to be modified by some twenty years of socialist critiques. A few Chartists, in turn, notably James Bronterre O'Brien, were sympathetic to socialism, and his later National Reform League provided an important bridge between the first generation of socialists and the revival of the 1880s. George Julian Harney and Ernest Jones also joined the chant for 'The Charter and Something More'.

The Queenwood community, however, proved to have poor agricultural land and never became profitable. Public opposition to Owenism mounted. Factory owners in some areas dismissed known Owenites from employment. The House of Lords debated socialist principles in 1840, and Owen was denounced by the bishop of Exeter. Riots occurred in some areas, and meeting halls were attacked. In 1842 one Owenite, George Jacob Holyoake, who would later develop Owen's ideas under the heading of 'Rationalism', was convicted of blasphemy and imprisoned for six months.

36 The *Sequel* is reprinted in Claeys (ed.), *Owenite Pamphlets*, vol. v. Bray's *Voyage* is reprinted in Gregory Claeys, *Modern British Utopias*, 8 vols. (London: Pickering & Chatto, 1997), vol. vii. Most of the pamphlets produced by the movement were collected by H. S. Foxwell and are currently housed in Senate House Library, University of London. Some 3,000 letters by and to Owen are preserved in the Co-operative Union Library, Manchester, a selection of which are printed in my *Owenite Pamphlets*, vols. ix–x.
37 *New Moral World* 6 (1839), p. 595.

By late 1844, after the expenditure of some £40,000, Queenwood was sinking, and by the summer of 1845 the most important communitarian experiment of the century in Britain had collapsed. Some branches emigrated collectively to the United States; many others dissolved. Owen had invested an immense amount in attempting to offer Queenwood as an example of the future socialist paradise, importing tropical hardwoods for the main building and constructing a dumb-waiter system for carrying food and dishes as elaborate as any in the best hotel in London, at a cost of some £15,000. There were stained-glass windows, and hot and cold water pipes. The aim was to demonstrate that socialism could attain a higher standard of living for the working classes: if there could be a working-class paradise, this would be it. There were lectures and instruction in French, science, arithmetic, and much else, plus dancing and singing. But there were too few agricultural labourers among the community's population to bear the expense, and too many craftsmen once the buildings were completed, and many former artisans worked at farm labour. John Finch's teetotal regime at the outset irritated many. (Some slipped out to the local village inn.) Private space was limited, and officers could enter married quarters (as at New Lanark). Dormitories housing eight were planned for single residents. Owen's insistence on 'superior class arrangements' for middle-class members rankled working-class colonists. The food was poor – half the inhabitants were evidently vegetarians – and the central heating malfunctioned. By 1841 the population, now only thirteen adults, was actually declining. But it rose again to about seventy-five full-time 'family' members in 1844. Most of the 150 members who resided at some point during the six-year period were working-class, with the majority coming from Manchester, Salford, Yorkshire, and London.[38] Relations with some branches, where membership was anyway declining, began to sour. By 1844, the farm was £10,000 in deficit and the end was nigh – less the millennium than, for Owenism, an apocalypse. Most of the branches folded soon thereafter, with the Manchester Hall being sold in 1851 to become the city's first public library.

Owen resigned at the 1844 congress, as Queenwood slid into bankruptcy. His personal influence dissipated rapidly after its collapse. He ran for Parliament several times, offering a programme that included proposals for a graduated property tax equal to the national expenditure; abolishing all other taxes; free trade; national education and national employment for those who desired them; liberty of speech, writing, and religious observance; and

38 Royle, *Robert Owen and the Commencement of the Millennium*, p. 129.

self-government to British dependencies. In the 1850s he turned to spiritualism, and was encouraged to find that his old friend, the duke of Kent, assured him that there were no titles in the hereafter. In 1857–8 he published his *Life*, still an indispensable source for its subject, though its late composition is unfortunate. He returned to Newtown in 1858 after an absence of seventy years, and died there at the Bear Inn, his son Robert Dale Owen at his side. He is buried in a ruined churchyard.

Legacies, 1845–1900

In the wake of the Queenwood disaster, Owenite energies dissipated. From 1844 a co-operative founded at Rochdale by a group of weavers developed a 'divi' scheme, where dividends are shared among consumers, thus founding the modern consumer co-operation movement. Efforts at producer co-operation, and acquiring land for communities, now receded in importance. A group from the Leeds Redemption Society attempted a Welsh colony in 1847 which lasted until 1855. Some former Owenites tried to reorganize; a 'Communist Committee' was formed out of the John Street branch in 1846; and as late as the 1860s there were still various community plans afoot, some projected for foreign colonies. The revolutionary year of 1848, which saw socialism/communism first widely placed on the agenda of modern politics, saw no revival of Owenism in Britain. The ideal of producer co-operation was, however, taken up by two of the most important mid-Victorian thinkers: John Stuart Mill, who regarded it as a key means of ensuring economic justice, and hoped that worker-owned enterprises electing their own managers would ultimately supplant the existing capitalist system; and Karl Marx, who regarded it as a halfway house to full communism.[39] Mill also crafted his theory of the self-formation of character as a means of countering Owenite necessitarianism, and embraced both atheism and birth control. The mid-Victorian critic John Ruskin made some use of Owenite theories of exchange in his influential critique of political economy, *Unto This Last* (1863), which had a profound influence on the late nineteenth-century labour movement. Owenism made a great impact on the co-founder of evolutionary theory, the socialist Alfred Russel Wallace, who first encountered secularism in the John Street branch in London. Many of the Fabians returned to Owen in the 1890s as a new

---

39 On Mill's trajectory here, see Gregory Claeys, *Mill and Paternalism* (Cambridge: Cambridge University Press, 2011), pp. 123–72.

generation began to confront his legacy, and weigh it against the more revolutionary ideals of H. M. Hyndman, who frequently referred to Owen, and others. By the late Victorian period, the radical republican Charles Bradlaugh commented, 'society now adopts the view which Robert Owen was the first to popularise, although not the first to enunciate – that man is better or worse according to the conditions surrounding the parents previous to the birth of the child, and those which surround the infant during its childhood, and accompany the boy or girl during youth'.[40] Leslie Stephen, who wrote the entry on Owen for the *Dictionary of National Biography* (1895) famously called him 'one of those intolerable bores who are the salt of the earth', and dismissed him as a man 'of one idea', 'that of himself and the Lanark cotton-mills'. In fact Owen was full of ideas: the centrality of environmental influence in character formation; the immense value of infant education; ideals of co-operation and communal sharing; a humane outlook on labour; and much else. The 'home colony' concept lived on in the schemes of 'General' William Booth, in some of William Morris' ideas, and in the Garden City movement.

Conclusion

Early accounts of Owen tended to stress the 'success' of the New Lanark years, portraying Owen as an enlightened capitalist, by contrast to 'the useless activity and hopeless ill-success of the latter half of his life, in William Lucas Sargant's description.[41] It was not until the Fabian Frank Podmore's two-volume biography of Owen, published in 1906, that he gained stature as a central figure in the modern history of socialism. The historiography of the movement as a whole became more sophisticated with the publication of Anton Menger's *The Right to the Whole Produce of Labour* (1899) and Esther Lowenthal's *The Ricardian Socialists* (1911), though it would not be until J. F. C. Harrison's *Robert Owen and the Owenites* (1969) that a fully fleshed-out account of the movement would become available.

Communitarian socialism assumed other forms in the later nineteenth and twentieth centuries, and the theme loomed large in the Soviet

---

40 C. Bradlaugh, *Five Dead Men I Knew When Living* (n.p., n.d.), p. 4.

41 W. L. Sargant, *Robert Owen and His Social Philosophy* (London: Smith and Elder, 1860), p. xxiii. More sympathetic accounts written by people who knew Owen well are L. Jones, *The Life, Times, and Labours of Robert Owen*, 2 vols. (London: Swan Sonnenschein, 1889–90); and G. J. Holyoake, *Life and Last Days of Robert Owen, of New Lanark* (London: Holyoake, 1859).

experiment, when thousands of communal apartments were built under Stalin, and even more in China under the early years of Mao's rule. Secularism remained a major theme in many subsequent socialist movements, as did birth control. The long-term influence of Owenism is best measured in terms of its critique of radical–liberal assumptions about the ability of 'free' markets and political democracy to provide opulence and justice for the majority. Following the lead of Charles Hall, Owenites made it clear that the example of the United States proved this was not the case. From Owen's theory of the concentration of wealth and propensity of capitalism to systemic cyclical crises emerged the much more influential Marxian account, which would dominate socialism in the twentieth century. Long after communitarianist socialism ceased to appeal, this critique of the limits of liberalism stood in good stead: economic problems did not have political solutions. But the 'social' modifications of democracy also entailed a commitment to solidarity and sociability that extended beyond communitarian aspirations. Firmly in the tradition of utopian idealism, it nonetheless suggests the possibility of a more supportive, just, and equal society – an ideal which doggedly refuses to disappear.

Further Reading

Bestor, Arthur, *Backwoods Utopias: The Sectarian Origins and the Owenite Phase of Communitarian Socialism in America: 1663–1829*, 2nd edn (Philadelphia: University of Pennsylvania Press, 1970).

Claeys, Gregory, *Citizens and Saints: Politics and Anti-Politics in Early British Socialism* (Cambridge: Cambridge University Press, 1989).

   Machinery, Money and the Millennium: From Moral Economy to Socialism 1815–1860 (Princeton: Princeton University Press, 1987).

   (ed.), *The Owenite Socialist Movement: Pamphlets and Correspondence*, 10 vols. (London: Routledge, 2005).

   (ed.), *Robert Owen: A New View of Society and Other Writings* (Harmondsworth: Penguin, 1991).

   (ed.), *The Selected Works of Robert Owen*, 4 vols. (London: Pickering and Chatto, 1993).

Garnett, R. G., *Co-operation and the Owenite Socialist Communities in Britain, 1825–1845* (Manchester: Manchester University Press, 1972).

Harrison, J. F. C., *Robert Owen and the Owenites in Britain and America: The Quest for the New Moral World* (London: Routledge & Kegan Paul, 1969).

Royle, Edward, *Robert Owen and the Commencement of the Millennium: A Study of the Harmony Community* (Manchester: Manchester University Press, 1998).

Siméon, Ophélie, *Robert Owen's Experiment at New Lanark: From Paternalism to Socialism* (London: Palgrave Macmillan, 2017).

7

Charles Fourier and Fourierism

JONATHAN BEECHER

Charles Fourier adamantly rejected the description of his work as 'utopian'. But, of all the early socialists, he is the only one for whom the designation 'utopian socialist' makes much sense. A social critic who advocated 'absolute deviation' from established philosophies and institutions, he distanced himself in every possible way from the society in which he lived. A psychologist who celebrated the passions as agents of human happiness, he carried to its ultimate conclusion the rejection of the doctrine of original sin that had long been a hallmark of the utopian tradition. A social prophet who drew up blueprints for everything from colour schemes for work uniforms to designs for nursery furniture, he was more concerned than any of his contemporaries to give precise definition to his conception of the good society. A visionary who foresaw an age in which oranges would grow in Warsaw and seawater would turn into lemonade, he had a faith in the power of human beings to shape their own world that was remarkable even in the age of Napoleon.

At the centre of Fourier's thought was a vision of what today would be called a non-repressive society, a society whose members would be free to obey the dictates of their passions and to seek pleasure and personal fulfilment when, where, and with whomever they pleased. This social vision was premised on the assumption that human behaviour is dictated by fundamental instinctual drives that cannot be permanently altered or suppressed. Fourier called these drives the 'passions', and he believed that one of his great accomplishments as a thinker had been to identify and define them and to analyse their functions. His argument with the thinkers of his own time was that they failed to recognize the power of the passions. For centuries, philosophers had been devising doctrines meant to curb the passions and thereby to alter human nature. In Fourier's view, the real task confronting the social theorist was to find a way to liberate and utilize these basic drives. Only when their primacy and immutability were recognized would it be possible to construct a society in which human beings could be free, happy, and productive.

The Shaping of the Theory

Charles Fourier was born in Besançon in Franche-Comté on 7 April 1772. He was thus a dozen years younger than Henri Saint-Simon and a contemporary of both Robert Owen and Napoleon. In later years he never tired of pointing out that he had been 'born and raised in the mercantile shops'. His father, who died in 1781, was a wealthy cloth merchant and his mother came from a prominent Besançon commercial family. As their only son, Fourier was expected to take charge of the family business. He had other ideas. He later claimed that he had sworn a 'Hannibalic oath' against commerce at the age of seven. But he could not escape the vocation for which his family had destined him. In 1791 he was apprenticed to a cloth merchant at Lyon. It was during these early years at Lyon that Fourier first began to wonder whether the economic practices of emerging capitalism were not so many calamities 'invented by God to punish the human race'.[1] When he turned twenty-one in 1793, Fourier collected half his patrimony. Investing it in colonial goods, he went into business for himself in Lyon as a merchant and importer.

A few months later Lyon rose up in arms against the revolutionary government. From August until November, the city was put to siege by the troops of the Convention. Fourier's goods were requisitioned without indemnity, and when Lyon capitulated he narrowly escaped execution. The experience of the Lyon insurrection was crucial for Fourier in two respects: it cost him much of his inheritance, and it left him with a lasting horror of political revolution and social turmoil.

If the Lyon insurrection disgusted Fourier with revolutionary politics, the financial chaos of the Directory shaped his economic views. The brief Jacobin experiment in a controlled economy was followed by the complete relaxation of economic controls, and the Directory was a period of skyrocketing inflation, industrial stagnation, and widespread food shortages. Fortunes were made overnight through speculation in paper money, profiteering in military supplies, and the creation of artificial food shortages. As a commercial

---

1 Charles Fourier, 'Politique et commerce' (1803), in *Publication des manuscrits de Charles Fourier*, 1 (Année 1851), in *Oeuvres complètes de Charles Fourier* (hereafter *OC*), 12 vols. (Paris: Editions Anthropos, 1966–8), vol. x, p. 274; Charles Fourier, 'Analyse du mécanisme d'agiotage', *La Phalange* 7 (1848), pp. 9–10; Charles Fourier, *Théorie des quatre mouvements et des destinées générales* (1808), in *OC*, vol. I, p. 5.

employee, first at Lyon and then at Marseille, Fourier saw these abuses at first hand. They strengthened his conviction that something was wrong with the whole economic system of free – or, as he called it, 'anarchic' – competition. He began to formulate a general critique of commercial capitalism that emphasized the parasitism of the merchant and middleman as the chief cause of economic ills. At the same time as Saint-Simon was developing his first schemes of social reorganization and Owen was making his first practical experiments in industrial reform, Fourier pondered the idea that a cure for the ills produced by free competition might be obtained through the establishment within the capitalist system of small self-sustaining co-operative communities or associations of producers and consumers.

In 1797 and 1798 Fourier's speculations took a bolder turn. He began to see the problems of cut-throat economic competition as symptoms of a deeper social sickness. The frustrations of his own life and the chaos of post-revolutionary society sufficed in his mind to demonstrate the futility of the revolution and to discredit the philosophical ideas that had inspired its leaders. As he saw it, the French Revolution was a spectacular proof of the vanity of the whole tradition of rationalist and 'enlightened' philosophy. The philosophers had attempted to impose rational norms on human behaviour, to stifle the passions. The cause of their failure was simply that they refused to accept man as he was. Institutions could be changed; human nature could not. The passions were God-given, and they were meant to be expressed.

Fourier's first efforts to bring together his initial speculations in a comprehensive view of human nature and society date from 1799. At that point he began to imagine his co-operative community as part of a larger theory of social organization designed to provide a useful outlet for every human passion. The task he set himself was to work out a scheme of 'natural association' within which the gratification of individual desires would serve the general good. In his sole surviving account of 'the indices and methods which led to the discovery', Fourier passed blithely over 'the stages of my research on the problem of natural association'. He merely observed that he eventually hit upon a scheme for the organization of a community – to be called the Phalanx – into small 'passional' groups and series of groups in which people would be inspired to work at socially useful tasks by 'rivalry, self-esteem, and other stimuli compatible with self-interest'.[2]

---

2 Fourier, *Quatre mouvements*, pp. 2–12. Here two definitions must be kept in mind. For Fourier a 'group' was not any collection of individuals but rather a gathering of at least three (ideally, seven to nine) people with a common passion. And a 'series' was

Fourier's crucial breakthrough came in April 1799. He was then employed as a merchant's clerk at Marseille. Quitting work, he travelled to Paris to undertake the scientific studies necessary to 'complete' his theory. He soon managed to persuade himself that he had hit upon the key to 'the riddle of the destinies'.[3] He had discovered the means to gratify and harmonize all the human passions. After less than a year of study, however, a number of 'misfortunes' – notably the loss of the remainder of his inheritance – compelled him to abandon his studies. In June 1800, shortly after the *coup d'état* that brought Napoleon to power, Fourier went back to work at Lyon.

During the fifteen years that followed his 'discovery' – the whole duration of the Napoleonic period – Fourier remained at Lyon and frequented its banks, its business houses, and its bourse. For a brief period he worked as cloth inspector in a military warehouse. Occasionally he did business for himself as an unlicensed commercial broker. But throughout most of the empire he was employed as a clerk and travelling salesman in the Lyon silk and textile industries. His 'home' in these years was the Quartier des Terreaux, a maze of dark, winding streets, shops, and ateliers at the centre of commercial Lyon. He lived in a succession of rented rooms: on the rue Saint-Côme 'chez Madame Guyonnet, marchande', the rue Clermont, and the place du Plâtre 'near the umbrella merchants'. Punctual at work, frugal in his habits, scrupulously neat in his dress, Fourier dined in the cheap *tables d'hôte* of the quarter and took his glass of white wine each morning at a small café on the rue Sainte-Marie-des-Terreaux.

For the rest of his life, Fourier devoted himself to the elaboration of the ideas that he had first formulated in 1799. Most days after work he would devote a few hours to his plans for the Phalanx and to the intricate theory of human motivation which he called 'the geometrical calculus of passionate attraction' and which, he claimed, was in 'complete accord' with Newton's theory of gravitational attraction. He had friends with whom he shared some of his ideas. But at work he hid behind the mask of a conscientious employee. As he confided later to an admirer, 'You are not aware that a man loses all credit, becomes an object of ridicule in a commercial establishment, if he gives the impression that he is writing a book.'[4]

a carefully stratified assemblage of groups of individuals differing in age, wealth, intelligence, and so forth, but sharing a common passion.

3 Charles Pellarin (ed.), *Lettre de Fourier au Grand Juge (4 nivôse an XII)* (Paris: Dentu, 1874), pp. 14–28.

4 Fourier, *Quatre mouvements*, p. 12; Charles Pellarin, *Charles Fourier. Sa vie et sa théorie*, 5th edn (Paris: Dentu, 1871), p. 89.

Fourier was indeed writing a book, and during the first decade of the century he was tormented by the question of how to reveal his 'discovery' to the world. Finally in 1808, after a number of fruitless 'announcements' in local newspapers, the book appeared at Lyon under an intentionally obscure title: *Théorie des quatre mouvements et des destinées générales* (*Theory of the Four Movements and the General Destinies*). Fearful that his ideas might be stolen, Fourier presented them in incomplete and parodistic form. In correspondence with his publisher he called the book a 'riddle'.[5] At the same time he flaunted his lack of academic credentials in the face of the intellectual establishment, chiding them for having left the discovery of passionate attraction to a 'near illiterate', a 'scientific pariah'. 'It is a *shop sergeant*', he boasted, 'who is going to confound all the weighty tomes of political and moral wisdom.'[6]

Not surprisingly, the book sold poorly, and the few reviews amounted to 'a litany of jeers'.[7] He inveighed against the critics in his notebooks, consoled himself with fantasies of revenge, and virtually abandoned his studies. In 1815, however, he managed to escape the 'jailhouse of commerce', taking up residence with relatives in the countryside. The next five years marked the most fruitful period in his intellectual life. He at last found the time and energy to set down on paper a comprehensive exposition of his ideas. The rudiments had been clear in his mind since 1799. But he now refined his earlier speculations and explored new branches of the doctrine. Spurred on by new discoveries, he focused on problems of love and sexuality. In four notebooks, collectively entitled *Le Nouveau monde amoureux* (*The New Amorous World*), he added a new dimension to his vision of the ideal community. By 1819, after three years of sustained intellectual activity, he had virtually completed the manuscript of a *Grand Traité* to be published in eight volumes.

In the course of his research, however, Fourier became convinced that the core of his theory could be presented in terms that would make possible a practical demonstration of the validity of his ideas. What was needed was an 'abridgement' which would persuade a potential 'founder' to finance the establishment of a 'trial Phalanx'. Fourier wrote such an abridgement, and in the spring of 1821 he returned to Besançon where, with the help of friends, he

---

5 A good selection of Fourier's writings on 'the riddle of the *Quatre mouvements*' may be found in the Fourierist periodical *La Phalange* 9 (1849), pp. 193–240. For excellent commentary on these texts and on the whole question of Fourier's guile, see F. Manuel, *The Prophets of Paris* (Cambridge, MA: Harvard University Press, 1962), pp. 243–8.

6 Fourier, *Quatre mouvements*, p. 102.

7 Fourier, 'Où l'auteur parle de lui-même', in *OC*, vol. I, pp. 24, 47, 49.

found a publisher. His 'shortened' version of the theory appeared in 1822 (in two 700-page volumes!) under the intentionally modest title of *Traité de l'association domestique-agricole* (*Treatise on Domestic–Agricultural Association*). Fourier was then just fifty years old and still at the height of his powers. But his growth as a thinker was over. For the rest of his life he sought to simplify his doctrine, to present it in a palatable form that would appeal to the *fondateur*.[8]

The Theory

'Civilization' was a pejorative term in Fourier's vocabulary, a synonym for perfidy and constraint. The attack he levelled against the institutions, ideologies, customs, and vices of civilization was both penetrating and comprehensive. In its scope, its intransigence, and its psychological insight, it recalls Jean-Jacques Rousseau's earlier challenges to civilized society and culture. But whereas Rousseau was concerned with the problem of how to live in a depraved society, Fourier's sole aim was to bring an end to civilization. His rules of method – Absolute Doubt and Absolute Deviation – implied a total rejection of civilization as a way of life. 'We must apply doubt to civilization', he wrote, 'we must doubt its necessity, its excellence, and its permanence.'[9]

There was no doubt much nonsense, pettiness, and prejudice in Fourier's indictment. His writing on civilization was punctuated by outbursts against the Jews, the English, the Parisians, and the 'philosophical cabal' which, he believed, was suppressing his ideas. His personal hatred of commerce was such that he often described the merchant as a villain whose machinations were the unique source of poverty and hunger. But, even at its most myopic, Fourier's attack on civilization had qualities not to be found in the work of any contemporary. His lack of education, his *déclassement*, and his sense of total alienation from the intellectual establishment were sources of insight as well as resentment. They heightened his contempt for conventional wisdom and shaped his awareness of ills which more successful and worldly men simply took for granted. For all its intellectual naivety and personal rancour, Fourier's social criticism was that of a man who absolutely refused to be

---

8 At a mere 500 pages, Fourier's *Le Nouveau monde industriel et sociétaire* (*The New Industrial and Social World*, 1829) came closer than the *Traité de l'association* to being the 'abridgement' that he desired. On his struggles to produce such a work, see his correspondence with Just Muiron in Pellarin, *Charles Fourier*, pp. 253–62.

9 Fourier, *Quatre mouvements*, pp. 3–5. See also C. Morilhat, *Charles Fourier, imaginaire et critique sociale* (Paris: Méridiens Klincksieck, 1991).

taken in by the lofty abstractions which others used to hide the physical suffering and emotional deprivation that were the lot of most people in civilization.

By 1808 Fourier had developed a panoramic vision of the thirty-two periods and eighteen creations that marked the whole course of human history. Within this theory, 'civilization' was the last of four 'subversive' stages that also included Savagery, Patriarchy, and Barbarism. But this elaborate cyclical-stadial picture of history played a largely decorative role in Fourier's thought. What he really cared about was the scientific analysis of the evils of civilization. This science usually consisted of what he thought was a revealing mathematical operation: enumeration. Civilization was characterized by 'seven scourges', and Fourier's science could discern thirty-six varieties of fraudulent bankruptcy and an equal number of types of cuckoldry. But at the beginning he focused on civilization's most obvious flaw: poverty.

What were the causes of poverty? In Fourier's analysis, the shameful poverty of civilization originated in the three branches of its economic system: commerce, distribution and consumption, and production. He began by exposing the roots of poverty in commerce. 'What is commerce?' he asked. His answer, subsequently the theme of infinite variations, was as straightforward as the question: 'It is falsehood in all its paraphernalia, bankruptcy, speculation, usury, and cheating.'[10] So, a major cause of poverty was the dishonesty of the merchant who abused public confidence through speculation, drove up prices by hoarding, and turned cheating into a fine art. Another cause was the waste that characterized distribution and consumption in civilization. Here the main problems were inept methods of distribution, the duplication of storage facilities, and the organization of production into 'isolated, incoherent households'. But the principal cause of poverty in civilization was the irrational organization of work. Free men justifiably abhorred work, Fourier believed, because civilization forced them to labour under conditions that ruined their health and stifled their spirit. Forced to work long hours at boring jobs in airless and dingy workshops, the urban worker inhabited a 'veritable industrial hell'. And agricultural workers were no better off. The sturdy peasants praised by writers were actually 'living automatons', sad and filthy creatures who subsisted on black bread and water.[11]

---

10 Fourier, *Quatre mouvements*, p. 227.
11 Ibid., pp. 67, 11, 121; and Charles Fourier, *Théorie de l'unité universelle*, in *OC*, vol. 11, p. 149.

Fourier's critique was not limited to the poverty, starvation, and wage slavery inflicted on the working class. He condemned all of civilization and pitied all of its victims, including the clerks and functionaries who toiled in offices and service occupations. These 'little people' were not starving, but they were prey to anxieties and emotional deprivation that were just as bad as physical suffering. Fourier's keen sense of the psychological costs of pinched, drab lives, insecurity, class jealousy, and the dread of *déclassement* on the part of the petite bourgeoisie separates him from almost all the social thinkers of his time.

Fourier's critique of civilization was all of a piece, and he regarded civilized sexual mores as marked by the same spirit of fraud, duplicity, and anarchic individualism that prevailed in the economic sphere. Just as the principle of laissez faire provided merchants with a sanction for dishonest business dealings, so, he insisted, had the institution of marriage sanctioned and institutionalized the practice of deceit in amorous relations. The lofty abstractions of political economy cloaked monopoly, exploitation, and social irresponsibility; but civilization's celebration of life in the 'happy family' barely concealed what everyone knew. Marriage was a state of 'domestic warfare' in which the 'virtuous wife' and the 'faithful husband' were no less determined to deceive one another than the parties to a business transaction. Since neither partner gained by the family system, it could only be described as 'the work of a third sex which seeks to torment the other two'. But the chief victims of monogamous marriage were women. Marriage was a 'mercantile calculation' in which a woman was 'a piece of merchandise offered to the highest bidder'. Once the transaction was concluded, she became in the eyes of the law her husband's property. Until that time civilization obliged her to remain chaste.[12]

Fourier's defence of women is one of the aspects of his thought for which he was and is best known. He was the first of the early European socialists to put a rigorous analysis of the situation of women at the centre of a comprehensive critique of his society.[13] His writings on the woman question were greatly admired by Flora Tristan, Jeanne Deroin, Désirée Véret, and other pioneering French feminists; and his followers did much to give currency to the idea of the emancipation of women within the socialist movement. This being the case, it is worth emphasizing one distinction.

12 Fourier, *Quatre mouvements*, pp. 110–33.
13 The most comprehensive and searching study of Fourier's approach to 'the woman question' is still, unfortunately, unpublished: B. Wilson, 'Charles Fourier (1772–1837) and Questions of Women', PhD dissertation, University of Cambridge, UK, 2002.

Unlike the position taken by the socialists of the 1840s, who argued for women's emancipation on humanitarian and moral grounds, the main thrust of Fourier's argument was utilitarian. He saw the servitude of women as a 'blunder' that wronged society as a whole and retarded its development in all spheres. 'The extension of the privileges of women', he wrote, 'is the fundamental cause of all social progress.'[14]

Everything in Fourier's speculations, down to the most minute details of life in his ideal community, was designed to ensure a life rich in gratified desire. The great discovery that would make such a life possible was the law of passionate attraction. He defined it in these terms in *Le Nouveau monde industriel*: 'Passionate attraction is the drive given us by nature prior to any reflection, and it persists despite the opposition of reason, duty, prejudice, etc.'[15] Although few eighteenth-century psychologists had denied that human beings are creatures of passion, most held that we are endowed with a rational faculty that enables us not only to organize our sense experience but also to impose checks on our passions. Breaking with this tradition, Fourier maintained that we are moved by instinctual forces which we cannot control. His primary concern as a psychologist was to specify and analyse these drives, for the passions were the 'mistresses of the world'; only when they had been recognized and allowed free expression could humans attain the happiness for which they were destined.

Although Fourier was acutely aware of the diversity of human instinctual promptings, he believed they could be subsumed within a basic classification of twelve recurring or 'radical' passions. In discussing them, he often employed the simile of a tree. From the trunk of the tree, which he called 'Unityism', sprang three branches. The first branch included five passions corresponding to the five senses. Fourier called these the 'luxurious' passions because their gratification depended on wealth as well as health – on the kind of material luxuries that only a rich man could afford in civilization. Fourier's second category included the four affective passions: Friendship, Love, Ambition, and Parenthood (or 'Familism'). These four passions tended to bring people together in groups. Like the other passions, they expressed themselves with varying degrees of intensity in different individuals. But, whereas the sensual drives remained relatively constant throughout the lifetime of a single individual, the strength of the affective passions varied

---

14 Fourier, *Quatre mouvements*, p. 133.
15 Fourier, *Nouveau monde industriel*, in *OC*, vol. VI, p. 47.

with a person's age. Children were dominated by friendship, young people by love, mature individuals by ambition, and old people by 'familism'.

The highest set of branches on Fourier's 'passional tree' included the three distributive or 'mechanizing' passions – so named because their free expression was essential for the gratification of the other nine. These were the cabalist or intriguing passion; the Butterfly or the passion for change and variety; and the Composite or the desire for the happiness to be found in the mixture of physical and spiritual pleasures. Useless and even harmful in civilization, these three distributive passions would become the 'mainsprings of the social mechanism' in the Phalanx. Their combined action would keep the other nine passions in equilibrium and permit the formation of the 'passionate series' which were to be the main forms of association within Fourier's ideal community.

While Fourier sometimes described the passions as the alphabet of his science, there was also a passional grammar with its own declensions, conjugations, and syntax. It delineated the various links that might be established among the different passions and the permutations they would undergo when combined. Without delving too deeply into the more subtle refinements, one can say that each of Fourier's passions could be divided into a host of nuances, each had its own 'exponential scale' of degrees of intensity, and each could manifest particular 'subversive' tendencies whenever the 'harmonic' tendency was repressed. Thus, repressed ambition could become destructive competition, and sadistic behaviour was a subversive manifestation of the passion of love.

Much of Fourier's writing was devoted to the detailed description of the life and institutions of his ideal society, the Phalanx. Fourier always imagined the Phalanx in a rural setting. Ideally, he wrote, it would be situated on a square league of land. The terrain would be hilly, the supply of water plentiful, and the climate suitable for the cultivation of a wide variety of crops. Visitors would be struck by the elegance and sheer vastness of the central building, the Phalanstery. Its lodgings, workshops, meeting rooms, and banquet halls would be built to accommodate roughly 1,600 people.

There would also be collective nurseries and classrooms, for an important facet of life in the Phalanx was a system of communal child-rearing and education in which children would be encouraged from an early age to develop vocations consistent with their instinctual (or 'passional') endowment. But the essential feature of the Phalanx was that all its institutions and practices were designed to promote the full and free expression of the passions. Fourier's plans focused particularly on the intrigues, rivalries, and alliances that would develop within what he called 'passionate' groups and series – small groups and series of groups in which people of different ages, classes, and passions would come together to work and play in conditions carefully calibrated to ensure that the gratification of individual desire led to collective happiness.

The great task of social thought, Fourier believed, was to show how work and the apparently incompatible desire for pleasure could be reconciled. Everyone agreed that in civilization workers laboured 'without ardour, slowly, and with loathing' and were driven to work only 'by the fear of famine and punishment'.[16] Surely, he insisted, there must be a better solution. That solution, devised by God and discovered by Fourier, was 'attractive labour'. Fourier laid down a number of conditions necessary to render labour attractive. Some of these conditions were not original. He proposed to replace wage labour with a system in which all members of the Phalanx would receive dividends proportional to their contributions in work, capital, and talent. He also insisted that the workshops, garden, and fields of the Phalanx had to be clean, well maintained, and even elegant. The other conditions are uniquely Fourier's. They constitute the mainsprings of attractive labour.

Labour would become truly attractive, Fourier argued, only if men and women could work at as many tasks as they chose – up to eight in the course of a day – in groups of friends and lovers who were spontaneously drawn together by fondness for the task at hand, for its product, and for each other. Thus, short and varied work sessions were a prerequisite of the working day in the Phalanx. So was the creation of groups and series of groups of workers, passionately bonded by a common liking for a particular task. But the most important condition for the realization of attractive labour was the granting of what Fourier called the 'social minimum'. This was a guaranteed income which would be given to people whether they worked or not. It was an absolutely essential component of attractive labour because, in addition to providing economic security, it made psychological liberation possible by freeing men and women from the necessity to work.

Fourier's Phalanx was an attempt to imagine a society from which the material and psychological pain long associated with work might be banished, a society in which work would be performed freely, at the urging of the passions. This vision of work as a source of passionate fulfilment has rarely been taken seriously. For most thinkers in the socialist tradition, Fourier's dream of an order in which work would become closely associated with

16 Fourier, *Unité universelle,* in *OC*, vol. III, p. 14.

erotic pleasure has seemed downright silly. Pierre-Joseph Proudhon could write scornfully about the dream of 'turning work into intrigue, love into gymnastics' and declared that work was actually 'the most powerful of anti-aphrodisiacs'. Almost a century later Antonio Gramsci used less colourful language to make a similar point, speaking of the need to create a new sexual ethic suited to the rationalized methods of production characteristic of a socialist economy: 'The truth is that the new type of man demanded by the rationalization of production and work cannot be developed until the sexual instinct has been suitably regulated and until it too has been rationalized.'[17]

It is true that Fourier's evocations of the Phalansterian working day had a certain appeal for the young Karl Marx and Friedrich Engels. They were clearly inspired by Fourier when, in *The German Ideology*, they looked forward to a communist society that would 'make it possible for me to do one thing today and another tomorrow, to hunt in the morning, fish in the afternoon, rear cattle in the evening, criticize after dinner, just as I like, without ever becoming a hunter, fisherman, shepherd, or critic'. In their later works, however, Marx and Engels came to reject the whole notion of 'attractive work'. Hints of this can be found in Marx's *Grundrisse* (1857–8) where he criticizes Fourier for treating a profound problem like a frivolous 'shop-girl' by claiming that labour can become 'mere fun, mere amusement'. In *Capital* Marx was emphatic. Stressing the distinction between free labour and labour determined by need and external purpose, Marx claimed that necessary work would one day be made immensely less arduous and fatiguing. Yet, he argued, all the improvements that technology and socialization might bring would not alter the fact that much of the work done in a socialist society would remain painful and unrewarding. He looked forward to the day when 'the development of machinery and automation' would enable men to develop their latent and unrealized capacities in their leisure hours. 'In fact', wrote Marx, 'the realm of freedom actually begins only where labor which is determined by necessity and mundane circumstances ceases', and the basis for the 'blossoming' of 'the true realm of freedom' was 'the shortening of the working day'. In passages like this, it is clear that the Fourierist vision of work has been left far behind.[18]

17 P.-J. Proudhon, *Système des contradictions économiques ou philosophie de la misère* (Paris: Marcel Rivière, 1923), vol. II, p. 371; A. Gramsci, *Selections from the Prison Notebooks* (New York: International Publishers, 1971), p. 297.
18 K. Marx and F. Engels, *The German Ideology*, in *Marx Engels Collected Works* (London: Lawrence & Wishart, 2010) (hereafter *MECW*), vol. V, p. 47; K. Marx, *Grundrisse*, trans.

The problem for Marx was that Fourier refused to take seriously the repugnant character of much of the work that had to be done in any society. But for Fourier there was no such thing as a natural aversion to work. This radically optimistic assessment of work was rooted in Fourier's denial of an irreconcilable antagonism between man and nature. He did not share Marx's Promethean vision of man as constantly engaged in wresting a living out of a hostile environment. For Fourier, *all* work was meant to be a source of pleasure and an instrument of human liberation; and the social theorist's task was to define the conditions under which work could at last become what it was meant to be.

If one of the central elements in Fourier's utopian plans was attractive work, the other was instinctual liberation. The ultimate goal of the Phalanx was to liberate the instincts, to assure all men and women an emotional and erotic life immeasurably richer than a repressive civilization could ever provide. In such a society, Fourier insisted, human relations would take on a new character, and the passion of love would undergo an extraordinary metamorphosis. No longer a diversion or a private affair, love could instead become an essential part of the collective life, a force for social harmony whose binding power would be felt even in the kitchens of the Phalanx and at its dinner tables. As Fourier wrote in a draft of *Le Nouveau monde amoureux,* 'love in the Phalanstery is no longer, as it is with us . . . a recreation that detracts from work; on the contrary it is the soul and the vehicle, the mainspring of all works and of the whole of universal attraction'.[19]

To realize this vision, Fourier argued, new laws and institutions were needed to promote the most diverse kinds of erotic gratification while at the same time integrating the sexual drives into the whole fabric of the community's collective life. This would entail the fulfilment of three conditions. First, recognition would have to be given to the sheer diversity of human sexual inclinations. According to Fourier, the failure of civilization to devise a tolerable 'amorous regime' resulted in large part from the belief that all men and women were essentially the same in their sexual wants. This belief, which amounted to a kind of 'erotic Jacobinism', was generally accompanied by the claim that the 'natural' sexual grouping was the heterosexual couple. If any generalization were to be made about human sexuality, Fourier argued, it would be that most people are polygamous in their inclinations. How else could one explain the ubiquity of adultery in civilized society? And how could

M. Nicolaus (New York: Vintage, 1973), p. 611; K. Marx, *Capital*, vol. III, in *MECW*, vol. XXXVII, p. 807.

19 Charles Fourier, 'Le Sphinx sans Oedipe', *La Phalange* 9 (1849), p. 200.

one ignore the sheer variety and inconstancy of human sexual proclivities? To force everyone into a single mould could only result in pain and frustration. Thus, the institutions of Fourier's new amorous world would promote the gratification of many desires that civilized society condemned as perversions. The goal was the liberation of all sexual minorities, so long as their activities did not involve the use or abuse of people against their will. Lesbians, 'sodomites', fetishists, and flagellants all figured prominently in Fourier's descriptions of amorous life in the higher stages of Harmony, and the highest ranks in the erotic hierarchy devised by Fourier were open only to individuals with a passionate attraction to members of both sexes.

The second vital element in Fourier's prescription for a new amorous world was a radical alteration in the position of women. As we have seen, Fourier argued forcefully in the *Théorie des quatre mouvements* that the emancipation of women was the key to social progress in all spheres. The most backward nations had always been those in which women were treated the worst, and social progress was 'a consequence of the progress of women towards freedom'. The third condition for the realization of Fourier's amorous utopia was the granting of what he called the 'sexual minimum'. In Harmony, he wrote, every mature man and woman must be granted a satisfying minimum of sexual pleasure. Whatever his or her age, and no matter how peculiar his or her desires, no Harmonian could go unsatisfied. Fourier maintained that this sexual minimum would play a role in the amorous world similar to that played by the social minimum in the world of work. Labour could become an instrument of human freedom and self-expression only when all members of the community were freed by a guaranteed income from the obligation to work. Similarly, love could become the liberating and binding force that it was meant to be only when the fear of deprivation had been removed.[20]

One result of the establishment of the sexual minimum, Fourier believed, would be to point the way beyond physical desire to a world of more subtle and complex relations that would become possible only when basic sexual needs were satisfied. One important aspect of this new world would be the awakening of sentimental or platonic love. '*L'amour céladonic*', he called it, invoking the name of Celadon, the chaste and faithful lover in Honoré d'Urfé's seventeenth-century novel, *L'Astrée*. In the civilization of the nineteenth century, Celadon was conceivable only as a figure of ridicule: a lover who failed to bring an amorous relationship to a physical consummation was

20 Fourier, *Nouveau monde amoureux*, in *OC*, vol. VII, pp. 439–45.

a natural butt of jokes. In Harmony, however, where physical gratification could be taken for granted, erotic ties would become more complex and more broadly diffused. The 'mania for exclusive possession' of a loved one would lose its force, and lovers would 'seek out refined sentimental relations to counterbalance their physical pleasures'.[21]

Fourier understood that 'civilized' minds would find this portion of his utopian vision difficult to accept. Thus, after offering readers of his first book a few glimpses of his amorous utopia, he said little about it in his subsequent published writings. But in 1818 he did write, for his own benefit, a treatise showing how the passion of love could flourish in a utopian future. The *Nouveau monde amoureux* describes a distant world, far beyond that of the Phalanx. In this world the amorous affairs of every community would be run by an elaborate hierarchy of officials – high priests, pontiffs, matrons, confessors, fairies, and fakirs. These dignitaries would officiate in the sessions of a Court of Love to be held in the evening after the children and the chaste Vestals had been put to bed. Both a judicial body and a recreational institution, the Court of Love organized fetes, orgies, and entertainments, and was also responsible for the application of a minutely detailed amorous code which facilitated sexual activity.[22]

In his first major work, Fourier devoted much attention to the more esoteric aspects of his doctrine. He discussed the sexual proclivities of the stars, predicted the emergence of wondrous new animal species, and chronicled the entire 80,000-year life-cycle of the earth from the first infection of the seas by stellar fluid to the moment when the planet would cease to rotate on its axis. The derision that greeted these prophecies convinced him to adopt a more circumspect tone in the presentation of his ideas. In his subsequent published writings he concentrated on his theory of social organization and attempted to pass off his esoteric speculations as mere 'entertainment for the ladies'. Fourier's earth-bound disciples went further: in their popularizations they practised what one of them described as a 'useful weeding out' of the doctrine. In simply purging it of its more extravagant elements, the disciples set a precedent that was long honoured by scholars interested in Fourier. Only in recent years, and thanks in part to the efforts of André Breton and the

---

21 Ibid., pp. 50, 98.
22 On the Court of Love and Festive Life in Fourier's amorous utopia, see T. Bouchet, 'L'Ecart absolu des festins. Fourier, Le Nouveau monde amoureux', *Australian Journal of French Studies* 43, 3 (2006), pp. 262–76; and J. Beecher, 'Parody and liberation in the *New Amorous World* of Charles Fourier', *History Workshop* 20 (Autumn 1985), pp. 125–33.

surrealists, has serious consideration been given to the imaginative qualities of Fourier's stellar reveries and his reflections on analogy.

It is still not clear exactly what one should make of Fourier's cosmogony and his theory of universal analogy. Perhaps they can best be seen as an attempt to make sense of a disorderly universe. 'EVERYTHING', he wrote, 'from the atoms to the stars, constitutes a tableau of the proper ties of the human passions.'[23] This affirmation of the correspondence between the passions and the material universe was Fourier's starting point. The theory of universal analogy rested on two premises: the universe is a unified system, and man is at its centre. Like the Christian cosmographers of the later Middle Ages, Fourier believed that everything that transpired in the human world had some echo in the world of nature. The seventy-two different 'commercial vices', for example, were represented by seventy-two different types of poisonous snakes. In the future these snakes, along with many other dangerous animals, would disappear. New creations would replace them with useful species whose existence would reflect the new-found harmony of the human passions.

Fourier's theory of analogy can be seen as a way of looking at the world so that nature lost its strangeness. 'Without analogy', he wrote, 'nature is no more than a vast patch of brambles.' With analogy, everything acquired a human dimension. The natural universe became comprehensible. To guide his readers through nature's tangled underbrush, Fourier drew up elaborate charts in which the analogies between passions, colours, metals, animals, plants, and geometrical forms were spelled out explicitly. He showed how different varieties of love could be represented by different flowers, and how one could represent different degrees of wit and stupidity by the heads of birds – their tufts, crests, plumes, and collars. But everything was grist for Fourier's mill, and he found as much to learn from an ear as from a head. 'Why does the lion have clipped ears?' he asked. The reason was that the lion represented the king: he was prevented by his courtiers from hearing the truth, just as the peasant, represented by the long-eared donkey, was forced to stand quietly listening to the worst insults.

Fourier knew that his civilized readers might regard all this as a waste of time. But it has a coherence and a poetry of its own. As gratuitous and arbitrary as it might seem, the theory of universal analogy was, like much else in Fourier's thought, an affirmation of underlying order and harmony in

---

23 Fourier, *Quatre mouvements*, pp. 31–2.

Fig. 7.1   Charles Fourier. (Encyclopaedia Britannica / Universal Images Group / Getty Images.)

a world of apparent disorder. It was one expression, among many, of Fourier's desire to end our separation from nature.[24]

The Fourierist Movement

Until the Bourbon restoration, Fourier was a solitary figure. It was only in 1816 that he acquired his first disciple. This was Just Muiron, a modest functionary at the prefecture of Besançon. Muiron, who was totally deaf, lacked all the qualities of creative imagination that he admired in Fourier's work. But he was an indefatigable publicist of Fourier's ideas. He arranged for the publication in 1823 of Fourier's *Traité de l'association domestique-agricole*.

---

24 On Fourier's cosmogony and his theory of universal analogy, see M. Nathan, *Le Ciel des fouriéristes. Habitants des étoiles et réincarnations de l'âme* (Lyon: Presses universitaires de Lyon, 1981); S. Debout-Oleszkiewicz, 'L'analogie ou "Le poème mathématique" de Charles Fourier', *Revue internationale de philosophie* 16, 60 (1962), pp. 176–99; and L. Rignol, *Les Hiéroglyphes de la nature. Le socialisme scientifique en France dans le premier xixe siècle* (Dijon: Les presses du réel, 2014).

And he gathered together at Besançon a group of admirers of Fourier, modest property-owners for the most part. The one remarkable member of this provincial sect was the *Polytechnicien* Victor Considerant. Not himself an original thinker, Considerant was a talented organizer and a brilliant publicist. In popularizing Fourier's ideas, Considerant simplified them and flattened them out. He also modernized them: while Fourier always imagined the Phalanx in a rural setting, Considerant focused on the problems of industrial society and the possibilities created by technological development. Fourier's work, with its irony, parody, and flights of fancy, was a kind of utopian poetry, whereas what Considerant offered was socialist prose. His *Destinée sociale* (*Social Destiny*, 3 vols., 1834–44) became the most important nineteenth-century popularization of Fourier's thought. In this work, which contained no trace of Fourier's 'new amorous world', the liberation of instinct gave way to the organization of labour.

What turned the small Fourierist group into a movement was a schism among the disciples of Henri Saint-Simon. Under the authoritarian leadership of Prosper Enfantin, the Saint-Simonian movement had become a religious cult; and when a schism broke out in 1832 some of Enfantin's most talented followers found a new prophet in Fourier. The working-class feminists Désirée Véret, Jeanne Deroin, and Suzanne Voilquin soon moved on from Fourier to the creation of a pioneering movement of their own. But the *Polytechniciens* Jules Lechevalier and Abel Transon were among the first refugees from the Saint-Simonian religion to be 'converted' to Fourierism. Together with Considerant, they organized public lectures on the doctrine and founded a weekly journal, *Le Phalanstère ou la Réforme industrielle* (*The Phalanstery or Industrial Reform*), intended to gain support for the establishment of a trial community. The journal's circulation remained modest, and it never came close to 'conquering Paris' as Fourier would have liked. But it did take Fourier's ideas to the provinces, where its articles were widely reprinted. The attempt to create a trial Phalanx at Condé-sur-Vesgre on the outskirts of the forest of Rambouillet never got off the ground. But an immediate, tangible achievement of the journal was to give Fourierism a life independent of Fourier himself, and of his Parisian disciples. This was most evident at Lyon, where, during the 1830s, a Fourierist movement developed among the silk-weavers or *canuts*, and where, between 1835 and 1838, the *chef d'atelier* Michel Derrion made the first significant attempt to create co-operative institutions based on Fourier's ideas.

The great period of the Fourierist movement was the decade prior to the Revolution of 1848. When Fourier died in October 1837, Victor Considerant was already widely recognized as the leader of the movement that now called itself the Ecole Sociétaire. A dissident group had surfaced in 1835 with the support of Just Muiron. Their main complaint about Considerant's leadership was that, after the debacle of the Colonie Sociétaire at Condé-sur-Vesgre, he gave up on efforts to create a trial Phalanx and focused all the resources of the movement on 'propaganda' – on the effort to reach a wide audience by means of the printed word.

In fact, Considerant and his associates succeeded in doing just what they set out to do. In the course of the 1840s they created an elaborate organization for the Fourierist movement: a share-holding company, a publishing house, an elegant Parisian office, a network of provincial bookstores and lending libraries, a stable of lecturers, a theoretical journal called *La Phalange* (*The Phalanx*), and a daily newspaper. The cornerstone of it all was the newspaper. Founded in 1843, *La Démocratie pacifique* (*Peaceful Democracy*) was one of the first socialist dailies; and its creation changed the character of the Ecole Sociétaire. The *école* never entirely lost its sectarian ambience and, despite the support of the Lyon *canuts*, Fourierism remained a largely bourgeois movement composed of doctors, lawyers, journalists, retired army officers, and petty functionaries. The movement never acquired a working-class following comparable to those gained by Etienne Cabet and Philippe Buchez. Still, by the mid-1840s the narrow group of disciples had become a social movement with a national reach.[25]

Charles Fourier had always been hostile to the revolutionary and republican traditions. His own experience in 1793 had marked him for life, and he presented his theory as an alternative to 'ridiculous' talk about political rights. Victor Considerant had no quarrel with Fourier initially on this point: in fact he dedicated the first edition of *Destinée sociale* to Louis-Philippe. But after 1845, influenced in part by detestation of the brutal conduct of the French army in Algeria, Considerant and most (not all) of his Fourierist colleagues joined the republican opposition to the monarchy.

During the Second Republic, most of the Fourierists threw themselves into the political arena, joining a democratic socialist movement committed both to the implementation of major social reforms and to the defence of republican institutions. Considerant, who was elected to the National Assembly in

---

25 There is no comprehensive study of the Fourierist movement in France. But the *Cahiers Charles Fourier*, published annually since 1990 by the Association d'Etudes Fouriéristes, constitute a mine of information on Fourier and Fourierism. Members of the association have also created an online *Dictionnaire biographique du fouriérisme* which contains more than 900 entries. See www.charlesfourier.fr.

April 1848, played a leading role in the *démoc-soc* movement. In the debate over the constitution of the Second Republic, he was the only member of the Assembly to argue for women's suffrage. But his participation in an abortive protest demonstration of 13 June 1849 forced him into an exile that was to last twenty years. He was joined in exile by many *démoc-soc* Fourierists (including François Cantagrel and Allyre Bureau). Others, notably Fourier's first biographer, Charles Pellarin, who had resisted the politicization of Fourierism, blamed Considerant and his followers for having split the movement.

Like most of the other socialist *écoles* that flourished in the 1840s, the Fourierist movement emerged from the Revolution of 1848 a shadow of its former self. It did not disappear. Its members, most of whom were now elderly and relatively well-to-do, continued to meet regularly, to maintain a publishing house, and to give their support to various co-operative experiments and to attempts to create Fourierist communities in Algeria, Normandy, Isère, and once again at Condé-sur-Vesgre. But none of these efforts proved enduring, and the most ambitious of them – the community of Réunion near Dallas, Texas, in 1855–6 – was a spectacular, and costly, failure. The one genuine success was the Familistère de Guise, a co-operative community created by J. B. A. Godin for the workers in his iron foundry. Godin was a visionary with practical skills, and the cast-iron stoves produced at the Familistère are still doing good service. But Godin was unique. What is striking about the Fourierists of this final phase is the modesty of their ambitions.[26]

By Fourier's standards the achievement of his disciples was limited. During the 1840s more than two dozen Fourierist Phalanxes were set up in the United States, but all of them were under-capitalized and short-lived, and none came close to approaching Fourier's exacting specifications. A more lasting aspect of his legacy was his influence on the development of the co-operative movement in France. Apart from such experiments in practical Fourierism, it can also be said that Fourier's ideas had a significant influence on the generation of European radicals and socialists who reached maturity in the 1840s. His analysis of the 'anarchic' character of early capitalist production and his brilliant depiction of the frauds of the marketplace were admired and assimilated not only by Considerant but also by Marx, Proudhon, Louis Blanc, Constantin Pecqueur, and many others. The demand for the right to work, which Fourier first voiced in 1806, became a battle cry in 1848. But, for

26 On the long, slow twilight of the Fourierist movement after 1848, see B. Desmars, *Militants de l'utopie? Les fouriéristes dans la seconde moitié du XIXe siècle* (Dijon: Presses du réel, 2010).

all its satirical verve, Fourier's critique of laissez faire economics was less penetrating than that developed by more sophisticated economists such as Jean Charles de Sismondi and the British Ricardian socialists.

It was as a critic of bourgeois society rather than of capitalist economics that Fourier made his most enduring contribution to radical thought. His indictment of 'civilized' morality, his attack on the family system, and his plea for the emancipation of women all made their way into the emerging socialist tradition. In a less obvious but equally important way his social criticism helped mould the mentality of the generation that fought on the barricades in 1848. His exposure of pain and suffering that others took for granted and his sympathy for all the outcasts of civilized society did much to give socialist thought the moral and humanitarian dimension that was its hallmark in 1848. His view of civilization as an order founded on the repression of basic instinctual drives may be more readily comprehensible in our post-Freudian age than it was to his contemporaries. But what nineteenth-century radicals could and did appreciate was the sense of moral outrage that informed even Fourier's driest commentary on the fraud and hypocrisy, the waste and needless suffering, of civilization.

Further Reading

Barthes, Roland, *Sade, Fourier, Loyola* (New York: Farrar, Straus and Giroux, 1976).

Beecher, Jonathan, *Charles Fourier: The Visionary and His World* (Berkeley: University of California Press, 1986).

 Victor Considerant and the Rise and Fall of French Romantic Socialism (Berkeley: University of California Press, 2001).

Debout, Simone, *L'Utopie de Charles Fourier. L'Illusion réelle* (Paris: Payot, 1978).

Desroche, Henri, *La Société festive. Du fouriérisme écrit au fouriérisme pratiqué* (Paris: Editions du Seuil, 1975).

Fourier, Charles, *Oeuvres complètes de Charles Fourier*, 12 vols. (Paris: Editions Anthropos, 1966–8).

 The Theory of the Four Movements, ed. G. S. Jones and I. Patterson (Cambridge: Cambridge University Press, 1996).

Guarneri, Carl J., *The Utopian Alternative: Fourierism in Nineteenth-Century America* (Ithaca: Cornell University Press, 1991).

Manuel, Frank E., and Fritzie P. Manuel, *Utopian Thought in the Western World* (Cambridge, MA: Belknap Press, 1979).

Schérer, René, *Charles Fourier ou la contestation globale* (Paris: Séguier, 1996).

Spencer, Michael C., *Charles Fourier* (Boston: Twayne Publishers, 1981).

8

Etienne Cabet and the Icarian Movement in France and the United States

CHRISTOPHER H. JOHNSON

'A spectre is haunting Europe – the spectre of Communism.'[1] Introducing the *Communist Manifesto*, Karl Marx and Friedrich Engels cast communism as an ill-defined force that allowed 'all the Powers in Europe' to tar all political opposition with its stigma. It was therefore 'high time ... to meet this nursery tale of the Spectre of Communism with a Manifesto of the party itself'. But communism was already much more than that. What the young revolutionaries in London ignored was a quite real and well-organized communist presence in France, the fruit of a movement launched in the 1840s by Etienne Cabet on behalf of his vision of *La Communauté* as inscribed in his hugely successful novel, *Voyage en Icarie (Travels in Icaria*, 1839). It was no accident that in 1848 his club drew the largest numbers of participants and gave full force to the social-democratic tenor of the early days of the revolution. Throughout France, Cabet had mobilized a following approaching 100,000 people, mostly working men and women. It was the first organized working-class movement of any scope in continental Europe, paralleled only by the Chartists in Britain. In their *Manifesto*, however, Marx and Engels made mention only of 'little Icarias' along with other useless utopian experiments. Cabet had indeed called for an 'emigration' of Icarians to the United States in 1847, thus allowing Marx and Engels to dismiss a movement that was in fact their chief rival. The reason was without question enshrined in the *Manifesto*'s opening line: 'The history of all hitherto existing society is the history of class struggles.' Cabet, though recognizing this reality, thought it could be overcome through persuasion of 'the bourgeoisie', not its violent overthrow. His star therefore faded rapidly as Marxist social democracy came to dominate the political left and the historiography of its development.

---

1 All quotations from the *Communist Manifesto* are from the 1883 English version in Robert C. Tucker (ed.), *The Marx–Engels Reader*, 2nd edn (New York and London: W. W. Norton, 1978), pp. 473–500.

When mentioned at all, Cabet was seen as the most utopian of the 'Utopian Socialists', in Engels' parlance. Only in the non-Marxist labour movement was there a glimmer of appreciation of Cabet as a communist forerunner. Reviewing Jules Prudhommeaux's detailed history of the American Icarian experience (1907), syndicalist intellectual Amédée Dunois wrote: 'the Cabet who counts for history is the Cabet of the years before 1848, the founder and leader of one of the first proletarian groupings, of a veritable workers' party'.[2]

Cabet *Républicain*

Etienne Cabet came from a comfortable artisan background (his father was a master barrel-maker in Dijon, the wine capital of Burgundy) and was well educated in local schools, receiving his doctorate in law in 1812 at the age of twenty-four. Typical for his town and social milieu, his family's politics were rooted in Jacobinism, and his key intellectual guides as a scholarship student at *lycée* and *faculté de droit* were pro-revolutionaries who accommodated Bonaparte, including his return to France after his banishment to Elba in 1815. In the aftermath, Cabet successfully defended key public figures tried by the Restoration government for their support of Napoleon's return. But he was suspended from the bar for a year for malpractice, which in fact further enhanced his reputation in liberal circles and occasioned his sponsored move to Paris, where he arrived shortly after the assassination of the heir to the throne, the duc de Berry, in early 1820. In this dark period of ultra-royalist reaction, he befriended the top echelon of the liberal opposition, including Marie-Joseph de Lafayette and Deputies Jacques-Antoine Manuel and Jacques-Charles Dupont de l'Eure, who found in him an ardent servant of their political agenda. He became a key figure in the Charbonnerie conspiracy (1821–2) and earned praise as an indefatigable organizer. Despite the suppression of the plot, Cabet had found his métier: a well-connected and vocal proponent of the republican vision.

In a widely circulated manuscript, he foresaw the Revolution of 1830 and at first, with Lafayette, supported the alleged 'monarchy with republican institutions' of Louis-Philippe. After a stint as the attorney-general of Corsica, Cabet was elected deputy for Dijon and sat with the moderate republican caucus led by Dupont. Not terribly effective in his new role, Cabet quickly

---

2 *L'Action directe*, 20 May 1908. See 'Further Reading' for an overview of the historiographical record.

turned to republican propaganda with a particular focus on direct interaction with the working masses, '*le peuple*', joining an explosion of popular unrest both in the streets and in the press. This 'heroic' period (1831–4) saw the reawakening of pro-Jacobin republican ideals that segued towards socialism (then just being named). Cabet, not yet willing to condemn capitalist private property, devoted himself to working-class enlightenment as secretary of the Association libre pour l'éducation du peuple (Free Society for the Education of the People) and above all via his weekly newspaper, *Le Populaire de 1833* (*Of the People, 1833*), which reached a national audience greater than any republican paper, focusing on issues concerning 'the needs and interests of the *classes laborieuses*'. The fundamental path to their 'amelioration' was the advent of universal (manhood) suffrage, the creation of 'national sovereignty'. His main line of argument was a relentless condemnation of the 'betrayal of July', holding the king directly responsible for the abandonment of any hint of 'republican institutions' in a regime where only the richest men in France had the right to vote. Cabet's virulence reached a peak in January 1834 when he accused Louis-Philippe of having innocent 'Frenchmen gunned down in the street' for peaceful protest. With his arrest and conviction for lèse-majesté, Cabet became a hero of the republican movement. Rather than accepting imprisonment, he chose a five-year exile, ending up in London. He was forty-six years old, but had the most eventful decades of his life still ahead of him. One should not, however, underestimate this long apprenticeship in republicanism, increasingly tilting towards popular Jacobinism, because it continued to serve as the root of his ultimate goal, a centralized communist republic in France.[3]

Cabet *Communiste*

Accompanied by his long-time Dijonnaise partner, now wife, Delphine, and their daughter Céline, Cabet settled in among other exiles, ultimately sharing a flat with neo-Babouvist Dr Camille Berrier-Fontaine. Documentation is lacking, but he had contact with British radicals, including Robert Owen. His own autobiographical notes, however, emphasize long days of reading and research at the British Museum, where, in the midst of a period of depression in later 1835 and a final

---

3 François Fourn dedicates the entire first half of his dissertation to Cabet's pre-communist years, underlining his republican foundation, which he never abandoned. See François Fourn, *Etienne Cabet (1788–1856). Une propagande républicaine*, vol. 1 (Villeneuve d'Ascq: Presses universitaires du septentrion, 1996).

diatribe against Louis-Philippe, he discovered Thomas More's *Utopia*.[4] Cabet described it as a lightning bolt of clarity in which private property replaced the king of France as the source of all evil. He thus bypassed the entire spectrum of social theories founded upon varying degrees of property-rights limitation – and became a communist. His other source of inspiration was Maximilien Robespierre, whose voice dominated the four-volume *Histoire populaire de la Révolution française* (*Popular History of the French Revolution*) that he undertook forthwith. German communist Karl Grün remarked simply: Cabet 'was the last consequence of '93'.[5] He also returned to a deep study of Christianity. Emerging from his earlier alienation, Cabet became convinced that Jesus Christ, the embodiment of love, human goodness, and equality, was a communist, an argument appearing in the *Voyage en Icarie* (1839) and expanded in *Vrai Christianisme* (*True Christianity*, 1846).

The French working men and women who read (or had read to them) *Lord Carisdall's Journey to Icaria*,[6] a novel modelled directly on More, found themselves in a serene world where not the least whisper of unhappiness, not the slightest ripple of discontent, troubled the lives of the inhabitants. They visualized themselves residing with their extended family in a single home, well fed and clothed with no hassles with shopkeepers and their faulty weights; their children went to school rather than the shop or mine; workdays were short, work easy and self-managed in spacious and healthy factories; much daylight remained for leisure-time activities at home with family and friends and outings in the beautiful countryside to picnic in spacious public parks reached without paying a fare on a vast system of public transportation; and no police to hound them wherever they were. All this via the simplest of measures: the abolition of private property.[7]

---

4 Cabet's *Lettre à Louis-Philippe* (London, 1835) was occasioned by the last straw of the king's betrayal of the two revolutions: the infamous Press Laws of September 1835, establishing Metternichian censorship.

5 Karl Grün, *Die soziale Bewegung in Frankreich und Belgien* (Darmstadt, 1845), p. 325.

6 *Voyage en Icarie* was published as a translation titled *Voyage et adventures de Lord William Carisdall en Icarie, traduit de l'anglais par Th. Dufruit* (Paris: Hippolyte Souverain, 1839). Cabet was initially worried that, even though he could enter the country legally in September, a publication under his name would immediately invite suspicion and scrutiny. It did not take long before word got around about who had written it and, in fact, there was nothing in this fantasy that was actionable under the Press Laws. It was first published under his name in 1842. He never explained why he chose the names Icar, the founder, and Icaria. The myth of Icarus is an unlikely candidate, given the hero's fate.

7 This image was what induced many workers to raise the necessary 600 francs to be admitted to the Icarian colony at Nauvoo once it was established and running in 1849,

'*La Communauté* is a mutual and universal guarantee, of all, for all. In return for moderate labor, [it] guarantees education, the possibility of marriage, food, housing; in a word, everything.'[8] 'Community' encompassed the totality of Cabet's ideal society. It is easy to move from this to 'totalitarian', as did J. M. Talmon in his effort to tag the entire French revolutionary tradition, of which he saw Cabet as the ultimate conclusion, with the roots of mid-twentieth-century horrors. But Cabet's world was not this simple-minded and, had it been, the working people who read *Voyage en Icarie* would have ignored it. Part of the ridicule it received from contemporary and ongoing intellectual commentary was founded upon a patronizing disdain of the ability of the members of '*la classe laborieuse/classe dangereuse*' to think beyond their most immediate needs. The positive reception it enjoyed among ordinary people was somehow an indicator of its inanity. That Cabet spoke their language, which he did here and in his journalism to promote it, made him intellectually suspect and, much worse, a pied piper to the land of totalitarian control. The curious reality is that his long-term influence rested in the arena of worker self-initiative in co-operation, and his strongest advocates at the time and later, men such as Martin Nadaud, Agricole Perdiguer, and Jean-Pierre Beluze, promoted a vision of an egalitarian society in which workers themselves would create their own world founded upon their own skills, talents, and intelligence. We must thank the scholars specializing in this period who took the thought of workers seriously for paving the way in French history to fulfil E. P. Thompson's challenge that we must rescue the voices and the visions of working people 'from the enormous condescension of posterity'.[9]

---

assuming that such a life awaited them. What they encountered instead led to inevitable disillusionment. J. Rancière's treatment in his *The Nights of Labor: The Workers' Dream in Nineteenth-Century France*, trans. J. Drury (Philadelphia: Temple University Press, 1989) of this and his unparalleled understanding of the *mentalités du peuple* in the '48 era underline the intelligent reception of the *Voyage*. The subject of leisure has had a difficult career in the history of socialism and communism, mainly because of its middle-class theorizers' heroic vision that workers, if their work were not alienated by exploitation, would freely embrace it and thrive in work towards unheard-of productivity. Cabet had no such illusions: mechanization would liberate them to have fun. On this subject, see André Gorz on the '*droit de la paresse*', an important theme in Gorz, *Paths to Paradise: On the Liberation from Work*, trans. M. Imrie (Boston: South End Press, 1985), and Gorz, *Critique of Economic Reason*, trans. G. Handyside and C. Turner (New York and London: Verso, 1989).

8 Etienne Cabet, *Voyage en Icarie*, 3rd edn (Paris, 1845), p. 568.

9 E. P. Thompson, *The Making of the English Working Class* (London: Gollancz, 1963), p. 12. In a cast of dozens, let us mention Jacques Rancière, Fernand Rude, Michelle Perrot, Maurice Agulhon, Yves Lequin, Laurence Fontaine, William Sewell, Joan Scott, Ronald Aminzade, Donald Reid, and John Merriman.

The most striking thing, perhaps, about the *Voyage* is its embrace of the promise of modern technology, which, it predicted, would multiply productivity while easing the burdens of work, leading to unheard-of prosperity. One might think, in light of Cabet's artisan origins and those of his base in the working class, that this picture of the future might be unwelcome. But, in fact, Cabet struck a nerve. Tailors, shoemakers, cabinet-makers, silk workers, stockingers, barrel-makers, handloom weavers, and many more flitting from job to job who flocked to his banner in response to life in Icaria were delighted with the security and stability they imagined. Alienation in work was not caused by the degradation of skills, but by the appropriation of their product by middlemen (for example, readymade clothing merchants in the case of tailors) between them and their customers. What could be better than actually owning, as a citizen of Icaria, the means of your own production if made by a machine you operated? They worked in a framework of *collective* creativity. Why should you not delight in your free time, having your extended family gathered close, food delivered to your doorstep, clothes in styles of your choice in appropriate sizes? Supplying these essentials was an elaborate system of distribution that began with an advanced railroad and canal grid serving mines, factories, and centralized agricultural hubs that family farmers could easily reach, delivering to giant warehouses near by in localities across the nation, hardly a far-fetched notion in the age of Amazon. Production at all levels was mechanized, with the latest inventions flowing from the polytechnical and higher scientific educational system. Farms remained under the control of individual families, a wise move by Cabet in which considerable variation in technique and organization was allowed, though farmers were supplied with the latest research by agronomists. Water and coal were the main sources of energy, and steam engines had reached new heights of perfection. Cabet allowed himself one fancy: a newly discovered energy source, called *sorub*, promised revolutionary improvement of efficiency and cleanliness. Altogether, then, the Saint-Simonian dream had been realized – but could be achieved only under communism based in co-operation, not competition.

Leisure time was spent with extended families who constantly intermingled with wider circles of neighbours and friends in various pleasures – playing games and organized sports, promenading and picnicking, and following artistic pursuits. Cabet made a special place for music, above all singing groups, that he thought best cemented *communauté*. Great public spectacles featuring gymnastic displays, large-scale theatrical performances, mass singing of patriotic songs, and fireworks created the spiritual foundation of Icarian life,

bonding citizens of all stripes. All of these activities were enjoyed and performed by men and women equally. Gender specialization here or in work was
not at all required, but Cabet assumed that each sex would follow their
'natural' inclinations in both domestic and work life. Herein lay the source of
ultimately fatal tension in Cabet's relationship to France's budding feminist
movement as well as within Icarianism itself.

Politically, all Icarians were citizens and had received a thorough civic
education in their twelve years of obligatory schooling. Upon joining the
active citizenry, all men and women participated in direct democracy in their
workplaces and their local communities to decide organizational issues,
develop innovations, and handle grievances. Serious infractions of the rules
of life and work were reported by one's peers ('nowhere is the police more
numerous') and judged in these assemblies, where calm debate led to 'nearly
unanimous' decisions.[10] A National Assembly of 2,000, whose representatives
were elected from the primary assemblies (two per commune) and renewed
every three years, governed the entire system, setting the policies that co-
ordinated the economic, social, cultural, and ludic life of the nation. It also
dealt with foreign policy and trade, which was quite extensive, making
certain that Icarians had access to products unavailable in their own land.[11]
Internal politics was indeed not about the governance of men, but the
administration of things, though Cabet did not put it as succinctly as did
Marx. Cabet's vision of politics ignored the myriad complications of its
arrangements, though he nobly thought, as did Nicolas de Condorcet, the
Girondist philosopher, that direct democracy could be effectuated. Of course,
Condorcet (bequeathing much to Henri Saint-Simon) rigged the system by
voting procedures that would result in an intellectual elite governing at the
highest level. Cabet blithely believed that all human beings were 'naturally'
equal in intelligence (as well as physical potential) and thought that those
most interested in higher-level political participation would rise to the
surface. Since there was no financial incentive to serve in these roles, sheer
talent in this particular kind of work would lead them into it, just as complex
machine operators were led to theirs. The whole question of how and why
Icarians gravitated to various roles after their primary education (which
begins at home: children 'taught by their mothers' – naturally – read and

10 On law and order in Icaria, see Cabet,*Voyage en Icarie*, pp. 128–35.
11 Unlike many utopias, Icaria was not autarchic. Cabet was convinced by arguments for
free trade then current especially in Great Britain, whose economists he read with
relish. He agreed with John Stuart Mill, Richard Cobden, and others that this would be
the foundation of world peace.

Fig. 8.1 Etienne Cabet. (Photo by Roger Viollet via Getty Images.)

wrote before they went to school at five) is exceedingly vague, though we are told that all forms of advanced education and training are abundant. But no skill, scientific, medical, humanistic, artistic, educational, mechanical, or custodial, was valued higher than any other. Cabet's view of human nature is virtually the opposite of Charles Fourier's. The latter's experiments failed because of too many choices, the former's because of too few. Cabet concluded the *Voyage en Icarie* with a long list of precursors in communism from Plato to Napoléon Bonaparte (*sic*), with a pithy quote from each, but his main antecedent was Robespierre and the Jacobin tradition that he, Cabet, was fulfilling.

Les Icariens Républicains-Communistes

Thus, armed with his utopia, his *Histoire populaire de la Révolution française*, and all the rest of History, Cabet weighed into the wars of republican politics of the 1840s. As he and his family settled in on the rue Jean-Jacques Rousseau in 1839–40, Paris was rocked with angry upheavals, large and small, motivated by the policies of the government of Louis-Philippe, still in lockdown mode.

Whatever the particulars of Cabet's ideal society and their many debatable elements, the identification of private property as the curse condemning people who had very little of it and lived on meagre wages or threatened income as petty tradesmen and -women was a revelation that rang true for them. For many, communism was the response. In 1840 it was more than a variation on social republican theory. In the words of Lorenz von Stein, the trenchant conservative critic of emerging 'industrial society': 'Socialism is the scientific expression of the interpretation of the social movement by an individual, while communism is the response of a whole class, the expression of a whole social situation', a kind of *Ur-Theorie* of the working class nurtured by the rapidly changing conditions of its existence.[12] But in the *Voyage en Icarie*, Cabet painted a serene picture of communism, of a world beyond the rage. This was the key to the success of his movement, which rapidly outflanked the followings of other communist writers such as Théodore Dézamy and Jacques Pillot, and millenialists Alphonse Esquiros and Abbé Constant, who tried to inflame the rage, hoping to organize for violent revolution.

His presses in place, Cabet's first major foray into opposition journalism arose from royal policy, guided by Adolphe Thiers, on the Eastern Question, which flared with the designs of Egyptian pasha Mohammed Ali on Syria. The British supported Istanbul, the French Cairo, where they had significant investments; fear of war and a British invasion loomed. During the second half of 1840, corresponding in time with a long strike that began in the building trades and spread to clothing, the main preoccupation was Thiers' proposal to rebuild the walls of Paris to defend the capital if besieged. Cabet thought it was a ruse to further control rebellious workers. Could not the cannons of these new 'bastilles' be turned 180 degrees? The main upshot was that the principal moderate republican newspaper, *Le National*, sided with Thiers. Cabet unloaded a polemic on this widely read paper, accusing it of abandoning *le peuple*. This created a rift that was never repaired – the first in a series of ruptures with most of the republican press.

Meanwhile, Cabet sorted out his relationship with the varied cohort of communist writers. Most were anchored in the Babouvist tradition,

---

12 L. von Stein, *Geschichte der sozialen Bewegung in Frankreich von 1789 bis auf unsere Tage* (Leipzig: Wigand, 1850), vol. II, pp. 334–5.

though the biblical Book of Revelations added melodrama to some of the writings.[13] Dézamy was the most thoughtful and collaborated for a while with Cabet before his position on violence broke them up. Pillot was the most strident: his *Ni châteaux, ni chaumières* (*Neither Castles nor Cottages*, 1840) sums up his Leveller perspective; he was also the most effective organizer among the communist crowd, hosting a series of '*Banquets communistes*' that drew overflow numbers. Cabet was invited and interactions were positive. Many participants had read the *Voyage en Icarie,* and he had won kudos for his attack on *Le National.* Cabet quickly outflanked most of the communists, but Dézamy's brochure attacking his sincerity and underlining his long career as a moderate republican[14] retained its salience throughout the decade, while a core of well-read communists led by Joseph Benoit in Lyon continued to resist Cabet's insistence that all true republicans, bourgeois included, could be brought into the communist fold through peaceful persuasion.[15]

Unlike his rivals, Cabet's mode of persuasion would be what worked so well in 1833: to build a mass movement of *le peuple* who shared his vision of a republican future, now in *Communauté.* This is where his unparalleled talents for organization and communication made all the difference. A revived *Le Populaire de 1841* became the vehicle for the project, enlivening and vastly expanding the network of contacts previously established, all now excited by a marvellous new vision of a world of plenty, harmony, and peace embedded in French revolutionary history. The newspaper's pages contain the history of this process, and the pages of police reports verify its claims. An analysis of both, along with the writings of friend and foe alike, reveals a remarkable picture of a working-class Icarian nation, centred in cities generally in the throes of economic distress occasioned by new capitalist practices, sometimes technological but more often organizational, that terminated the direct exchange between producer and consumer. To be sure, middle-class professionals and intellectuals rallied to Cabet, but they were few in number and often turned out to be unreliable.

---

13 See C. H. Johnson, *Utopian Communism in France: Cabet and the Icarians, 1839–1851* (Ithaca: Cornell University Press, 1974), pp. 68–73, for a survey.

14 T. Dézamy, *Calomnies et politique de M. Cabet. Réfutation par des faits et par sa biographie* (Paris: Prévost, 1842).

15 See Christopher H. Johnson, 'Deux lettres inédites de cinq ouvriers Lyonnais à Cabet et Dézamy', *Revue d'histoire économique et sociale* 47, 4 (1969), pp. 529–39.

After a slow start, but fortified by the polemic with *Le National, Le Populaire* soon became a leading journal in the democratic socialist galaxy, outselling all of them by 1846. Unlike the Fourierist press, the Saint-Simonian *Atelier* (*Workshop*), or the Babouvist *Fraternité* (*Fraternity*), it spent little time on ideology, referring its readers to the *Voyage* and more recent pamphlets. Instead it was a *news*paper for and by working people and their sympathizers. As the Icarian stonemason Martin Nadaud put it, these others 'treated social questions from a point of view so elevated that only the best-educated workers could read' them.[16] *Le Populaire* was divided into two main sections, '*la politique*' and '*la sociale*', with plenty of room for letters from adherents and interchanges about the growth and issues of the movement. Cabet occasionally included feuilletons, such as the novellas about working-class misery by Félix Lamb (pseud. Jenny d'Héricourt). The former section dealt with both domestic and international politics interpreted from Cabet's left perspective while the latter reported on police repression, strikes, trials, and especially the conditions of existence of French workers. Here he also defended communism against his critics, mainstream and left-wing. Although he occasionally made incisive comments about social structure and the broad problems of the working class, generalizations were kept to a minimum. Cabet's real forte was to recount hundreds of specific incidents of working-class oppression, stories of murders and accidents, of starving children and fallen women, of moral decay within the upper classes, of the hardships of competition among businesses, of the consequences of technological and organizational restructuring in capitalist industry, and of the corruption of government officials and other political scandals. Compared with the arid analyses of his rivals, such tales grabbed attention immediately. Cabet always concluded simply: 'None of this in Icaria!'[17]

Le Populaire was much more than a newspaper, however. It had an organizational structure headed by Cabet that began with a council of principal shareholders[18] who oversaw the financial operations of the paper and signed off (after debate at regular meetings) on the principal decisions and ideological orientations of the movement. The day-to-day business of the

---

16 Quoted in A. Cuvillier, *Un Journal d'ouvriers. 'L'Atelier' (1840–1850)* (Paris: Ed. Ouvrières, 1954), p. 179, n. 1.

17 For examples, see Johnson, *Utopian Communism*, pp. 85–6.

18 The financial structure of the paper was organized as a *société en commandite*, and shares cost 100 francs but could be gathered into coupons of 10 francs each after the sale of the first 100, the '*actionnaires principaux*', which meant that many were master artisans, small business-owners, and professionals, often Jacobin democrats, convinced by Cabet's equation with communist fulfilment.

journal and oversight of press and distribution work was led by Firman Favard, a tailor, who, especially with his marriage to Cabet's daughter Cécile, emerged as second-in-command and would be later succeeded by cabinet-maker Jean-Pierre Beluze, both as business manager (*gérant*) and as son-in-law. Early provincial expansion relied significantly on former agents of *Le Populaire de 1833*, now republican–communists. Among them was Chameroy, a travelling salesman for a Lyonnais commercial house, who at every stop distributed the paper and sold Cabet's works, and sought with great success *'correspondants'* to serve as local chiefs of the movement.[19] Cabet called him his 'Saint Paul', and Chameroy attributed his conversion to his Christian values. He was disappointed, however, that few of his fellow *commerçants* saw the light, for he had hoped, like Fourier, that 'if the rich and the powerful understood the situation as I do, how they would give themselves to the enlightenment of the people and strive to know its thoughts'. Nonetheless, his work produced an enthusiastic response among educated craftsmen. The process is illustrated by the example of Reims, one of the major strongholds of Icarianism. A merchant customer of Chameroy employed a clerk named Mauvais who had a circle of friends among artisans and office workers. Mauvais' propaganda touched a chord among shoemakers via 'citizen Jandon ... very well qualified in terms of his erudition, his subtlety of mind, his elocution'.[20] Word of mouth created a solid core of believers in his circle, where troubling trends within their craft stimulated visions of new forms of social organization among a particularly literate and thoughtful group. Chameroy also promoted another weapon in the Icarian arsenal: the publication of an almanac. Popular almanacs – containing facts and figures on a multitude of subjects, home remedies, practical advice on legal matters, and tips to consumers, as well as political and social discussions – were common. Cabet immediately took up the idea and in November 1842 brought out the first *Almanach icarien* (*Icarian Almanac*), which proved an instant success and was followed annually until 1848, selling 10,000 copies in the last three years.

By mid-1842, the national structure of the Icarian movement had become visible. Correspondents of *Le Populaire* were being selected for each department where Cabet's ideas resonated. They oversaw distribution, sold Cabet's works, and organized meetings to discuss local economic and political conditions. An inner cadre formed around them and became emissaries for

---

19 See J. Prudhommeaux, 'Un commis-voyager en communism icarienne. Chameroy, disciple de Cabet', *La Révolution de 1848 et les révolutions du xixe siècle* 24, 120 (March–May 1927), pp. 25–30, and 24, 122 (September–November 1927), pp. 146–71.

20 Ibid., 24, pp. 65–6, and 25, p. 165.

the Icarian cause elsewhere. The core was Lyon and its region, but virtually all corners of the hexagon were reached as dozens of 'Icarian cities' dotted the map. In the west, radiating from Nantes, an oval including Rennes, Tours, Niort, and Angoulême, arose. Around Niort, correspondent Paul Guay travelled throughout Charente and the Vendée. Reims and Toulon served as centres of influence in their rapidly industrializing departments, while Toulouse sent out tendrils to much of Languedoc. In 1847, authorities discovered Icarian ties among the textile towns of the Aisne, promoted by propagandists from Reims. Around Paris, obviously still the hub with thousands of '*adèptes*', major centres emerged, including Versailles and Choisy-le-Roi.

Lyon was the second city of Icarianism. Its regional network outdistanced the capital's. Lyon was already the heart of communist propaganda and competing programmes, with the tradition of 'secret societies' still strong. Cabet's campaign against them had been partially effective, but the depth of intelligent historical analysis by his adversaries posed a continuing roadblock. Several visits on his part and the work of his advocates, chef-d'atelier Chapius and shoemaker Faucon, cleared the way to an agreement that the ultimate goal was a greater positive than the means to get there and that all commun-ists could work harmoniously for now. This placed Icarianism at the heart of the overall movement – and made it the principal target of government scrutiny. Lyonnais Icarians numbered some two thousand plus, and while the movement's power remained strongest in the Croix Rousse and the silk industry, it had significant support from the crafts, especially, as elsewhere, among tailors and shoemakers. Several dozen activists travelled widely in the region proselytizing the doctrine. The *Voyage en Icarie*, in its third edition by 1845, turned up in police searches in towns roundabout, and multiple sub-scriptions to *Le Populaire* reached as far as Annonay in the northern Ardèche, Grenoble in the Isère, and Rive-de-Gier in the Loire. The most vibrant centre was Vienne (Isère) southward on the Rhône, a woollens town undergoing industrialization, where Vincent Coëffé, a shoe-form maker from Lyon, became one of the leading figures in provincial Icarianism. Fernand Rude, who studied both city and movement, including editing a text by two Viennois workers who ventured to the United States, estimated that Icarian communism held sway over '400 to 500 workers'.[21] Icarian missionaries from Lyon also travelled with other radicals to the coal basin of the Loire, which

---

21 Rude, the great historian of the insurrections of Lyon in the early 1830s, became fascinated with Vienne after his discovery of this manuscript. See 'Further Reading'.

produced more than half of the coal in France, during the great strike of 1844 and found many converts in an industry hitherto untouched.[22]

By 1846, Icarian communism had established a nationwide presence. Based on subscriptions to *Le Populaire* alone, seventy-eight of eighty-six departments were represented. There were several other measures of areas of concentrated support, including petitions, the Eugène Sue medal contributions, and tributes to Cabet, which far outstripped the paid subscription total. It is impossible to estimate the total number of Icarian communists in France, though I worked out a ratio of 1 sale to 20 supporters, about 70,000 nationwide, of which about one-third were concentrated in Paris and its banlieues. The remarkable provincial following was unparalleled on the left. Officials were most concerned about the communist 'infection' of Lyon and its region, and rightly so, but Icarian communism established strong footholds in many other towns in the nation, led early on by Toulouse. The latter enclave was due in large measure to the tireless propaganda and organizational skill of the painter Adolphe Gouhenant, who traversed dozens of localities peddling his artwork. A flamboyant personality and spellbinding speaker, his work also convinced the Ministry of Justice that a conspiracy of secret societies was afoot. The highly publicized trial of a dozen men, including a prominent Catalan revolutionary exile, in mid-1843 brought nationwide attention and wide sympathy from the left-wing press, especially Alexandre Auguste Ledru-Rollin's *La Réforme* (*Reform*). The tide of public opinion turned against the government, and acquittal soon followed. In the words of the local *L'Emancipation* (*Emancipation*), it was 'the triumph of communism at Toulouse'. Cabet rightly said that his movement had 'crossed the Rubicon'.[23] Most importantly, he felt that future co-operation with the entire republican camp was at hand. In this, he would be sorely disappointed.

As it turned out, the place of Toulouse in Icarian history was more symbolic than substantive, as support there languished in the later 1840s.[24] Cabet expected it to be the nucleus of growth in a populous region, but in reality Upper Languedoc was heavily agricultural, rural France, where Icarianism rarely registered. Throughout Lower Languedoc and Provence, prosperous (though contentious) woollens and agriculture dominated the economic landscape; Marseille qualifies

22 See F. Fourn's excellent analysis, *Etienne Cabet ou le temps de l'utopie* (Paris: Vendémiaire, 2014), pp. 139–47.
23 *Le Populaire*, 12 November 1843.
24 See Johnson, *Utopian Communism*, pp. 127–34, 202–3; and Fourn, *Etienne Cabet ou le temps de l'utopie*, pp. 126–31.

as a workers' city, but its diverse and shifting population seemed unreceptive. Toulon alone was a true *'ville ouvrière'*, in the words of the great historian Maurice Agulhon. There, Icarianism found fertile ground, with the largest proportional presence throughout the south at fifty-four subscribers. In Toulon, a whirlwind of rapid industrial change, especially in the naval arsenal, and an unrivalled population boom created a variety of pressures affecting many occupations and neighbourhoods as rents and prices outpaced wages. Structural change in the social relations of production was rooted more in new technologies than in organizational concentration, though the latter still affected traditional crafts such as tailoring and shoemaking. The Icarian correspondent, Fraysée, was a locksmith and as such bridged the two sectors. Agulhon argues convincingly that both Saint-Simonism and Icarianism benefited from bourgeois 'democratic patronage' of workers, raising hopes that patient propaganda could yield a communist republic inclusive of all.[25]

In the west of France, the networks of activist tailors from Nantes, who had organized one of the first multi-craft trade union movements in the nation, promoted Icarianism throughout the region. Although connections spread in all directions, the small town of Niort in the Deux-Sèvres showed a particular affinity for Icarian ideas, and its typicality is worth a pause. Niort had been a leading centre in France in the production of chamois. Besides a worldwide commerce in fine gloves, Niort supplied the cavalry of the Old Régime with similar chaps and gloves. The revolutionary military was less selective, often substituting wool and cotton, and the long decline in the industry unfolded, bottoming out during the parsimonious July Monarchy. The other trades affected were shoes, boots, and clothing, which were rapidly overtaken by the readymade revolution then rampant. Niort workers, in concert with bourgeois republicans, veterans of the struggle against the dominant regional Legitimism, became radicalized, creating a popular 'demonstrative politics' in the 1840s that brought social republicans to power even before 1848. This was the seedbed of Icarianism's second-largest proportionate contingent in France. Paul Guay, a fine-shoemaker and a long-time advocate of worker 'association' in trade unions and producer co-operatives, was Cabet's correspondent and regional missionary. In 1846, *Le Populaire* had 24 paying subscribers, 124 signed a petition of 'adherence', and the *Almanach* was eagerly awaited by hundreds of recipients.

25 M. Agulhon, *Une ville ouvrière au temps du socialism utopique. Toulon de 1815 à 1851* (Paris and The Hague: Mouton, 1970), pp. 183–5 and 271–3; Johnson, *Utopian Communism*, pp. 202–4.

Communists were by no means the only force on the left, as Saint-Simonians and Réformistes flourished, in co-operation with them, as well. Niort, along with Toulon, can perhaps be thought of as a microcosm of what France might have been in 1848.[26]

How can one summarize the bases of Icarian support? Clearly Cabet's following was overwhelmingly working-class, though largely from trades suffering from the impact of new capitalist practices, if not necessarily significant technological innovation; the new working class of factory indus-try was still in its infancy in France, and the relative absence of Icarians in textile towns in the north speaks to this point. In general, those undermined by new modes of production, such as hand-loom weavers, far outnumbered machine spinners in large factories. Insecurity of employment and downward pressure on wages in the face of capitalist structural reorganization charac-terized the lot of most Icarians. At the same time, most were relatively well educated, having passed through apprenticeships, and many were in crafts, such as tailoring, shoemaking, cabinet-making, musical instrument making (for example, Mirecourt), and locksmithing which allowed long periods of contemplation.[27] Many of the Lyonnais Jacquard-loom silk weavers (both chefs d'atelier and journeymen) who filled Icarian ranks were well versed in the social ideas of the age and argued toe to toe with Cabet, Dézamy, Victor Considerant, Pierre Leroux, or Flora Tristan about their visions of a new world and means to achieve it. But virtually all were being pressured towards poverty (la misère in the dramatic language of the day) by the relentless shifts in the economy of the July Monarchy and railed against the vast inequalities that marked the era.[28]

The grand problem within the Icarian movement, as with others, was that the national leadership was not observing what was happening on the ground. In Paris, sectarian rivalries were faithfully polemicized by the ideo-logues in Le Populaire, L'Atelier, La Démocratie pacifique (Peaceful Democracy), and La Réforme. At the same time, a trend was occurring within segments of Icarianism towards sectarian bonding manifested in cultural activities of group gatherings, often in the countryside, of picnicking, song, ritual readings

---

26 For Niort and the relevant archival citations, see Johnson, *Utopian Communism*, pp. 198–202.
27 This is a point made by E. Hobsbawm and J. W. Scott in 'Political shoemakers', *Past and Present* 89 (November 1980), pp. 87–114.
28 It must be said that François Fourn's effort to dismiss my deep and nationwide research that unearthed the scope of the Icarian base as somehow 'Marxist' is simply untenable and has been laid to rest in reviews of his book, above all that of V. Robert in *Le Mouvement social* No. 251 (April–June 2015), pp. 162–6.

from the *Voyage*, and long homages prepared and sent to their venerated leader, now increasingly addressed as 'Père' Cabet.[29] Moreover, in 1845 he was hard at work on *Vrai Christianisme* and increasingly referencing in *Le Populaire* Christian precedents of communism and talking of his own work as a 'mission'. Coupled with this was his feeling that Icarianism was under siege from the Saint-Simonians, Fourierists, and Ledru-Rollin's Jacobin social democrats, and that his efforts to convince them all that the ultimate republic would be communist were fruitless. His acerbic debate with Ledru via *La Réforme* late in 1845 convinced Cabet that 'if the Bourgeoisie persists in rejecting us', so be it; 'let us close our ranks; let us march separately on our own side'. Verging in a direction that Marx and Engels were taking at that very moment, Cabet then hesitated, saying that communists should form a 'rear guard: let us allow the Bourgeoisie to engage itself, and we will throw ourselves in only to decide and to direct the victory to our profit as to its'.[30] But communist rank and file made the central point, embracing, if need be, class antagonism: twenty 'proletarians' in a 'Parisian workshop' wrote that 'communists are pacific, but are conscious of their power; they will know how to use it when the time comes ... if society were separated into two camps, if there was a struggle, the victory would not be in doubt: the bourgeoisie, egotistical, skilful in the wiles of trade, impotent as to the production of the wealth it amasses, would not struggle against the strong arms of the producers'. Cabet published this manifesto in *Le Populaire* on 22 November 1845. Solidarity of a different, more militant sort seemed to be brewing.

Effectively, the movement remained torn between basking in visions of a beautiful future and the realities of working-class life amidst an economy and a polity tearing it asunder. For Cabet personally, options narrowed between two choices: admit that revolutionary communists had assessed current conditions correctly and declare for confrontational class struggle; or think of an escape to experimental community-building as promoted by the Fourierists and Owenites to 'prove' the viability of that vision. What he ignored was the work of his own people in places such as Toulon and Niort (and indeed almost anywhere, including Paris and Lyon), in building progressive coalitions on behalf of a social republic with all like-minded activists. In 1845–7, class-conscious working people and middle-class social republicans stood ready to compromise ideology for *results*.

29 See S. Commissaire, *Mémoires et souvenirs*, 2 vols. (Lyon: Meton, 1888), vol. I, pp. 98–9.
30 Etienne Cabet, *Salut par l'union ou ruine par la division, la paix ou la guerre entre le 'Populaire' et la 'Réforme'* (Paris: Bureau du 'Populaire', 1846), p. 50.

But Père Cabet chose the second option. He had long decried the notion of small, 'experimental' communities, so on 9 May 1847 he summoned the faithful with the call *Allons en Icarie!* It would be instead a mass *émigration* to the New World. The electrifying news was accompanied by appropriate biblical quotations, and the fervent responses of the true believers poured in. They would 'realize' Icaria across the seas in the here and now. It is impossible, from existing documentation, to determine what motivated Cabet to allow himself to evolve into a semi-messianic visionary. We are left with a controlling personality who could not bear to abandon his hard-earned reputation as the leading communist advocate against secret societies and violent revolution.

In later 1847, the movement underwent a tumultuous upheaval as thousands of pragmatic activists opposed the departure and sought to stay the course in a France consumed with ecological and economic disaster; but thousands more flocked to the millenarian call.[31] The New Icaria turned out to be a desolate area in Texas where crooked land agents sold mile-square *non-contiguous* lots to Cabet's English real estate agents. Nevertheless, on 3 February 1848, the advance party of sixty-nine (each having paid 600 francs, meaning few 'workers', for whom that was an annual income, joined) and led by Gouhenant, the Toulouse artist, took off for New Orleans to the strains of a rewritten 'Chant de départ' of revolutionary lore. Three weeks later, France roiled in a new revolution.

Revolution and the United States

'*Quelle Révolution!*' blared *Le Populaire* on 23 February as if it were the one Cabet had predicted. In reality it was the one foreseen by the 'rear guard', which rapidly emerged as Parisian Icarians, urged on by Martin Nadaud and many others of the inner circle, clamoured for their leader to enter the fray. Although there was considerable popular support for Cabet to be named to the Provisional Government, only Louis Blanc and the 'worker' Albert joined Ledru-Rollin as its left flank under the shaky command of the romantic poet Alphonse de Lamartine, whose elevation was already smiled upon by the forces of reaction.[32] But Icarians leapt into action, forming a club called the

---

31 See Johnson, 'From Movement to Sect, 1846–1847', chapter 5 of *Utopian Communism*, pp. 207–59.
32 See J. Beecher, 'Lamartine, the Girondins, and 1848', in D. S. Maggoch and G. S. Jones (eds.), *The 1848 Revolutions and European Political Thought* (Cambridge: Cambridge University Press, 2018), pp. 14–38.

Société Fraternelle Centrale (Central Fraternal Society) that quickly became the largest in Paris, giving Cabet a purchase that promised the impossible dream: to lead the nation to a communist republic. His principal focus was to democratize the National Guard, especially by providing uniforms free of charge and paying realistic salaries to its members, and delaying elections of officers until its ranks, traditionally dominated by bourgeois, were filled by working men. Defending and advancing revolutionary goals 'by the People themselves' became the watchword. Ironically, the 'pacific' Cabet knew precisely where revolutionary power resided: with force of arms. Cabet, along with Auguste Blanqui, Blanc, Leroux, and François-Vincent Raspail, used his newspaper and club to organize a giant rally on 17 March on behalf of a people's National Guard and postponement of the elections for the National Assembly. Never had his star shone so bright.

Elsewhere in France, Icarians, whether Cabet loyalists enthusiastic about the emigration or Icarians sceptical of this grand shift, jumped into the revolutionary mix, but tended to split along familiar lines: the sceptics encouraging confrontation, the 'loyalists' trying to tone it down, seeking avenues of communication and co-operation with the bourgeois *républicains de lendemain*' who largely took command of makeshift provisional local governments. Many local histories of the revolution document the significant role of Icarians of both stripes in the upheaval and then note their ongoing disappointments and reorientations, to joining the emigration to be sure, but also, especially in the Lyonnais region, towards the co-operative movement.

But what happened in Paris was paramount. Cabet's very prominence became a vehicle to rally the forces of reaction set in motion behind an ominous cry that continued to ring across France that year (and indeed for a century to come whenever the power of wealth was threatened): *à bas les communistes!* As it engulfed the revolution and as Cabet's followers fell victim to it, the shift towards counter-revolution unfolded, and the familiar story of the unravelling of European democracy's seemingly magic moment played out to 'farce' in France and 'blood and iron' elsewhere. Personally, Cabet was hounded with death threats and, finally, driven out of his residence, though ultimately given refuge by Lamartine. This brave act of fraternity was characteristic of the weeks leading to the derailment of the hopes of the left ending with the premature elections for the national assembly on 23 April when rural France overwhelmingly voted for the defenders of private property, responding to their fantasies of a communist 'agrarian law'. After the failure of 17 March, then of the more virulent 16 April demonstrations, and the ultra-conservative outcome of the elections, all capped off by the June Days, the slide towards reaction was relentless.[33]

While Cabet continued to contribute critical commentary in *Le Populaire*, the energies of his movement returned to the emigration. And here a whole set of new problems had arisen. The Texas expedition had become a total disaster. A majority of the avant-garde were ill equipped to deal with the rigours of the frontier, and fatigue and disease overtook them. Like their leader Gouhenant, many were bourgeois and better-off artisans with no rural or even direct hand-working experience. Gouhenant, always the visionary optimist, had sent letters vastly overstating their prospects. The truth was finally revealed in a collective letter dated 20 August 1848 signed by fifty-two members of the group. The 'second avant-garde', organized after Cabet's defeat in the June election, found a demoralized Icaria and immediately decided that the only avenue was to abandon the project and retreat to New Orleans. Gouhenant, who was blamed for the failure and accused of being an 'agent of the Jesuits', stayed behind and went on to become a founding father of Dallas.[34] Cabet met the returning faithful in New Orleans on 28 January 1849 and began a search for another location. He was in luck. The town of Nauvoo, Illinois, on the Mississippi River was available at a bargain price. After the murder of Joseph Smith, Brigham Young had led his Latter-Day Saints away from the land of sin to their permanent haven in Utah in 1846. This time, an entire infrastructure already existed, with dwellings and the meeting hall built in. Suddenly, the immediate establishment of the Icarian dream seemed in reach. With a troop of Icarians, some veterans, most recently arrived, Cabet was able to purchase and occupy sizeable tracts in town and some 2,000 acres of already worked river-bottom farmland.

The promise of the venue paid off, despite setbacks, as the Icarians put their skills to work immediately with masons, carpenters, seamstresses, laundresses, tailors, and the whole range of urban occupations deployed joyfully. Children (the next wave of emigrants included entire families) began their schooling by autumn 1849 even as a new school was being constructed. Farmers were trained by hired locals, many of whom welcomed the newcomers. In a year, the Icarian population was more than 250, still

---

33 On all this see Johnson, *Utopian Communism*, pp. 280–2, esp. n. 61. See also Fourn, *Etienne Cabet ou le temps de l'utopie*, pp. 206–31.

34 See Fourn, *Etienne Cabet ou le temps de l'utopie*, pp. 238–46; J. Beecher, *Victor Considerant: The Rise and Fall of French Romantic Socialism* (Berkeley: University of California Press, 2001), pp. 309–10, for the Fourierist's meeting with Gouhenant in 1852.

a minority in a town happy to have communitarians not threatening their religious beliefs. Politically, it was a 'democratic republic' with an assembly elected yearly by universal (read male) suffrage that passed legislation literally administering things usually proposed by the elected president and then signed into law by the same: 'Père' Cabet (alias Le Bon Icar) by name. It was as if the *Voyage en Icarie* was being enacted. The supply of new recruits multiplied as J.-P. Beluze took over the Paris office while the contributions poured in. Cabet was satisfied enough with where things stood to return to France in late 1850 to stand trial – and be exonerated – on fraud charges. He also tried to revamp *Le Populaire*, which Ludwik Krolikowski had allowed to lose its Icarian identity altogether. In some respects, this was inevitable since the Icarian movement in France was virtually non-existent, having become little more than a recruitment society. But Cabet still dreamed, it appeared, of a democratic socialist republic in France itself, trying to launch with Louis Blanc and Pierre Leroux an opposition newpaper to stand bravely against the reaction now fully crystallizing around Louis-Napoléon Bonaparte, President (soon for life) of the Second Republic. When this effort failed to get off the ground, he converted *Le Populaire* into *Le Républicain populaire et social* (*The Popular and Social Republican*) to which his colleagues gave their support. It hearkened to the deepest social-republican traditions of his entire career. It lasted two months, snuffed out by the *coup d'état* of 2 December 1851. Although Cabet was imprisoned briefly after the nationwide resistance, there is no evidence that he was actively involved; after a perfunctory hearing, he was ordered to leave for London.

Cabet returned to Nauvoo on 20 July 1852. Even without their Father, the Icarians had carried out many of the plans legislated before he left.[35] One can imagine the excitement as Icarians recreated their Icaria. The centrepiece was the vast refectory, constructed by their artisans, where they gathered and bonded daily in a long dinner break from their labours. A stage at one end doubled as a venue for plays and musical events, often modelled on scenes from the *Voyage*. In many respects, the making of Icaria seemed to flow easily. Housing posed problems because so much still needed to be done. But in general they persevered, perhaps recalling a prescient line from the guide in the *Voyage* that 'Icarians may have been happier in the building' of their utopia than after its realization. This of course suggests the core of any philosophical argument about the meaning of utopia in human existence,

---

35 R. Sutton's chapter 'The *Communauté de Biens* at Nauvoo' summarizes incisively the essentials: Sutton, *Les Icariens: The Utopian Dream in Europe and America* (Urbana: University of Illinois Press, 1994), pp. 72–81.

but Icarians were living the transition and deeply engaged in the project. Visitors were impressed, and the flow of newcomers (and the accommodation of those who wished to leave) signalled that this might become the most successful of all the secular utopian experiments in the United States to date. The pleasures of Icaria were many and mirrored the vision on the *Voyage*, with concerts, plays, and promenades in the country animating their Sundays and after-work moments. The countryside along the Mississippi was beautiful.

However, Cabet arrived in July 1852 to growing reports of disaffection. There were workshops to cover most essential needs and others for specialized production, but Cabet had assigned jobs that did not necessarily match skills, and workers were often moved from one to another. Above all, work was highly regimented with regard to time and procedures. The military precision of it all rankled growing numbers of people. Grievances also flowed from restrictions on what many considered their private lives, above all strictures against smoking and drinking. Cabet's response, essentially, was to crack down even more. As his dream for France was now shattered, Icaria had to succeed. Thus began a confrontation between an increasingly dictatorial and puritanical president and members of the assembly, who were airing the grievances of the discontents.

As Diana Garno has shown, *les citoyennes* of Icaria were a key element in the confrontation, both as targets of Cabet's wrath and as active participants in his overthrow. Women had been an important force in the emigration project, many motivated by Christian values. The realities of their lives in Nauvoo, however, did not match its egalitarian promise. Icaria was highly segregated by sex. Women did 'women's work': cooking, the dishes, communal laundry, child care (until the school age of five, mothers were relieved of other duties to ready their babies for Icarian life, which Cabet saw as paramount in the making of *Communauté*), and the single craft role of seamstress, in which all girls were trained to clothe all Icarians. For Cabet and most of his male followers, this work was deemed foundational to the entire project. Women could attend assembly meetings and have their voices heard, but they could vote only on issues that pertained to them. Cabet had written a long pamphlet called *La Femme* (*Woman*, 1843) in which he declared his belief in the total equality of all human beings and therefore of men and women. Curiously, however, while he strained credulity by arguing the essential equality of human physical and mental capacities, he differentiated the reproductive functions of the two genders as fundamental, and argued that, while women should never be treated as inferior to men, they must be 'elevated' to equality *because* of their function. 'Respect' and 'honour' abound in his vocabulary. This did not change. In 1848, the great feminist Jeanne Deroin came to his club meetings to urge his endorsement of women's right to vote and hold office in a democratic republic. Cabet's response was 'of course', but only after the populace (male) had been educated in the principles of *communauté*. His own ally, Jenny d'Héricourt, turned on him. In Nauvoo, he was challenged, after his return, by an increasingly vocal cadre of women, most of them those venerated mothers, who demanded full political rights and access, derivative of their equal education in the philosophy of communism (girls and boys had separate but equal education to the age of seventeen and eighteen respectively), to all professions that they might follow, whether in the crafts or intellectual pursuits. Tensions built, and a large minority of the women were added to the scores of men who chafed under the restrictions and regimentation imposed and defended by an increasingly authoritarian Cabet. Thus it was that the grand Schism of Icarian Nauvoo came about in 1855–6. After a long and complicated debate, the opposition prevailed, and Cabet was deposed by a narrow margin. He led his supporters to a new New Icaria outside St Louis, but lived only two months, felled by a stroke. His overwrought, but immensely productive, brain finally gave out.[36]

The majority, 219 strong, relaxed the stringent regulations and enjoyed the open spaces left behind. But finances were in disarray as they moved ahead to a plan already in the making, to sell up and move to open land near Corning, in south-east Iowa. There, they created, in Robert Sutton's words, a 'rural commune', They retained the Icarian principles of fraternity, equality, and goodwill, but bowed to the realities of the market and of individual differences and rights. Corning would remain an outpost of French culture and social-democratic principles, welcoming exiles from the Second Empire such as Jules Leroux, who published a Franco-American newspaper, and thereafter refugees from the Paris Commune. Its numbers never went far beyond the 400 at Nauvoo. One essential point: after the Commune, this commune finally granted women full political equality.[37]

This tragic ending only underlined the fundamental contradiction of Cabet's life's work. Although certainly one of the most ardent and effective activists in the pursuit of a republican France grounded in popular sovereignty that was crowned by an infectious vision of a communist utopia, when

36 Sutton, *Les Icariens*, pp. 81–102; D. Garno, *Citoyennes and Icaria* (Lanham, MD: University Press of America, 2005), pp. 124–53.
37 Garno, *Citoyennes and Icaria*, pp. 172–207.

his tireless efforts came to fruition in 1846 as a mass working-class movement nationwide, he allowed his role as its leader and ideological keeper of the faith to overwhelm his practicality (which had been so fundamental in the building of this amazing achievement). Rather than cede ideological ground to his rivals in the name of social republican unity and view his vision as a long-term goal, as many of his followers were doing in their locales, he fell victim to what might be called the 'utopian disease', seeing himself as the embodiment of that utopia and taking literally his role as the Father of all Icarians, and thus 'True Christianity', whose 'converts', persecuted in one country, would flee to another to build the New Jerusalem. The movement splintered, and the parodied communist ideology became a vehicle for the conservative reaction to snatch away the promise of the social republic that the February Revolution had seemed to portend.

The Legacy

Although the Icarian movement in France effectively disappeared after the Second Republic, its heritage was lasting within various strands of the working-class movement thereafter. I would emphasize three general components. The first is worker self-determination, especially as manifested in *associationisme* (labour unions) and consumer and producer co-operation; Cabet's followers saw both as crucial preliminary steps towards the creation of a communist society. Jean Gaumont, the pre-eminent historian of co-operation, cites dozens of Icarians who contributed to each, one the foundation of the other. Lyon, an Icarian stronghold, was at the heart of it. Parisian J.-P. Beluze, Cabet's chief lieutenant and second son-in-law who ran recruitment for the colony until 1860, moved on to found Le Crédit de Travail, which financed co-operative ventures throughout the nation. French syndicalism (as represented by Amédée Dunois' assessment of Cabet's contribution to the French labour movement) combined the two forces and saw the general strike as the basis for the creation of an egalitarian society (though one quite different from Cabet's, shedding his authoritarianism entirely). The second component, also captured in Dunois' statement, was the influence of Cabet's dictum, *'point d'indifférence politique'*, by which he meant that workers must develop a general consciousness of their own power as a class and express it in political organization and action. Martin Nadaud perfectly represents this tradition, standing tall in the Revolution of 1848 and running for and holding office as a social republican during a long career thereafter. There is no question that Cabet organized the first 'veritable workers' party' in the 1840s, with Nadaud and dozens of other workers in its leadership nationwide, which Cabet argued would become the dominant force in a republic based on popular sovereignty and lead to communism. This, of course, also became the maxim of Marxist social democracy everywhere in the later nineteenth and early twentieth centuries, best represented by Jean Jaurès, who, like Cabet, embraced the Jacobin tradition as the root of a potential workers' egalitarian republic. Finally, let us return to Cabet's *Icarie*: like all such utopias, it provided (in this case often in delightful detail) a vision of what life might be like in a communist society. Although Cabet and his more fervent followers were dedicated to its creation in their lifetime and in the end opted for an experiment to prove its viability, the clear majority of Icarians saw it as a distant ideal, as a model of a communist society worth striving for, a 'not impossible' dream – and that authoritarian regimentation would destroy the entire project. This prescient perspective emerged, even for Cabet himself, within the movement as the Revolution of 1848 unfolded, only to be dashed by the distortion of its own rhetoric. Obviously, however, the ideal persisted, continuing to animate generations of struggle for democratic socialism.[38]

Further Reading

Agulhon, Maurice, *The Republican Experiment, 1848–1852*, trans. Janet Lloyd (Cambridge: Cambridge University Press, 1983).

Angrand, Pierre, *Etienne Cabet et la République de 1848* (Paris: Presses universitaires de France, 1948).

Beecher, Jonathan, *Victor Considerant and the Rise and Fall of French Romantic Socialism* (Berkeley: University of California Press, 2001).

Cabet, Etienne, *History and Constitution of the Icarian Community*, trans. Thomas Teakle (New York: AMS Press, 1975).

  Travels in Icaria, trans. Leslie J. Roberts, with introduction by Robert Sutton (Syracuse: Syracuse University Press, 2003).

Cordillot, Michel, *Utopistes et exilés du Nouveau Monde. Des Français aux Etats-Unis de 1848 à la Commune* (Paris: Vendémiaire, 2013).

Crétinon, Jean-François, and François-Marie Lacour, *Voyage en Icarie. Deux ouvriers viennois aux Etats-Unis en 1855*, ed. F. Rude (Grenoble: Presses universitaires de Grenoble, 1980).

Fourn, François, *Etienne Cabet ou le temps de l'utopie* (Paris: Vendémiaire, 2014).

Garno, Diana, *Citoyennes and Icaria* (Lanham, MD: University Press of America, 2005).

---

38 For a trenchant analysis of the utopian impulse, see F. Jameson, *Archaeologies of the Future: The Desire Called Utopia and Other Science Fictions* (London and New York: Verso, 2005).

Johnson, Christopher H., *Utopian Communism in France: Cabet and the Icarians, 1839–1851* (Ithaca: Cornell University Press, 1974).

Rancière, Jacques, *The Nights of Labor: The Workers' Dream in Nineteenth-Century France*, trans. John Drury, with introduction by Donald Reid (Philadelphia: Temple University Press, 1989).

Sutton, Robert P., *Les Icariens: The Utopian Dream in Europe and America* (Urbana: University of Illinois Press, 1994).

9

Wilhelm Weitling and Early German Socialism

BERTEL NYGAARD

Socialist ideas, practices, and discourses first took shape in the bustling politico-cultural environment of Paris and the British centres of industrial development. But, since these places had the attention of the rest of urban Europe, it did not take long before the question of socialism was hotly debated there too. In many cases, socialism was not only passively received as a set of foreign ideas, but also actively redefined and adapted to particular social contexts or intellectual mores. Germany, though not yet united as a nation in politico-institutional terms, was the main site of such redefinitions and adaptions during the 1830s and 1840s. Soon it became a hub of early socialism in its own right, with German ideas of socialism disseminating in neighbouring regions outside the three dominant nationalities of Europe.

In retrospect, of course, the most influential and well-known version of German socialism was the one founded by Karl Marx and Friedrich Engels during the 1840s. And some of Marx's and Engels' writings did gain some attention during the latter part of that decade (particularly Engels' *The Condition of the Working Class in England*). But the codification of Marxism as a comprehensive, systematic outlook with a strong position in the labour movement was several decades away. While Marx and Engels' *Communist Manifesto* from 1848 was later disseminated in millions of copies in innumerable languages, its first editions gained very little attention during that year of revolutionary turmoil.[1]

---

1 B. Andréas, 'Marx et Engels et la gauche hégelienne', *Annali dell'Istituto Giangiacomo Feltrinelli* 7 (1965), pp. 353–526; W. Mönke, *Die heilige Familie. Zur ersten Gemeinschaftsarbeit von Karl Marx und Friedrich Engels* (Berlin: Akademie-Verlag, 1972); B. Andréas, *Le Manifeste communiste de Marx et Engels. Histoire et bibliographie 1848–1918* (Milan: G. Feltrinelli, 1963); G. Haupt, *Aspects of International Socialism, 1871–1914: Essays* (Cambridge: Cambridge University Press, 1986); P. Anderson, *Considerations on Western Marxism* (London: New Left Books, 1976); E. J. Hobsbawm, *How to Change the World: Reflections on Marx and Marxism* (London: Abacus, 2012), pp. 16–47, 101–20, 176–96.

Other notable figures personified socialism to German-speaking Europe before Marx and Engels, and they remained prominent throughout the 1840s. The most important German among them, and the most scandalous to bourgeois public opinion of his time, was the tailor Wilhelm Weitling. Most other prominent German socialists and radicals of the 1840s were intellectuals, typically approaching socialism and the cause of labour in philosophical terms before proceeding to political engagement or organizational projects. By contrast, Weitling integrated his own experience of workers' lives in the early nineteenth century in his approach to the various pre-existing trends of European left-wing politics, and he constantly did so with an eye to the unity of theory, organization, and transformative practice. Thus, Weitling's life, intellectual development, and active engagement in the cause of the workers may provide insight into early (pre-Marxist) German approaches to socialism and communism as such. This will be the purpose of this chapter.

German Workers in Paris

Born in 1808, the son of a poor, unmarried woman in Magdeburg and a French captain passing through, Weitling trained as a tailor.[2] Travelling around Europe for some years as a journeyman (in German *Wandergeselle*), as was customary at that time, he stopped to work in Dresden, Vienna, and several smaller Bohemian and Moravian cities. In 1835, he finally settled in Paris, 'the wide sorcerer's pot in which world history lives', as the prominent political exile and Young Hegelian philosopher Arnold Ruge put it a few years later.[3]

Under the young, comparatively liberal July Monarchy, scores of people from other parts of Europe sought the French capital, seeking escape from political persecution or economic misery. The number of German exiles in Paris grew from fewer than 7,000 in the early 1830s to approximately 60,000 in the latter half of the 1840s. This influx of exiles and foreign workers

---

2 W. Seidel-Höppner, *Wilhelm Weitling (1808–1871). Eine politische Biographie*, 2 vols. (Frankfurt am Main: Peter Lang, 2014). See also L. Knatz, *Utopie und Wissenschaft im frühen deutschen Sozialismus. Theoriebildung und Wissenschaftsbegriff bei Wilhelm Weitling* (Frankfurt am Main: Peter Lang, 1984); H.-A. Marsiske, *'Wider die Umsonstfresser'. Der Handwerkerkommunist Wilhelm Weitling* (Hamburg: Ergebnisse, 1986); L. Knatz and H.-A. Marsiske (eds.), *Wilhelm Weitling. Ein deutscher Arbeiterkommunist* (Hamburg: Ergebnisse, 1989); C. Wittke, *The Utopian Communist: A Biography of Wilhelm Weitling, Nineteenth-Century Reformer* (Baton Rouge: Louisiana State University Press, 1950).

3 A. Ruge, *Zwei Jahre in Paris. Erster Theil* (Leipzig: Wilhelm Jurany, 1846), p. 4.

contributed to keeping living expenses high and wages low, but there was also a thriving culture of worker solidarity, protest, and – at least among a significant minority – political organization.[4] In Paris, 'no one becomes so poor as to lose one's hope of dying in the fight against the oppressors', Weitling later reminisced.[5]

In his new hometown, Weitling joined the Bund der Geächteten (League of Outcasts). This organization of expatriate Germans was founded in Paris in May 1834 with about 500 members. The previous organization of Germans in France, the Deutscher Volksverein (German People's Association), had by then dissolved as a result of the general government ban on all organizations suspected of belonging to the republican opposition, introduced in the aftermath of the failed republican uprising of April 1834.

Following the examples of the Charbonnerie Démocratique Universelle (Universal Democratic Charbonnerie; led during the late 1820s by Filippo Buonarroti, former collaborator of François-Noël Babeuf in the Conspiracy of the Equals and later the editor of Babeuf's writings), as well as contemporary regroupments of French republican forces in new organizations such as Auguste Blanqui's Société des Familles (Society of Families), the Bund der Geächteten was organized as a secret society. Its leadership structures were secretive and authoritarian, but its political principles were more radical than those of earlier organizations. Its declaration of purpose centred on a Jacobin interpretation of human and civil rights beyond mere liberalism, emphasizing the 'right to exist' (that is, the right to a certain socio-economically defined level of existence) and the 'right to work'. To some extent, this radical political programme reflected the broad range of members of the Bund der Geächteten as well as numerous French secret societies: along with the radical intellectuals traditionally dominant in politics, there were also many artisans and journeymen like Weitling voicing grievances of their own. But, while the French secret societies naturally focused on overturning the French social order, the Bund der Geächteten combined that aim with working as a German republican opposition in exile, communicating in German and striving to establish contacts in their native countries.[6]

---

4 J. Grandjonc, 'Les étrangers à Paris sous la Monarchie de Juillet et la Seconde République', *Population* 29 (1974), pp. 61–8; L. S. Kramer, *Threshold of a New World: Intellectuals and the Exile Experience in Paris, 1830–1848* (Ithaca: Cornell University Press, 1988).
5 Quoted in Seidel-Höppner, *Wilhelm Weitling*, p. 203.
6 J. Höppner and W. Seidel-Höppner, 'Der Bund der Geächteten und der Bund der Gerechtigkeit', in H. Reinalter (ed.), *Politische Vereine, Gesellschaften und Parteien in Zentraleuropa 1815–1848/9* (Frankfurt am Main: Peter Lang, 2005), pp. 89–153; M. Hundt,

As Weitling joined the Bund der Geächteten, bitter international debates had arisen concerning political aims, but also involving questions of rank-and-file influence on such politics, including the rights of manual labourers to participate in such debates on an equal footing with intellectuals. One faction within the Bund defended its traditional conception of political reform as the prime immediate aim of the movement and a distinct stage of development. That achievement would then make it possible to fight economic inequality and the poverty of the workers. The opposing faction of the Bund saw it the other way around: social reform was a precondition and an integral part of any progressive political reform. Such political differentiations, too, followed main trends in the French republican societies, in which the most radical parts were beginning to revive the notions of communal property developed by Babeuf and the Conspiracy of the Equals four decades earlier. Thus, gradually, the more radical wing of the Bund der Geächteten began to conceive of a social revolution overturning inequality and attacking private property in the means of production.[7]

This internal strife about fundamental objectives proved too much for one organization. Some hundreds of members of the Bund der Geächteten left the organization during the next couple of years in order to establish a new

Geschichte des Bundes der Kommunisten 1836 bis 1852 (Frankfurt am Main: Peter Lang, 1993); J. Schmidt, Brüder, Bürger und Genossen. Die deutsche Arbeiterbewegung zwischen Klassenkampf und Bürgergesellschaft 1830–1870 (Bonn: Dietz, 2018), pp. 103–50; W. Schieder, Anfänge der deutschen Arbeiterbewegung. Die Auslandsvereine im Jahrzehnt nach der Julirevolution von 1830 (Stuttgart: Ernst Klett, 1963); J. Harsin, Barricades: The War of the Streets in Revolutionary Paris, 1830–1848 (New York: Palgrave, 2002), esp. pp. 65–123; T. Bouchet, 'Les sociétés secrètes pendant la monarchie censitaire', in J. J. Becker and G. Candar (eds.), Histoire des gauches en France, vol. I, L'héritage du XIXe siècle (Paris: La Découverte, 2005), pp. 161–8; J.-N. Tardy, 'Des catacombes à l'insurrection. Signes de reconnaissance, signes de ralliement des sociétés secrètes en France (1821–1851)', Hypothèses 10, 1 (2007), pp. 45–54. See also W. Kowalski (ed.), Vom kleinbürgerlichen Demokratismus zum Kommunismus. Zeitschriften aus der Frühzeit der deutschen Arbeiterbewegung (1834–1847) (Berlin: Akademie-Verlag, 1967); W. Kowalski (ed.), Vom kleinbürgerlichen Demokratismus zum Kommunismus. Die Hauptberichte der Bundeszentralbehörde in Frankfurt am Main von 1838 bis 1842 über die deutsche revolutionäre Bewegung (Berlin: Akademie-Verlag, 1978); H.-J. Ruckhäberle (ed.), Frühproletarische Literatur. Die Flugschriften der deutschen Handwerksgesellenvereine in Paris 1832–1839 (Kronberg: Scriptor Verlag, 1977); O. Büsch, Die frühsozialistischen Bünde in der Geschichte der deutschen Arbeiterbewegung (Berlin: Colloquium Verlag, 1975); E. Schraepler, Handwerkerbünde und Arbeitervereine 1830–1853. Die politische Tätigkeit deutscher Sozialisten von Wilhelm Weitling bis Karl Marx (Berlin: De Gruyter, 1972); H. Förder et al. (eds.), Der Bund der Kommunisten. Dokumenten und Materialien, vol. I, 1836–1849 (Berlin: Institut für Marxismus-Leninismus, 1970).

7 Höppner and Seidel-Höppner, 'Der Bund', pp. 63–70; Seidel-Höppner, Wilhelm Weitling, pp. 77–87; Harsin, Barricades, pp. 188–208; A. Maillard, La communauté des égaux. La communisme néo-babouviste dans la France des années 1840 (Paris: Kimé, 1999); G. Sencier, Le babouvisme après Babeuf (Paris: Marcel Rivière & Cie, 1912).

one: the Bund der Gerechtigkeit (League of Justice, often misleadingly referred to as the Bund der Gerechten, that is, League of the Just). The latter organization evolved from an elitist revolutionary conspiracy towards a propaganda group with a much larger degree of membership democracy, appealing – as far as circumstances permitted – to broad sections of the working class with the purpose of stirring them into action. Weitling quickly became the most prominent person in the organization, and in 1838, he authored its programme, published illegally as *Die Menschheit, wie sie ist und wie sie sein sollte (Humanity as It Is and as It Should Be)*.[8]

Radicalizing and specifying the conceptions of social rights only loosely described in the programme of the Bund der Geächteten, Weitling's text conceived of equality in the conditions of work, consumption, education and political participation, and equal rights and duties for men and women alike, as well as the fullest possible freedom of speech and action. The core aim, however, was not the introduction of complete equality, but the creation of a community based on the abolition of private property and money. This would allow the full flowering of the potential of each individual, beyond the present oppressive power of the egoism of a select few – and not on a narrowly national scale, but all over the world. Emancipation from the rule of private property and moneyed interests would make 'the world into one garden and humanity into one family'.[9]

The programme also warned against competing strategies in the struggle against modern pauperism: the comparatively moderate aim of distributing capital more equally among individual producers would only result in the solidification of moneyed interests in a wealthy middle class. And apparent shortcuts in the struggle, such as machine-wrecking, assassinations of individual rulers, or *coups d'état*, would only prove counterproductive. The only road to emancipation was that of organizing and educating the mass of workers to a sense of collective consciousness and agency.[10]

As the historian Waltraud Seidel-Höppner has emphasized, Weitling's programme of 1838 and his expanded exposition of his thoughts in what became his most important book, *Garantien der Harmonie und Freiheit*

---

8 Seidel-Höppner, *Wilhelm Weitling*, pp. 94–129; Höppner and Seidel-Höppner, 'Der Bund', pp. 70–6; W. Seidel-Höppner, 'Unter falschem Namen. Der Bund der Gerechtigkeit und sein Namenswandel', *Jahrbuch für Forschungen zur Geschichte der Arbeiterbewegung* no. 1 (2013), pp. 47–57.

9 W. Weitling, *Die Menschheit, wie sie ist und wie sie sein sollte* (Bern: Jenni, 1845 (2nd edn); 1st edn. 1838), https://archive.org/details/diemenschheitwie00weit, p. 54; see also pp. 19–20 and 33–4.

10 Ibid., pp. 7–9, 13–15.

(*Guarantees of Harmony and Liberty*) from 1842, adopted the ideal of a community of goods propounded by the French Babouvists while transcending their ascetic egalitarianism by means of an anthropology of human urges reminiscent of Charles Fourier's thoughts. And, while Weitling's writings were generally short on specific historical references, there was an overall philosophical approach to historical development in his writings on social problems, revealing not only the theories of stages of social development commonplace in liberal social theory of the nineteenth century, but also more specific influences from a Saint-Simonian conception of history as aiming towards future potentials of the acknowledgement of the importance of labour.[11]

These and other theoretical influences reveal more than just a remarkable breadth of reading and intellectual orientation. Comparing each of these strands of French social thought to Weitling's first book, we may also see how he – probably to a large degree through intense discussions with his comrades in the Bund der Gerechtigkeit – did not simply borrow and combine elements of each of them. Instead, Weitling and the Bund der Gerechtigkeit developed new approaches to social reality, critically engaging with the pre-existing French positions and theories, but re-evaluating such theories from their own experiences as German manual workers and labour organizers.

Weitling's first book served as the programme of the Bund der Gerechtigkeit for close to ten years, only to be replaced by the *Communist Manifesto* by Marx and Engels in 1848, as the organization was renamed the Bund der Kommunisten (League of Communists). With the first edition printed – secretly – in 2,000 copies and being reprinted five times over the next sixteen years, alongside a Hungarian edition from 1840, it is clear that the Bund der Gerechtigkeit did much to propagate their ideas, not only among German-speaking exiles, but also among workers in the member states of the German League. And while the programme text indicated a project of propaganda and education focusing on long-term aims of social change, the Bund der Gerechtigkeit also immersed itself in the shorter-term struggles of the workers, particularly during the great strike among tailors – many of them Germans – in the fashion centre of Paris during the summer of 1840. Weitling was a member of the strike leadership and appealed to German-speaking workers in Paris and many cities in the German League for solidarity. To many people involved in these struggles, French and German alike,

---

11 Seidel-Höppner, *Wilhelm Weitling*, pp. 129–53, 301–8, and *passim*.

the strikes of 1840 were a turning point in their shift from identifying as artisans within a particular trade to identifying as workers and as members of an international working class.[12]

Proletarian Politics and Religious Discourse

Weitling developed his position on workers' organization further in 1841, as he relocated to Geneva to organize the Bund der Gerechtigkeit among German-speaking artisans and journeymen in Switzerland. Though the political and cultural climate of Switzerland was a far cry from Paris, with the latter's sense of world history in the making, this endeavour did meet with some success, as pre-existing circles of German-speaking workers associated with Young Germany proved more open to the new organization than in most other places, and from early 1841 until late 1842 the membership of the Swiss section of the Bund der Gerechtigkeit grew from around 300 to around 750 or 800.[13]

In collaboration with the journalists August Becker and Sebastian Keller, among others, Weitling founded the first German workers' paper in Geneva, initially under the name of *Der Hülferuf der deutschen Jugend* (*German Youth's Call for Help*), later under the less cumbersome name of *Die junge Generation* (*The Young Generation*). As the literary scholar Patrick Eiden-Offe has emphasized, this journal became a crucial site of Weitling's articulation of a new proletarian political discourse and an innovative set of class narratives supporting an 'imaginary self-discovery' of the proletariat as proletariat, a 'class poetry' which, however, still revealed its roots in the 'spirit of the old journeyman language'.[14] In the opening declaration of purpose of *Der Hülferuf der deutschen Jugend* in 1841, Weitling declared that all manual labourers asserted a shared identity as *workers*, and in this capacity claimed the right to play a political role: 'We, too, claim a voice in public deliberations concerning the wellbeing of mankind; for we, the people wearing smocks, jackets, kilts, and capes, are the most numerous, the most useful, and the strongest people on God's wide Earth.'[15]

---

12 J.-P. Aguet, *Contribution à l'étude du mouvement ouvrier français. Les grèves sous la Monarchie de Juillet (1830–1847)* (Geneva: E. Droz, 1954); Seidel-Höppner, *Wilhelm Weitling*, pp. 167–78.
13 Höppner and Seidel-Höppner, 'Der Bund', p. 77.
14 P. Eiden-Offe, *Die Poesie der Klasse. Romantischer Antikapitalismus und die Erfindung des Proletariats* (Berlin: Matthes & Seitz, 2017), p. 79; see also pp. 77–93.
15 'Aufruf an Alle welche der deutschen Sprache angehören', *Der Hülferuf der Deutschen Jugend* I, 1 (1841), p. 3 (reprinted in *Der Hülferuf der deutschen Jugend. Die junge Generation. 1841–1843* (Leipzig: Zentralantiquariat der deutschen demokratischen Republik, 1972)).

He was quick to acknowledge that intellectuals possessed insights crucial to the struggle for emancipation. But against dominant assumptions that intellectuals should think, speak, and act on behalf of those working with their hands, he stressed the necessity of letting the workers speak for themselves, reflecting their own, class-specific experiences: 'Those who want to assess workers' conditions correctly need to be workers themselves; otherwise they can have no notion of the kind of toil involved.'[16] In other words, labour politics was not only politics *for* workers, but also politics *by* workers.

At first glance, this commitment to class struggle and very concrete proletarian grievances might seem at odds with the markedly religious discourse often invoked in Weitling's writings: 'A new Messiah shall come to make the teachings of the first Messiah a reality. He shall destroy the rotten construction of the old world order, lead the sources of tears into the lake of oblivion, and transform Earth into Paradise', he claimed in *Garantien der Harmonie und Freiheit*.[17] This and many other Weitling texts are full of biblical references.

Defending religion against the prevailing assumption among Young Hegelian intellectuals that the destruction of religious belief was the necessary precondition of human emancipation as such, Weitling was certainly a diligent reader of the Bible. He interpreted it earnestly, assisted by previous religious heretics such as the sixteenth-century German revolutionary Thomas Müntzer and the nineteenth-century social-Catholic preacher Félicité de Lamennais. But it would be a mistake to regard his revolutionary politics merely as a reflection of a messianic Christian vision in the century-long history of chiliasm or millennialism. Rather, it was the other way around: Weitling used biblical discourse and images to justify and convey his basically secular conception of communism as the result of workers' self-emancipation. What he gained from Müntzer was an interpretation of Christianity as sympathetic to the poor. What he gained from Lamennais had little to do with theological doctrines, but consisted, rather, in the very act of protesting social power through Christian dogma.

In addition, Weitling's religious discourse was an important part of his attempt to establish a dialogue with the manual labourers at large, starting from discourses and imaginaries already familiar to them, overcoming the scepticism against agitators and against communism instilled into workers by

---

16 'Aufruf', p. 4.
17 W. Weitling, *Garantien der Harmonie und Freiheit* (Vivis: published by the author, 1842), *Bayerische Staatsbibliothek*, https://reader.digitale-sammlungen.de/de/fs1/object/display/bsb10862497_00009.html, p. 260.

the authorities: 'Religion is not to be destroyed, but may be *used* to liberate human beings. Christianity is the religion of liberty, modesty, and enjoyment . . . Christ is the prophet of freedom, his teaching is liberty and love', he wrote in his most concerted treatment of religious questions, the book *Das Evangelium eines armen Sünders* (*The Poor Sinner's Gospel*) from 1843. In that respect, Weitling's religious discourse was a way of democratizing not only the content of social ideals, but also the strategy for constructing that future society.[18]

Praise and Persecution

Weitling's *Garantien der Harmonie und Freiheit* was disseminated through local branches of the Bund der Gerechtigkeit, was widely discussed among German radicals, and was translated into Hungarian and Norwegian during the 1840s. That book, more than anything else, secured Weitling's position as 'the founding father of German communism', as Engels put it in 1843. The young Marx was at least as jubilant. In Weitling's 'immeasurable and brilliant debut', the German proletariat had found its first crucial voice, Marx wrote in the summer of 1844, during his Parisian exile.

But the same ideas that evoked such enthusiasm in Marx caused scandal among the authorities. Under pressure from Prussia, the Swiss authorities had Weitling arrested. He was charged with blasphemy and outrage against religion, but during the course of the trial the public prosecutor emphasized Weitling's revolutionary endeavours and his participation in secret societies. This was a show trial, and its findings were publicized to great effect by the leading prosecutor Johann Caspar Bluntschi, associating Weitling and his comrades with the spectre of violent communist conspiracy and thus, in effect, announcing the existence of communism among German workers to Europe at large. Weitling was convicted and incarcerated in horrible conditions for a year, until in May 1844 he was deported to Prussia and the authorities there. He was allowed a short stay in the free city of Hamburg on condition that he would continue his journey to London and subsequently the United States.[19] Thus, Weitling became more widely known just as he was forced from the scene of action.

18 W. Weitling, *Das Evangelium eines armen Sünders* (Bern: Jenni, 1845), p. 17, *Bayerische Staatsbibliothek*, http://reader.digitale-sammlungen.de/de/fs1/object/display/bs b10777308_00005.html; Seidel-Höppner, *Wilhelm Weitling*, pp. 129–53 and 677–764; Schieder, *Anfänge*, pp. 263–300; A. Jansson, '"The pure teachings of Jesus": on the Christian language of Wilhelm Weitling's communism', *Praktyka Teoretyczna* 3 (2018), pp. 31–48.
19 F. Engels, 'Progress of Social Reform on the Continent' (1843), in *Marx Engels Collected Works* (London: Lawrence & Wishart, 2010) (hereafter *MECW*), vol. III, pp. 392–408;

Fig. 9.1   Wilhelm Weitling, 1845. (Photo by Ullstein Bild/Ullstein Bild via Getty Images.)

The trial against Weitling, and the public attention accorded that trial, also reflected a growing concern with the entire spectrum of new political positions emerging far to the left of the established framework of political debate. Weitling's ideal of a future society, as well as the strategy for reaching it, amounted to a distinct position within the debates on similar questions arising in other parts of the German-speaking public. By mapping the main positions within this field, we may gain not only a broader outlook, but also

K. Marx, 'Critical Marginal Notes on the Article "The King of Prussia and Social Reform. By a Prussian"' (1844), in *MECW*, vol. III, pp. 189–206; J. C. Bluntschi [anonymously], *Die Kommunisten in der Schweiz* (Zurich: Orell, Füssli & Co., 1843); Seidel-Höppner, *Wilhelm Weitling*, pp. 490–518, 597–659; J. Haefelin, *Wilhelm Weitling. Biographie und Theorie. Der Zürcher Kommunistenprozess von 1843* (Bern: Peter Lang, 1986); T. Pryser, 'Internasjonale "revolusjonære" strømninger i Norge 1847–1849', *Historisk Tidsskrift* 60 (1981), pp. 105–32; B. Nygaard, 'Der wichtigste kommunistische Anführer. Wilhelm Weitling und die frühe Arbeiterbewegung', in R. Hecker (ed.), *Marx, Engels und utopische Sozialisten. Beiträge zur Marx-Engels-Forschung Neue Folge 2016/17* (Hamburg: Argument, 2018), pp. 167–86; E. Gamby, *Per Götrek och 1800-talets svenska arbetarrörelse* (Stockholm: Tidens förlag, 1978), pp. 173–4 and 207.

a better grasp of the context in which Weitling strove to combine theoretical development with concrete transformative practice on the part of the workers.

Concepts: Socialism and Communism

The idea of a society characterized by a community of goods, equally shared by all members, had been around for centuries. But its restatement in a modern social context gave it new historical implications, as was evident already in Weitling's programme of the Bund der Gerechtigkeit. No longer simply a principle to be imagined or assessed on moral grounds, nor a feature of a mythical lost golden age, it was now conceived as a future stage beyond the bourgeois order. That is, the society of equality and the community of goods were conceived as an extension of the same conception of progressive social development by which bourgeois society legitimized itself against the old aristocratic or feudal order. Though it was possible at first for outside observers to dismiss the phenomenon of socialism as a purely French (or, more specifically, Parisian) problem, it was clear to many commentators that French problems very often also became problems of European civilization.

This wider historical dynamic had already been prominent in the first appearances of Saint-Simonism from the early 1830s. Not long after reports of the Saint-Simonian movement in Paris appeared in the German press, some of their core viewpoints were incorporated in public debates on the so-called social question outside France as well. In Germany, Heinrich Heine and other authors associated with the Young German movement adopted Saint-Simonian social critique, their demands for the 'rehabilitation of the flesh', and their vision of a future beyond the current denigration of labour. Similarly, Eduard Gans, the editor of Hegel's *Philosophy of Right* and a liberal professor of law in Berlin with a strong public presence even beyond German-speaking Europe, incorporated a Saint-Simonian critique of the poverty of modern workers into his overarching Hegelian account of the progressive development of state forms.[20]

20 E. M. Butler, *The Saint-Simonian Religion in Germany: A Study of the Young German Movement* (Cambridge: Cambridge University Press, 1926); S. Siebers-Gfaller, *Deutsche Pressestimmen zum Saint-Simonismus 1830–1836* (Frankfurt am Main: Peter Lang, 1992); T. Petermann, *Der Saint-Simonismus in Deutschland. Bemerkungen zur Wirkungsgeschichte* (Frankfurt am Main: Peter Lang, 1983); M. Bienenstock, 'Die "soziale Frage" im französisch-deutschen Kulturaustausch. Gans, Marx und die deutsche Saint-Simon Rezeption', in R. Blänkner et al. (eds.), *Eduard Gans (1791–1839). Politischer Professor*

The Saint-Simonians of the 1830s had used the term 'industrial association' to characterize their vision of a superior, more cohesive ('organic') society of the future. The early texts of Weitling as well as those of his closest French and German allies had described their common social aim as the community of goods (*Gütergemeinschaft*) or simply as the principle of community (*Gemeinschaft*).[21] But, around 1840, two words conceptualizing this type of society began to circulate and gain notoriety around Europe, both shaped by their specifically French uses: 'socialism' and 'communism'.

While the two concepts were often used interchangeably – as they frequently are today – they also had distinct references. 'Socialism' was predominantly associated with the Fourierist school of thought along with differing ideas of producers' co-operatives (as projected by Louis Blanc, Philippe Buchez, and others) aimed at defending independent artisanal production and the interests of consumers on more or less equal terms against big capital. 'Communism' signified the more radical ideal of the abolition of private property in favour of a true community of goods, as the French Neo-Babouvists demanded, and as Etienne Cabet idealized in his account of the utopian society Icaria. In the German-speaking parts of Europe, this distinction was reaffirmed and codified in the most authoritative account of the new French proletarian currents, Lorenz von Stein's 500-page reflective survey *Der Socialismus und Communismus des heutigen Frankreichs* (*Socialism and Communism in Present-Day France*) from 1842.[22] Weitling himself began explicitly identifying his outlook with communism around the same time, though he complained that Stein was grossly misrepresenting this principle, focusing exclusively on its violent negation of core values of established civilization and describing it only on the basis of a limited amount of publications without any real knowledge of the movements. To Weitling, this was quite contrary to the aims of true communists: 'We are not struggling against the persons, but against property.'[23]

zwischen Restauration und Vormärz (Leipzig: Leipziger Universitäts-Verlag, 2002), pp. 153–75; W. Breckman, 'Eduard Gans and the crisis of Hegelianism', *Journal of the History of Ideas* 62, 3 (2001), pp. 543–64.

21 See, for example, Weitling, *Die Menschheit*, p. 23; Weitling, *Garantien*, p. 204.

22 L. von Stein, *Der Socialismus und Communismus des heutigen Frankreichs* (Leipzig: Otto Wigand, 1842). See also J. Grandjonc, *Communisme/Kommunismus/Communism. Origine et développement international de la terminologie communautaire prémarxiste des utopistes aux néo-babouvistes*, Schriften aus dem Karl-Marx-Haus 39, 2 vols. (Trier: Karl-Marx-Haus, 1989); W. Schieder, 'Sozialismus', and W. Schieder, 'Kommunismus', in O. Brunner et al. (eds.), *Geschichtliche Grundbegriffe*, 8 vols. (Stuttgart: Klett Cotta, 1974–97), vol. v, pp. 923–96, and vol. iii, pp. 455–529. See also Chapter 8 in this volume.

23 A. Ruge, 'Zur Verständigung der Deutschen und Franzosen. Von einem Publizisten in der Fremde' (1843), in H. Pepperle and I. Pepperle (eds.), *Die hegelsche Linke. Dokumente*

The Marginalization of Artisan Communism

After his imprisonment and deportation from Switzerland, Weitling still had a following and, for most of the next decade, he was able to organize new groups of workers. But, in the wake of numerous setbacks, rival projects began to challenge his position within the Bund der Gerechtigkeit around the mid-1840s. Adherents of 'true socialism' as well as of Cabet's pacifist Icarian communism argued against revolutionary strategy and the immediate mobilization of workers. And, despite their early praise for Weitling and their basic agreement with him on questions of class struggle and communist principles, Marx and Engels also found an axe to grind with him.

This became clear during the first personal encounter between Weitling and Marx in Brussels in the spring of 1846. Though Marx had invited Weitling there to engage in the work of the newly established Communist Correspondence Committee, and relations had seemed amicable enough during the first weeks of his stay, things came to a head at a meeting of the committee on 30 March 1846. According to the memoirs of the Russian literary critic Pavel Annenkov, a non-member witnessing the meeting at Marx's invitation, Engels opened the meeting with a call for building a communist movement on 'firm theoretical foundations', only to be interrupted by Marx's inquisitive questioning of the theoretical foundations of Weitling's preachings to German workers. At first perplexed, Weitling finally retorted that his own work of preparation might prove more important to the entire cause than any armchair critique of theories far removed from the needs of the people. At this point, Annenkov recalled, Marx became so agitated that he slammed his fists onto the table, yelling: 'Ignorance never helped anyone!'[24]

Frequently recounted in later biographies of Marx and accounts of the history of socialism, this episode has been interpreted either as a decisive moment in the assertion of scientific socialism against pre-Marxist dilettantism or, conversely, as an intellectualist rejection 'from above' of the modes of thought characterizing early German proletarian communists: 'wild',

zu Philosophie und Politik im deutschen Vormärz (Leipzig: Reclam, 1985), esp. pp. 718–19; W. Weitling [anonymously], 'Ueber Komunismus und Socialismus', Die Junge Generation 2, 3 (1843) p. 36 (reprinted in Der Hülferuf der deutschen Jugend); Seidel-Höppner, Wilhelm Weitling, pp. 253 and 503–6; B. Nygaard, Det røde spøgelse. Kommunismen og 1840'ernes danske politiske kultur (Copenhagen: SFAH, 2014), pp. 79–91.
24 'Bericht P. W. Annenkows über eine Sitzung des Kommunistischen Korrespondenzkomitees in Brüssel 30. März 1846' (1880), in Förder et al. (eds.), Bund der Kommunisten, pp. 301–5.

experience-based, practice-oriented, emotional, and collectively independent 'from below'.[25]

Judging from Annenkov's account exclusively, such generalizing contrasts may appear convincing. However, his memoirs were finalized more than three decades later, and in retrospect Annenkov clearly emphasized certain elements of the events for dramatic effect. It can be difficult to square his account with the fact that Weitling had actually been rather extensively preoccupied with social theories, as noted above. More specifically, a contextual analysis of events and Weitling's own account of the specific confrontation with Marx, in a letter written to the communist intellectual Moses Hess the very day after the meeting, indicate a more complex set of reasons for the conflict with Marx.[26]

First of all, a number of more or less trivial issues made for mutual miscomprehension. Not only did Weitling and Marx only know each other's thoughts and writings very selectively. In addition, Weitling's journey to Brussels came in the wake of a longstanding campaign of slander against him carried out by his rivals within the Paris and London branches of the Bund der Gerechtigkeit – rivals who, incidentally, held views much further from Marx's than did Weitling. Even if Marx himself seemed to reject the accusations against Weitling, this campaign did some damage to the latter's reputation among communist circles in European cities. Weitling also seemed unaware that acute financial problems were haunting both Marx personally and the work of the Communist Correspondence Committee, which simply lacked the means of realizing its ambitious publication plans and was thus desperately looking for ways of attracting a sponsor. On top of all that came a certain lack of personal chemistry between the experienced, self-confident 38-year-old veteran labour organizer and the no less assertive and self-confident Engels and Marx, both about ten years younger. The latter friction was certainly to some extent rooted in the powerful tradition of separation of intellectuals from manual labourers in nineteenth-century Europe at large.[27]

---

25 See, for example, Sven-Eric Liedman, *A World to Win: The Life and Works of Karl Marx* (London: Verso, 2018), pp. 201–2; D. McLellan, *Karl Marx: His Life and Thought* (New York: Harper Colophon, 1977), pp. 155–8; Gareth Stedman Jones, *Karl Marx: Greatness and Illusion* (London: Allen Lane, 2016), pp. 212–16. The latter line of interpretation is developed most extensively in W. Schäfer, *Die unvertraute Moderne. Historische Umrisse einer andren Natur- und Sozialgeschichte* (Frankfurt am Main: Fischer, 1985), pp. 68–111.

26 Förder et al. (eds.), *Bund der Kommunisten*, pp. 305–8.

27 Seidel-Höppner, *Wilhelm Weitling*, pp. 832–60, 910–11, 926–9, 937–43; Liedman, *A World to Win*, pp. 166–72, 196–218.

There were also elements of substantial disagreement at play here, concerning differences of social analysis, strategy, and temporality. In 1846, Marx had only fairly recently realized the importance of that comprehensive critique of political economy which was to take up so much of his remaining life. Weitling had not reached similar conclusions, nor could he have known much about Marx's discoveries in those fields, since these were still mainly contained in unpublished notes and manuscripts – and in Marx's mind.

For related reasons as well as for the sake of building political alliances, Marx and Engels now rejected those strategic conceptions that had led to their initial unreserved admiration for Weitling and his achievements in the first place. In his conversion to communism in 1844, Marx had characterized communist (or 'human') revolution as the necessary condition of any real emancipation. By 1846, he and Engels were developing a strategy of distinct stages of revolution, according to which a proletarian communist revolution necessitated a prior bourgeois–democratic revolution, which, consequently, they now conceived as the immediate task of communists.[28] This would appear intuitively unacceptable to Weitling and his supporters, whose entire political *raison d'être* since the break with the bourgeois-republican faction of the Bund der Geächteten in the 1830s had been based on the social and political independence of communist workers from the bourgeoisie.

All of this, finally, was linked to differences of temporality in approaches to social analyses as well as to political strategy in general. Weitling's politics basically proceeded from workers' experiences in and of their own time, and his core political purpose was that of organizing them and establishing a dialogue with them on the basis of such experiences and their grievances. Marx and Engels were looking ahead to workers' experience and struggles under the conditions of a developed industrial capitalism, based on their own grasp of the basic contradictions and developmental tendencies of the capitalist mode of production.

A detailed reading of Marx and Engels' *Communist Manifesto* of 1848 shows agreement with Weitling on most core points. It also reveals some important elements of specific, though implicit, debt to the earlier writings of Weitling and the Bund der Gerechtigkeit – particularly concerning proletarian self-emancipation and internationalism. It is also significant, though often overlooked, that Marx proved remarkably forthcoming towards Weitling during their last encounter in London

---

28 Cf. H. Draper, *Karl Marx's Theory of Revolution*, vol. II, *The Politics of Social Classes* (New York: Monthly Review Press, 1978), pp. 177–200.

in 1849, at a time when Marx himself was moving away from his strategic conception of the necessity of a distinct stage of bourgeois–democratic revolution in favour of new conceptions of permanent revolution and proletarian class independence. Nevertheless, disagreements remained between Marx and Weitling. In addition to the above-mentioned issues, Weitling explicitly contested Marx's and Engels' conceptions of the party as organized around a sharply defined set of theoretical conceptions. By contrast, Weitling thought of the party as 'the revolutionary party of workers', that is, a less restrictively defined political grouping of the workers based on their sum of different, though related, experiences. Finally, against Marx's and Engels' anti-utopian reluctance to convey a utopian imaginary of post-capitalist society, Weitling defended the politically productive effects of appealing to workers' fantasies of social possibilities.[29]

Such differences became crucial to the marginalization of Weitling's brand of artisan communism. During 1846–7, the Bund der Gerechtigkeit leaned towards Marx and Engels. Under their auspices, the organization was renamed the Bund der Kommunisten in 1847. Disappointed, Weitling travelled on to New York, proceeding to organize German workers in the United States in a newly established Befreiungsbund (League for Liberation) that managed to acquire a few hundred members.

When the revolution broke out in Prussia in March 1848, Weitling and other militant labour leaders rose to action. He immediately made for his old home country to join the revolutionary left wing. But Berlin was not ready for Weitling's far-reaching plans. Nor did he gain support from the participants at the Congress of Democrats in that city in October 1848. Things went slightly better for him when, after General Friedrich von Wrangel had entered Berlin, he quickly made his way to Hamburg, where he managed to gather some hundreds of supporters in his German–American Befreiungsbund. But when, a few months later, the Hamburg authorities launched a campaign against heresy, he saw no other solution than to return to the United States.[30]

---

29 Seidel-Höppner, *Wilhelm Weitling*, pp. 1231–40; quote from 'Unsere Parthei', *Republik der Arbeiter*, 21 June 1851, p. 79, ibid., p. 1236.

30 Ibid., pp. 1093–1231; H.-A. Marsiske, *Eine Republik der Arbeiter ist möglich. Der Beitrag Wilhelm Weitlings zur Arbeiterbewegung in den Vereinigten Staaten von Amerika, 1846–1856* (Hamburg: Hamburger Institut für Sozialforschung, 1990), available at www.virtuella.net/ham/diss.html).

German Communism in the Diaspora

After the defeat of the 1848–9 revolutions, and with the ensuing persecution of democrats and socialists on the European continent, many German radicals resettled in London or the United States. Some continued their internal debates in increasingly marginalized emigrant circles. Others retreated from their radical positions or from politics altogether. At first, Weitling maintained his commitment to labour politics. During the first years of the 1850s, he fared comparatively well, too.

His New York-based monthly, later weekly, journal *Republik der Arbeiter* (*Republic of Workers*) began publication in January 1850 with a thousand subscribers and remained in circulation for more than five years, longer than any comparable journal. It had several corresponding writers across Europe and the Americas.[31] Concurrently, he strove to unite German workers on both sides of the Atlantic, while also revising his earlier communist doctrines along co-operativist and syndicalist lines. He played a key role in the building of a German–American fraternity, later reformed as the Arbeiterbund (Workers' League), in conjunction with a co-operative loan bank and a health insurance society for workers. And, whereas he had once rejected Fourierist and Icarian–communist strategies of building colonies as small exemplary enclaves of a better society, he now joined the small Fourierist settlement Communia in Iowa, encouraging members of the Arbeiterbund to support and invest in the settlement, thus in effect coupling Communia and the Arbeiterbund with himself as the leader of both bodies. This proved an unhappy marriage, causing friction in both quarters, and led Weitling to flee Communia and leave his role as a labour organizer behind.[32]

From the mid-1850s Weitling virtually gave up on politics, settling down with his new family and finding work as a tailor once again. Just as other veterans of German socialism and radicalism of the 1840s found solace in scientific endeavours, he began to apply his intellect to studying nature and astronomy, but had no success in convincing the world of the importance of his discoveries. His long endeavours to found a new, more rational universal language now came to fruition in a complete manuscript which, however, was only published long after his death. He corresponded with prominent

---

31 Seidel-Höppner, *Wilhelm Weitling*, pp. 1303–42. See also the complete reprint of *Republik der Arbeiter* (Vaduz: Topos Verlag, 1979).
32 Marsiske, *Eine Republik*, pp. 57–177; Seidel-Höppner, *Wilhelm Weitling*, pp. 1241–1569; Wittke, *Utopian Communist*, pp. 237–75; G. Schulz-Behrend, 'Communia, Iowa: a nineteenth-century German–American utopia', *Iowa Journal of History* 48 (1950), pp. 27–54.

scientists in the hope of earning acknowledgement for his theories of the universe and its principles. He also strove to make it as the inventor of smart additions to the new sewing machines emerging at that time, including a mechanism for sewing buttonholes and making lace – once again with little luck.[33]

Not until 1871, as the labour movement was experiencing new progress, did he re-establish contact with the movement. He was featured as a speaker at a labour meeting in New York shortly before his death in the same year. Obituaries in the new labour press were respectful, but few. While never completely forgotten as a part of the pre-history of the socialist labour movements during the following decades, he remained a rather marginal memory, too often distorted in hindsight.[34] In that respect, too, he was emblematic of early German socialism.

Further Reading

Breckman, Warren, *Marx, the Young Hegelians, and the Origins of Radical Social Theory: Dethroning the Self* (Cambridge: Cambridge University Press, 1999).

Lattek, Christine, *Refugees: German Socialism in Britain, 1840–1860* (London and New York: Routledge, 2006).

Liedman, Sven-Eric, *A World to Win: The Life and Works of Karl Marx* (London: Verso, 2018).

Schmidt, Jürgen, *Brüder, Bürger und Genossen. Die deutsche Arbeiterbewegung zwischen Klassenkampf und Bürgergesellschaft 1830–1870* (Bonn: Dietz, 2018).

Seidel-Höppner, Waltraud, *Wilhelm Weitling (1808–1871). Eine politische Biographie*, 2 vols. (Frankfurt am Main: Peter Lang, 2014).

Stedman Jones, Gareth, *Karl Marx: Greatness and Illusion* (London: Allen Lane, 2016).

Wittke, Carl, *The Utopian Communist: A Biography of Wilhelm Weitling, Nineteenth-Century Reformer* (Baton Rouge: Louisiana State University, 1950).

33 W. Weitling, *Grundzüge einer allgemeinen Denk- und Sprachlehre* (Frankfurt am Main: Peter Lang, 1991); Wittke, *Utopian Communist*, pp. 298–316; Knatz, *Utopie*, pp. 127–217; Seidel-Höppner, *Wilhelm Weitling*, pp. 1485–1560. See also C. Lattek, *Revolutionary Refugees: German Socialism in Britain, 1840–1860* (London and New York: Routledge, 2006); S. Freitag (ed.), *Exiles from European Revolutions: Refugees in Mid-Victorian England* (New York: Berghahn, 2003); C. Wittke, *Refugees of Revolution: The German Forty-Eighters in America* (Philadelphia: University of Pennsylvania Press, 1952).

34 See the brief survey of early Weitling historiography in Schäfer, *Die unvertraute Moderne*, pp. 18–41.

THE ARRIVAL OF THE HOSTILE SIBLINGS: MARXISM AND ANARCHISM

———

10

The International Working Men's Association (1864–1876/7)

FABRICE BENSIMON

The International Working Men's Association (IWMA) was the first truly international working-class organization. It was founded before the development of mass working-class parties, and it mostly gathered trade unions which numbered a few hundred or few thousand members, associations, co-operatives, and individual members. It favoured various forms of solidarity among workers: co-ordination between unions to prevent the international circulation of strike-breakers, financial support for strikes, support for political refugees. It debated and passed resolutions on many issues: some stemmed from social and economic preoccupations – from production co-operatives to land ownership and socialism, from the machine question to children's and women's labour, from the eight-hour day to universal compulsory education. It also addressed issues of international politics: it backed the Union against the Confederates in the American Civil War; it supported the emancipation of Poland and Ireland and the unification of Italy and Germany; and it opposed Germany's annexation policy in the Franco-Prussian War. It supported the 1871 Paris Commune, which was denounced by all governments. The IWMA held a foundation meeting (1864), two international conferences (1865 and 1871), and five international congresses (1866, 1867, 1868, 1869, 1872), plus several conferences that met after the split

The author thanks Michel Cordillot, Detlev Mares, Jeanne Moisand, Iorwerth Prothero, Rachel Rogers, and Marcel van der Linden for their valuable comments on earlier versions of this text.

between the 'centralists' and the 'autonomists' in 1872. Though the branches of the IWMA were largely autonomous, it had a leadership, a General Council (GC) that met weekly in London until 1872.

For a long period of time, the historiography focused on the political debates: there were Marxist and Bakuninist histories of the association, trying to establish the responsibilities for its failure.[1] The International has also been studied through the biographical works on Karl Marx and Mikhail Bakunin. A centenary conference in 1964 marked a transition to a history of the rank and file of the association.[2] Since then, an attempt to write a social and cultural history has been pursued with a series of monographs on different countries.[3] There have also been several syntheses.[4] In the socialist tradition, the association was often studied as the first in a series, in the 'age of Internationals' (1864–1943).[5] But the protagonists of the IWMA did not see it as the 'First', just as 'the' International. On the one hand, sources are plentiful. During its lifetime, the IWMA published many documents, and others were published by its enemies. Since then, the minutes of the GC and the debates of the international congresses have been published. The histories of some branches, for example, in Lyon, are also well substantiated by local records. Several newspapers were directly related to the IWMA, and they also offer some valuable insight into the lives of the sections. The material culture of the IWMA was obviously rich, with banners, flags, membership cards (see Figure 10.1), pottery, and embroidery. At the same time, we have little knowledge of the inner life of the IWMA and the workings of its branches. Few of the strikes it backed, and even fewer unions or associations, have been studied. Much has survived but it is largely scattered and often not very accessible. Although several dictionaries now

1 J. Guillaume, *L'Internationale. Documents et souvenirs (1864–1878)* (Paris: P.-V. Stock, 1905–10; reprint Vaduz: Topos Verlag, 1979); G. M. Stekloff, *History of the First International* (London: M. Lawrence, 1928).

2 *La Première Internationale. L'institution, l'implantation, le rayonnement* (Paris: CNRS, 1968).

3 H. Collins and C. Abramsky, *Karl Marx and the British Labour Movement: Years of the First International* (London: Macmillan, 1965); J. P. W. Archer, *The First International in France, 1864–1871* (Lanham, MD: University Press of America, 1997); H. Perrier, 'Idées et mouvement socialistes aux Etats-Unis, 1864–1890', PhD dissertation, Paris 8 University, France, 1984; T. Messer-Kruse, *The Yankee International: Marxism and the American Tradition, 1848–1876* (Chapel Hill: University of North Carolina Press, 1998).

4 J. Braunthal, *History of the International*, vol. 1 (London: Nelson, 1967); H. Katz, *The Emancipation of Labor: A History of the First International* (Westport, CT: Greenwood Press, 1992); M. Léonard, *L'Emancipation des travailleurs. Une histoire de la Première Internationale* (Paris: La Fabrique, 2011); M. Musto (ed.), *Workers Unite! The International 150 Years Later* (London: Bloomsbury Academic, 2014).

5 M. M. Drachkovitch (ed.), *The Revolutionary Internationals, 1864–1943* (Stanford: Stanford University Press, 1966).

include numerous members of the IWMA, there has been no prosopography, even of the GC, whose membership is known, not to mention the different branches, whose records have usually disappeared.[6] And some categories of its members, such as women, agricultural labourers, and non-workers, are little known.

This chapter summarizes what we know about the IWMA, including new perspectives on its social history. It begins with the making of the association and its original features. It then tries to sketch its growth and main developments, including in the extra-European world. It considers how the IWMA addressed international issues, and its stance on women's work and female membership. Last, it deals with the new challenges raised by the Franco-Prussian War, the Paris Commune, the rift between Marx and Bakunin, and its ultimate demise.

A New Brand of Organization

In the twenty years before the establishment of the IWMA, some attempts were made in London to gather democrats, radicals, and socialists from different countries: the Fraternal Democrats (1845–8), the International Committee (1854–6), and the International Association (1856–9).[7] But these failed to expand beyond the circles of refugees and British Chartists. While the comparative success of the IWMA from 1864 was traditionally explained by individual factors or political circumstances, structural factors are now being considered.[8] In the 1850s, the Industrial Revolution spread from Britain and Belgium to the rest of the continent, especially France and the German states. Between 1848 and 1864, much of the world was reshaped by technology and trade. Cotton production more than doubled. The global economy expanded. Telegraph cables, steamships, and railroads made both nation-states and the world smaller. International organizations such as the Red

6 E. Gianni, *L'internazionale italiana fra libertari ed evoluzionisti. I congressi della Federazione italiana e della Federazione Alta Italia dell'Associazione internazionale dei lavoratori, 1872–1880* (Milan: Pantarei, 2008); *Le Maitron. Dictionnaire biographique. Mouvement ouvrier. Mouvement social*, https://maitron.fr/; M. Cordillot, *La sociale en Amérique. Dictionnaire du mouvement social francophone aux Etats-Unis, 1848–1922* (Paris: Editions de l'Atelier, 2002); *The Dictionary of Labour Biography*, 15 vols. (London: Macmillan, 1972–2020); *The Biographical Dictionary of Modern British Radicals*, 3 vols. (Brighton: Harvester Press, 1979–88).
7 C. Lattek, *Revolutionary Refugees: German Socialism in Britain, 1840–1860* (London: Routledge, 2006); M. C. Finn, *After Chartism: Class and Nation in English Radical Politics 1848–1874* (Cambridge: Cambridge University Press, 2003).
8 M. van der Linden, 'The Rise and Fall of the First International: An Interpretation', in F. L. van Holthoon and M. van der Linden (eds.), *Internationalism in the Labour Movement, 1830–1940*, 2 vols. (Leiden: Brill, 1988), vol. I, pp. 323–35.

Cross (1863), the League of Peace and Freedom (1867), and the Universal Postal Union (1874) were created. The working and living conditions of artisans were increasingly challenged by the rise of factory production, and even in non-manufacturing sectors machinery gained ground – a much-debated issue within the IWMA. Broader economic shifts and cycles were increasingly interconnected: the 1847–8 crisis had been European, and it is often argued that the 1857 downturn was worldwide. It has even been controversially argued that a mid-century world political crisis began with the 1848–9 European revolutions, reaching China in 1851 with the Taiping rebellion, India in 1857 with the Great Mutiny, and the USA in 1861–5 with the Civil War.[9] European industrialization and urbanization also speeded up the transnational migration of workers. In the 1850s, more than 2 million people emigrated from Europe, and in the 1860s, more than 2.7 million. Intra-European migration also rose. By 1860, there were half a million foreigners in France. German workers were also numerous in Britain, Belgium, and Switzerland. An international labour market was in the making in western Europe and across the Atlantic, and in 1860 a free trade treaty was signed between France and Britain. The recruitment of strike-breaking labour overseas became established practice in Britain, for example during the strikes of the London tailors and pianoforte-makers in 1850, of the tin-plate workers in Wolverhampton in 1851 and Birmingham in 1853, and of the gas-stokers in 1859.

Trade unions and strikes multiplied in Britain, France, Belgium, and Switzerland with implications for international solidarity. In 1859, in London, the building trades went on strike and, when the employers responded by threatening to import foreign workers, the strikers wrote to foreign workingmen's associations; the Paris building workers sent help.[10] The London Society of Compositors had sent money to its counterpart in Paris both in 1852 and 1862. There had also been some attempts at bilingual journals, such as *Gutenberg* for the printers, and *The Innovator or Boot and Shoemaker's Monitor*.[11] In the spring of 1864, there was also a strike of the Limoges porcelain makers who appealed to the Staffordshire potters for help. Learning about the struggle from a socialist in exile, newspapers such as *The Bee-Hive* (London) and organizations such as the London Trades' Council

9 C. Bayly, *The Birth of the Modern World 1780–1914: Global Connections and Comparisons* (Oxford: Blackwell, 2004).
10 *The Bee-Hive*, 16 July 1864, p. 5.
11 I. Prothero, *Radical Artisans in England and France, 1830–1870* (Cambridge: Cambridge University Press, 1997), p. 116.

took up the case. In May 1864 in France, the Ollivier law recognized the *'droit de coalition'*, the right to strike, which had existed in Britain since 1824.

International exhibitions were another feature of the age. In 1862, for the Great London Exposition, Napoleon III sponsored the travel costs of French workers. Some of them met British trade unionists there, and these contacts continued to be maintained. Some causes also played a unifying role. Polish independence and the Italian *Risorgimento* were common sources of indignation and grounds for protest. Following the Polish Rising of 1863, a National League for Polish Independence was set up in London and organized a meeting on 22 July, attended by some French delegates, including Henri Tolain, a bronze-chaser with Proudhonist leanings. In 1864, when Giuseppe Garibaldi visited Britain, he was welcomed by huge crowds, including a French delegation, shouting 'Garibaldi forever'. In November 1863, the leaders of the trade unions in London published a statement, 'To the Workmen of France from the Working Men of England'.[12] There had been similar texts before, and the issue raised by the document – 'to bring up the wages of the ill paid to as near a level as possible with those who are better remunerated' – had limited appeal in the French labour movement, which was still heavily dominated by artisans with little taste for strike action. In Tolain's reply, the issue was couched in terms of the independent artisan threatened by high finance. Yet, despite such divergences, he expressed class solidarity.

The founding meeting of the IWMA in St Martin's Hall, London, on 28 September 1864 had been convened by George Odger, secretary of the London Trades Council. It gathered some 2,000 people, including French delegates such as Tolain, Blaise Perrachon, and Antoine Limousin, French refugees such as Victor Le Lubez, German refugees such as Johann Eccarius and Marx, and, for the London Italian Workingmen's Association, Louis Wolff and G. P. Fontana. It was chaired by history professor Edward Spenser Beesly, a positivist with early anti-imperialist views.[13] The British trade union leaders (Odger, but also the bricklayer George Howell and the carpenter Randal Cremer), Owenites such as John Weston, and former Chartists also took part. The meeting went largely unnoticed, and *The Times* derisively reported that 'good wishes were expressed for all the oppressed of the earth, from the Irish to the Hindoos, and one speaker went so far as to advocate the

---

12 *The Bee-Hive*, 5 December 1863.

13 G. Claeys, *Imperial Sceptics: British Critics of Empire 1850–1920* (Cambridge: Cambridge University Press, 2010).

restoration of Gibraltar to Spain'.[14] Those gathered had decided to create the IWMA, which was to be based in London, with a committee to write a programme and a constitution.

Quite soon, the *Inaugural Address of the IWMA* was circulated. The text, written by Marx with wit and vigour, was both political and economic.[15] It argued that 'everywhere the great mass of the working classes were sinking down to a lower depth, at the same rate at least that those above them were rising in the social scale'. It denounced 'British industry, which, vampirelike, could but live by sucking blood, and children's blood, too', as well as the 'infamous crusade for the perpetuation and propagation of slavery' in the United States and 'heroic Poland being assassinated by Russia'. In some respects, it resembled the 1848 *Communist Manifesto* which Marx had written with Friedrich Engels for the Communist League, and it ended with the same war cry: 'Proletarians of all countries, unite!'[16] The emphasis on class was to play a part in the dynamism of the association, but also meant that some, such as Giuseppe Mazzini, Louis Blanc, or neo-Babouvist worker Joseph Benoit, refused to join, as they thought that all social classes should unite. At the same time, the address acknowledged the political diversity of the embryonic IWMA. It paid tribute to the Owenites and the 'co-operative movement', which showed that, 'to bear fruit, the means of labour need not be monopolised as a means of dominion over, and of extortion against, the labouring man himself', while highlighting its limits. The address ended with a rallying call to the working classes to 'conquer political power'.

In October 1864, Marx also wrote some provisional general rules, a brief text beginning with the famous formula, 'that the emancipation of the working classes must be conquered by the working classes themselves, that the struggle for the emancipation of the working classes means not a struggle for class privileges and monopolies, but for equal rights and duties, and the abolition of all class rule'.[17] Among other things, the rules stipulated that an annual congress with delegates should meet, and a GC elected by the congress and composed of 'workingmen from the different counties' would be created. The GC was to act as 'an internal agency' for information and mutual support. Societies that joined the IWMA could 'preserve their

---

14 *The Times*, 5 October 1864, p. 9.
15 *Inaugural Address and Provisional Rules of the International Working Men's Association, along with the 'General Rules'* (London, 1864).
16 Often rendered in English as 'Workers of the world, unite!'
17 *Address and Provisional Rules of the Working Men's International Association* (London, November 1864).

existent organizations intact'. In the absence of a British section, the GC also oversaw the activities of the association in Britain. Out of a total of fifty members, it first numbered twenty-one British, ten Germans, nine Frenchmen, six Italians, two Poles, and two Swiss. Its membership changed considerably over time.

Though Marx was not the initiator of the IWMA, he played a leading role from its inception. In London, he had mostly stayed aloof from refugee circles. In 1864 he decided to get involved: 'I knew that on this occasion "people who really count" were appearing, both from London and from Paris, and I therefore decided to waive my usual standing rule to decline any such invitations . . . there is now evidently a revival of the working classes taking place.'[18] From then on, and until 1872, he was a prominent figure of the GC and the main inspiration of the International.

However, the IWMA was not 'Marxist'. Many in the different branches and in the GC held differing views. Marx held no official position, and in 1866 he declined an invitation to become its president.[19] He attended the conferences in 1865 and 1871 and the congress in 1872 and, although he was absent from the four congresses from 1866 to 1869, his politics was nevertheless influential in these. He attended the meetings of the GC, corresponded with many activists, and wrote several of the most important texts. He presented arguments in a dynamic, sometimes moving way. He wrote virtually all the policy documents issued by the GC. He both determined key topics and gave some meaning to events.[20] Although he was little known to the members of the different sections, except among the London trade unionists and among the German refugees, he became the driving force of the organization. He was also a point of convergence between different trends, bringing together disparate strands of the movement. At the same time, Marx never backed away when he thought the issue was important. And he was involved in the practical, day-to-day business of the International. In 1865, while organizing international solidarity in many cases, he argued that 'the working class ought not to exaggerate to themselves the ultimate working of these

18 Marx to Engels, 4 November 1864, in K. Marx and F. Engels, *Marx Engels Collected Works* (London: Lawrence & Wishart, 2010) (hereafter *MECW*), vol. XLII, p. 16.

19 *Marx–Engels Gesamtausgabe* (Berlin: Dietz, 1975) (hereafter *MEGA*²), vol. I/21, pp. 1200–18, quoted in J. Herres, 'Karl Marx and the IWMA Revisited', in F. Bensimon, Q. Deluermoz, and J. Moisand (eds.), *'Arise Ye Wretched of the Earth': The First International in a Global Perspective* (Leiden and Boston: Brill, 2018), p. 305.

20 Herres, 'Karl Marx and the IWMA Revisited', pp. 299–312; D. Mares, 'Dialektische Endlosspirale. Karl Marx in der Internationalen Arbeiterassoziation (1864–1872)', in M. Endreß and C. Jansen (eds.), *Karl Marx im 21. Jahrhundert. Bilanz und Perspektiven* (Frankfurt and New York: Campus, 2020), pp. 155–79.

everyday struggles': 'Instead of the *conservative* motto: *A fair day's wage for a fair day's work!*', he argued, 'they ought to inscribe on their banner the *revolutionary* watchword: *'Abolition of the wages system!'*[21] He helped the members to transcend their local, national, or trade identities, as printers, shoemakers, or carpenters, to forge a sense of class cohesion.

A Resistible Growth

Periodizing the history of the IWMA is tricky, as each national branch had a separate chronology. However, the association had its own dynamics, which depended on its membership and geographical reach across the continent, and on its inner workings. Most members joined in groups, especially in trade unions. There were no real working-class parties then, if one excepts the Lassallean Allgemeiner Deutscher Arbeiter-Verein (German Workers' General Association, ADAV) in Germany, which did not join. At the same time, trade unions already counted some 800,000 members in Britain, and were making progress in many countries; 'the unions mesmerise the masses of the workers', Marx noted.[22] The association was first and foremost made of these burgeoning unions. Marcello Musto has suggested four stages:

(1) the early days, from its foundation to the first congress in Geneva in September 1866;
(2) the period of expansion (1866–70);
(3) the revolutionary surge and the repression following the Paris Commune (1871–2);
(4) the split and crisis (1872–7).[23]

This is a starting point for considering the stages of development of the IWMA.

From 1864 to 1867, the association, which was – according to French internationalist Auguste Bibal – 'a child born in the Paris workshops and nursed in London', expanded mostly in these two countries. In Britain, of the forty-one member trade unions, three joined in 1865, twenty in 1866, and twelve in 1867.[24] All in all, by 1867, the IWMA may have numbered 40,000

21 K. Marx, *Value, Price and Profit*, which was originally a report read by Marx to the GC on 20 and 27 June 1865: *MECW*, vol. xx, pp. 101–49.
22 *MEGA²*, vol. 1/21, pp. 906–7 and 2141–4, quoted in Herres, 'Karl Marx and the IWMA Revisited', p. 307.
23 M. Musto, 'Introduction', in Musto (ed.), *Workers Unite!*
24 Cited in Edouard Fribourg, *L'Association internationale des travailleurs* (Paris: A. Le Chevalier, 1871), no. 10, p. 151; K. Robinson, 'Karl Marx, the International Working

members in Britain, and fewer than 1,000 in Ireland.[25] In France, seven branches were founded in 1865, at least seventeen in 1866, and eleven in 1867, though many of these were very small or short-lived.[26] Paris numbered between 500 and 1,000 members; Lyon, Vienne, and Caen each had about 500 in 1867, and other towns had a few dozen members at most. In 1865, the IWMA held a conference in London (25–9 September) which prepared the later congress, and debated Poland and religion. In September 1866, the first congress was held in Geneva. A major dispute occurred over trade unions and strikes. While the British members of the GC thought such events were integral to workers' emancipation, many Proudhonists, who had a strong following in France, Romandy, Wallonia, and Brussels, opposed strike action, instead advocating the establishment of co-operatives and a central people's bank.[27] In 1866, Marx – in the name of the GC – drew attention to the limits of 'the co-operative system [which] will never transform capitalist society'.[28] The GC also insisted on the struggle for the eight-hour working day, for restrictions on nightwork, and for the rights of 'children and juvenile persons', whose labour, driven by capitalism, was 'an abomination' and whose parents were turned into 'slave-holders, sellers of their own children'. This direction was approved at the Geneva Congress (1866), putting the Proudhonists into a minority.

From 1866 to 1870, the IWMA benefited from the upturn in working-class militancy, with strikes taking place in Britain (tailors in 1866), France, Belgium (Marchiennes miners in 1867, Charleroi miners in 1868, Seraing puddlers in 1869), and Switzerland (Geneva construction workers in 1868). Support lent to the bronze workers (1867) and the Paris tailors gave the IWMA great prestige. In 1869, the strike of the Paris leather-dressers drew support from Paris trades and radicals.[29] The association gained new

Men's Association, and London Radicalism, 1864–1872', PhD dissertation, University of Manchester, UK, 1976, pp. 75–6.

25 Ibid., p. 79.

26 J. Rougerie, 'Les sections françaises de l'Association internationale des travailleurs', in La Première Internationale, p. 97.

27 P. J. Proudhon, De la capacité politique des classes ouvrières (Paris: n. p., 1865), p. 428; S. Hayat, 'The Construction of Proudhonism within the IWMA', in Bensimon et al. (eds.), 'Arise Ye Wretched of the Earth', pp. 313–31.

28 K. Marx, 'Instructions for the Delegates of the Provisional General Council', first published in Der Vorbote, Nos. 10 and 11, October and November 1866, and International Courier Nos. 6/7, 20 February 1867, and Nos. 8/10, 13 March 1867, in MECW, vol. XX, pp. 185–94.

29 A. Dalotel, A. Faure, and J.-C. Freiermuth, Aux origines de la Commune. Le mouvement des réunions publiques à Paris 1868–1870 (Paris: Maspero, 1980); M. Cordillot, Aux origines du socialisme moderne. La première internationale, la Commune de Paris, l'exil (Paris: Editions de l'Atelier/Editions ouvrières, 2010); J. Rougerie, Eugène Varlin. Aux origines du mouvement ouvrier (Paris: Editions du Détour, 2019).

branches and new members. In France, it reached a peak in 1869, with a few tens of thousands.[30] In Switzerland, it made rapid progress, thanks to the presence of many exiles and the activity of the German Johann Philipp Becker. First created in Geneva, the association then spread to Romandy and the threatened watch industry. When it met in Geneva in September 1866, the sixty delegates came from Britain, France, Germany, and Switzerland. In two years, the association had gathered some 100 different unions and, by 1870, it totalled some 6,000 members.

In Belgium, the first steps had been made in 1865. The main socialist thinker, César De Paepe, a typographer and proof-reader, had attended the London Conference. By 1867, there were still only two branches, in Brussels and Patignies. It was in 1868 that the International took off, thanks to the Brussels Conference, which numbered fifty-eight 'Belgian' delegates, but above all following strikes at L'Epine and Charleroi, where ten workers were killed by the army. Brussels activists created fifteen sections in the Hainaut, with Verviers, a large manufacturing centre, becoming the most important group. By the spring of 1869, there were some 10,000 members.

In Germany, the development of the association did not rely on unions as much as on the political propaganda within the ADAV and the Sächsische Volkspartei (Saxon People's Party). Along with Marx, August Bebel and Wilhelm Liebknecht in 1869 founded the Sozialdemokratische Arbeiterpartei Deutschlands (Social Democratic Workers' Party, SDAP), which sympathized with the IWMA. Due to legal restrictions, it called on its 14,000 members to join individually.

The third congress in Brussels (6–13 September 1868) also drew delegates from Italy and Spain. In Spain, the IWMA had been reported on from 1865, but the first groups were created following the September 1868 revolution, especially in Barcelona and Madrid. Italian activist Giuseppe Fanelli was sent by the Geneva branch (led by Bakunin) and played a prominent part in the establishment of the first groups late in 1868 and early in 1869. In 1870, a workers' conference in Barcelona created the Spanish Regional Federation, the FRE-IWMA, which was boosted by the Paris Commune and remained active until 1881. Its principal base was Catalonia, especially Barcelona, and it remained predominantly led by anarchists. It numbered 10,000 members by April 1872.[31] In Italy, Mazzini and his circle were critical of

---

30 Rougerie, 'Les sections françaises', p. 111.
31 A. Garcia-Balañà, '1871 in Spain: Transnational and Local History in the Formation of the FRE-IWMA', in Bensimon et al. (eds.), 'Arise Ye Wretched of the Earth', pp. 221–37.

the IWMA, but Garibaldi was supportive, especially from 1871. The first section was created in 1869, and the inaugural conference was held in 1872, followed by other conferences until 1880. The most notable period of growth also followed the Commune when sections and regional federations created a dense web, especially in the towns of Tuscany and the Romagna, and in the industrializing environments of Milan, Biella, and more marginally Turin. Based in Naples from 1871, Carlo Cafiero was the GC's correspondent in Italy. He later translated *Capital* in an abridged Italian version but, insisting on the autonomy of the branches, he became disillusioned with Marx and Engels and followed Bakunin in 1872 (see below). By 1874, Italy officially boasted 32,450 IWMA members.[32]

The 1868 Brussels Congress moved the IWMA in a socialist direction by passing resolutions on the collectivization of the means of production. This was confirmed in the following congress in Basel (5–12 September 1869). In France, the IWMA was now dominated by the collectivists (or communists), rather than the mutualists, who favoured a co-operative system and opposed political intervention and strike action. In his struggle against mutualists, Marx had been able to rely upon the British trade unionists. By the late 1860s, however, the growth of the association in Britain was limited. Among the French, while a few delegates, including Tolain, voted against a text which declared that 'society has the right to abolish individual ownership of the land and to make it part of the community',[33] a majority voted for it. The French federation was now led by men such as Eugène Varlin and Benoît Malon. New sections were created in Marseille, Aix-en-Provence, La Ciotat, and elsewhere in the south, in Lille, Roubaix, and Tourcoing in the north, in several towns around Rouen, and in Le Creusot, following a strike of the steelworkers in March 1870.

By then, the IWMA had created a network of communications, with letters, articles, and texts being circulated among the different branches. With the membership of unions and branches, it was soon not just cosmopolitan but truly international. Whereas in its early years the IWMA had aroused little interest from governments, by the late 1860s it was raising alarm among those who believed that it was responsible for domestic strife. The leaders of the Paris branch were prosecuted in November 1867, May 1868, and May 1870. In Belgium, in 1869, following several strikes,

32 C. Levy, 'The Italians and the IWMA', in Bensimon et al. (eds.), '*Arise Ye Wretched of the Earth*', p. 209.
33 J. Freymond, *La Première Internationale. Recueil de documents* (Geneva: Droz, 1962), vol. II, p. 74.

Charles-Victor de Bavay, Brussels' public prosecutor, wanted to 'strike the bandits hard' and close the IWMA; several leaders were arrested, and branches were searched.[34] The association had now become more than a scapegoat, a bit like a 'spectre haunting Europe'. Police spy Oscar Testut argued in 1871 that it had become 'a real state, with its central government, its budget, its loans, its ministers, its ambassadors, its representatives, its states general, its cantonal, provincial or regional assembles, its ballots, its civil servants with special prerogatives'.[35]

What was the total membership of the IWMA? By 1871–2, estimates varied from 800,000 to 2.5 million members, and Testut predicted it would rise to 5 million.[36] It is difficult to establish reliable figures. In fact, by 1871–2, the IWMA probably did not exceed a cumulative total of 150,000 members. This is smaller than the figure commonly cited; for instance, well-informed historian Jan Dhondt in 1968 estimated 100,000 Belgian members, whereas more recently Jean Puissant and Freddy Joris put the number at no more than 10,000.[37] This discrepancy and others can be explained by different levels of involvement. Michel Cordillot suggests a distinction between three circles: first, a few tens of thousands of individual members who paid dues; second, hundreds of thousands who joined collectively and often temporarily through their union, or with a vote in a strike; third, large masses of workers who, without being members, sympathized with the IWMA and were ready to call upon it for help.

The IWMA was mostly rooted in France, Britain, Belgium, Switzerland, Italy, and Spain, and in the United States, although it included some small groups in the Netherlands (fewer than 1,000 members in 1872), Denmark and Austria-Hungary (a few thousand each), and Portugal (fewer than 1,000).[38] It also hosted refugees from eastern Europe (Poland, Russia,

34 J. Puissant, 'The IWMA in Belgium (1865–1875)', in Bensimon et al. (eds.), *'Arise Ye Wretched of the Earth'*, pp. 152–3.

35 O. Testut, *Le Livre bleu de l'Internationale* (Paris: E. Lachaud, 1871); O. Testut, *L'Internationale. Son origine, son but, son caractère* (Paris: E. Lachaud, 1871).

36 O. Testut, *L'Association internationale des travailleurs* (Lyon: Vingtrinier, 1870), p. 310.

37 J. Dhondt and C. Oukhow, 'Belgique', in *La Première Internationale*, pp. 151–65; Puissant, 'The IWMA in Belgium', p. 151.

38 J. Giele, *De Eerste Internationale in Nederland. Een onderzoek naar het ontstaan van de Nederlandse arbeidersbeweging van 1868 tot 1876* (Nijmegen: SUN, 1973); J. Engberg (ed.), *Den Internationale Arbejderforening for Danmark*, 2 vols. (Copenhagen: Selskabet til forskning i arbejderbevaegelsens historie, 1985, 1992); S. Daly, *Ireland and the First International* (Cork: Tower Books, 1984); H. Steiner, 'Die Internationale Arbeiter Association und die österreichische Arbeiterbewegung', *Archiv für Sozialgeschichte* 4 (1964), pp. 447–513; C. Da Fonseca, *A Origem de la Internacional em Lisboa* (Lisbon: Estampa, 1978); B. Bayerlein, 'La Première Internationale au Portugal, vue à travers la correspondance internationale, particulièrement celle avec le Conseil général', in

Austria-Hungary) within its ranks. In addition, it had branches in Montevideo, Uruguay, from 1872, in Argentina in Buenos Aires from 1870, and in Mexico from 1871. In these three countries, printers played a significant role.[39] In 1872, W. E. Harcourt, a delegate from the Democratic Association, in Victoria, Australia, attended meetings of the GC in London; other Australian colonies were not represented. Some Italian anarchists also founded a section in Egypt, though only in 1876.[40]

Gaining members was not enough. Right from the start, the GC was also busy securing the publication of newspapers. As early as November 1864, it adopted *The Bee-Hive* as the official organ for IWMA publications. When the GC was dissatisfied with its content, they tried and failed to take it over, and they acquired a less influential paper which they renamed *Commonwealth* – which was in fact edited by the leaders of the London Trades Council.[41] In Belgium, a weekly paper published in Verviers became the 'organ of the IWMA' from December 1867; Flemish papers such as *De Werker* (*The Worker*, Antwerp) and *Peper en Zout* (*Pepper and Salt*, Bruges) were also linked to the IWMA. In Switzerland, *Der Vorbote* (*The Harbinger*, 1866), *L'Egalité* (*Equality*, 1869), and *Tagwacht* (*The Daytime Vigil*, 1870) were created by different local sections of the IWMA. In France, *La Tribune ouvrière* (*The Workers' Tribune*), *Le Courrier français* (*The French Post*), *Le Travail* (*Labour*), *La République des travailleurs* (*The Workers' Republic*), and *La Marseillaise* (a daily with a print-run of 50,000) were either published by the Internationalists or offered them free copies. In the USA, the periodicals the *International Herald* and *Woodhull and Claflin's Weekly* were mouthpieces for the IWMA, though the first advocated spiritualism, international languages, and the colonization of Mars, and the latter reported spirit manifestations, and espoused mesmerism and supernaturalism.[42] *La Federación* (*The Federation*) was published by workers' societies in Barcelona from 1869, and *La Solidaridad* (*Solidarity*)

Fondation Calouste Gulbenkian, *Utopie et socialisme au Portugal au xixe siècle* (Paris: Touzot, 1982), pp. 479–534.
39 H. Tarcus, 'The First International in Latin America', in Bensimon et al. (eds.), *'Arise Ye Wretched of the Earth'*, pp. 253–69.
40 A. Gorman, '"Diverse in Race, Religion and Nationality . . . But United in Aspirations of Civil Progress": The Anarchist Movement in Egypt 1860–1940', in S. Hirsch and L. van der Walt (eds.), *Anarchism and Syndicalism in the Colonial and Postcolonial World, 1870–1940* (Leiden: Brill, 2011), pp. 1–31.
41 D. Mares, 'Little Local Difficulties? The General Council of the IWMA as an Arena for British Radical Politics', in Bensimon et al. (eds.), *'Arise Ye Wretched of the Earth'*, p. 49.
42 A. Taylor, '"Sectarian Secret Wisdom" and Nineteenth-Century Radicalism: The IWMA in London and New York', in Bensimon et al. (eds.), *'Arise Ye Wretched of the Earth'*, p. 290.

from 1871. The heterogeneity of the IWMA press reflected the diversity of the association.[43] But it was essential in strengthening a movement that was public and open for the most part. I will return to the later developments of the IWMA, but I now want to focus on two of these: strike solidarity and international politics.

Organizing Solidarity, Addressing International Issues

Strike solidarity was one of the main benefits of the IWMA to workers. After all, capital was international, and transfers of money across borders were part and parcel of the solidarity that the IWMA wanted to implement among workers. However, money issues raised certain questions and surfaced again and again in internal discussions. First, the GC tried to raise some funds of its own. These sums were not huge. In 1866–7, the British sections contributed £56 (equivalent to the annual wages of a skilled worker), the French £30, and the Swiss £8.[44] Although the rules stated that there are 'no rights without duties, no duties without rights', General Secretary Eccarius explained in 1871 that 'there are many sections that feature more in the minutes than in the accounting books'.[45] In theory, workers contributed to their sections and to the GC, which required that each member should contribute one penny a year; in practice, the GC was pragmatic and granted discounts when the expansion of the association was at stake.

The finances of the GC were only part of a much wider circulation of money via the IWMA. It organized mutual assistance in the form of aid and donations. The GC circulated information, co-ordinated subscriptions among branches, and issued loans. Loans were often seen as a more egalitarian practice than donations, as they were more respectful of the autonomy of the groups.[46] But they had to be repaid, which sometimes proved difficult. Money matters were also complicated by the debates between the centralists and the autonomists, that is, between the followers of Marx and those of Bakunin. Just like the police in several countries, which believed the IWMA had huge reserves, some branches overestimated the capacity of the GC. At

---

43 *Répertoire international des sources pour l'étude des mouvements sociaux aux xixe et xxe siècle*, vol. i, in *La Première Internationale. Périodiques 1864–1877* (Paris: A. Colin, 1958).

44 Freymond, *La Première Internationale*, vol. i, pp. 163–73.   45 Ibid., vol. ii, p. 177.

46 N. Delalande, 'Transnational Solidarity in the Making: Labour Strikes, Money Flows, and the First International, 1864–1872', in Bensimon et al. (eds.), *'Arise Ye Wretched of the Earth'*, p. 84; N. Delalande, *La Lutte et l'Entraide. L'âge des solidarités ouvrières* (Paris: Editions du Seuil, 2019).

the same time, the GC also wanted to contribute – this was in line with efforts to prevent strike-breaking through the mobilization of foreign labour; during the Creusot strike of 1870, for instance, Marx noted that 'from everywhere money was sent, and it would have a bad effect if London sent only words'.[47] When a strike occurred in Sotteville-lès-Rouen in 1869, 2,500 francs (£100) was collected, including 500 (£20) from London. There were also practical obstacles, as it took time to physically transfer the money, especially when activists were under police surveillance. And trustworthy intermediaries had to be found. All in all, the circulation of money proved to be a protracted issue. But such flows 'produced bonds of solidarity and interdependence', particularly at a time when most labour movements were in their infancy.[48] The IWMA gradually disseminated the idea of transnational solidarity, to the point that some strikers joined the association to benefit from financial solidarity.[49]

The cigar-makers constitute a good case study: they operated within a transnational labour market, especially in Britain, Germany, Belgium, the Netherlands, and the USA. They travelled a lot, both nationally and internationally. Like other workers whose independent status was threatened, they were politicized. They tried to regulate their cross-border labour market; that is why they were active in the IWMA, to prevent both strike-breaking and wage-cutting from abroad. They featured prominently in the local branches of Amsterdam, Antwerp, London, and New York. One of them, James Cohn, was a member of the GC. Several of their strikes benefited from international solidarity.[50]

The IWMA did not focus solely on workers' struggles. It addressed international issues such as national emancipation, slavery and the civil war in the USA, war and peace, the republic in France, and the Paris Commune. At the time interest in international politics was widespread across Europe. This was fostered by the rise of literacy, the growth of newspapers with a wide circulation, and the development of the telegraph network. But there was more. As we have seen, supporting the Polish cause was part and parcel

47 Meeting of 26 April 1870, in *The General Council of the First International* (Moscow: Foreign Languages Publishing House, 1970), vol. IV, p. 229.
48 Delalande, 'Transnational Solidarity'.
49 C. Auzias and A. Houel, *La grève des ovalistes. Lyon, juin–juillet 1869* (Paris: Atelier de création libertaire, 1982).
50 A. Knotter, 'Transnational cigar-makers: cross-border labour markets, strikes, and solidarity at the time of the First International (1864–1873)', *International Review of Social History* 59 (2014), pp. 409–42.

of the creation of the IWMA. In a way, it was not just the result of the blossoming labour movement, but also the belated product of the 'spring-time of the peoples', with its aspirations to national emancipation. The *Inaugural Address* insisted that 'The fight for such a foreign policy forms part of the general struggle for the emancipation of the working classes.'[51] However, the Polish cause became a bone of contention. Marx and the British trade unionists believed that the alliance of Russia, Austria, and Prussia was essential to preserving the old order in Europe. Pierre-Joseph Proudhon had opposed the reconstruction of independent Poland and argued that its partition was a historical necessity, and after 1865 Proudhonists refused any 'political' involvement.[52] This was debated during the 1865 conference, when several delegates unsuccessfully opposed the association's stance supporting the emancipation of Poland. At least ten Poles belonged to the GC and were signatories of key documents, although they did not belong to its leading circles.[53] The members of the Polish section in London were the most radical democrats within the Polish community in exile, and had devised a programme of national reconstruction and socialism.

More unexpectedly, given the support within British public opinion of the British hold on Ireland, the IWMA also supported the sovereignty of Ireland, although there was little consensus on the means of achieving it. In 1867, when a short-lived Fenian insurrection took place, the GC was presented with a resolution asserting 'Ireland's right to autonomy', yet dissenting voices rejected political violence. The issue was raised again two years later when British prime minister William Gladstone refused to grant amnesty to Fenian prisoners. Such disagreements probably limited the capacity of the association to act on Ireland, but its official position remained: 'Therefore the International Association's attitude to the Irish question is absolutely clear. Its first need is to press on with the social revolution in England, and to that end, the major blow must be struck in Ireland.'[54]

When the IWMA was created, the American Civil War was still raging. While the British government had leaned towards the Confederates, there

51 *Inaugural Address.*
52 P. J. Proudhon, *Si les traités de 1815 ont cessé d'exister. Actes du futur congrès* (Paris: n.p., 1863).
53 K. Marchlewicz, 'For Independent Poland and Emancipation of the Working Class: The Poles in the IWMA, 1864–1876', in Bensimon et al. (eds,), *'Arise Ye Wretched of the Earth'*, p. 185.
54 'The General Council to the Federal Council of French Switzerland', 1 January 1870, first published in *Les prétendues scissions dans l'Internationale*, 1872. On the Irish question, see Mares, 'Little Local Difficulties?', pp. 42–5, and Daly, *Ireland and the First International.*

had been widespread support from the trade unions for the cause of the Union, despite the impact of the blockade on imports of Confederate cotton, which resulted in a major crisis in Lancashire. Following John Brown's attempted uprising and a slave rebellion in Missouri, Marx had written that 'the most momentous thing happening in the world today is the slave movement'.[55] When President Abraham Lincoln was re-elected in November 1864, the GC approved a congratulatory message: 'the triumphant war cry of your re-election is Death to Slavery'.[56] And when he was assassinated, the IWMA sent another address to his successor, Andrew Johnson, castigating the 'sycophants who … stick to their Sisyphus work of morally assassinating Abraham Lincoln … rival with each other to strew rhetorical flowers on his open grave'.[57] The association congratulated the people of the USA for abolishing slavery, while calling for a further step: 'We warn you then, as brothers in the common cause, to remove every shackle from freedom's limb, and your victory will be complete'.[58] Although the IWMA did not specifically try to organize African-Americans, several of its members were prominent in the fight against segregation.[59] When internationalist Victoria Woodhull ran for president, former slave Frederick Douglass was nominated by the Equal Rights Party as her running mate, a nomination he did not accept.

Where did the IWMA stand on colonialism? In its day, anti-colonialism existed neither as a structured political tendency, nor as a defined political ideology. Those who, in the UK or France, opposed colonial expansion did so on the ground of cost v. benefit. Marx was critical of colonial atrocities, such as in India in 1857, and at the same time he believed that extra-European societies could move forward if they followed Europe's path of industrial development.[60] The IWMA did not denounce the colonial system as such. But it denounced Russian, Austrian, and Prussian rule in Poland, as well as British rule in Ireland. It did not have branches in other colonial spaces. When a rising of former slaves

55 Marx to Engels, 11 January 1860, in *MECW*, vol. XLI, p. 3.
56 K. Marx, 'To Abraham Lincoln, President of the United States of America', approved by the GC on 29 November 1864 and first published in *The Daily News*, 23 December 1864, in *MECW*, vol. XX, p. 19.
57 K. Marx, 'Address from the IWMA to President Johnson', approved by the GC on 9 May 1865 and published in *The Bee-Hive*, 20 May 1865, in *MECW*, vol. XX, p. 99.
58 'To the People of the United States of America', *The Workman's Advocate*, 14 October 1865, reproduced in *The General Council of the First International*, vol. I, p. 312.
59 R. Blackburn, *An Unfinished Revolution: Karl Marx and Abraham Lincoln* (London and New York: Verso, 2011).
60 G. S. Jones, 'Radicalism and the Extra-European World: The Case of Karl Marx', in D. Bell (ed.), *Victorian Visions of Global Order: Empire and International Relations in Nineteenth-Century Political Thought* (Cambridge: Cambridge University Press, 2009), pp. 186–214.

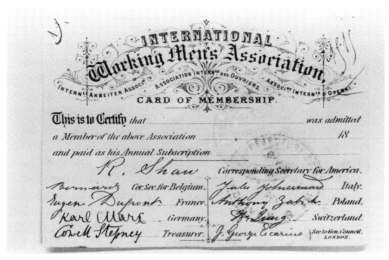

Fig. 10.1 Hermann Jung's IWMA membership card, 1869. Jung (1830–1901), who paid two shillings for his annual subscription in 1869, was a Swiss watchmaker who had emigrated to London after the 1848–9 revolution in Germany in which he had been involved. (Hermann Jung Papers, International Institute of Social History, Amsterdam.)

was brutally suppressed by the governor of Jamaica in 1865, the *International Herald* campaigned against the British government's meeting the governor's legal fees.[61] In Cuba, a separatist insurgency lasted for ten years (1868–78) and was defeated only by a contingent of 180,000 Spanish soldiers; the Spanish Federation failed to establish contact with Cuban workers, but internationalists in New York sent 'a message of solidarity' to the insurgents.[62] There was an insurrection of former slaves against white land-owners in Martinique in September 1870, and a major anti-colonial uprising in Algeria in 1871. The IWMA does not appear to have had branches in either of these territories. Spanish sailors involved in the cantonalist insurrection of July 1873 in Cartagena and in the IWMA were imprisoned for insubordination in the penal colony of La Havana; 71 cantonalists and former members of the IWMA were deported to Fernando Po, and 1,076 others to the Philippines, where they were put into the service of the colonial navy, suppressing natives' attempts to resist

---

61 Taylor, '"Sectarian Secret Wisdom"', p. 294.
62 J. Moisand, 'Revolutions, Republics and the IWMA in the Spanish Empire (around 1873)', in Bensimon et al. (eds.), '*Arise Ye Wretched of the Earth*', p. 249.

colonization.[63] But, as in the case of the Communards deported to New Caledonia, this was beyond the reach of the IWMA.

In a nutshell, the IWMA, whose members were mostly based in industrializing countries, was not dedicated to the struggle against colonialism. But when it did address these issues, its stance was more progressive than other sections of society. This was also the case in relation to women.

Women and Gender in the Association

In 1864, in western Europe and the USA, elections and parliamentary politics were male preserves. The women's movement was just in the making, with some groups, usually middle-class activists, campaigning on issues such as voting rights, accession to the professions, domestic violence, education for girls, and legislation on venereal diseases. Like most progressive and democratic organizations of the period, the IWMA was created by men. Most of its members were skilled artisans from the urban crafts, who were predominantly men. As far as women were concerned, two issues were raised: could women become members? What was the stance of the association on paid work for women?

On the question of female labour, the IWMA was divided. While in France women accounted for a third of the workforce, and sometimes more, for example in textiles, Proudhon had fiercely opposed woman's work. Women could be either 'courtesans or housewives', he wrote.[64] Many of his followers believed that women's work competed with men's and would lead to lower wages. In the 1866 congress, the delegates discussed the prohibition of female paid work. Four Frenchmen proposed: 'Woman is not made to work; her position is in the family household; she is the natural educator of the child; she alone can prepare him for a free, male, and civil existence.' The British considered this to be nonsense: women were already part and parcel of the industrial workforce.[65] Varlin argued that, if women were to be saved from prostitution, they had to have the means of earning a living. Marx opposed the resolution to ban women from paid employment: 'Everyone who knows anything of history also knows that great social revolutions are impossible without the feminine ferment.'[66] This was the majority position, though some unions still refused to admit women. Women's groups remain under-

---

63 Ibid., p. 249.
64 P. J. Proudhon, *Contradictions économiques* (Paris: Garnier, 1846), p. 254.
65 See Freymond, *La Première Internationale*, vol. I, pp. 31–50.
66 Marx to Kugelmann, 12 December 1868, in *MECW*, vol. XLIII, p. 185.

researched, however. The 'ovalists', female silk workers in Lyons, went on strike in 1869 to be paid according to time, just like men. Somewhere between 4,000 and 8,000 women, mostly young and single, and about 2,000 strikers decided to join the IWMA.[67] In Cadiz, a women's club, the Mariana Pineda Club, was formed in 1869 and joined the local branch of the IWMA. These women were involved in grassroots militancy, in peasant protests, and in the wave of strikes that intensified in 1873. There were then perhaps 5,000 women who belonged to or sympathized with the FRE-IWMA.[68]

Although the IWMA remained an overwhelmingly male movement, hundreds, maybe thousands, of women were nevertheless active in the International. In this respect as in others, it reflected the debates and contradictions of the emerging labour movement. In France, Proudhon opposed women's participation in politics, as did most Proudhonists, though others, following Varlin, evolved on the issue. Several women became active: Virginie Barbet, a Bakuninist publican in Lyon; André Léo, a novelist and advocate of women's rights in Paris; Polish journalist Paule Mink; bookbinder and strike leader Nathalie Le Mel. During the Commune, the GC sent young Russian exile Elizabeth Dmitrieff to Paris, as an emissary. On 12 April, with others, such as Le Mel, she set up the Union des femmes pour la défense de Paris et les soins aux blessés (membership around 300). This union campaigned for women's right to work and to divorce, for education for girls, and for equal pay, before fighting against the Versaillais on the barricades. In Britain, some trades and their unions ruled out the participation of women.

'Ladies are admitted', Marx wrote, suggesting to Engels that his partner Lizzie Burns join the IWMA.[69] The issue was discussed at the 1871 London Conference and, following Marx's proposal, women were allowed to form their own sections.[70] Some women were involved in the association's leadership. Harriet Law (1867–9) and Marie Huleck (1868) belonged to the GC. Law was a British secularist who believed that women were the equals of men. Marie Huleck (born Marie-Louise David) was the daughter of a French exile, who lived in London and belonged to the London French branch of the IWMA; she joined the GC with her husband, the Forty-Eighter Huleck, before emigrating to the USA, and was involved in the IWMA in New York, where

67 Auzias and Houel, *La grève des ovalistes*.
68 G. Espigado, 'Las mujeres en el anarquismo español (1869–1939)', *Ayer* 45 (2002), p. 45; L. Sanfeliu, 'Republicanismo y ciudadanía femenina en el Sexenio Democrático', *Bulletin d'Histoire Contemporaine de l'Espagne* no. 46 (2011), pp. 91–110.
69 Marx to Engels, 25 January 1865, in *MECW*, vol. XLII, p. 67.
70 Freymond, *La Première Internationale*, vol. II, p. 167, n. 11.

she proposed setting up an international feminist league.[71] There, suffrage advocates Victoria Woodhull and her sister Tennessee Claflin belonged to the IWMA. Woodhull was controversial: she had been some sort of prostitute and had become an advocate of free love and of the abolition of marriage laws, as well as a suffragist who in 1872 ran for president of the USA. She edited *Woodhull and Claflin's Weekly*, which published an English translation of the *Communist Manifesto*, before opposing the centralist German section and eventually getting expelled from the association. At the same time, she had set up the first female brokerage firm in Wall Street with her sister. In other places, such as Geneva, some women were active in sections: for example, Désirée Gay, a Saint-Simonian since 1832, who had founded several newspapers for women and had been an advocate of women's rights, at some stages with Jeanne Deroin and Eugénie Niboyet; she belonged to the IWMA in Geneva, where she lived with her exiled husband in 1868–9, and where there was an active women's section.[72] Guillermina Rojas y Orgis, a schoolteacher, moved from Cadiz (where she had led the Mariana Pineda Club) to Madrid, where she earned a living as a seamstress. She took part in workers' meetings, wrote articles for the press, and came to occupy the position of secretary in the local council of the Federation of Madrid. She publicly criticized received views on family organization, which caused an outcry from the liberal and conservative papers.[73]

There is a lot we do not know about gendered forms of involvement. Probably, women were more often sewing the banners and men were more often on the hustings or writing for newspapers. There might have been anonymous female translators of texts, such as the Russian Communard Anna Jaclard, who likely translated the *Inaugural Address* into Russian. In Brussels, several women organized subscriptions for and helped refugees.[74] They sang democratic songs such as the 'Marseillaise de l'Internationale'. But some women were also IWMA activists, and in

71 See https://maitron.fr/spip.php?article56662, entry for 'DAVID Marie-Louise (HULECK Marie)' by M. Cordillot.
72 See https://maitron.fr/spip.php?article208779, entry for 'GAY Jeanne, Désirée, née Véret' by Jacques Cana; A. Schrupp, 'Bringing Together Feminism and Socialism in the First International: Four Examples', in Bensimon et al. (eds.), 'Arise Ye Wretched of the Earth', pp. 343–54; A. Schrupp, *Nicht Marxistin und auch nicht Anarchistin. Frauen in der Ersten Internationale* (Königstein: Ulrike Helmer Verlag, 1999).
73 Espigado, 'Las mujeres'; and G. Espigado Tocino, 'Mujeres "radicales". Utópicas, republicanas e internacionalistas en España (1848–1874)', *Ayer* 60 (2005), pp. 15–43.
74 On Belgian women, I am following F. Loriaux, 'Femmes et exil durant la Première Internationale', *Carhop*, August 2008, www.carhop.be/images/femmes_exil_premiere_internationale_f.loriaux_2008.pdf.

this respect the IWMA was ahead of other political forces. Marie Iatskévitch was the treasurer of the Paris branch; she met Belgian internationalist Eugène Hins, and followed him to Brussels, Verviers, and eventually Russia. Victorine Brocher's memoirs offer a rare insight into a rank-and-file woman's experience in the IWMA. A boot-stitcher in Paris, she was involved in the creation of a co-op bakery in 1867 and in the Commune in 1871: 'When I joined the association, I understood the immense impact of this union. In the meetings of our small group, we heard the impassioned speeches of our comrades, we were carried away by our faith, we were swept away by our ideal.'[75] Wilhelmine Müller (Mina Pucinelli) joined in Belgium, after fighting with Garibaldi, in the Franco-Prussian War, and in the Paris Commune. She spoke passionately for the republic and the International, for example on 2 November 1871 in Dison, addressing 500–600 people, including about 50 women. 'She seemed to me a first-rank member of the Commune as she reports on some facts that happened then', a police officer wrote after listening to her in Verviers. 'This woman is dangerous and I believe that, if she gave a few lectures, she would carry on with her all the female workers of our small town, because she speaks with such eloquence she may reach the heart of these wretched internationalists.'[76] She died in fighting in Valencia in 1873. She may have recruited Marie Mineur, a Belgian textile worker who had started work at the age of eight in Verviers. After the Commune, Mineur created a female section of the IWMA, which numbered 300 members in 1873 and remained active until 1878. She often spoke from the platform and wrote in a local revolutionary newspaper, *Le Mirabeau*, for the emancipation of workers and of women and against the clergy. Her last recorded activity was when she attended a meeting of a local atheist circle. After this she vanished until she was recovered from oblivion by second-wave feminists in the 1970s.[77] Oblivion and the scarcity of sources are common problems for an unknown number of female IWMA activists.

75 V. Brocher, *Souvenirs d'une morte-vivante. Une femme du peuple dans la Commune de 1871* (Montreuil: Libertalia, 2020 [1909]), pp. 78–9.

76 'Rapport d'un agent de police au commissaire de Verviers, 27 octobre 1871', in H. Wouters (ed.), *Documenten betreffende de geschiedenis der arbeidersbeweging ten tijde van de 1e Internationale (1866–1880)* (Leuven/Louvain: Ed. Nauwelaerts and Paris: Béatrice-Nauwelaerts, 1971), p. 427.

77 F. Joris, *Marie Mineur, Marie rebelle. Une pionnière féministe en milieu ouvrier au XIXe siècle* (Waterloo: Avant-Propos Editions, 2013).

New Challenges

The Franco-Prussian War (July 1870–January 1871), the Paris Commune (March–May 1871), and the brutal suppression of the latter challenged the very existence of the IWMA. It had already discussed the issue of a war, and insisted on 'uniting the working classes of all countries in a perpetual bond of fraternal cooperation'.[78] It had denounced wars, such as the colonial expeditions in the Dutch East Indies, a 'battle to seize a source of Oriental products'.[79] As Varlin explained to a judge in 1866, the IWMA 'opposed the right to work to the right to arms; it considered the alliance between workers was above the hostility between governments'.[80] And in 1867 it adopted an address to the Congress of Peace, arguing that 'to put an end to war, it is not enough to do away with armies, but it is further necessary to change the social organization in the direction of an ever more equitable distribution of production'.[81] On 19 July 1870, soon after the Franco-Prussian War broke out, a first address of the GC especially denounced the responsibility of 'Louis Bonaparte', noting that on the German side 'the war [was] a war of defence'. At the same time, it denounced Chancellor Otto von Bismarck for conspiring with Bonaparte 'for the purpose of crushing popular opposition at home, and annexing Germany to the Hohenzollern dynasty'. And it repeated its rallying cry, 'Proletarians of all countries, unite!' After the major French defeat at Sedan on 2 September and Napoleon III's abdication on 4 September, the GC issued another address (again, like the first one, written by Marx) which advocated immediate peace without any annexation of territory.[82] In parliament and in *Der Volksstaat*, Bebel and Liebknecht agitated against the war and the annexation of Alsace-Lorraine, were arrested for treason, and spent two years in jail.

Although a workers' insurrection in Paris could have been foreseen from 4 September 1870, the 18 March 1871 rising against the Versailles government was unexpected. In Britain, there was widespread condemnation of the

78 Text sent by the GC to the Operative Bricklayers Society, on 7 February 1865, after approving their admission to the IWMA. The full version is in *The General Council of the First International, 1864–1872: Minutes*, 5 vols. (Moscow: Foreign Languages Publishing House, 1963–9), vol. II, pp. 261–2.
79 César De Paepe, speech on 7 September 1868 at the Brussels Congress, reproduced in Musto (ed.), *Workers Unite!*, p. 231.
80 M. Audin, *Eugène Varlin. Ouvrier relieur 1839–1871* (Montreuil: Libertalia, 2019), p. 156.
81 Hafner, ['The Real Causes of the War'], published in the 1867 Lausanne Congress papers, reproduced in Musto (ed.), *Workers Unite!*, pp. 233–4.
82 'Working Men and the War', First Address of the General Council of the International Working Men's Association on the Franco-Prussian War, 23 July 1870, *The Pall Mall Gazette* 28 July 1870, p. 3.

events, barring comments in a few papers. Despite their earlier reservations about a Parisian uprising, Marx and Engels were immediately supportive. In Paris, among the eighty-five members of the Commune elected on 26 March, there were seventeen members of the IWMA, including Eugène Varlin, Hungarian-born Léo Frankel, Edouard Vaillant, and Benoît Malon. They were a minority in the council, which was dominated by Jacobins, and they did not act as a party. But they gave the Commune its socialist dimension, within the Commission on Labour and Exchange, which promoted a series of transformations. The Commune was crushed, however, and the IWMA was targeted with repression. Several activists were killed, and the others had to leave Paris. The association was outlawed in France. The address, which Marx read to the GC on 30 May, understood the Commune as 'the first revolution in which the working class was openly acknowledged as the only class capable of social initiative'.[83] It did not delve too far into the measures that were implemented: 'The great social measure of the Commune was its own working existence.' It completed the programme of the IWMA: 'The working class cannot simply lay hold of the ready-made state machinery and wield it for its own purposes.' While trying to draw lessons, it was a powerful apology for the first working-class government: 'Working Men's Paris, with its Commune, will be forever celebrated as the glorious harbinger of a new society. Its martyrs are enshrined in the great heart of the working class.' The text was adopted by the GC and published as a booklet, soon translated and widely disseminated. However, in Britain, the barrage of criticism from the press and the authorities had some effect. George Jacob Holyoake attacked Marx's address in *The Daily News* (20 June), and several union leaders, such as Thomas Dunning of the bookbinders, disapproved of his defence of the Commune against charges of atrocities and incendiarism. Odger and Benjamin Lucraft resigned from the GC. It was the first split, and the conservative press rejoiced.

The Commune had another impact on the association: its French section was decimated, and it would take a decade for working-class organizations to be properly revived. Varlin was one of their protagonists: he had joined the International early in 1865 and, although he never belonged to the GC, he took part in several conferences and congresses. He belonged to the federal council in Paris (1865–8). A bookbinder, he spent the last years of the Second Empire organizing workers in different trades. With a few friends, he set up a co-op restaurant with newspapers, La Marmite, in 1868, and a consumers'

---

83 'The Civil War in France', 30 May 1871, in *MECW*, vol. XXII, p. 336.

co-op, La Ménagère, in 1869. He was involved in the Paris Commune and was executed. The generation of Varlin was decimated.[84]

From 1869 until The Hague Congress in September 1872, the IWMA was plagued by the divide between the centralists and the autonomists. By the mid-1860s, Bakunin had become an opponent not just of religion and the existing governments, but of the state itself. He had first tried to convince the League of Peace and Freedom – created in 1867 by pacifists such as Emile Acollas, John Stuart Mill, and Elisée Reclus – to subscribe to the IWMA, but the League would embark on no such change. Bakunin became the co-founder of the International Alliance for Socialist Democracy (IASD), which then applied to join the IWMA. The GC initially turned down the application: the IASD was itself an organization, and it advocated the 'equalization of classes', while the IWMA stood for the 'abolition of classes'. Bakunin joined the Geneva section and from there started building a power base among the French-speaking Swiss branches against Marx's leadership. He took part in the proceedings of the 1869 Basel Congress as a delegate. His supporters in the IWMA criticised the GC for allegedly diverting from the original aims and procedures of the association. The French-speaking Swiss federation split during its congress in La Chaux-de-Fonds (3–4 April 1870), each of the two wings now claiming to be the true *Fédération romande*. Marc Vuilleumier has argued that in Geneva there was no unanimity for Bakunin – far from it.[85] But Bakunin's opposition to the IWMA leadership made progress in Switzerland and France (in Lyon, for example) as well as in Italy and Spain, where the IWMA was young and expanding. The 'autonomists' or 'federalists' could rely on the aspirations of sections to be independent from the authority of the GC. Marx and Engels were determined to counter this progress. They disagreed with Bakunin's anarchist agenda of state abolition and opposed his establishment of secret societies, which they considered the antithesis of the IWMA's successful claim at establishing itself as a public association with access to the press, rising membership, and an open organization of workers. Bakunin had indeed been associated with Sergei Nechaev, a Russian conspirator who wanted to assassinate the tsar, who had killed a dissenting member of his group, and whose *Catechism of a Revolutionary* (1869) advocated the 'merciless destruction' of society and the state.

84 On Varlin, see M. Cordillot, *Eugène Varlin. Internationaliste et communard* (Paris: Spartacus, 2016); Audin, *Eugène Varlin*; and Rougerie, *Eugène Varlin*.
85 M. Vuilleumier, 'The First International in Switzerland: A Few Observations', in Bensimon et al. (ed.), *'Arise Ye Wretched of the Earth'*, pp. 165–80.

The congress in The Hague (1–7 September 1872) was the setting for an open confrontation between the two wings. It was attended by sixty-five delegates from fourteen countries. Marx and Engels relied on their authority to defeat the Bakuninist proposal that the GC be just an office for correspondence and statistics. The congress ended with the expulsion of Bakunin and his Swiss follower James Guillaume from the IWMA; the autonomists withdrew from the association. The split would cast a long shadow over the IWMA, although rank-and-file members mostly did not know about it. The Blanquists, who had joined after the events of 1870 in Paris, and were now also present in New York, quit the association as well.

The Hague Congress also adopted Engels' proposal to transfer the seat of the GC to New York. Why Marx and Engels proposed this has been a matter of debate. The autonomists argued it was a manoeuvre that would imply the end of the leadership of the International in most struggles, for example in Europe. Marx and Engels lamented that conflicts in London had reached such a level that the transfer was necessary, but they also contended that the USA was the new home of the labour movement. It was true that following the victory of the Union in the civil war, and the rapid industrialization of the country, labour had made rapid progress there. The number of sections rose from six in May 1871 to thirty-five by November, reaching forty-seven in 1872. All in all, the IWMA numbered 60 US sections and 4,000 members in 25 towns. In order to honour the Paris Commune, the French Internationalists organized a march in New York on 17 December 1871, which gathered 10,000 people and impressed the country. But the transfer of the GC was to prove a failure. In the USA, the International was riddled with division between two rival factions, which did not mirror the split in Europe. Unlike Marx, the US centralists refused any form of political or electoral activity; and, unlike Bakunin, the US autonomists did not want to destroy the state, just democratize it. There were also rifts between German-, English-, and French-speaking members. The labour movement had suffered a setback on the eight-hour movement, and many unions wanted to distance themselves from the 'communists'. The socialist movement in New York mostly consisted of a handful of German-speaking unions.[86] Following the beginning of an economic crisis in 1873 and rising unemployment, the internationalists organized a demonstration on 13 January 1874, which met with the brutal

---

86 M. Cordillot, 'Socialism v. Democracy? The IWMA in the USA, 1869–1876', in Bensimon et al. (eds.), 'Arise Ye Wretched of the Earth', p. 276.

repression of the authorities. On 15 July 1876, ten delegates representing thirteen German sections voted for the final dissolution of the IWMA.

As for the autonomists, in the week following the Hague Congress, they met in Saint-Imier in Switzerland, and created an 'anti-authoritarian' International.[87] They organized the 'sixth' congress in Geneva (1–6 September 1873). The thirty-two delegates decided to abolish the GC, and they debated new political perspectives, such as anarchism and the general strike. The 'seventh' congress was held in Brussels in 1874 (7–13 September) with sixteen delegates, fourteen of whom were from Belgium; it agreed on the fact that it was up to 'any federation and socialist democratic party in each country to decide which political line it thought it should follow'.[88] The 'eighth' congress (Bern, 26–30 October 1876) was also marked by major disagreements, notably between the line of De Paepe and that of Guillaume. The last congress of the autonomist wing was held in Verviers (6–8 September 1877), with twenty-two delegates, mostly anarchists, in attendance.

*

Since the 1870s, the reasons for the ultimate failure of the IWMA have been the subject of debate. As we have seen, several leading British trade unionists quit in 1871. Its French section suffered from the repression following the Commune. The disagreements between the centralists and the autonomists turned into an open rift. As a result, the experience of the IWMA is often associated with a long-term divide between working-class organizations. Socio-economic explanations also had their part to play: from 1873, Britain, Germany, and the USA went through an economic crisis. In Britain, the founding of the Trades Union Congress in 1868 and the Trades Union Act in 1871 gave the unions a better legal status. In France and Germany, following the Franco-Prussian War, 'the working classes entered into a closer relationship with the nation states' (elementary education, military service, public monuments).[89] The workers' parties that the Second (New) International could rely upon in 1889 did not exist at the time of the IWMA.

The prestige of the IWMA far outreached its real strength. Its treasure chest was a myth, and so was its impressive membership. In the countries (France, Britain, Belgium, Switzerland, Spain) where it was more influential,

---

87 M. Enckell, 'Bakunin and the Jura Federation', in Bensimon et al. (eds.), 'Arise Ye Wretched of the Earth', p. 360.
88 Freymond, La Première Internationale, vol. IV, p. 350.
89 Van der Linden, 'The Rise and Fall', p. 332.

it only appealed to a small section of organized workers and an even smaller section of non-organized workers. In Britain, while the trade unions gathered some 800,000 members, the membership of those unions that joined the IWMA did not exceed 50,000. Many of the member branches were small and short-lived. A large number of members were probably not aware of the debates and conflicts between the collectivists and the mutualists, between the centralists and the autonomists. We know little about how the rank and file experienced membership. However, the few autobiographies or memoirs that are available suggest that belonging to 'the International' was something important for the members, not just for those who attended congresses.

Despite its limits, the IWMA was a landmark in the history of labour and eventually of socialism. Its strength was derived from the rise of the working-class movement in several European countries, and from its beginnings in North and South America. In many respects, the IWMA was less a rigid organization than a meeting place for trade unions, friendly societies, and co-ops, where people created bonds of comradeship.[90] It promoted some basic ideas of financial solidarity and mutual assistance among workers, at a time when 'in order to oppose their workers, the employers either bring in workers from abroad or else transfer manufacture to countries where there is a cheap labour force'.[91]

The most lasting effect of the association perhaps was its spreading of concepts: the strength of the workers was not local – it was global. If manufacturers could rely on resources from without, workers could do the same. Workers shared common interests with people who had different occupations, who lived in other countries, who spoke other languages. In our days of rising nationalism and scarce international workers' solidarity, reading the debates of the IWMA can be refreshing. Women's and children's work; machinery and technical progress; landed property; strike action; the struggles for national emancipation and against slavery; attitudes regarding war and the environment: there is still much to be learnt from the history of the first international organization of the labour movement.

Further Reading

Archer, Julian P. W., *The First International in France, 1864–1871* (Lanham, MD: University Press of America, 1997).

90 Cordillot, *Eugène Varlin*.
91 'To Members, Affiliated Societies and All Workers', in *MECW*, vol. XX, p. 421. This was adopted by the GC on 9 July 1867 for the Lausanne Congress.

Bensimon, Fabrice, Quentin Deluermoz, and Jeanne Moisand (eds.), *'Arise Ye Wretched of the Earth': The First International in a Global Perspective* (Leiden and Boston: Brill, 2018).

Collins, Henry, and Chimen Abramsky, *Karl Marx and the British Labour Movement: Years of the First International* (London: Macmillan, 1965).

Eckhardt, Wolfgang (ed.), *The First Socialist Schism: Bakunin vs Marx in the International Working Men's Association* (Oakland, CA: PM Press, 2016).

The General Council of the First International, 1864–1872: Minutes, 5 vols. (Moscow: Foreign Languages Publishing House, 1963–9).

The Hague Congress of the First International: September 2–7, 1872, 2 vols. (Moscow: Progress, 1976–8).

Katz, Henryk, *The Emancipation of Labor: A History of the First International* (Westport, CT: Greenwood Press, 1992).

Messer-Kruse, Timothy, *The Yankee International: Marxism and the American Tradition, 1848–1876* (Chapel Hill: University of North Carolina Press, 1998).

Musto, Marcello (ed.), *Workers Unite! The International 150 Years Later* (London: Bloomsbury Academic, 2014).

La Première Internationale. L'institution, l'implantation, le rayonnement (Paris: Editions du Centre national de la recherche scientifique, 1968).

11

Karl Marx, Friedrich Engels, and Early Workers' Movements

LUCIA PRADELLA

Introduction

Karl Marx's (1818–83) and Friedrich Engels' (1820–95) critique of political economy developed through different individual trajectories, but for both it was more than an intellectual project: it was part of their involvement in national and international workers' movements.

Both Marx and Engels came from the Rhineland, but their family backgrounds – respectively the secularized Jewish middle class and the Pietistic industrial bourgeoisie – were very different. The Rhineland experienced an abrupt shift from liberal reforms under French rule to the imposition of Prussian absolutism after Napoleon's defeat in 1813–15. Together with the advent of early industrialization, this may explain the region's importance in the 1848 revolution, in which both Marx and Engels would play a part.[1]

Their youth coincided with a period of acute class struggle in a number of west European countries in the wake of France's July 1830 revolution and the uprisings of the Lyon weavers in 1831 and 1834. In England and Wales, the class struggle gained in intensity after the 1832 Great Reform Act, which paved the way to power for the industrial bourgeoisie and led to the rise of Chartism: the workers' own movement for universal male suffrage. In Prussia, the reactionary policies pursued by King Friedrich Wilhelm IV after his accession in 1840 radicalized the democratic opposition. Both Marx and Engels rallied to this opposition as young intellectuals.

In late 1842, Engels, already philosophically a communist, was sent to work at his father's part-owned factory in Manchester, the centre of the Industrial

---

1 For biographical information, see M. Heinrich, *Karl Marx and the Birth of Modern Society: The Life of Marx and the Development of His Work*, vol. 1, *1818–1841* (New York: Monthly Review, 2019); G. Mayer, *Friedrich Engels: A Biography* (London: Chapman & Hall, 1935); J. Sperber, *Karl Marx: A Nineteenth-Century Life* (New York: W. W. Norton & Co, 2013); and E. A. Stepanova, *Engels: A Short Biography* (Moscow: Progress Publishers, 1984).

Revolution, when it was still shaken by the General Strike (or Plug Riots) that August. There Engels met Mary Burns, an Irish working woman with whom he fell in love and who walked him through the workers' districts and the enraging humiliations of pauperism. In the Preface to *The Condition of the Working Class in England* (1845), Engels addressed 'The Working Classes of Great Britain': 'I wanted to see you in your own homes, to observe you in your everyday life, to chat with you on your condition and grievances, to witness your struggles against the social and political power of your oppressors.'[2]

In Manchester Engels 'openly aligned himself with the Chartist movement'.[3] Chartism offered Engels, and through him Marx, a model of how the new industrial working class could develop from economic struggles into a political movement. In Germany, where a proletariat was still in the making, Marx's defence of peasants' and workers' rights to existence exposed the limits of liberalism and pushed him towards communism. When Marx and Engels met in Paris in September 1844, they had already embraced communism and the idea that in civil society lay the secret of politics and ideas and that 'the anatomy of this civil society . . . has to be sought in political economy'.[4] In Paris, their lifelong friendship began, and the critique of political economy became their common project.

This chapter traces Marx's and Engels' political and theoretical activities from the early 1840s to the consolidation of European social democracy in the 1890s. It looks both at the development of the labour movements in Europe and the United States and at Marx's and Engels' evolving assessment of the peasant, colonial, and women's questions. In the second section I trace the links between their critique of political economy and their political activity before and during the 1848 revolution. The next section then follows their further reflections in the first years of their English exile. The fourth section focuses on the return of critique after the global economic crisis of 1857 and the first steps of the International Working Men's Association: a political engagement that inspired Marx's work for *Capital*, Volume I. Marx thought of *Capital* as a theoretical tool for the working class, and constantly revised it in the light of significant political developments, such as the evolution of the

2 Friedrich Engels, 'The Condition of the Working Class in England: From Personal Observation and Authentic Sources', in *Marx and Engels Collected Works* (London: Lawrence & Wishart, 2010) (hereafter *MECW*), vol. IV, p. 299.
3 Friedrich Engels, ['On Poland'] (1847), in *MECW*, vol. VI, p. 389.
4 Karl Marx, 'A Contribution to the Critique of Political Economy' (1859), in *MECW*, vol. XXIX, p. 262.

Irish question in the late 1860s, which I discuss in the fifth section. The sixth section then turns to the Paris Commune and the subsequent disintegration of the International. The following two sections focus on two aspects of Marx's and Engels' activity after 1872: their engagement within the working-class movements and the formation of mass political parties in Europe, and their engagement with Russian revolutionaries and their studies of world history. The link between these two aspects of their activity sheds light on the global dimension of Marx's writings on the women's question, then reworked by Engels, and on the challenges and opportunities raised by the development of mass working-class parties in western Europe.

The Coming Revolution

It was Engels who took the first steps in what would prove Marx's lifelong project, in his 'Outlines of a Critique of Political Economy' (1844). Inspired by the Chartist movement, the two friends linked developing this theoretical critique with promoting a working-class movement which, they believed, had to aspire to the abolition of private property. In the spring of 1845 Engels joined Marx in Brussels, where they applied themselves to the detailed elaboration of the new conception of history emerging from their critique of political economy – the theory of historical materialism and the programme of revolutionary socialism – first in the manuscripts published after their deaths as *The German Ideology* (and attributed to their sole authorship) and in Marx's critique of the rival socialist thinker Pierre-Joseph Proudhon, *The Poverty of Philosophy* (1847). Marx's 'Theses on Feuerbach' (1845) outlined their view of the role of revolutionary praxis in transforming and understanding the world.

In the summer of 1845, the two friends went on a six-week visit to Britain, where they examined economic literature unavailable in Brussels and where Marx acquainted himself with the working-class movement. After their stay in Manchester, they went to London, where they met left-wing Chartists and members of the League of Justice, a secret organization of German communist workers. A joint meeting of the two organizations and of democrats of different nationalities resident in London decided, with Marx's and Engels' active intervention, to set up an international society of democrats: 'The proletarians in all countries have one and the same interest, one and the same enemy, and one and the same struggle.'[5]

---

5 Friedrich Engels, 'The Festival of Nations in London' (1845), in *MECW*, vol. vi, p. 6.

Chartism's rapid ascent filled Marx and Engels with revolutionary optimism. Thanks to the combined development of British industry, French politics, and German philosophy, they believed, social revolution was imminent in western Europe and could not be stopped by any bourgeois advance.[6] To this end, in January 1846 they founded the Communist Correspondence Committee, which maintained contacts with socialists and workers' movements in different countries. Their goal was to reach consensus on the fundamentals of the communist movement, in opposition to the more utopian currents of socialism, what they regarded as Proudhon's petty bourgeois radicalism, and the insurrectionist communism of Gracchus Babeuf and Auguste Blanqui, which was a strong influence on the League of Justice.

In June 1847 the committee and the League of Justice merged, giving birth to the International Communist League. They changed their motto from 'All men are brothers' into 'Workers of all countries, unite!', which expressed the principles of proletarian internationalism. The League was, in Engels' eyes, the *'first international movement of the working class'*.[7] It comprised members of the League of Justice, the Communist Correspondence Committee, British Chartists, and German refugees dispersed across Europe. Marx and Engels were tasked with writing its programme: what would become the *Communist Manifesto*. The *Manifesto* sketched the worldview and programme of the communist movement: denouncing the limited achievements of the bourgeois revolution, it stressed the centrality of the conscious activity of the working class. If the capitalist mode of production led to the impoverishment and exploitation of an increasing number of workers all over the planet, and to the subordination and oppression of entire nations under its system of division of labour, the same system had also laid the conditions for its revolutionary supersession. The bourgeoisie 'produces, above all, its own grave-diggers'.[8]

Unlike earlier socialist thinkers, Marx and Engels saw the working class not only as a victim, but also as an active agent in the transformation of society. Despite its expansion, capitalism could neither escape crises of overproduction nor stop wages from declining towards the absolute

---

6 Friedrich Engels, 'Rapid Progress of Communism in Germany' (1844), in *MECW*, vol. IV, p. 238.
7 Friedrich Engels, 'On the History of the Communist League' (1885), in *MECW*, vol. XXVI, p. 312.
8 Karl Marx and Friedrich Engels, *Manifesto of the Communist Party* (1848), in *MECW*, vol. VI, p. 496.

minimum.[9] The inevitable growth of pauperism in industrial societies would turn trade union struggles into struggles for the abolition of capitalism. And 'in proportion as the exploitation of one individual by another is put to an end', they believed, 'the exploitation of one nation by another will also be put an end to'.[10] 'In place of the old bourgeois society, with its classes and class antagonisms, we shall have an association, in which the free development of each is the condition for the free development of all.'[11]

The published version of the *Manifesto*, finalized by Marx, took a negative view of the petty bourgeoisie and did not even mention the existence of a specific peasant question.[12] Colonized peoples were not recognized as autonomous political actors.[13] This reflected Marx's and Engels' excessive economic pessimism at the time and resulting revolutionary optimism. At the end of 1847 Marx had proclaimed that the imminent social revolution in Britain would also allow Polish independence.[14] Engels rejoiced at the US conquest of Mexico[15] and the French conquest of Algeria, which he saw 'as an important and fortunate fact for the progress of civilisation'.[16] But this does not mean that Marx and Engels believed in the progressive role of colonialism in promoting development, as Kevin Anderson and others maintain.[17] On the contrary, they assumed that capitalism was exhausting its developmental possibilities: revolution was imminent and, with it, human emancipation.

Revolution was indeed imminent. In February, when the *Manifesto* was published, it flared up throughout continental Europe, setting the order of the Vienna Congress ablaze. Marx's and Engels' participation in it played a key role in the development of their ideas. Expelled from Brussels and Paris, Marx moved to Cologne, where he set up the *Neue Rheinische Zeitung* (*New Rhenish Times*, NRZ) with Engels. Convinced that the revolution had first to abolish absolutism in order to create the preconditions for overthrowing capitalism, Marx stopped operating through the Communist League and

---

9 E. Mandel, *The Formation of the Economic Thought of Karl Marx: 1843 to Capital* (London: New Left Books, 1972), p. 58.
10 Marx and Engels, *Manifesto*, p. 503. 11 Ibid., p. 506.
12 H. Draper, *Karl Marx's Theory of Revolution*, vol. II, *The Politics of Social Classes* (New York, Monthly Review Press, 1978), p. 364.
13 Marx and Engels, *Manifesto*, p. 488.
14 Karl Marx quoted in Friedrich Engels, ['The Anniversary of the Polish Revolution of 1830'] (1847), in *MECW*, vol. VI, pp. 391–2.
15 Friedrich Engels, 'The Movements of 1847' (1848), in *MECW*, vol. VI, pp. 527–8.
16 Friedrich Engels, 'Extraordinary Revelations – Abd-El-Kader – Guizot's Foreign Policy' (1848), in *MECW*, vol. VI, pp. 471–2.
17 K. Anderson, *Marx at the Margins: On Nationalism, Ethnicity, and Non-Western Societies* (Chicago: University of Chicago Press, 2010), p. 8.

started to work with the Rhenish liberal bourgeoisie.[18] In the course of the revolution, the *NRZ* group elaborated their programme and put into practice an alliance between workers, the petty bourgeoisie, and small peasants. This alliance became more and more important as the liberal bourgeoisie in Frankfurt and Berlin moved rightwards.[19]

The *NRZ* group also aligned themselves with democratic struggles in the rest of Europe. Engels developed the theory of the 'great historic nations' – this supported national self-determination in Germany, Hungary, Poland, and Italy, where it threatened the absolute monarchies of Prussia, Austria, and Russia, but labelled the Czech and southern Slavic peoples as 'counter-revolutionary'[20] because the Habsburg and Romanov regimes used their national movements for their reactionary aims. This approach, however, meant abandoning the peasant masses rebelling against the nobility and feudalism in these countries, letting them become instruments of the counter-revolution.[21] And, from the east, in the wake of the repression of the June 1848 insurrection in Paris, the counter-revolution advanced in western Europe, facilitated by the absence of social revolution in Britain and by peasant support for Louis Bonaparte (later Napoleon III) in France.

(Anti-)Imperial Vantage Points

Expelled from both Germany and France, in the summer of 1849 Marx and then his family moved to London, where they initially faced poverty, debt, and deprivation. Marx convinced Engels to leave his refuge in Switzerland and move to London, where they tried, to no avail, to make the *Neue Rheinische Zeitung* a source of income. Initially they took upon themselves the job of reorganizing the Communist League, still hoping for a revival of the revolution. But by autumn 1850 they realized that the situation had changed. The crisis had been overcome by a period of industrial prosperity, which postponed the conditions for a new crisis and revolutionary movement.[22] Withdrawing from the faction-ridden Communist League, Marx and Engels focused on analysing the lessons of the revolutions. Marx published *The Class Struggles in France* (1850), *The Eighteenth Brumaire of Louis Bonaparte* (1852), and *Revelations Concerning the Communist Trial in Cologne*

---

18 Draper, *Karl Marx's Theory of Revolution*, vol. ii, p. 196.   19 Ibid., pp. 372–5.
20 Friedrich Engels, 'The Magyar Struggle' (1849), in *MECW*, vol. viii, p. 234.
21 R. Rosdolsky, *Engels and the 'Nonhistoric' Peoples: The National Question in the Revolution of 1848* (Glasgow: Critique Books, 1987).
22 Karl Marx and Friedrich Engels, 'Review: May to October [1850]', in *MECW*, vol. x, p. 510.

(1853), while Engels wrote *The Peasant War in Germany* (1850) and *Revolution and Counter-Revolution in Germany* (1851–2).

They also further elaborated the theory of permanent revolution, that is, of the fusion of democratic and socialist struggles, which Marx had initially sketched in 1844 and then temporarily abandoned in 1848.[23] In *The Class Struggles in France*, Marx explained how the French peasantry – groaning under the burden of mortgage debt, 'interest slavery', and taxation – channelled their frustration into support for Napoleon and the reaction. But, for the same reasons, the peasantry might be radicalized by continuing tax burden and rebel against the provisional government. He was echoed by Engels' *The Peasant War in Germany*, a historical work on the great anti-feudal peasant uprising in 1525. This was inspired by the awareness that in countries like Germany a worker–peasant alliance was key to the success of social revolution. As Marx put it in a letter to Engels of 6 April 1856: 'The whole thing in Germany will depend on whether it is possible to back the Proletarian revolution by some second edition of the Peasants' war. In which case the affair should go swimmingly.'[24]

Marx and Engels started to elaborate a more concrete understanding of the revolutionary movements not just in France and Germany, but around the world. Importantly, they changed their previous unidirectional view of international revolution, recognizing the autonomous role of non-European peoples. If in January 1849 Marx had concluded that 'The defeat of the working class in France and the victory of the French bourgeoisie was the victory of the East over the West, the defeat of civilisation by barbarism',[25] after only one year Marx and Engels greeted the first steps of the Taiping Rebellion, imagining reactionaries fleeing revolution in Europe just to find written on the Great Wall of China, 'RÉPUBLIQUE CHINOISE: LIBERTÉ, EGALITÉ, FRATERNITÉ'.[26]

In November 1850, Engels returned to his father's factory in Manchester, and could thus give financial support to the Marxes as well as to a number of other less-well-off revolutionaries. Marx started his studies at the British Museum and in August 1851 received an offer to work for the *New York Tribune*, the most important progressive newspaper in the United States.

---

23 Draper, *Karl Marx's Theory of Revolution*, p. 174. See also H. Mehringer, *Permanente Revolution und Russische Revolution* (Frankfurt am Main: Peter Lang, 1978).
24 Marx to Engels, 16 April 1856, in *MECW*, vol. XL, p. 41.
25 Karl Marx and Friedrich Engels, 'The Revolutionary Movement' (1848), in *MECW*, vol. VIII, p. 214.
26 *NRZ*, 31 January 1850: Marx and Engels, 'Review: January–February [1850]', in *MECW*, vol. X, p. 267.

London, as Marx put it, was a 'convenient vantage point for the observation of bourgeois society',[27] where he went back to his studies of political economy. He wanted to understand why social revolution had been defeated in Europe, and the economic crisis that triggered it overcome by a new period of prosperity. His collaboration with the *New York Tribune* further enriched the global scope and depth of his critique of political economy – as it pushed him to write about a large spectrum of contemporary issues, from British politics, workers' struggles, and strikes to financial policy, the Crimean War, British colonialism, the Spanish revolution, and the American Civil War.

His *London Notebooks* (1850–3) document that Marx put in question some of his previous convictions, like the quantity theory of money and the iron law of wages, which had hampered his analysis of the international process of capital accumulation. He also studied the history of pre-capitalist societies, the impact of colonization, and the evolution of the condition of women in society. During the 1852–3 parliamentary debates on the renewal of the East India Company's charter, Marx delved into the debate on land ownership in India and realized that village communities were not just the foundations of Asiatic despotism: he found that traces of the ancient communal property were at the basis of the Asiatic form and that democratic structures still prevailed in some parts of India.[28] He thus began to question his previous dichotomous view of a 'democratic West' and a 'despotic East'.

These theoretical achievements were closely linked to his revolutionary work. After the dispersal of their demonstration in London in April 1848, the Chartist movement was experiencing a period of decline and adaptation. Marx and Engels urged the left Chartists, headed by Julian Harney and Ernest Charles Jones, to break with those who were making compromises with the liberal bourgeoisie. They drew closer to Jones and helped him launch *Notes to the People*, and both contributed to it.[29] As recent scholarship has shown, Jones' emphatic internationalism and support for anti-colonial struggles may have influenced Marx.[30] But Marx and Engels had supported the first steps of

---

27 Marx, 'A Contribution to the Critique of Political Economy', p. 264.
28 See L. Pradella, *Globalisation and the Critique of Political Economy: New Insights from Marx's Writings* (Abingdon and New York: Routledge, 2015), pp. 92–125.
29 According to the editors of the *Marx–Engels Gesamtausgabe* (*MEGA²*), Marx co-wrote with Jones at least six articles for the *Notes to the People*: MEGA² 1/10, pp. 641–7; 1/10, pp. 648–54; 1/11, pp. 464–9; 1/11, pp. 470–2; 1/11, pp. 473–7; 1/11, pp. 492–4. Engels contributed prolifically to the Chartist newspapers *Notes to the People* and *The People's Paper*.
30 See T. Drapeau, '"Look at our colonial struggles": Ernest Jones and the anti-colonialist challenge to Marx's conception of history', *Critical Sociology* 45, 7–8 (2019), pp. 1195–1208.

the Taiping Rebellion before moving to London. When Jones allied with the bourgeois Radicals in Parliament, moreover, they broke with him. Despite their anti-colonial rhetoric, the Radicals were in favour of free trade expansion.[31]

Marx, by contrast, radicalized his support for anti-imperialist struggles, hoping that movements like the Taiping Rebellion would trigger economic crisis and revolution in Europe.[32] He also saw, for the first time, two different paths towards national liberation in India: not only a proletarian revolution in Britain, but also an independent national struggle in India itself. Given the strength of the mode of production in countries like China, where the power of the state had not been seized by the colonizers, he came to the conclusion, rightly, that Western colonization of China was unlikely to be successful.[33]

Following the wave of strikes centred on Bradford in northern England in 1853, moreover, Marx openly criticized the iron law of wages.[34] In Britain workers had claimed and achieved a share in the prosperity generated by free trade. 'Under certain circumstances, there is for the workman no other means of ascertaining whether he is or not paid to the actual market value of his labour, but to strike or to threaten to do so.'[35] Thanks to productivity increases and imperial exploitation, the class struggle in imperialist countries could lead to material improvements for the working class. As Engels wrote to Marx on 7 October 1858, this generated new challenges for the international labour movement:[36]

> There is in fact a connection between Jones' new move . . . and the fact that the English proletariat is actually becoming more and more bourgeois, so that the ultimate aim of this most bourgeois of all nations would appear to be

31 See M. Taylor, *Ernest Jones, Chartism, and the Romance of Politics 1819–1869* (Oxford: Oxford University Press, 2003), esp. ch. 5. An interesting discussion of the Chartist press's reports on empire, which also presents Harney's shift from an internationalist to a pro-imperialist stance, is G. Vargo, 'Outworks of the citadel of corruption: the Chartist press reports the empire', *Victorian Studies* 52, 2 (2012), pp. 227–53.
32 Karl Marx, 'Revolution in China and in Europe' (1853), in *MECW*, vol. xxii, pp. 93–100.
33 Karl Marx, 'The Future Results of British Rule in India' (1853), in *MECW*, vol. xxii, p. 218; Marx to Engels, 8 October 1858, in *MECW*, vol. xl, p. 347.
34 K. Lapides, *Marx's Wage Theory in Historical Perspective: Its Origins, Development, and Interpretation* (Westport, CT: Praeger, 1998), p. 140.
35 Karl Marx, 'Panic on the London Stock Exchange – Strikes' (1853), in *MECW*, vol. xxii, pp. 332–3.
36 In the 1892 edition of *The Condition of the Working Class in England*, Engels argued that the working class had achieved long-lasting gains, especially two better-protected sections – adult male factory workers and members of big trade unions, who represented an 'aristocracy among the working class'. See Friedrich Engels, 'Preface [to the 1892 Edition of *The Condition of the Working Class in England in 1844*]' (1892), in *MECW*, vol. xxvii, p. 266.

the possession, *alongside* the bourgeoisie, of a bourgeois aristocracy and a bourgeois proletariat. In the case of a nation which exploits the entire world this is, of course, justified to some extent.[37]

Returns of Critique

When the Indian population stood up against colonialism in 1857, Marx and Engels supported their struggle – whatever the consciousness of the rebels, for Marx, this had a national character. The general uprisings of 'the great Asiatic nations' against British colonialism – he noted in his *Books on Crisis* – aggravated the 1857 global economic crisis and contributed to a revival of social movements: in Russia and the United States, for the abolition of serfdom and slavery; in Europe against bourgeois attempts to make workers bear the burden of the crisis and break strikes by importing immigrant workers. In response, workers started to mobilize both at the trade union level and at the political level, with workers' committees and trade unions establishing links in different countries.

The 1860s also marked the revival of movements for national unification in Italy and Germany; the Civil War in the United States (1861–5) was also, among other things, a struggle for national unification. This revival of democratic national movements contributed to the political awakening of the working class. Marx and Engels supported German and Italian unification, but on an internationalist basis and with a view to strengthening democratic and working-class interests. They were highly suspicious of Napoleon III's Italian policy and bitterly opposed to the architect of German unification, the Prussian prime minister Otto von Bismarck. They disagreed with Ferdinand Lassalle, the main organizer and theoretician of the workers' party in Germany, whom Bismarck hoodwinked into believing he could trade working-class support for the Prussian regime and its programme of territorial expansion in exchange for manhood suffrage and social reforms.

In January 1860 Marx wrote to Engels that 'the most momentous thing happening in the world . . . [was] the slave movement – on the one hand, in America, started by the death of [John] Brown, and in Russia, on the other'.[38] The movement in Russia had a major political significance:

> [The serfs] are surer than ever to rise. And if they do, the Russian 1793 will be at hand; the reign of terror of these half-Asiatic serfs will be something

37 Engels to Marx, 7 October 1858, in *MECW*, vol. xl, p. 344.
38 Marx to Engels, after 11 January 1860, in *MECW*, vol. xli, p. 4.

Fig. 11.1 Karl Marx (right), with his daughters Jenny, Eleanor, and Laura, and Friedrich Engels (left), 1860. (Photo by Ullstein Bild/Ullstein Bild via Getty Images.)

unequalled in history; but it will be the second turning point in Russian history, and finally place real and general civilization in the place of that sham and show introduced by Peter the Great.[39]

39 Karl Marx, 'The Emancipation Question' (1858), in *MECW*, vol. xvi, p. 147.

The war against slavery in the United States, on the other hand, expressed the antagonism between two social systems: an industrial north and a slavery-based south integrated into the British industrial system. As African-American enslaved workers were a pillar of the British industrial system, on them depended the outcome of the war.[40] This is why, from the outset, Marx was confident the north would win. Northern capital, in his view, was developed enough to unify the country, and in order to do so the Union would be forced to wage the war by revolutionary means, either by mobilizing black troops or by encouraging a slave uprising.[41] This would have set in motion a movement against white supremacy in the north too.[42] This position reflected that of American abolitionists such as Frederick Douglass and of German émigré socialists in the Mississippi Valley close to Marx, who came to play leading roles in the Union Army, and immediately attacked slavery, welcoming fugitives among their ranks as fellow soldiers.[43] And soon internal tensions and the movement of fugitives – what W. E. B. Du Bois called a 'general strike' against the plantation system – 'propelled a reluctant white America down to the road to abolition'.[44] As Marx predicted, organizing black military troops was key to the Union's victory.

Confirming Marx's view of the interconnection of anti-colonial and labour struggles, the Civil War caused 'the greatest economic catastrophe' that had ever threatened Britain and 'sounded the alarm bell' for the European working class.[45] In England, the campaigns for British military intervention in support of the south by the cotton manufacturers, the press, and the government did not find supporters among the industrial working class, who admirably supported the emancipation of the slaves.[46] It was because of pressure from below, Marx noted in February 1862, that 'not a single public war meeting could be held in the United Kingdom', not even in Manchester.[47]

40 W. E. B. Du Bois, *Black Reconstruction in America 1860–1880* (New York: Atheneum, 1969), p. 57.
41 Marx to Engels, 7 August 1862, in *MECW*, vol. XLI, p. 400.
42 Marx to Lion Philips, 6 May 1861, in *MECW*, vol. XLI, p. 277.
43 A. Zimmerman (ed.), 'From the Second American Revolution to the First International and Back Again', in G. P. Downs and K. Masur (eds.), *The World the Civil War Made* (Chapel Hill: University of North Carolina Press, 2015), p. 314.
44 E. Foner, *Reconstruction: America's Unfinished Revolution 1863–1867* (New York: Harper Perennial, 2014), p. 3.
45 Karl Marx, *Capital*, vol. I, trans. Ben Fowkes (Harmondsworth: Penguin, 1976), p. 91.
46 Workers repeatedly proclaimed 'their warmest sympathy for the endeavours of the Abolitionists to bring about a final solution of the question of slavery'. See Karl Marx, 'A London Workers' Meeting' (1862), in *MECW*, vol. XIX, p. 156.
47 Karl Marx, 'English Public Opinion' (1862), in *MECW*, vol. XIX, p. 137; see also Marx, 'A London Workers' Meeting', p. 154.

It was in the wake of this great example of workers' international and anti-racist solidarity that the International Working Men's Association (IWMA, or First International) was founded on 28 September 1864. Even more striking was the international solidarity displayed by the proletariat during the Polish uprising against Russian domination of 1863–4. In July 1864, at an international meeting in London in solidarity with the Polish insurrection, British trade unionists and French workers agreed to found an association aimed at the co-ordination of working-class activities in different countries. The founding meeting of the International Working Men's Association on 28 September was also attended by Italian followers of Giuseppe Mazzini, French socialists and Blanquists, Polish revolutionaries, and members of the former Communist League, including Marx. His activity in the IWMA was central, aimed at reinforcing international solidarity which, according to the *Inaugural Address* he wrote, was the condition for the conquest of political power and the emancipation of the proletariat.[48]

Unlike the Communist League, the First International was not a predominantly political and propagandistic organization; it also had strong support from the powerful British trade unions.[49] The International grew vigorously in its first years of activity, partly as a consequence of the strike movements following the upswing of 1868. It gained new members and spread to new countries. In the same period, the political standing of Marx and Engels increased sharply. The IMWA embraced a wide range of political tendencies, from British trade unionists allied to the Liberals to followers of the anarchist leader Mikhail Bakunin.[50] Marx expected that the revival of the movement, together with the struggle that he and Engels were waging, would enable the workers to develop a revolutionary consciousness.[51] 'Every step of real movement is worth a dozen programmes', he told Wilhelm Bracke.[52] He was aided in this by the formation in 1869 of the Social Democratic Workers' Party, led by his allies Wilhelm Liebknecht and August Bebel.

In 1864, the General Council of the IMWA issued an address, written by Marx, congratulating US president Abraham Lincoln on his re-election and welcoming the struggle against slavery as part of its own struggle for

---

48 'The General Council of the International Working Men's Association on the Lausanne Congress' (1867), in *MECW*, vol. xx, p. 422.
49 Marx to Joseph Weydemeyer, 29 November 1864, in *MECW*, vol. xlii, p. 44.
50 See Chapter 10 in this volume.
51 Marx to Engels, 4 November 1864, in *MECW*, vol. xlii, p. 18.
52 Marx to Wilhelm Bracke, 5 May 1875, in *MECW*, vol. xlv, p. 70.

emancipation.[53] Indeed, as Marx wrote in *Capital*, Volume I, 'labour in white skin cannot emancipate itself when it is branded in a black skin'.[54] In the aftermath of the US Civil War, there was a wave of working-class revolt and a new militant spirit among freed slaves. The truly 'multi-national' working classes of the United States embraced the struggle for the eight-hour day, which soon became a key demand of the First International. But Marx was well aware of the challenges facing the labour movement in the United States. If US citizens did not immediately declare black people 'free and equal, without any reserve', they would 'sooner or later face a new struggle which will once more drench [their] country in blood'.[55] Such was the revolutionary potential of this movement, in his eyes, that in the 1867 Preface to *Capital* Marx declared that the US Civil War 'sounded the tocsin' for the European working class.[56]

Ireland and the National Question

In 1868 the International's Brussels Congress passed a resolution recommending workers to read the first volume of *Capital*. 'As long as there have been capitalists and workers on earth', Engels stated, 'no book has appeared which is of as much importance for the workers as the one before us.'[57] Central in it was the exposition of the theory of surplus value, which laid bare the secret of capitalist exploitation and the laws of development of capitalism as a global system. Since 'capital is dead labour, which, vampire-like, lives only by sucking living labour' and relies on labour co-operation, for Marx, capital also creates the conditions for its own supersession, for the 'expropriation of the expropriators' that paves the way to the future human society.

After Lassalle's secret negotiations with Bismarck were exposed, Engels complained to Marx that he had 'given the movement a Tory–Chartist character, which it will be difficult to get rid of and which has given rise to a tendency in Germany which was previously unheard of by the workers. This nauseating toadying to the reaction comes through everywhere. We shall have some trouble with that.'[58] The problem was not just explicit

---

53 See R. Blackburn, *An Unfinished Revolution: Karl Marx and Abraham Lincoln* (London and New York: Verso, 2011).

54 Marx, *Capital*, vol. I, p. 414.

55 Institute of Marxism-Leninism (ed.), *General Council of the First International, 1864–1866, Minutes* (Moscow: Progress Publishers, 1962), pp. 311–13; cf. Du Bois, *Black Reconstruction in America*, p. 354, and Anderson, *Marx at the Margins*, p. 114.

56 Marx, *Capital*, vol. I, p. 91.

57 Friedrich Engels, '[Review of Volume I of *Capital* for the *Demokratisches Wochenblatt*]' (1868), in *MECW*, vol. XX, p. 231.

58 Engels to Marx, 13 February 1865, in *MECW*, vol. XLII, p. 88.

capitulation to ruling-class nationalism, but also the refusal (represented by Proudhon and his followers) to recognize the significance of the national question.

In the late 1860s, the intensification of the struggle for Irish independence and Marx's disappointment in Reconstruction in the US south pushed him to reconsider his position on the colonial question[59] and better to appreciate the strength of racism in propping up class domination as Western imperialism continued its worldwide expansion.[60] Marx and Engels affirmed the right of the Irish workers to have an independent organization within the International (Ireland was then an unwilling part of the United Kingdom). Marx also sought by any means to incite the International, English workers in particular, to lend support to the Fenians, who were waging an armed struggle for independence, and to sideline those trade union leaders who had been outspoken against slavery but then backtracked on Ireland.[61] After a number of Fenians were sentenced to death in Manchester in September 1867, just a few days before the publication of *Capital*, Volume I, the International launched a solidarity campaign and 20,000 workers gathered in London to petition for mercy. For Marx, the General Council had to distinguish its position from British interests, treating 'the Irish like the English would treat the Polish'.[62] Irish separation had become inevitable and the working class in England had to support it, including 'protective tariffs against England'.[63]

Two years later, on 24 October 1869, a mass demonstration organized by Fenian supporters took place in London, the largest demonstration since the days of Chartism. For Marx, the participation of English workers showed that 'at least a part of the English working class had lost their prejudice against the Irish'.[64] Marx and Engels did not cease to support the Irish struggle even when they disapproved of its tactics. In November 1869, the General Council supported the resolution Marx drafted giving unconditional solidarity to the

---

59 In Du Bois' eyes (*Black Reconstruction in America*, p. 360), the International took no real root in the United States: one of its main mistakes was to concentrate its activity in the north and fail to realize the centrality of the 'new political power of the Southern worker'.

60 A. Zimmerman in Karl Marx and Friedrich Engels, *The Civil War in the United States*, ed. Andrew Zimmerman (New York: International Publishers, 2016), p. 201.

61 Anderson, *Marx at the Margins*, p. 126.

62 'Record of Marx's Speeches on the Policy of the British Government with Respect to the Irish Prisoners' (1869), in *MECW*, vol. XXI, p. 412.

63 Marx to Engels, 30 November 1867, in *MECW*, vol. XLII, p. 487.

64 Institute of Marxism-Leninism (ed.), *General Council of the First International, 1868–1870, Minutes* (Moscow: Progress Publishers, 1966), p. 172.

Irish. A month later, in a letter to Engels, he declared that he had changed his mind on the relationship between the labour movement in England and the Irish anti-colonial struggle: the lever for the emancipation of the English working class had to be applied primarily in Ireland rather than England. Irish independence, in his view, could severely damage the British ruling classes, deal a blow to landlordism, and accelerate social revolution in Britain, where a transition to socialism was possible:

> For a long time, I believed that it would be possible to overthrow the Irish regime by English working class ascendancy ... Deeper study has now convinced me of the opposite. The English working class will *never accomplish anything* before it has got rid of Ireland. The lever must be applied in Ireland.[65]

According to August Nimtz, this was Marx's most significant turn because it placed the primary revolutionary lever in a colonized country rather than in the metropolis.[66] In Marx's view, even more important than the economic consequences of Irish independence, which he probably overestimated,[67] was the possibility of overcoming the antagonism between English and Irish workers:

> And most important of all! All industrial and commercial centres in England now have a working class *divided* into two *hostile* camps, English proletarians and Irish proletarians. The ordinary English worker hates the Irish worker as a competitor who lowers his standard of life. In relation to the Irish worker he regards himself as a member of the *ruling* nation and consequently he becomes a tool of the English aristocrats and capitalists against Ireland, thus strengthening their domination *over himself*. He cherishes religious, social, and national prejudices against the Irish worker.

Significantly, Marx compared the attitude of the English worker towards the Irish workers to the attitude of the poor white population towards black people in the former slave states of the American Union:

> The Irishman pays him back with interest in his own money. He sees in the English worker both the accomplice and the stupid tool of the *English rule in Ireland*. This antagonism is artificially kept alive and intensified by the press, the pulpit, the comic papers, in short, by all the means at the disposal of the ruling classes. *This antagonism is the secret of the English working class's*

---

65 Marx to Engels, 10 December 1869, in *MECW*, vol. XLIII, p. 398.
66 A. H. Nimtz, *Marx and Engels: Their Contribution to the Democratic Breakthrough* (Albany: State University of New York Press, 2000), p. 104.
67 A. Callinicos, 'Marx's politics', *International Socialism* 2, 58 (2018), pp. 55–8.

impotence, despite its organisation. It is the secret of the maintenance of power by the capitalist class. And the latter is quite aware of this.[68]

Marx and Engels welcomed the possible economic damage Irish independence would inflict on British imperialism and thought it imperative for the British proletariat to distance itself from its own ruling classes. The IWMA General Council had a crucial role in making English workers aware that Irish emancipation was 'not a question of abstract justice or humanitarian sentiment, but the first condition of their own social emancipation'.[69] Workers' support for it was the condition for undermining anti-Irish racism and building solidarity between Irish and English workers. Such solidarity could also open a wedge inside the Irish anti-colonial movement. In private correspondence, Marx and Engels criticized Irish nationalists for attempting to conceal English workers' support for Ireland: for Engels, this was a 'calculated policy' aimed 'to maintain their domination over the peasants'.[70] According to Hal Draper, 'under Marx's guidance, the International became a considerable force for cementing an alliance between the Irish peasant revolution and the English working class struggle'.[71] Years later, Marx noted that, thanks to the attention articles on the Fenian prisoners by his daughter Jenny had drawn to the International, its first section was created inside Ireland.[72]

The Paris Commune and the Break-up of the International

In March 1871, after six months of hunger and ruin caused by the war between France and Prussia, the working people in arms took control of Paris and ruled the city for two months. Initially Marx was not convinced about the prospects of the Commune. In his eyes, the Communards did not have enough national support and their tactics were too moderate: they did not seize the Banque de France or march on Versailles, overthrowing the official government and generalizing the civil war. But Marx supported the Commune wholeheartedly and called it 'the most glorious deed of our Party since the June insurrection in Paris'.[73] In line with what Marx and Engels wrote in the *Manifesto*, the Commune had proved that workers could take political power, destroying the existing military bureaucratic apparatus and replacing it with a state of their

---

68 Marx to Sigfrid Meyer and August Vogt, 9 April 1870, in *MECW*, vol. XLIII, pp. 474–5.
69 Ibid., p. 475.   70 Engels to Marx, 9 December 1869, in *MECW*, vol. XLIII, p. 394.
71 Draper, *Karl Marx's Theory of Revolution*, p. 400.
72 See Anderson, *Marx at the Margins*, p. 152.
73 Marx to Ludwig Kugelmann, 12 April 1871, in *MECW*, vol. XLIV, p. 132.

own. While the Commune was still struggling to survive, Marx developed a programme of peasant demands for the Commune that would be able to cement an alliance with the countryside.[74] But the Commune was bloodily repressed in May, and many revolutionaries were forced to leave Paris.

Whatever the immediate result, for Marx, the Commune was 'a new point of departure of world-historic importance'.[75] In the midst of the fighting on the barricades in Paris, he wrote the 'Address' of the General Council of the International, *The Civil War in France*. Marx reaffirmed his earlier thesis that the proletariat, upon coming to power, should demolish the old state apparatus. Marx and Engels attached such importance to this point that in an 1872 preface to the *Communist Manifesto* they described it as a further development of the principles first laid down in it. The Commune was the 'political form at last discovered under which to work out the economical emancipation of Labour'.[76]

Marx's growing international influence was reflected also in his personal circumstances. After the workers took power in Paris, he was witch-hunted in the press and denounced as the 'head of a vast conspiracy'. Marx even threatened the editor of the *Pall Mall Gazette* with a duel if he did not retract the paper's charges. In spite of this, Marx enjoyed his notoriety, writing to Ludwig Kugelmann that he was 'the best calumniated and the most menaced man in London. That really does one good after a tedious twenty years' idyll in the backwoods.'[77] Italian revolutionaries meeting in Rome in September 1871 offered a toast to 'Carlo Marx, the indefatigable instrument' of the working class. In Macerata, a workers' society chose its three honorary presidents: Giuseppe Garibaldi, Giuseppe Mazzini, and Karl Marx. But in the short term the Commune accelerated the disintegration of the IMWA, as the respectable British trade union leaders abandoned it, the International lost forces in France and Germany, and Bakunin and his followers sought to wrest control.

Social Democracy, World History, and the Women's Question: Crossing the Divides

Despite the defeat of the Commune, the labour movement made a huge leap forward during what Eric Hobsbawm called the Age of Empire (1875–1914): 'Wherever democratic and electoral politics allowed it, mass parties based on the working class, for the most part inspired by an ideology of revolutionary

74 Draper, *Karl Marx's Theory of Revolution*, pp. 392–3.
75 Marx to Ludwig Kugelmann, 17 April 1871, in *MECW*, vol. XLIV, p. 137.
76 Karl Marx, 'The Civil War in France' (1871), in *MECW*, vol. XXII, p. 334.
77 Marx to Ludwig Kugelmann, 18 June 1871, in *MECW*, vol. XLIV, p. 158.

socialism (for all socialism was by definition seen as revolutionary) and led by men – and even sometimes by women – who believed in such an ideology, appeared on the scene and grew with startling rapidity.'[78] The emergence of these mass parties was expressed in the formation of the Second International in 1889.

This advance was a massive vindication of the perspective of growing working-class self-organization outlined in the *Manifesto*. But the task Marx – and more particularly Engels after the former's death in 1883 – faced was that of seeking to guide parties constituted at the national level and operating on the terrain of electoral and parliamentary politics, which created very powerful pressures for socialist leaders to adapt to the existing order. Furthermore, the international context was increasingly shaped by the imperialist expansion by the great powers, which gave rise to dangerous arms races. This confronted the rising socialist movement with increasingly difficult political choices.

Marx and Engels faced the resulting problems first when the most import-ant of these parties, the Social Democratic Party of Germany (SPD), was formed in 1875 as a result of a fusion between their followers and those of Lassalle. While Marx and Engels welcomed the creation of a united workers' party, they were highly critical of the theoretical concessions Liebknecht had made to Lassalle's statist socialism. They criticized the programme adopted at the founding Gotha Congress of the party for its acceptance of the iron law of wages, its silence on trade unions, and its dismissal of non-proletarian classes such as the petty bourgeoisie and the peasantry as forming 'one reactionary mass'. Engels complained to Bebel that 'the principle that the workers' movement is an international one is, to all intents and purposes, utterly denied in respect of the present, and this by men who, for the space of five years and under the most difficult conditions, upheld that principle in the most laudable manner'.[79]

In his 'Critique of the Gotha Programme' Marx, in challenging Lassalle's statism, sought to draw the lessons of the Commune, which he had already called in the drafts to *The Civil War in France* 'a Revolution against the State itself, this supernaturalist abortion of society, a resumption by the people for the people, of its own social life'.[80] Ridiculing the idea of a 'free people's state', he insisted that 'Freedom consists in converting the state from an organ superimposed upon society

<hr/>

78 E. J. Hobsbawm, *The Age of Empire 1875–1914* (London: Weidenfeld & Nicolson, 1987), p. 116.
79 Engels to August Bebel, 18–28 March 1875, in *MECW*, vol. XLV, p. 61.
80 Karl Marx, ['First Draft of *The Civil War in France*'] (1871), in *MECW*, vol. XXII, p. 486.

into one completely subordinate to it.'[81] He distinguished between higher and lower stages of communist society governed by different distributive principles – 'To each according to their labour', which reflected the legacy of capitalism, and the full communist principle, 'From each according to their abilities, to each according to their needs.' Achieving full communism was a historical process: 'Between capitalist and communist society lies the period of the revolutionary transformation of the one into the other. Corresponding to this is also a political transition period in which the state can be nothing but *the revolutionary dictatorship of the proletariat*.'[82]

The implication was that, in transition to full communism, even the radically democratic form of state pioneered by the Commune would cease to be necessary. As Engels puts it, '*It dies out*.'[83] His and Marx's interest in these later years in pre-capitalist communal social forms was intended to vindicate this perspective historically. Engels suggested to Bebel that in the Gotha programme '*Gemeinwesen* [community] be universally substituted for *state*; it is a good old German word that can very well do service for the French "Commune"'.[84] But it was Marx who explored this theme in most depth. In the 1870s his studies became more focused on world history: he deepened his research on pre-capitalist societies, colonialism, and the condition of women in history; reflected on the historical developments of agricultural production; traced the evolution of different forms of communal landed property; and expected to rewrite the section on ground rent in the third volume of *Capital*, in which Russia would occupy a central role as a historical model. Marx investigated communal social forms from Russia and Ireland to Asia, Latin America, and North Africa. In his *Notes on Indian History (664–1858)*, he traced the country's long history of resistance to different colonizers. Marx also studied recent developments in archaeology, ethnology, and anthropology, denouncing the influence of imperialist interests on their development.

These notebooks, as Raya Dunayevskaya noted, document Marx's increasing hostility to colonialism, racism, and gender oppression.[85] In the *Ethnological Notebooks* published by Lawrence Krader, for example, Marx

---

81 Karl Marx, 'Marginal Notes on the Programme of the German Workers' Party' (1875), in *MECW*, vol. XXIV, p. 94.
82 Ibid., p. 95.
83 Friedrich Engels, 'Herr Eugen Dühring's Revolution in Science' (1878), in *MECW*, vol. XXV, p. 268.
84 Engels to Bebel, 18–28 March 1875, p. 64.
85 R. Dunayevskaya, *Women's Liberation and the Dialectic of Revolution: Reaching for the Future* (Atlantic Highlands, NJ: Humanities Press, 1985), pp. 218–19.

rejected racial theories of social progress and refuted the view of the Indo-Europeans as a single race, racial categories, and the concept of the Aryan race itself. He also drew on the works of Lewis Henry Morgan and Johann Bachofen and argued for the historical priority of the gens and the matrilinear lineage, ridiculing the view that the patriarchal family was the original form of family. Imperialist representations, he denounced, projected forms of despotism into primitive institutions in order to naturalize them.[86]

These studies were not a distraction from Marx's central preoccupations of completing his critique of political economy, supervising the translations and revisions of *Capital* in different languages, and promoting the development of the international labour movement. As David N. Smith argued,[87] near the end of his life, Marx felt the need to study even more concretely the resistance that capital confronted in its global expansion. Although he did believe that the capitalist system tended to expand itself globally, he rejected the view that each people had to go through it in order to reach communism.[88] The connection between a peasant revolution in Russia and an anti-capitalist revolution in western Europe, for example, would have allowed Russia to transition towards socialism without the violent dispossession of 'primitive accumulation', unavoidable if the Russian Revolution remained isolated.[89] It is not unrealistic to argue that Marx saw similar possibilities for revolutionary interconnection elsewhere.

Marx's interest in the evolution of the condition of women, for example, was informed by pressing political issues. Women had become more involved in the labour movement, leading Marx to declare that 'major social transformations are impossible without ferment among women'.[90] He argued in favour of women's equality within the First International and praised the 'noble and prominent part' women workers played in the strikes in France in 1868[91] and during the Paris Commune: 'the women of Paris joyfully give up their lives at the barricades and on the places of execution'.[92] France's 1880 Workers' Party programme, which Marx contributed to

---

86 L. Krader (ed.), *The Ethnological Notebooks of Karl Marx* (Assen, Netherlands: Van Gorcum, 1972), pp. 430, 479.
87 D. N. Smith, 'Accumulation and the clash of cultures: Marx's ethnology in context', *Rethinking Marxism* 14, 4 (2002), pp. 79–80.
88 Marx, Letter to *Otechestvennye Zapiski* (1877), in *MECW*, vol. xxiv, p. 200.
89 Karl Marx and Friedrich Engels, 'Preface to the Second Russian Edition of the *Manifesto of the Communist Party*' (1882), in *MECW*, vol. xxiv, p. 426.
90 Marx to Ludwig Kugelmann, 12 December 1868, in *MECW*, vol. xliii, p. 184.
91 Institute of Marxism-Leninism (ed.), *General Council of the First International, 1868–1870, Minutes*, p. 336; H. A. Brown, *Marx on Gender and the Family: A Critical Study* (Leiden and Boston: Brill, 2012), pp. 116, 121.
92 K. Marx, *The Civil War in France* (1871), in *MECW*, vol. xxii, p. 350.

drafting, included demands for the end of women's inferiority in relation to men and for societal responsibility for the care of the elderly and those with disabilities. In this, different *Gemeinwesen* could offer positive models for the struggle ahead. Marx's study of pre-capitalist societies, therefore, was driven by the urgency of international solidarity in the Age of Empire: a motive that Engels did not fully reflect in drawing on these notebooks to write the more evolutionist *The Origin of the Family, Private Property and the State* (1884).

Marxism after Marx

Marx's death left Engels with the task of guiding the rapidly growing international socialist movement. He had described their role to Bebel when he criticized the Gotha Programme: 'People imagine that we run the whole show from here, whereas you know as well as I do that we have hardly ever interfered in the least with internal party affairs, and then only in an attempt to make good, as far as possible, what we considered to have been blunders – and *only theoretical* blunders at that.'[93] *Anti-Dühring* (1879), Engels' defence of Marx against a German academic critic, and its spin-off *Socialism Utopian and Scientific* played an enormous role in educating the swelling ranks of socialist activists in what was now known as Marxism. 'Now for the first time a real Marxist school, a real Marxist tradition, was created on the Continent', writes Gustav Mayer.[94]

While preoccupied with the immense task of editing the second and third volumes of *Capital* (Volume III appeared not long before Engels' death in August 1895), he conducted an extensive correspondence with socialist politicians and intellectuals all over the world. His two guiding principles remained the same as Marx's: insistence on participation in real movements of the working class and unwavering opposition to 'opportunist' adaptations to liberal–bourgeois parliamentary politics. Engels impatiently pressed the Marxist sects in Britain and the United States (he complained that they had 'changed the concept of our movement into a rigid dogma to be learned by rote')[95] to get involved in strikes such as that of the London dockers in 1889. But, after an SPD deputy disavowed the idea of the dictatorship of the proletariat in the Reichstag, Engels riposted: 'Well and good, gentlemen, do you want to know what this dictatorship looks like?

---

93 Engels to Bebel, 18–28 March 1875, p. 65.
94 G. Mayer, *Friedrich Engels: A Biography* (London: Chapman & Hall, 1935), p. 224.
95 Engels to Friedrich Adolph Sorge, 10 June 1891, in *MECW*, vol. XLIX, p. 197.

Look at the Paris Commune. That was the Dictatorship of the Proletariat.'[96]

It is, however, open to question how much practical influence Engels had even on the SPD. After all, his and Marx's criticisms of the Gotha Programme were ignored. After his death, his former secretary Eduard Bernstein argued in *The Preconditions of Socialism* (1899)[97] that the party should abandon its revolutionary Marxist inspiration and openly avow its commitment to reformist gradualism. He was strongly challenged by another of Engels' proteges, Karl Kautsky, as well as by the young and brilliant Polish Social Democrat Rosa Luxemburg, but received much support from the powerful SPD right wing. The party leadership balanced between the different factions. Kautsky ruefully admitted to Bebel in January 1903: 'If Bernstein had written his *Voraussetzungen* [*Preconditions*] when Engels was still alive, the General would not have treated him as delicately as we have, but would have dispatched him with a kick and a cry of "Out, scoundrel."'[98] Indeed, less than ten years earlier Engels had complained to the same Kautsky about how the party leadership had bowdlerized his Introduction to Marx's *Class Struggles in France* when publishing it in their paper *Vorwärts* (*Forward*) 'to present me as a peace-loving proponent of legality *quand même*'.[99]

Where the tension between revolutionary programme and increasingly reformist practice in the SPD and other parties of the Second International reached breaking point was of course in their attitude to the outbreak of the First World War. By the 1890s the risk of a general war was evidently growing, notably with the arms race developing between imperial Germany and the alliance of republican France and tsarist Russia. Engels struggled in his efforts to advise the leaders of the SPD, whose growing delegation of deputies in the Reichstag confronted them with decisions on how to vote on the ballooning military budget. He was hampered by using the political framework that he and Marx had forged during the struggle for democracy and national unification between 1848 and 1871. Then they had seen (sometimes to and beyond the point of exaggeration) tsarist Russia as the citadel of European reaction and France under Napoleon III as its agent. As Vladimir Lenin later pointed out, this problematic no longer fitted the

---

96 F. Engels, 'Introduction to K. Marx's *The Civil War in France*' (1891), in *MECW*, vol. XXVII, p. 191.
97 E. Bernstein, *The Preconditions of Socialism* (Cambridge: Cambridge University Press, 1993).
98 M. Salvadori, *Karl Kautsky and the Socialist Revolution 1880–1938* (London: New Left Books, 1979), p. 79.
99 Engels to Karl Kautsky, 1 April 1895, in *MECW*, vol. L, p. 486.

inter-imperial competition that came to dominate world politics in the years before 1914.

In a letter of 13 October 1891, with a new Franco-Russian alliance in prospect, Engels told Bebel that if a two-front war were imminent the SPD might be justified in voting war credits to the regime:

> Should the threat of war increase, we can then tell the government that we should be prepared, if enabled to do so by decent treatment, to support them against a foreign enemy, provided they prosecuted the war ruthlessly and with all available means, including revolutionary ones. Should Germany be attacked from the east and west, all means of defence would be justified. It is a question not only of the nation's existence but also, in our own case, of asserting the position and the future prospects for which we have fought. The more revolutionary the prosecution of the war, the more it will be waged in accordance with our ideas.[100]

But, even when contemplating unwarranted concessions to the Wilhelmine monarchy, Engels still judged the prospect of war from the point of view of its impact on the revolutionary movement in Germany and elsewhere. He also consistently warned of the hugely destructive and unpredictable consequences of a general war. In *Can Europe Disarm?* (1893) he argued that Germany should propose the gradual conversion of Europe's huge and growing standing armies into people's militias. But Bebel dismissed this plan as not practical politics.[101]

Little more than twenty years later, the SPD's decision to vote for war credits in August 1914 would blow the Second International apart and create the conditions for the formation of the Communist International after the Russian Revolution of October 1917. In justifying this break Lenin drew heavily on the insights that Marx had gained when building the First International – both the necessity of building an international workers' movement based on resisting not merely exploitation but also national, racial, and gender oppression and the objective of what Lenin called the 'Commune State' as the precondition for communism. Despite the development of what has been described as a 'thousand Marxisms', the globality of Marx's and Engels' critique of political economy still offers us untouched resources for confronting the twenty-first century.

---

100 Engels to August Bebel, 13 October 1891, in *MECW*, vol. XLIX, p. 258.
101 Mayer, *Friedrich Engels*, pp. 292–5.

Further Reading

Anderson, Kevin, *Marx at the Margins: On Nationalism, Ethnicity, and Non-Western Societies* (Chicago: University of Chicago Press, 2010).

Brown, Heather A., *Marx on Gender and the Family: A Critical Study* (Leiden and Boston: Brill, 2012).

Callinicos, Alex, Stathis Kouvelakis, and Lucia Pradella (eds.), *Routledge Handbook of Marxism and Post-Marxism* (New York: Routledge, 2020).

Draper, Hal, *Karl Marx's Theory of Revolution*, vol. II, *The Politics of Social Classes* (New York: Monthly Review Press, 1978).

Dunayevskaya, Raya, *Women's Liberation and the Dialectic of Revolution: Reaching for the Future* (Atlantic Highlands, NJ: Humanities Press, 1985).

Krader, Lawrence (ed.), *The Ethnological Notebooks of Karl Marx* (Assen, Netherlands: Van Gorcum, 1972).

Marx, Karl, *Notes on Indian History (664–1858)* (Honolulu: University Press of the Pacific, 2001).

Nimtz, August H., *Marx and Engels: Their Contribution to the Democratic Breakthrough* (Albany: State University of New York Press, 2002).

Pierre-Joseph Proudhon's Mutualist Social Science

ALEX PRICHARD

Introduction

Pierre-Joseph Proudhon was born in Besançon, the capital of the Franche Comté region of France, on 15 January 1809. These were formative times for France and Europe. The Napoleonic wars were turning in favour of the Holy Alliance, and it was the beginning of the end of the First Republic. In 1814, a year before the fall of Napoleon, the Austrians laid siege to Besançon and, following the end of the war, the city was struck by successive waves of famine, compounding the Proudhon family's poverty. Pierre-Joseph's father was a cooper and taverner, who infamously refused to profit from his customers, and his mother was from a modest peasant background. These deprivations made completing a timely, formal education impossible. Nevertheless, his intellect stood out, and his father urged him to take an apprenticeship as a proof-reader and typesetter for a local press, which was highly skilled intellectual work at the time.

The press printed two types of texts in huge quantities, both of which would have a lasting influence on Proudhon's intellectual development and his socialism. The first was the Bible and the endless theological commentaries on it, which prompted him to learn Hebrew at the age of twenty and, later in life, to proclaim theology to be 'the science of the infinitely absurd'.[1] The second was the works of his compatriot from Besançon, Charles Fourier, in particular the *Nouveau Monde Industrielle* (*New Industrial World*, 1829). This text, in all its erratic, neologistic splendour, was a harbinger of bourgeois industrialism and socialist communalism. Its combination of feminist (a term he probably coined), anti-rationalist, anti-clerical, industrial, and communalist futurism, which would also

---

1 P.-J. Proudhon, *What Is Property? Or, an Inquiry into the Principle of Right and of Government*, trans. D. R. Kelley, ed. B. G. Smith (Cambridge: Cambridge University Press, 1994), p. 25.

become so central to the Saint-Simonian movement that followed, was the pole star of Proudhon's socialism in his early years. He melded this set of influences with the debates about republicanism and scientific positivism, to develop his own *science sociale*, which became federalist anti-statism in the final fifteen years of his life. It was also during these last years that he turned back to the Napoleonic wars that had so structured his life. Uniquely among socialists, Proudhon extensively theorized the relationship of international relations to the possibility of freedom from domination.

Throughout this intellectual evolution, Proudhon's primary concern would be the arbitrary and stifling domination of the church, the state, the emerging structures of bourgeois French capitalism. The turn to federalism and international relations, from 1851, developed a unique and insightful account of the ways in which religion, state, and capitalism were being transformed by war, and shaping revolutionary possibilities in turn. As I will show, even though he came to it last, in many respects international relations were analytically primary for Proudhon: the possibility of revolutionary social change at the end of the nineteenth century was determined by the balance of European great power politics. Without international peace and stability, the social revolution would be impossible, he argued. This theory led him to defend the Concert of Europe, reject the Italian *Risorgimento* and the unification of Poland, and dismiss national unity as a focus for revolutionary socialism. Needless to say, this attracted considerable criticism.

This theory of international relations was also underpinned by a sophisticated political philosophy and social science. It foregrounded a scientific understanding of emancipation born of the correct organization of society, predicated on a philosophical, even Heracletian understanding of change and impermanence, the equivalence of exchange relations, the irreducibility and infinite collective plurality of human life, and the moral autonomy and agency of 'natural groups'. Natural groups were any collection of individuals that developed a 'collective consciousness', moral collective personhood, and a *puissance* or force of their own. These forces could be collective ideas, actions, or products. The product of labour is an emergent property, irreducible to any one individual in the process. This produce of collective endeavour was rightfully the group's to exchange as they chose, democratically. Under liberal bourgeois property relations, this product, including any surplus,[2] becomes the

---

2 For a fuller discussion, see I. McKay (ed.), *Property Is Theft! A Pierre-Joseph Proudhon Anthology* (Edinburgh: AK Press, 2011), Introduction and p. 796. Note that where English translations of Proudhon's works are available I have used those and refer to them using

property of the title-holder or capitalist, not the workers who produced it, and title-holders are free to transfer that title as they please. Proudhon located this historic injustice at the heart of *dominium*, the symbiotic relation between states and proprietors, one born out of expropriation and perpetuated through the normalization of liberal theories of sovereignty and property.[3]

In what follows, I will flesh out these key ideas. The chapter has five sections. In the first I briefly discuss the historiography of Proudhon's thought. In the second section I set out the origins and general contours of Proudhon's social science. I then show how this links to his mutualist socialism in the third section before turning to his federalist theory of international relations in the fourth section. In the final section, I turn to his anti-feminism and antisemitism. Proudhon was neither the first nor the last patriarchal racist in the history of socialism, but the epithets have stuck to him more tenaciously. I link both to his wider social theory, to show how they were integral to, but self-evidently a fundamental contradiction of, his thought. I conclude by showing how these main aspects of Proudhon's social theory were engaged, by the right and left, after his death.

The Contested Oeuvre of Pierre-Joseph Proudhon

Proudhon was a self-taught public intellectual who gained mainstream, academic, and popular recognition, and lived solely by the income he generated from his prolific output. Publish or perish was very much the literal reality of his life, and from 1851 he was writing to support his wife and two children. And he was prolific. Proudhon's collected works now span more than fifty volumes. These include the definitive twenty-six volumes of his published works, the *Oeuvres Complètes* (*Complete Works*), eight posthumous works, and eighteen volumes of letters and notebooks, with many more new editions now available, in print and online, thanks to the work of Edward Castleton and others.[4] This collection does not include his commissioned newspaper articles, nor his own publishing ventures, including multiple journals and newspapers. Even his most systematic and extensive works, like *De la justice dans la révolution et dans l'église* (*On Justice in the Revolution and*

---

their translated English title. Translations into English from the original texts are my own.

3 For more on this, see R. Kinna and A. Prichard, 'Anarchism and non-domination', *Journal of Political Ideologies* 24 (2019), pp. 221–40.

4 Edward Castleton has archived and generated facsimiles of Proudhon's unpublished notebooks, manuscripts, and letters, which are publicly available online from the Besançon municipal library: http://memoirevive.besancon.fr, last accessed 13 August 2020.

the Church, 1858), which comes in at 2,358 pages, and *La Guerre et la paix* (*War and Peace*, 1861), at more than 194,000 words, sold tens of thousands of copies each, with works such as *What Is Property?* (1840) and *The Principle of Federation* (1863) not eclipsed until decades later by Marx's *Capital*. By the time of his death in 1865, Proudhon was without doubt one of the most significant socialist theorists in Europe. Nevertheless, like almost all writers, he was always on the verge of poverty, and lacking a benefactor and permanent library, moving periodically, being jailed for three years, and being twice forced into exile, with no let-up in output, meant his writings had to be based on borrowed books and notes collected sometimes decades before in his indispensable, but rambling *carnets*. This explains some of the inconsistency across his writings.

In the English language much of the reception of Proudhon's writings is filtered through Marx's *Poverty of Philosophy* (1847), a riposte to *System of Economical Contradictions, or the Philosophy of Poverty* (1846). This book was certainly an interesting marker in the development of Marx's thinking, but a careful and considered reconstruction and engagement with Proudhon's ideas it is not. Based on this text, and much of the Marxist-inspired secondary literature, many English-language commentators persist with the myth that Proudhon was impenetrably incoherent and/or a liberal individualist.[5] These myths have no doubt been off-putting for a number of would-be novice researchers. Thankfully, more recent contextualist histories of Proudhon's thought have reset our understanding of Proudhon's place in the history of socialism.[6] What these show is that, while Proudhon's ideas inevitably developed over time, and in such prolific output there is inevitably some contradiction, his underlying social philosophy was nevertheless remarkably consistent and coherent. This said, his theory is always shrouded in contemporary detail, which gave it popular appeal at the time, but which means it also dated quickly, and now demands considerable knowledge of the historical context in order to make sense of it. Nevertheless, this speaks to the politically engaged nature of his political theory.

---

5 See, for example, P. Thomas, *Karl Marx and the Anarchists* (London: Routledge, 1980), and A. Ritter, *The Political Thought of Pierre-Joseph Proudhon* (Princeton: Princeton University Press, 1969). For a set of criticisms of Marx's reading of Proudhon, see I. McKay, 'Proudhon's constituted value and the myth of labour notes', *Anarchist Studies* 25, 1 (2017), pp. 32–67.
6 The standard text is K. S. Vincent, *Pierre-Joseph Proudhon and the Rise of French Republican Socialism* (Oxford: Oxford University Press, 1984).

Socialism v. *Science Sociale*

It is often claimed that Proudhon was not a socialist. But it is more accurate to show that Proudhon associated socialism with communism and Jacobinism, and both almost entirely with the writings of Louis Blanc. As an anti-statist, he could not associate with this Jacobin republicanism. In *System of Economical Contradictions*, he defines socialism as an immature political ideology, ill defined and imprecise, but always the child of Blanc's Jacobinism. In his 'Manifesto for Election' in 1848, he remarked that, 'For us, socialism is not a system: it is, quite simply, a protest.'[7] What socialism lacked was any scientific underpinning, resulting in a doctrine of authority, not unlike a religion. Proudhon's social science, which he spent the rest of his life trying to set out, sought out a more secure scientific basis for the emancipatory organization of labour.

Three intellectual tendencies in Restoration France made the most telling impact on Proudhon's social science. These were the various inflections of Saint-Simonism, which includes the ideas of Charles Fourier and Auguste Comte and the communalism of Etienne Cabet; the liberalism of Adam Smith, Benjamin Constant, Jean Baptiste Say, Jules Barni, and others; and the radical republicanism of the Jacobins, including, most notably for Proudhon and for European politics generally, Jean-Jacques Rousseau and his followers, including Immanuel Kant. However, his first and lasting adversary was the Catholic Church. These intellectual foils can be clearly seen in his first three publications.

Proudhon's first published piece was the prize-winning *De la célébration du dimanche* (*On the Celebration of the Sabbath*, 1839). This essay explored the social, communal function of the observance of the Sabbath. For Proudhon, the Sabbath could be retooled in republican ways by appealing to a secular communion. The promise of religion, he argued, could be truly realized only in a secular, egalitarian society. In almost every book he published subsequently, this primordial and primitive nature of theodicy was the philosophical and historical genesis of secular and republican modernity. It was not a transcendence, but a humanization, of religion. He soon proclaimed himself an anti-theist, not just denying the plural ideas societies hold of gods, or their social function, but rejecting the notion of god as such. For Proudhon, religion served a social and intellectual function in the early stages of our development: it is what you get when you do not have better empirical

---

7 Pierre-Joseph Proudhon, 'Manifesto for Election', in McKay (ed.), *Property Is Theft!*, p. 372.

explanations. Piercing the divine, the originary philosophy, as he put in *La Guerre et la paix*, is the object of science.[8]

Proudhon's second book was the product of the prize scholarship that *De la célébration du dimanche* won him. *What Is Property? Or an Inquiry into the Principle of Right and of Government* (1840) remains Proudhon's most famous book in the English language, giving birth to anarchism as a political ideology, but also arguably socialism as such. Marx is surely right that this was the first scientific treatment of the concept of property in history. In brief, Proudhon argued that the exclusive right to a thing, dominium, was impossible to defend by recourse to nature or reason. It could only be sustained, in practice, by the state in the interests of proprietors, those who profit from rent, usury, debt, and the labour of others. Because the state is imperative to the enforcement of property rights, and needs proprietors to fund its activities in turn, the one could not be removed without the removal of the other. Private property is impossible, even with state force, because the state itself demands its share. The reality, Proudhon argued, was that all property was usufruct, mutually agreed use, and what was needed was more egalitarian rules to govern this necessarily social relation. Calling for the removal of the state, Proudhon declared himself an 'anarchist',[9] the enemy of all domination, material and ideal, from slavery to the ontological absolute, which was at this time primarily associated with the idea of God.

For Proudhon, the promise of the republic was a 'positive anarchy',[10] not only freedom from slavery, but also an enabling set of federated institutions that protected the maximal freedoms agreed, directly, by all. Proudhon's anarchism was the heir and logical conclusion of nineteenth-century republicanism, in particular the ideas of Rousseau. From Rousseau he developed ideas of communal self-governance, an explicit rejection of church and the *ancien régime*, and an account of constitutional republicanism that could harness the will of the collective, protect the moral dignity of the individual, and throw off the shackles of domination. But, unlike Rousseau, Proudhon celebrated communal autonomy and rejected the centralization and the mythological construction of the nation. Universal male suffrage was designed to elide social pluralism or factions, he thought. Proudhon objected to it on these terms, arguing that democracy ought to be the direct voice of all social groups as well.

By the mid-nineteenth century, the conjoining of the state and the people was being described as a 'Supreme Being', the metaphysical colossus of the

---

8 P.-J. Proudhon, *La Guerre et la paix. Recherches sur la principe et la constitution du droit des gens*, 2 vols. (Paris: Editions Tops, 1998), vol. I, p. 40.
9 Proudhon, *What Is Property?* (1994), p. 205.
10 Cited in Vincent, *Pierre-Joseph Proudhon*, p. 170.

revolution. The state was the aggregation of the will of the people. Proudhon's objection was that the state ran roughshod over the constituent groups of society, which were more immediately and tangibly real than the metaphysical monster the Jacobins sought to construct. Proudhon's third book, *De la création de l'ordre dans l'humanité* (*On the Creation of Order in Humanity*, 1843), was directed primarily to refuting Saint-Simonian and Jacobin ideas such as these, but Fourier's account of order was the main object of attack.

The essence of Fourier and the Saint-Simonians' argument was that humans had natural proclivities, aptitudes, and gifts, determined by biology, which would find their fullest expression in a social order that encouraged and nurtured them. For Fourier, the communalists, Icarians, and the communists, the collective was superior to the sum of the individual wills, and had an autonomous personality. But to realize this supreme being demanded the design of fantastically intricate utopias, all of which were closed communities, hierarchically organized, in which individual autonomy, the egoist pathology at the heart of society, could be sublimated into the communal whole. In Comte's *System of Positive Politics* (1851), arguably the nadir of this line of argument, these communities would stretch to national borders and be administered by a cadre of 'Priest Scientists', with the bourgeoisie below, guiding a docile and happy labouring class to the ends of social harmony. All other social factions would vanish: 'the government of things replaces that of men', and the state eventually withers away.[11]

In nearly all his subsequent works, Proudhon objects to and develops his critique of this type of hierarchical and arbitrary authority, in which individuality vanishes from the philosophy of history and politics. In response, he drew on Kant and the liberals to defend the moral dignity of the individual and developed a philosophy of history around an idea of 'immanence'.[12] As he put it in *De la justice*, to talk in terms of immanence makes one 'a true anarchist'.[13]

11 A. Comte, 'Plan of the Scientific Work Necessary for the Reorganisation of Society', in H. S. Jones (ed.), *Comte: Early Political Writings* (Cambridge: Cambridge University Press, 1998), p. 108. In 1852, Auguste Comte sent Proudhon a copy of his *System of Positive Politics*, with a request to join Comte in proselytizing the positivist religion, which Proudhon declined for the same reasons he turned down Marx in 1846: he objected to the idea of Comte's Priest Scientists, among other things.

12 The significance of this latter concept is often underestimated in the existing secondary literature. For an exception, see J. S. Cohn, *Anarchism and the Crisis of Representation: Hermeneutics, Aesthetics, Politics* (Selinsgrove, PA: Susquehanna University Press, 2006), pp. 73–6.

13 P.-J. Proudhon, *De la justice dans la révolution et dans l'église* (Paris: Fayard, 1988–91), p. 637.

For Proudhon, if something is immanent it is latent within and emerges out of concrete social processes, realized in and through purposeful, directed individual and collective human agency. Where he differed from Comte was in arguing that there was no necessary directionality to this process, because individual agency was, philosophically at least, free. Comte famously argued that the positivist future is pre-ordained in the material structures of history. The correct scientific understanding of time, he said, should proceed from the past, to the future, to the present: 'the dead rule the living', as he famously put it.

Developing liberal ideas, in particular Adam Smith's theory of the division of labour, Proudhon argued that human ingenuity and initiative were central to the production of history.[14] Production is free when it tends towards the increasing division of labour, to specialization, to artistry, and to co-operation and co-ordination, and the free exchange of ideas and materials to this end. As he detailed in *The Philosophy of Progress* (1853), progress was not the fulfilment of a telos, end, or utopia. Progress was, indeed ought to be, the conscious development of social and political systems that enabled the utmost freedom for individuals and groups. Progress was the development of openness, not the realization of a transcendent ideal. Anything that constrains this free flow of human initiative, purposefully or unintentionally, is unjust and by definition antithetical to the possibility of progress.[15] Teleological and transcendent accounts of history are as unjust as direct domination, because, being false, they arbitrarily close down the scope of free thought and agency.

Following Kant, Proudhon argued that the dynamism of history emerged from a perpetual rebalancing of the 'antinomies' in new social and historical contexts. For Kant, the antinomies were noumenal, ideal, and free, but had no corollary in the material world, which was mechanical and deterministic. Proudhon, by contrast, developed a metaphysics he called 'ideo-realism', which posited that ideas are phenomenal, born of both nature and context, and also, in turn, enabling human agency. Proudhon argued that the ideas were not lenses, which once polished sufficiently would give us a perfect understanding of reality. Rather, following Comte's biological naturalism, he argued that our ideas were generated by our physical being, in society. Our bodies are 'moral organs', as he put it in

14 See McKay (ed.), *Property Is Theft!*, pp. 180, 289, 546, 658, 668.
15 P.-J. Proudhon, *The Philosophy of Progress* (2012 [1853]), trans. S. Wilbur, www.libertar ian-labyrinth.org/working-translations/the-philosophy-of-progress-revised-transla tion/, last accessed 13 August 2020.

De la justice.[16] In other words, ideas are real and are as shaped by society as shaping of it. This was a nuanced argument for the 1850s, where materialist structuralism, or liberal idealism, predominated.

Justice was the historically evolving product of human agency. It was codified in law, as right, but not reducible to it. Justice evolves, he argued, and so then must our laws, as we rebalance the poles of the antinomy. For example, good and evil are not only intellectual categories: for Proudhon they are real and realized or institutionalized in society. Society makes us, and our ideas of the good, but we have a purposeful ability to shape social facts in line with new equilibria between our conscience and the discoveries of science. Collectively, then, we establish temporary equilibria between the poles of the antinomies, like good and evil, liberty and authority, (re-) reconciling one with the other, with appeal to, or by reshaping, the prevailing wisdom of that historical era and our conscience.

In *Du principe fédératif* (*The Federative Principle*, 1863), he argues that it is not only that the balance between the needs or relative virtues of liberty and authority changes over time, but also that the very nature and meaning of the terms themselves change too.[17] The resolution is immanent to our intellect and society, shaped but not preordained by history. In constructing our own ideas about the world and balancing the inevitable antinomies of thought and of life, we come to make our own histories. Whether this is progress or not depends on whether it widens the scope of freedom and initiative, not whether it fulfils a historic ideal or telos.[18]

The antinomy between individual and community is another central antinomy in Proudhon's philosophy. Crucially, the individual neither thinks nor acts in isolation, but always in communion. Proudhon called the communities that individuals join or form 'natural groups'. They were natural insofar as they emerged out of the organic needs and actions of individuals. These groups are empirical, real, self-directing, and collectively conscious, an idea he adapted from Comte's theory of 'social facts'. These communities or associations are, *inter alia*, functional, affective, compelled, instrumental, accidental, but always supervenient, collective consciousnesses. He objected to the metaphysical claim that social groups were somehow superior, because different from people. As he put it, 'how can

---

16 Proudhon, *De la justice*, p. 2057.
17 P.-J. Proudhon, *The Principle of Federation*, trans. R. Vernon (Toronto: University of Toronto Press, 1979).
18 For more on this, see H. De Lubac, *Un-Marxian Socialist: A Study of Proudhon*, trans. R. E. Scantlebury (London: Sheed and Ward, 1948).

the genus possess a quality that is not in the individual?'[19] Individuals are the moral basis for groups, not vice versa.

Mutualism

Mutualism, another of Proudhon's neologisms, can be understood as the mature articulation of his social science. On the basis that society is onto-logically complex and irreducible to any one individual, but nevertheless structured historically by the division of labour and collective forces, he demanded a general egalitarian principle of reciprocity between everything from individual behaviour through to the federal constitutional relations of peoples in a global society. In *The Political Capacity of the Working Class* (1865), his last book, mutualism implied:

> mutual insurance, mutual credit, mutual aid, mutual education, reciprocal guarantees of job opportunities and markets, of exchange, of labour, of the good quality and fair pricing of goods, etc. This is what mutualism intends to create, with the help of certain institutions, a principle of the State, a law of the State, I even would say a sort of religion of the State, the practice of which is as easy for citizens as it is beneficial to them; one which requires neither police, nor repression, nor constraints, and cannot, under any condi-tions, for anyone, become a cause of deception and ruin.[20]

This is not a state we would recognize today. Proudhon is calling for the full, transparent participation of citizens in all public affairs, localized in their respective, linked and overlapping, groups, with responsibility shared by all. This 'positive anarchy' is any social order in which there is no final point of authority, because authority is mutualized. In the absence of hierarchical authority relations, it is incumbent on the constituent groups to organize their relations in ways that maintain their mutual freedoms, and these relations must of course be reciprocal, because, as Kant put it, for one to be

---

19 Cited in M. C. Behrent, 'Pluralism's Political Conditions: Social Realism and the Revolutionary Tradition in Pierre Leroux, P.-J. Proudhon and Alfred Fouillée', in J. Wright and H. S. Jones (eds.), *Pluralism and the Idea of the Republic in France* (London: Palgrave Macmillan, 2012), p. 110. For Constance Margaret Hall, Proudhon was one of the first to theorize an equilibrium between the collective and the individual in this way: C. M. Hall, *The Sociology of Pierre-Joseph Proudhon, 1809–1865* (New York: Philosophical Library, 1971). For more on the theory of collective intentionality, see A. Prichard, 'Collective intentionality, complex pluralism and the problem of anarchy', *Journal of International Political Theory* 13, 3 (2017), pp. 360–77.
20 McKay (ed.), *Property Is Theft!*, p. 730.

free, all must be free. Anarchist or mutualist politics becomes a quintessentially constitutional politics, setting out and then institutionalizing the relative powers and responsibilities of groups and individuals, functionally and in accordance with the prevailing or historical norms of justice, themselves transformed by the findings of science and education. As such, mutualism can be understood as a 'permanent revolution', another term he probably coined.[21]

Proudhon's politics was revolutionary insofar as it implied the constant search for, and overthrow of, all arbitrary systems of domination. The most common form of arbitrary domination is that which results within and from the formation of any collective or association, the arbitrary domination of one individual by another, or by groups of others. Groups become dominating when minorities and majorities dominate without any intermediary group, constitutional provision, or democratic voice to explicitly justify it. The French economy was a case in point. Proudhon described the emerging economy as 'industrial feudalism' and *militarisme*. The former denoted the arbitrary powers industrialists had over the workers once the factory doors were closed, and the second referred to the conjoining of state and military industry to the ends of general exploitation and war.[22] Proprietors, politicians, military industrialists, monarchs, and emperors exercised arbitrary power over workers, subjects, and citizens, and universal suffrage could not resolve this, he argued. Universal suffrage was more akin to a plebiscite on a general system of injustice pre-arranged by elites.

Ironically, Proudhon stood for election to the National Assembly, twice, succeeding the second time in 1848, and campaigned on a mutualist platform. Once elected, he participated in the infamous Committee of Finance, alongside Adolphe Thiers, who would later turn state guns on the people of Paris during the June Days of 1848 and then again in 1871. Proudhon objected to the national workshops programme. Established in response to public protests for 'the right to work', these workshops, Proudhon argued, would centralize power and would leave the underlying social origins of the problem of unemployment untouched.

His protests against one of the earliest examples of social democracy failed, and if he was not an anarchist beforehand, he certainly became one then. He redoubled his critique of private property, much to the chagrin of the Parisian

21 Vincent, *Pierre-Joseph Proudhon*, p. 186.
22 '*Militarisme*' was another of Proudhon's neologisms. See V. R. Berghahn, *Militarism: The History of an Intellectual Debate 1861–1971* (Leamington Spa: Berg Publishers, 1981), p. 1.

bourgeoisie, arguing that private capital should be liquidated through mutual exchange banks. He argued that the only way to gradually make property a social product, and to allow labour to organize itself, was to institute interest rates at, or as near as possible to, zero and to develop mutual exchange banks to serve as autonomously worker-run associations. This last system he later called *'autogestion'*, an idea revived by French radicals seventy years later. Once these groups were the economic base of society, the state would resemble a regional delegate assembly with strict mandates, initiating large infrastructure projects, but otherwise stepping out of the economic and political organization of society, which would be left to the federations of worker assemblies, the latter therefore the 'toothing stone of universal republic'.[23] He was jailed for these ideas in 1849.

International Relations and the Future of the Revolution

It was not until his final years that Proudhon properly theorized the 'universal republic'. His ideas took root while he was incarcerated in Sainte-Pélagie (1849 and 1852). It was during this time, and over the subsequent years, that he adopted the term 'federalism' to define his politics, too, and generalized this mutualist theory to European politics and the philosophy of war and peace.

While incarcerated, he struck up an enduring friendship with Giuseppe Ferrari, the celebrated Italian federalist, who published one of his most important works, *The Republican Federation*, in 1851. Ferrari, Alexander Herzen, the painter Gustave Courbet and Charles Beslay (two future leaders of the Paris Commune), and Alfred Darimon came to visit him in jail, and would spend their evenings discussing the failure of the Second Republic, the Battle of the Sonderbund to defend the Swiss Confederation in 1847, and the debates over the unification of Poland, Germany, and Italy.[24] Proudhon's ideas developed over the following years and were nourished by the ideas of Jules Michelet, the celebrated French historian, whose lectures Proudhon

---

23 Cited in E. Castleton, 'Association, mutualism, and corporate form in the published and unpublished writings of Pierre-Joseph Proudhon', *History of Economic Ideas* 25, 1 (2017), p. 164.

24 A not insignificant footnote to this period of incarceration is Proudhon courting and marrying his wife, Euphraise, fathering his first child, and writing three more books before release. For more on the productive and enduring friendship between Proudhon and Ferrari, see C. M. Lovett, *Giuseppe Ferrari and the Italian Revolution* (Chapel Hill: University of North Carolina Press, 1979).

attended in 1839. Michelet sent Proudhon a copy of his *History of the French Revolution* in 1853. His argument that the Jacobins had destroyed the organically federal nature of French society would resonate strongly with Proudhon.[25]

This federalist theory was crystallized during his five years in exile, between 1858 and 1863. After the collapse of the Second Republic, Marx, Mazzini, Louis Blanc, Pierre Leroux, and others fled to London. Proudhon, by contrast, went into exile in francophone Brussels for two months in 1849, but returned to face the music and was incarcerated in Sainte-Pélagie later that year. Nine years later, when the publication of his magnum opus *De la justice* prompted a fine, censorship, and then the threat of imprisonment, Proudhon again chose exile in Brussels. This divergence was hugely significant for Proudhon's social theory. Unlike his contemporaries, Proudhon turned to international rather than class conflict. On the one hand, this is unsurprising because there was no mass working-class movement to speak of at the time but, on the other hand, it is also striking how little attention his contemporaries paid to the subject of war and European politics.

Between 1858 and 1863, Proudhon completed *La Guerre et la paix*, two books on the unification of Italy, one on the post-war settlement of 1815, and manuscripts on the unification of Poland and the concept of natural borders, the latter published posthumously in 1875. In these works, Proudhon developed his ideas of collective force and natural groups to their logical conclusions. He argued that the epitome of collective force in history was war. War had historically been understood as a 'divine' expression of social agency, shaping the most profound storytelling, from the Iliad to the Bible, justifying empire and religion. But the brutality of war, he argued, contravened the 'divine' principles it sought to realize. The philosophers rationalized this historical evil in terms of a secular theodicy. Kant, his foil here, had argued that good would inevitably emerge out of the evil of war, fulfilling the telos of history and the structures of reason.[26] Proudhon was not so sure.

25 Michelet included Proudhon's thank-you note as the preface to the second, 1868 edition. See G. Navet, 'P.-J. Proudhon: Pluralism, Justice and Society', in Wright and Jones (eds.), *Pluralism and the Idea of the Republic in France*, pp. 85–98.

26 On Proudhon's international theory, see A. Prichard, *Justice, Order and Anarchy: The International Political Theory of Pierre-Joseph Proudhon* (Abingdon: Routledge, 2013); F. Ferretti and E. Castleton, 'Fédéralisme, identités nationales et critique des frontières naturelles. Pierre-Joseph Proudhon (1809–1865), géographe des "Etats-Unis d'Europe"', *Cybergeo: European Journal of Geography* (2016), pp. 1–23, DOI: https://doi.org/10.4000/cybergeo.27639; E. Castleton 'Pierre-Joseph Proudhon's *War and Peace*: The Right of Force Revisited', in B. Kapossy, I. Kakhimovsky, and R. Whatmore (eds.), *Commerce*

Proudhon argued that the inevitability of perpetual peace was guaranteed only if the martial impulse could be retooled to productive ends. Industrialization was the key, but progress could be guaranteed only if production and politics were diversified not centralized, communalized not militarized. The signs were not great. He argued that the militarist capabilities of states were enabling unification and centralization in unprecedented ways. For this reason, Proudhon advocated federalism, not unification, as a working-class revolutionary politics. His final works were appeals to revolutionaries such as Mazzini and statesmen such as Napoleon III to draw back from the tendency to unification, and to celebrate and constitute regional federal autonomy. Federalism could constrain states, enable a sophisticated division of labour, and give political voice to the groups necessary to reconstitute society from the bottom up. Rather than advocate for the end of the 1815 treaties signed at the Congress of Vienna, as his radical compatriots had, Proudhon argued for the embedding of its secular, quasi-constitutional international architecture as the precondition of revolutionary domestic reforms. The congress balanced French power through treaty and military force; it did not seek to destroy France. And this was precisely how Proudhon understood federalism: balancing forces through pacts. Without this international stability, progress and justice in places such as Italy or Poland would be impossible, he argued. Unifying states would make them prizes for the more powerful to seize, whether from outside, as in the case of Poland, or internally in the case of Italy.[27]

Proudhon modelled his future for Europe on the cantonal and communal autonomy enshrined in the Swiss constitution, arguments championed by Proudhonists in the League of Peace and Freedom, particularly the Bern congress (1868), and the meetings of the International Working Men's Association in the years immediately before and following his death (1864–8).[28] Interestingly, Mazzini, Proudhon's foil here, left Switzerland out of his map of the future Europe of Nations, believing the country too diverse to survive the revolutionary period. Proudhon was on the right side of history, but the wrong side of the argument; as he prophetically put it: 'the twentieth century must open the era of federations, or else humanity will resume a thousand years of purgatory'.[29]

and Peace in the Enlightenment (Cambridge: Cambridge University Press, 2017), pp. 272–99.

27 For more on this, see A. Prichard, 'Deepening anarchism: international relations and the anarchist ideal', Anarchist Studies 18 (2010), pp. 29–57.

28 E. Castleton, 'The origins of "collectivism": Pierre-Joseph Proudhon's contested legacy and the debate about property in the International Workingmen's Association and the League of Peace and Freedom', Global Intellectual History 2 (2017), pp. 169–95.

29 P.-J. Proudhon, 'The Federative Principle', in McKay (ed.), Property Is Theft!, pp. 710–11.

Fig. 12.1 Pierre-Joseph Proudhon, 1850. (Photo by Apic/Getty Images.)

Anti-Feminism and Antisemitism

Proudhon's mutualist socialism was, for all its ingenuity, also deeply sexist and racist. He actively and systematically promoted a provincial patriarchal, sexist politics and the antisemitic and racist tropes that suffused socialism at this time. These views surface throughout his writings, but in unequal measure. While his antisemitism never reached the systematic exposition of Marx's pamphlet 'On the Jewish Question' (1846), for example, this cannot be said for his anti-feminism, which was the subject of three books. Two were published as the eleventh and twelfth études of his magnum opus, *De la justice dans la révolution et dans l'église* (1858), titled 'Love and Marriage' and 'Women', and the third was penned during his final, sick, and often deranged days, published posthumously in 1875 as *La Pornocratie. Ou, les femmes dans les temps modernes* (*Pornocratie, or Women in Modern Times*). Including this discussion here is as much a warning to contemporary socialists as it is an uncovering of the past, and reconstructing this aspect of Proudhon's thought helps illustrate, via a concrete example, the pros and cons of his wider theory.

My summary of Proudhon's place in the history of socialism comes full circle at this point, because his antisemitism and anti-feminism have similar intellectual foils: Saint-Simonism. What makes this so much more painful for the progressive and sympathetic reader of Proudhon's work is that the Saint-Simonian movement was a welcome home for radical feminists, both men and women, and black and Jewish radical intellectuals. Indeed, some of the most progressive parts of French politics stemmed from this group, most of whom graduated from the new Ecole Polytechnique during the July Monarchy. These highly educated public intellectuals and reformers were also economists, financiers, and bankers by training, and often by family heritage, with many subsequently becoming senior figures in a range of posts in the republican and imperial governments, including Michel Chevalier, who would negotiate the Cobden–Chevalier free trade treaty in 1860, Pierre Leroux, and many others. This professional evolution would fuel antisemitic conspiracy theories throughout the period.

The feminist movement at this time also emerged out of, indeed, could be seen as synonymous with, Saint-Simonism and was largely a male movement. Alongside Fourier, and Saint-Simon's search for the 'Female Messiah' (pursued enthusiastically by Prosper Enfantin and Auguste Comte), there were also the writings and activism of the female Saint-Simonians, including Jenny D'Héricourt and Jeanne Derroin, among others.[30] Both were active in caring for women left destitute by the exploitation of men, including concubines, prostitutes, and abandoned wives and their children, as well as leading radical publishing initiatives and political campaigning. While the men focused their energies on *Le Globe*, the women ran journals such as *La Voix des femmes* (*The Voice of Women*) and *Opinion des femmes* (*The Opinion of Women*). *Tribune des femmes* (*Women's Tribune*), which originally had a unisex editorial team, was later run as a wholly independent journal for women by women. Also, Flora Tristan, grandmother of the artist Paul Gauguin, was an active feminist campaigner on women's issues, who called on workers to emancipate themselves through unionization four years prior to the publication of the *Communist Manifesto*.

Combining his anti-feminism with standard antisemitic tropes of Jewish conspiracies, Proudhon believed that neither D'Héricourt nor Derroin had

---

30 K. Offen, 'A nineteenth-century French feminist rediscovered: Jenny P. D'Héricourt, 1809–1875', *Signs* 13 (1987), pp. 144–58. See also S. Wilbur, www.libertarian-labyrinth .org/the-sex-question/welcome-anarchy-sex-question/, last accessed 6 August 2020.

the intellectual capacity or philosophical acumen necessary to properly articulate their critiques themselves, and implied that Prosper Enfantin was the figure behind their writings. This paranoid, conspiratorial view of the influence of the Saint-Simonians was also reflected in his writings about the path beyond liberal bourgeois property relations. His view was that the Saint-Simonians were singularly unable to deliver on their promises because they were, at root, Jewish and bankers. Saint-Simonism was doomed for many reasons, Proudhon believed, but one of them was because, he argued, Jesus was a Christian, not a Jew.[31] The attempt by these socialists to liberate women, Proudhon argued, would simply result in communalizing them, replicating the 'bank-ocracy' central to conspiratorial antisemitism of the time with a porn-ocracy.

Proudhon more often extolled the opposite of racism, that all men are equal. Women too. But between the two there was no equality. Men were, he argued, physiologically superior to women, which, corresponding to his general theory of force, underpinned the social distinction of roles between men and women too. Proudhon argued that men and women had fixed biological traits, derived primarily from their sex organs, that fundamentally shaped their social capacities and functions. This was by no means an original or unique idea. Indeed, the Saint-Simonians, such as Comte, had said much the same thing about the fixed biological and intellectual capacities of the workers, industrialists and scientists, and women (even Marx, a Jew himself, had said the same of 'Jewishness'). Women, he thought, were the passive recipient of 'the germ' during the act of procreation, having no seed or active role of their own.[32] He assumed men were virile and women beautiful; indeed, women were physically inferior to men to a ratio of 28:7, their brains on average four ounces lighter, and so on.[33]

Building on this phrenology, one of the precursors to race science, Proudhon followed the Saint-Simonians in arguing that these differences demanded social institutions to equalize natural inequalities. Proudhon's solution was an almost misogynistic paternalism. He followed the Greeks in arguing that the family was the generative origin of collective

31 For more on this topic, see R. S. Wistrich, 'Radical antisemitism in France and Germany (1840–1880)', *Modern Judaism* 15 (1995), pp. 109–35; M. Battini, *Socialism of Fools: Capitalism and Modern Antisemitism*, trans. N. Mazhar and I. Vergnano (New York: Columbia University Press, 2016).

32 P. Haubtmann, *Pierre-Joseph Proudhon. Sa vie et sa pensée 1849–1865* (Paris: Relié, 1987), p. 67.

33 P.-J. Proudhon, *La Pornocratie. Ou, les femmes dans les temps modernes* (Paris: A. Lacroix, 1875), p. 35.

consciousness, the *oikos*. Here, due to immutable biological differences, the father is the natural leader and the first to appropriate and lead this social *puissance*, protecting the public face of the family, while the wife manages the social economy within. Proudhon understood patriarchy as a 'law of nature', where the strongest must guide the weaker sex.[34]

This primal appropriation had to be balanced by other familial obligations, most importantly love.[35] But this is only possible, Proudhon argued, in the institution of marriage. Marriage is the harmonization of the sexual or biological antinomy. Sex is for procreation alone, and lust the basest of vices. As far as Proudhon was concerned, in seeking to destroy the marriage contract, the Saint-Simonians were undermining society itself. For him, marriage was an institution that gives social force to affective virtues; love is, he thought, the true emotional bond that binds men and women together, giving us the family, on which all social order must rest. The family is the incarnation of justice because it is the immanent equilibrium of difference that consecrates a balance of affections, roles, and duties; it is where the androgyny of humanity is realized in microcosm. Interestingly, Proudhon accepts homosexual love, but not as the incarnation of justice. Homosexuality falls short of the transcendent equilibrium of the sexual antinomy between opposite sexes.[36]

The Saint-Simonians, and their female feminist followers, were, for Proudhon, leading society towards a 'pornocracy'. Proudhon defines a pornocracy as a social order which combines the enfranchisement of women with general promiscuity.[37] The general acceptance of concubinage within Parisian middle- and upper-class male society was the polar opposite of his maternal peasant upbringing.[38] Proudhon also denounced divorce because it consecrated the power of the church, and left women abandoned to servitude and prostitution.[39]

To enfranchise women without protecting the social conditions necessary for them to thrive (that is, the family) would be to cast them into the unknown, without support or public function, leading inevitably, he thought,

---

34 Proudhon, *De la justice*, p. 706.   35 Ibid.
36 Daniel Guérin speculated that Proudhon may have repressed his own homosexual feelings. For more on this, see A. Copley, 'Pierre-Joseph Proudhon: a reassessment of his role as a moralist', *French History* 3 (1989), pp. 206–7.
37 Proudhon, *La Pornocratie*, p. 74.
38 For more on the gendered nature of the peasant family, see M. Segalen, *Love and Power in the Peasant Family: Rural France in the Nineteenth Century* (Oxford: Basil Blackwell, 1983).
39 Proudhon, *La Pornocratie*, p. 52.

to prostitution. This argument bears comparison to his argument in favour of the confederalists of the southern states of America, in *La Guerre et la paix*. Proudhon argues that the true friend of the slave is one who would nurture and educate them to freedom, rather than simply enfranchise them and leave them to the rapacious whims of industrial capitalism and wage slavery.[40] But, even with such social support, a woman, he argued, could never be a man's associate or a fellow citizen, while black male slaves could be the equals of white men.

Underpinning all of this is a vitalist and biological conception of force. While might does not make right, he argues, no right can exist without force to sustain it, either the force of arms or force of will. But Proudhon argues that only men have this public, combative role, derived mainly from their superior strength. Women cannot be soldiers, cannot be combatants, and so cannot have a public role.[41] Proudhon's logic, his prejudices, and his reading of history, of the Bible, and of the history of war led him to a degree of ambivalence around wartime sexual violence, which is deeply upsetting. Proudhon argues that temperance, honour, and chastity ought to be the guiding virtues of military men but that, because of the structural pressures of conflict, they routinely fail to reach this ideal. Citing liberally from the book of Exodus (22:21), Proudhon points out how historically women become the property of the victor, 'the soldier's conquest',[42] for three reasons. First, because assimilation of property or territory is the *sine qua non* of war. Secondly, because men's sexual appetites are excited on the battlefield. And, finally, he argues, because women are naturally enamoured of the virility of the soldier. It is only if war and society are transformed that women will no longer be seen as objects of male domination and exploitation.[43]

Jenny D'Héricourt should have the final word:

> You wish to subordinate women because in general they have less muscular force than you; but at this rate the weak men ought not to be the equals of the strong, and you combat this consequence yourself in your first 'Memoir on Property' where you say: 'Social equilibrium is the equalization of the strong and the weak.'[44]

---

40 Proudhon, *La Guerre et la paix*, vol. I, pp. 182–5.   41 Ibid., p. 68, n. 106.
42 Ibid., p. 272.
43 Ibid., p. 271.
44 J. D'Héricourt, *A Woman's Philosophy of Woman or, Woman Affranchised: An Answer to Michelet, Proudhon, Girardin, Legouvé, Comte, and Other Modern Innovators* (Westport, CT: Hyperion Press, 1981), p. 34.

D'Héricourt sought to develop his sensible ideas and to correct him: an immanent critique. Recall that, in Proudhon's view, social and intellectual antinomies are dynamic and complex, and sex differences are not solely responsible for defining human potential. But Proudhon's categorical anti-feminism contradicts all of this. As D'Héricourt puts it: 'You have naively mistaken the scalpel of your imagination for that of science.'[45] Proudhon wilfully ignored the latest scientific evidence that contradicted his claims regarding women's role in reproduction, the biological basis of his account of sex differences and patriarchy. D'Héricourt continues:

> You say ... she cannot be a political leader ... And history shows us a great number of empresses, queens, regents, sovereign princesses who governed wisely, gloriously, proving themselves vastly superior to many sovereigns ... [You say] [w]omen cannot be philosophers or professors ... [but] Hypatia, massacred by the Christians, professed philosophy brilliantly ... in France at present, many graduates of the Ecole polytechnique set great store in [the] geometrician Sophie Germain, who dared to understand Kant ... The argument presented by Mr Proudhon is, as we have just seen, contradicted by science and fact.[46]

In this case, Proudhon was on the wrong side of history and the argument. Indeed, it is instructive that Switzerland, Proudhon's idealized constitutional order, was the last state in Europe to introduce universal suffrage, in 1991, waiting on its smallest canton, Appenzell Innerrhoden.

Conclusion

More than any other thinker of that time, Proudhon's prodigious output, the sheer complexity of the revolutionary times in which he took part and then wrote about, and the historical distance between him and us make him irreducible to 'Proudhonism', 'socialism', or 'anarchism'. But interrogating all three in context can help us understand the origins of the socialist movement and its multiple lines of flight. Proudhon's socialism was predicated on a sophisticated social theory, an anti-Jacobin and pluralist politics, with a philosophy of history that was open, balancing agency and structure to the ends of justice.

---

45 Ibid., p. 58.
46 Cited in A. Primi, 'Women's history according to Jenny P. D'Héricourt (1809–1875), "Daughter of Her Century"', *Gender and History* 18 (2006), p. 154.

There is no doubt that Proudhon's thought was, like all such grand theorizing, flawed, and often deeply so. We should object to it on the basis that it is anti-feminist and antisemitic, and these criticisms hold more water than the Stalinist and Leninist critiques of Proudhon's ideas. He cannot be accurately described as a petty bourgeois nor can we argue, as others have done, that he was a proto-fascist, quite simply because he was an anti-statist and anti-capitalist.[47] These three sets of criticisms are used to justify ignoring what is otherwise a unique anti-statist contribution to the history of socialism. However, the Cercle Proudhon and Action Française were both able to ignore this simple fact, and claim Proudhon as an intellectual forebear to their antisemitic, chauvinist, and nationalist politics. Likewise, the doctrine of national syndicalism, led by a group of French monarchists, would also claim Proudhon to their cause. Proudhon's federalism was also evoked by the French Republican Federation, a right-wing parliamentary coalition, which opposed the Jacobin, dirigiste tendency in France, and the defence of Dreyfus.

In the English language, Proudhon's positive legacy is still to be properly uncovered. While his links to late nineteenth- and twentieth-century anarchism have been made abundantly clear, more remains to be said about the influence of Proudhon on mainstream European constitutional politics. Francisco Pi y Margall became president of the first Spanish Republic in 1875, and had translated three of Proudhon's constitutional works into Spanish. Four years prior to this, the anarchistic Proudhonists shaped the Paris Commune, then the IWMA, and thirty years later Proudhonism would become central to Georges Sorel's theory of revolutionary anarcho-syndicalism. The functionalist and jurisprudential writings of David Mitrany and Harold Laski were deeply influenced by Proudhon's federalism, and more has yet to be written about Proudhon's influence on the Russian anarchist movement too, in particular Leo Tolstoy, who came to visit him for a fortnight in 1860, in Brussels, while he was writing *La Guerre et la paix*. The evidence suggests Tolstoy eventually took more than the title for his own magnum opus and for the development of his Christian anarchism.[48]

This said, for all the careful re-reading and historical reconstruction and contextualization, Proudhon's place in the history of socialism will probably always be contested, but the effort to understand his ideas, and their

47 J. S. Schapiro, 'Pierre-Joseph Proudhon, harbinger of fascism', *American Historical Review* 50, 4 (July 1945), pp. 714–37.
48 B. Eikhenbaum, *Tolstoi in the Sixties*, trans. D. White (Ann Arbor, MI: Ardis, 1982).

reception, is hugely rewarding. Diligent and meticulous scholars are charting the path for others to follow. But in spite of this, indeed, perhaps because of these new careful histories, and the insights we gain, the definitive Proudhon is likely to remain elusive.

Further Reading

Bouchet, Thomas, et al. (eds.), *Quand les socialistes inventaient l'avenir, 1825–1860* (Paris: La Découverte, 2015).

Chambost, Anne-Sophie, *Proudhon. L'Enfant terrible du socialisme* (Paris: Armand Colin, 2009).

Haubtmann, Pierre, *Pierre-Joseph Proudhon. Sa vie et sa pensée, 1809–1849* (Paris: Relié, 1982).
Pierre-Joseph Proudhon. Sa vie et sa pensée 1849–1865, 2 vols. (Paris: Relié, 1987).
Proudhon, Marx et la pensée allemande (Grenoble: Presses Universitaires de Grenoble, 1981).

Hoffman, Robert L., *Revolutionary Justice: The Social and Political Theory of P.-J. Proudhon* (London: University of Illinois Press, 1972).

Jennings, Jeremy, *Revolution and the Republic: A History of Political Thought in France since the Eighteenth Century* (Oxford: Oxford University Press, 2011).

McKay, Ian (ed.), *Property Is Theft! A Pierre-Joseph Proudhon Anthology* (Edinburgh: AK Press, 2011).

Woodcock, George, *Pierre-Joseph Proudhon: A Biography* (London: Routledge and Kegan Paul, 1956).

13

Mikhail Bakunin and Social Anarchism

WOLFGANG ECKHARDT

The Russian revolutionary Mikhail Aleksandrovich Bakunin was one of the great European socialists of the nineteenth century. Unlike most of his colleagues he does not, however, belong to the tradition of social democratic or party-communist state socialism. Together with Pierre-Joseph Proudhon, he is instead one of the founders of an *anti-statist* and *social revolutionary* socialism from which anarchism emerged. This current is anti-statist because it rejects government; it is social revolutionary in its conviction that the goals of socialism can be obtained only by refusing to participate in existing power structures, destroying them, and creating new forms of community.

Bakunin's contributions to the history of political ideas have long been underestimated. To this day, he is known to large parts of the academic world at best as an anarchist revolutionary, and at worst as a conspirator and adventurist. Yet, a few free spirits have always held Bakunin in high regard: Noam Chomsky's 'intellectual pedigree' includes not only Wilhelm von Humboldt and Rudolf Rocker, but also Bakunin, and Paul Feyerabend said the thinkers from whom he had learned were not Theodor W. Adorno and Karl Popper – 'Philosophical mayflies like these are of no interest to me' – but Protagoras, Søren Kierkegaard, John Stuart Mill, and Bakunin.[1]

Life

Bakunin came from an old Russian noble family. His father, Aleksandr Bakunin, was an enlightened nobleman and head of the Priamukhino family estate (Tver Governorate, north-west of Moscow) with at least 500 serfs. The

---

1 S. Harbord, 'Extracts from "An Historian's Appraisal of the Political Writings of Noam Chomsky"', in C. P. Otero (ed.), *Noam Chomsky: Critical Assessments*, 4 vols. (London: Routledge, 1994), vol. III.2, p. 487; P. Feyerabend, 'Rückblick', in H. P. Duerr (ed.), *Versuchungen. Aufsätze zur Philosophie Paul Feyerabends*, 2 vols. (Frankfurt am Main: Suhrkamp, 1980–1), vol. II, p. 368.

Bakunin home was open to the educated and progressive personalities of the time, which gave family life (Aleksandr married Varvara Muraveva in 1810) an unusual spiritual and cultural level and also had a positive effect on the eleven children who resulted from the marriage.

Bakunin was born on 30 May (18 May according to the Julian calendar) 1814 in the quiet countryside as the third child after two daughters. He spent a happy and secure childhood separated from Russian reality, which was marked by despotism and serfdom. He was eleven years old when Russian nobles rebelled in vain against the tsar in the Decembrist revolt of 1825. Bakunin's father had friends and relatives among the conspirators and belonged to a group involved in the uprising. In the aftermath, he relied on unconditional loyalty to the tsar and sent his eldest son Mikhail to the St Petersburg Artillery School in December 1828: Bakunin was to pursue a military career in keeping with his class.

Away from his cultivated milieu, Bakunin could only feel extreme revulsion towards the military bull-headedness and monotonous drills. He became an officer in January 1833 and used the freedom that came along with the rank to immerse himself in the social life of St Petersburg, but without finding satisfaction in it. His neglect of his studies at the Artillery School resulted in a reprimand; as punishment he was transferred to Belarus and Lithuania in February 1834. Bored with his service in the dreary provinces, he tried to give his life new meaning by reading academic works in his spare time, which brought him into contact with philosophy. When he was sent on an official mission near the family estate in Priamukhino, he did not return to his regiment, and he narrowly escaped arrest for desertion through the influence of his powerful relatives. He was finally discharged from the army at his own request in December 1835.

After rejecting his father's demand to accept a post in the civil service, he left his parents' house abruptly in February 1836 and moved to Moscow, where he planned to make a living teaching mathematics. There he joined the circle around Nikolai Stankevich, who had met Bakunin the year before and introduced him to German philosophy. After reading Immanuel Kant, Bakunin turned his attention to Johann Gottlieb Fichte under Stankevich's guidance, but he was even more fascinated by Georg Wilhelm Friedrich Hegel, whose philosophy he successfully mastered through intensive study: by the time Stankevich went abroad at the end of 1837, Bakunin was already considered the leading Hegel expert in Russia and the spokesperson of the Moscow circle. The first authentic Hegelian text in Russian appeared in 1838 in the magazine *Moskovskii Nabliudatel* (*Moscow Observer*): the *Gymnasium*

Lectures, translated by Bakunin with an introduction which can be considered the programme of the circle. He published another spectacular article, 'On Philosophy', in the journal *Otechestvennye Zapiski* (*Notes of the Fatherland*), in the spring of 1840, but then left Russia in July to continue his studies in Berlin, financially supported by his lifelong friend Alexander Herzen (Aleksandr Gertsen), in order to prepare for a professorship in Moscow.

Bakunin attended Berlin University from the end of September 1840 and through the influence of Left Hegelianism increasingly turned to political topics. After the winter semester 1841/2 he left the university and moved to Dresden, where he met the radical Left Hegelian Arnold Ruge. In the meantime Bakunin had abandoned his plan for a university career in Moscow: on 9 October 1842, he told his brother Nikolai that he would not return to Russia. Two weeks later, Ruge's *Deutsche Jahrbücher für Wissenschaft und Kunst* (*German Yearbooks for Science and Art*) published Bakunin's epochal article 'The Reaction in Germany' under the pseudonym Jules Elysard, in which he developed antithetical dialectics and – still in Hegelian jargon – made the transition from philosophy to direct discussion of the revolutionary question.[2] In January 1843, after attracting the attention of Russian secret agents because of his political connections, he left for Zurich, where he met the communist Wilhelm Weitling. After Weitling's sudden arrest and the publication of the papers found on him, Bakunin came under the scrutiny of the Russian embassy in Bern. When he did not comply with an order to return to Russia, the Russian Senate sentenced him in absentia in November 1844 to the loss of his rights of nobility, expropriation, and deportation to Siberia. Nevertheless, Bakunin travelled via Brussels to Paris, where he protested against tsarism in the democratic newspaper *La Réforme* (*Reform*) on 27 January 1845. He socialized with the international Parisian emigrant community, became friends with Proudhon, and met Karl Marx and many French socialists.

However, Bakunin did not become politically active himself until he came into closer contact with Polish émigrés in Paris, following an article on Poland and Belarus.[3] At their invitation, he delivered a speech on 29 November 1847 on the seventeenth anniversary of the Polish uprising of 1830, in which he called on the Poles to form a revolutionary alliance with

2 Jules Elysard [Bakunin], 'Die Reaction in Deutschland. Ein Fragment von einem Franzosen', *Deutsche Jahrbücher für Wissenschaft und Kunst* 5 (1842), pp. 985–7, 989–91, 993–5, 997–9, 1001–2.
3 M. Bakounine, ['Lettre au sujet des religieuses basiliennes et de la note récemment publiée par M. de Boutenieff'], *Le Constitutionnel* no. 78, 19 March 1846, pp. 1–2.

Russian democrats to overthrow tsarism. This speech made Bakunin famous throughout Europe, but led to his expulsion from France at the request of the Russian ambassador. After only two months in Brussels, the February Revolution of 1848 brought him back to Paris. However, at the end of March, he set off for Poland, where he wanted to join General Ludwik Mierosławski's revolutionary peasant army and participate in a planned attack against the Russian Empire. Bakunin crossed revolutionary Germany on the way, but he made it only as far as Wrocław (then Breslau) because the Polish forces had already been suppressed by Prussian troops. He participated in the Prague Slav Congress in June as well as the uprising that followed, which was defeated by the Austrian army. Back in Wrocław, Bakunin was struck 'as if by a brick to the head'[4] by the false report circulated by Marx's *Neue Rheinische Zeitung* (*New Rhenish Newspaper*) on 6 July 1848: according to the French writer George Sand, Bakunin was a Russian secret agent. But Sand, who had met Bakunin in Paris, knew nothing about it. When Bakunin sent her the report, she replied with a firm counter-statement. After his surprise expulsion from Prussia and Saxony in October, Bakunin spent the winter in the Duchy of Anhalt, where he developed his frequently attacked project of a union of all European democrats, summarized in his pamphlet *Appeal to the Slavs*. In May 1849, he assumed the military leadership of the revolutionary government in Dresden, which had forced the Saxon king to flee but was soon confronted by a Prussian invasion. His comrades-in-arms, Richard Wagner among them, later acknowledged his calm determination and his considerable organizational talent; during the retreat, he was arrested in Chemnitz.

He was sentenced to death in Saxony, but was then pardoned and extradited to Austria in June 1850, where he was sentenced to death by hanging and then to a life sentence in a dungeon. Austrian authorities finally extradited him to Russia in May 1851, where he was held without trial in two fortress prisons. Here, at the request of Tsar Nicholas I, he wrote the so-called *Confession*, the contents of which he later called 'Poetry and Truth', alluding to Johann Wolfgang von Goethe's memoirs.[5] Bakunin did not, as is sometimes claimed, exhibit moral bankruptcy in the *Confession*: in February 1854, in a letter smuggled past the gendarmes, he confided to his sister Tatiana that he hoped in any case, 'to be able take up once again what brought me to this

---

4 M. Bakounine, 'Rapports personnels avec Marx. Pièces justificatives No. 2', p. 13, in M. Bakounine, *Oeuvres complètes*, CD-ROM (Amsterdam: International Institute of Social History, 2000).
5 Bakunin to Herzen, 8 (20) December 1860, p. 7, ibid.

point, only perhaps with more wisdom and foresight'.[6] Bakunin did not reveal anything that was not already known through other evidence in the previous investigations in Dresden and Prague, but tried to avert a real investigation against himself by means of a colourful description of his activities. He did not achieve the goal of improving his desperate situation by making superficial concessions in the form of the report; only after another six years and a petition to the new tsar, Alexander II, was the prison sentence commuted to exile in Siberia in March 1857. He found a job in a trading company there (he refused to enter the civil service) and married a Polish woman, Antonia Kwiatkowska. In June 1861, he travelled, allegedly on business, to the Amur region in eastern Siberia, where he managed to escape via Japan and the United States to Europe. Antonia was later able to leave the country legally via Moscow, and the two were reunited in April 1863.

After his arrival in London (27 December 1861), Bakunin first worked with Herzen and Nikolai Ogarev on the publication of the Russian opposition newspaper *Kolokol* (*The Bell*). At the same time, he tried to get in touch with opposition groups in Russia. He participated in a naval expedition in the Baltic Sea in March 1863 in support of Polish revolutionaries, which failed. Following a tour of Sweden, England, Belgium, and France, he settled in Italy from 1864 to 1867, where he founded his first fluctuating secret societies. At the end of August 1867, he travelled to Geneva to attend the founding congress of the League of Peace and Liberty, to which democrats and radicals from all over Europe had been invited to develop a joint programme. In his speech to the congress on 10 September, Bakunin declared a lasting peace between the existing military states impossible and called for the dissolution of states based on despotism and conquest. He was elected to the committee of the League, for which he wrote a summary of his ideas, which would probably have been titled *The Revolutionary Question: Federalism, Socialism, and Anti-Theologism*, but remained unpublished during his lifetime. However, at the second congress of the League (held in Bern in September 1868) Bakunin's views were rejected by a majority. With a letter of protest, Bakunin and seventeen other participants quit the League. Bakunin, who had been a member of the International Working Men's Association (First International, 1864–76/7) since June–July 1868, suggested to the departing League members in Bern that they join the International and continue their personal association as a secret society under the name International Alliance

6 Bakunin to his sister Tatiana, February 1854, p. 2, ibid.

of Socialist Democracy. It was finally decided, however, that the alliance should also constitute itself publicly as an independent organization within and alongside the International, although Bakunin cautioned that it 'would compete in a most undesirable way' with the International.[7] In fact, the Geneva Alliance group was admitted to the International only after the umbrella organization was dissolved.

Upon Bakunin's initiative, Giuseppe Fanelli, a friend from the alliance, undertook an agitation tour of Spain in the winter of 1868–9, whereupon the first Spanish sections of the International were established. Bakunin himself worked actively in the Geneva sections of the International and became editor of *Egalité* (*Equality*), the organ of the Romance Federation (Fédération Romande) of the International in Switzerland. In February and May 1869, he undertook lecture tours to the Jura, where he became friends with activists, including James Guillaume. After attending the fourth congress of the International (September 1869 in Basel), Bakunin left Geneva for family reasons and moved to Locarno in November. In April of that year, Bakunin became acquainted with Sergei Nechaev, an unscrupulous revolutionary who posed as the representative of a secret Moscow action committee and whose fervent energy temporarily won Bakunin over. Bakunin parted ways with him in June 1870 when it became apparent that Nechaev was trying to dominate those around him with rigorous methods. This episode did Bakunin a great deal of harm; among other things, various pamphlets by Nechaev (for example, his *Catechism of a Revolutionary*) were wrongly attributed to Bakunin and used against him.

Bakunin intently followed the news about the start of the Franco-Prussian War in July 1870. In his opinion, the war would end in an unstable situation, in which armed uprisings in the provinces could instigate a general revolution. To this end, he went to Lyon in September. However, the revolution he and his friends attempted to foment failed due to a lack of support. He was forced to flee the country secretly via Marseille. Upon his return to Locarno, Bakunin set about giving the ideas inspired by his recent experience a final form in a comprehensive book. Of many manuscripts, however, only *The Knouto-Germanic Empire and the Social Revolution: First Instalment* was published in April 1871. Other parts were published posthumously by Elisée Reclus, including a fragment that Reclus published under the title *God and the State* (1882), which has since become one of Bakunin's most famous writings and one of the most popular works of anarchist literature. Bakunin wholeheartedly

7 M. Bakounine, 'L'Alliance internationale des sociaux-révolutionnaires', p. 12, ibid.

welcomed the uprising of the Paris Commune in March 1871 and went to visit his friends in the Jura in April to prepare a relief operation. When the Italian republican Giuseppe Mazzini attacked the Paris Commune and the International, Bakunin replied within four days with his *Response of a Member of the International to Mazzini* (August 1871), which was again followed by longer manuscripts, the bulk of which appeared in December under the title *The Political Theology of Mazzini and the International*. The polemics caused a great stir, leading to the rise of the International in Italy, bringing Errico Malatesta, among others, into Bakunin's circle. After Bakunin had already given the impetus for the foundation of the International in Spain, the movement in Italy also developed in a similar manner due to his influence.

Marx, the leading figure in the London-based General Council of the International, followed Bakunin's activities from the moment he joined the International with extraordinary suspicion and hatred. Thus, from 1868 onwards, Marx's correspondence only ever refers to Bakunin as 'that intriguer', 'brute', or 'this damned Muscovite'. 'He should be careful', Marx announced to Friedrich Engels ominously as early as July 1869, 'otherwise he will be officially excommunicated.'[8] Even today, the bias which Marx laid bare in his bitter polemics against Bakunin is astonishing, particularly at a time when the historical difference between Marxism and anarchism was becoming apparent and when a debate based on principles would have been important. The conflict reached its climax in 1872 at the International's congress in The Hague, the composition of which, as modern research shows, had been manipulated. Marx and Engels denounced Bakunin there, in his absence, and let the majority vote to expel him, while enshrining their state-socialist doctrine – the constitution of the working class as a political party and the conquest of political power – within the rules of the International, thus eliminating the previous pluralism. These decisions were subsequently declared null and void by sections and federations of the International in Italy, Spain, the Swiss Jura, France, Belgium, Britain, the Netherlands, and the United States. In this way, Marx's victory at The Hague quickly became a defeat: in the years that followed, the International went its own way almost entirely without Marx and the General Council.[9]

---

8 Marx to Kugelmann, 17 February 1870, in *Marx Engels Collected Works* (London: Lawrence & Wishart, 2010) (hereafter *MECW*), vol. XLIII, p. 436; Marx to Engels, 10 February 1870, ibid., p. 424; Marx to Paul Lafargue, 19 April 1870, ibid., p. 493; Marx to Engels, 27 July 1869, ibid., p. 333.

9 W. Eckhardt, *The First Socialist Schism: Bakunin vs Marx in the International Working Men's Association* (Oakland, CA: PM Press, 2016), chs. 15–20.

Fig. 13.1   Mikhail Bakunin, 1863. Artist: Sergei Levitsky. (Photo by Fine Art Images/
Heritage Images/Getty Images.)

For Bakunin, who supported the actions of the sections and federations to
the best of his ability, Russian and Italian connections were particularly
important in the last years of his life. He visited the Russian student colony
in Zurich in the summer of 1872 and established numerous contacts there. In
1873, he and a few members of the colony founded a print shop which printed
Statism and Anarchy, his most extensive work published during his lifetime. In
August 1874, Bakunin took part in the uprising in Bologna. However, he
retired from the movement afterwards, exhausted. On 1 July 1876, he died in
Bern at the age of sixty-two.

Ideas

The basic impulse of Bakunin's political thought is the idea of a community in
which its members can freely develop all their powers of action and all their
faculties without exercising power over one another. In this sense, freedom

meant to Bakunin an *emancipatory community*, 'the unique environment within which the intelligence, dignity, and happiness of mankind may develop and increase'. Bakunin attached great importance to such an environment ('I don't want to be *Me*, I want to be *We*'), and he demonstratively acknowledged such communities on the front pages of some of his writings ('Member of the Slav Congress in Prague', 'Member of the International Working Men's Association'). The idea of an emancipatory community reaches far back into his youth in the idyllic Priamukhino, in that world full of feelings and fantasies, where he had a close relationship with his ten siblings, which became the 'model for all his organizations and his conception of a free and happy life for humanity in general'.[10]

Bakunin first tried to find this community in the spiritual union with God, then in philosophy, but finally turned away from both. Bakunin's development was inspired by Ruge's Left Hegelianism, Ludwig Feuerbach's philosophical humanism, Weitling's communism, and Proudhon's early anarchism, among others. He wrote to his brother Pavel on 29 March 1845:

> I am still the same as before – a notorious enemy of the current reality, with the only difference that I have stopped being a theoretician and that I have at last overcome the metaphysics and philosophy in me and wholeheartedly thrust myself into the practical world ... Emancipating man is the only legitimate and beneficial form of influence. – Down with all religious and philosophical dogmas, – they are nothing but lies; – truth is not a theory, but a fact, life itself, – it is the community of free and independent men.[11]

At that time, Bakunin remained isolated in his support of these ideas and was not able to cultivate any intense political relations except with Proudhon. He became politically active only when his close collaboration with Polish emigrants began in 1846–7. This opened up a sphere of action for him that he extended to the whole Slavic world after his participation in the Prague Slav Congress (June 1848): the creation of an anti-tsarist federation for the national liberation of the Slavic peoples.

After the fiasco of the Polish naval expedition (1863), Bakunin began to reconsider his Slavic nationalist activities and returned to his earlier idea of an emancipatory community. From 1864 onwards, Bakunin founded various

---

10 M. Bakunin, *Selected Writings*, ed. A. Lehning (London: Cape, 1973), p. 196; Bakunin to Lodovico Nabruzzi, 3 January 1872, p. 8, in Bakounine, *Oeuvres complètes*; Bakunin to Albert Richard, 7 February 1870, p. 4, ibid.; M. Nettlau, 'Mikhail Bakunin: A Biographical Sketch', in G. P. Maximoff (ed.), *The Political Philosophy of Bakunin: Scientific Anarchism* (Glencoe, IL: Free Press, 1953), p. 30.
11 Bakunin to his brother Pavel, 29 March 1845, pp. 3, 5, in Bakounine, *Oeuvres complètes*.

secret societies with diverse names (Fraternité Internationale / International Brotherhood, Société Internationale Secrète de l'Emancipation de l'Humanité / International Secret Society for the Emancipation of Humanity, and so on). However, these societies (with strictly vertical organizational structures and ranks of membership) that he invented in several *drafts of statutes* only ever existed on paper. In reality, Bakunin's friends and acquaintances formed these fluctuating groups, which relied on their personal rapport and not on a secret hierarchy to maintain their internal cohesion. On the other hand, the theoretical revolutionary reflections Bakunin developed in his *draft programmes* played a significant role in the development of his political ideas. His new springboard was the vision of an international revolution, through which all state institutions and social coercion throughout the world would be eliminated. This historical upheaval was by no means meant to be the work of a tiny leadership clique or vanguard. Rather, the revolution was to be carried out by the most vibrant awakening from below, by the people, and lead to new forms of social organization: the administration of public life by committees of delegates, the formation of independent communities (municipalities and districts), a large-scale federation of all initiatives – in other words, an emancipatory community, where the following was to apply:

> *Freedom* is the absolute right of every man or woman who has come of age to seek no other sanction for their acts than their own conscience and their own reason, to determine these according to their own will alone, and consequently to be solely responsible for these first of all to themselves, and then to the society of which they are a part.[12]

According to Bakunin, emancipation could only ever be realized in such a community, not in a reformed bourgeois or (supposedly temporary) revolutionary state. Therefore, the members of the secret society were to work towards a revolution in which they would have one negative task above all else: they should not seize power, but rather prevent the emergence of any new power, which would always be opposed to the people. With these draft programmes (various versions as far back as 1864 still exist),[13] Bakunin laid the groundwork for his anarchist worldview, to which

12 Bakounine, 'Principes et organisation de la société internationale révolutionnaire. I. Objet. II. Catéchisme Révolutionnaire', p. 2, ibid.
13 See, for example, Bakounine, 'Société internationale secrète de la Révolution. Programme provisoirement arrêté par les frères fondateurs', ibid.; M. Bakunin, 'Programme and Purpose of the Revolutionary Organization of International Brothers', in Bakunin, *Selected Writings*, pp. 166–72.

he now dedicated himself entirely; on 8 September 1867, in the magazine *Libertà e giustizia (Liberty and Justice)*, he called himself an 'anarchist' for the first time.

Bakunin's critics never tired of stressing that he was not a systematic thinker. While Bakunin did not formulate any large-scale system or theoretical constructs, his thinking was nevertheless coherent: based on the idea of an emancipatory community, he developed his concept of *freedom*, which he anchored in community ('Man is truly free only among equally free men; . . . the slavery of even one man in the world, as an offence against the very principle of humanity, is a negation of the freedom of all')[14] and *equality*, in particular that all members of society should have the same basis and starting point, which led him to educational concepts, a critique of inheritance law, and feminist demands: 'Woman, *differing from man* but *not inferior to him, intelligent, industrious and free like him, is declared his equal both in rights and in all political and social functions and duties.'*[15] Furthermore, as an atheist and anarchist, Bakunin developed a profound critique of religious and political power structures and their ideologies – in particular a *critique of the state, expertocracy*, and *Marxism*.

Critique of the State

Bakunin understood the two major institutions of church and state as the opposite of an emancipatory community because both dictate 'that the masses, *ever* incapable of governing themselves, must at all times bear the beneficent yoke of a wisdom and a justice which, in one or another manner, shall be imposed on them from above'. The state has therefore always been 'the patrimony of some privileged class' and is nothing 'but this domination and exploitation, regulated and systematized'; 'to exploit and to govern mean the same thing'.[16]

But Bakunin's critique was not limited to the autocratic systems that were dominant during his time: he made short work of such archaic forms of the legitimation of power as divine right, national myths, and so forth. Bakunin dedicated much more energy to a critique of modern concepts of the state, such as Jean-Jacques Rousseau's theory of the social contract and

---

14 Bakounine, 'Principes et organisation', pp. 2–3.   15 Bakunin, *Selected Writings*, p. 83.
16 Bakounine, 'Fédéralisme, socialisme et antithéologisme', pp. 85, 87, in Bakounine, *Oeuvres complètes*; M. Bakunin, *From out of the Dustbin: Bakunin's Basic Writings, 1869–1871*, ed. Robert M. Cutler (Ann Arbor, MI: Ardis, 1985), p. 177; M. Bakounine, 'L'Empire Knouto-Germanique et la Révolution Sociale. Suite. Dieu et l'Etat. 4', p. 62, in Bakounine, *Oeuvres complètes*.

contemporary democratic and parliamentary forms of government. The fact that republican forms of rule could also be quite despotic had already been made clear by the two catastrophes for the socialist movement of the nineteenth century: the suppression of both the Parisian popular movement of June 1848 and the Paris Commune of 1871. These had been bloodily put down not by violent absolutist regimes, but by elected republican govern-ments. Modern monarchies and republics, Bakunin explained, were equally characterized by strict military and bureaucratic centralization, so that today's despotism no longer manifested itself only 'in the *form* of the State' but 'in the *principle* of the State and of political Power'.[17]

In Bakunin's opinion, modern institutions of power are in any case stronger than the will of the individual and cannot be reformed from within; the corresponding pressure to conform is already exerted by

> the extraordinary temptations to which all men who hold power are infal-libly exposed, the effect of the enormous ambitions, rivalries, jealousies, and cupidities which besiege precisely the highest positions day and night, and against which neither intelligence nor often even virtue is guaranteed, – for the virtue of the isolated man is a fragile thing.[18]

According to Bakunin, such ideas are rightly advocated by anarchists, who are 'enemies of all power, knowing that power corrupts those invested with it just as much as those compelled to submit to it'.[19]

'But does this also apply to democratic states?' Bakunin asked rhetorically. In a democratic state, he answered, one might think 'the people will choose only the good men. But how will they recognize them? ... [The politicians] live in a society different from their own; they doff their hat to Their Majesty the sovereign people only at election-time, and once elected they turn their backs.'[20] The problem starts with the system of representation itself: it is hypocritical because it is based on the premise 'that a power and a legislative chamber resulting from a popular election absolutely must or even can represent the real will of the people'. In reality, this had never happened in history and the supposed representation of the people remains fictitious. The people represent social reality, whereas politics is only a negative abstraction

17 Bakounine, 'L'Empire Knouto-Germanique et la Révolution Sociale. La révolution sociale ou la dictature militaire', p. 34, in Bakounine, *Oeuvres complètes*.
18 Bakounine, 'Fédéralisme, socialisme et antithéologisme', p. 84.
19 Michael Bakunin, *Statism and Anarchy*, ed. Marshall Shatz (Cambridge: Cambridge University Press, 1990 [1873]), p. 136.
20 Bakunin, *From out of the Dustbin*, p. 51.

of this reality; an elected politician is in reality 'a representative of abstractions'.[21]

Critique of Expertocracy

In Bakunin's opinion, science would certainly be important and useful for emancipatory communities, but not a government of experts. As a rule, this would amount to the domination of the majority by a privileged minority – only this time 'in the name of the presumed stupidity of the one and the presumed intelligence of the other'. After all, science is the compass of life, but not life itself; its mission is only 'to enlighten life, not to govern it'.[22] Intellectual work does not require privileges, since it already carries its own rewards; isolation from society is even quite detrimental to science.

Bakunin explained that, in an emancipatory community, he would have no problem with the authority of specialists:

> In the matter of boots, I refer to the authority of the bootmaker; concerning houses, canals, or railroads, I consult that of the architect or engineer. For such or such special knowledge I apply to such or such a *savant*. But I allow neither the bootmaker nor the architect nor the *savant* to impose his authority upon me. I listen to them freely and with all the respect merited by their intelligence, their character, their knowledge, reserving always my incontestable right of criticism and censure ... The greatest intelligence would not be equal to a comprehension of the whole. Thence results, for science as well as for industry, the necessity of the division and association of labour. I receive and I give – such is human life. Each directs and is directed in his turn. Therefore there is no fixed and constant authority, but a continual exchange of mutual, temporary, and, above all, voluntary authority and subordination.[23]

Critique of Marxism

Aspects of his critique of the state and of expertocracy also came to bear in Bakunin's confrontation with Marx and Engels. In his critique, Bakunin referred to their contemporary political documents, such as the *Communist Manifesto* (1848) and the *Inaugural Address* (1864), to the resolutions which Marx and Engels pushed through at the London Conference (1871) and the

---

21 M. Bakounine, 'Les Ours de Berne et l'ours de St-Pétersbourg', p. 11, in Bakounine, *Oeuvres complètes*; Bakounine, 'La théologie politique de Mazzini et l'Internationale. Deuxième partie: fragments et variantes. Fragment M', p. 31, ibid.
22 Bakunin, *Statism and Anarchy*, p. 137; Michael Bakunin, *God and the State* (London: Freedom Press, 1910), p. 38.
23 Bakunin, *God and the State*, pp. 19–20.

Hague Congress (1872) of the First International, and to their support for political–parliamentary activities as practised – for example – by the Social-Democratic Workers' Party in Germany by way of participation in elections and parliamentarianism.[24] In contrast, Bakunin said that participation in state power always has the same result, even under socialists, namely the

> government of the vast majority of the people by a privileged minority. But this minority, the Marxists say, will consist of workers. Yes, perhaps of *former* workers, who, as soon as they become rulers or representatives of the people will cease to be workers and will begin to look upon the whole workers' world from the heights of the state. They will no longer represent the people but themselves and their own pretensions to govern the people.[25]

Bakunin's scathing conclusion: 'Take the fiercest revolutionary and instal him on the All-Russian throne ... and in a year he will become worse than [the current tsar] Alexander himself.'[26]

A further difference with Marx becomes apparent around the question of the subject of revolutionary change: instead of a strict organization of the industrial workers (into a working-class party), Bakunin relied on the spontaneous and continued action of the proletariat of the country and the cities, including 'that destitute proletariat to which Marx and Engels, and, following them, the whole school of German social democrats, refer with the utmost contempt'.[27]

In Bakunin's critique of Marxism, besides clear-sighted analyses, there are also anti-German and anti-Jewish resentments that seem to have been triggered by the conflict in the International since they date mainly from the years 1869 to 1874, the time of his conflict with Marx. At the same time, Bakunin was very analytical in his resistance to the Marxist vision of the state, as developed in the *Communist Manifesto*: according to that document, the political rule of the proletariat would 'centralise all instruments of production in the hands of the State, *i.e.*, of the proletariat organised as the ruling class', and this rule would be organized through 'centralisation of credit in the hands of the State', 'equal liability of all to labour. Establishment of industrial armies, especially for agriculture', and so on.[28] According to this theory, Bakunin commented sarcastically, the people should not only abstain from destroying the state during their revolution, but also

---

24 Eckhardt, *The First Socialist Schism*, pp. 94, 97, 477.
25 Bakunin, *Statism and Anarchy*, p. 178.
26 M. Bakounine, 'La science et la question vitale de la révolution', p. 17, in Bakounine, *Oeuvres complètes*.
27 Bakunin, *Statism and Anarchy*, p. 7. 28 *MECW*, vol. VI, pp. 504–5.

they must fortify it and strengthen it, and in this form place it at the complete disposal of their benefactors, guardians, and teachers – the leaders of the communist party, in a word, Marx and his friends, who will begin to liberate them in their own way. They will concentrate the reins of government in a strong hand, because the ignorant people require strong supervision. They will create a single state bank, concentrating in their own hands all commercial, industrial, agricultural, and even scientific production, and will divide the people into two armies, one industrial and one agrarian, under the direct command of state engineers, who will form a new privileged scientific and political class.[29]

Precisely such prophetic warnings by Bakunin about a new class of socialist officials, a 'red bureaucracy' in socialism,[30] were well received by thinkers such as Milovan Djilas and Noam Chomsky in the twentieth century after the existence of such a class of privileged party cadres became apparent in 'actually existing socialism'.

'They are governmentalists, we are really anarchists',[31] Bakunin stated, and this could not be belied by the Marxist promise that the state would wither away over the long term, as expressed in the *Communist Manifesto*, for example, according to which the *abolition* of political power would result nearly automatically from the *conquest* of political power and the change in the conditions of production.[32] Bakunin commented on this dialectical connection of *conquest* and *abolition* of the state with the words:

> They say that this state yoke, this dictatorship, is a necessary transitional device for achieving the total liberation of the people: anarchy, or freedom, is the goal, and the state, or dictatorship, the means. Thus, for the masses to be liberated they must first be enslaved . . . We reply that no dictatorship can have any other objective than to perpetuate itself, and that it can engender and nurture only slavery in the people who endure it. Liberty can be created only by liberty, by an insurrection of all the people and the voluntary organization of the workers from below upward.[33]

Liberty without socialism, Bakunin argued, is privilege and injustice; socialism without liberty is slavery and brutality.[34]

---

29 Bakunin, *Statism and Anarchy*, p. 181.
30 Bakunin to Herzen and Ogarev, 19 July 1866, p. 6, in Bakounine, *Oeuvres complètes*.
31 Bakounine, 'Lettre au journal *La Liberté* de Bruxelles', p. 3, ibid.
32 *MECW*, vol. VI, pp. 505–6.   33 Bakunin, *Statism and Anarchy*, p. 179.
34 Bakunin, *Selected Writings*, p. 110.

Impact

Bakunin is one of the central figures in anarchism's founding phase and can be regarded as its first organizer. With Bakunin, anarchism developed into a mass movement for the first time. In Italy and Spain, socialism even arrived in the anti-statist and social-revolutionary form propagated by Bakunin. Bakunin's broad impact can best be explained by three influential factors which were bundled together in his life.

An International Bridging Role

Bakunin's kindly manners and his talent for making contacts were often mentioned by his contemporaries. Because he spent a large part of his life as an emigrant, he had many opportunities to meet protagonists from various countries and so cultivated an international network of contacts. In the Paris of the 1840s alone, Bakunin met numerous Polish, German, Italian, and Russian emigrants in addition to the French radicals. After the March Revolution of 1848, Bakunin identified with the ideals of the 'Springtime of the Peoples' (national self-determination, political freedom, and international solidarity) and continued to hold fast to them even after public opinion in various countries turned to nationalism over the course of that revolutionary year, when even democratic milieux were seized by national resentments. To counteract this trend, he published his pamphlet *Appeal to the Slavs* in December 1848, in which he demanded a settlement between Hungarians, Slavs, and Germans, declaring: 'It is a sacred duty for all of us, champions of the revolution, democrats of *all* countries, to unite our forces.'[35] Since the strengthening of reactionary forces at the beginning of 1849 had already prompted many protagonists in the democratic movement to reconsider their stance, Bakunin's appeal for co-operation was well received. In this situation, in the spring of 1849, Bakunin was one of the few people whose international network was still intact, able to bring the protagonists of the Polish, Czech, and German movements together to initiate a project of international co-operation.

Fifteen years later, in 1864, Bakunin tried to unify his international network in an organizational framework. Perhaps the desire to create an emancipatory community, which meant so much to Bakunin, again stood in the foreground, for he called the members of the planned secret societies 'brothers [*frères*]' – although there was a great deal of fluctuation in the groups, in

---

35 M. Bakounine, 'Appel aux Slaves par un patriote russe', p. 6, in Bakounine, *Oeuvres complètes*.

terms of both people and organization. Later, when Bakunin befriended James Guillaume and other socialists from the Swiss Jura as well as the Spanish delegates to the Basel Congress in September 1869, Rafael Farga Pellicer and Gaspar Sentiñón, the organizational framework was even more informal. Together with Bakunin's long-time acquaintances, such as Carlo Gambuzzi and Mikhail Sazhin (Ross), they formed a revolutionary network whose function Bakunin described as 'the necessary bridge between the propaganda of socialist theories and revolutionary practice'.[36] Defamed by the Marxists at the Hague Congress as a secret society under Bakunin's strict dictatorship, this network in reality functioned largely autonomously, as can be seen from their decisions on various controversial issues that contradicted Bakunin's wishes.[37] This network continued to exist even after Bakunin's withdrawal in 1874 and after his death; Peter Kropotkin became its secretary in 1877.[38] In this way, Bakunin's idea of community had a continuing effect on the international anarchist network.

The Russian Revolutionary Movement

Statism and Anarchy was smuggled into Russia in large numbers in 1874, ensuring that Bakunin's ideas spread widely in his homeland. His reputation continued to grow in the populist movement (*narodnichestvo*) in the years that followed. Bakunin became one of the most important initiators of the anti-tsarist liberation struggle and influenced the entire generation of the 1870s – even Georgii Plekhanov was a 'Bakuninist' at the beginning of his political career. Marxist polemics against Bakunin initially had little effect in Russia: Eduard Bernstein wrote in 1910 that every Russian socialist he ever met was more or less strongly opposed to it.[39] The first anarcho-communist groups that emerged in Russia around 1900 were committed to upholding Bakunin's values. There was renewed interest in Bakunin during the Revolutions of 1905 and 1917. His name was on everyone's lips as the embodiment of the Russian revolutionary tradition: the anarchists claimed him for themselves, Vladimir Lenin included Bakunin in his plan for monumental propaganda in 1918, Nestor Makhno's followers declared their leader the second Bakunin, and the Mensheviks disparagingly called

---

36 Bakunin to Celso Ceretti, 13–27 March 1872, p. 21, ibid.
37 Various examples in Eckhardt, *The First Socialist Schism*, p. 319.
38 M. Nettlau, *La Première Internationale en Espagne (1868–1888)*, ed. Renée Lamberet (Dordrecht: M. Nijhoff, 1969), p. 295.
39 E. Bernstein, 'Karl Marx und Michael Bakunin. Unter Benutzung neuerer Veröffentlichungen', *Archiv für Sozialwissenschaft und Sozialpolitik* 30 (1910), p. 5.

Lenin the new Bakunin.[40] Even in the 1920s, when anarchists were increasingly persecuted, the leading Bolshevik historians often did not know whether to celebrate Bakunin as the forerunner of the Russian Revolution or to demonize him as the opponent of Marx in the First International. On the fiftieth anniversary of Bakunin's death in 1926, this historical–political crisis culminated in anarchists and Bolsheviks each preparing their own commemorative events, whereupon the secret police confiscated the excellent collection of essays on Bakunin published by anarchists to mark the anniversary[41] – the last anarchist publication in Russia for more than six decades. Finally, Joseph Stalin put an abrupt end to Bakunin's tradition, research, and researchers alike in the mid-1930s.

Co-Founder of Anarchism

In the process of socialism's diversification into social democracy, communism, and anarchism in the last third of the nineteenth century, Marx and Bakunin became exponents of opposing currents. The First International was a decisive setting for this. In the first years it offered an open forum for the different socialist tendencies of the day. Opposing theoretical viewpoints were exchanged at the organization's annual congresses, which ensured that the International could accommodate a broad spectrum of ideas. These positive effects were further enhanced by the federalist internal organization of the International, which guaranteed programmatic autonomy for each individual section.

Several national federations of the International, which were to a large extent shaped by the idea of the autonomous workers' culture and association, were therefore surprised in September 1871 when the London Conference of the International, prepared by Marx and Engels, adopted the notorious Resolution no. 9, enshrining the constitution of the working class as a political party and the conquest of political power as a goal. The desire to impose this minority programme upon the International inevitably brought Marx and Engels into conflict with its federations, which preferred trade union forms of struggle and rejected the formation of parties and any involvement in parliamentarianism. Marx and Engels' motion was tantamount to a complete break with

40 See J. F. Goodwin, 'Russian anarchism and the Bolshevization of Bakunin in the early Soviet period', *Kritika: Explorations in Russian and Eurasian History* 8 (2007), pp. 535–9.
41 A. Borovoi (ed.), *Mikhailu Bakuninu 1876–1926. Ocherki istorii anarkhicheskogo dvizheniia v Rossii* [To Mikhail Bakunin, 1876–1926: Sketches of the History of the Anarchist Movement in Russia] (Moscow: Golos Truda, 1926).

the established working-class culture: 'Apparently, political action, such
as the founding of a political party, could only be interpreted as joining
the enemy, through their kind of organization, by participating in bodies
and organizations ruled by the enemy', notes historian Daisy Devreese.[42]
Of course, the national federations insisted on their autonomy, which
was a natural expression of the established federalist internal organization
of the International, and rejected obligations imposed from above, such
as those of the London Conference.

Bakunin's criticism on that matter was also fundamental: instead of promoting workers' self-determination and their autonomous culture of resistance, Marx and Engels advocated the commitment of the labour movement
to the methods (parties) and forums (parliament) of bourgeois and statist
politics. According to Bakunin, this political–parliamentary strategy would
lead to compromises and alliances with bourgeois parties, which they
believed they would exploit – in reality, however, the workers in parliament,
removed from their traditional lifestyle, would be demoralized and become
bourgeois themselves:

> The worker-deputies, transplanted into a bourgeois environment, into an
> atmosphere of purely bourgeois political ideas, will in fact cease to be
> workers and, becoming Statesmen, they will become bourgeois, and perhaps
> even more bourgeois than the Bourgeois themselves. For men do not make
> their situations; on the contrary, men are made by them.[43]

Bakunin argued that the autonomous workers' culture would be destroyed
should the labour movement take part in parliament, instead of being
strengthened as an emancipatory community and the seed of a future free
society that it should be:

> the proletariat already carries within itself all the seeds of its future
> organization in the natural organization of the trades and the various
> workers' associations which sooner or later will necessarily have to
> embrace all human work, both manual and intellectual, each man having
> to become, according to justice, at once a worker of the brain and the
> hands; moreover, each will freely adapt himself in a more specific way to
> the kind of work that suits him best. The completely free organization,
> without any protection or permission from the State, of all labour,

42 D. E. Devreese, 'An Inquiry into the Causes and Nature of Organization: Some
Observations on the International Working Men's Association, 1864–1872/6', in
F. L. van Holthoon and M. van der Linden (eds.), *Internationalism in the Labour
Movement 1830–1940*, 2 vols. (Leiden: Brill, 1988), vol. I, p. 297.
43 Bakunin, *From out of the Dustbin*, p. 108.

scientific, artistic, agricultural, and industrial associations, on the basis of collective property, with fair remuneration for the work of each individual; and their equally spontaneous and free federation, from the bottom up, in the communes, in the regions, in the nations and in all Internationality . . . – this is the future of humanity.[44]

The conflict regarding internal organization and pluralism within the International was clearly expressed in the *Sonvillier Circular* of November 1871 by the sections of the Swiss Jura and the section of the Commune refugees in Geneva, which together formed the Jura Federation: they asserted that the International was a free federation of autonomous groups and not a centralist organization with a predetermined political line. The *Circular* spread discussions about the orientation of the International to more and more European countries. The international federations defending their autonomy became aware of what separated them from the social democratic movement influenced by Marx, which relied on centralist organizational forms, the establishment of national labour parties, and the conquest of political power. This can be seen as a decisive moment in the history of political ideas: the split between centralist party politics and federalist grassroots movement.

Bakunin was a relevant participant in this debate on federalist or centralist socialism. Through his close contacts in the Jura, Italy, and Spain, he was able to provide analysis and substantial debate – for example, by applying his critique of the state to Marx's 'government of the International'[45] or on the subject of the relationship between goal and means, which has become characteristic of anarchism in general. Even if the conflict as a whole was not yet carried out under the banner of anarchism v. Marxism, the terms 'anarchist' and 'anarchy' were used here to describe the opposition in the International over the course of this dispute, thus identifying a movement critical of power for the first time.

In the process of emergence of the social democratic, communist, and anarchist currents of socialism, Bakunin thus assumed a pioneering role: while communism and social democracy can be traced back to Marx and Engels, and both state-socialist approaches did indeed find loud proponents in them, the socialist current critical of power would perhaps have been culled from the outset without Bakunin. His contribution, however, secured a place for anti-statist and social revolutionary socialism and paved the way for anarchism.

44 M. Bakounine, 'L'Italie et le Conseil général de l'Association internationale des travailleurs', pp. 5–6, in Bakounine, *Oeuvres complètes*.
45 Bakounine, 'Lettre au journal *La Liberté* de Bruxelles', p. 8.

In this sense, Bakunin's ideas belong to all the variants of socialism that are critical of power. They form, so to speak, the bedrock of anti-authoritarian thought. Political–ideological constructs that only consider Bakunin a forefather of a pure 'social anarchism' (as opposed to an 'individualist anarchism'), or an exclusively syndicalist orientation, often fall short in their explanations. In reality – despite their differences – such diverse theorists as the individual anarchist Benjamin Tucker, but also Kropotkin, the pacifist anarchist Ferdinand Domela Nieuwenhuis, and Johann Most held Bakunin in high esteem.

It is also difficult to classify Bakunin's ideas because he referred to democratic, communist, and collectivist concepts during most of his lifetime, that is, before the different socialist currents and their labels emerged. Only three years before his death, Bakunin formulated a coherent definition of anarchy as

> the free and independent organisation of all the units and parts of the community and their voluntary federation from below upward, not by the orders of any authority, even an elected one, and not by the dictates of any scientific theory, but as a result of the natural development of all the varied demands put forth by life itself.[46]

In view of the three factors outlined here (international bridging role, importance in the Russian revolutionary movement, and status as cofounder of anarchism) and the resulting broad impact Bakunin had, it is astonishing how small a role he plays in political discourse. One explanation is that his influence is diminished due to at least three factors, including himself. Bakunin regularly set down his ideas and views in written form, mostly in unpublished manuscripts, seldom in published articles and pamphlets, but mostly in long letters, of which only a fraction have survived. While the surviving texts are full of extraordinary ideas and insights, they were written by Bakunin primarily in the course of his intensive study of his times and in connection with his revolutionary activities. He made countless statements on contemporary events, but left hardly any abstract ideological constructions behind for scholars to examine. Moreover, the surviving texts are often only hastily edited and sometimes reveal a provocative ambiguity, for example, when the atheist Bakunin describes himself and his political friends as 'our church – if I may be permitted to use for a moment an expression which I so detest', or when he writes that the secret society

---

46 Bakunin, *Statism and Anarchy*, p. 198.

struggling against any power amounts to a 'dictatorship without insignia, titles or official rights'.[47] There are whole texts that are ambiguous, such as the *Confession to the Tsar*, a complex document full of subtext, and even ambiguous collaborations such as the one with the unscrupulous revolutionary Nechaev, which raise various questions of authorship. An authoritative edition of Bakunin's writings therefore requires the inclusion of numerous contemporary sources and biographical contextual material, which make such editions a difficult read.

A second detrimental factor for an unbiased understanding of Bakunin is the continuing influence of polemics from the distant past. Marx and Engels were for the most part unwilling or unable to grasp the growing difference between anarchism and Marxism in the history of ideas; they simply denounced the *alternative concept of socialism* formulated by Bakunin's anarchism as nonsense, 'empty babblings, a garland of ostensibly horrifying hollow fancies', and so on.[48] In the social sciences, which have been influenced partly by Marxism, the study of a debased figure such as Bakunin has long been regarded as disreputable; this has led to several shortfalls in research, so that a lack of reliable knowledge even about existing sources can be found in many papers. The difficult research situation, on the one hand, and the easy availability of historical polemics on the other lead authors to believe that they can make far-reaching judgements based on a brief and completely superficial study of Bakunin.[49] Even a modern tendency such as post-structuralist anarchist philosophy, in which numerous anarchist thinkers have been reconsidered, continues to bash Bakunin without a second thought.[50]

Finally, Bakunin's influence is also affected by the fact that he did not establish a special school or organization. Posterity has used Bakunin primarily as a source of inspiration, and thus the paths of reception run rather below the surface: we see renewed interest in Bakunin emerge naturally during uprisings, as can be seen in the Russian Revolutions of 1905 and 1917, the Spanish Revolution of 1936, and the worldwide revolt of 1968. And free spirits – such as Karl Korsch, Albert Camus, Walter Benjamin, Huey Newton, and others in the past – will continue to pay tribute to him in the future.

---

47 Bakunin, *God and the State*, p. 21; Bakunin, *Selected Writings*, p. 180.
48 *MECW*, vol. XXI, p. 113.
49 A few prominent examples are analysed in P. McLaughlin, *Mikhail Bakunin: The Philosophical Basis of His Anarchism* (New York: Algora, 2002), pp. 2–12.
50 See G. Kuhn, 'Bakunin vs Postanarchismus', *Bakunin Almanach* 1 (2007), pp. 140–76.

Further Reading

Bakounine, Michel A. [Mikhail Bakunin], *Archives Bakounine*, 7 vols. (Leiden: Brill, 1961–81). A more recent edition of Bakunin's later writings and letters in the original languages, which provides the required intense contextualization of his writings.

Oeuvres complètes, CD-ROM (Amsterdam: Internationaal Instituut voor Sociale Geschiedenis, 2000). The first complete but totally unannotated edition of Bakunin's works on CD-ROM.

Carr, Edward Hallett, *Michael Bakunin* (London: Macmillan, 1937). This book – a reassessment and synthesis of Nettlau's and Steklov's biographies, which together have long ceased to represent the current state of research, but form the basis of most of the modern Bakunin biographies – may suffer in many places from Carr's delight in sensational details, but it still represents an uncomplicated and well-documented look at Bakunin's life.

Nettlau, Max, *Michael Bakunin. Eine Biographie*, 4 vols. (1924–6), manuscript at the Internationaal Instituut voor Sociale Geschiedenis in Amsterdam (Max Nettlau Papers, nos. 1706–1713). Nettlau personally interviewed many former friends and acquaintances of Bakunin, collected a large amount of material from and about Bakunin, and incorporated his research results into several biographical works, available only in handwriting; the most cited is his biography from 1896–1900; the above-mentioned is the most elaborated manuscript.

Steklov, Yurii, *Mikhail Aleksandrovich Bakunin. Ego zhizn i deiatelnost* [Mikhail Aleksandrovich Bakunin: His Life and Work], 4 vols. (Moscow: Izdatelstvo Kommunisticheskoi Akademii, 1926–7). This biography by a Bolshevik historian is a biased work, which can be understood only in the context of the Soviet Bakunin research of the two post-revolutionary decades.

New biographical material is provided by many specialized studies, notably some drawing on sources from the former Central Party Archives in Moscow, which were largely inaccessible before 1990.

14

Peter Kropotkin and Communist Anarchism

RUTH KINNA

Peter Kropotkin (1842–1921) is remembered as a theoretician of anarchism and one of the leading exponents of anarcho-communism, a doctrine he helped to elaborate with his comrades Carlo Cafiero and Elisée Reclus in the late 1870s. He grew up in what he described as Moscow's Faubourg Saint-Germain, into considerable privilege, and attended the prestigious corps of pages, an elite military academy in St Petersburg, from 1857. In 1860 he edited his first revolutionary paper, then as a constitutionalist. Two years later, looking for more outlets for his rebellious instincts, Kropotkin passed up the opportunity of a glittering career at the imperial court and joined the Cossacks stationed in the far east of Russia. He spent the next five years in Siberia. Further radicalized by his experiences, he left the military in 1867 to study geography at St Petersburg University. Five years later, encouraged by a trip to western Europe, Kropotkin became an anarchist. On his return to Russia. he joined the revolutionary Chaikovsky Circle. Soon imprisoned as a result of his activities, he escaped from the prison infirmary of the Peter–Paul Fortress in 1876 and began his life in exile in western Europe. He did not go back to Russia until 1917.

Able to turn his mind to virtually any issue, Kropotkin published on topics ranging from gardening to X-rays to the migratory habits of Siberian tigers. For many of his admirers, his reputation hangs on his book *Mutual Aid: A Factor of Evolution* (1902), a critique of the Social Darwinian view of the natural world as a sphere governed by competitive struggle for individual advantage. Yet this book belongs to a more extensive body of work which he elaborated as both an intellectual and a pamphleteer to defend anarchist communism: *Appeal to the Young*, *Modern Science and Anarchism*, *Anarchism: Its Philosophy and Ideal*, *The State: Its Historic Role*, *Anarchist Morality*, and the posthumously published *Ethics* were all part of this project. *Fields, Factories and Workshops* and *The Conquest of Bread* outlined an accompanying anarchist

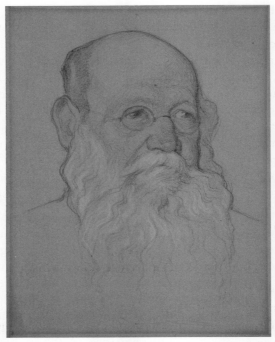

Fig. 14.1 Peter Kropotkin, 1920–1. Artist: Nikolai Andreevich Andreev (1873–1932). (Photo by Fine Art Images/Heritage Images/Getty Images.)

economics, and his influential account of the French Revolution explored the sociological forces active in nineteenth-century Europe and the dilemmas they presented.

Kropotkin's ethics of mutual aid bore the stamp of Russian populism. In his autobiography, *Memoirs of a Revolutionist*, Kropotkin records how the Chaikovsky Circle adopted mutual respect, honesty, transparency, equality, and care as organizational principles. Referencing the Chaikovskists in later discussions of mutual aid, he tied anarchist ethics to non-reciprocal giving, voluntary co-operation, and compassion. Communism, the principle of distribution according to need, was a necessary corollary of anarchist ethics, and it provided the best institutional safeguard against private accumulation and the re-appearance of centralized systems of state regulation. Its operation required the close integration of agriculture and industry and the careful, creative application of technology to facilitate local self-sufficiency.

Kropotkin believed that the success of anarchist communism depended on the extension of mutual aid in all areas of social life. His hope was that individuals would find ways of bypassing the state and resisting its colonizing processes by acting 'for themselves', as he put it. Should these anarchizing initiatives fail, Kropotkin predicted Caesarism: following the Prussian model, European states were tending towards greater militarization, industrial monopoly, and social control. Kropotkin's binary analysis was divisive because he placed Marxist social democracy in the same Caesarist camp as the autocracies all socialists attacked. When his concern to resist the drift towards Caesarism led him to support the Entente powers in 1914, it caused a rift in the anarchist movement, too. Yet when he went back to Russia in 1917, his reputation badly tarnished, Kropotkin continued to advocate anarchist communism. In a short and tense encounter with Vladimir Lenin in 1919, he argued forcefully that Marxist communism was a poor alternative to the anarchist ideal.

The Politics of Anarchist Communism

In 1848, Karl Marx and Friedrich Engels famously described communism as a spectre haunting Europe. Their *Manifesto* was written to dispel fears about inevitable, impending social transformation and to outline the 'views ... aims ... tendencies' of those who best understood it.[1] For Kropotkin, too, communism was a cause of trepidation as well as liberation. The difference was that Kropotkin's strategy was infused with hope, not spirit: his worry was that the transformation that Marx predicted would be far from liberating. Presented by Marx as a cure-all for the ills of capitalism, communism obviously appealed to workers' innate sense of injustice; the idea also had a prominent place in the socialist lexicon. But, for Kropotkin, as long as it lacked clear political expression, energetic justification, and imaginative description, it was unlikely to inspire genuinely emancipatory projects.[2] The task, Kropotkin believed, was to explain what 'anarchist communism' entailed. In 1886, nearly ten years after anarchists had formally embraced communism, he told his friend, the anti-parliamentary socialist William Morris, that anarchism was still a 'new system of thought'.[3] There was still

---

1 K. Marx and F. Engels, *Manifesto of the Communist Party*, in *Marx Engels Collected Works* (London: Lawrence & Wishart, 2010), vol. VI, p. 481.
2 P. Kropotkin, 'The Necessity of Communism', repr. in P. Kropotkin, *Act for Yourselves*, ed. N. Walter and H. Becker (London: Freedom Press, 1987 [1887]), p. 63.
3 Kropotkin to William Morris, 11 April 1886, William Morris Papers, British Library Add. MS. 45345, fol. 109.

'so much work to do for elaborating the principles of our Anarchist philosophy'.[4]

To recall the context: coming to anarchism in the 1870s when divisions between anarchist 'anti-authoritarians' and Marxian 'authoritarian socialists' were beginning to emerge in the First International, Kropotkin had joined forces with Cafiero and Reclus, formerly members of Mikhail Bakunin's inner circle, to press 'anti-authoritarians' organized in the anarchist Jura Federation to commit to communism.[5] Much later, he acknowledged in a letter to James Guillaume, a leading Bakuninist and member of the Jura Federation, that his stance had been controversial. After all, Pierre-Joseph Proudhon had been a vocal anti-communist, associating communism with monasticism.[6] The proposed change also appeared to distance anarchism from collectivism, the rubric which Bakunin had adopted. Against this, Kropotkin wrote at considerable length to persuade Guillaume that 'free communism' – 'libertarian anarchist and anti-militarist' – was entirely consistent with Proudhon's critique and the position that anti-authoritarians had espoused as collectivists.[7] Similarly, communism was compatible with Spanish anarchism, which had always been termed 'collectivist'. Even though Spanish comrades continued to organize as 'collectivists', Kropotkin remarked that they were nevertheless anarchists and communists: federalists and communalists who believed that groups of workers should be free to manage their affairs as they wished.[8] There was no tension between his view and theirs.

Kropotkin's willingness to placate collectivists had its limits, however. He told Guillaume that there was no point in an anarchist revolution without communism: communism was the only answer to the problem of private accumulation and government regulation. As a propagandist for communism, he used the term both descriptively – to explore overlaps with other anarchist currents (notably 'cultural' and 'Christian' anarchism) – and strategically to attack two rival positions: anarchist individualism and Marxism.

Sidelining the work of some of the most influential anarchist individualists of the nineteenth century (notably Emile Armand, Voltairine de Cleyre, and Moses Helman), Kropotkin picked Benjamin Tucker, the editor of *Liberty*, as

4 Ibid.
5 M. Nettlau, 'Introduction', in *Oeuvres Bakounine*, vol. 1 (Paris: P.-V. Stock, 1972 [1895]), p. 20.
6 P. Kropotkin, 'Communist-Anarchism', in Kropotkin, *Act for Yourselves*, p. 98.
7 Peter Kropotkin to James Guillaume, Max Nettlau Papers, International Institute of Social History (hereafter IISH), ARCH01001700, 12 June 1903 https://search.iisg.amsterdam/Record/ARCH01001.
8 Kropotkin to Guillaume, 11 February 1904, IISH ARCH01001700.

the exemplar for anarchist individualism. The choice perfectly suited Kropotkin's lukewarm appreciation of individualism as a form of American Proudhonism. Kropotkin held Tucker's intellectual precursors, a group including Josiah Warren and Stephen Pearl Andrews, in high regard. Yet he warned that Tucker's individualism veered too far towards Herbert Spencer's bourgeois anti-statism and that it lacked mechanisms to counter the growing trends towards corporate monopoly.[9]

Kropotkin's critique of Marxism was more hostile still. He told Guillaume that one of the main reasons he had pressed the Jura Federation to give up collectivism for communism was because the emergence of Marxism had entirely altered the meaning of 'collectivism'. Unsurprisingly, he identified the collapse of the First International in 1871–2 as the watershed moment in its rise, since this event had formalized hostilities between 'authoritarian' and 'anti-authoritarian' socialists. His novel argument was that the division of the socialist movement had also catalysed significant changes in political discourse. These were encapsulated in a series of policy revisions and restatements of position. As anarchists, anti-authoritarians had reaffirmed the International's traditional policy – the direct struggle against capital for social revolution. In contrast, authoritarians had started to espouse a new doctrine, namely social democracy or 'Marxism'. Kropotkin described this as a badly digested mishmash of Fourierism, Hegelianism, and collectivism.[10] How far he also considered it a deviation from Marx's philosophy is difficult to assess; Kropotkin rarely had anything good to say about Marx and was happy to repeat his comrade Varlam Cherkezishvili's view that the *Manifesto* had been plagiarized.[11] If it was possible to think of communist anarchism as a synthesis of Marx and Proudhon, as Kropotkin once grudgingly conceded,[12] this was only because he believed that Marx had added nothing to socialism, except his impoverished metaphysical 'science', which anarchists like him totally rejected. Either way, the important point was that the International's demise had brought about a split in the socialist movement which the anarchist advocacy of 'collectivism' threatened to conceal. Proudhonist and Bakuninist anti-authoritarians had not immediately understood this but, Kropotkin argued, the risk of confusion was obvious.

---

9   See P. Kropotkin, *Modern Science and Anarchism* (London: Freedom Press, 1912), pp. 70–1; P. Kropotkin, 'Anarchism', in Peter Kropotkin, *Two Essays: Anarchism and Anarchist Communism* (London: Freedom Press, 1987 [1910]), p. 18.
10 Kropotkin to Guillaume, 11 February 1904.
11 Kropotkin to Guillaume, 23 December 1902, IISH ARCH010012700.
12 Kropotkin to Guillaume, 11 February 1904.

In a letter to Guillaume, Kropotkin identified three social theorists, Charles Pecqueur, Hippolyte Colins, and Albert Schäffle, as the key influences on social democracy. In this, he followed the ex-Communard, historian, and politician Benoît Malon. However, unlike Malon, who distinguished nine types of collectivist,[13] Kropotkin emphasized their commonality, finding this in the 'idea of the State as Capitalist'.[14] In his view, this formulation was totally wrongheaded because it suggested that the state could be decoupled from capitalism and refashioned as socialist. Kropotkin responded by branding social democracy 'state-socialist' and, believing the state's detachment from capitalist exploitation nonsensical, concluded that *collectivism is state capitalism*.[15] Similarly – much to the irritation of H. M. Hyndman, leader of the British Social Democratic Federation – Kropotkin refused to accept that Marxists were or could be 'communist'.[16] Though he conceded that they promoted the communist principle of distribution according to need, their 'communism' was negated by the three-point programme of nationalization, state regulation, and wage-work. This presupposed the existence of predatory and tyrannical institutions. Once it was decoupled from anarchy, communism was a numbing and repressive prospect. His succinct message to Guillaume was that *anarchy is the principle that makes communism possible*.[17]

Kropotkin thought that prevailing late nineteenth-century ideational and sociological trends made the alignment of anarchy to communism vital. Like Proudhon and Bakunin before him, he rejected materialist history because it wrongly accepted capitalism's centralizing, monopolizing, and bureaucratizing forces into socialism. Here, Kropotkin echoed Bakunin, who had argued that Marx's materialist history played to the inherent conservatism of German socialists, explaining their misguided faith in the revolutionary potential of a 'peoples' state'.[18] Kropotkin also anticipated Gustav Landauer's blistering attack on Marxism as a dispiriting, 'unspirited' philistinism.[19] Like Landauer, he argued that Marx's dismissal of the 'idiocy

13 K. S. Vincent, *Between Marxism and Anarchism: Benoît Malon and French Reformist Socialism* (Berkeley: University of California Press, 1992), p. 97.
14 P. Kropotkin, *The Great French Revolution, 1789–1793*, trans. N. F. Dryhurst (New York: Vanguard Press, 1927 [1909]), p. 11.
15 Kropotkin to Guillaume, 11 February 1904.
16 H. M. Hyndman, 'Social-Democrat or Socialist?', *The Social-Democrat* 8 (August 1897), p. 229.
17 Kropotkin to Guillaume, 12 June 1903.
18 M. Bakunin, *Statism and Anarchy*, ed. Marshall Shatz (Cambridge: Cambridge University Press, 1990 [1873]), pp. 177, 193.
19 G. Landauer, *For Socialism*, trans. David J. Parent (St Louis: Telos Press, 1978 [1911]), p. 60.

of rural life' made the dystopian implications of scientific socialism plain. In Russia he observed that the risks of this analysis could hardly be more serious: the abolition of village communes would reduce millions of rural workers to absolute misery.[20] Marxist materialist history was totally at odds with the idea of social revolution organized 'from the bottom up'. He told Guillaume, *their metaphysics is authoritarian*'.[21]

Kropotkin's reflections on this historical context provide an important lead for the analysis of anarchist communism. His efforts to anarchize 'communism' were designed to safeguard the libertarian principles he shared with individualists and at the same time replace the deadening, mechanical processes that Marxism promoted with creative, anarchist forms of utopianism. Commenting that original thought issued not from without but within social movements, Kropotkin also suggested that revolutionaries had a role to play in explaining and disseminating ideas useful to them.[22] This involved elaborating key concepts and showing the suitability of anarchist communist definitions. But it did not involve the production of a scholarly mapping or hierarchical arrangement of concepts, as leading modern scholars of political ideology recommend.[23] Indeed, Kropotkin's attempt to promote anarchist thinking considerably complicated this task, since it involved the articulation of new concepts ('mutual aid', 'free agreement'), the rejection of concepts such as 'law' that had been fashioned by the historical experience of the European state, and the recuperation of others, for example 'justice', which he believed had been distorted by state institutions.[24] This theoretical modelling was unconventional, as was his approach to political philosophy. Here, Kropotkin departed from the rigorous analytical standards set by liberal theorists such as J. S. Mill by deliberately refusing to give his terms precise meanings.[25] For example, he used 'mutual aid' variously as a statement of anarchy in the language of science, an analytical tool capable of deconstructing all natural and social sciences, and a springboard for the construction of

20 Kropotkin to Guillaume, 23 December 1902.
21 Kropotkin to Guillaume, 12 June 1903.
22 P. Kropotkin to A. Atabekian, 5 May 1920, in *Kropotkine Publication du 'Groupe de Propagande par l'écrit'*, No. 8 (n.p.: Victor Robinson, Imp. Toulousiane, 1920), p. 23.
23 B. Franks, N. Jun, and L. Williams, *Anarchism: A Conceptual Approach* (New York and London: Routledge, 2018), pp. 1–13.
24 See, for example, P. Kropotkin, 'La Loi et l'autorité', in P. Kropotkin, *Paroles d'un Révolté* (Paris: Librairie Marpon et Flammarion, n.d.), p. 216; P. Kropotkin, *Organised Vengeance Called 'Justice'* (London: Freedom Press, 1902), p. 7.
25 J. S. Mill, *The Collected Works of John Stuart Mill*, vol. VIII, *A System of Logic Ratiocinative and Inductive*, Part II, ed. John M. Robson (Toronto: University of Toronto Press, and London: Routledge and Kegan Paul, 1963–91), ch. IV, para. 1, p. 698.

a new social-voluntarist ethics.[26] While Kropotkin's unorthodox approach makes conventional analysis of his political thought difficult, his sense of the interconnections of conceptual and structural change provides a firmer lead into his understanding of anarchist communism.[27] In what follows, I therefore consider how Kropotkin outlined anarchist communism to attack political rivals and how he expected or hoped that it would alter social norms and practices.

When Kropotkin reflected on his own contribution to anarchism, he pinpointed five themes: (i) the use of natural sciences to examine the prospects for anarchy, (ii) the systematic analysis of sociological trends, (iii) the development of anarchist ethics, (iv) the defence of socialist organization, and (v) the development of practical planning.[28] To indicate how these helped Kropotkin distinguish anarchist from non-anarchist communism, I integrate his science of mutual aid into an opening discussion of ethics, before examining his sociology and idea of social justice. This leads to an exploration of Kropotkin's thinking about socialist organization and planning and his approach to internationalism in the context of his anti-Jacobinism. Rather than offer a general account of anarchist communism or ask what a commitment to it entails, my aim is to explain Kropotkin's interventions in nineteenth- and early twentieth-century socialist debates and outline the social choices he recommended.

Anarchist Communism and Ethics

Kropotkin told a story about a drowning child to explain the ethics of anarchist communism. In one version, four men stand on the river bank: a 'partisan of "Each one for himself"', a 'religious moralist', a utilitarian, and 'a plain man of the people'. A second version eliminates the first character (the representative of middle-class commerce who remains stock-still), to concentrate on the motives of the other three. While all attempt to save the child, the religious moralist and the utilitarian both calculate the expected benefits. The former anticipates both heavenly and earthly reward while the latter estimates the intensity and durability of his pleasure after the rescue. Although they set aside considerations of pure material gain, unlike the commercialist, they are 'egoists' just the same. Only the last man behaves

26 Kropotkin to Guillaume, 12 June 1903.
27 Adapting insights from M. Richter in 'Begriffsgeschichte and the history of ideas', Journal of the History of Ideas 48 (1987), pp. 247–63.
28 Kropotkin, 'Anarchism', pp. 19–20.

ethically. Brought up 'from his childhood to feel himself *one* with the rest of humanity', he acts instinctively, prompted by empathy. When he returns the child to its mother, he says: 'Why! I could not do otherwise than I did.'[29] The response exemplified the ethics of anarchist communism: mutual aid.

Kropotkin began to explore mutual aid with Reclus and his fellow geographer Léon Metchnikoff in the 1870s, incorporating insights he had gained during his expeditions in northern Manchuria in the 1860s.[30] His first comprehensive statements in the 1890s were followed by the book *Mutual Aid: A Factor of Evolution*.[31] It presented an evolutionary sociology that linked ethics to environment. Rejecting as unscientific the Social Darwinist image of 'nature' as 'red in tooth and claw', Kropotkin also dismissed the unvarnished neo-Hobbesian hypothesis of competition. In addition, he rejected T. H. Huxley's philosophical review, which accepted the validity of the Social Darwinist hypothesis but disputed the conclusions, wrongly suggesting that ethics lay in the realm of the divine or supernatural.[32]

Mutual aid chimed in with a fraternal ideal that was often proclaimed in the socialist movement, as well as in anarchist communist circles. Kropotkin's comrade Errico Malatesta summed this up when he spoke of the 'feeling of sympathy, tolerance, of love . . . which aims at making society a true gathering of brothers and friends all working for the common good'.[33] In Malatesta's vision, anarchy would end 'the domination and exploitation of man by man' and unite men 'as brothers by a conscious and desired solidarity, all co-operating voluntarily for the well-being of all . . . bread, freedom, love and science for everybody'.[34] Kropotkin generally used a different register, focusing on the nature of co-operation and the social mechanisms that normalized co-operative practices. Communism was one of these: 'Communist customs and institutions are of absolute necessity for society . . . to maintain and develop social customs that bring men in contact

---

29 P. Kropotkin, 'Anarchist Communism', in Kropotkin, *Two Essays: Anarchism and Anarchist Communism*, p. 58. See also P. Kropotkin, *The Place of Anarchism in Socialistic Evolution: An Address Delivered in Paris*. trans. Henry Glasse (London: William Reeves, 1886).

30 F. Ferretti, 'Organisation and formal activism: insights from the anarchist tradition', *International Journal of Sociology and Social Policy* 36 (2016), pp. 726–40.

31 P. Kropotkin, 'Introduction', in P. Kropotkin, *Mutual Aid: A Factor of Evolution* (Boston: Extending Horizons Books, n.d.), pp. vii–xix.

32 T. H. Huxley, *Evolution and Ethics: The Romanes Lecture* (London: n.p., 1893). For a discussion, see Ruth Kinna, 'Kropotkin's theory of mutual aid in historical context', *International Review of Social History* 40 (1995), pp. 259–83.

33 E. Malatesta, *Life and Ideas*, ed. Vernon Richards (London: Freedom Press, 1977), p. 74.

34 Ibid., pp. 197–8.

with one another' and for 'establishing such relations between men that the interest of each should be the interest of all'.[35]

He developed the argument in different texts: *Mutual Aid* mapped the biologically rooted capacity for co-operation to a variety of social systems and their enduring solidaristic practices. *The State: Its Historic Role* linked the erosion of mutual aid to the acculturation of competitive individualism and concomitant processes of modern state formation – territorialization, centralization, bureaucratization, and legal codification. Yet Kropotkin was not just interested in showing how material conditions, or what he called *'culture'*, affected co-operation. He was also concerned with 'the development of the intellectual and the spiritual organization of society', or *'civilization'*.[36] As his story about the drowning child indicated, he wanted to understand the imperatives for ethical action and how these were encouraged.

His last book *Ethics* (posthumously published) can be read as a history of civilizations, which examined ethics zoologically, anthropologically, and philosophically. It pitted anarchist communist ethics against two alternatives: 'religious' and 'realist'. Religion explained ethics as the acceptance of externally imposed rules to achieve predetermined ideas of moral good, while realism linked ethics to human psychology or inward drivers. His argument was that both accounts were partial and, consequently, their conclusions about practice and human wellbeing were distorted. Religious ethicists were openly prescriptive about moral duties and obligations, relying on obedience and command to ensure compliance. Realists avoided overt prescription but were unable to explain either how practice dovetailed with moral principle or how norms varied over time and space. Kropotkin's conclusion mirrored his story: religion and realism were two sides of the same coin. Realism, whether materialist or Kantian, effectively secularized ethics, introducing internalized principles of obligation which generated universal conceptions of the good that were remarkably similar to religion. Similarly, both gave rise to egoism and a bundle of values that the bourgeoisie felt it their mission to impose. This was civilization of sorts, but it was not one that anarchists could accept because their model sprang from the values of those made vulnerable by this mission.

Kropotkin acknowledged that the flaws of conventional moral philosophy had already been exposed by Friedrich Nietzsche, but he worried that

---

35 P. Kropotkin, *Anarchism: Its Philosophy and Ideal*, 4th issue (London: Freedom Press, 1907), p. 23.
36 P. Kropotkin, *Ethics: Origin and Development*, trans. Louis S. Friedland and Joseph R. Piroshnikoff (New York and London: Benjamin Blom, 1968), p. 272.

Nietzsche's poetic challenge to bourgeois values had stimulated a new type of amoral egoism. This, too, risked losing the complex interplay of social and individual drivers. To formulate his alternative, Kropotkin turned back to Proudhon, using the moral philosophy of Jean-Marie Guyau to rework Proudhon's conception of immanent justice. Borrowing Guyau's framing of morality 'without compulsion or authority', Kropotkin argued that anarchist communism provided the cultural conditions for co-operation while allowing groups and individuals to specify moral rules flexibly by their daring, life-affirming actions.

Anarchist ethics was a virtuous disposition directed towards social well-being, not unlike a modern feminist ethics of care.[37] Kropotkin had described its three central tenets in his 1882 essay, *An Appeal to the Young*: the acknowledgement of individual responsibility and social interdependence, a concern for the most defenceless or those in the greatest need, and a willingness to tackle injustice. And, later noting that women and children were habitually subjected to the intimidations of authoritative male rulers in both 'primitive' and bourgeois societies, he described women's behaviours to illustrate it.[38] Spanish women revolutionaries who goaded 'the soldiery' while standing 'in the front ranks of the insurrection' provided a dramatic example.[39] But he identified the same ethics in more mundane situations, too. In the family, the lead was taken by mothers who inculcated a sense of justice in their children, directed their menfolk to join socialist causes, and set domesticity aside to participate directly in social struggles.[40] Each case showed how individual risk-taking could re-create social rules. This was the nub of Kropotkin's ethics.

Kropotkin concluded that anarchy was communism's necessary complement because it enshrined Proudhon's and Guyau's ideas of permanent contestation. As he put it in *Anarchism: Its Philosophy and Ideal*, anarchy recognized the 'separate faculties, autonomous tendencies, equal among themselves, performing their functions independently, balancing, opposing one another continually'.[41] The interplay was crucial in any social environment because ethical development depended on the willingness of individuals to test social norms and modify social relationships where these were found wanting. Such assertions of individual sovereignty were essential for

37 V. Held, *The Ethics of Care* (Oxford: Oxford University Press, 2006).
38 Kropotkin, *Ethics*, pp. 301, 335.
39 P. Kropotkin, *An Appeal to the Young* (London: William Reeves, n.d.), p. 15.   40 Ibid.
41 Kropotkin, *Anarchism: Philosophy and Ideal*, p. 5.

'*sociality*', the abandonment of obligation, and the avoidance of unfettered egoism.

Anarchist Communism and Social Justice

Communism, Kropotkin noted, was an ancient social practice, familiar to anthropologists; as a principle of social justice, it meant distribution according to need: 'common possession of the necessaries for production' and 'common enjoyment of the fruits of common production'. For Kropotkin, it necessarily entailed the abandonment of individual ownership of social capital (land, housing, raw materials, and the instruments of production) and 'of every wage system'.[42] These principles constituted the 'mother idea' of socialism.

In this modern form, Kropotkin observed that communism was one of the main currents to emerge from the French Revolution. Anarchists had not played a special role in its theorization. That owed most to the actions of the *sans-culottes* who had continually pressed the revolutionary government to meet their economic demands. However, socialists – Charles Fourier, William Godwin, Robert Owen, and Proudhon[43] – had transmitted the idea, and anarchism had become communism's most dependable bearer. Rival radicals, social democrats, and various other socialists had proposed various mixed or partial schemes of collective ownership. But all of these guaranteed individual property in one way or another, notably through the maintenance of a wage system.[44] Kropotkin, by contrast, aligned anarchism to full communism by means of expropriation.

One of the misconceptions Kropotkin was keen to correct was the idea that socialism was compatible with amelioration by benevolent state action. This was the 'socialist' policy pursued by politicians such as the French radical Léon Gambetta. Kropotkin described their manoeuvres as 'stealing': detaching socialism from communism, just as an earlier generation of politicians had 'stolen' republicanism by rooting governance in law.[45] However, his primary justification for communism was that it was the only sure defence against the rise of inequality and egoism. A hundred years after Jacques

---

42 Kropotkin, 'Anarchist Communism', p. 43.
43 Kropotkin, *Great French Revolution*, p. 373.
44 P. Kropotkin, 'Communism and the Wage System: A Speech Delivered by P. Kropotkin at the Freedom Group Meeting 13 July 1888', in Kropotkin, *Act for Yourselves*, pp. 103–13; P. Kropotkin, *The Wage System* (Sheffield: Pirate Press, n.d. [1889]).
45 P. Kropotkin, 'Tous socialistes!', in Kropotkin, *Paroles d'un Révolté*, pp. 268–9.

Roux's 'anarchist' *Enragés* had made the point, Kropotkin observed that US anti-trust activists were also discovering that the 'democratic Republic' was impossible for 'as long as there was no protection against the monstrous inequality of incomes'.[46] This was his charge against anarchist individualists. Their defence of individual rights – 'a confused term handed over from past ages, meaning nothing at all or too much' – failed to take account of the monopolizing tendencies of capitalism. And it contained no answer to the problem of uneven accumulation which, Kropotkin argued, pointed only to the reconstruction of 'tribunals and legal punishments, even to the penalty of death', or, in other words, the reintroduction of the state.[47]

Pressing this argument, Kropotkin described individualism – liberal or anarchist – as outmoded. To show this, he analysed the dynamics of communism, sketching the outlines of his conception in two essays originally published in 1887.[48] He began with the proposition that anarchist communism was 'the only equitable solution' to the problem of distribution, adding that the 'tendency of modern society' was towards 'free communism' or 'no-government'. Confronting the strength of countervailing pressures favouring management, surveillance, and regulation, he maintained that a plethora of non-state organizations driven by local initiatives worked against 'Capital and the State'.[49]

In *The Conquest of Bread* Kropotkin made interconnectedness a leading theme: socio-economic trends revealed the latency of anarchist communism, anchoring social equality and the co-operative practices associated with mutual aid. The argument had two related parts: first, the trends of international production and trade were towards increasing global complexity; secondly, these demonstrated the advantages of co-operation while making any calculation of individual effort near impossible. In sum, both economic analysis and anarchist–communist principles of social interdependence removed the sociological defence of private property as a bastion of liberty. That still left a philosophical defence of individual property intact. But the individualist vision had been nullified by global dynamics. For Kropotkin, it was now obvious that those who still held it fell into one of two camps. Some

---

46 Kropotkin, *Great French Revolution*, p. 373.
47 P. Kropotkin, 'Communism and Anarchy' (1901), repr. in Iain McKay (ed.), *Direct Struggle against Capital: A Peter Kropotkin Anthology* (Oakland, CA: AK Press, 2014), p. 638.
48 P. Kropotkin, 'The scientific basis of anarchy', *The Nineteenth Century* 21 (February 1887), pp. 238–52; P. Kropotkin, 'The coming anarchy', *The Nineteenth Century* 22 (August 1887), pp. 149–64. The essays were re-worked as *Anarchist Communism*.
49 Kropotkin, 'The coming anarchy', p. 151.

were ideologically wedded to the perpetuation of egoism, slavery, and exploitation. Others were hoodwinked by ideologues to believe that socialism represented a threat to liberty and that individual ownership provided the best bulwark against it.[50]

Kropotkin's detailed analysis of 'no-government ethics' and 'no-capital economics' followed in *Fields, Factories and Workshops*, published in 1899. The problem it addressed was how to empower local communities to meet their need while dispensing with planning. By planning, Kropotkin meant the economic 'laws' of market exchange, originally devised by eighteenth-century academic economists and subsequently absorbed into Marxist critique. These linked social wellbeing to profit and its strict management and regulation. In industrialized capitalist states, planning laws had stimulated an organizational principle of divided labour which had two aspects. On the one hand, it patterned individual work-time through minute job specification. Workers became industrial cogs, while being classified as autonomous service providers, free to enter into 'enforced contracts (under threat of hunger)'.[51] On the other, it structured international power relations based on specialization. This instituted a permanent specialization of states and their colonial possessions as manufacturers, mono-cultures, or natural resource providers. In combination, planning normalized industrialized production based on ruthless exploitation of labour and natural resources to meet the insatiable demands of capitalist speculation and profiteering.

Kropotkin produced a wealth of evidence to show how states and corporations were implicated in global interconnectedness. The implication was that advocates of laissez faire and the regulatory state could take more comfort from his analysis than anarchist communists. Yet the point for Kropotkin was that changes in the global economy concealed the possibility of anarchist alternatives while providing compelling reasons for revolutionary action. The impact of interconnectedness on either the liberal or the social democratic model would be disastrous. Directing global trends towards the realization of anarchist communist alternatives would be an enormous task, but it was not impossible.

In attending to these changes, Kropotkin's recommendations were largely directed towards simplification: increased production on a local level, to be achieved by the integration of agriculture and industry and the recalibration of needs. A new physiology of society would focus on the provision of food,

50 P. Kropotkin, *The Conquest of Bread* (London: Chapman and Hall, 1906), pp. 31–9.
51 Kropotkin, 'Communism and Anarchy', p. 638.

housing, clothing, and small luxuries 'with *the least expenditure of energy*'.[52] The old measures based on production for profit, which perpetually inflated consumption, would be abandoned. However, in other ways, Kropotkin's proposals were as complex as the systems they were designed to arrest. He imagined a world in which local units were federated, territorially and functionally, creating networks of mutual aid sustained by intricate bilateral and multilateral agreements. This arrangement would alleviate the distress caused by periodic disruptions of supply and problems of production resulting from constraints imposed by the physical environment. It would also modify subsistence economics by facilitating knowledge exchange about technological innovations and scientific experimentation.

Kropotkin dismissed objections that his model would fail as a result of free-riding or under the weight of demands for social compliance. He believed that the first objection reflected a deeply entrenched class prejudice, reminiscent of the racism of former slave-owners. It was based on the view that hard work was a function of the whip or, as Niccolo Machiavelli once remarked, hunger and poverty. Kropotkin argued, to the contrary, that the most powerful inducement to work was 'the enjoyment of the produce of one's labour'. The abolition of workers' enslavement to property-owning masters was a first step to this accomplishment.[53]

Kropotkin made two points against the criticism that communism would saddle individuals with unbearable social responsibilities. On the one hand, he acknowledged that communism was intimately tied to mutual aid and individual self-sacrifice. The readiness of sailors to take initiatives to rescue stranded seafarers was one of his favourite examples of the communist spirit. On the other, he deemed that all systems of social justice required individuals to balance their interests against the interests of others. Anarchist communism used free agreement as the mechanism. In keeping with his ethics, this meant that social rules were never regarded as fixed or naturally patterned and that they were instead understood to be continuously enacted. There was no primary one-off commitment – a social contract – that established a permanent framework for rights and obligations. Secondly, free agreements were secured by constantly shifting power alignments. There was no external or independent system of enforcement. Kropotkin argued that all associations, irrespective of their size or complexity – 'cohabitation', 'the family', or the 'co-operation of two persons in gardening or in bringing out a paper' – were

52 Kropotkin, *Modern Science and Anarchism*, p. 78.
53 P. Kropotkin, 'Are We Good Enough?', in Kropotkin, *Act for Yourselves*, p. 84.

potentially enslaving.[54] Recognizing the potential for power entrenchment was the first step in challenging it. Anarchist communism removed the material inequalities that hampered co-operation but recognized that individuals were brought into social arrangements that were always unequal. They had to be open to adjustment. There was no greater good beyond the relationships that communism stimulated and sustained.

The most significant weakness of anarchist communism, which Kropotkin accepted, was that he might be wrong about its potential and that 'State Capitalism and the Collectivist Wages System'[55] might emerge as liberalism's chief challenger. His hope was that anarchist communists could rival Marxism and neutralize appeals made by would-be leaders to deliver liberation. 'The Revolution is a question of ideas to be acted upon, and of force to enable us to act upon them.'[56] The anarchists' role was to assist communities, unions, co-operatives, and other movements to build independent micro-economies. To provide a libertarian social structure for the coming anarchy, these would have to be strong enough to withstand the privations created by trade dislocation and White Terror. Anarchy was a hard struggle. Yet, taking confidence from 'history and science', Kropotkin argued that 'we need in no way lack the additional incentive that we are thereby building up freedom and welfare for those who shall follow us'.[57]

Communism and Jacobinism

Contrary to Marx, Kropotkin saw not communism but Jacobinism as the spectre haunting Europe. Unless it was resisted, the world would be condemned to live with one form of terror or another. Acknowledging that intellectuals, activists, and politicians were divided in their responses to Jacobinism, Kropotkin suggested that post-revolutionary systems of government could be judged by their capacity to advance or resist it. Representative government, the ideal preferred by liberals and radicals, appeared to provide a bulwark. But this was an illusion. As an instrument of bourgeois rule, representative government was designed to maintain capitalism by domination. It would always be faced with internal conflict and, whenever this arose, liberals would restrict general liberty to protect elite power, adopting

54 Kropotkin, 'Communism and Anarchy', p. 635.
55 Kropotkin, *Modern Science and Anarchism*, p. 79.
56 P. Kropotkin, 'The Permanence of Society after the Revolution', in Kropotkin, *Act for Yourselves*, p. 87.
57 Ibid., p. 91.

Jacobin methods to do so. Kropotkin proposed 'communalism' as the appropriate organizational form for anarchist communism.[58] This would eradicate the inequalities embedded in liberal constitutionalism and, in doing so, provide the most robust defence against Jacobinism.

References to Jacobininsm appear throughout Kropotkin's writing; *The Great French Revolution* contains his sustained analysis. In this history of the French Revolution, he identified Jacobinism with two modes of government. Both were derived from Rousseauian republicanism. One, exemplified by Maximilien Robespierre, prioritized liberty for the achievement of equality and proposed the introduction of a constitutional monarchy on the English model. The king would be 'a mere enregistering scribe . . . chiefly to act as the symbol of national unity'.[59] The other, espoused by François-Noël 'Gracchus' Babeuf, was conspiratorial. It made equality the key to liberty and plotted the imposition of communism by means of dictatorship, transferring individual rights of ownership to the nation.[60]

For Kropotkin, both expressions of Jacobinism were flawed. In Robespierre's case, the weaknesses were revealed in his growing resistance to popular actions directed at the equalization and communalization of property. Robespierre's concern to alleviate the 'sufferings of the people'[61] had been sincere but, like the nineteenth-century radicals who followed him, he was fearful that the people might 'become masters of the situation'.[62] In this respect, he was naive; he failed to understand that his regime had provided the model for a string of illiberal successors.[63] As for Babeuf, he had taken the next step, openly advocating proletarian dictatorship for the purpose of emancipation. His plan resuscitated Caesarism for the modern era and 'paved the way for Bonaparte' and 'the faith in a Napoleon or a Disraeli – the faith in a saviour which still persists to this day'.[64]

Acknowledging these variations, Kropotkin identified two associated processes within Jacobinism, one towards centralization and the other towards policing. In the first instance, Jacobinism accelerated the controlling mechanisms that monarchy had put in motion before the revolution, 'depriving . . . popular organisations of such rights and the nomination of the judges and the administration of relief work, as well as of all other administrative

58 P. Kropotkin, 'Le Gouvernement réprésentatif', in Kropotkin, *Paroles d'un Révolté*, p. 171.
59 Kropotkin, *Great French Revolution*, p. 7.   60 Ibid., p. 494.   61 Ibid., p. 362.
62 Ibid., p. 257.
63 P. Kropotkin, 'Le Gouvernement révolutionnaire', in Kropotkin, *Paroles d'un Révolté*, p. 255.
64 Kropotkin, *Great French Revolution*, p. 492.

functions'.[65] During the revolution, this practice had led to the destruction of the 'sections' in Paris – the relatively autonomous administrative units that had enacted the democratic republican programme of the Constituent Assembly.[66] Borrowing from Jules Michelet's *History of the French Revolution*, Kropotkin noted that the power of the sections' general assemblies was ceded by force to Jacobin revolutionary committees, unelected bodies comprising 'groups of officials nominated by the authorities'.[67]

The second development, the 'concentration of police functions', occurred within this broad process. Kropotkin called it the 'leading idea of the Jacobin government'.[68] Policing had been one of the many functions of the sections, organized by the citizens in their districts. A series of laws had converted them into 'police bureaux' and, 'by disciplining them to obedience', had weakened and 'transformed them into machinery of the State'. Jacobinism thus revived 'one of the worst traditions of the *ancien régime*', clearing a path for the creation of the Committee of Supervision and the Committee of Public Safety.[69] The Terror – 'always a weapon of government'[70] – was the most spectacular result of this change. In Kropotkin's eyes, it was less an aberration of the revolution than a symptom of the contradictions of Jacobinism: the combination of democracy with aristocratic government and the obsession of the leadership to protect 'the revolution' (variously identified with the state or the nation) from its enemies. These tensions dogged the post-revolutionary European state system, too, and they would continue to do so until Jacobinism itself was halted.

The ramifications of the revolution had been felt across Europe. Kropotkin noted that the abolition of serfdom had been its major achievement, observing, too, that the manner of its accomplishment had also been significant. Popular rebellion in France ensured that 'the change ... acted against the lords ... to the advantage of the great mass of the peasants'. In Russia and Prussia, where the abolition had been achieved 'bureaucratically', it reinforced the economic power of the lords and 'ruined' the peasantry.[71] The unevenness of abolition was mirrored in the institutionalization of the wage system and in the instability of European politics: while the sway of absolutism had been reduced as a result of the revolution, it endured nonetheless, creating a source of political tension in Europe that complicated inter-state rivalries.

65 Ibid., p. 532.   66 Ibid., p. 215.   67 Ibid., p. 532.   68 Ibid., p. 530.   69 Ibid., p. 531.
70 Ibid., p. 535.   71 Ibid., p. 431.

Yet Caesarism and the 'Republic strongly centralised'[72] were the revolution's lasting ideological legacies. Like Bakunin, Kropotkin argued that this revolutionary idea had importantly set the template for the new German state. Unification represented 'the triumph of military and political despotism ... the worship of the State, of authority and of State Socialism'.[73] But Caesarism was a prejudice that extended far beyond the borders of the new Germany. Prussia's victory over France in 1871 marked its triumph 'in the European mind', equally moulding Marxism and the 'Socialism of Herr Bismarck'.[74] The European predicament was stark: bourgeois liberal values, entrenched in representative government, were being squeezed by Babouvist Jacobinism. Kropotkin concluded that the vigour of libertarian politics depended on the extension of communalist self-rule and anarchist–communist federation.

Turning to the anarchist alternative, Kropotkin described communalism as the process against dictatorship and a social order. Just as he linked Jacobinism to the progressive smothering of the aspiration for self-government, he associated communalism with popular resistance to saviour models of leadership. One of the lessons he took from his study of the Paris Commune was that communalists had to dispense with the 'fetish' of government and reject the paraphernalia that went with it. This included systems of representation, elections, and voting. Solutions to organizational problems would emerge only in the course of revolution and from 'the people in action'.[75] Kropotkin's seeming vagueness on this point reflected his assessment that 'Everywhere and always a revolution is made by minorities.'[76] Forming constitutional councils or calling for votes on programmes and policies would inevitably play into the hands of the few who had already decided what the best course of action should be, thus entrenching the domination of revolutionary government. He presented the same ideas in the Russian revolutionary context: 'in every factory, in every building yard, every workshop, and every mine, *establish yourselves the order of things which, by common accord, you will find proper to establish* ... Don't allow others to interfere! It is *your* affair, and *you* have to settle it.'[77]

---

72 P. Kropotkin 'Parliamentary Rule', in Kropotkin, *Act for Yourselves*, p. 40.
73 P. Kropotkin, 'Caesarism', *Freedom*, June 1899.
74 P. Kropotkin, 'What We Must Do', in Kropotkin, *Act for Yourselves*, p. 31.
75 Kropotkin, 'Le Gouvernement révolutionnaire', p. 251.
76 Kropotkin, *Great French Revolution*, p. 363.
77 Peter Kropotkin, letter to *Freedom*, 3 November 1905 (repr. as 'The Revolution in Russia', in McKay (ed.), *Direct Struggle against Capital*, pp. 455–7), p. 457.

Kropotkin argued that Fourier had set out the 'essential' organizational hallmarks of communalism fifty years earlier, when he imagined small territorial units federating regionally and nationally to organize production, consumption and exchange, and the abandonment of forced labour.[78] Kropotkin also looked at practical revolutionary experiments to refine these ideas. Seeing a precursor in the 1789 Paris Commune, he was most enthusiastic about the 1871 Commune and other nineteenth-century manifestations, notably the 'Federative Republic and Commune in Spain and Italy and the Unitarian Democratic Republic in Germany'.[79] These movements bucked the trend towards European Caesarism, inspiring anarchist and cantonalist movements in France, Spain, Italy, and Switzerland.[80] None was perfect, but each modelled a form of communalism that was anti-bourgeois, anti-clerical, anti-capitalist, and internationalist. They were quite different from the parochial, medieval communes of the past.[81]

Kropotkin pinpointed the organizational strength of communalism in the development of decentralized federation. To explain the process, he compared communalism to municipal socialism. Like the municipalities, communes were self-governing. He imagined 'thousands of cities and villages' expressing 'their own interests' and being recognized as 'the best judges of those interests'.[82] However, communalism used expropriation as an instrument of change, departing from the municipal model, which relied on law. And, whereas municipalism promoted local service provision, communalism shifted power down to the smallest possible units – individuals – to reconfigure social organization 'from the bottom up' while respecting sovereignty.

Kropotkin anticipated that communalist experiments would most probably occur in bounded spaces. Yet interconnectedness meant that the inevitable disruption of international trade would likely have a domino effect. Revolution, Kropotkin argued, was the spread of rebellion for the achievement of the *'welfare of all'*[83] by mimicry and solidarity. Kropotkin found an analogy in British politics, where the principle of Home Rule had already spread from Ireland to Scotland and Wales.[84] It could easily take root in London or any other metropolitan area, albeit in a different form. These

78 Kropotkin, *Modern Science and Anarchism*, p. 59.
79 P. Kropotkin, 'Before the Storm: A Speech Delivered by P. Kropotkine at the Meeting Held at South Place, November 29, to Bid Farewell to Mrs Parsons', in R. Kinna (ed.), *Early Writings on Terrorism* (London: Routledge, 2006), p. 376.
80 Kropotkin, 'Parliamentary Rule', p. 40.
81 P. Kropotkin, 'La Commune', in Kropotkin, *Paroles d'un Révolté*, pp. 105–18.
82 P. Kropotkin, 'A General View', in Kropotkin, *Act for Yourselves*, p. 79.
83 Kropotkin, *Great French Revolution*, p. 563.   84 Kropotkin, 'Parliamentary Rule', p. 39.

tangible examples of resistance were all-important for the advancement of anarchism against Jacobinism. 'All human progress' could be explained by the 'practical application of new principles'. Indeed, implementation was the only means of 'convincing most people of their applicability'.[85]

Kropotkin imagined that communalist internationalism would evolve through the federation and mutual support of local units. In 1914, he told Luigi Bertoni, editor of *Il Risveglio/Le Réveil* (*The Awakening*) and a comrade who rejected his stance on the war, that he took the resolutions of the 1872 Saint-Imier Congress of the Jura Federation as his model.[86] These enshrined the full independence of sections united by mutual friendship and mutual defence. One upshot was that federation implied variety. 'To dream that the next revolution may follow one single programme' was a mistake. While Kropotkin talked about a new decentralized federal 'nation' – a 'federation of . . . free organisms, economically and politically free' – he argued that this would reflect the complex multi-formity of existing human associations.[87] A second implication was that internationalism assumed permanent contestation and that defence pacts provided the best security against the threat of domination. Kropotkin's commentary on Herbert Spencer hinted at the principle: 'that which constitutes an evil in society includes all acts of aggression of one member of society against the other'. Toleration of aggression obviously diluted 'the stability of the social bond'. Anarchist order thus relied on 'mutual coöperation' and if this was not 'practiced for the defence of the group' notions of common welfare would be undermined in local sections, too, and communist principles would also be enfeebled.[88]

Conclusion

Kropotkin presented anarchist communism as a framework for social organization capable of reconfiguring social relations on the basis of equality. This framework would resist structural domination and empower co-operation. Sadly, Kropotkin's estimation of the relative strength of anarchism and Marxism proved to be accurate. Yet his justification for revolutionary change anticipated critiques of globalization and chimed with today's campaigns for the development of alternatives. Similarly, Kropotkin's understanding of revolutionary processes, replication, and local experimentation resonates

---

85 P. Kropotkin 'Local Action', in Kropotkin, *Act for Yourselves*, pp. 44–5.
86 P. Kropotkin to Luigi Bertoni, 30 November 1914, Max Nettlau Papers, IISH, ARCH010012698.
87 Kropotkin, 'A General View', p. 80.   88 Kropotkin, *Ethics*, p. 302.

RUTH KINNA

with recent waves of pro-democracy campaigning, notably the international solidarities expressed by activists with counterparts in other parts of the world. At the same time, Kropotkin appears out of step with modern social justice campaigns. He avoided the language of democracy to advance social change, perhaps fearing that this would reinforce the prestige of bourgeois representative institutions that were then becoming increasingly central to its interpretation. He also attached little importance to the inscription of anarchist communism on activists' banners.[89] The problems posed by anarchist communism would not be solved by making anarchists. The practical conundrum was how to sustain and empower actions tending towards transformative change. Famine, he warned, 'will result in Caesarism',[90] no substitute for the conquest of bread. It was a hard message, but the economic model it inspired dovetails with modern degrowth agendas.[91]

Kropotkin's internationalist vision was perhaps the most controversial aspect of his revolutionary politics. Noting in his correspondence with Bertoni that workers were not natural revolutionaries and that soldiers and Pinkertons were for the most part workers, too, he rejected the idea that international solidarity rested on the harmonization of class interest. Rather, the impulse to rise in defence of those resisting domination – an expression of mutual aid – was also central. His rose-tinted view of the war was informed by this view and, above all, his fear of the entrenchment of Caesarism. In 1915 he was sure that, 'in proportion as the atrocities committed in Belgium will become known', workers 'will better see the danger afforded by a powerful military state in the centre of Europe, bent upon conquering new territories and armies for its own expansion'. Referring to his history of the French Revolution, he continued: 'One sees there what importance the *sections* of Paris acquired for imposing their will in political and economical matters' and, 'when war broke out in 1792', in determining 'the choice of the volunteers, their equipment, their . . . correspondence with them, the supply of labour to the unemployed and so on'. Kropotkin believed that 'something . . . on a much smaller state [*sic*]' was taking place 'in the Society at large' and that 'peasants and intellectuals alike' were learning both how 'to live through this calamity' and how to 'affirm their rights of reconstructing society'. He was wrong. The war did not 'bear fruit'.[92] Nevertheless,

89 Kropotkin, 'The Necessity of Communism', p. 63.
90 P. Kropotkin, 'Revolution and Famine', in Kropotkin, *Act for Yourselves*, p. 68.
91 S. Latouch, *Farewell to Growth*, trans. D. Macey (Cambridge: Polity, 2009); G. Kallis, *Degrowth* (Bath: Agenda, 2018).
92 Copy by Nettlau of 'Lettres sur les questions actuelles' by P. Kropotkin, 7 January 1915, Max Nettlau Papers, IISH, ARCH010012706.

his warnings about the inherent weakness of liberal democracy, the fragility of the pacts that rulers make with the ruled to share the benefits of 'growth', and the attendant risks of Caesarism seem prescient. And his defence of anarchist communism achieved 'from the bottom up' remains attractive.

Further Reading

Adams, Matthew, *Kropotkin, Read, and the Intellectual History of British Anarchism: Between Reason and Romanticism* (London: Palgrave Macmillan, 2015).

Cahm, Caroline, *Kropotkin and the Rise of Revolutionary Anarchism 1872–1886* (Cambridge: Cambridge University Press, 1989).

Kinna, Ruth, *Kropotkin: Reviewing the Classical Anarchist Tradition* (Edinburgh: Edinburgh University Press, 2016).

Miller, Martin, *Kropotkin* (Chicago: University of Chicago Press, 1976).

Morris, Brian, *Kropotkin: The Politics of Community* (New York: Humanity Books, 2004).

PART II

NEGATING STATE POWER

———

15

Anarchism and Syndicalism in France

ALEXANDER VARIAS

'The Communist's emphasis is always on centralism and efficiency, the Anarchist's on liberty and equality.'[1] With these words George Orwell contrasted two allied forces alongside which he fought, attempting to save the republic from the fascist-supported army of Francisco Franco during the Spanish Civil War. Division between these 'allies' was strong, involving unresolvable differences, and convincing them to work in harmony was a formidable task. Orwell was not alone in his awareness of that division. In revolutionary circles, the anarchist and socialist personalities have been sharply distinguished in temperament and approach – anarchists preferring undeterred freedom and disliking government while the more organized socialists prioritize cohesion, success, and the ability to change course. Anarchists express an aspirational and dreamlike vision of ending social division and authority, but attuned to concerns for culture, psychology, and the human relationship to nature. Anarchists' character is assumed to cross national boundaries. Yet national setting could matter, as in France, where the contrast with socialism was furthered by a different relationship to the French Revolution. Anarchism may stress internationalism and denounce nationalism, but emotions tied to the French context need consideration.

Anarchists and the French Revolution

The word 'anarchist' is often used in vague, accusatory, and confused ways. Conservatives attach 'terrorist', 'troublemaker', 'disorder', and 'chaos' to it. In their view, the only thing that seems to motivate anarchist actions and thoughts is the tendency to destroy with no reason other than destruction. Anarchists, it is said, act only to tear down existing society, leaving behind all

To Lorraine.
1 G. Orwell, *Homage to Catalonia* (New York: Harcourt, 1938).

semblance of balance and morality. Such a view is not confined to conservatives. Rival opposition movements brand anarchism as irrational and purposeless, universally the same and not dependent on circumstances, regardless of national context or political situation. One must ask: can different contexts reveal variations in anarchist movements, and are they only marked by disorder and destruction? Is there an anarchist ideal not exclusively bound to destruction?

Modern French anarchism did not emerge in a vacuum. Anarchists and their fellow socialists placed themselves in the context of the French Revolution but differed in the way they viewed their relation to it. Socialists saw the new era as marking a distinct break, while anarchists felt continuity and aspired to complete and update the revolution.[2]

Another major factor shaping French anarchism was Paris, the stage for much of the revolution's drama and later nineteenth-century upheavals. Its overarching and mutating political and cultural character was magnetic, although it was a paradox for anarchists, drawn to the rural world, to be entranced by a city. But in France, especially in Paris, the revolution was keenly felt, its storehouse of memories and examples of action vivid as models. Alongside earlier ideals and emotions, nineteenth-century French anarchism developed out of a national tradition of revolutionary activity. Revolutionary currents remained vivid and set French anarchism off from varieties of the movement elsewhere. Anarchists frequently interpreted later events as repetitions of the revolution, seeking to imitate its violence, which was seen as necessary for a just and egalitarian society, and scorning compromise and moderation. Later rebels were also stirred by the revolution's idealistic aspirations. Popular action to combat authority and tradition; the development of the concept of 'citizen'; passionate devotion to liberty, equality, and fraternity: such developments represented a new phase to generations of future revolutionaries. Despite frustration at the revolution's disintegration and unachieved goals, anarchists felt connected to it, reliving the drama while aiming for a happier end.

Throughout Europe and the Americas, notwithstanding its undeniable internal conflicts, the revolution was perceived as an attack by the oppressed on the power and legacy of the Bourbons. Nineteenth-century political and social movements were affected by the revolution, which cast a glow among succeeding generations of rebels while evoking a sense of splintering and

2 A. Varias, *Paris and the Anarchists: Aesthetes and Subversives during the Fin de Siècle* (New York: St Martin's Press, 1996).

fragmentation. The effects were universal and their revolutionary influence obvious. While other nineteenth-century reformers and revolutionaries clearly contrasted their rhetoric and goals to those of the revolution, anarchists tended to cling to its emotional inspiration. Less transfixed, liberals, republicans, and socialists throughout western Europe consciously sought to channel the ideals of 1789–93 into new historical conditions. Anarchists never forgot the revolution's ardour, but they emphasized hatred of the state – a departure from the revolution's devotion to *l'état* – which caused them to define their positions in an oblique and often vague manner. Anarchists may have inherited a broader and older tradition from the revolution, but history offered new situations to which they connected their rebellion.

French anarchism emerged in the early nineteenth century. Countering it and other movements, modern conservatism developed during and after the revolution as words such as 'tradition' and 'authority' registered in the slogans of thinkers such as Edmund Burke and Joseph de Maistre to reverse the course of events. Nineteenth-century anarchists were inspired by, among others, Pierre-Joseph Proudhon's federalist programme involving small co-operative voluntary communities. The provincial reality of France furthered the local nature of anarchism even as a more international character emerged in Lyon, near the Swiss Jura, where Mikhail Bakunin championed anarchist goals within the boundaries of the International in an uneasy relationship with Karl Marx between the failed 1848 revolutions and the 1870s.

Anarchists continued to be radical, angry, and challenging. That the events of the French revolutionary era were driven by the *mentalité* of anger and irrepressible crowd violence has been well documented by Timothy Tackett.[3] Such anger did not subside, but continued to stir rebels into putting up barricades, as dramatized in early Romantic novels. French anarchists especially drew upon that well of emotion. Associated with hatred of the state and capitalism, esteem for individual freedom, spontaneous protest and destruction, and crowd uprisings, anarchism seemed an especially emotional follow-up to the revolution.

Anarchist Engagement in Paris

Making his way through the city's neighbourhoods before the 1848 revolution, the exiled Russian dissident Alexander Herzen emotionally relived

---

3 T. Tackett, *The Coming of the Terror in the French Revolution* (Cambridge, MA: Harvard University Press, 2015).

Paris's rebellious past and its illustrious 'grand events', humanizing the usual sweeping continental and international perspective.[4] Just as significant as the Parisian past was the great city's nineteenth-century complex cultural, intellectual, and social transformation in 'modernity'. Baron Haussmann's rebuilding added a more modern accent in the 1850s, involving demolition of older quarters of the city and replacement with linear streets and boulevards amenable to the dominant bourgeoisie – especially in central Paris. Anarchists had to live and work within confined spaces in other quarters. In the dialogue over local issues, Parisian anarchists contributed their share to the city's tumultuous history, becoming, in time, immersed in the transformed environment of political, social, and cultural controversies.

In this setting, anarchists walked a metaphorical tightrope as they contested both the established order and competing opposition movements. Combining hostility to the state and to capitalism with a mystique for the freedom of the individual, anarchism lacked a core, its adherents filled with varying centrifugal degrees of ardour. Countless individual situations, however, defying any final position after heated argument, tested anarchists' beliefs.

During the 1850s and 1860s, anarchism attracted little attention, as just one of several opposition forces within the Second Empire. Over time, workers' organizations emerged in and around various parts of Paris, such as Belleville.[5] Such movements worked across neighbourhood lines, finding support in the more intellectual pockets in the vicinity of the Sorbonne/Latin Quarter. This undercurrent was evident in both the Second Empire and the Third Republic. The Commune of 1871, following on the heels of a failed Bakunin-inspired uprising in Lyon, sent shockwaves through France and remained in the collective memory of the lower classes. The Second Empire did come to an end after the defeat by Prussia. Paris regained its revolutionary position, although this was tempered by the catastrophic crushing of the Commune. But its suppression did not end dissent. What had ended was one form of authoritarian government, but was the newest republic any more satisfying? As the Second Empire receded into the past, the new government encountered opposition from the anarchists, among other quarters – crestfallen as they may have been as they returned from exile.

Late nineteenth-century anarchists strayed from the French revolutionary tradition as the authority being challenged was not an absolutist monarchy,

4 A. Herzen, *My Past and Thoughts* (London: Faber and Faber, 2008).
5 J. Merriman, *Massacre: The Life and Death of the Paris Commune* (New York: Basic Books, 2014).

but the Third Republic, the emblem of which, Marianne, hearkened back to the revolution. Some anarchists lowered their hostility to republican life, but others did not. The wide contrast between a theoretical republic and its contemporary practice was disorienting. Since 1793, the vision of republicanism had been radical. The destruction of monarchy, growth of popular sovereignty, and local power exerted by the *sans-culottes*: all were comfortably under the umbrella of the republic's radical legacies. Restoration authorities saw republicanism as a radical force, one to fear. So it appeared in the early days of the 1848 revolution as the republican ideal swept across the continent.

Nevertheless, during the early years of the Third Republic, memories resurfaced of recent measures under the republic intended primarily to secure upper-class rule, beginning with the Terror, continuing with the June Days of 1848, and culminating in the crushing of the Commune. The legacy of the French revolutionary tradition was double-edged. Oppressive authorities and exploitative classes had been removed but were replaced by new authoritarians and exploiters. As Alexis de Tocqueville noted in *L'Ancien Régime et la Révolution* (*The Old Regime and the Revolution*), by the time of Napoleon, the state's authoritarian power would have been envied by the Bourbons. Anarchists' dislike of the Third Republic was especially pronounced, given their scorn for bourgeois republics and socialists' and radicals' accommodation of them.

Anarchists viewed the newly created 'monarchist' republic with its military ethos as another hateful state to be opposed. The slide into the 'opportunist' era did not assuage their feelings. While Marxists and anarchists alike thought that the republics of 1793 and 1848 were flawed, they still saw glimmers of good intentions. In contrast, anarchists condemned the Third Republic for its authoritarian baggage carried over from the Second Empire. The massacres of the Commune and the resulting shattered streets and quarters of Paris suggested a direct link to the June Days of 1848 rather than to the 'glorious' days of the Bastille and the storming of the Tuileries. Such critics found the Third Republic's first centre in Versailles symbolic of its repressive nature. In fact, in their eyes, Adolphe Thiers' national army resembled the monarchy's in its attack on Paris's historic neighbourhoods. Radicals were at best ambiguous, extolling the Communards as working-class heroes, while excoriating republican authorities as repressive murderers. A walk through the city revealed rubble in recently rebuilt quarters. In this setting, anarchists regrouped.

With the Law on Freedom of the Press of 29 July 1881 (the Lisbonne Law), Parisian anarchism became increasingly vocalized in newspapers as education expanded and literacy grew.[6] The model was the French revolutionary press, which had seemingly moved the masses at its whim – as in Jean-Paul Marat's articles calling for Parisians to carry out the September Prison Massacres of 1792. The press could either emulate such violent rhetoric or display more restraint and reasoned persuasion, bound to the revolution but moving with the times as the century went on.

Anarchist journalism emanated from various Parisian locales where publicists with diverging concerns, tones, even languages operated. The Dreyfus Affair, terrorist attacks, unions, and bohemian irrationalism drew French anarchists into the labyrinth of Third Republic politics. Such geographical fragmentation corresponded to contrasting views of Jean Grave, Emile Pouget, Louise Michel, Sébastien Faure, and Henri Rochefort, among others. In apparent imitation of the pattern set by the *sans-culottes*, clubs within the various neighbourhoods emerged, seemingly generated by the familiarity of locals with similar views, a small number since police estimated that throughout Paris there were only five hundred anarchists connected to such clubs.[7] Clubs, not surprisingly, were named in ways corresponding to their locale or focus, thus: Les Antipatriotes, Les Antipropriétaires, La Justice Sociale, L'Egalité, La Lutte, La Panthéon, La Vengeance, Les Libertaires, Le Drapeau Noir, Le Groupe Anarchiste du Père Lachaise, and Le Groupe Anarchiste de Belleville. Intimacy, yes, but ensured by the small numbers.[8]

During the 1880s and 1890s, Grave, a former *cordonnier* and the foremost advocate of the earlier movement, published *La Révolte* (*The Revolt*), *Le Révolté* (*The Rebel*), and *Les Temps Nouveaux* (*The New Times*) from rue Mouffetarde. While committed to workers' causes, he emphasized an intellectual and theoretical approach – reinforced by his proximity to the Sorbonne, Panthéon, and Latin Quarter. Carrying the epithet 'Pope of rue Mouffetard', Grave bridged two worlds, addressing the working classes while acknowledging the area's official intellectual and artistic life, seemingly emblazoned in the surrounding neo-classical architecture. Intellectuals such as the renowned geographer Elisée Reclus were part of this 'academic' circle, defining anarchist ideas as laws of nature.

6 E. Weber, *Peasants into Frenchmen* (Stanford: Stanford University Press, 1976).
7 J. Maitron, *Le mouvement anarchiste en France*, vol. I, *Des origines à 1914* (Paris: François Maspero, 1983), p. 452.
8 Varias, *Paris and the Anarchists*. The club names are The Antipatriots, Those Against Property, Social Justice, Equality, The Struggle, The Pantheon, Vengeance, The Libertarians, The Black Flag, The Anarchist Group of Père Lachaise, and The Anarchist Group of Belleville.

Those anarchists, however, who addressed Grave as 'Pope' represented a different Parisian world. They operated and lived in remote decaying neighbourhoods with narrow streets where the architectural ambience was provided by old crumbling buildings. Such an area was the newly absorbed enclave of Montmartre perched on a hill, detached from the centre, sharing only the Parisian identity. From there, Pouget espoused syndicalism and, striving to raise their anger, in *Père Peinard* addressed workers in street slang and vulgar language. Inspiring this publication was Jacques René Hébert's French revolutionary newspaper, *Père Duchesne*, which fed the *sans-culottes* a hearty denunciation of the wealthy in *argot*. Pouget's popular tone and violent rhetoric, aimed at workers, opposed Grave's caution and highlighted the volatility of anarchism, which changed from moment to moment, mimicking the revolution.

The allure of Bohemia, with its legacy immortalized in both the Latin Quarter and Montmartre, drew more culturally inclined anarchists, who challenged official artistic centres such as the Salon. The Moulin Rouge especially represented the outcast culture of Montmartre with its artistic enclaves and erotic clubs and cafés, reflecting the exotic fringes of the city. Neighbouring Place Pigalle was saturated with clubs such as the Café du Néant – oriented around the macabre and where coffins functioned as tables, on which drinks and hors d'oeuvres were served.

Belleville was another popular area, sharing with Montmartre a vocal street life, vaudeville, and popular entertainment that exuded vibrant rebelliousness. During the Commune, the area was a centre for some of the concluding battles, especially in nearby Père Lachaise cemetery and memorialized in popular legends and memory. From Belleville, Sébastien Faure published his journals in support of Dreyfus.

Various debates highlighted European socialism during the Second International. After the initial and often turbulent course set by the International Working Men's Association, socialists became more attached to mass organized parties. But they also were divided, and the most obvious schism was between orthodox Marxists and revisionists who wanted to pursue compromise and less violent means. Germany was the most dramatic example of this dispute. In France, socialists (Jean Jaurès and Jules Guesde, among others) would eventually work within the framework of the republic, which anarchists rejected, maintaining an outsider position, their eyes always on revolution. However, they found themselves compelled to engage key issues, at times feeling uncomfortably drawn into indirect participation. Socialists had their own dialogue on participating but felt less compromised.

For the anarchists, this controversy involved language, ideas, and emotions at the heart of the movement. The ensuing division made for tentativeness and a wavering presence in the politics of the republic.

Parisian anarchism was partly shaped by the Commune's revolutionary legends – especially after the exiles' return. It was difficult for the 're-engaged rebels' to separate the contemporary movement from the Commune. Past and present seemed one in the examples offered of Parisian courage and engagement. French revolutionary memories of 1789–93 aroused Parisian action against large, hostile forces, as was also true in 1870. Parisians' refusal to abide by the Versailles government's surrender to the Germans was a reminder of the French revolutionary wars. Communards such as Louise Michel achieved revolutionary renown, but they were also sent into exile to New Caledonia. In exile, Michel met the young Charles Malato and both 'converted' to anarchism, sympathizing with the native New Caledonians and advocating their liberation from French rule. Returning to Paris, they attached their sympathy for the non-European world to their revolutionary activism.

Michel, known as the 'Red Virgin', publicized the roles of women in social and political life. Accused of being one of the 'incendiary women' of the Commune, during the trial she maintained an especially calm and stoic manner that impressed her fellow 'incendiaries' and public officials. She exploited the moment, praising courageous revolutionary women who challenged traditional male authority. Anarchism itself was marred by the patriarchal chauvinism of Proudhon, but at the other extreme Michel mocked Jules Michelet's idolization of women. While her ideas and actions reflected growing female activism, they did not extend to suffrage and feminism.[9]

In the interlude, exiles had developed politically in ways that were often not so predictable. Some veered further to the left and came to identify with anarchism. After returning to Paris, they worked within local clubs. Others were less staunchly leftist and drifted into other currents, sometimes of a more nationalistic nature. These figures updated their vision of anarchism with personal versions of freedom and equality.

Anarchism and the Cultural Slant

Baron Haussmann's rebuilding of Paris reconfigured the city's structure with a superimposed imperial façade more pleasing to Napoleon III. Improved

9 E. Thomas, *Louise Michel ou la Velleda de l'anarchie* (Paris: Gallimard, 1971), p. 159.

sanitation and health standards were complemented by the tearing down of the city's labyrinthine streets and replacement by wider modern boulevards in keeping with military preferences and bourgeois proclivities for leisure and for law and order.

Such change was accompanied by one involving art and culture, which in the new Paris also offered new perspectives for anarchists. Symbiotically, rebellious avant-garde artists and critics found sustenance in anarchist individual freedom while some anarchists themselves were drawn to the aesthetic issues of the day complementing their political slant.

At the centre of this situation was the official government-supported Salon and the challenge to it from rebellious newer artists influenced by the bohemian underground and deemed 'avant-garde'. Painting was central to this artistic revolution, although poets such as Charles Baudelaire and musicians such as Hector Berlioz also contributed to the aesthetic mood. Style and content varied, as Gustave Courbet emphasized realistic subjects whereas Impressionists such as Claude Monet and Camille Pissarro (an anarchist) went further, depicting the enigmatic interplay of colour and light. As a result, the entire Parisian cultural world of painting, music, and literature was shaken as angry debate among critics and the public at large ensued. Not hidden from view was the reality of modernity suggested in works that could be described as exhilarating or alienating. Artistic audiences, preferring uplifting historic, religious, or mythological subjects found such paintings of ordinary subjects disappointing.

Such individualistic defiance drew anarchist support in this cultural–political relationship. Courbet and Pissarro were prominent in emphasizing political rebellion. But another component of the 'anarchist creed' figured into the situation. Besides the social, economic, and political concerns of Peter Kropotkin and Jean Grave, anarchism included a deeply irrational commitment to individualism, 'egoism', derived from the ideas of Max Stirner. Egoists were drawn to the anarchist attack on social and political ills but did little to explain apparent contradictions in emphasizing unrestricted individualism over social concerns.

A tangential side is found in the aimless, drifting *flâneur* portrayed by the later cultural critic Walter Benjamin – one transfixed by the anonymity of modern urban life found in the modern boulevards where store windows beckoned, inviting momentary escape from the humdrum of life. The stroller is also a dreaming consumer. Politics was not central to the *flâneur* but not necessarily excluded. Such individuals found themselves unconsciously invited into the anarchist fold. Personality and artistic perception could be especially key to the emergence of such an individual.[10]

From Montmartre, the art critic and aesthete Félix Fénéon promoted works of avant-garde painters such as Georges Seurat. Fénéon also connected his artistic rebellion to a strong condemnation of the French state and bourgeois life. Writing under various pseudonyms, he carried on the life of aesthete, dandy, and angry, scornful critic in a manner echoing Baudelaire, though more overtly political. Fénéon was both an art critic promoting neo-Impressionism and a supporter of anarchism and terrorism. He is suspected of having taken part in some of the terrorist attacks in Paris and having known some of the more notorious culprits such as Emile Henry. Fénéon's devotion to art was matched by his tirades against an oppressive system. Idealism and contempt complemented each other. Fénéon inhabited both worlds, not secluding himself in either. His defiance of convention of any kind was directed both at state authorities and at other revolutionary groups. This enigma provided one more accent to Parisian anarchism: defiance of the mechanical world of convention. Condemning order and regimentation, Fénéon noted that Marxists 'prefer the complexity of the clock, to that of a living body'.[11]

Bohemians emphasized their marginality, projecting an outcast identity and way of life. Their urban identity was a given, but anarchism also provided the perfect support for naturalist clubs inspired by Jean-Jacques Rousseau and the back-to-nature movement. Fénéon's 'living body' reflected such an anarchist bond. Meeting in Montmartre, directed by Henri Zisly, the *Naturiens* emphasized vegetarianism, closeness to the soil, adoration of the primitive, and hostility to civilization loosely justified in the name of anarchism but described by Grave as excessive.

Anarchism and Current Issues

Parisian anarchism was espoused and disputed throughout the city in local clubs and informal meetings, and adherents publicized views in a variety of journals and newspapers. In their clashing Parisian clubs, anarchists addressed current inescapable issues, often making them feel entangled in

10 W. Benjamin, 'Paris, Capital of the Nineteenth Century' (1938), in W. Benjamin, *Reflections: Essays, Aphorisms, Autobiographical Writing*, ed. P. Demetz (New York: Schocken Books, 1986), pp. 156–62.
11 J. Halperin, *Félix Fénéon: Aesthete and Anarchist in Fin-de-Siècle Paris* (New Haven: Yale University Press, 1988), p. 241.

a spider's web. Debates over such international, national, or local matters concerned methods and aims at the heart of anarchism, which was thus engrossed in the politics of early Third Republic France and Europe.

The pitch of anarchist rhetoric, both orally and printed, could be violently intense or theoretical and balanced. At times, apocalyptic overtones crept in. Recalling the revolution's string of executions on the guillotine, *compagnons* at *séances* wondered about the number of dead necessary for a successful revolution, singing refrains from 'Dame Dynamite'. During the height of terrorist attacks, supportive cries for Ravachol or Emile Henry included images of blood.

Unexpected trouble arose when rival dissidents decided to work within the government. Anarchists consequently had to decide whether to do so occasionally as well and nuance their usual proud self-regard as outsiders. Anarchists' unequivocal hostility to government, even when non-authoritarian, was well known. Nevertheless, as socialists increasingly participated in the Third Republic, anarchists debated their alternatives. Electoral participation was an unpopular option since anarchists lacked socialists' accommodating flexibility. Anarchists enjoyed the freedom of assembly and press guaranteed by the state yet contemptuously attacked its 'bourgeois' and 'authoritarian' character. The fact that their meetings were spied upon by police agents reinforced this inclination.

Nonetheless, anarchists addressed such questions and sometimes restrained their rhetoric. Paul Brousse complicated the situation as he moved from militant anarchism to endorsing elections through 'Possibilism'. As a former radical, Brousse's change of direction brought new divisions as he confronted resistance from the 'older flank' anarchists who rejected reforms dependent on the republic.[12]

Anarchists did grudgingly take part in the public dialogue and acknowledged some role for the state in issues affecting French workers. It was not that anarchists completely accepted the need to participate. Their temperamental and theoretical resistance remained. However, a gradual flexibility emerged as certain issues drew anarchists into the arena of Third Republic politics. While the number of activists was never great, the nature of their rhetoric projected their voice loudly.

It was a challenge for the more publicly active anarchists to endorse or condemn 'propaganda by deed'. In the wake of the Russian Narodniks' assassination of Tsar Alexander II, anarchist terror in France made waves.

---

12 P. Avrich, *Anarchist Portraits* (Princeton: Princeton University Press, 1988).

Between 1890 and 1894, a series of attacks shook France, including a series of bombings carried out by Ravachol, Auguste Vaillant throwing a bomb in the Chamber of Deputies, Emile Henry hurling a bomb into the Café Terminus at Gare St Lazare, and the assassination of President Sadi Carnot by an Italian anarchist, Sante Geronimo Caserio. While they did not necessarily subscribe to the anarchist cause, such terrorists reflected the movement's emphasis on individualism and the legacy of French political violence since the revolution.

Various hopes were attached to the attacks. Ecstatic visionaries anticipated a single attack setting off a conflagration. Other terrorists were simply sending a message, making a statement, and releasing pent-up passions bound to frustration. As some of the terrorists attached themselves to the movement, the attacks became a focus of anarchists. Anarchist clubs and journals reflected this contest of views. The more ardent and angry members supported the swift, spontaneous, and destructive attacks. Others, like Grave, endorsed a more constructive and patient approach and expressed revulsion at the loss of life and fear of damage in public opinion. During and after the Trial of the Thirty in 1894–5, when the state prosecuted prominent activists and intellectuals for terrorist involvement, anarchists began to see the need for caution. While the trial ended in a general acquittal (excepting a few individuals), police scrutiny compelled anarchists to soften their rhetoric, to be less threatening to authorities and the public. The trial was a political filter separating the volatile part of the movement from the more practical and theoretical side and heralded a new era.

Anarchists could not evade Captain Alfred Dreyfus' court-martial and sentence to Devil's Island over false charges of handing military secrets to Germany. Division was fierce as Dreyfusards and anti-Dreyfusards dominated Parisian life in the 1890s. In engaging the issue, anarchists were bound to disagree, once they overcame their disdain for official politics and the larger press. Some saw the matter as involving just another capitalist and militarist. As one of them stated: 'un capitulo est un capitulo'. Captain Dreyfus' cause also ran up against prevailing anarchist distaste for his military status and prejudice inherited from Proudhon's antisemitism, which was at the heart of the case as Dreyfus was Jewish. Mass feeling against him was due to such racism. Ironically, Dreyfus' alleged treason fuelled further hatred of Germany even with the general anarchist inclination towards anti-militarism. However, patriotic fervour against Germany, central to the Commune, negated anarchist instincts in the lead-up to the Great War.

Other anarchists supporting universal human rights condemned Dreyfus' scapegoating. The press was vocal on both sides of the debate. Edouard Drumont's reactionary and nationalist *Le Libre Parole* (*The Free Word*, with a circulation exceeding 100,000) viciously condemned Dreyfus through fierce, right-wing, antisemitic stereotypes. Such depictions made their way into loud and divisive anarchist rhetoric. Henri Rochefort, a former Communard, and at the time an anarchist, fomented anti-Dreyfusard views in *L'Intransigéant* (*The Intrasigent*). Rochefort's political shift from left to right reflected the extreme nationalism and racism intruding on the revolutionary mindset. Under the later leadership of Léon Bailby in 1906, *L'Intransigéant* reached a circulation of 50,000. The presence of right-wing, racially focused, and nationalistic movements was a shock to those on the left who believed that mass-driven politics was their exclusive domain. Grave and Zo d'Axa (the pseudonym of Alphonse Gallaud), even with their differing orientations, both condemned Rochefort's antisemitism.

In the forefront of anarchist publications supporting Dreyfus but with a smaller circulation was *Le Journal du Peuple* (*The Journal of the People*), edited by Sébastien Faure, who had previously co-founded (with Louise Michel) the weekly *Le Libertaire* (*The Libertarian*) from his base in Montmartre. Faure had been led to the Dreyfusard side by his Zionist friend Bernard Lazare, a convert to anarchism. Circulation hovered between 7,000 and 10,000. Nearly all the writing in *Le Journal du Peuple* was devoted to the Dreyfus Affair, which Emile Zola in *J'accuse* (*I Accuse*) exposed in the popular press.[13]

Syndicalism

Following the public and internal anarchist uproar over terrorism and the Trial of the Thirty, alternative approaches were considered. It was clear to some anarchists that their movement was in danger of fragmenting into too many parts and that more co-ordination and structure were needed even if these conflicted with the movement's principles. In city-wide dialogues, anarchists were more divided and began to search for unity or co-ordination.

They also needed to address the situation of labourers. With its central position in French history, the setting and context of Paris's revolutionary past figured greatly in the discussion. The intimacy of Paris's neighbourhoods and streets made it stand out to labourers as it contrasted to urban sprawl and

---

13 C. Bellanger, J. Godechot, P. Guiral, and F. Terrou, *Histoire générale de la presse française*, vol. III, *De 1871 à 1940* (Paris: Presses Universitaires de France, 1972), pp. 341–5, 379.

the world of the anonymous factory that German observers called 'Manchesterism' and attracted those resisting dislocation and alienation. Even after its expansion and structural modernization, Paris exuded its past, seeming to preserve an internal revolutionary essence attractive to anarchists.

Complementing the size and scale of the city, workshops and factories tended to be on a smaller scale. This reality had other social and political consequences. Paris's traditional essence as a city where artisanal work still flourished reinforced its revolutionary aura. Kropotkin himself described Paris as a 'beehive' of active artisans devoted to traditional crafts and its neighbourhoods distinct from the centre, seemingly a separate world. The *sans-culottes* thrived in such an atmosphere during the revolution, which later haunted Parisian radicals attached to their local clubs.

A historical undercurrent also affected the social environment. Long-enduring medieval guilds had provided security and employment to workers within the various crafts. While hierarchical and often religiously based, guilds afforded workers reassurance and confidence. Workers also learned social communication and mutual understanding. Guilds were later complemented by the fraternal *compagnonnages* that furthered workers' associationism. With all its commitment to fraternity, the revolution undercut the support system in place with the Le Chapelier law of 1791, which prohibited all medieval associations including guilds – as workers involved in the manufacture of luxury goods lost employment due to collapsing markets. Artisans' estrangement from a revolution for which they had fought thus made the *sans-culottes'* position ambiguous at best.

As they considered labourers' concerns, anarchists viewed 'trade unions' as localized, small-scale gatherings in accordance with smaller French workshops and factories rather than the larger, more bureaucratic British trade unions. The relatively archaic and smaller factories made the move into trade unionism different in all respects and gave an immediate sense of definition to the French labour scene.

Aversion to organization separated anarchists from socialists. Accordingly, syndicalism sparked controversy as a new vehicle for anarchist and labour action. There were two obstacles: the anarchist insistence on individualism and suspicion of the British trade unions. Representing factory workers, trade unions sought better working conditions, increased salaries, and shorter hours, adding up to a non-revolutionary purpose. Syndicalism, alternatively, would revive revolutionary anarchism and avoid compromise.

Anarchists' debate over syndicates was nuanced by another emotional and divisive question: whether to rely on strikes or to engage politically within parties. Was action in the factories or behind-the-scenes negotiation preferred? Instinct and practical considerations shaped the ways such choices were viewed. Workers welcomed unions as potentially militant forces challenging employers, but they feared subsequent compromise and disappointment. Was it better to desire the collapse of the entire system or to agree to piecemeal reforms? To be revolutionary or compromise? These questions were more troubling to anarchists as (unlike socialists) they still asked whether republics represented revolutionary fervour or craven betrayal.

Discord arose from the very idea of organization, as scepticism stemming from their ideas of action divided anarchists. Some saw the order, organization, and centralized bureaucracy of syndicalism as necessary while others were hostile. From the beginning, anarchists had been fighting not only authoritarian states but also related popular movements that favoured central organization.

Such apprehension surfaced in this discussion. There were so many points of concern about syndicalism that it was a challenge for anarchists to accept. Anarchists of the 'old school' felt that their movement was ideally one of free individuals acting on their own. Syndicalism threatened to impose organization and centralized bureaucracy on clubs where heated rhetoric flourished – a disturbing possibility reminding anarchists of socialists' obsession with central control. Contrary to anarchist inclinations as well was the participation of revisionist socialists in elections that negated revolution.

Nevertheless, frustration at their low numbers provoked anarchists to expand and modernize their movement. Among those Parisian anarchists promoting syndicalism were Fernand Pelloutier, Paul Delasalle, and Emile Pouget, each with a different way of speaking, but together attempting to connect anarchism to the modern work setting. Confronting the subject, Pelloutier wondered why anarchists would not resort to organization, which had benefited rival movements.

Within syndicalism, division was evident. Some endorsed co-operation with left-wing parties. Other anarchists saw the sole hope for syndicalist goals in revolutionary actions. In other words, anarcho-syndicalism was to be achieved either by political co-operation (as was true of socialists) or exclusively by radical means, paralysing the economy and reshaping society through the general strike.

During the Second International, socialist revisionists contested orthodox Marxism's demand for violent worker insurrections. German socialists

August Bebel and Eduard Bernstein saw workers' progress and improved economic status as linked to democracy and labour unions. In France, organized socialism, led by Jaurès and Guesde with their diverging rhetoric and strategy, worked within the Third Republic. Jaurès' charismatic humanitarian support for Dreyfus drew French voters. Flexible anarchists saw a similar approach as being in keeping with their own position, since syndicalism and political co-operation could strengthen and expand the workers' movement.[14]

Contrary to Vladimir Lenin's elitist manipulation of the masses in the Bolshevik Revolution, anti-revisionist socialists in Germany such as Rosa Luxemburg placed more faith in the general strike. Their aim was to embolden the masses, emphasizing the consciousness, instincts, anger, and readiness of workers for revolutionary action. Workers' collective determination, it was felt, was far more reliable as a weapon than elitist manipulation.

Anarcho-syndicalism itself emerged against this labour-defined background but was also shaped by anarchists' frustrated ambitions and realization that their numbers were insufficient and divided, and needed to be expanded and co-ordinated. Syndicalists promised expansion, which would give anarchists more prominence without socialist bureaucracy. Pelloutier with his Fédération des Bourses du Travail (Labour Exchange) envisaged organizing labourers around anarchist principles and workplace action. The Bourses, founded in 1892, were inspired by anarchist revolutionary theory, with local centres co-operating in a federated manner, although not in alliance with political parties. Their purpose was to educate workers about their plight and the ways they could overcome it. As anarchist bastions, they were local and decentralized, with little emphasis on a director.

The Confédération Générale du Travail (General Confederation of Labour, CGT) merged with the Bourses in 1895. While in the background initially, it became dominant in anarcho-syndicalism, being more centralized and national in orientation, with a secretary general serving an executive role. Generally, the Confédération indicated a move away from anarchist principles and towards practical goals. However, with the general strike envisioned as the key to revolutionary transformation, a shift towards practical gains in working conditions and pay became evident. The focus was on individual factories and industrial action emanating from them. Over time, membership in the CGT grew and declined – corresponding to different

---

14 J. Joll, *The Second International* (London: Routledge, 1974); L. Kolakowski, *Main Currents of Marxism*, vol. II, *The Golden Age* (Oxford: Oxford University Press, 1978).

Fig. 15.1 Button-makers on strike with a CGT flag, Meru (Oise), May Day 1909. (Photo by Branger/Roger Viollet via Getty Images.)

situations such as labour grievances, the onset of the First World War, and the effects of the Bolshevik Revolution[15] Various questions divided the anarcho-syndicalists. As usual, some wanted to keep the movement free of political parties, while others supported such a linkage. There was also the divide between those who wanted to keep anarchist goals intact and others seeing more value in bonding the syndicates to trade union concerns and arousing workers' militancy in that way. As noted, the CGT was always evolving its positions.[16] Various congresses were held to try to iron out the differences. All led up ultimately to the Charter of Amiens in 1907 which discouraged linking syndicalist activity to political parties. While individual *compagnons* were free to go in that direction individually, the movement generally would stay detached. Anarcho-syndicalists used industrial action

---

15 For instance, 402,125 in 1893, 400,000 in 1895, 614,000 in 1902, 200,000 in 1904, 687,463 in 1911, 213, 968 in 1914, 35,000 in 1915, 1,200,000 in 1919, and 2,460,000 in 1920. These figures are from B. Mitchell, *The Practical Revolutionaries: A New Interpretation of the French Anarchosyndicalists* (Westport, CT: Greenwood, 1987).
16 M. Dreyfus, *Histoire de la CGT. Cent ans de syndicalisme en France* (Paris: Editions Complexe, 1995).

and strikes in fighting for their ends and were at their height of success between 1906 and 1908. Ardent anarchists were reassured by continued reliance on workers' spontaneity, which kept bureaucracy minimal. Separation from political parties' reformist efforts suggested more revolutionary rhetoric and goals. Strikes resulted in both success and suppression, but decline ensued, and syndicalism emerged a less revolutionary, more negotiation-oriented force. Outwardly, the pronounced goals and rhetoric may have been revolutionary, but the movement towards achieving practical goals was unmistakable, and the 1907 Anarchist International Congress in Amsterdam witnessed similar disputes among the advocates of syndicalism.

Individual leadership also offered contrasts. Victor Griffuelhes, who headed the CGT between 1902 and 1909, provided aggressive militant leadership. He was succeeded by the more reformist and conciliatory Léon Jouhaux, who had a much longer tenure. While the aim of revolutionary ends was intrinsic to the movement, anarchists feared co-option.

Political parties brought similar controversy and promise. Anarchists were not alone in being mistrustful. So were many syndicalists. Such mistrust was fuelled by fear of the possible diminishing of revolutionary fervour. Delasalle sought a synthesis in discussions he directed in local meetings. But contrary directions were indicated by the French irrationalist thinker, Georges Sorel, who invoked mythic visions of workers, collective violence, and eventually nationalism to keep the revolutionary aspect of syndicalism alive. Although the general strike remained a focus of revolutionary planning, irrational mythic visions of violence took centre-stage in the call to action.

The decline of French anarchism was intensified by the Russian Revolution and the creation of the French Communist Party. Such continued to be the case in the 1930s and during the Second World War because the Communists were so instrumental to the Resistance. The CGTU (Confédération Générale du Travail Unitaire (United Confederation of Labour)) formed by the Communists overcame the CGT as the strongest and most vocal labour force. Indeed, the overall picture was complicated. There was not only the mainstream CGT and the Communist-driven CGTU, but the radical CGT–SR (Confédération Générale du Travail – Syndicaliste Révolutionnaire (General Confederation of Labour – Revolutionary Syndicalism)) as well, representing revolutionary anarcho-syndicalism. In league with the Confederación Nacional del Trabajo (National Confederation of Labour, CNT) of Spain, it came into being as a movement that would continue to represent the fading anarchist front as political parties, Soviet dominance, and immersion in practical goals for workers overtook syndicalism. Strikes and other activities could be directed by the three groups, but workers could also carry out acts spontaneously without organizational direction. CGT leaders did not necessarily call strikes, which workers did on their own. The massive sit-down strikes in factories during the Popular Front government of the socialist Léon Blum were such examples. Spontaneous actions were the key to the strikes, and ideology seems a minimal factor as Blum's coalition included socialists and communists. Most striking at the time was the confrontation of left-wing workers with a left-wing government in the Popular Front. In the end, the Matignon Agreements resulted in gains for workers – not only in pay but also in the eight-hour day and the forty-hour work week. We are far from the days of pre-Great War revolutionary syndicalism.

Sorel's move to the right and to nationalism, irredentism, and the cusp of fascism presented yet another challenge to syndicalism. Even with the general strike serving as a central strategy for syndicalism, workers' attention was diverted by military tensions before the First World War, the surge of nationalism, French military concerns, and the Union Sacrée – intended to overcome internal divisions. Antipathy to Germany was as powerful as that to capitalism. *Révanche* and patriotic fervour were difficult to overcome – even among the working classes – especially as tensions increased. Jouhaux sought to stem the challenge, organizing anti-war protests, while Jaurès worked feverishly to prevent the cataclysm. Such a challenge at the political level was complemented by intellectual swerves like Sorel's. The war itself consumed workers as it did people generally. It was not yet clear what Jaurès was intending to do – oppose the war or gather patriotic support for it. But his assassination ended the suspense. Anarchists tended to oppose the war, but some, like Sébastien Faure, were less adamant and moderate, running counter to the more radical opponents. By contrast, Grave and Kropotkin both ended up supporting France's entry into the war on the side of the Triple Entente.

*

Other issues also confronted anarchists, such as the rise of Nazism and the outbreak of the Spanish Civil War in 1936. In the latter conflict, anarchists had a role in combating Franco, who received support from fascist Italy and Nazi Germany. In contrast, the Spanish Republic received little outside support from nations and relied on voluntary support from socialists, democrats, anarchists, and disaffected intellectuals. All ended in the defeat of the republic, which in retrospect would appear as one of the steps leading to the Second

World War. One of the most striking moments in Orwell's *Homage to Catalonia* is his observation that the communist forces fighting Franco resented and betrayed their allies (most notably the Trotskyite POUM – Partido Obrero de Unificación Marxista (Workers' Party of Marxist Unification) – and the anarchists) revealing their party-driven obsession not to be outflanked by other left-wing forces. Not surprisingly, the communists' totalitarian concern for power superseded the anarchists' idealistic fight for freedom. Emerging from the conflict was anarchists' view that they alone worked for truly revolutionary ends while the communists worked with republican leaders to suppress those to their left.

With the collapse of the Third Republic, Nazi occupation of northern France, and the Vichy regime, the Resistance arose, spearheaded by General Charles de Gaulle's Free France movement and the communists. After the war, under the Fourth Republic's weak executive and active parliament, the economy itself revived and soon worked within the European Common Market. Serious issues such as Algeria and Indochina confronted France. Existentialism – with its philosophy of anxiety, responsibility, and freedom of action – represented the time, as Jean-Paul Sartre and Albert Camus, among others, restated in contemporary language their definition of the human dilemma. De Gaulle's replacement of the Fourth Republic with a Fifth gave him wider powers as president within a more centralized France. Anarchism remained a silent force as the communists and the socialists contested De Gaulle. This silent force resurfaced during the events of May 1968.

1968

The development that goes under the name of '1968' was French, and especially Parisian, in character. But it cannot be separated from events internationally in the era of the Vietnam War protests, the Cold War and attendant fears of nuclear devastation (most acutely felt during the Cuban Missile Crisis of 1962), the American civil rights movement, urban rioting in the United States, the free speech movement on American college campuses, assassinations of American political leaders, the Prague Spring movement, anti-colonialism, and the violent chaos of the Democratic Convention in Chicago. Looming large in the upheavals was the role of the New Left – a largely youthful phenomenon opposing the capitalist and political establishment in the West but also distanced from the Soviet Union and Marxism generally and following the words of some opposition elders. Whereas previous critics of the West had seen the Soviet Union as an alternative to the capitalist West, this was no longer the case after the revelation of Joseph Stalin's mass murder campaigns. Some turned to Maoism (which of course was equally, if not more, murderous) or looked to Third World societies.

The New Left was critical not only of the West but also of the economic determinism dominating Marxism. Culture, having long been viewed as secondary by Marx, re-emerged as a central force for the New Left. Philosophers such as Herbert Marcuse and Erich Fromm re-evoked Sigmund Freud among other psychological theorists. Love and emotional and spiritual fulfilment were rediscovered as goals in the age of the Beatles and on the eve of Woodstock. Along with sexual liberation, feminism was another powerful current with the influential and incisive writings of Betty Friedan and Simone de Beauvoir. Works of early nineteenth-century utopian socialists such as Charles Fourier were rediscovered and added to the climate with a more abstract outline of the perfect society as an escape from time. Less focused on contemporary reality and more on idealized future societies, utopians had blueprints for happiness that inspired the establishment of certain short-lived communities. Ignoring the clock, they differed from the more time-bound Marxists and from anarchists. In the rebellion against technological oppression, pre-modern lifestyles were idealized. Reminiscent of the *Naturiens*, protesters branded civilization as overrated, seeking a return to basics. With a new economic and anti-capitalist accent, support grew for workers' control of the workplace. Nevertheless, the emphasis was on a universal form of happiness and the end of alienation – from society, from nature, from the self. There was no single central aim, just an abstract, idealistic voice for fulfilment.[17]

When May '68 erupted, observers searched for causes – De Gaulle's authoritarian style, capitalist exploitation, anti-colonialism, unhappiness with conventional life, patriarchal dominance, and so forth. Universities were influenced by the Berkeley Free Speech movement as students demonstrated – first at Nanterre, then at the Sorbonne. Events seemed to mimic those on American college campuses, with Daniel Cohn-Bendit as one of the charismatic leaders at the heart of the moment. Anarchist and other slogans seemed to define the upheaval. Youth was a dominant feature of the protesters, but the rising took an unexpected direction when the students were joined by workers expressing their own discontent in a rebellion of seismic

17 M. Seidman, *The Imaginary Revolution: Parisian Students and Workers in 1968* (New York: Berghahn Books, 2004).

proportions, uniting unrelated parts of the society. This union of students and workers brought 1848 to mind, as social grievance and cultural rebellion merged. Protests were massive, dominating Parisian life, and the events drove De Gaulle into hiding. But the movement fizzled out and the government survived. De Gaulle would resign within a year, student leaders went back to their careers, and it seemed that not much had been accomplished. Was this just another instance of 'Revolution for the hell of it' as Abbie Hoffman would note? Regardless, May '68 assumed a place in popular memory as a final burst of anarchist fervour bringing back the emotional embrace of ways and ideals from the time just after the French Revolution. It would be defined as utopian, in this sense meaning 'unrealistic' and 'overly idealistic', but reflected the times, and its vibrancy still resurfaces at moments in the popular world.[18]

Viewed in that context, May 1968 belonged to a decade of continual unrest, naive idealism, and disappointed purpose. That anarchism came to the fore revealed that somehow it was still vibrant and accommodating to contemporary realities. Its unique reawakening was symbolic of and reflective of an already turbulent decade. Freedom was the most ardent of demands, linked to the issues addressed in the streets – whether civil rights, sexual freedom, identity, or resistance to the draft. For those few weeks in May, Paris was the centre of the struggle and united the disparate themes. May '68 brought back a familiar tone. Paris was experiencing a revolutionary situation and living up to a legacy begun in 1789, bringing to light the aphorism 'when Paris sneezes, Europe catches a cold'. In this case, Paris caught something from abroad, but May '68 confirmed its history of the last two centuries.

Americans had ignited a universal feeling of protest and made freedom a strong concern of the counter-culture. Perhaps the words of George Hanson (the lawyer portrayed by Jack Nicholson in the cult 1960s film *Easy Rider*) state the struggle for freedom most succinctly. Responding to the strong view about the need for freedom held by his co-rider, Billy, George replies:

> Oh, yeah, that's right. That's what's it's all about, all right. But talkin' about it and bein' it, that's two different things. I mean, it's real hard to be free when you are bought and sold in the marketplace. Of course, don't ever tell anybody that they're not free, 'cause then they're gonna get real busy killin' and maimin' to prove to you that they are. Oh, yeah, they're gonna talk to

18 T. Judt, *Postwar: A History of Europe since 1945* (New York: Penguin, 2005), p. 411.

you, and talk to you, and talk to you about individual freedom. But they see a free individual, it's gonna scare 'em.[19]

Zo d'Axa's decision earlier in the century to stop protesting and take to the road on his bicycle was an interesting prelude to the 1960s mentality. Protest still mattered but other forms of freedom beckoned as well. Such attachment to freedom can transcend the boundaries of politics. Travel as a private alternative led one along roads to wherever they might lead. By 1968, Parisian students and workers felt the desire for 'real freedom' as a trans-Atlantic current between Paris and American campuses emerged to connect the cultures. Freedom continued to be seen in contrasting ways, but anarchism, long dormant, resurfaced to add a historical connection. The words and slogans of anarchism continue to be heard and testify to human character as attached to activism – even when its advocates are unsuccessful at creating a new order. That search for freedom reveals them as powerless – for sure – but vocal and heard, which is the main point. Such is the enigma of anarchism which there is no Oedipus to solve.

Further Reading

Halperin, Joan U., *Félix Fénéon: Aesthete and Anarchist in Fin-de-Siècle Paris* (New Haven: Yale University Press, 1988).

Herbert, Eugenia W., *The Artist and Social Reform* (New Haven: Yale University Press, 1961).

Joll, James, *The Anarchists* (London: Methuen, 1969).

van der Linden, Marcel, and Wayne Thorpe (eds.), *Revolutionary Syndicalism: An International Perspective* (Brookfield, VT: Gower Publishing Company, 1990).

Maitron, Jean, *Le mouvement anarchiste en France*, 2 vols. (Paris: François Maspero, 1983).

Merriman, John, *The Dynamite Club* (Boston: Houghton Mifflin, 2009).

Mitchell, Barbara, *The Practical Revolutionaries: A New Interpretation of the French Anarchosyndicalists* (Westport, CT: Greenwood, 1987).

Sonn, Richard D., *Anarchism and Cultural Politics in Fin de Siècle France* (Lincoln: University of Nebraska Press, 1989).

Thomas, Edith, *Louise Michel ou la Velleda de l'anarchie* (Paris: Gallimard, 1971).

Varias, Alexander, *Paris and the Anarchists: Aesthetes and Subversives during the Fin de Siècle* (New York: St Martin's Press, 1996).

Woodcock, George, *Anarchism* (New York: Penguin Books, 1962).

---

19 *Easy Rider*, dir. Dennis Hopper, written by Peter Fonda, Dennis Hopper, and Terry Southern, Columbia Pictures, 1969.

16

Spain in Revolt: The Revolutionary Legacy of Anarchism and Anarcho-Syndicalism

GEORGE ESENWEIN

Although anarchism was introduced to Spain during the last quarter of the nineteenth century, it was not until the First World War that it attained the proportions of a mass movement. Following a brief review of the ideological development of anarchism up to the time of the Second Republic (1931–6), this chapter examines two competing tendencies that dominated the movement during the 1930s, namely, the syndicalists (*treintistas*) and the ultra-revolutionaries (*faístas*). Because it was during the Spanish Revolution and Civil War between July 1936 and March 1939 that anarcho-syndicalism experienced the apogee of its development in Spain, the central focus of this chapter will be on those aspects of anarchist wartime activities that illuminate both the strengths and the weaknesses of Spanish libertarianism. A concluding section will examine the fate of the movement during Francisco Franco's dictatorship (1939–75) and in the post-Franco era (1977–2010).

Spanish Anarchism: The Formative Years

Despite the persistence of the belief – for many years promoted by liberal and Marxist historians – that Spanish anarchism remained virtually unchanged from its beginnings in 1869 until the Spanish Civil War, the fact is that over the years the doctrine itself experienced significant transformations. Anarchism, as it was first formulated in Spain, was a mixture of Proudhonian federalism and Bakuninist collectivism. Founded on the principles of the International Working Men's Association (IWMA), as well as on the articles of Mikhail Bakunin's own secret brotherhood, the Alliance of Social Democracy (Alianza de la Democracia Socialista), the Spanish anarchist movement was launched during the tumultuous days of the 'Glorious Revolution' of 1868.

Working surreptitiously through the Alianza, the Spanish counterpart to Bakunin's brotherhood, Bakunin's disciples rapidly became the driving and controlling force of the First International's Spanish Section (Federación Regional Española, FRE). From its inception in 1870, the FRE was based on a trade union structure. Its leaders organized the federation according to anarchist principles, making certain that there were no hierarchies and that power flowed from the bottom upwards. Thus, each craft union (*oficio*) – the basic unit of the FRE – was not bound to any decision made at the regional or national levels. The flexible nature of the FRE also had the advantage of allowing it to expand or contract according to the prevailing circumstances. For example, when the FRE was forced underground for seven years, its membership dropped precipitously, from around 30,000 in 1874 to fewer than 3,000 in 1881. But, by the end of 1882, the FRE – then called the Federación de Trabajadores de la Región Española (Federation of Workers of the Spanish Region, FTRE) – comprised 218 federations: 663 sections with a membership of more than 57,000.[1]

Throughout this period, the anarchist movement itself was frequently paralysed by incessant and often bitter doctrinal disputes. Beginning in 1878, a militant tendency emerged and began challenging the FRE's commitment to organizing the workers into unions. Adherents to this group argued that the social revolution would be made not by building a massive trade union organization, but by tearing away the fabric of bourgeois society by direct action tactics or 'propaganda by the deed'.

When the theory of anarchist communism – a variant of anarchist doctrine largely derived from the writings of Peter Kropotkin, Errico Malatesta, and Elisée Reclus – finally penetrated Spain in the mid-1880s, the FTRE split into rival theoretical camps. On the one side were the collectivists, who believed that the revolution could be advanced by organizing Spain's workers into anarchist-dominated unions. On the other side were the 'communists', who argued that the pro-syndicalist ideas that had informed the revolutionary strategy of the national movement for many years placed too much emphasis on unionizing workers and operating openly in public spaces. Rather than use unions as vehicles of class struggle, the communists insisted that the revolutionary movement consist exclusively of radicals who embraced direct action tactics. The 'communists' scored a decisive victory at the Valencia Congress of 1888, when it was decided to dissolve the FTRE and organize adherents

---

1 See A. Lorenzo, *El Proletariado Militante*, introduction and notes by J. Alvarez Junco (Madrid: Alianza, 1974).

along the lines of loosely federated anarchist cells (*grupos de afinidad*). Significantly, this shift in the overall strategy of the movement tended to undermine the anarchists' presence in trade union-sponsored social and cultural forms – union halls, for example – that formed an integral part of the associational life found in most working-class communities.

It was at this time that yet another current of anarchist thinking came to the fore. During the late 1880s and continuing into the 1890s, libertarian intellectuals such as Ricardo Mella and Tarrida del Mármol attempted to combat the dogmatic elements within both the collectivist and the communist camps by promoting an ecumenical form of anarchism that later became known as 'anarchism without adjectives'. Believing that anarchist doctrine could accommodate a variety of viewpoints, adherents to this group sought to synthesize a broad spectrum of libertarian ideas that included strands of Pierre-Joseph Proudhon's mutualism, Bakunin's collectivism, Kropotkin's communism, and individualist perspectives.[2]

Apart from the ideological sectarianism referred to here, the most serious problem facing anarchism throughout the late nineteenth century was the threat of government repression. During the 1880s and 1890s, the anarchist movement passed through one of its most violent and, consequently, debilitating phases. A cycle of small-scale rebellions, bombings, assassinations, and other violent acts that came to be identified with the tactic known as 'propaganda by the deed' provoked the Spanish authorities into conducting a ruthless campaign of persecution against anarchists as well as anyone identified with their cause.

Anarcho-Syndicalism in Spain

Anarchist communism remained in the ascendancy until the turn of the century. Then, instead of being abandoned, it was fused with the syndicalist ideas of French and Italian revolutionaries – Fernand Pelloutier and Emile Pouget, and Arturo Labriola – that were being imported into Spain in the closing years of the nineteenth century.[3] The end product of this marriage of ideas was the doctrine of anarcho-syndicalism as conceived and practised in

---

2 See G. Esenwein, 'Anarchist Intellectuals: The Utopian Legacy of Ricardo Mella, 1861–1925', in S. L. Vilaseca (ed.), *Anarchist Socialism in Early Twentieth-Century Spain: A Ricardo Mella Anthology* (Cham: Palgrave Macmillan, 2020), pp. xxix–xlviii.
3 See A. Bar, *La CNT en los años rojos. Del sindicalismo revolucionario al anarcosindicalismo, 1910–1926* (Madrid: Akal, 1981); and X. Cuadrat, *Socialismo y anarquismo en Cataluña. Los orígenes de la CNT (1899–1911)* (Madrid: Revista de trabajo, 1976).

Spain during the twentieth century. According to the new theory, violence was to be retained in the revolutionary strategy, but this time it was to be conducted primarily through the trade unions in the form of general strikes, sabotage, and the like. Anarcho-syndicalism was officially inaugurated with the formation of the National Confederation of Labour (Confederación Nacional del Trabajo, CNT) in late 1910. At first the CNT grew slowly, but, with the outbreak of the First World War, its membership soared, climbing from 15,000 in 1915 to more than 700,000 by the end of 1919. Although its spectacular growth was undoubtedly a result of the social and economic circumstances brought on by the war – such as rising prices and falling wages – the real success of the CNT lay in its syndicalist formula and in the brilliant organizing efforts of men such as Salvador Seguí and Angel Pestaña.

The structural problems attendant upon the CNT's rapid development were partially resolved at the Catalan Regional Congress (Sans) of 1918. The congress decided to abandon the practice of organizing workers along craft lines in favour of a form of industrial unionism. According to this, workers would be grouped into large unions (*sindicatos únicos*), which would include all the workers in a particular industry. A local federation would now consist of the various *sindicatos únicos* of a given town; then there would be a grouping of local federations on a district (*comarcal*) level; and, finally, the district federations would be bound by a regional one, such as the Catalan or Andalusian Regional Federation. These kinds of modifications not only made it possible for the CNT to expand its industrial base, but they also preserved the federalist and anti-authoritarian character of its trade union movement. At a National CNT Congress held in Madrid in 1919, the idea of the *sindicato único* was formally adopted, and it was to remain a feature of the organization up to the period of the Civil War, 1936–9.[4]

Parallel to these structural changes, rank-and-file members of the CNT (*cenetistas*) were becoming increasingly radicalized. The structural features of the *sindicato* – which delegated power to shop stewards and other lower-ranking union officials – may have contributed to the organization's radicalization insofar as there were now fewer bureaucratic obstacles to the calling of strikes, work stoppages, and other forms of direct action tactics. At all events, the revolutionary sentiments of the workers themselves had been running high since 1917. The Bolshevik Revolution made a tremendous impact on the young militants of the CNT, particularly those belonging to

4 J. Romero-Maura, 'The Spanish Case', in J. Joll and D. E. Apter (eds.), *Anarchism Today* (Garden City, NY: Doubleday, 1972), pp. 60–83. See also J. Brademas, *Anarcosindicalismo y revolución en España, 1930–1937* (Barcelona: Ariel, 1974).

action groups Los Solidarios (Solidarity) and the 'anarcho-bolsheviks' led by Manuel Buenacasa. Their efforts to emulate the Bolsheviks threw them into conflict with the syndicalist leaders, giving rise to numerous heated discussions concerning the direction the movement was going to take. 'Anarchobolshevik' influence climaxed at the Madrid Congress of 1919. Thanks to Buenacasa and the militant factions, most syndicalist-backed proposals, such as Seguí's plan to fuse the rival CNT and the socialist Unión General de Trabajadores (General Union of Workers, UGT) organizations, were rejected. The militants' crowning achievement came at the end of the congress, when the majority of *cenetistas* proclaimed their provisional adherence to the Comintern.[5]

Between 1919 and 1923, leading syndicalists struggled in vain to control the extreme elements of the movement. But, against the background of general strikes, employers' lock-outs, the rise of company 'free unions' or *sindicatos libres*, and a brand of inter-union warfare known as '*pistolerismo*', they had little hope of winning the CNT over to a moderate position. In the latter case, the organizing efforts of CNT officials were overshadowed by a string of deadly shootings undertaken by radical action groups who were responding to an employer-backed terrorist campaign aimed at CNT militants. The anarcho-syndicalist movement as a whole paid an exorbitant price for this cycle of violence. Not only were dozens of *cenetistas* assassinated by hired gunmen who belonged to the *sindicatos libres*, but an even greater number of those detained by the authorities fell victim to the notorious extra-judicial killings – referred to by the left as the '*ley de fugas*' – carried out against those who were allegedly trying to escape from prison. The gang-related murders of Evelio Boal – the secretary general of the CNT – in 1921 and Salvador Seguí in 1923 symbolized the position the syndicalists held at the end of this historical phase of anarcho-syndicalist development.

Miguel Primo de Rivera's dictatorship (1923–30) brought the post-First World War era of working-class violence to a rapid close. In the next few years the CNT, now forced to operate underground, virtually collapsed, and did not revive until it emerged from clandestinity in 1931. During the Primo years, sectarianism continued to plague the CNT, but this time out of the

---

5 See R. Martínez Fraile, 'Comentarios a la Revolución Rusa aparecidos en "Solidaridad Obrera" durante el año 1917', *Cuadernos de Historia Economica de Cataluna* 12 (1974), pp. 146–83. See also G. Meaker, *The Revolutionary Left in Spain* (Stanford: Stanford University Press, 1974), pp. 233–48, and M. Buenacasa's autobiographical *El movimiento obrero español, 1886–1926* (Gijon, 1977), pp. 59–72.

debates crystallized two mutually opposed tendencies which were to dominate the course of the movement throughout the 1930s.

The first can be broadly classified as the syndicalist wing. We have seen how the syndicalists rose to prominence after the formation of the CNT in 1910. By 1924, they constituted the largest single group within the anarcho-syndicalist movement. With few exceptions, the syndicalists were a homogeneous group of anarchists who, like the collectivists of the 1880s and 1890s, saw the revolution as a distant goal of the working classes. Trade unions were regarded as the basic building blocks in the syndicalists' plan to erect an anarchist society alongside the existing bourgeois order, serving as the apex around which working-class life would revolve. Through working-class clubs, community-based *ateneos* (usually the local dance or recreational hall that also served as a library and school), and similar trade union-sponsored organizations, the CNT could not only exercise a hegemony over the cultural and economic affairs of workers, but also insulate them from what were perceived to be the 'evil' influences of bourgeois institutions. On another level, the trade union was seen as the only effective vehicle for conducting class warfare. Strikes, sabotage, and other trade union weapons were to be employed in the daily struggle to improve the lot of the worker, whereas the general strike was to be reserved for those occasions when social revolution seemed imminent. Once the CNT had established itself throughout Spain and was capable of sustaining its own working-class society, the belief was that it remained only to mobilize a general strike, and the state and bourgeois society would be easily overturned.

During Primo's dictatorship, the syndicalists suffered a series of blows from which they never wholly recovered. Beginning in 1925, Angel Pestaña's leadership of the CNT was increasingly challenged by a growing number of radicals, who were particularly angered by Pestaña's attempts to divorce the CNT from the anarchist-dominated affinity groups. The formation of the *comités paritarios* – government-controlled arbitration boards that favoured socialist participation – in 1926 threw this conflict into sharper relief. Responding to this development, Pestaña began advocating for a 'possibilist' (reformist) line of action which, among other things, promoted the CNT's co-operation with these bodies. This time his swing to the right provoked a split within syndicalist ranks, further undermining their dominant position within the CNT.

In response both to Pestaña's possibilism and to the deteriorating strength of the CNT under Primo's repressive rule, there emerged at this time what I shall term the FAI (Federación Anarquista Ibérica) tendency – the anarchist 'purists' who pictured themselves as the custodians of anarchist doctrine. This was composed of militant anarcho-syndicalists who fell, roughly, into two categories. The first was the FAI itself, which came into being in July 1927.[6] Founded by exiled ultra-radical dissidents within the CNT who were intractably opposed to the reformist-minded members of the syndicalist wing and by a cadre of émigré Portuguese anarchists (hence the peninsular nature of the name), the FAI was in many ways the reincarnation of Bakunin's secret Alianza: it was to function clandestinely with the expressed aim of preserving the revolutionary spirit and anarchist character of the CNT. Where the FAI differed from its nineteenth-century predecessor was in its emphasis on forming a '*trabazón*' or organic bond with the anarchist-dominated syndicates or unions. The FAI was to be organized along the lines of the CNT: members of a locality were grouped into local or district federations, and these were linked by a regional committee, with all of the regional committees converging at the Peninsular Committee. In order to inoculate itself against *agents provocateurs* as well as anti-revolutionary elements, the kernel of the FAI, the *agrupación* (formerly known as an 'affinity' group), was to consist of five to ten members. The second group within the FAI tendency included an assortment of radical *cenetistas* and independent-minded libertarians who were sympathetic to FAI policies. The most notable members of this latter group were the Montsenys, the well-known anarchist dynasty consisting of Juan (Federico Urales), Soledad Gustavo (Teresa Mañé), and their daughter Federica, who was so closely identified with the radical elements of the anarchist movement during the early 1930s that she earned the sobriquet 'Miss FAI' in 1932, despite the fact that she did not join the FAI until July 1936.[7]

The Birth of the Second Republic: Syndicalists
v. *Faístas*

When the CNT resurfaced from the underground in 1930, the FAI was a relatively obscure entity, exercising little influence among the working

---

6 On the FAI, see *El movimiento libertario español. Pasado, presente y futuro* (Paris: Ruedo Ibérico, 1974); S. Christie, *We, the Anarchists! A Study of the Iberian Anarchist Federation (FAI) 1927–1937* (Hastings, UK: Meltzer, 2000); and J. Gomez Casas, *Historia de la FAI. Aproximación a la historia de la organización específica del anarquismo y sus antecendentes de la Alianza de la Democracia Socialista*, 3rd edn (Madrid: Fundación Anselmo Lorenzo, 1977).

7 F. Montseny, letter to Burnett Bolloten (July 1981), Bolloten Papers, Hoover Institution, Stanford University, Stanford, CA. See also A. Pons, *Converses amb Frederica* [*sic*] *Montseny* (Barcelona: Laia, 1977), p. 132.

classes. At the III CNT National Congress held in Madrid in June 1931, the FAI participated for the first time in a public debate with its syndicalist rivals. But, in what turned out to be a pro-syndicalist congress, the FAI's ultra-revolutionary stance proved to be unpopular. Later that summer, however, a dramatic turn of events sparked a rapid rise in the FAI's strength and influence. From then onward, the FAI was to play a decisive role in shaping the fate of the anarcho-syndicalist movement.[8]

Beginning in July, a quick succession of highly disruptive strikes jolted the newly established republic (1931–6). As the strike movement gained momentum in the following months it became increasingly apparent that the strikes themselves were running out of control. The syndicalist leaders struck a defensive posture, blaming the FAI for perpetuating the chaotic cycle of strikes. Through the CNT-controlled press they appealed for a moratorium on activity, arguing that wildcat strikes would only invite further government repression. On the other hand, the *faístas'* interpretation of events pointed to a different understanding of the nature of revolution. For them the strikes signified a revolutionary drive that had to be spontaneous in order to bring down the republic.

Given that the *faístas* constituted a minority within the anarcho-syndicalist movement, they faced the problem of how to implement their strategy and remain consistent with their anti-authoritarian principles. Critics of the FAI have long contended that the organization conquered the CNT by imposing its own 'dictatorship'. While it is true that some *faístas* often resorted to anti-democratic methods, the federal structure of the FAI did not lend itself to the establishment of such a dictatorship. In fact, the process by which the FAI established its hegemony within the CNT was more complicated than its critics have suggested. As a former CNT member and FAI critic explained, the *faístas* won a *sindicato* over to their position by working within it as a unit. Accordingly, pro-FAI proposals stood a good chance of being adopted by the *sindicato* simply because the *faístas* always voted as a bloc. The FAI also exercised considerable influence through the *comités de defensa* (Defence Committees) and the *comités pro-presos* (Pro-Prisoner Committees).[9] The former served as the basic building blocks for the infrastructure of the

8 See M. Losada Uriguen et al., *El hilo. Rojinegro de la prensa confederal (1932–2012). 80 aniversario del periódico CNT* (Madrid: Fundación Anselmo Lorenzo, 2012).

9 J. García Oliver examines the role of the comités de defensa in his *El eco de los pasos* (Barcelona: Planeta, 1978), pp. 118–37. See also R. Sanz, *El sindicalismo y la política* (Toulouse: Dulaurier, 1966), pp. 157–76; and A. Guillamón, *Ready for Revolution: The CNT Defense Committees in Barcelona, 1933–1938* (Oakland, CA, and Edinburgh: AK Press, 2014).

anarchists' military apparatus. The latter of these was particularly useful for promoting the FAI's image as a defender of workers' rights. By dedicating themselves wholeheartedly to the cause of imprisoned workers, *faístas* and militants who were sympathetic to the FAI, such as Buenaventura Durruti and Francisco Ascaso, not only kept the spirit of revolution alive during times of repression, but also won the respect and allegiance of the rank and file.

No less a contributing factor to the FAI's rise to prominence within the CNT was its highly successful propaganda programme. The FAI carried out its propaganda work not only on the shop-floors of the *sindicatos* but also in the numerous *ateneos* and social clubs, like the Juventudes Libertarias (Libertarian Youth), that formed part of the rich fabric of associational life in the urban centres. Although the *ateneos* were, traditionally, the main focus of anarchist educational activities, they were during the 1930s largely under the influence of radical action groups and *faístas* working through the CNT. Outside the major cities, where associational life was less well developed, *ateneos* or *centros obreros* – union meeting halls that also served as cultural centres – were, more often than not, the only places were a worker could learn to read. As these were usually under the direction of the CNT, it is hardly surprising that anarchist doctrine became so popular.

Of all the militant groups of this period, the FAI was probably the most successful at putting across its ideas in the multitudinous weeklies and dailies read by the workers. This was especially true after 1933 when Diego Abad de Santillán – an anarchist theorist and organizer who had recently emigrated from Argentina – used the widely circulated *Tierra y Libertad* (*Land and Freedom*) and his own theoretical journal, *Tiempos Nuevos* (*New Times*), to promulgate the *faísta* line. Simultaneously, thousands of anarchist '*folletos* [pamphlets]' and books were published with the FAI imprimatur. In this way, those workers who were introduced to anarchist literature could readily associate the FAI with the standard tracts of Peter Kropotkin, Errico Malatesta, Sébastien Faure, and other libertarian thinkers.[10]

Most *faístas* of this period believed the revolution was so near at hand that there was not time for the formal development of the worker's mind.[11] Indeed, as labour agitation intensified during the 1930s, the maxim '1 act = 1,000 pamphlets' gained currency within the CNT. While not abandoning its written propaganda programme, after 1932 the FAI's

---

10 D. Abad de Santillán, *Memorias, 1897–1936* (Barcelona: Planeta, 1977), p. 186.
11 A. Paz, *Durruti: The People Armed* (Nottingham: Spokesman, 1976).

campaign to topple the government through a series of interlinking strikes and 'cycle of insurrections' took centre-stage.

By means of a tactic they referred to as 'revolutionary gymnastics', the practice of staging social revolts, the *faístas* hoped to awaken the rebellious instincts of the masses and thereby accelerate their drive towards the establishment of a stateless form of anti-authoritarian communism: *'comunismo libertario'*. The principal agents of the 'revolutionary gymnastics' were the FAI's *agrupaciónes*, which were to agitate for revolution within the respective CNT *sindicatos*, while the paramilitary *comités de defensa* were to serve both as the dynamic force and as the sustaining element of the cycle of revolts.[12]

The first and most representative of these insurrections occurred in January 1932 in the mining districts of Alto Llobregat and Cardona.[13] A general strike that was called in the town of Figols triggered work stoppages in neighbouring villages and towns. Soon afterwards, anarchists rose up throughout the region, declaring their intention to establish *comunismo libertario*. Though suppressed by government troops only a week after it had begun, the Figols rebellion quickly passed into anarchist legend as an example of the people's resolve to usher in the dawn of the social revolution. Figols was indeed the harbinger of numerous such risings which erupted throughout Spain during the so-called Red years between 1932 and the outbreak of the Civil War.

The cycle of anarchist-inspired revolts reached its apogee one year later in the tiny Andalusian village of Casas Viejas. Like so many of the FAI's exercises in 'revolutionary gymnastics', the Casas Viejas rising was the product of a failed general strike movement. In this case, the ill-fated rebellion was ruthlessly put down by the government: Civil Guards and Assault Guards stormed the tiny village, killing some twenty anarcho-syndicalists and *campesinos* (peasants). Far from furthering the anarchist cause in the region, the Casas Viejas incident actually eroded the very organizational foundation of the workers which the CNT and FAI were striving to establish so that their strike campaigns could be successful.[14]

While risings like that of Casas Viejas exacted a heavy toll on the anarcho-syndicalist movement, the FAI nonetheless capitalized on the revolutionary

---

12 García Oliver, *El eco de los pasos*, p. 129.

13 See C. Borderias and M. Vilanova, 'Cronología de una insurrección. Figols en 1932', *Estudios de Historia Social* 24–5 (January–June 1983), pp. 187–99; and P. Flores, *Las luchas sociales en el Alto Llobregat y Cardoner* (Barcelona: the author, 1981).

14 See J. Mintz, *The Anarchists of Casas Viejas* (Bloomington: Indiana University Press, 2004). See also G. Brey and J. Maurice, 'Casas Viejas. Reformisme et anarchisme en Andalousie (1870–1933)', *Le Mouvement Social* 83 (1973), pp. 95–135.

atmosphere such events inevitably produced. During their impressive absten-
tionist (¡No Votad!) campaign of 1933, for example, faístas skilfully exploited
the wave of public indignation and outrage against the government which
had arisen as a result of the Casas Viejas episode. The fact that a significant
number of workers – perhaps close to a million – boycotted the November
elections attested to the FAI's success in gaining widespread support for its
slogan: '¡Frente a las urnas, la Revolución Social! [Social Revolution instead of
the ballot boxes!]')[15]

By the end of 1933, the FAI had become the predominant force in the CNT.
As we have seen, until then only a critical current of cenetistas – the treintistas –
had offered vigorous opposition to the FAI's insurrectionary methods. This
group had emerged at the end of the turbulent summer of 1931, when several
leading syndicalists, including Angel Pestaña, Juan López, and Juan Peiró,
publicly issued an anti-FAI manifesto, the 'Manifesto of the Thirty'.
Afterwards, they, along with anyone else who opposed the FAI, were dubbed
treintistas. From the outset, though, circumstances appeared to conspire
against their plan to prevent the CNT from pursuing an ultra-revolutionary
path. In October of that year they lost editorial control of the important daily
Solidaridad Obrera (Workers' Solidarity), and the following year saw the exodus
of thousands of treintistas, who had either resigned or, more commonly, been
expelled from the CNT. After 1932, the majority of treintistas hoped to exert
a constraining influence on the FAI by operating outside the CNT, and
accordingly they established their own ateneos (for example, Ateneo
Sindicalista Libertario, the Liberatarian Syndicalist Athenaeum, founded in
1932), circulated a rival newspaper, La Cultura Libertaria (Libertarian Culture),
and in January 1933 constituted a syndicalist organization in opposition to the
CNT, the Sindicatos de Oposición (Opposition Syndicates). With the possible
exception of the Sindicatos de Oposición, which by 1936 had attained
a membership of approximately 40,000, none of these measures ever threatened to undermine the FAI's position within the CNT.[16]

The general elections of 1933 marked the beginning of two years of
reactionary rule, which came to be known to the left as el bienio negro ('the
two black years'). Throughout this period, the left as a whole suffered the
consequences of a regime that energetically pursued a course of action chiefly
aimed at dismantling the pro-labour legislation introduced in the first bienio as

15 Quoted in J. Joll, The Anarchists (London: Methuen, 1982), p. 232.
16 See E. Vega, El trentisme a Catalunya (Barcelona: Editorial Curial, 1980); and A. Bar
Cendón, 'La Confederación Nacional del Trabajo Frente a la II República', in M. Ramirez
(ed.), Estudios sobre la II República Española (Madrid: Editorial Tecnos, 1975), pp. 217–49.

well as at checking the growing power of revolutionary groups such as the CNT and FAI. It was within this context of heightening class tensions that various left-wing groups moved rapidly towards the adoption of a revolutionary strategy that would strengthen their position vis-à-vis the forces of the right.

In the aftermath of the Casas Viejas debacle, it had become apparent that the anarcho-syndicalists by themselves could no longer sustain the cycle of insurrections to which they had been committed since the birth of the Second Republic. This was clearly demonstrated first in December 1933 when a national strike movement mounted by the CNT collapsed and again in March–April 1934 when a massive general strike staged in Zaragoza also proved abortive. In fact, the most important workers' rebellion to take place during the *bienio negro*, the October 1934 revolution in Asturias, was not a result of 'revolutionary gymnastics' but rather was largely a product of a socialist-led coalition of workers' organizations known as the Alianza Obrera (Workers' Alliance, AO).[17] Though it was brutally put down and resulted in the mass arrest of thousands of left-wing workers, the Asturian uprising was widely seen on the left as the Spanish workers' clarion call for revolution, becoming for some Spain's Paris Commune. Out of the commune experience was born the phrase 'United Proletarian Brothers' (Unidad de Hermanos Proletarios, UHP), which gave expression to the working classes' hope for a united front against their enemies on the right.

Despite the fact that the CNT and FAI failed to mount any successful offensives against the state between 1934 and July 1936, they nonetheless can be credited for having initiated and then reinforced the revolutionary trajectory of the Spanish workers, which inevitably led them first to Asturias and then to civil war.

Revolution and Civil War: Anarcho-Syndicalism, 1936–1939

At the beginning of the Civil War, the anarcho-syndicalists of the CNT–FAI emerged as the chief promoters of a popularly based revolutionary movement that swept through vast areas of republican territory. In regions such as Catalonia, hastily organized people's militias immediately took to the streets. Along with the local police and national military units loyal to the republic,

17 V. Alba, *La Alianza Obrera. Historia y análisis de una táctica de unidad en España* (Madrid and Gijon: Jucar, 1978).

these civilian units managed to quash the rebel troops who were attempting to seize control of the region. In the aftermath of the bloody street clashes between these opposing groups in Barcelona, the anarcho-syndicalists emerged as the primary victors. But rather than seize the power that lay within their grasp, the leaders of the CNT–FAI decided to allow the regional government, the Generalitat, to remain standing alongside a parallel ruling body, the Central Anti-Fascist Militias Committee (Comité Central de Milícies Antifeixistes de Catalunya, CCMA), in which the CNT–FAI would share power with other leftist working-class and middle-class parties.

Though the wider implications of this unprecedented move were impossible to foresee, at the time anarcho-syndicalist leaders justified their impromptu decision on the grounds that the 'realities of the moment' demanded that the CNT–FAI join other republican factions in a collective effort to defeat fascism. The alternative in their eyes was to use the leverage that pro-revolutionary organizations wielded at the outset of the conflict to impose a libertarian dictatorship, a prospect that was not only objectionable from a doctrinal standpoint but also unrealistic given that the anarchists themselves lacked a programme of their own for exercising power.[18] In the event, on 23 July the CCMA came into existence, the first government body ever established in which anarcho-syndicalists were represented. According to Abad de Santillán, the person most closely identified with the CNT–FAI's ad hoc collaborationist strategy, the main work of this provisional ruling body was to maintain a rearguard as well as to raise militia forces for the defence of the Aragon front. CNT–FAI representatives also oversaw committees concerned with public order, transportation, and the economy.

Once it became apparent that a civil war had broken out and that the power of the workers was in the ascendant, the revolutionaries of the CNT–FAI insisted that work begin immediately on laying the foundation for the establishment of *comunismo libertario*. Their attempts to radically restructure society along libertarian lines were both guided and propelled by the belief that fascism could be defeated only by waging war and revolution simultaneously. Their first decisive step in this direction was to undertake a thoroughgoing collectivization programme embracing both land (agriculture) and industry. In urban areas throughout Catalonia, Aragon, and the Levante all types of enterprise were quickly brought under the control of the CNT–FAI and other left-wing unions. In factories, small businesses, and

18 J. Balius, *Hacia la nueva revolución* (Barcelona: La Agrupación de Los Amigos de Durruti, 1976 [c. 1938]), p. 15.

workshops where they had already established a firm foothold or where the owners and their management had fled the scene, the revolutionaries encountered little difficulty in completely taking over their operations. Those enterprises not dominated by the unions were either partially administered by worker (control) committees or simply declared to be part of the emerging revolutionary economy.

Elsewhere, especially in the villages of the countryside, anarchists and left-socialists of the UGT immediately set about collectivizing farms and the economic structures of rural communities. The new order was established in a variety of ways. For example, in republican-held eastern Aragon, where nearly three-quarters of the land was collectivized, the anarcho-syndicalists would sometimes use the threat of their militias to impose their economic will on small proprietors and farmers. As we shall see, such heavy-handed methods quickly earned the anarchist-dominated Council of Aragon and similar de facto ruling bodies set up in order to co-ordinate the collectivization process the reputation of being dictatorial. But many other collectivist efforts in Aragon and elsewhere were not forced upon the local inhabitants. In fact, an untold number sprang up spontaneously and enjoyed popular consent. Particularly for Spain's downtrodden and 'have-nots', the economic revolution was a liberating affair.

Since mid-July the largely spontaneous revolutionary movement led by the CNT–FAI had developed along federalist lines. Having co-operated with other Popular Front forces to put down the military rebellion, the anarcho-syndicalists managed to exercise power through their own military columns or militia, through the numerous industrial and agricultural collectivist enterprises they had established throughout the republican zone, and through the de facto ruling bodies which they dominated in regions such as Aragon (Council of Aragon) and Catalonia (CCMA). By the end of the summer of 1936, however, the revolutionaries were forced to confront the fact that, unless they were able to consolidate their revolutionary gains, their movement would inevitably founder. Several developments at both the regional and national levels brought this issue into sharper focus. The formation of a new Popular Front government in Madrid on 4 September paved the way for the re-establishment of central authority, and it also provided impetus for the Generalitat to reassert its authority over Catalonia.

After Francisco Largo Caballero formed his cabinet in September 1936, a certain number of anarchists decided it was time to react to the latest turn of events. At a plenary session called in mid-September, the CNT–FAI representatives sought to replace the central government with a revolutionary ruling body, the National Council of Defence (Consejo Nacional de Defensa). But, like all other anarchist initiatives aimed at leveraging their power and influence in the regional and central government structures, this proposal failed to win support among the other republican factions. Facing intractable opposition from the non-revolutionary leftist parties as well as from the radical elements of their own organizations, the pragmatic leaders of the CNT–FAI decided in the end to negotiate for anarchist representation in Caballero's government. Although they asked for portfolios in five ministries, Caballero granted them only four: justice, industry, commerce, and health. As a result, on 3 November 1936 Spain's anarcho-syndicalists took the unprecedented step of joining a national government. The entry of a female into Largo's cabinet was also momentous in that Federica Montseny, the new minister in charge of public health and assistance, was one of the first females in Europe to be named to such a high-ranking government post.[19]

Another major setback to the revolutionary movement came when the central government in Madrid began promulgating measures aimed at militarizing the anarchist-controlled people's militias. In sharp contrast to traditional military units, these improvised militias or 'columns' operated according to libertarian principles. Thus, in the anarchist militias there was no strictly enforced military discipline or hierarchical regimentation. Recognizing that the numerous defects of the anarcho-syndicalist militias had resulted in a growing number of casualties at the front, Buenaventura Durruti, Cipriano Mera, and other anarchist military leaders soon became resigned to the fact that the adoption of certain traditional military values – such as discipline and order – was necessary in order to wage war effectively.

Meanwhile, Largo Caballero's administration moved quickly to incorporate the popular militias into a state-controlled Popular Army. Countering that such a development not only challenged their inveterate anti-militarism but also directly threatened the power they wielded over their revolutionary projects, some anarcho-syndicalists – the members of the dissident 'Iron Column', for example – lashed out against the CNT–FAI officials who were defending the government's efforts to militarize the militias. Yet their resistance was fatally undermined by the fact that the arms and manpower the recalcitrant elements of the anarcho-syndicalist movement required to sustain their independent fighting units were under the control of the central government's war ministry. Starved of essential supplies and unable to convince the regional committees and other official bodies of the CNT–FAI

19 Montseny oversaw domestic issues and other rearguard activities.

to come to their aid, maverick libertarian units such as the Iron Column soon found themselves isolated and, to all intents and purposes, rendered impotent.

In the wake of the July military uprising, the breakdown of traditional forms of civil authority – the courts, police services, and so on – in the republican zone led directly to a wave of working-class vigilantism, much of which was spearheaded by the anarcho-syndicalists of the CNT–FAI. Throughout the cities and countryside, revolutionary labour groups attempted to ferret out anti-republican elements by rounding up suspected rebels and their sympathizers. Known members of right-wing organizations were primary targets, as were priests, nuns, and other representatives of the Catholic Church. In addition to these targeted groups, many innocent bystanders also fell victim to the street justice that was being meted out in the heat of the moment.

The impromptu creation of a variety of 'investigation committees' or popular tribunals presided over by representatives from the CNT–FAI and other left-wing groups helped to regularize the process of identifying, prosecuting, and then summarily punishing suspected class enemies. However, these improvised 'judicial' bodies did little to prevent the nightly parade of killings (popularly known as *'paseos'*) that occurred in many locations during the high tide of revolutionary eruptions.

But while it is true that Spain's anarcho-syndicalists played a central role in both promoting and sustaining the violence that accompanied the opening phases of civil war, it should be noted that the vast majority of the atrocities committed during this period were inspired not by anarchist ideas and beliefs, but by an intense and deeply ingrained class and religious hatred that had long divided Spanish society.[20] This is not to deny the anarcho-syndicalists' moral responsibility for the widespread and sometimes indiscriminate bloodletting that accompanied the onset of revolution and civil war. Rather it is to say that such violence was not a cornerstone of their revolutionary doctrine.

This latter point is borne out by the fact that moderate leaders of the CNT–FAI were among the first republicans to call for a halt to the excesses of the revolution. As early as August 1936, they began calling for a halt to arbitrary or revenge killings, particularly those that were motivated by vendettas and personal greed and that were being carried out largely by criminals and street gangs.

---

20 See, for example, J. Ruíz, *The 'Red Terror' and the Spanish Civil War: Revolutionary Violence in Madrid* (New York: Cambridge University Press, 2014).

Fig. 16.1 Women snipers fighting on the government side during the Spanish Civil War, 1936. (Photo by Keystone/Getty Images.)

Anarcho-Syndicalism and Gender

While the doctrine of anarcho-syndicalism was above all centred around the strategy and tactics of revolutionary trade union organizations, the movement itself encompassed a far greater radius of social, cultural, and economic activities relating to the development of the libertarian community as a whole. In fact, since the late nineteenth century, libertarian men and women such as Teresa Claramunt had been promoting the idea of organizing women workers and treating them as men's equals.

However committed anarchists of both sexes may have been to egalitarian principles, the fact is that, until the outbreak of civil war in 1936, women were more often than not consigned to a secondary status in the movement. This was in large measure due to the patronizing attitudes deeply engrained in all working-class communities. Catholic values permeated Spanish society, and even libertarian men seemed unaware of how their 'Catholic' home life and conservative relations with their wives or *compañeras* could affect their views on gender questions. According to the anarchist activist Enriqueta Rovira, the persistence of traditional views of women who belonged to libertarian circles inevitably imposed limits on female participation in the revolutionary movement.[21]

Foremost among the anarcho-syndicalist groups addressing the gender question during the civil war was the Mujeres Libres (Free Women), a feminist organization independent of both the CNT and the FAI, which focused on educational and cultural programmes promoting anarchist ideas and social practices.[22] Established in May 1936, Mujeres Libres' main agenda was to raise a revolutionary consciousness among women that could empower them to liberate themselves from state oppression, illiteracy, and exploitation in the workplace. To this end, members set up a decentralized system of chapters in regions dominated by the left, with major centres established in Madrid, Barcelona and its environs, and Valencia.

A certain number of women transgressed well-established gender lines by enlisting in the popular militias that were being organized and directed by affiliates of the CNT–FAI, POUM (Partido Obrero de Unificación Marxista (Workers' Party of Marxist Unification)), and other revolutionary organizations. While many Spaniards saw this as shockingly inappropriate behaviour, libertarian women in particular did not hesitate to answer the call to fight. For the most part, these were spontaneous responses to the outbreak of civil war, which occurred during the period when the traditional lines of political and military authority in republican Spain had been all but erased. The motives of those who sought to become women warriors were mixed. As one historian has pointed out, some of these daring women were already active in left-wing circles and organizations, and they simply joined militias to which their friends, lovers, and husbands belonged.[23]

Almost overnight, it seemed as though the republic had embraced the idea of women serving in the military. Posters, pamphlets, and popular slogans featured women in their new role.[24] By the end of the summer of 1936, however, the initial enthusiasm expressed for women taking up arms had all but evaporated. From September 1936 on, the movement to restrict women's participation in the army was due to the restoration of male-dominated

21 Quoted in M. Ackelsberg, *Free Women of Spain: Anarchism and the Struggle for the Emancipation of Women* (Bloomington: Indiana University Press, 1991), p. 203.
22 Mujeres Libres rejected both the practice and the ideas associated with the liberal feminist cause. Nationalism – *catalanismo*, for example – provided a further dividing line among female groups.
23 Mary Nash, *Defying Male Civilization: Women in the Spanish Civil War* (Denver: Arden Press, 1995), pp. 105–97.
24 See Mary Nash, '"Milicianas" and homefront heroines: images of women in revolutionary Spain (1936–1939)', *History of European Ideas* 11, 1–6 (1980), pp. 235–44.

military structures. Having women fight alongside men reflected a radical conception of the war, something that was diametrically opposed to the ideas of militarization being promoted by the Largo Caballero government. Following the formation of the People's Army in the autumn of 1936, women were no longer welcome at the front.

Given the many-sided character of republican women groups, clashes over gender-related policies among different feminist organizations inevitably occurred. One of the main functions of Mujeres Libres was, in the words of Martha Ackelsberg, 'to compete with socialist organizations for the allegiance of the Spanish working woman'.[25] Their challenge was further complicated by the fact that splintering of women's voices occurred even within the anarchist movement itself. For example, Mujeres Libres was at odds with the female branch of the Iberian Federation of Libertarian Youth (Federación Ibérica de Juventudes Libertarias, FIJL) over the question of whether an independent female organization was necessary. Moreover, the Women's Secretariat of the FIJL insisted that Mujeres Libres confine its recruitment to women over the age of thirty despite the fact that the latter did not see itself as an organization comprising only 'adult' women.[26] Even more problematic were the ideological differences among the various women's groups. Politically, the communist Agrupación de Mujeres Antifascistas (Anti-Fascist Women's Group, AMA) and Unió de Dones de Catalunya (Union of Catalan Women, UDC) supported the Popular Front stance taken by their anti-revolutionary political affiliates. As such, they were adamantly opposed to the radical policies being promoted by both the women's section of the POUM and Mujeres Libres. The latter, for example, rejected the Popular Front idea calling for the fusion of all women's organizations on the grounds that the social advances of women relied on the diversity of opinion.

In the end, it proved impossible for women's organizations to transcend the effects of the over-arching political struggle that dominated republican affairs. Nor were women able in such a short time span to thoroughly dispel the male chauvinistic attitudes that prevailed among the working classes. As a result, women's issues tended to be pushed into the background for most of the war. On a practical level, the greatest obstacle to the forward progress of women even within the anarcho-syndicalist movement itself seems to have been entrenched sexist attitudes and behaviour. Attempts to emancipate females on many fronts revealed just how much men continued to draw

25 Ackelsberg, *Free Women of Spain*, p. 144.
26 See D. Evans, *Revolution and the State: Anarchism in the Spanish Civil War, 1936–1939* (Chico, CA: AK Press, 2020), pp. 180–1.

upon pre-existing definitions of male/female relations. This was largely because the public and private identities of most women were shaped and conditioned by deeply rooted social conventions. Male attitudes towards prostitution were particularly illustrative of the double standards that persisted even during the high tide of revolutionary changes. According to one eyewitness, in sharp contrast to spokespersons of Mujeres Libres, anarchist militiamen returning from the front were not anxious to end prostitution, believing that it was necessary to change the 'mentality of women' first before the issue could be definitively addressed.[27]

Spanish Anarcho-Syndicalism in the International Arena

Given the scope and depth of the popular revolution that was unfolding during the first months of the civil war, it is scarcely surprising that anarchist activities during this period attracted international attention, particularly among individuals and groups in both Europe and the Americas that had longstanding ties to Spain's libertarian movement. Upon hearing news of the outbreak of civil war, for example, dozens of left-wing activists and anarchist émigrés living in the United States, France, the UK, and elsewhere demonstrated their solidarity with their Spanish comrades. While many began raising money for the anarchist cause, others volunteered to go to Spain in order to lend their support to revolutionary developments as well as to join what they perceived as an anti-fascist struggle.

Thanks in part to the CNT–FAI's well-established links to the international revolutionary labour movement, including its longstanding affiliation with the syndicalist International Working Men's Association (IWMA), a number of prominent foreign anarchists also made their way to Spain. Some, like the Italian anarchist intellectual Camillo Berneri, went to fight as well as to promote the revolutionary movement.[28] In the latter case, he used his journal, *Guerra di classe* (*Class War*), as a mouthpiece for defending the Spanish Revolution against the pragmatic policies identified with the leaders of the CNT–FAI.[29]

---

27 See M. Low, *Red Spanish Notebook* (n.p.: Secker & Warburg, 1937), pp. 196–7; and M. Gadant (ed.), *Women of the Mediterranean* (London and Atlantic Highlands, NJ: Zed Books, 1986), p. 52.

28 Berneri himself helped to organize an Italian militia column, 'Giustizia e Libertà [Justice and Liberty]'.

29 See Berneri, 'Open Letter to Comrade Federica Montseny', *Guerra di classe* No. 12 (14 April 1937). Berneri was murdered by his political enemies during the notorious disturbances of May 1937.

Another influential and outspoken critic of the collaborationist tendencies of the CNT–FAI was the Russian émigré Alexander Schapiro. Having spent some time in Spain as a representative of the IWMA during the Second Republic, Schapiro was one of the few foreigners observing events inside the country who had an intimate knowledge of both the strengths and the shortcomings of the strategy and tactics of the CNT–FAI. As he made clear in an open letter to the CNT published in 1937, Schapiro strongly objected to the leadership's minimalist 'war programme', which gave primacy to fighting at the front rather than to the revolutionary restructuring of Spain's social and economic structures in the rear.[30] According to him, this policy was self-defeating, not least because it played into the hands of the bourgeois and Marxist factions whose policies were unequivocally aimed at thwarting the power and influence that the anarcho-syndicalists wielded through their organizations.

The impact these critical assessments had on the Spanish anarcho-syndicalist movement as a whole is exceedingly difficult to determine. At the very least these views, coming as they did from leading representatives of international anarchism, most likely stoked the resentments and stiffened the resistance among anarchist 'purists' who increasingly bridled at the collab-orationist tendencies of the CNT–FAI leadership. As far as the leadership of the CNT–FAI was concerned, however, their decision to pursue a pragmatic strategy was a correct one. As a result, they sought to minimize the influence of foreigners by refusing to invest them with any meaningful control over their internal or external affairs. An example of this can be found in the CNT–FAI's conflicted relationship with the German anarchist Helmut Rüdiger, who served throughout most of the Civil War as the assistant secretary of the IWMA based in Spain. Because he saw revolutionary developments in Spain as a projection of the ideas and goals of both the Spanish and the international anarchist movements, Rüdiger believed that the IWMA should take charge of the CNT–FAI's propaganda programme aimed at countries abroad. However, his Spanish comrades saw things differently. Thus, when the national committee of the CNT decided to set up a foreign propaganda secretariat of their own, they made certain that control of international propaganda would be in the hands of their representatives and not those of outsiders.

30 See A. Schapiro, 'Open Letter to the CNT', *The One Big Union Monthly* 1, 8 (August 1937), pp. 6–7.

The debates and discussions that revolved around the role foreign anarchists should be playing during the Civil War highlighted the fact that, even though the Spanish anarchists and their supporters in Europe and the Americas may have shared fundamental doctrinal principles, they were nonetheless divided over strategy and tactics. This is not to deny the strong sense of solidarity and support that prominent foreign anarchists who were critical of the CNT–FAI's wartime policies demonstrated towards their Spanish counterparts. Despite his differences with the 'collaborationists', Rüdiger did not hesitate to come to their defence when he sensed they were being unfairly maligned by radical sections of the IWMA. For Rüdiger, Emma Goldman, and other critical observers of events in Spain, the CNT–FAI leadership may have deviated from the path of revolution but, in the light of the challenging circumstances in which they found themselves, their decision to do so was defensible.[31]

Political Manoeuvrings against Anarcho-Syndicalism in the Republican Camp

More problematic for the CNT–FAI members who had opted for a policy of collaboration were their avowed political opponents on the left who, despite their own political differences, collectively strove to undermine the anarchists' position in the government. Over time, the communists of the PCE (Partido Comunista de España, Spanish Communist Party) became the principal ideological and political enemies of the CNT–FAI. This was true despite the fact that, in anarchist-dominated regions such as Catalonia, communists initially adopted a conciliatory stance towards the pragmatic elements of the CNT–FAI.[32] But at the same time they were attempting to 'strengthen fraternal relations' with the moderate sections of the CNT–FAI, the communists did not refrain from publicly challenging the radical members of the anarcho-syndicalist movement. Often referred to in communist publications and in public speeches as 'uncontrollables', gangsters, mavericks, and *agents provocateurs*, anarchists who opposed the collaboration

---

31 See Emma Goldman's address to the IWMA in December 1937, 'Address to the International Working Men's Association Congress', excerpted in A. K. Shulman (ed.), *Red Emma Speaks: Selected Writings and Speeches by Emma Goldman* (New York: Random, 1979), pp. 375–6.
32 See the 'Resolution of the ECCI (Executive Committee of the Communist International) Presidium on the Activities of the Spanish Communist Party, 28 December 1936', in *The Communist International, 1919–1943, Documents*, vol. III (Oxford: Oxford University Press, 1965), pp. 396–400.

policies being pursued by the CNT–FAI leadership were denounced as major stumbling blocks to the anti-fascist unity needed to defeat the Nationalists. Communist propaganda of this sort was mostly directed at the libertarian movement in Catalonia, where neighbourhood defence committees and other anarchist organizations were largely under the sway of militant anti-collaborationists.

The communists' campaign to end the dual system of authority in Barcelona where the anarchists had established their hegemony was focused on their efforts to dismantle the revolutionary *barrio* committees, especially those which maintained an extensive food supply and distribution network in the city.[33] Besides seeking to dissolve the *barrio* committees that controlled the wholesale food trade in the region, the communists sought to create a single security force. In this way, they hoped to eliminate the forces of public order under working-class control – such as the *patrullas de control* – which the anarcho-syndicalists had always regarded as one of the main bulwarks of their revolutionary movement.

Reacting to these blatant manoeuvrings, the general mood of the rank and file of the CNT–FAI in the region as well as the left wing of the anti-Stalinist POUM grew increasingly belligerent. At first their disquietude was limited to a war of words in publications such as the FAI's *Tierra y Libertad* and the POUM's daily *La Batalla* (*The Struggle*), but, by late spring of 1937, there were growing signs that a showdown between the opposing sides was imminent.

More than any other single event during the Spanish Civil War, the May disturbances of 1937 marked a turning point for the revolutionary movement in the republican zone. In the weeks leading up to this watershed episode, there were visible signs within the anarcho-syndicalist movement itself of growing resistance to the collaborationist policies that had been adopted by the CNT–FAI leadership. In early March, for example, militants returning from the Gelsa front set up the Friends of Durruti (Los Amigos de Durruti) – named after the iconic anarchist leader Buenaventura Durruti. Besides opposing the militarization of the militias, the Friends objected strongly to the central (Valencian) and regional (Generalitat) governments' efforts to dissolve the defence committees and *patrullas de control*, grassroots organizations that the anarchists used to exert their power and influence in the *barrios* of working-class communities.

---

33 The Central Supplies Committee – later superseded by the Liaison Committee – served as the hub for the *barrios'* defence committees.

At the beginning of May, the power struggle that had been simmering for months – between the militant factions on the left and their anti-revolutionary opponents in the government – came to a head. On the one side of this conflict stood the Partit Socialist Unificat de Catalunya (Unified Socialist Party of Catalonia, PSUC), the republican separatist party, the Esquerra Republicana (Republican Left (of Catalonia)), and various government security forces, which included republican Assault Guards, Civil Guards, and the autonomous Catalan police or Mossos de Esquadra. Arrayed against these anti-revolutionary groups were the militant sections of the CNT–FAI and FIJL along with the anti-Stalinist POUM.

Following the erection of barricades in working-class districts, skirmishes broke out between opposing factions. Attempts to resolve the crisis began on 4 May, but fighting between the two sides did not end until 6 May. Dissension and defeatism within the ranks of the anarcho-syndicalist movement itself were fomented not just by the escalation of military measures taken by the Generalitat and Valencia governments, but also by the refusal of leading anarchist officials to endorse the militants manning the barricades. At the height of the hostilities, Federica Montseny, Jacinto Toryho, and other prominent representatives of the CNT–FAI began calling for a ceasefire. By the early morning hours of the 7th it was clear that the government forces had prevailed and that the rebellious sentiments that had previously animated the radical elements of the anarcho-syndicalist movement in the region had been spent.

For the next several weeks, fallout from the May Events reverberated throughout the republican zone. Not least of the repercussions was the ousting of the republic's left-socialist prime minister, Largo Caballero, who was forced to step down as premier on 17 May. As far as the anarcho-syndicalists were concerned, the defeat of the revolutionaries at the barricades came as a crushing blow, above all because the May Events had exposed the longstanding strains and fractures of their movement.

Emboldened by the fact that the power of the revolutionaries in Catalonia had been broken during the May disturbances, in the late spring and early summer of 1937 the communists and their anti-revolutionary allies dramatically escalated their efforts to extend the Valencia government's centralized control over what remained of the republican zone. The communists played a key role in this campaign by spearheading an all-out military assault against the Council of Aragon, an anarchist-dominated provincial ruling body that had been set up in Caspe during the first months of the Civil War. Because the Madrid government had invested it with considerable authority, the council functioned in many respects as a separate political entity.[34]

The council itself collapsed on the 11th of August, the day when the official government decree declaring its dissolution appeared in the official *Gaceta de la República* (*Gazette of the Republic*). In the following days and weeks the former head of the council, Joaquín Ascaso, along with several hundred anarcho-syndicalists regarded as 'uncontrollables' by the authorities, were rounded up and imprisoned. Force was also applied in the ensuing campaign to dismantle the collectives themselves. The brutality shown in these 'clean-up' operations was disturbing to many, including some communists who had previously welcomed the end of the 'Anarchist dictatorship'.[35]

While it is true the communist assault against the collectives in Aragon accelerated the demise of the revolutionary forces in the republican camp, the final destruction of the power of the anarcho-syndicalist movement came about as a result of the growing dissension within the CNT–FAI itself. Ironically, it was the repression vigorously carried out by the communists and anti-revolutionary parties in government that deepened the schisms that were already splintering the libertarian movement into opposing factions. Militant groups – such as the Friends of Durruti mentioned earlier – attempted to provoke the CNT–FAI leadership into resisting the communist-inspired repression in the villages and towns. But their efforts were in vain, not least because the official representatives of the anarcho-syndicalists were by now single-mindedly pursuing a 'possibilist' agenda. The belief held by Horacio Prieto, Mariano Vásquez, and others was that the political and military crises facing the republicans at this stage in the war demanded a pragmatic rather than a revolutionary response. By this time even leading *faístas* such as Abad de Santillán were promoting a political role for the FAI. Just how far the FAI itself had drifted from its pre-war hostility towards politics was clearly reflected in the dictums passed at a plenum held in July 1937, the tenth anniversary of the founding of this ultra-revolutionary organization. At this meeting it was announced that the FAI was to undergo a transformation, becoming what was called a 'new organic structure [*nueva estructura orgánica*]'. In its new form, the FAI would become a mass organization, one open not just to the disciples of a militant form of anarchism, but to all who were willing to abide by the resolutions of the FAI plenums.

34 See J. Casanovas, 'Anarchism and revolution in Aragon, 1936–1939', *European Historical Quarterly* 17, 4 (1987), p. 435.
35 See José Silva's report quoted in B. Bolloten, *The Spanish Civil War* (Chapel Hill: University of North Carolina Press, 2015), p. 530.

The underlying significance of this reorganization did not escape the notice of the radical current of anarcho-syndicalists, who had long opposed the politicalization of the libertarian movement. At a regional plenary of the FAI held a month after the Valencia Conference, representatives of this group inveighed against the restructuring of the FAI, dubbing it a 'new government party'.

Clearly the fragmented nature of the opposition tendency posed a major obstacle to them. In the main, their resistance lacked focus in that there were no formal organizational links among the different locally based opposition groups. Unable to act as one body, they were in no position to challenge forcefully the upper echelons of the CNT–FAI organizations. Moreover, the commonly held belief that unity was paramount in order to defeat fascism undoubtedly inhibited many of the militants from waging an all-out struggle against the official representatives of the anarcho-syndicalist movement. In the event, given the declining strength of the anarcho-syndicalists, it came as no surprise when these attempts to endow the CNT–FAI with political respectability were virtually ignored by the republican parties.

Anarcho-Syndicalism during the Franco Years, 1939–1975

The Francoist victory in April 1939 marked an end to the CNT's role as the leading revolutionary trade union in Spain. Rather than face persecution and summary execution at home, an estimated 80,000 CNT–FAI militants and activists left Spain in the closing weeks of the war.[36] Many joined the great 'La Retirada [retreat]' of refugees who crossed over the Pyrenees into France, where they were forced to endure the hardships of the dreary internment camps that had been hastily constructed in the south-west region as a way of absorbing the huge number of displaced individuals fleeing Nationalist Spain. Within a few months, the mettle of the republican exiles was further tested when France was invaded, conquered by Nazi Germany, and then split in two. The creation of the right-wing Vichy regime in the south-central zones of the country meant that the majority of Spanish anarcho-syndicalists – like other republicans confined to camps – would be subjected to further trials and tribulations. Some, such as the former minister of industry in the republican government and two-time secretary general of the CNT, Joan

---

36 See S. Gemie, 'The ballad of Bourg-Madame: memory, exiles and the Spanish republican refugees of the "Retirada"', *International Review of Social History* 51, 1 (2006), pp. 1–40.

Peiró, would be forcibly repatriated to Spain where they met a grim fate.[37] Most were imprisoned, and the less fortunate ones among them, including Peiró, were tried for war crimes and then executed. Yet a certain number of anarcho-syndicalists escaped their captivity and joined the armed struggle of the anti-Nazi French resistance (maquis) in Vichy France and North Africa for the duration of the war.

It was not until the Second World War ended in 1945 that it was possible for the much-reduced number of Spanish anarcho-syndicalists living in France to recover the remnants of their movement.[38] But, despite these efforts to resurrect the CNT, exiled libertarians were not able to re-establish the movement's links to organized labour. This was true in part because its ties to the Spanish labour movement had been effectively severed and in part because, on foreign soil, the CNT could no longer function as a vehicle for (revolutionary) syndicalist activity. Bereft of local federations and other workers' associations that had previously formed the core of the anarcho-syndicalist community in Spain, the CNT experienced a steep decline in its popular base. Between 1947 and 1961, for example, membership in the organization dropped from a high of around 24,000 to some 7,000.[39]

Meanwhile, inside Spain, the CNT failed to mount an effective underground resistance to Franco's regime. Unable to adapt their traditions and methods to the harsh conditions imposed by the dictatorship, and still divided over whether they should form political alliances with other anti-Franco forces or pursue violent, insurrectionary tactics, anarcho-syndicalists inevitably lost their former position of leadership within the unions they once represented. The movement itself also suffered from the debilitating blows dealt by a ruthlessly oppressive dictatorship. Between 1945 and 1947 the police intensified their campaign of repression against anarchists, arresting scores of activists and forcing the closure of several national committees of the CNT. The regime's relentless persecution of the CNT's fragile organizational infrastructure – which initiated the precipitous decline in its membership – eventually brought about the full eclipse of a once powerful and influential syndicalist movement.

---

37 Some anarcho-syndicalists were marked for deportation to German concentration camps.
38 See C. Ealham 's essay, 'Spanish Anarcho-Syndicalists in Toulouse: The Red-and-Black Counter City in Exile', in S. Belenguer (ed.), Getting It Wrong in Spain (New York and London: Routledge, 2017), pp. 95–114.
39 C. Eahlam, Living Anarchism: José Peirats and the Spanish Anarcho-Syndicalism Movement (Oakland, CA, and Edinburgh: AK Press, 2015), pp. 180–1.

The demise of the CNT's reciprocal relationship with trade union structures did not bring an end to anarchist activities in Spain. Throughout the 1960s, for example, a cadre of Spanish anarchists who were in contact with militant members of exiled CNT–FAI groups operating in France, Mexico, and other countries decided to wage an armed struggle against the dictatorship. Co-ordinating their activities with members of the Spanish Libertarian Movement (Movimiento Libertario Español, MLE), these dedicated revolutionaries formed a clandestine Interior Defence Committee (Defensa Interior) in 1961 which, among other things, launched several failed attempts to assassinate Franco.[40]

With the CNT shorn of its *raison d'être* as a trade union organization, the relevance of Spanish anarcho-syndicalism in the post-Second World War era both inside and outside Spain was largely confined to the cultural sphere. Publications such as *Espoir* and *Cenit* (*Hope* and *Zenith*, both from Toulouse) as well as the memoir literature produced by veterans of the Spanish anarchist movement living in exile communities in Europe and the Americas spoke mostly of the past failures and accomplishments of a moribund syndicalist movement. Nonetheless, anarchism's power to inspire a younger generation of radicals was in evidence during the European protest movements of the late 1960s. The New Left's attraction to libertarian ideas and other ideologies that had been for many years consigned by Marxists, liberals, and conservatives to the 'dustbin' of history served briefly to revive the revolutionary legacy of Spanish anarcho-syndicalism.[41]

'Propaganda by the deed' and other violent tactics associated with anarcho-syndicalism's past struggles also appealed to the more militant elements of the protest generation. But during the 1970s and 1980s, when extremist left-wing organizations in Europe and the Americas resorted to bombings, assassinations, kidnappings, and robberies, it became apparent that revolutionary violence of this sort that had long been identified with Spanish anarchism had changed its meaning in the course of the Cold War era. The majority of the violent acts committed in the name of revolution at this time were part and parcel of the armed struggle being conducted by maverick Marxist organizations. The extremist wings of the separatist Basque ETA

---

40 The resurgence of a violent current within the Spanish anarcho-syndicalist movement was opposed by leaders of the Toulouse-based CNT and FAI. See, for example, Ealham's *Living Anarchism*, chs. 7–8.

41 See J. Vadillo Muñoz, *Historia de la CNT. Utopía, pragmatismo y revolución* (Madrid: Los Libros de la Catarata, 2019).

(Euskadi Ta Askatasuna, Basque Homeland and Liberty), the Provisional Irish Republican Army (PIRA), the Red Army Faction (Rote Armee Fraktion, RAF) in Germany, and the Brigate Rosse (Red Brigades, BR) in Italy were all operating according to a Marxist understanding of the role violence played in the class struggle. At least during the 1970s and 1980s anarcho-syndicalism was no longer viewed as the sole or most prominent revolutionary movement that saw the overthrow of capitalism in apocalyptic terms.

The End of Anarcho-Syndicalism? 1976–2020

Following the death of Francisco Franco in November 1975, there was a brief resurgence of the CNT–FAI's trade union movement inside Spain. The demise of the dictatorship between 1976 and 1978 was accompanied by a general amnesty for political exiles of all stripes, including anarchists who had fled the country at the end of the Civil War. In the ensuing months, surviving libertarian luminaries such as Abad de Santillán, José Peirats, and Federica Montseny were warmly received by throngs of students, workers, and intellectuals who saw their return as marking the beginning of a freer, more democratic era for Spanish society. In the months immediately following its legalization in 1977, the CNT's membership soared to around 300,000, and it became the third-largest trade union in the country.

Yet it did not take long before the nostalgia associated with the historical legacy of Spain's oldest revolutionary organization began to fade. There were a number of reasons why this was the case. First and foremost was the fact that the movement's unswerving commitment to direct action tactics and the principles of revolutionary syndicalism placed the CNT in opposition to Spain's other leading trade unions, the socialist UGT and the communist-dominated Workers' Commissions (Comisiones Obreras, CCOO). Both of these bodies showed a willingness to collaborate with politicians seeking a peaceful path towards democratization. In October 1977 every major working-class organization except the CNT signed on to the Moncloa Pacts, inter-class agreements that obliged the unions to rein in labour agitation and keep wages below the level of inflation in exchange for promised economic and political reforms.

By opting out of the reformist model of re-democratization, the militants of the CNT believed it was possible to win over dissident workers who opposed the idea of harnessing unions to middle-class parties. Yet their hopes in this regard were soon disappointed. At the beginning of 1978, a deadly petrol bombing at a Barcelona nightclub (Scala) popular with workers was blamed on radical elements of the FAI. Now viewed by the general population as a terrorist threat to the democratic process that was unfolding across the country, the CNT began experiencing a steady decline in its membership. This reversal of fortunes was further exacerbated by growing tensions within the CNT movement itself. At its first openly held national congress in December 1979, FAI groups that adamantly opposed modifying anarcho-syndicalist practices in light of the ever-evolving circumstances drove a deep wedge between themselves and the majority of *cenetistas*. Over the course of the next decade, the schism that surfaced at this congress resulted in a formal split in Spain's anarcho-syndicalist movement. The group known as 'renovadores' decided to form a breakaway organization, the General Confederation of Labour (Confederación General del Trabajo, CGT). Since then, the CNT has seen its base of affiliated members shrink, while the CGT has maintained a strong presence among workers in the transportation and communication sectors, claiming a membership of some 100,000 as late as 2018.

The CNT's downward spiral at this time also owed a great deal to two other overarching factors. First and foremost was the fact that Spain's transition to democracy had been accompanied by a steady decline in trade union membership, including nationally and regionally based unions such as the UGT, CCOO, and USO (Union Sindical Obrera, Workers' Trade Union).[42] Over this same period, the anarcho-syndicalist movement itself was in the throes of a generational crisis. Most of its core members were over fifty, and leaders like Montseny were in their seventies and eighties. Spain's younger generation of trade union activists – particularly those under the age of forty – were mostly forward-looking and therefore not preoccupied with the same social and political issues that informed the strategy and tactics of the 'old guard' of anarcho-syndicalists. Thus, while younger members of the 'reborn' CNT saw the organization as a vehicle for addressing modern social problems such as the equality of the sexes and rights for homosexuals in the workplace, veterans such as José Peirats viewed these concerns with disdain. For this older group, it was nonsensical for *cenetistas* to embrace a broadly defined cultural agenda, not least because this only served to dilute the identity of what, in their eyes, a militant syndicalist should stand for. This group's inability to see how their prejudices reflected old-fashioned attitudes

---

42 Despite having experienced some spurts of growth in the following years, trade union membership in Spain has decreased in recent years (2010–), to the point that unionism as a whole is considered by most to be in a state of crisis.

and an otiose mindset made it, if not impossible, exceedingly difficult to bridge the chasm between generations.

Though still committed to the idea that an anarcho-syndicalist organization should be organized from the bottom up and that all representatives were answerable to the rank and file, the 'new' CNT/CGT is nevertheless representative of a very different kind of trade union movement than it had been during its earlier phases of development. Rather than promote a revolutionary agenda like their predecessors, post-Franco anarchists have insisted that their unions should protect workers' rights in a democratic environment by promoting the principles of self-management, federalism, and mutual aid. To most members of the new generation of activists, then, today's anarcho-syndicalist movement represents a modern iteration of Spain's long tradition of libertarianism.

Further Reading

Alexander, Robert, *The Anarchists in the Spanish Civil War*, vols. I–II (London: Janus Publishing, 1998).

Bolloten, Burnett, *The Spanish Civil War: Revolution and Counter-Revolution*, new intro. by George Esenwein (Chapel Hill and London: University of North Carolina Press, 2015).

Casanova, Julián, *Anarchism, the Republic and Civil War in Spain: 1936–1939*, trans. Andrew Dowling and Graham Pollok (revised by Paul Preston) (Abingdon and New York: Routledge and Taylor & Francis, 1997).

Ealham, Chris, *Living Anarchism: José Peirats and the Spanish Anarcho-Syndicalist Movement* (Edinburgh and Oakland, CA: AK Press, 2015).

Evans, Danny, *Revolution and the State: Anarchism in the Spanish Civil War, 1936–1939* (London and New York: Routledge, 2018).

Gómez Casas, Juan, *Anarchist Organization: The History of the FAI*, trans. Abe Bluestein (Montreal and Buffalo: Black Rose Books, 1986).

Leval, Gaston, *Collectives in the Spanish Revolution*, trans. Vernon Richards (London: Freedom Press, 1975).

Nash, Mary, *Defying Male Civilization: Women in the Spanish Civil War* (Denver: Arden Press, 1995).

Peirats, José, *La CNT en la Revolución Española*, vols. I–III (Toulouse: Ediciones CNT, 1951–3) (English edition published in three volumes, edited by Chris Ealham, *The CNT in the Spanish Revolution*, trans. Paul Sharkey and Chris Ealham (Hastings: ChristieBooks/PM Press, 2005–11)).

Ruíz, Julius, *The 'Red Terror' and the Spanish Civil War: Revolutionary Violence in Madrid* (New York: Cambridge University Press, 2014).

Anarchism and Syndicalism in Italy

CARL LEVY

This chapter will present an overview of Italian anarchism and syndicalism during the era of liberal Italy and the fascist era (1870–1945) and will conclude with a discussion of the contrasting period after 1945. It will examine the personalities, the political culture, the conviviality and artistic manifestations, the social geography, gender relations, and emotional contexts, and the doctrines of Italian anarchism and syndicalism. This chapter employs a synoptic historical overview in order to understand how the anarchists retained a strong presence in the quotidian life of the Italian left in the era of liberal Italy even as the socialists were predominant and explains their relative marginalization after 1945.

The First International (1860s–Early 1880s)

The First International drew its strength from radicalized and disenchanted members of the *Risorgimento*, usually followers of Giuseppe Mazzini's republicanism, and younger men and women coming of age in the late 1860s and early 1870s, too young to have participated, but disillusioned with unified Italy.[1] As we will see, the First International in Italy directly and indirectly influenced the left well into the 1880s, rather longer than in other national cases. The birth of self-conscious, direct action anarchist collectivism can be partially traced to Mikhail Bakunin's sojourns in Italy during the 1860s, in which he interacted with these Italians. Whether or not the socio-political ideas of the martyred hero of the *Risorgimento*, Carlo Pisacane, were a direct influence on Bakunin or the Italians remains controversial. Pisacane called for a social *Risorgimento* involving peasant seizure of the land, a federalized Italy

---

1 The most recent overview is C. Levy, 'The Italians and the IWMA', in F. Bensimon, D. Quentin, and J. Moisand (eds.), *'Arise Ye Wretched of the Earth': The First International in a Global Perspective* (Leiden and Boston: Brill, 2018), pp. 207–20.

ruled by communes, which ran parallel to Bakunin's suggestions a decade later.

The growth of the International in Italy occurred in the wake of the Paris Commune, from 1871 to 1874, with official membership reaching 32,450.[2] The initial predominance of the south was lost to the small and medium-sized towns of Tuscany, Emilia, and the Romagna. There was also growth in the Federation of Upper Italy, in the industrializing northern cities. The Internationalists brought socialism to the Po Valley, attracting increasing numbers of *braccianti* (landless labourers), but by the 1880s and 1890s these numerous followers were mostly lost to the socialists and socialist trade unionists. The patterns of anarchist predominance were set in the 1870s: the towns and villages of the Marches, Emilia-Romagna, Umbria, Liguria, and Rome and its surroundings were strongholds of Italian anarchism until the 1920s. Noted for their fierce anti-clericalism and militant republicanism, due to the memories of the Papal Legations in some of these localities, the International was also the first modern political party in Italy, which transcended the personality-based and clan-like organization that characterized the republicans and the consortia of the historic right and historic left.

The Italian Internationalists played a tangential role in the battle with the 'Marxist' London council. Indeed, Carlo Cafiero and Emilio Covelli criticized the authoritarian politics of Karl Marx and Friedrich Engels, but they were fascinated by their political economy and were the first translators of Marx's work in Italy. Unlike Bakunin, the Italian anarchists were pioneers in embracing anarcho-communism. Advocates of direct action, they formulated the concept of 'propaganda by the deed', originally inspired by the insurrectional acts of the *Risorgimento* and the myriad acts of unrest which shook the unstable Savoyard–Italian monarchy throughout the 1860s.

An insurrectional attempt in central Italy (1874) was centred on urban areas, but the second attempt in 1877 played out in the mountainous Matese, south of Naples. The aim was to perform demonstrative acts in isolated villages, overthrowing the local authorities, burning the tax registers, and inciting the peasantry to seize land, fight a guerrilla war, and establish an insurgent zone.[3] This was disastrous and, along with a series of mysterious bomb explosions and an attempt on the king's life by a deranged republican, led to the banning of the International and the splintering of the movement in

---

2 Ibid., p. 209.
3 N. Pernicone, *Italian Anarchism, 1864–1892* (Princeton: Princeton University Press, 1992), pp. 82–128; B. Tomastiello, *La Banda del Matese 1876–1878. I documenti, le testimonianze, la stampa dell'epoca* (Casalvelino Scalo: Galzerano, 2009).

the 1880s and 1890s. Over the next twenty years, the concept of propaganda by the deed was transformed from insurgent guerrilla warfare to regicide, to the bombing of symbolic property and public events, and to random acts of mass terrorism. Arguments raged about the meaning of propaganda by the deed and also over the practice of 'illegalism', igniting fierce internal polemics and limiting the growth of a formally organized, mass movement.[4]

The Interregnum: Proto-Syndicalism, Terrorism, and Social Unrest (1880s–1890s)

The second phase, the pre-history of syndicalism, foreshadowed developments which unfolded during the Giolittian period before the First World War. After the destruction of the International, the anarchists did not succeed in establishing a continuous national organization until after the First World War. Classified as either terrorists or insurrectionists, the anarchists were targeted with greater ferocity by the state than the emergent parliamentary Partito Socialista Italiano (Italian Socialist Party, PSI). However, during the 1880s and 1890s, the state and civil society suffered myriad crises (economic, financial, ecological, political, and diplomatic), which were accompanied by the authoritarian governments of the former Mazzinian radical Francesco Crispi and General Luigi Pelloux (the hammers of the anarchists, socialists, and at times republicans and radicals, too). In this time of distress, the anarchists faced fluctuating fortunes.[5]

Tensions inherent in the International burst out in the 1880s, thus the *fasci operai* (workers' organizations) were alienated by the insurrectional tactics and heated rhetoric of prominent middle-class Internationalists. The anarchists' attempts to reconstruct the International at Chiasso in 1880 came to naught because the reformist Federation of Upper Italy could not be reconciled with the anarchists, many of whom in any case embarked on diasporic odysseys, which meant that for much of the period before 1914 the centre of gravity for Italian anarchism became the global diaspora, not Italy itself.[6]

---

4 P. C. Masini, *Storia degli anarchici italiani dal Bakunin a Malatesta* (Milan: Rizzoli, 1974), pp. 166–8.
5 P. Brunello, *Storie di anarchici e di spie* (Rome: Donzelli, 2009); S. di Corato Tachetti, *Anarchici, governo, magistrati in Italia, 1876–1892* (Turin: Carocci, 2009); D. Turcato, *Making Sense of Anarchism: Errico Malatesta's Experiments with Revolution, 1889–1900* (Basingstoke: Palgrave Macmillan, 2012), pp. 71–126; G. Sacchetti (ed.), *Nel fosco fin del secolo morente. L'anarchismo italiano nella crisi di fine secolo* (Milan: Biblion, 2013).
6 D. Turcato, 'Italian anarchism as a transnational movement, 1885–1915', *International Review of Social History* 52, 3 (2007), pp. 407–44; K. Zimmer, *Immigrants against the State:*

Former anarchists maintained a libertarian valence, however, and thus can be better understood as pragmatic partisans of the electoral weapon. The politics of Enrico Bignami, Osvaldo Gnocchi-Viani, and Benoît Malon (an exiled French Communard) were not dismissive of Internationalist legacies, but advanced an electorally oriented libertarian gas-and-water socialism. But younger first-generation anarchists, such as Errico Malatesta, engaged in ferocious polemics over the use of the electoral tactic. Andrea Costa's departure from the anarchist path was rooted in the politics of his birthplace, establishing the Revolutionary Socialist Party of the Romagna, contesting local and then national ballots, in which the minimum programme was collectivism but the maximal goal still retained radical objectives.[7]

The ill-defined radical Amilcare Cipriani gained widespread notoriety in the 1880s and 1890s, and his biography illustrates the effects of anarchist and 'anarchoid' patterns of political culture in Italy before 1914. Cipriani personified the anti-dynastic 'subversive': a volunteer with Giuseppe Garibaldi at a tender age, a colonel in the Paris Commune, transported to New Caledonia, later imprisoned in Italy for a murky incident resulting in a triple murder in Egypt many years previously, he was finally granted his freedom in 1888 following a massive campaign organized by the anarchists in conjunction with radical liberals, socialists, and republicans. However, some anarchists thought him impulsive and muddle-headed and, furthermore, his close ties to French republicans, his advocacy of a League of Latin Peoples against the German threat, and his unbridled support of the Cretan revolt of 1897, considered by critics as too close to the Greek monarchy's interests, foreshadowed the left-wing war interventionism of 1914–15.[8]

The examples of Costa and Cipriani demonstrate a broader-based form of populism or *sovversivismo* in Italian left political culture in which the anarchists and cognate movements could exercise greater influence than sheer numbers would lead one to conclude. The previously mentioned libertarian gas-and-water socialism was interwoven with the northern Partito Operaio

Yiddish and Italian Anarchism in America (Urbana: University of Illinois Press, 2015); T. Tomchuk, *Transnational Radicals: Italian Anarchists in Canada and the US, 1915–1940* (Winnipeg: University of Manitoba Press, 2015); E. Bignami, *In viaggio dall'utopia al Brasile. Gli anarchici italiani nella migrazione transoceanica (1876–1919)* (Bologna: Bononia University Press, 2017).

7 Pernicone, *Italian Anarchism*, pp. 165–79.
8 C. Levy, 'Italian Anarchism, 1870–1926', in D. Goodway (ed.), *For Anarchism: History, Theory, and Practice* (London and New York: Routledge), pp. 42–3; C. Levy, '"Sovversivismo": the radical political culture of otherness in liberal Italy', *Journal of Political Ideologies* 12, 2 (2007), pp. 147–61; M. Sassi, *Amilcare Cipriani il rivoluzionario* (Rimini: Bookstones, 2019).

Fig. 17.1 Errico Malatesta (1853–1932), anarchist activist and thinker. (DeAgostini/Getty Images.)

Italiano (Italian Workers' Party, POI). Workerist anarchists could mix easily here, but the young, highly educated Luigi Galleani helped form small trade unions of rice-weeders, bakers, builders, and factory workers in Lombardy and Piedmont.[9] In any case, it would be misleading to argue that anarchist insurrectionists of the 1870s were not attracted to organizing workers and peasants into resistance leagues. Errico Malatesta organized workers in Naples and Florence and later in exile in Argentina, and he became a skilled trade unionist, indeed one of the founders of the modern labour movement in the South American republic.

Therefore, when Italy entered its decade of crises in the 1890s, the anarchists were present in many formats and organizations in the peninsula and islands, albeit co-ordination and focus were lacking. Organizationalist

9 A. Senta, *Luigi Galleani. L'anarchico più pericoloso d'America* (Rome: Nova Delphi Libri, 2018), pp. 29–53.

anarchists, such as Malatesta, sought to revive the spirit of the International, drawing together anarchists and allies under the banner of anarchist socialism. But a congress in the Swiss border town of Capolago in 1891 failed to produce a convincing result. However, the anarchists persisted and sought working alliances with the POI at the first congresses, which eventually gave birth to the parliamentary Italian Socialist Party in the early 1890s, while Malatesta seconded their efforts at the London Congress of the Second International in 1896. The dual expulsion from the PSI and the Second International, plus the impressive electoral successes in Germany of the parliamentary Sozialdemokratische Partei Deutschlands (SPD) and more modest, if encouraging successes of their Italian political cousins, isolated the anarchists, the workerists, and proto-syndicalists at both the national and international levels.[10]

Nevertheless, the Italian anarchists still made their presence felt. In the south the Fasci Siciliani were influenced by anarchists at the leadership and cadre levels; albeit far from being a purely anarchist social movement, the Fasci Siciliani demanded fairer taxes, land for the poor, free trade unions, and an open and equitable legal system, mixing at the grassroots images of the Madonna with red and black flags. Mass protests in Sicily were alternatively conciliated and repressed by the government, while the anarchists sought to link the Sicilian movement to the northern Partito Operaio.[11] When the Fasci Siciliani were suppressed by the military in 1894, the anarchist marble quarry miners of Carrara and the Lunigiana rose in solidarity in armed insurrection but were rapidly quashed.[12]

Concurrently came the rise of an Italian anarcho-communist so-called anti-organizationalism: in fact a doctrine and practice of decentralized organization, employing a determinist reading of Peter Kropotkin (championed by the charismatic Luigi Galleani in Italy and in exile in North America after 1900, though he remained close to Malatesta), fostering sectarianism and inflexible spectacular forms of direct action, and making focused activities far more difficult for the nationally oriented federal organizationalists.[13]

10 Turcato, *Making Sense of Anarchism*, pp. 128–75; Pernicone, *Italian Anarchism*, pp. 258–94.
11 P. Schneider, 'Rural artisans and peasant mobilisation in the Socialist International: the *fasci siciliani*', *Journal of Peasant Studies* 13, 3 (1986), pp. 61–81; Turcato, *Making Sense of Anarchism*, pp. 108–22.
12 G. Vatteroni, '*Abbasso i dazi, viva la Sicilia*'. *Storia dell'insurrezione carraese del 1894* (Sarzana: Zappa, 1993).
13 Senta, *Luigi Galleani*, pp. 74–89, 154–6, 165–7, 174–7.

The Italian anarchists were notable in the era of *attentati* (assassinations). Sante Geronimo Caserio stabbed to death Sadi Carnot, President of France, in 1894; Michele Angiolillo murdered Antonio Cánovas del Castillo, Prime Minister of Spain, in 1897; Luigi Luccheni stabbed to death the innocuous Empress Elizabeth of Austria in 1898; and Gaetano Bresci assassinated King Umberto of Italy in 1900. An embarrassed Italian government called an International Anti-Anarchist Conference in Rome in 1898, which accomplished little (but one can trace the origins of Interpol from it).[14]

Anarchists such as Malatesta challenged the terrorism of Ravachol and his Italian followers and argued for a distinct difference between regicide and mass terrorism, and Malatesta rallied liberal and socialist opinion against the authoritarian excesses of Crispi, including the mysterious deaths of anarchists in prison and his widespread use of *agents provocateurs*. Many anarchists also sought alliances with liberals, radicals, and socialists against the executive's dictatorial plotting of the 1890s, which saw the prison islands rapidly fill up with militants and prominent personalities of the entire Italian left.

Based in Ancona (to which he would return in 1913–14), Malatesta organized the local working classes into resistance leagues, and in a series of articles in the 1890s Malatesta invoked London's Great Dock Strike of 1889 as a new syndicalist strategy for anarchists caught in profitless cycles of hopeless insurrections or terrorist plotting, concurrently converting the French anarchist pioneers of revolutionary syndicalism, Fernand Pelloutier and Emile Pouget, to this approach during their London exile of the 1890s, where Malatesta lived on and off for thirty years.[15] In May 1898 Milan rose against the high price of bread caused by the Spanish–American War. At least eighty civilians (probably many more) were mown down by cannonades and gunfire.[16] The king awarded a medal to the general in charge, which caused Gaetano Bresci to return from the 'anarchist town' of Paterson, New Jersey, to murder Umberto. The liberal turn of the Giolittian era ushered in the third phase of anarchist history.

14 E. Diemoz, *A morte il tiranno. Anarchia e violenza da Crispi a Mussolini* (Turin: Einaudi, 2011), pp. 3–266; N. Pernicone and F. M. Ottanelli, *Assassins against the Old Order: Italian Anarchist Violence in Fin-de-Siècle Europe* (Urbana: University of Illinois Press, 2018).

15 C. Levy, 'The Rooted Cosmopolitan: Errico Malatesta, Syndicalism, Transnationalism and the International Labour Movement', in D. Berry and C. Bantman (eds.), *New Perspectives on Anarchism, Labour and Syndicalism: The Individual, the National and the Transnational* (Newcastle upon Tyne: Cambridge Scholars, 2010), pp. 61–79.

16 L. A. Tilly, '*I fatti di maggio*: The Working Class of Milan and the Rebellion of 1898', in R. J. Bezucha (ed.), *Modern European Social History* (Lexington, MA: D. C. Heath, 1972), pp. 124–60; C. Levy, 'The centre and the suburbs: social protest and modernization in Milan and Turin, 1898–1917', *Modern Italy* 7, 2 (2002), pp. 171–88.

The Giolittian Era: Libertarian Culture and the Rise of Syndicalism (1900–1910)

Giovanni Giolitti's liberal experiment accompanied the first wave of mass industrialization in Milan, Genoa, and Turin. The Piedmontese statesman permitted trade unionization (albeit industrial disputes were peppered with 'proletarian massacres'), but still targeted socialist intransigents, the syndicalists and the anarchists, who could be arrested under a series of restrictive press and association laws. He was perfectly prepared to support certain strikes, but he and his network of provincial prefects ordered the arrest on a regular basis of anarchists and syndicalists. The anarchists were no match for the continuity and density of socialist networks and, as socialist political and trade union power grew before the First World War, the anarchists failed to maintain a continuous national organization, albeit national conferences were held in 1891, 1907, and 1915. It might appear that the first decade of the twentieth century was an era of stasis for the anarchists, but this would be misleading. Although leading figures, such as Malatesta and Galleani, spent most of their time in the Italian anarchist diaspora, the unique and resilient shape of pre-fascist Italian anarchism was set.[17]

The modulated repression of the Giolittian era and the intense doctrinal disputes between organizationalists, anti-organizationalists, and individualist Stirnerite–Nietzschean anarchists seemed to threaten the extinction of the movement. However, the anarchist strongholds identified previously (Tuscany, the Marches, the Romagna, Liguria, and Rome) retained their vibrancy through a mixture of oral and print traditions rooted in urban neighbourhoods and peripheral suburbs, and 'cadres' who linked popular movements with exiles such as Malatesta and others abroad through a global republic of newspapers and single-issue broadsheets.[18] This libertarian culture is illustrated by the career of Pietro Gori (lawyer, sociologist, criminologist, playwright, poet, troubadour, and nomad).[19] He fused advertising, melodrama, residues of Christianity, folklore, and personal charisma. Gori

17 G. Berti, *Errico Malatesta e il movimento anarchico italiano e internazionale, 1872–1932* (Milan: Franco Angeli, 2003), pp. 389–478; F. Giulietti, *Storia degli anarchici italiani in età giolittiana* (Milan: Franco Angeli, 2012).

18 Levy, 'Italian Anarchism', pp. 33–4; M. Manfredi, *Emozioni, cultura popolare e transnazionalismo. Le origini della cultura anarchica in Italia (1880–1914)* (Milan: Mondadori Education, 2017).

19 M. Antonioli, F. Bertolucci, and R. Giulianelli (eds.), *Nostra patria è il mondo intero. Pietro Gori nel movimento operario e libertario italiano e internazionale* (Pisa: BFS, 2012); E. Minuto, 'Pietro Gori's anarchism: politics and spectacle (1895–1900)', *International Review of Social History* 62, 3 (2017), pp. 425–50.

employed the courtroom speech, the well-crafted tune, and the political play to fashion a politics of redemptive emotional drama which appealed far beyond anarchist heartlands.

But the anarchists also modernized their appeal by adopting syndicalist arguments and seeking shelter in the labour movement, particularly in the Chambers of Labour (*camere del lavoro*). Like the French *bourses du travail*, at first subsidized by municipal authorities as places for class reconciliation, they became radical exemplars of class autonomy for the urban and rural working classes on a territorial basis and sought to control the local labour market, which was plagued by periodic underemployment, reinforcing their presence with the promotion of boycotts and sympathy strikes. The chambers gave the working classes a taste for self-management; they were associated with older traditions of 'workerism [*operaismo*]', localism, and anti-parliamentary politics. They overlapped politics, economics, and culture, running educational programmes and centres of conviviality for neighbourhood, city, and provincial life (giving shelter to anti-clerical, anti-militarist, and neo-Malthusian movements). The political will of the chambers was expressed through the *comizio* held to commemorate past struggles, to protest against 'proletarian massacres', or in solidarity with the national and international labour movements. The will of the meeting was expressed through resolutions (*ordini del giorno*), which were treated as plebiscites: indeed one can trace the life and death of waves of popular unrest through their outcomes. In this arena of direct democracy, the anarchists thrived.[20] This discussion leads us on to the complex and contentious relationship of the anarchists to Italian syndicalism.

Compared to most syndicalist movements before 1914, the Italian variation was anomalous. While I have had cause to discuss varieties of proto-syndicalism, in the Giolittian era syndicalism as a self-identifying movement may have drawn on these strands of proletarian élan, but its first adherents and publicists were from within the PSI itself, from intransigents fearful that Giolitti would seduce the party leadership with cabinet posts and incorporate the northern proletariat into the undemocratic, monarchical state. The first generation of syndicalists were expelled from the PSI in 1908, limiting their political effect. The formation of the socialist-dominated General Confederation of Labour (Confederazione Generale del Lavoro, CGL) also saw greater efforts to exercise control of the general strike weapon and restrict the activities of

20 Levy, 'Italian Anarchism', pp. 48–51.

radicals in the Chambers of Labour. These institutions thus became the central battleground for the second generation of syndicalism.

This second generation of syndicalists had a leadership of more lower-middle-class provenance and excelled in organizing a series of spectacular agricultural strikes (Parma in 1907; Ferrara in 1908), but then threw caution to the winds and antagonized allies and enemies alike (frightening former sharecropper allies), and forcing employers to create more effective sectoral organizations in response. The CGL and the Federterra (National Federation of Land Workers) increased their prestige in the Po Valley, and the second generation of syndicalists scattered in many directions, bidding as independent candidates for parliament, embracing the more irrational nostrums of Georges Sorel, and joining forces with nationalists, or even re-entering the PSI.

A third episode in the history of syndicalism was stimulated by a more aggressive attitude from agrarians and industrialists, who ditched Giolitti's even-handed approach, and sought to modernize production, undermine experiments in industrial democracy, and link up with the nationalists in a programme of social imperialism and increased military expenditure, which ushered in bitter strikes in the company towns of Piombino and Terni in 1910–11, followed by strikes in the automobile and engineering industries of Milan and Turin in 1912 and 1913. Although these intense industrial disputes were short-lived, in all these cases anarchists on the shop-floor and in working-class neighbourhoods gained a renewed prestige there as well as in the newly formed Unione Sindacale Italiana (Italian Syndical Union, USI; founded in 1912). This was an amalgamation of older agriculturally based Chambers of Labour with a new stratum of organizers, promoting industrial unions. Whereas the CGL was larger than the USI, due to the hegemony of the Federterra in the countryside, in the most modern centres of industry (Turin, Milan, Genoa), workers briefly went over *en masse* to the USI. Whereas the industrial unionists plumped for greater centralization, the older Chambers of Labour sought confederation. The anarchists could be found among the chambers, in the newly born industrial unions, and in the leadership positions of such strategic if independent unions, such as those of the railway and port workers.[21]

But the anarchists expressed concerns about full-fledged syndicalism.[22] Malatesta demanded autonomy for the anarchists, albeit he advocated

---

21 For the discussion of the complex subject of syndicalism, see C. Levy, 'Currents of Italian syndicalism before 1926', *International Review of Social History* 45, 2 (2000), pp. 209–50.

22 M. Antonioli, *Azione diretta e organizzazione operaia. Sindacalismo rivioluzionario e anarchismo tra la fine dell'Ottocento e il fascismo* (Manduria: Piero Lacaita, 1990);

trade union unity, and argued that they should enter all working-class organizations as ginger groups. Syndicalism was a tactic that allowed anarchism to be a serious alternative for workers but never remained an end in itself. The general strike could be smashed by the state and vigilantes, or otherwise the strikers could be starved into submission. In any case, the social revolution would only be accomplished through a general strike, which mutated into an armed insurrection: the armed general strike.[23] Trade unions, even syndicalist trade unions, exhibited oligarchical tendencies similar to those of parliamentary socialist parties. The libertarian ginger groups had to struggle for grassroots union democracy and the rotation of worker-wage paid officials, and guard against corporatist tendencies; the aim was libertarian anarcho-communism, which went beyond class-based arguments. Although Malatesta engaged in the class struggle as a tried-and-tested tactic, he was a revolutionary humanist, not a class warrior.[24]

By the early twentieth century Malatesta had shaped a unique form of ideology and practice, influenced by his intellectual collaborators, Francesco Saverio Merlino[25] in the 1880s and 1890s, and Luigi Fabbri[26] from the early 1900s to his own death in 1932. Malatesta joined together three generations of anarchists from the era of Bakunin to that of Vladimir Lenin and Benito Mussolini. Anarchism was recognized as a minority movement, and Malatesta's form of non-sectarian anarcho-communism sought to establish a distinct anarchist party as a spur to direct revolutionary action by the entire left. After the insurrection, the anarchists would be the conscience of the revolution during reconstruction, edging towards an anarchist society through example and education. Malatestan anarchists were sharp critics of determinism. Like Kropotkin, Malatesta endorsed the scientific experimental method and became self-critical of his youthful embrace of Marxist sociology and political economy, following lines laid down by the Russian and Merlino. But Malatesta was disturbed by Kropotkin's mixture of biology, ethics, and

M. Antonioli, *Figli dell'officina. Anarchismo, sindacalismo e movimento operaio tra Ottocento e Novecento* (Pisa: BFS, 2012).

23 E. Malatesta, 'Lo sciopero generale', *Lo Sciopero Generale* (London), 2 June 1902; C. Levy, 'Da Bresci a Wormwood Scrubs. Il "capo" dell'anarchismo mondiale a Londra', in D. Turcato (ed.), *Errico Malatesta, 'Lo Sciopero Armato'. Il lungo esilio londinese 1900–1913* (Milan and Ragusa: Zero in Condotta and Edizioni La Fiaccola, 2015), pp. xv–xxx.

24 Berti, *Errico Malatesta*, pp. 242–57, 377–88; Levy, 'The Rooted Cosmopolitan'.

25 G. Berti, *Francesco Saverio Merlino. Dall'anarchismo socialista al socialismo liberale (1856–1930)* (Milan: Franco Angeli, 1993).

26 M. Antonioli and R. Giulieanelli (eds.), *Da Fabriano a Montevideo. Luigi Fabbri, vita e idee di un intellettuale anarchico e antifascista* (Pisa: BFS, 2006); S. Fedeli, *Luigi Fabbri. Un libertario contro il bolscevismo e il fascismo* (Pisa: BFS, 2006).

politics. Kropotkin's form of the bio-politics of altruistic mutual aid was another form of determinism, he argued, which avoided hard questions and dampened organizational activity, and infused the sporadic spontaneity of his friend, Luigi Galleani.[27] A sharp critic of social imperialism and popular militarism, Malatesta understood (from his own biography) the attractions of Mazzinian republican and Garibaldian traditions: the imperatives of international volunteering, the ethical struggle against non-domination, and the fight against the monarchical form of government, even if the 'Free Country', the American Republic, was little better than the imperial Old World.

Revolution, Counter-Revolution, and Fascist Regime: 1910–1926

The fourth phase in the history of the Italian anarchists saw the whipsaw interaction of the movement with the threats and opportunities of anti-militarism and war, revolutionary upheaval and counter-revolutionary backlash. These sixteen years saw the anarchists and cognate syndicalist organizations serve as key networkers behind the Red Week of 1914 and the political and social earthquake of the *Biennio Rosso* (1919–20), and as an alternative basis to the anti-fascist fightback in 1921 and 1922. Anarchists had their greatest national impact since the International, but unlike in the 1870s they were no longer numerically the major force on the extreme left, though they were the catalyst for broader social movements, which they embodied but did not lead strategically. The number of anarchists in Italy probably ranged from 10,000 in 1914 to a height of 30,000 in 1920.[28] In order to understand how the libertarians, in a brief age of universal manhood suffrage and rapidly expanding membership in unions and the PSI, were so significant, we have to take a closer look at waves of social protest.

The Red Week[29] in June 1914 was connected to an anti-militarist campaign closely co-ordinated by the Chambers of Labour. Anarchists had been in the forefront of Italian anti-militarism since the imperialist adventures in Eritrea and Abyssinia in the 1880s and 1890s, had opposed persistent 'proletarian massacres' in the Giolittian era, and now objected to the Italian invasion of

---

27 For a good example of Malatesta's critique of Kropotkin's approach, see E. Malatesta, 'Pietro Kropotkin: Recollections and Criticisms by One of His Old Friends', in D. Turcato (ed.), *The Method of Freedom: An Errico Malatesta Reader* (Oakland, CA: AK Press, 2014), pp. 511–21.

28 A. Senta, *Utopia e azione. Per una storia dell'anarchismo in Italia (1848–1984)* (Milan: Eléuthera, 2015), p. 133.

29 L. Lotti, *La Settimana Rossa* (Florence: Le Monnier, 1965); C. Rosati, *Il processo alla Settimana Rossa* (Milan: Affinità Elettive, 2014).

Libya on 19 September 1911, which touched off inflation and a renewal of militant industrial disputes. A massive campaign was mounted for the fate of two anti-militarist conscripts (one was charged with the wounding of his commanding officer and sent to a psychiatric hospital) and the brutal punishment battalions of the Italian army.[30] A small group of libertarian anti-militarists, assisted by the radical Socialist Youth Federation, had grown to a national organization of 20,000. The anarchists forged an anti-dynastic alliance with younger and bolder republicans, 'rebel' socialists, whose paladin was the then Blanquist-like socialist firebrand Benito Mussolini, and the syndicalists of the USI, which had been foreshadowed in the 1909 wave of protest after the execution of the Catalan anarchist militant and educationalist Francisco Ferrer i Guardia, an alliance at the time which also stretched to middle-class free-thinkers of left–liberal leanings.[31] At the apex of this evolving movement was Malatesta, who had returned from his London exile and through frenetic activity sought to coalesce non-sectarian alliances (like those of 1897–8 and later in 1920). A protest on the anniversary of the Savoyard Constitutional Statute in the anarchist stronghold Ancona led to three deaths and the spread of spontaneous protest across the centre of the peninsula, nearly cutting Italy in two, witnessing the declaration of social republics in the small towns of the Marches and the Romagna and the raising of 'trees of liberty' throughout central Italy. But the events lacked forward movement because the socialists and the CGL dampened down an uprising reminiscent of 1848.

Within months the rebel alliance was riven by the debate over the intervention of Italy into the First World War. Antebellum anti-militarism was not pacifism: for the anarchists, revolutions involved violence, and anti-imperialist wars might be legitimate. Anti-militarism was associated with opposition to dynastic wars and imperialist adventures but did not dismiss the people in arms. Along with the socialist Mussolini, a limited number of well-known anarchists and syndicalists melded nostalgia for the French Republic with Mazzinian and Sorelian themes. Although most anarchists were not attracted, a group of Stirnerite and Nietzschean anarchists – noted publicists who mixed in the bohemian milieux of Milan, Rome, and Florence, in which Futurists were inspired by anarchist ideas for their painterly themes and

30 G. Cerrito, *Dall'insurrezionalismo alla settimana rossa. Per una storia dell'anarchismo in Italia (1881/1914)* (Florence: CP Editore, 1977), pp. 117–60; L. De Marco, *Il soldato che disse no alla guerra. Storia dell' anarchico August Masetti (1886–1966)* (Santa Maria Capua Vetere: Spartaco, 2003).
31 M. Antonioli (ed.), *Contro la chiesa. I moti pro Ferrer del 1909 in Italia* (Pisa: BFS, 2009).

styles – were ferociously pro-interventionist. This loud, if small, group served as a political life raft for Mussolini on his journey to radical authoritarian nationalist populism (along with the lubricative effects of funds supplied by the British and French governments and Italian industrialists).[32] The USI also divided into interventionist and anti-interventionist wings and, after a complex series of events, the Romagnole anarchist Armando Borghi assumed leadership of the now purged and much reduced, if more openly anarchist-tinged USI.[33]

Italy entered the war in May 1915, but by 1916–17 a transversal alliance of radical opponents to the war was forged with the anarchists, anti-war syndicalists, and radical socialists. At the grassroots, militarized factory discipline chafed, and galloping inflation stirred the industrial suburbs of Genoa, Milan, and Turin. Some limited anarchist smuggling of deserters to Switzerland occurred, and anarchist anti-war leaflets reached the front lines, but the largely apolitical peasant infantry were immune to these arguments, and the military collapse at Caporetto in the autumn of 1917 had nothing to do with their agitation. Earlier, a rising in Turin in August 1917 was spurred on by the breakdown in bread supplies, the news from Russia, and granular industrial disputes at the factory level. Once this largely spontaneous revolt of harried housewives and male and female factory workers gained traction, small groups of anarchists did assist in organizing defences against the security forces. Similar anarchist involvement in other protests in the war years happened, but for the most part the anarchist press was muzzled, leading figures were sent into internal exile, and activity was carried out at the semi-clandestine level.[34]

Global anti-war agitation interlinked with libertarian–left socialist alliances in Rome, Milan, Turin, and Genoa, although attempts to fashion *fasci rivoluzionari* were limited by party boundaries and the persistence of socialist parliamentary strategies. But due to shared sovietist interpretations of the Bolshevik Revolution the socialist left and the libertarians drew closer.

32 A. Luparini, *Anarchici di Mussolini. Dalla sinistra al fascismo, tra rivoluzione e revisionismo* (Montespertoli: MIR, 2001); M. Antonioli, *Sentinelle perdute. Gli anarchici, la morte, la guerra* (Pisa: BFS, 2009); C. Levy, 'Malatesta and the War Interventionist Debate, 1914–1917: From "Red Week" to the Russian Revolutions', in R. Kinna and M. Adams (eds.), *Anarchism 1914–1918: Internationalism, Antimilitarism and War* (Manchester: Manchester University Press, 2017), pp. 69–92.

33 M. Antonioli, *Armando Borghi e l'Unione Sindacale Italiana* (Manduria: Piero Lacaita, 1990).

34 C. Levy, *Gramsci and the Anarchists* (Oxford and New York: Berg, 1999), pp. 85–94; F. Giulietti, *Gli anarchici italiani della Grande Guerra al fascismo* (Milan: Franco Angeli, 2015), part I.

Camillo Berneri described the Russian Soviet Republic as *autodemocrazia*.[35] Antonio Gramsci, who worked closely with the group of anarchists involved in the 1917 Turinese rising, at least until the summer of 1920, imagined the party not as a Leninist vanguard of 'scientific socialists' but as a co-ordinating force guiding the rank and file's factory councils. In Gramsci's anti-Jacobin councilism the factory internal commission, transformed into a dual-power factory council, would carry out Pierre-Joseph Proudhon's 'war of the workshops'. Lenin led by charismatic example, not by dogma or implacable terror.[36] Many anarchists agreed, although Malatesta dissented: Lenin was the new Maximilien Robespierre, who even with good intentions would set in motion a chain of circumstances in which the revolution would devour its own children.[37] In any case, attempts by anarchists and syndicalists to form anti-war or revolutionary alliances were stymied by veteran maximalist socialists and the Young Turks, such as Amadeo Bordiga and Gramsci, who cleaved to the tradition of the party and Marxism, and viewed anarchist ideology with contempt. At war's end, an atmosphere of revolutionary anticipation swept the anarchists and syndicalists, and thrust them back in the forefront of new alliances, reminiscent of the Red Week and grassroots wartime endeavours.

The *Biennio Rosso* was characterized by high levels of unionization, the dramatic growth of the Socialist Party, and the signal role of the socialists and Catholic *popolari* in parliament: the discredited liberal and conservative notables could no longer rule effectively alone. There were northern industrial strikes and factory occupations, massive agrarian strikes in the Po Valley, and widespread peasant land occupations in the south. Large sectors of the *ceti medi* (middle classes), disgruntled and fired up with frustrated nationalist longings, were attracted to authoritarian nationalist populism.[38] Governments during the *Biennio Rosso* were concerned that the anarchists and syndicalists, guided by Malatesta and Armando Borghi, might supply a leadership to co-ordinate social unrest at the grassroots, with newly reborn alliances of the maximalist socialists, the libertarian left, and interventionist national populists threatening the

35 C. Berneri, 'L'autodemocrazia', *Volontà* 1, 1 June 1919.   36 Levy, *Gramsci*, pp. 197–206.
37 Although published elsewhere, Malatesta's complete letter (30 July 1919) to Luigi Fabbri is in the Fabbri Papers of the International Institute of Social History (Amsterdam). For the Italian anarchists on the Russian Revolution, see S. Fedeli, *Una breve illusione. Gli anarchici italiani e la Russia sovietica, 1917–1939* (Milan: Franco Angeli, 1996); F. Bertolucci, *A oriente sorge il sol dell'avvenire. Gli anarchici italiani e la rivoluzione russa 1917–1922* (Pisa: BFS, 2017).
38 R. Vivarelli, *Storia delle origini del fascismo. L'Italia della Grande Guerra alla marcia su Roma* (Bologna: Il Mulino, 1991), vols. I–II.

established order. But once again the anarchists were 'go-betweens' and mobilizers but lacked the numbers or tactical and strategic vision to execute a revolutionary insurrection. By 1920, there were perhaps 30,000 anarchists, with the lion's share affiliated with the Unione Anarchica Italiana (Italian Anarchist Union, UAI) and, on paper, 500,000 trade unionists of the USI, but concurrently the CGL grew to 2,000,000 trade unionists and the PSI to 250,000 party members.

Four issues were congenial for the anarchists in 1919–20. First, inflation stimulated cost-of-living demonstrations and bread riots in the spring of 1919 and early summer of 1920. The spring 1919 riots were the most revolutionary moment because, like the Red Week of 1914, dual power briefly was vested in the hands of the Chambers of Labour. But, just as in the Red Week, the anarchists were ginger groups and notable first-movers in restricted localities but did not master the situation.[39] Secondly, frustrated interventionists melded with older libertarian traditions of anti-militarism and anti-imperialism. The 'Bard of Italy', Gabriele D'Annunzio, led a mutiny to seize control of the contested city of Fiume on the Yugoslav border, and some of his military followers were 'social' interventionists, former anarchists, and syndicalists.[40] With the return of Malatesta at Christmas 1919, a march on Rome was discussed by D'Annunzio's followers, the maximalist wing of the PSI, the anarchists, the USI, the seamen's union, and the anarchist-led railway workers' union. Nothing came of this unlikely alliance, but in June 1920 at Ancona soldiers mutinied against being sent to Albania, and local anarchists (with arms from the base) engaged in a local but doomed insurrection suppressed by naval cannon fire. Thirdly, the arrival of Malatesta served as a catalyst in a highly charged charismatic moment. The elderly anarchist was acclaimed the 'Lenin of Italy' and the 'Socialist Garibaldi', and was central to the formation of the UAI and the launch of a mass daily newspaper in Milan, Umanità Nova (New Humanity), which threatened to overshadow the circulation of the socialist daily Avanti! (Forward!).[41] Fourthly, the growing strength of the factory council movement (with, as I mentioned, anarchist input) led to a stand-off between the engineering and automobile factory owners and the socialist union Federazione Impiegati Operai Metallurgici

39 Levy, 'Italian Anarchism', pp. 61–8.
40 C. Salaris, Alla festa della rivoluzione. Artisti e libertari con D'Annunzio a Fiume (Bologna: Il Mulino, 2002); E. S. Longhi, Alceste De Ambris. L'utopia concreta di un rivoluzionario sindacalista (Milan: Franco Angeli, 2011).
41 C. Levy, 'Charisma and social movements: Errico Malatesta and Italian anarchism', Modern Italy 3, 2 (1998), pp. 205–17; Berti, Errico Malatesta, pp. 639–705.

(Italian Federation of Metal Workers, FIOM) and the USI. A general strike in Turin in April 1920 was followed by a threatened national lock-out and an ensuing occupation of the factories in September, which potentially placed on the table the question of who ruled. Marooned in their factory strong-holds, the occupiers were not co-ordinated with rural unrest or isolated mutinous moments in the armed forces, nor did the occupiers fashion networks to restart production on libertarian principles, as Malatesta sug-gested they do. The reformist FIOM outmanoeuvred the USI and anarchists and, within the FIOM, anarchists were isolated once the Giolitti government fashioned a vague and never-implemented plan for workers' control (a form of corporatist co-determination), while satisfying other bread-and-butter issues.[42]

In October 1920 Giolitti arrested the entire leadership of the USI and the UAI but the socialists did not respond: they were distracted by the wave of motorized fascist attacks on their strongholds in the Po Valley, while the post-war boom turned to bust and worker demobilization was effectuated through unemployment. The anarchists and their allies organized a new transversal alliance to free the hunger-striking Malatesta and comrades from prison or bring them to trial (they were acquitted some months later). But a burgeoning alliance of 'subversives' was cut short by a misdirected anarch-ist terrorist bombing, which killed more than two dozen spectators in a Milanese theatre, and the fascists sacked the Milan offices of *Umanità Nova*.[43] The anarchists and the USI (who on the left were disproportionately affected by fascist squad violence) remained in the forefront of direct action united front reaction to the violence of the fascists. While the internally riven socialists engaged communists in disputes, and the left was simultaneously battered by fascist assaults on crucial cultural and institutional networks, the anarchists helped establish the Arditi del Popolo (anti-fascist veteran officers and soldiers) to defend working-class districts in Rome and elsewhere.[44] Due to the libertarians' connections with disillusioned 'social' interventionists, who included officer veterans of the Great War, military expertise could on

---

42 Levy, *Gramsci*, pp. 142–76, 221.
43 V. Mantovani, *Anarchici alla sbarra. La strage del Diana tra primo dopoguerra e fascismo* (Milan: Il Saggiatore, 2007).
44 G. Furlotti, *Parma libertaria* (Parma: BFA, 2001); A. Sonnessa, 'Working-class defence organization, anti-fascist resistance and the *Arditi del Popolo* in Turin, 1919–1922', *European History Quarterly* 33, 2 (2003), pp. 183–218; V. Gentili, *Roma combattente. Dal 'biennio rosso' agli Arditi del Popolo, la storia mai raccontata delle organizzazioni che inventarono la lotta armata in Italia* (Rome: Alberto Castelvecchi, 2010); M. Rossi, *Arditi, non gendarmi! Dalle trincee alle barricate: arditismo di guerra e arditi del popolo (1917–1922)* (Pisa: BFS, 2011).

occasion counter the favouritism that the forces of law and order bestowed on the fascist squads, so in Parma in 1922 fascists required the outright intervention of the state's threadbare 'monopoly of legitimate violence' to settle the matter. The timidity of the socialists and the sectarianism of the communists stymied the Arditi del Popolo. The anarchists, syndicalists, and the railway workers' union also supported the broadly left Labour Alliance in 1922, but this lacked unity and was too little, too late.

The anarchists were outclassed during the *Biennio Rosso*: inconsistent strength was joined by the limited tradition of armed struggle in liberal Italy (unlike Russia or Spain), and the socialists had a strong tradition of peaceful evangelical politics; thus the cycles of mass demonstrations and riots did not threaten the existence of the liberal constitutional state. But, unlike the cycles of exile and return from the 1880s to the 1920s, the libertarians were confronted with a profoundly different enemy. At first anarchists did not understand Mussolini's movement and his regime: fascism was not merely a preventative counter-revolution, as the anarchist Luigi Fabbri argued in one of the earliest analyses of fascism (1922),[45] nor was Mussolini a new 'Crispi', as Borghi suggested in 1924.[46] The fascists were a militia movement originating in civil society, which colluded with the forces of law and order, and annihilated labour and popular cultural institutions, simultaneously replacing them with fascist counterparts. Fascism was a secular mass movement, which adopted the techniques and cultural tropes of the subversive left married to a secularized religiosity borrowed from the Catholic world, resulting in an authoritarian national populism. Between 1922 and 1926 Mussolini shaped his totalitarian regime, punctuated by failed assassination attempts on his person,[47] including the anarchist Gino Lucetti's near success in 1924, and Anteo Zamboni's far more mysterious affair (1926), which may have been a set-up job.[48] In November 1926, using the pretext of the supposed attempt by the teenager Zamboni (who was lynched), Mussolini destroyed the last vestiges of the liberal state.

45 L. Fabbri, *La controrivoluzione preventiva. Reflessioni sul fascismo* (Bologna: Cappelli, 1922).

46 A. Borghi, *L'Italia tra due Crispi* (Paris: Libreria Internazionale, 1924).

47 C. Levy, 'The Anarchist Assassin in Italian History, 1870s–1930s', in S. Gundle and L. Rinaldi (eds.), *Assassinations and Murder in Modern Italy: Transformations in Society and Culture* (New York and London: Palgrave Macmillan, 2007), pp. 207–21; Diemoz, *A morte il tiranno*, pp. 267–364.

48 B. dalla Casa, *Attentato al duce. Le molte storie del caso Zamboni* (Bologna: Il Mulino, 2001).

In exile, the libertarian left retained its role as link between the socialists and the former disenchanted interventionists or anti-fascist 'Fascists of the First Hour'. They were involved in a series of failed attempts on the Duce and they joined with Carlo Rosselli's federalist and libertarian socialist Giustizia e Libertà (Justice and Freedom) movement, during Catalonia's anarchist season of 1936–7, fighting for the republic before the communist-dominated International Brigades and the militarization of the Spanish anarchist militias made life more uncertain: Camillo Berneri was murdered by Stalinist agents during Barcelona's May Day events of 1937.[49]

Berneri[50] was in the 'class' of the last generation of anarchists before fascism, the last with an organic link to the workers and peasants of Italy. He was the 'Merlino' of the 1920s and 1930s. He analysed mass society and politics employing Freudian psychology in his studies of fascism, Nazism, and Stalinism. He noted a new murderous form of antisemitism which fed off industrialized warfare, the cults of dictators, and totalitarianism. His pen skewered the holy cows of 'worker worship' and dogmatic atheism (he was agnostic). He argued for competitive forms of alternative economics during post-revolutionary reconstruction and thus remained sceptical of anarcho-communism. But he was far from an ivory tower intellectual. In his conspiracies against Mussolini, he was driven from pillar to post: the most deported man in exile Europe. He died an activist intellectual anticipating the libertarian existentialism of Albert Camus and other mavericks after 1945.

As the distinguished historian Claudio Pavone noted, the Resistance (1943–5) – with its mini-partisan republics of the north, clandestine self-management in the factories, the collapse of the Italian state's monopoly of legitimate violence, and initial anti-militarism in its armed units – created the space for an anarchist atmosphere that far outstripped self-declared anarchist resisters.[51] Although the anarchists did not join the national CLN (Comitato di Liberazione Nazionale, National Liberation Committee) or the CLNAI (Comitato di Liberazione Nazionale Alta Italia, National Committee for the Liberation of Northern Italy), they were prominent locally. Anarchist units were folded into socialist brigades, the Action Party, and communist-dominated partisan groups: indeed some anarchists commanded thousands of fighters in the Garibaldi Brigades, and in the old anarchist seedbeds they held executive roles during the liminal period

---

49 L. Di Lembo, *L'anarchismo in Italia dal biennio rosso alla Guerra di Spagna (1919–1939)* (Pisa: BFS, 2001), pp. 161–222.
50 C. De Maria, *Camillo Berneri. Tra anarchismo e liberalismo* (Milan: Franco Angeli, 2004).
51 As quoted in Fabrizio Giulietti, *Il movimento anarchico italiano nella lotta contra il fascismo 1927–1945* (Manduria: Piero Laciata, 2004), pp. 348–9.

spanning the Resistance, the liberation, and the reordering of post-war Italy (Carrara, Pistoia, Imola, and so on.). Some anarchists found common cause with disenchanted dissident communists, socialists, and resistance partisans in the late 1940s, even engaging in brief returns to the mountains in 1946–7,[52] but the era of anarchism after 1945 is a different story and deserves its own discrete treatment further on in this chapter.[53]

Analysis: The Marginalization of the Anarchists and Syndicalists in Italy

When did the anarchists and the syndicalists become marginalized in the broader social and labour movement of Italy? Anarchism began to lose its grip on local political cultures in the 1920s. Anarchism was not biologically reproduced in its heartlands (the local leadership in Carrara, Piombino, and Imola, for example, lost their grip on the Chambers of Labour by the late 1940s); the movement was splintered between returning exiles and internees, between those in the Allied-occupied 'Kingdom of the South' and those who experienced the resistance in the puppet Salò Republic, between the veterans of the Spanish Civil War deeply suspicious of the communists and youngsters who had no such inhibitions. Although there was a brief upsurge of youthful anarchists of the resistance generation (aged between eighteen and twenty-seven), most drifted away from the movement in the late 1940s, being drawn to the communists, the socialists, or their variations once the Cold War broke out. In the anarchist heartlands, the communists married class struggle and national populism and tamed the subversive tradition, sweeping the anarchists aside, albeit local communist leaderships were briefly concerned that the mass of new recruits might be distracted by anarchists who badged themselves libertarian communists. The communists inherited the 'second socialist culture', the institutions such as the Camera del Lavoro, the wave-like spread of nearly insurrectional general strikes, localism, anti-statism, and *operaismo* (workerism), channelling these energies into the party and its cultural and collateral organizations. Global replenishing of activists and financial aid from the anarchist diaspora was cut short by a twenty-year hiatus and could not compete with communist

52 M. Rossi, *Ribelli senza congedo. Rivolte partigiane dopo la liberazione, 1945–1947* (Milan: Zero in Condotta, 2009).
53 Giulietti, *Il movimento anarchico italiano*, pp. 299–387; P. Iuso, *Gli anarchici nell'età repubblicana. Dalla Resistenza agli anni della Contestazione 1943–1968* (Pisa: BFS, 2014); M. De Agostini and F. Schirone, *Per la rivoluzione sociale. Gli anarchici nella Resistenza a Milano (1943–1945)* (Milan: Zero in Condotta, 2015); E. Minuto, *Frammenti dell'anarchismo italiano, 1944–1946* (Pisa: ETS, 2011); Senta, *Utopia e azione*, pp. 167–86.

international networks. Cold War polarities squeezed the anarchists out of the Italian political cockpit. Fascism destroyed the continuity of cultural and institutional memory for the anarchists, habituating Italians to party and corporatist political culture, and at the same time, after the fall of the regime, an acceptance of the democratic republic of parties. Thus the fairly healthy movement of 1945 shrank fast. Unlike notable figures, the anarchist rank and file participated in the referendum to establish the republic and the constitutional constituent assembly, and then many of them participated in the watershed general election of 1948, voting on the left against the Christian Democrats, but never returning to the anarchist movement. The gradual appearance of mass consumer culture, and geographical and social mobility, undermined the viability of the libertarian alternative to the party form, albeit, as we shall see, crises in the Italian Republic would allow anarchist-like political and cultural behaviour to persist.[54]

Women and Italian Anarchism in the Liberal and Fascist Eras

It has been asserted that women played a minor role in the Italian anarchist and syndicalist movements because few were found in the diasporic, national, and provincial leaderships or in the public sphere of congressional and journalist activities. While male social networks pre-dominated, the intellectual, physical, and emotional labour of women managed and organized the lectures, festivals, picnics, choral events, theatrical performances, and activities for May Day (considered a family holiday). Women ran shops, publishing houses, boarding houses (in the diaspora), and other social spaces, which knitted the anarchist community together. During times of repression (in the 1890s, the First World War, the American Red Scare, and the rise of fascism and the fascist regime), women distributed leaflets and newspapers and kept funding drives afloat by canvassing neighbours; women replaced male partners in leading roles during periods of repression.[55]

Excluded from the male gatherings in social circles, cafés, and hostelries, women created all-female circles; invisible to the public gaze and dismissed by male comrades, these were key to the continuity of the movement. At

54 Levy, 'Italian Anarchism', pp. 74–5.
55 L. Bignami, 'Le schiave degli schiavi'. Le 'questione femminile' dal socialismo utopisco all'anarchismo italiano (1825–1917) (Bologna: Clueb, 2011); L. Bignami (ed.), Le donne nel Novecento anarchico italiano: 1871–1956 (Sesto San Giovanni: Mimesis, 2018).

times men deemed it necessary to spread anarchism to women so as to forestall clerical infiltration of the anarchist family: complete oblivion was replaced by grating paternalism, in which men were the keepers, dispensers, and educators of the anarchist tradition to their companions. There were many exceptions to the rule. The partnership of Maria Roda and the Catalan Pedro Estreve, in *La Questione Sociale* (*The Social Question*, published in the 'anarchist town' of Paterson, New Jersey) became a focal point for feminist discussions from 1899 to 1906. On the other hand, *L'Adunata dei Refattari* (*The Gathering of the Refractories*), of a slightly later era, had a noticeable absence of women participants, reflecting a similar trend in the masculinist tropes of syndicalist organizers on both sides of the Atlantic.[56] Violence and violent rhetoric were not limited to men, however; the *galleanisti* were decidedly top-heavy with males but there were certainly some notable women; for example, 'Dynamite Girl', as screaming American headlines dubbed Gabriella Antolini.[57] Elena Melli (Malatesta's partner from 1919 to his death in 1932) was a key if nebulous figure in a circle of young terrorists in the febrile Milan of the *Biennio Rosso*.[58]

Many female anarchists' 'conversion stories' featured a break with the tyrannical Catholic family order or antediluvian education by teaching orders. But transmuted imagery from Catholicism invoked a form of natural spiritualism to promote the 'beautiful idea'. For Leda Rafanelli, anarchists should embrace 'femininity' rather than feminism, thus women (*donne*) were the persona of females in the public sphere but females (*femmine*) connoted their gender and sexuality.[59] There were few examples of the questioning of gender binaries or discussion of lesbianism in women's identity.

Like their male counterparts, youthful friendship circles embodied in the politics of revolutionary friendship and intimacy were steps in women's biographies of anarchist militancy, but the favoured male position could lead to a replication of exploitative contexts in open relationships.[60] Few women anarchists argued for waged housework, and many households were plagued by male violence (although on occasion male anarchists pleaded for

56 J. Guglielmo, *Living the Revolution: Italian Women's Resistance and Radicalism in New York City, 1880–1945* (Chapel Hill: University of North Carolina Press, 2010).
57 F. Manganaro, *Dynamite Girl. Gabriella Antolini e gli anarchici italiani in America* (Rome: New Delphi, 2013).
58 M. Lunardelli, *Dieci pericolissime anarchiche* (Turin: Blu Edizioni, 2012), pp. 92–3.
59 A. Pakieser, *I Belong to Myself: The Life and Writings of Leda Rafanelli* (Oakland, CA: AK Press, 2014).
60 C. B. Angelini, *Amore e anarchica. Francesco Pezzi e Luisa Minguzzi, due ravennati nella seconda metà dell'Ottocento* (Ravenna: Angelo Longo, 2004).

comrades to fight their inner domestic tyrant). However, the biological reproduction of anarchism was, as I have suggested, central to its historical continuity. Many women were born into anarchism or partnered or married an anarchist man. The *Risorgimento* trope of the mother of the nation and the consoler of her menfolk was adapted by the anarchists. Most women anarchists criticized feminism as a ploy by middle- and upper-class women to retain their privileges. The women anarchists, with variations on the theme, advocated human emancipation from the church, capital, and the state and did not theorize an overarching and oppressive patriarchy. Free love meant love not sanctioned by the church or the state; women were allies of men; they were not their slaves but they still might be their consolers and home-makers. The anarchist couple was (in principle if not practice) based on emotional intimacy, erotic pleasure, and a partnership of equals. But some were more equal than others: the libertarian mother was the natural nurturer, the educator of libertarian children; thus women were considered as perfect teachers in anarchist educational experiments.[61]

Women were usually excluded from the decision-making forums of the anarchists, given that these were located in bars, social circles, and centres of conviviality. However, women were very apparent during social protests, from everyday resistance on the shop-floor of textile and spinning mills (in Paterson or Biella) to the rice fields of Vercelli, and most spectacularly in the cost-of-living demonstrations and insurrections in Milan (1898) and Turin (1917).[62] Even with the presence of masculinist syndicalism, successful organizing demanded the participation of women workers. Thus the presence of women in the First International, and its *fasci operai*: Annunziata Gufoni and hundreds if not thousands of cigarette workers in Florence in the 1870s. There were women sections of the International in Florence, Aquila, Imola, Perugia, Carrara, and Prato. Vincenza Matteuzi and Luisa Minguzzi played key roles in the Marchigan–Umbrian and Tuscan Federations respectively. Women were also noticeably prominent in the Fasci Siciliani (see above) in the 1890s.[63] Italian anarchism between 1900 and 1914 cannot be understood without the participation of women as social actors. The intertwining of anti-militarism, neo-Malthusianism, anarchist education informed by Ferrer's educational programmes, and revolutionary syndicalism was reliant upon the efforts of a group of extraordinary women mainly centred in Florence and

---

61 Bignami, '*Le schiave degli schiavi*', pp. 252–80.   62 Levy, 'Centre'.
63 Bignami, '*Le schiave degli schiavi*', pp. 149–200.

Milan (Nella Giacomelli, Leda Rafanelli, Aida Latini, Irma Pagliai, Maria Rossi, and Maria Rygier, to name a few prominent individuals).[64]

Some women could command public events: they were celebrities, orators, and public performers in much the same manner as Emma Goldman, the 'most dangerous woman in America'. They tended to be educated, usually former schoolteachers, the children or partners of renowned male comrades, or of foreign birth or descent. Thus the 'Louise Michel' of Italian anarchism, Maria Rygier, was of Polish middle-class origin, and her abode in Milan served as a melting pot for Futurists, syndicalists, anarchists, and anti-militarists during the years leading up to the Red Week. She was a key figure in the anti-militarist alliance-building, which – as we saw – allowed the anarchists to punch above their weight in June 1914.[65] Leda Rafanelli, an orientalized mixture of Islam and gypsy fancy dress, was joined by a thoughtful presentation of ethically infused Stirnerite pacifist anarchism. Working with her partners in Florence (Luigi Polli) and Milan (Giuseppe Monanni), as a trained typographer and self-taught intellectual, Rafanelli published classic anarchist texts, Futurist drawings and texts (she was also the partner of Carlo Carrà), modern foreign novels, a series of anarchist newspapers, and a vast array of her own novels, poems, and children's stories, many of which were an engaging anarchist 'pulp fiction'.[66] Maria Rossi, the partner of another Milanese anarchist, Carlo Molaschi, helped establish the Ferrer School.[67] The poet Virgilia D'Andrea, a natural replacement for the deceased Pietro Gori, was an equally magnetic and alluring female bard of the anarchist movement.[68]

The liberation of anarchist women in the antebellum and wartime era was halted after 1918. The fascist squads destroyed the anarchist republic of print, a prime space for women anarchists. In the anti-fascist diaspora, Luce

---

64 Bignami, 'Le schiave degli schiavi', p. 231; Fausto Buttà, Living like Nomads: The Milanese Anarchist Movement before Fascism (Newcastle upon Tyne: Cambridge Scholars, 2015), pp. 153, 163, 167–8, 171; M. Scriboni, 'Anarchiche e antimilitarismo in età giolittiana', in E. Bignami (ed.), Le donne nel movimento anarchico italiano (1871–1956) (Milan: Mimesis, 2018), pp. 41–60.

65 B. Montesi, Un 'anarchica monarchica'. Vita di Maria Rygier (1885–1953) (Rome and Naples: Edizioni Scientifiche Italiane, 2013).

66 Pakieser, I Belong to Myself; B. Spackman, Accidental Orientalists: Modern Italian Travellers in Ottoman Lands (Liverpool: Liverpool University Press, 2017), pp. 154–210.

67 M. Granata, Lettere d'amore e d'amicizia. La corrispondenza di Leda Rafanelli, Carlo Molaschi e Maria Rossi per una storia dell'anarchismo milanese (1913–1919) (Pisa: BFS, 2008).

68 F. Piccioli, Virgilia D'Andrea. Storia di un'anarchico (Chieti: Centro Studi Libertari Camillo Di Sciullo, 2002); F. Iacovetta and L. Stradiotti, 'Betrayal, vengeance and the anarchist ideal: Virgilia D'Andrea's radical antifascism in (American) exile', Journal of Women's History 25, 1 (2013), pp. 85–110.

Fabbri[69] and Marie-Louise Berneri[70] have been pictured as the anarchist daughter-torchbearers for renowned anarchist fathers (Luigi Fabbri and Camillo Berneri, respectively). This is extremely misleading. In London, Marie-Louise Berneri became a prominent intellectual figure in the post-war British anarchist movement and the author of studies of wartime bombardment of civilians, the spread of totalitarianism, East and West, and Wilhelm Reich, and an insightful account of utopias. Maria Luisa (or Marie-Louise), her mother Giovanna Caleffi Berneri, and Camillo's mother Adalgisa Fochi Berneri were historical personalities in their own right, not merely the daughter, wife, and mother of Camillo.[71] Adalgisa was a direct connection to the legacies of the radical and romantic strands of the *Risorgimento*. Marie-Louise was essential for the rebirth of British anarchism, and Giovanna was a major figure in Italian anarchism in the post-1945 era as editor of *Volontà* (*Will*). Marie-Louise, Giovanna, and Luce were leading intellectuals, and increasingly they are placed in a framework with their contemporaries Hannah Arendt and Simone Weil, sharing a libertarian anti-totalitarianism and seeking out mavericks who were uncomfortable with East and West.[72]

Italian Anarchism and Syndicalism after 1945: New Contexts, New Paradigms, New Anarchism(s)

From the 1940s to the 1990s, certain parameters limited the expansion of self-declared anarchism in the Italian context. The language, politics, and vision of Marxism predominated on the left. Thus the dissident communists of the 1940s, the disillusioned communists after the events in Hungary in 1956, the New Left of the 1950 to 1970s, and even most of the unorthodox varieties of Workers' Autonomy (Autonomia Operaia) in the 1970s, as well as the militarized left-wing guerrilla groups of the 'Years of Lead', endorsed Marxism. Most of the non-terrorist left eventually endorsed electoral

---

69 M. Rago, *Tra la storia e la libertà. Luce Fabbri e l'anarchismo contemparaneo* (Milan: Zero in Condotta, 2008).
70 C. De Maria (ed.), *Maria Luisa Berneri e l'anarchismo inglese* (Reggio Emilia: Biblioteca Panizzi, 2013); G. Sacchetti, 'Una donna contro i totalitarismi. Maria Luisa Berneri (Arezzo 1918–Londra 1949)', in Bignami (ed.), *Le donne nel movimento anarchico italiano (1871–1956)*, pp. 99–116.
71 See also Chapter 18 in this volume.
72 C. De Maria, *Una famiglia anarchica. La vita dei Berneri tra affetti, impegno ed esilio nell'Europa del Novecento* (Rome: Viella, 2019).

strategies and the party form; support for the dictatorship of the proletariat was universal among these groups.[73]

On the other hand, mass 'spontaneous' movements of peasants, workers, and, later, students, the radicalized white-collar workers, and young professionals of '1968' engaged in events that echoed, if in new contexts, the contentious risings of 1898, the Red Week of 1914, the *Biennio Rosso* (1919–20), and aspects of the Resistance. This is evident after the failed assassination attempt on the leader of the PCI, Palmiro Togliatti, in 1948;[74] the violent demonstrations in Genoa, Reggio Emilia, and elsewhere when the Christian Democrats attempted to form a government with the neo-fascists in 1960;[75] and the revolt of car workers in Turin in 1962.[76] These events foreshadowed the much more widespread mass movements of students in 1968 and workers in 1969 – the 'Hot Autumn' of mass production 'Fordist' young southern migrant workers in the northern factories – both of which led to Italy's 'Creeping May of the 1970s'[77] and the movement of 1977, an amalgam of precarious students and workers.[78]

Through to the early 1990s, the entire New Left, whether it liked it or not, was affected by the gravitational pull of the communists and the socialists and their various and numerous offshoots and factions. The disenchantment with the Stalinists and post-Stalinists after 1956, the failure of the socialists to carry out reforms as the junior partners of the Christian Democrats in the 1960s, and the rise and fall of the communists' 'Historic Compromise' with the

---

73 For a general overview of Italy since 1945, see P. Ginsborg, *A History of Contemporary Italy: Society and Politics 1943–1988* (London: Penguin Books, 1990); P. Ginsborg, *Italy and Its Discontents, 1980–2001* (London: Allen Lane, 2001); J. Foot, *The Archipelago: Italy since 1945* (London: Bloomsbury, 2018).
74 Witness the insurrectional risings at the old anarchist strongholds of Piombino and Abbadia San Salvatore. See M. Ilari, *Parole in libertà. Il giornale anarchico Umanità Nova (1944–1953)* (Milan: Zero in Condotta, 2009), pp. 74–5.
75 There was a small but vibrant presence of anarchists in Liguria and Genoa during the 1950s. For the events, see P. Cooke, *Luglio 1960. Tambroni e la repression fallita* (Milan: Teti, 2000); M. Franzinelli and A. Giacone, *1960. L'Italia sull'orlo della guerra civile: il racconto di una pagina oscura della Repubblica* (Milan: Mondadori, 2020).
76 The anarchist newspaper *L'Agitazione del Sud* noted the participation of a new type of uncontrollable young southern worker in Turin. See Senta, *Utopia e azione*, p. 205; and D. Lanzardo, *La rivolta di Piazza di Statuto* (Milan: Feltrinelli, 1979).
77 In reference to the events of May 1968 in France, the student and worker occupations, which nearly brought down the Gaullist regime.
78 For '1968', the 'Hot Autumn of 1969', and Italy's 'Creeping May' of the 1970s, see S. Tarrow, *Democracy and Disorder: Protest and Politics in Italy, 1965–1975* (Oxford: Clarendon, 1989); R. Lumley, *States of Emergency: Cultures of Revolt in Italy from 1968 to 1978* (London: Verso, 1990); S. Wright, *Storming Heaven: Class Composition and Struggle in Italian Autonomist Marxism* (London: Pluto, 2002); A. Ventrone, *Vogliamo tutto. Perché due generazioni hanno creduto nella rivoluzione, 1960–1988* (Bari: Laterza, 2012).

Christian Democrats in the 1970s offered opportunity structures for the New Left. At the same time, an anarchist-like *Zeitgeist* manifested itself in direct action and self-management movements in factories and popular neighbourhoods: in contrast to the established unions, workers who were organized at the grassroots in *Comitati unitari di base* (CUBs or Unitary Base Committees), together with students grouped into assemblies, demanded egalitarian wages, launched scattergun internal short-term work stoppages, engaged in sabotage, promoted rent strikes and price self-reduction movements in popular neighbourhoods, and so on.

So, to summarize, self-declared anarchists played a complex role in shaping the direction and tone of politics in Italy but they were part and parcel of a left culture which, however, had its centre of gravity in Marxist parties. But in terms of formal membership for both the anarchists and the New Left, and of votes for New Left parties that engaged in electoral politics, they all were as minnows to the Communist whale. The combined membership of the galaxy of New Left and dissident left parties never exceeded several tens of thousands, and when they ventured into electoral politics they never exceeded, on the generous side, 10 per cent of the national vote.

There were two souls in the movements of the 1960s and 1970s. On the one hand, the theorists and popularizers of the various iterations of autonomy argued that Italy was the weak link in Western capitalism, and revolution was possible in Europe; one did not have to wait for or serve as allies to the Third World, so long as it happened in the here and now before the Leviathan carceral and cybernetic imperialist state shut down further possibilities for action.[79]

On the other hand, the meaning of 1968 and its aftermath can also be interpreted as the de-fascistization and democratization of civil society, or in other words the expansion of social and political citizenship beyond the formal and patchily realized promises of the post-fascist constitution. The struggle to democratize civil society was associated with the rise of New Social Movements, which interacted with political parties and the state, and employed the national referendum to achieve change.[80] The result was the Workers' Statute, the legalization of divorce and abortion, the critique of total institutions, such as the asylum, the spread of the anti-psychiatry movement,[81] and the democratization of the school and the university, albeit the lack of

79 Ventrone, *Vogliamo tutto*, pp. 333–5.
80 D. Della Porta, *Movimenti collettivi e sistema politico in Italia, 1960–1995* (Bari: Laterza, 1996).
81 J. Foot, *The Man Who Closed the Asylums: Franco Basaglia and the Revolution in Mental Health Care* (London: Verso, 2015).

funds for the latter meant the students of the mass university, in the wake of the widening of participation from 1969, were short-changed.[82] This struggle can also be seen in the fight by libertarian architects against planning blight and unbridled motorization in the land of Fiat and the Agnellis, or the formation of a liberated culture that was secular but also attractive to Catholic dissidents. Within this context, the anarchists had limited but important influence.

Italian Second Wave feminism had an anarchist valence in its consciousness-raising affinity groups, the critique of the hegemonic patriarchy as a form of male power not dependent on the control of the means of production, wages for housework,[83] and a probing of male violence, a critique of double standards and masculinist presuppositions of that nucleus of Italian life, the family. Many feminists were escapees from the male-dominated Marxist New Left; they refused their roles as 'angels of the mimeograph machine'. Unfortunately, the anarchist organizations were equally plagued and dominated by male chauvinist 'know-it-alls'.[84]

In what follows I will present an overview of Italian anarchism's organizational structure after 1945 and return for a closer look at the direct effect of anarchism on the 1960s and 1970s. The Federazione Anarchica Italiana (Italian Anarchist Federation, FAI) was founded at the Carrara Congress of 1945. Various libertarian communist splits occurred almost immediately, but the next major breakaway was the Gruppi Anarchici di Azione Proletaria (Anarchist Groups of Proletarian Action, GAAP) in 1951. A further two groups were established in 1965: the Gruppi di Iniziativa Anarchica (Groups of Anarchist Initiative, GIA) and the Gruppi Giovanili Anarchici Federati (Federated Anarchist Youth Groups, GGAF), transformed in 1970 to the Gruppi Anarchici Federati (Federated Anarchist Groups, GAF). Over these twenty-five years, longstanding and cross-cutting divisions were apparent: class-based militants v. humanists, anti-organizationalists v. federal organizationalists, individualists v. collectivists, and classical anarchists v. the New Anarchists.[85]

---

82 S. J. Hilwig, *Italy and 1968: Youthful Unrest and Democratic Culture* (Basingstoke and New York: Palgrave Macmillan, 2009); B. Mercer, *Student Revolt in 1968: France, Italy and West Germany* (Cambridge: Cambridge University Press, 2019).

83 P. Cunninghame, '"Hot Autumn": Italy's Factory Councils and Autonomous Workers' Assemblies, 1970s', in I. Ness and D. Azzellini (eds.), *Ours to Master and to Own: Workers' Control from the Commune to the Present* (Chicago: Haymarket Books, 2011), pp. 322–37.

84 Senta, *Utopia e azione*, p. 220.

85 G. Sacchetti, 'Eretici e libertari. Il movimento anarchico in Italia (1945–1973)', *Diacronie* 9, 1 (2012), pp. 1–16; Iuso, *Gli anarchici nell'età repubblicana*; F. Giulietti, *L'anarchismo in Italia, 1945–1960* (Casalvelino Scalo: Galzerano, 2018).

By 1950, if truth be told, the local federal units of the FAI were run by a restricted group of activists, with the rest of the membership becoming increasingly passive. The young militants of the GAAP sought to marry their anarchism with varieties of dissident communism and, most interestingly, the rediscovery of the council communist tradition of the *Biennio Rosso*, with a libertarian reading of the young Antonio Gramsci to boost their theory.[86] But the organization failed to make headway in the polarized and balkanized trade union federations of the high Cold War.

The crisis in the Communist Party after the Soviet assault on the Hungarian Revolution in 1956, Algeria and Cuba, and the transformative powers of the Italian Miracle were the background to a generational shift in anarchism. The Federazione Anarchica Giovanile Italiana (Italian Anarchist Youth Federation, FAGI) and the GGAF played key roles in the dissemination of a politicized, if initially restricted youth culture, which was the forerunner to the student movement of 1968 and the long 1970s. Their 'neo-anarchism' questioned established forms of sexuality (but not in practice masculinity and masculinism) and promoted cheeky insubordination, which began to 'infect' Italian society. FAGI staged 'Happenings', anti-conscription, anti-Vietnam War, anti-fascist, and anti-Franco demonstrations:[87] they promoted methods of direct democracy via assemblies, soon to be widespread in universities and factories.

But these unorthodox indulgences were met with a dusty response by the old guard of the FAI. In turn the young anarchists mocked their elders: this was the anarchists' own 'generation gap', made more glaring because the forty-year-olds were missing, the lost generation of the vanished youth of the Resistance. It all came to a head at the international anarchist conference held in Carrara in September 1968. A generational turnover occurred shortly afterwards; youth renewed the FAI and its newspaper, *Umanità Nova*: in 1968 20 per cent of those who attended were deemed youth, but at the 1971 congress that had risen to 80 per cent.[88]

The movement of 1977, a 'strange movement of strange students', recruited its base from the generation which came of age, or played a secondary role, in the events of 1968 and 1969.[89] The base for '1977' consisted

86 P. C. Masini, *Antonio Gramsci e l'Ordine Nuovo visti da un libertario* (Livorno: L'impulso edizioni, 1956).
87 In 1962, young anarchists kidnapped the Spanish consul in Genoa in order to prevent the imminent execution of a Spanish anarchist. At their trial they were acquitted.
88 Senta, *Utopia e azione*, p. 215.
89 G. Lerner et al., *Uno strano movimento di strani studenti* (Milan: Feltrinelli, 1978).

of radicalized secondary school students and entrants into the creaking post-1969 universities, and the most militant workers from hotspots such as the immense Mirafiori car plant in Turin, Pirelli in Milan, and the chemical plants in Porto Marghera on the Venetian lagoon, which did not accept the replacement of the free-wheeling factory assemblies with union-dominated factory councils.[90]

A new generation of anarchists arose in the context of this confused and rapidly shifting scenario.[91] This anarchism of affinity groups (exemplified in the GAF), squats, and street warfare attracted the young and very young, who mixed the older ideology of the veterans, New Marxism, autonomism, and Situationism. These 'children' of 1968 promoted new analyses and new political languages. They spread their anarchism via street graffiti, theatre, readings, concerts, and the galaxy of free radio stations (which had sprung up after a ruling in the Constitutional Court threw out the state monopoly of broadcasting).[92] Mass youth culture was the sea in which they swam. The Italian version of the politicized 'Woodstock Nation' of the American Yippies of the late 1960s arrived in Italy when its American incarnation was already becoming part of the nostalgia industry in the USA. Thus Metropolitan Indians, fancy dress and orientalized 'American Indians', carried out Dadaist 'Happenings' and poked fun at the pious militancy of the Leninist New Left: Potere Operaio (Workers' Power), was renamed Potere Dromedario (Dromedary Power).[93]

The other source of mobilization was the constant clashes with neo-fascists and the overwhelming fear that the state would mount a fascist/authoritarian coup. The 'red thread' narrative of a sinister state-sponsored 'Strategy of Tension' or fear[94] was embodied in the fates of the Milanese 'anarchist ballet dancer' Pietro Valpreda and the 'martyred' railway worker Giuseppe Pinelli,[95] yet this story was narrated most loudly and effectively by the New Left, not the organized anarchist movement.

The far-right 'Strategy of Tension' sought to discredit and generate fear in the left, finish off the Christian Democrat/socialist government in the 1960s,

90 Cunninghame, '"Hot Autumn"'.
91 A. Cardella and L. Fenech, *Senza tregua. Per una storia della Federazione anarchica italiana dal 1970 al 1980* (Milan: Zero in Condotta, 2005).
92 D. Pollard, 'Radio Alice and Italy's Movement of 1977: Polyvocality, Sonority and Space', *Sound Studies*, 7, 2 (2021), pp. 151–72, DOI: 10.1080/20551940.2020.1759979.
93 Ventrone, *Vogliamo tutto*, p. 349.
94 A. Ventrone, *La strategia della paura. Eversione e stragismo del Novecento* (Milan: Mondadori, 2019).
95 L. Lanza, *Secrets and Bombs* (Hastings, UK: Christie Books, 2012).

and prevent the communists from being too close to power in the 1970s. The aim was either to precipitate a fascist government on the model of the Greek colonels or Augusto Pinochet's Chile, or to instal an authoritarian version of Gaullism, a 'guided' democracy in which the Communist Party and the New Left would be banned. A series of bomb blasts caused widespread casualties in piazzas, banks, railway carriages, and railway stations.

In the wake of the 'Hot Autumn', on 12 December 1969, sixteen persons died and eighty-seven were wounded in a series of bomb blasts at banks in the centre of Milan. Valepreda was imprisoned and released several years later, whereas Pinelli 'accidentally' fell to his death from police headquarters after three days of interrogation. After countless twists and turns, the Supreme Court of Cassation in 2005 acknowledged that the real culprits were neo-fascist terrorists who worked with the Italian secret services.

The anarchists mobilized the Italian left in Milan and elsewhere. The events were reminiscent of the Dreyfus Affair and the Sacco–Vanzetti campaign. But the movement of 1977 was isolated from the broader streams of Italian society, which had assimilated the waves of democratization and consumer subjectivity that the 1960s had touched off.

The promotion of 'class egoism' in the Fordist factory and 'radical subjectivity' in the 'social factory' had paradoxical effects, including the undermining of traditional forms of working-class solidarity, which paved the way for a hedonistic individualism of the consumer-driven 1980s.[96] However, the world of precarious labour, small to medium-sized enterprises, robots in Fiat plants, and 'immaterial labour' – the dawn of globalized capitalism – did demonstrate the prescience of the autonomists' predictions.[97] The 1968 movement promised a better world, while '1977' advanced the ethic of negativity or 'weak thought'; thus the aim of these politics was not militancy and sacrifice, but the realization of one's own needs and desires as well as a libertarian critique of the Leviathan state.

Since the 1990s, the Marxist whale has disappeared, and the Italian anarchists of the late twentieth and twenty-first centuries have been part and parcel of New and the Newest Social Movements.[98] Prefiguration, communitarianism, affinity groups, and the practice of Temporary Autonomous Zones

96 P. Morando, *Dancing Days, 1978–1979. I due anni che hanno cambiato l'Italia* (Bari: Laterza, 2009).
97 Cunninghame, '"Hot Autumn"'.
98 A. Poma and T. Gravante, 'Beyond the state and capitalism: the current anarchist movement in Italy', *Journal for the Study of Radicalism* 11, 1 (2017), pp. 1–27. For an interpretation that argues that anarchism is 'dead', see G. Berti, *Contro la storia. Cinquant'anni di anarchismo in Italia (1962–2012)* (Milan: Biblion, 2016).

inform their practice and ideology. Anarchists have been present in the grassroots unions, COBAS (Confederazione dei Comitati di Base, Confederation of Base Committees), the descendants of the CUBs of the 1960s/1970s, in the squatted urban social centres (*centri sociali*), in the alter-global movements (at the notorious harsh repression of the mass demonstration against the G-8 in Genoa in 2001), and their successors, the post-2008–10 anti-austerity and anti-Euro movements. They are present in movements which have embraced 'Exodus', the rural communes such as Urupia and those of Genuino Clandestino (an alter-global organic farming movement).

The Newest Social Movements are informed by self-organization, anti-hierarchical decision-making via consensus, direct action, and a DIY ethos. Militants can be found in territorially based movements to prevent the high-speed train line from Lyon to north-west Italy and the bridge from Calabria to Sicily[99] and anti-racist, no-borders, and refugee rescue projects on land and in the Mediterranean.

Italy has witnessed a surge of populism since the 1990s, which has thrived on a politics of anti-politics, a critique of *partitocrazia* ('partitocracy') and manipulations of the 'elites', a discontent with an opaque judicial system and an inefficient civil service, and lacklustre economic performance, but anarchism and the populisms of the twenty-first century are like chalk and cheese: populism relies on authoritarian leadership, cronyism, the failure to differentiate the public from the private, and the scapegoating of defenceless 'Others'.[100] The anarchists' political ethics of socialized subjectivity, prefiguration, and practising quotidian democracy on the ground are profoundly different from the populists' offer.

Further Reading

Giulietti, Fabrizio, *Gli anarchici italiani della Grande Guerra al fascismo* (Milan: Franco Angeli, 2015).

Il movimento anarchico italiano nella lotta contro il fascismo, 1927–1945 (Manduria and Rome: Piero Lacaita, 2004).

Storia degli anarchici italiani in età giolittiana (Milan: Franco Angeli, 2012).

Levy, Carl, 'Italian Anarchism, 1870–1926', in D. Goodway (ed.), *For Anarchism: History, Theory, and Practice* (London: Routledge, 1989), pp. 24–78.

Masini, Pier Carlo, *Storia degli anarchici italiani dal Bakunin a Malatesta* (Milan: Rizzoli, 1974).

99 D. Della Porta and G. Piazza, *Voices of the Valley, Voices of the Straits: How Protest Creates Communities* (New York and Oxford: Berghahn Books, 2008).

100 M. Tarchi, *Italia populista. Dal Qualunquismo a Beppe Grillo* (Bologna: Il Mulino, 2015).

Storia degli anarchici italiani nell'epoca degli attentati (Milan: Rizzoli, 1981).

Pernicone, Nunzio, *Italian Anarchism, 1864–1892* (Oakland, CA: AK Press, 2009).

Pernicone, Nunzio, and Fraser M. Ottanelli, *Assassins against the Old Order: Italian Anarchist Violence in Fin-de-Siècle Europe* (Urbana: University of Illinois Press, 2018).

Santarelli, Enzo, *Il socialismo anarchico in Italia* (Milan: Feltrinelli, 1977).

Senta, Antonio, *Utopia e azione. Per una storia dell'anarchismo in Italia (1848–1984)* (Milan: Eléuthera, 2015).

18

Anarchism and Syndicalism in the United Kingdom

DAVID GOODWAY

For a century and a half anarchists have been overwhelmingly socialist, despite the concurrent existence of small numbers of individualists in Europe and the USA. Yet a fruitful, though neglected, approach to under-standing anarchism is to recognize its thoroughly socialist critique of capital-ism, while emphasizing that this has been combined with a liberal critique of socialism, anarchists being united with liberals in their advocacy of autono-mous associations and the freedom of the individual, even exceeding them in their opposition to statism. The apparent paradox, perhaps particularly for the British, is therefore that anarchism has historically been a type of social-ism but simultaneously closely related to liberal thought. This bipolar nature of anarchism helps, in fact, to explain anarchism's failure to flourish in the United Kingdom, with its deeply entrenched liberal traditions and a strong radical liberalism. John Stuart Mill, the great theorist of liberalism, and Herbert Spencer, a major exponent of laissez-faire individualism, whose writings appealed immensely to the Spanish anarchists, can be – and have been – rightly designated as 'libertarians'.[1] Victorian liberalism, shading into libertarianism, was the dominant ideology in Britain during the second half of the nineteenth century; and working-class liberalism was a mass force, the radical electors enfranchised in 1867 and 1884 voting enthusiastically for the Gladstonian party. In these circumstances, the revival of socialism saw those hostile to the existing order largely opting for its statist forms, social demo-cratic and/or Marxist.

Consequently, anarchism as a social movement never amounted to much in Britain, except among the Yiddish-speaking Jews of East London and – for reasons still to be explored – on Clydeside, where a tenacious libertarian tradition existed in the twentieth century among Glaswegian workers. It was

---

1 P. Marshall, *Demanding the Impossible: A History of Anarchism* (London: Harper Perennial, 2008), pp. 163–8.

in countries with despotic or centralizing states that anarchism flourished: France after the bloody suppression in 1871 of the Commune and the criminalizing of anarchist activity with *les lois scélérates* of 1893–4; the ram-shackle, semi-feudal empires of Russia, where political parties and trade unions were completely illegal before 1906 and unions only a little less so until the February Revolution, and Spain, where the Confederación Nacional del Trabajo (National Confederation of Labour, CNT) was banned between 1923 and 1930; and Italy with a heavy-handed new state, attempting to assert itself in the aftermath of the unification of 1870 and periodically subjecting anarchist militants to *domicilio coatto* – confinement in prison or banishment to penal islands – especially from 1894 to 1900. The liberal, minimal statism of Britain, even though the powers of the state, both national and local, were increasing after 1867, principally for reasons of social reform, was situated in a world apart from these turbulent and sanguinary histories.

The other common characteristic of the anarchist cultures is that they were embedded in the artisan response to industrialization, first in France, followed by Italy, and finally, in the early twentieth century, by Russia and Spain. The equivalent period in Britain ran from the Jacobinism of the 1790s through Luddism to Chartism, but had terminated with the latter's disappearance after 1848. Had anarchist, or indeed Marxist, ideology been available in those decades British history might have been very different, but it would still have had to contend with the constitutionalism of the 'free-born Englishman' (or true-born Briton), as depicted with typical brilliance by E. P. Thompson.

Although for these reasons mass, proletarian anarchism failed to erupt in the British Isles, there was all the same a distinguished minority intellectual, overwhelmingly literary, anarchist – and rather broader and still more distinguished libertarian – tradition. William Morris, Edward Carpenter, G. D. H. Cole, and George Orwell were notable libertarian socialists; the writings of Oscar Wilde and the still underrated John Cowper Powys were strikingly original; while Herbert Read, Alex Comfort, and Colin Ward identified as anarchists. Morris became a pre-eminent libertarian, near-anarchist thinker, while strenuously distancing himself from anarchism, his theoretical achievement contrasting starkly with the practical insignificance of the surrounding movement.

William Morris

The first indigenous anarchist groups and journals in Britain date only from the 1880s and the belated revival of socialism – 'revival' because Owenite socialism had flourished in the 1830s and 1840s. London, in particular, afforded sanctuary in the late Victorian and Edwardian decades for militants from continental Europe fleeing repression by their governments, and there was much interaction between them and the tiny numbers of local anarchists, whom initially they often converted. Henry Seymour, a Proudhonist and admirer of Benjamin Tucker, brought out the *Anarchist* in 1885–6. Peter Kropotkin, who from 1877 had lived in Switzerland and France – including three years in a French prison – moved to England in 1886, when he co-founded *Freedom* with Charlotte Wilson and others. The Labour Emancipation League had been founded in East London in 1882 and, while never calling itself anarchist, was always libertarian socialist and became anti-parliamentarian, as expressed in Joseph Lane's notable *An Anti-Statist, Communist Manifesto* of 1887. Meanwhile the Democratic Federation had been inaugurated by H. M. Hyndman in 1881, became committed to socialism in 1883, and modified its name to the Social Democratic Federation (SDF) the following year, when the Labour Emancipation League began working with it. The SDF was to be Marxist, whereas the Fabian Society, dating from 1884 and of which Wilson was also a prominent member, rapidly developed its peculiarly British form of evolutionary socialism, rejecting Marxist economics – accepting instead the neo-classical marginalist criticism of the labour theory of value – and appealing to the equally home-grown political and philosophical example of the utilitarians of the first half of the nineteenth century.

Morris had joined the Democratic Federation, as it still was, early in 1883 and was almost immediately elected treasurer, just before the June conference at which a socialist programme was adopted. Already recognized as a designer and craftsman of genius, concurrently he was an acclaimed poet. Perry Anderson has astutely related the quality of his utopian vision to the fact that he was

> a practising artist of the highest gifts, for whom ordinary work was daily creation ... Moreover, the major fields of Morris' practice were plastic arts, which are themselves distinctive within the forms of aesthetic composition for eluding the division between mental and manual labour. Yet at the same time, he was also a poet and a writer. Thus one might say that in his figurations of the future, Morris was able to draw on unique resources in his *present*, which brought him tangibly nearer to the conditions he imagined than any of his communist contemporaries: secure wealth, creative work, polymathic skills.[2]

2 P. Anderson, *Arguments within English Marxism* (London: Verso, 1980), pp. 163–4 (emphasis in original).

Morris began to deliver in 1877 speeches and lectures in forceful, unadorned language on art, art and society, and finally socialism. He gave the last in the year of his death, 1896, bringing the total to 197. To understand the content of the lectures and Morris' thought generally, the indebtedness to John Ruskin needs to be appreciated. 'The Nature of Gothic', a chapter in *The Stones of Venice*, Morris considered so important that he printed it separately in 1892 as one of his Kelmscott Press books. In his discussion of the worker's place in the productive process Ruskin rivals for radical profundity Karl Marx's analysis of alienation:

> You must either make a tool of the creature, or a man of him. You cannot make both. Men were not intended to work with the accuracy of tools, to be precise and perfect in all their actions. If you will have that precision out of them, and make their fingers measure degrees like cog-wheels, and their arms strike curves like compasses, you must unhumanize them ... On the other hand, if you will make a man of the working creature, you cannot make a tool. Let him but begin to imagine, to think, to try to do something worth doing; and the engine-turned precision is lost at once. Out come all his roughness, all his dulness, all his incapability ... but out comes the whole majesty of him also.[3]

In his 1892 preface, Morris comments that Ruskin's teaching is 'that art is the expression of man's pleasure in labour; that it is possible for man to rejoice in his work ... and lastly, that unless man's work once again becomes a pleasure to him ... all but the worthless must toil in pain, and therefore live in pain'. Morris concludes that 'the hallowing of labour by art is the one aim for us at the present day' and 'if Politics are to be anything less than an empty game ... it is towards this goal of the happiness of labour that they must make'.[4] It was therefore left for Morris to go beyond Ruskin, using the latter's thought as a foundation for the highly distinctive socialism he was to develop himself.

The principal drawback to the SDF was Hyndman's autocratic personality; and so it was that, as early as 1884, the organization was split, with Morris leading a breakaway including Eleanor Marx, Edward Aveling, Walter Crane, and Joseph Lane, complaining of arbitrary rule, to form on the last day of the year the Socialist League. Karl Marx had died in 1883, but Friedrich Engels supported the dissidents from the outside. The weekly *Commonweal* was

---

3 J. Ruskin, *The Stones of Venice*, 3 vols. (New York: Merrill and Baker, n.d. [1851–3]), vol. II, pp. 161–2.
4 May Morris, *William Morris: Artist, Writer, Socialist*, 2 vols. (Oxford: Basil Blackwell, 1936), vol. I, pp. 292–3.

Fig. 18.1   William Morris. (Stock Photo/Getty Images.)

launched as the organ of the Socialist League, with Morris both editing and financing it.

In the early years of the socialist revival, boundaries between the various societies were blurred and there was much overlapping. An example is Charlotte Wilson, the first editor of *Freedom*, also being a member of the Fabian Society. From the mid-1880s this fluidity began to change considerably as, for instance, Fabian doctrine was elaborated. Similarly, Morris between 1885 and 1890, the years he was involved with the Socialist League, thought through his socialism. This he did in his lectures and the prolific journalism he contributed to *Commonweal*, preceded by a year's worth to the SDF's paper *Justice*. He had already read Marx's *Capital* in the French translation, he continued to study it, and E. P. Thompson was convincingly to claim him for Marxism. That is, Morris' mature socialism both fits within and extends Marx's thought, and George Bernard Shaw, who came to know him well from 1884, had no doubt that he was 'on the side of Karl Marx *contra mundum*'.[5]

During 1890 Morris serialized in *Commonweal* his great utopian novel, *News from Nowhere; or, An Epoch of Rest*, in reaction to the state-socialist and highly regimented society depicted in *Looking Backward* by the American Edward Bellamy. It is unique as a utopia written by a major socialist theorist and exceptionally unusual as a utopia in which it would actually be pleasurable to live. 'Nowhere' is indeed a stateless society without government and representative institutions.

There can be no doubt that *News from Nowhere* depicts an anarchist society; but Morris was not an anarchist. The novel opens with William Guest returning from a meeting of 'the League' at which 'there were six persons present, and consequently six sections of the party were represented, four of which had strong but divergent Anarchist opinions'.[6] Morris *knew* about anarchism, for anarchists became preponderant in the Socialist League in the late 1880s, and such was his disagreement with them that he withdrew in 1890. Thereafter his political activity was restricted to a local body, the Hammersmith Socialist Society (formerly the Hammersmith branch of the Socialist League). He frequently, consistently, and vehemently denied that he was an anarchist. He described himself as a 'Communist' and, although he maintained that 'Communist-Anarchists' often could not 'differentiate themselves from Communists', he considered that 'Anarchism and Communism, notwithstanding our friend Kropotkin, are incompatible in principle.' He also stated, with some bitterness: 'Such finish to what of education in practical Socialism that I am capable of I received ... from some of my Anarchist friends, from whom I learned, quite against their intention, that Anarchism was impossible.'[7]

Morris gave two sets of reasons for his rejection of anarchism: its violence and its individualism. Although he appreciated that not every anarchist advocated extreme violence, he had no sympathy with the terrorism that engulfed anarchism internationally in the 1880s and 1890s, nor with the obsessive emphasis on violent revolution as opposed to propaganda by the

5 George Bernard Shaw, 'Morris as I Knew Him', ibid., vol. II, p. ix.
6 May Morris (ed.), *The Collected Works of William Morris*, 24 vols. (London: Longmans, Green, 1910–15), vol. XVI, p. 3.
7 W. Morris, *Political Writings: Contributions to* Justice *and* Commonweal, *1883–1890*, ed. N. Salmon (Bristol: Thoemmes Press, 1994), p. 448; J. B. Glasier, *William Morris and the Early Days of the Socialist Movement* (London: Longmans, Green, 1921), p. 63; May Morris (ed.), *Collected Works of William Morris*, vol. XXIII, p. 278 ('How I Became a Socialist').

word: 'For I cannot for the life of me see how [the principles of anarchy], which propose the abolition of compulsion, can admit of promiscuous slaughter as a means of converting people.'[8] Both the Socialist League and eventually *Commonweal* were to be extinguished, as early as the mid-1890s, through their association with and support for terrorism. (The brother-in-law of a leading member of the league was killed in 1894 when his bomb exploded prematurely outside Greenwich Observatory; and previously entrapment at Walsall by an *agent provocateur* resulted in swingeing prison sentences for four men enamoured of dynamite.) And while Morris celebrated *individuality* – for its self-restraint, fearlessness, tolerance, and pride – he abhorred the selfishness and egotism which he considered *individualism* entailed.

Morris was then an anti-statist and during the 1880s he eschewed parliamentarianism. His lecture of 1887, 'The Policy of Abstention', although only delivered twice and never published in his lifetime, was to be commended by Herbert Read as 'the best statement of the case against parliamentary action ever made in English'.[9] Although he moderated his opposition to parliamentary participation from 1890 with the thwarting of his revolutionary hopes and his abandonment of the Socialist League, he did so reluctantly and retained extreme distaste for conventional politics.

Despite the early disappearance of the Socialist League, Morris' influence was considerable within the British working-class movement. Tom Mann, indefatigable socialist and trade unionist militant over half a century, had never been a member of the Socialist League, but he was deeply indebted to Morris, whom he acknowledged as enabling him to 'get a really healthy contempt for Parliamentary institutions and scheming politicians'. Although he was appointed national secretary of the newly formed Independent Labour Party (ILP), he never believed in political action as the exclusive means of attaining socialism – and concluded his 1894 pamphlet *What the ILP Is Driving At* with the 'grand words of William Morris, "Come hither, lads and hearten/for a tale there is to tell/of the wonderful days a-coming/when all shall be better than well . . . "'[10] The historian of British syndicalism considers that the principal indigenous influence on emergent syndicalism, 1900–10, came from 'the anti-state traditions of William Morris and the Socialist League'. And Mann, who was to become the leading syndicalist in Britain,

8 *The Collected Letters of William Morris*, 4 vols., ed. N. Kelvin (Princeton: Princeton University Press, 1984–96), vol. IV, p. 113.
9 H. Read, *The Politics of the Unpolitical* (London: George Routledge, 1943), p. 3.
10 C. Tsuzuki, *Tom Mann, 1856–1941: The Challenges of Labour* (Oxford: Clarendon Press, 1991), p. 74; J. White, *Tom Mann* (Manchester: Manchester University Press, 1991), p. 88.

was to write in 1914: 'Grand old William Morris taught the true doctrine, and slow though we are, there are multitudes not far from salvation. To be free from state dictatorship to function as joint co-operative controllers of industry through our industrial organizations – this is the conception needed.'[11]

There was always ready acceptance and indeed prominence of women in anarchist groups. Charlotte Wilson and, in the 1940s, Marie-Louise Berneri occupied especially prominent roles, although also notable were Louisa Bevington, a prolific contributor to the anarchist press, yet who died as early as 1895, and Nannie Dryhurst, translator of Kropotkin's *The Great French Revolution*.

The Labour Movement

The only mass following that anarchism was able to attract was among the Jewish workers packed into a small area of inner East London: Spitalfields, Whitechapel, Stepney. They were refugees from persecution in the Russian Empire, fleeing the frequent pogroms. More than half of those who settled in England and Wales did so in London, where the number increased eightfold over thirty years – from 8,700 in 1881 through 26,700 (1891) and 53,500 (1901), to 63,100 in 1911; 45 per cent worked in tailoring or dressmaking, and 12 per cent in boot- and shoe- or slipper-making. They were employed predominantly in small workshops, sweated by fellow Jews. In these circumstances unionization was fitful and explosive.

A strike of the East End tailors in which socialists and anarchists were equally prominent in 1889 was fiercely resisted by their employers, whom public opinion finally compelled to concede a reduction in the working day, meal breaks, and the regulation of overtime. In the new century anarchism pulled ahead, much aided by the charisma of Rudolf Rocker, a German Gentile who settled permanently in Britain and became fluent in Yiddish. He edited the revived *Der Arbayter Fraynd* (*The Workers' Friend*) from 1903 and, two years later, *Germinal*, a cultural magazine with an international readership, becoming an eloquent lecturer at the Jubilee Street club after its foundation in 1906. He was the representative of the London movement in 1907 at the International Anarchist Congress in Amsterdam and was chosen as a member of the International Anarchist Bureau established there. The high

11 B. Holton, *British Syndicalism, 1900–1914: Myths and Realities* (London: Pluto Press, 1976), pp. 37–8, 139.

point came in 1912 with an all-London strike of tailoring workers for increased wages and improved conditions, resulting in (nominal) victory for all, including 13,000 in East London, predominantly Jewish and galvanized by Rocker's leadership. On the outbreak of war Rocker was interned for its duration – and in 1918 immediately deported to his native Germany, where he was to be the primary mover in the creation of the syndicalist International Working Men's Association (IWMA-AIT).

Anarchism's impact on the wider labour movement was otherwise imperceptible. The great flowering of British libertarianism in the second decade of the twentieth century, most readily identified in 'the Labour Unrest of 1910–14' but in fact lasting until after the First World War ended, had its origins largely in specific industrial problems. Even so, it had the greatest potential for effecting radical change in British society since Chartism. Yet there was a social gulf between the anarchists, who were frequently middle-class or, if proletarian, indifferent to trade unionism (John Turner was the sole prominent anarchist unionist), and the unions.

Syndicalism proper, although never a coherent, organized movement, erupted in Britain from 1910 to be terminated by the coming of war. It was principally an import from France, where from the late 1890s trade unionists, as members of the Confédération Générale du Travail (General Confederation of Labour, CGT), were overwhelmingly syndicalist. The word 'syndicalism' indeed is derived from 'syndicalisme', which simply means 'trade unionism', the French equivalent for the English 'syndicalism' being 'syndicalisme révolutionnaire': revolutionary trade unionism. When Mann returned to England in May 1910 after eight years in Australasia, Guy Bowman was one of the group who met him at the Royal Victoria Dock, London. Virtually the first thing Mann said to the francophone Bowman was 'Let's go and see the men of Direct Action', and within three weeks the two men were in Paris talking to leading members of the CGT.[12] Mann and Bowman launched the monthly Industrial Syndicalist in July with the propagandist Industrial Syndicalist Education League following in December.

Of equal importance to French syndicalism was the influence of American industrial unionism: of the Industrial Workers of the World (IWW), founded in 1905, and of Daniel De Leon's semi-parliamentarian, semi-syndicalist Socialist Labor Party. A Socialist Labour Party (SLP) had been launched in Britain in 1903 as a breakaway from the SDF's Scottish section; and, centred

12 G. Brown, 'Introduction', in The Industrial Syndicalist (Nottingham: Spokesman Books, 1974), pp. 11–13.

on Clydeside, it was to be of decisive importance in the wartime shop stewards' movement. Initially advocating 'dual unionism', only during the war did it relax its prohibition of members accepting union office. William Paul, a leading theoretician of the SLP, was in 1917 to subject the Fabian and ILP programme of municipal and state enterprise to a cogent critique, maintaining that the extension of state control would merely reinforce capitalism and 'bring with it armies of official bureaucrats, who will only be able to maintain their posts by tyrannizing and limiting the freedom of the workers', the proletariat becoming little better than serfs. In contrast he advocated industry being 'democratically owned and controlled by the workers electing directly from their own ranks industrial administrative committees', leading to the replacement of 'the capitalist political or geo-graphical State' by a 'central industrial administrative committee'.[13] Concurrently, the movement for amalgamation, seeking the merger of existing organizations into industrial unions, was not simply pursued by its political advocates but took place as the natural byproduct of enormous trade union growth.

Britain experienced a series of massive strikes during 'the Labour Unrest': in the docks, on the railways, where an amalgamated union was being formed – leading to the first national rail strike – and in the mines also with a national stoppage. Particularly dramatic was a general transport strike on Merseyside in August 1911, bringing together the dockers, carters, railwaymen, and seamen. This was an intercontinental stoppage in which dockers from Belgium, the Netherlands, Denmark, and the eastern seaboard of the USA participated. Mann's presence, as secretary of the district committee of the Transport Workers Federation (a recent, albeit as yet loose, formation), led to his being dubbed 'Dictator of Liverpool'; and police, troops, and gunboats were moved to the port. After a break of several months the *Industrial Syndicalist* was succeeded in January 1912 by the *Syndicalist* (later *Syndicalist and Amalgamation News*), now edited by Bowman and published by Mann. In the first issue they reprinted an 'Open Letter to British Soldiers', dubbed 'Don't Shoot', appealing to the military not to intervene in industrial disputes:

> WHEN WE go on Strike to better OUR lot, which is the lot also of YOUR FATHERS, MOTHERS, BROTHERS and SISTERS, YOU are called upon by your officers to MURDER US ... BOYS, DON'T DO IT![14]

---

13 William Paul, *The State: Its Origin and Function* (Glasgow: Socialist Labour Press, n.d.), pp. 183, 197–8.
14 *Syndicalist*, January 1912.

This had originated as a leaflet written by a syndicalist stonemason and had already appeared in Larkin's *Irish Worker*, but it was Mann and Bowman who were prosecuted under the Incitement to Mutiny Act of 1797, and each was sentenced to six months' imprisonment. The very well-informed G. D. H. Cole regarded Mann as 'at the moment, the most striking personality in the Trade Union world', but insisted correctly that he

> did not in any sense cause the strikes or the unrest: he contributed a great deal to the direction they took and to the guiding of the 'unrest' into definite and constructive channels, but he cannot be said to have caused it. He utilized an existing state of affairs with an eye to a wider future as well as to the present ... The time was ripe, and it was his fortune and privilege to be the spark to set the train alight.[15]

The first dispute with a syndicalist dimension had been a lock-out at a colliery in Tonypandy, in the Rhondda, from September 1910. In November miners employed in the five other pits controlled by the Cambrian Combine went on strike in sympathy, 13,000 men staying out until August, when they returned to work on terms they could have had before the strike began. The conflict originated in grievances peculiar to the Rhondda Valleys, but was exacerbated by the contempt of the younger socialist miners for the official union leaders of the South Wales Miners' Federation (SWMF), at least three of whom had been Lib–Lab MPs, wedded to conciliation with the coal-owners. These conditions generated the remarkable home-grown syndicalism of *The Miners' Next Step* of the (South Wales Miners) Unofficial Reform Committee, published in 1912. The document argued against leadership in principle, with 'officials or leaders ... excluded from all power on the executive, which becomes a purely administrative body ... directly elected by the men'. It proposed that: 'The old policy of identity of interest between employers and ourselves be abolished, and a policy of open hostility installed' and stated that the objective was 'to build up an organization, that will ultimately take over the mining industry, and carry it on in the interests of the workers'. Ownership of the mines by the state was rejected.[16]

The Miners' Next Step was the work of eight men, only four to six (the evidence is conflicting) actively contributing to the drafting. Of the latter group five had been students at Ruskin College, Oxford, and/or later

15 G. D. H. Cole, *The World of Labour: A Discussion of the Present and Future of Trade Unionism* (London: G. Bell, 1913), pp. 40–1.
16 Unofficial Reform Committee, *The Miners' Next Step: Being a Suggested Scheme for the Reorganization of the Federation* (London: Pluto Press, 1973 [1912]), pp. 26, 29–30.

supported the formation of the Plebs League of 1908 and the breakaway from Ruskin of the Central Labour College (initially funded by only the SWMF and the National Union of Railwaymen). The league, promoting an 'independent working-class education', achieved immediate success in South Wales with classes throughout the coalfield. It derived its name from a pamphlet by De Leon, *Two Pages from Roman History*, and De Leonism was rampant in the new initiative, yet *The Miners' Next Step* was not hobbled by the purism of its definite influence, advocating instead industrial, not dual, unionism and opposing nationalization.

There is consensus that the primary shaper of *The Miners' Next Step* was Noah Ablett, a checkweighman at Mardy (a village that became a 'Little Moscow' during the interwar years). A writer well qualified to judge considers he was 'the most outstanding organic intellectual to emerge from the south Wales coalfield' and that 'his thinking shaped a generation of miner activists'.[17] It is noteworthy that Ablett never joined the Communist Party, while declining the invitation to stand as a prospective Labour MP. Syndicalism was important also in County Durham, the coalfield outside South Wales where its influence was greatest.

One of the final outbreaks occurred in Dublin, where for six months in 1913–14 there was a bitter, violent lock-out of the Irish Transport and General Workers' Union, which was under the inspirational leadership of James Larkin, a quasi-syndicalist, and James Connolly, a major theorist of industrial unionism who had been an organizer for the SLP and IWW in Scotland and the USA respectively. The Citizen Army, a militia formed to protect strikers from the police, was to be a key component of the Easter Rising of 1916.

Immediately after the declaration of war, the trade union leadership declared an 'industrial truce' in August 1914, and this was supplemented the following year by the Munitions of War Act, which made arbitration compulsory and suspended union customs in all industries supplying vital war needs. In the face of the growing labour shortage and the need to change over to the production of weapons, employers were obliged to reorganize their workshops and – in a process known as 'dilution' – to employ less-skilled men as well as women in jobs previously reserved for skilled male workers. In these conditions, power in the factories and mines fell into the hands of unofficial movements. The heirs of pre-war syndicalism were to be the amalgamation committee movement, seeking the creation of an industrial

17 Hywel Francis, entry on Noah Ablett (2004), *Oxford Dictionary of National Biography*.

union in engineering as the first step in the attainment of workers' control, and especially the shop stewards' movement, shop stewards leading many unofficial strikes in opposition to both the government and the trade union officials.

Clydeside had the largest concentration of the production of munitions in the British Isles and has been viewed as the cockpit for a struggle over dilution, a considerable mythology being generated around the self-appointed Clyde Workers' Committee as the spearhead of the shop stewards' movement, a narrative for which the intellectually impressive J. T. Murphy, of the Sheffield Workers' Committee, bears much responsibility. The Clyde Workers' Committee, which was dominated by the sectarians of the SLP, appreciated that resistance to dilution *per se* was socially regressive, and developed the policy not only to accept dilution but also to assist in its implementation, in exchange for 'an ever-increasing control over conditions', that is, a share in the control of the industry.[18] Its struggle over dilution was lost when a strike of March 1916 was broken with the fining of strikers, the deportation of ten of the leaders, and the imprisonment of five others. Leadership of the movement then shifted towards Sheffield. In August 1917 the Shop Stewards' and Workers' Committee Movement was inaugurated at a national conference in Manchester; and five more conferences were held before the end of the war, at which at least thirty-three towns were represented. There was a weekly paper, the *Worker*, published in Glasgow, and a monthly, *Solidarity*, in London. The movement was to disintegrate rapidly with the coming of peace, as war production ended and former militants found themselves unemployed. Its remnants were to form a constituent – a section of the SLP, with which it overlapped, was another – when the Communist Party of Great Britain was founded in 1920.

With respect to gender, there was a glaring absence of women in the libertarian industrial movements of c. 1910–19, although it should be noted that the massive increase in unionization during the decade – density grew threefold – saw the proportion of females in total trade union membership almost doubling.

In this first period negligible interest was displayed in matters of empire, the principal exception being the Boer War – yet here the issues were the jingoistic fervour, concern for the white settlers, and war in itself. Most

---

18 Quoted by B. Pribićević, *The Shop Stewards' Movement and Workers' Control, 1910–1922* (Oxford: Basil Blackwell, 1959), p. 124.

anarchists opposed the First World War, other than a minority following Kropotkin.

Guild Socialism

Another variety of libertarian socialism also became prominent during the second decade of the twentieth century. This was the exclusively British guild socialism. The *Syndicalist*, of which Bowman was editor, complained:

> 'Guild Socialism' stands forth as the latest lucubration of the middle-class mind. It is a 'cool steal' of the leading ideas of Syndicalism and a deliberate perversion of them.
>
> We do not so much object to the term 'guild' as applied to the various autonomous industries, linked together for the service of the common weal, such as advocated by Syndicalism. But we do protest against the 'State' idea which is associated with it in Guild Socialism.[19]

There is considerable justice in these criticisms of what was undeniably a very middle-class form of socialism, though guild socialism was theoretically more important than they could allow, since it was to become more radical and eventually non-statist.

Guild socialism emerged in the columns of the *New Age* with the publication in 1912–13 of a series of articles by S. G. Hobson, which the paper's editor, A. R. Orage, collected as a book entitled *National Guilds*. Hobson envisaged the trade unions converting themselves into enormous national guilds which would take over the running of modern productive industry as well as distribution and exchange. This was, as the *Syndicalist* observed, entirely compatible with syndicalism; but alongside and independent of the 'Guild Congress' the state would remain 'with its Government, its Parliament, and its civil and military machinery ... Certainly independent; probably even supreme.'[20]

While Hobson seems to have been responsible for initiating the primary features of guild socialism, its outstanding thinker (with the possible exception of Ramiro de Maeztu, a Spaniard then living in London and writing for the *New Age*) was to be G. D. H. Cole, a very young Oxford Fellow before the war and unpaid research officer to the Amalgamated Society of Engineers

---

19 *Syndicalist*, February 1914.
20 A. R. Orage (ed.), *National Guilds: An Inquiry into the Wage System and the Way Out* (London: G. Bell, 1914), p. 263.

during it. Cole, a prolific author throughout his life, was particularly fecund between 1917 and 1920, when he published four books on guild socialism – *Self-Government in Industry, Social Theory, Chaos and Order in Industry*, and, the most systematic exposition, *Guild Socialism Re-stated* – another four with major guild socialist bearings, several pamphlets, and many articles. He developed a theory of functional democracy, rejecting democratic representative government in favour of a pluralistic society in which representation would be functional – that is, derived from all the functional groups of which the individual is a member (the most important are named as political, vocational, appetitive, religious, provident, philanthropic, sociable, and theoretical), final decisions having to emerge as a consensus between the different groups, not as the fiats of a sovereign authority:

> there must be . . . as many separately elected groups of representatives as there are distinct essential groups of functions to be performed. Smith cannot represent Brown, Jones and Robinson as human beings; for a human being, as an individual, is fundamentally incapable of being represented. He can only represent the common point of view which Brown, Jones and Robinson hold in relation to some definite social purpose, or group of connected purposes. Brown, Jones and Robinson must therefore have, not one vote each, but as many different functional votes as there are different questions calling for associative action in which they are interested.[21]

Much of Cole's conception of a fully participatory society had its origins in Jean-Jacques Rousseau, though Morris, whom he described as 'of the same blood as National Guildsmen', was the major lifelong influence on Cole.[22]

Although many of his fellow guild socialists – together they had converted the Fabian Research Department into the Labour Research Department – were to become communists, Cole himself stuck with the Labour Party while remaining a guild socialist and a libertarian. He could write as late as 1941: 'One man cannot really represent another – that's flat. The odd thing is that anyone should have supposed he could.' Similarly he believed that 'every good democrat is a bit of an anarchist when he's scratched'.[23] At the end of his life he concluded his monumental history of socialist thought with a forthright statement:

> I am neither a Communist nor a Social Democrat, because I regard both as creeds of centralization and bureaucracy, whereas I feel sure that a Socialist

21 G. D. H. Cole, *Guild Socialism Re-Stated* (London: Leonard Parsons, 1920), p. 33.
22 G. D. H. Cole, *Self-Government in Industry* (London: G. Bell, 1917), p. 121.
23 G. D. H. Cole, *Essays in Social Theory* (London: Macmillan, 1950), pp. 98, 100.

society that is to be true to its equalitarian principles of human brotherhood must rest on the widest participation of as many as possible of its citizens in the tasks of democratic self-government.[24]

The National Guilds League had been set up belatedly in 1915 and from 1916 published the *Guildsman* (initially from Clydeside, significantly). R. H. Tawney became a member, and one of his most impressive works, *The Acquisitive Society* of 1921, bears the imprint of the guild socialist emphasis on function. Bertrand Russell, of a Whig family, the godson of J. S. Mill, and a member of the Fabian Society from the 1890s, was another eminent member of the National Guilds League, serving on its executive.

Working guilds were set up in 1920 in the building industry, one in London, another in Manchester, followed by many other towns. They were to tender for local authority housing under the breakthrough Act of 1919, provide continuous pay regardless of weather, and allow their operatives ultimate control of the organizations for which they worked. While they initially prospered, attracting much support and enthusiasm, they were to be wound up as early as 1923 on account of mismanagement, the involvement of the high-handed Hobson and, crushingly, the repeal of the Addison Act.

Maurice Reckitt, who had been a prominent guild socialist, believed that 'syndicalism was so plainly an importation without any organic relation to English tradition or the industrial situation here, that apart from its effect in giving an impulse to the trade union amalgamation movement, its direct influence was very slight'. 'The anti-collectivist and anti-political trend found', he considered, 'its true tongue in quite other quarters.' One of these was the *New Age* in general and Hobson's articles in particular; the other was the critique by Hilaire Belloc, Liberal MP for Salford South, 1906–10, of the Liberals' innovative social legislation culminating in the National Insurance Act of 1911, originating in his articles for the *New Age* and published as *The Servile State* in 1912. 'I cannot overestimate the impact of this book upon my mind', Reckitt recalled:

> Belloc argued . . . that the whole allegedly Socialist trend, which the Fabians were so fond of boasting that they had grafted upon Liberalism, was leading not to a community of free and equal citizens, not even to any true collectivism, but to the imposition upon the masses as the price of the reforms by which their social condition was to be ameliorated, of a servile

24 G. D. H. Cole, *A History of Socialist Thought*, 5 vols. (London: Macmillan, 1953–60), vol. v, p. 337.

status, definitely sundering them from the condition of those more prosperous members of the community not requiring to be subjected to any such legislation.[25]

Belloc was to develop with G. K. Chesterton the theory of distributism, urging the creation of a nation of small proprietors through the widest possible distribution of property: 'the re-establishment of a Distributive State in which the mass of citizens should severally own the means of production'. Syndicalists, industrial unionists, and guild socialists, supplemented during wartime by the leadership of the Shop Stewards' Movement, had no sympathy for this political programme, yet were impressed by Belloc's analysis, sharing his rejection of 'the servile state'.[26] Belloc's political origins in liberalism help to explain the apparent paradox that in their anti-statism the revolutionary socialists had drawn very near to the concerns of the radical–liberal 'Old Unionists' who had been resisting state socialism since the 1890s and continued to represent a major current within the trade unions, and hence also within the early Labour Party (established in 1900–6).

By the end of the war the mental landscape of much of the labour movement had been, although only temporarily, transformed. As Tawney commented in 1920:

It is a commonplace that during the past six years the discussion of industrial and social problems has shifted its centre. Prior to the war students and reformers were principally occupied with questions of poverty. Today their main interest appears to be the government of industry. An increasing number of trade unionists regard poverty as a symptom of a more deeply rooted malady which they would describe as industrial autocracy and demand 'control'.[27]

But the traditional moderation of British trade unions was soon to reassert itself; the first phase of the interwar depression arrived during the second half of 1920, overwhelming the chances of success for militant action; and the Labour Party's electoral advances, above all the breakthrough in the election of 1922, went far to restore faith in parliamentarianism and to set the British working class, after the decade-long dalliance of some of its sections with libertarian alternatives, firmly on the parliamentary road to socialism. Cole

25 M. B. Reckitt, *As It Happened: An Autobiography* (London: J. M. Dent, 1941), pp. 107–8.
26 H. Belloc, *The Servile State* (London and Edinburgh: T. N. Foulis, 1912), pp. 5–6.
27 R. H. Tawney, 'Foreword', to C. L. Goodrich, *The Frontier of Control: A Study in British Workshop Politics* (New York: Harcourt, Brace and Howe, 1920), p. vii.

and his wife Margaret had from 1919 edited the *Guildsman*, which they kept going as the *Guild Socialist* down to 1923, and then brought out their own *New Standards* until they were obliged to admit defeat the following year, overwhelmed by the statism of both the Labour Party and the Communist Party. The 1920s and the first half of the 1930s were therefore exceptionally unfavourable years for left libertarianism, the current only reviving in 1936 with the initial success of the Spanish Revolution.

Revival

Freedom had appeared monthly since 1886, a sober and thoughtful journal that survived while other publications appeared and soon folded in the tempestuous and often violent world of contemporary anarchist activism. Articles were largely unsigned but, in addition to Kropotkin and Wilson, prominent contributors over the years included the poet L. S. Bevington; the journalist H. W. Nevinson; Varlaam Cherkezov (Varlam Cherkezishvili), a close associate of Kropotkin; Errico Malatesta, the notable Italian anarchist; Max Nettlau; John Turner, pioneer of shop assistants' trade unionism and eventually a lone anarchist member of the TUC General Council; and William C. Owen, a journalist much influenced by the experience of Mexico, 1910–16, and collaboration in Los Angeles with the Magón brothers on the English-language section of their *Regeneración*. Yet the dwindling of anarchism after the First World War was to lead to the suspension of the paper in 1927. The composer Tom Keell, its editor since 1913, withdrew with the stock of Freedom Press to the Whiteway Colony in Gloucestershire, from where he produced irregularly fifteen issues of a *Freedom Bulletin* until 1932, but thereafter nothing. He commented: 'The *Bulletin* has just faded out of existence . . . I feel the loss of a link with old comrades, but without money it had to be broken.'[28]

It was the Spanish Revolution and outbreak of the Civil War in 1936 which were to revive the modest fortunes of anarchism in Britain. The young Vernon Richards, born Vero Recchioni, the son of an old comrade of Malatesta, began to bring out *Spain and the World*, which Keell anointed as the true successor to *Freedom* (a dissident group, supporters of Kropotkin during the First World War, had been publishing a rival *Freedom*). With the Nationalist victory, *Spain and the World* was renamed for six issues *Revolt!*,

28 Quoted by H. Becker, 'Notes on Freedom and the Freedom Press, 1886–1928', *The Raven* no. 1 [1987], pp. 23–4.

becoming *War Commentary* for the duration of the Second World War, and in 1945 resurrecting the title of *Freedom* (initially as *Freedom through Anarchism*).

In 1937 Richards had been joined in London by Marie-Louise (originally Maria Luisa), daughter of the Italian anarchist philosopher, Camillo Berneri, assassinated in Barcelona that year, almost certainly by the communists. The family backgrounds of Richards and Berneri induced fierce loyalty among anarchists, particularly those of Italian origin. The Freedom Press Group that gathered around Richards and Berneri was young, energetic, and talented – it was to include George Woodcock and Colin Ward – and they wrote the bulk of the paper. In addition, Herbert Read (until his acceptance of a knighthood in 1953 brought anarchism into significant disrepute on the left), Alex Comfort, and later the political scientist Geoffrey Ostergaard could be called upon to contribute articles. The brilliantly gifted Berneri was said to be the principal theoretical influence behind *War Commentary* and *Freedom* – down to her premature death in 1949.

A vicious split had occurred towards the end of the war between syndical-ists, supported by Spanish exiles belonging to the CNT, and the anarchist communists gathered around Berneri and Richards, who had inherited Malatesta's scepticism of the revolutionary potential of syndicalism. But the revived *Freedom* was to be notable for its inclusiveness, its pages open not merely to Malatestan communists, but to anarchists of all kinds: syndicalists, individualists, pacifists, even Buddhists.

War Commentary had fared relatively well in wartime on account of the solidarity and intercourse between the small anti-war groups, principally *Peace News*, but also the ILP with its *New Leader*. An important minority current of anarchist pacifism emerged in the 1930s, and this world war had been met with resolute resistance. With the end of the war and Labour's electoral triumph in 1945, the anarchists were to become very isolated indeed, Freedom Press being unswervingly hostile to the Labour govern-ments and their nationalization and welfare legislation. Berneri considered, very reasonably, in the late 1940s: 'The paper gets better and better, and fewer and fewer people read it.'[29] In a review of the 1950s Ward was to observe:

> The anarchist movement throughout the world can hardly be said to have increased its influence during the decade . . . Yet the relevance of anarchist ideas was never so great . . . For the anarchists the problem of the nineteen-sixties is

---

29 Interview with Colin Ward by David Goodway, Kersey Uplands, Suffolk, UK, 29 June 1997.

simply that of how to put anarchism back into the intellectual bloodstream, into the field of ideas which are taken seriously.[30]

The empire and decolonization had become major preoccupations for the Freedom Press Group, first with the mandate in Palestine, later with Africa. For example, the annual volumes of selected articles from *Freedom* were entitled *Colonialism on Trial* in 1953 and *The Tragedy of Africa* in 1960.

During the 1940s *War Commentary* followed by *Freedom* had been fortnightly, but from 1951 the paper went weekly (until 1975, when fortnightly production was resumed). Richards' optimistic hope was always for a daily newspaper. It was to break from the treadmill of weekly production that Ward began to urge the case for a monthly, more reflective *Freedom*; and eventually his fellow editors responded by giving him his head with the monthly *Anarchy* in 1961, while they continued to bring out *Freedom* for the other three weeks of each month. *Anarchy* ran for 118 issues, culminating in 1970. Sales never exceeded 2,800 per issue, no advance on *Freedom*'s 2,000–3,000.

As editor of *Anarchy*, Ward did have some success in putting anarchist ideas 'back into the intellectual bloodstream', largely because of propitious political and social changes. The rise of the New Left and the nuclear disarmament movement in the late 1950s, culminating in the student radicalism and general libertarianism of the 1960s, meant that a new audience receptive to anarchist attitudes came into existence. By 1968 Ward himself could say: 'I think that social attitudes have changed ... Anarchism perhaps is becoming almost modish. I think that there is a certain anarchy in the air today.'[31] Nuclear disarmament attracted deep anarchist involvement: in the constitutionalist CND (Campaign for Nuclear Disarmament), its precursor the Direct Action Committee, and the near-anarchist, direct action Committee of 100.

It was Richards who, for both good and ill, was the principal force behind *Freedom* following Berneri's death. He was to withdraw from the editorship of the paper; but he continued to take a close interest in the running of *Freedom*, intervening directly whenever he thought essential until his official retirement from its affairs in 1995. There had been for several decades an acrimonious dispute with Albert Meltzer, originally a loyal member of the Freedom Press Group in the late 1940s and early 1950s, who brought out the cantankerously militant *Black Flag* from 1970 in opposition to *Freedom*. After Meltzer's death in 1995 and Richards' in 2001 the supporters of the opposing

30 *Freedom*, 26 December 1959.
31 R. Boston, 'Conversations about Anarchism', *Anarchy* no. 85 (March 1968), p. 74.

papers reached a very welcome rapprochement, yet this did not provide *Freedom* with a necessary fillip and, ironically, *Black Flag* expired as a monthly several years before its rival. *Freedom*, by then almost certainly the longest-running left periodical in Britain, announced that the issue of February–March 2014 was its last.

It was the passing of Vernon Richards that contributed decisively to *Freedom*'s decline. For many years (until his death in 2000) Nicolas Walter, whose name always signified quality, had been a contributor, and there was also Ward's 'Anarchist Notebook' column. The nurturing of Colin Ward's distinctive anarchism was probably *Freedom*'s greatest achievement, Freedom Press publishing no fewer than nine of his books in addition to voluminous journalism. Given the break in publication of the 1930s, the *Freedom* of Richards and Ward clearly originated in 1936 with *Spain and the World*, not – despite its constant assertion – with Kropotkin's and Wilson's journal of 1886.

Another noteworthy efflorescence came with the libertarian socialist Solidarity group, 1960–92, which, while inspired by *Socialisme ou Barbarie* (*Socialism or Barbarism*) and the ideas of Cornelius Castoriadis, developed its own character, distinctive and admired, publishing *Solidarity*, more than sixty pamphlets, and the translations and writings of Christopher Pallis (a.k.a. Maurice Brinton). Intimately connected with Solidarity were 'The Spies for Peace' who in 1963 revealed the system of regional government that would rule the country in the event of nuclear war. This caused a sensation, yet no 'spy' was ever unmasked and prosecuted. Solidarity's politics and publications were almost certainly more influential on the libertarian left than any orthodox anarchism.

Further Reading

Clegg, Hugh Armstrong, *A History of British Trade Unions since 1889*, vol. II, *1911–1933* (Oxford: Clarendon Press, 1985).

Goodway, David (ed.), *For Workers' Power: The Selected Writings of Maurice Brinton*, 2nd edn (Chico, CA: AK Press, 2020).

Hinton, James, *The First Shop Stewards' Movement* (London: George Allen & Unwin, 1973).

Holton, Bob, *British Syndicalism, 1900–1914: Myths and Realities* (London: Pluto Press, 1976).

Mates, Lewis H., *The Great Labour Unrest: Rank-and-File Movements and Political Change in the Durham Coalfield* (Manchester: Manchester University Press, 2016).

Price, Richard, 'Contextualizing British syndicalism, c. 1907–c. 1920', *Labour History Review* 63 (1998), pp. 261–76.

Ray, Rob, *A Beautiful Idea: History of the Freedom Press Anarchists* (London: Freedom Press, 2018).

Reid, Alastair, 'Dilution, Trade Unionism and the State during the First World War', in S. Tolliday and J. Zeitlin (eds.), *Shop Floor Bargaining and the State: Historical and Comparative Perspectives* (Cambridge: Cambridge University Press, 1985), pp. 46–74.

Thompson, E. P., *William Morris: Romantic to Revolutionary*, 2nd edn (London: Merlin Press, 1977).

Wright, Anthony W., 'Guild socialism revisited', *Journal of Contemporary History* 9, 1 (January 1974), pp. 165–80 (reprinted in Tony Wright, *Doing Politics* (London, Backbite, 2012)).

19

Anarchism and Syndicalism in the United States

KENYON ZIMMER

Both anarchism and syndicalism built upon pre-existing American traditions, while simultaneously adapting new ideas and tactics from Europe and elsewhere. Recognizably anarchist doctrines began to circulate in the decades before the American Civil War (1861–5), but a large-scale anarchist movement emerged only in the 1880s. The first and only major American syndicalist organization, the Industrial Workers of the World (IWW), appeared in 1905, influenced by American strains of Marxism and unionism as well as anarchism. Nevertheless, there was much overlap and mutual influence between the two movements, and each peaked in size and power around the time of the First World War. Despite subsequent declines, syndicalism and, even more so, anarchism continued to significantly influence American intellectual, cultural, and social movements, and both have survived into the twenty-first century.

Precursors and Individualist Anarchism, 1830s–1880s

American libertarianism has deep and diverse roots. Many indigenous societies practised forms of decentralized decision-making and non-hierarchical organization, as did maroon communities composed of fugitive slaves, Native Americans, and, in some cases, runaway European indentured servants; the same is true of the Atlantic's mutinous sailors and pirates. Radical Protestantism likewise inspired antinomian movements that rejected all earthly authorities.[1] Even the classical liberalism of the United States' founders distrusted centralized power. In the nineteenth century, transcendentalist writers such as Ralph Waldo Emerson (1802–82) and Henry David

---

1 The classic overview of these interconnected radical traditions is P. Linebaugh and M. Rediker, *The Many-Headed Hydra: Sailors, Slaves, Commoners, and the Hidden History of the Revolutionary Atlantic* (Boston: Beacon Press, 2000).

Thoreau (1817–62) emphasized self-reliance, the individual will, and civil disobedience, and the 'immediatist' wing of the abolitionist movement drew on radical Christian tradition to oppose the legal sanction of slavery and advocate non-violent resistance to it.[2]

Inventor Josiah Warren (1798–1874) is often labelled the 'first American anarchist' (although he never used that term himself, instead preferring 'Democrat'). A former member of the utopian socialist commune of New Harmony, Indiana, in the 1820s and 1830s Warren developed a libertarian political system based on individual autonomy and a mutualist economic system based upon the labour theory of value. Under Warren's scheme, producers would exchange 'labour notes' denominating hours of work and the 'repugnance' of the labour performed, and have interest-free access to mutual credit banks. Rent and wage labour would be eliminated, but private possession of property and market exchanges would remain, albeit under the dictum 'Cost the limit of price', thereby abolishing surplus value. Warren's ideas anticipated those advanced a decade later in France by Pierre-Joseph Proudhon (1809–65), but also reflected the agrarian and artisanal character of the United States' antebellum economy.[3] Over the next three decades a scattering of former abolitionists and champions of an eclectic variety of other causes embraced the ideas of Warren and Proudhon, and eventually began to call themselves 'individualist anarchists', though some later adopted the label 'egoists' after discovering the writing of German ultra-individualist Max Stirner (1806–56) in the 1880s.[4]

These mostly American-born men and women founded newspapers such as *The Word* (1871–93), *Liberty* (1881–1908), and *Lucifer* (1883–1907), which reached between 1,000 and 2,000 readers at their respective heights. These publications promoted a variety of interlinked causes, including monetary and land reform, feminism and 'free love' (that is,

---

2 Anarchists often invoked such antecedents; for examples see V. de Cleyre, 'Anarchism and American Traditions', in *Selected Works of Voltairine de Cleyre*, ed. A. Berkman (New York: Mother Earth Publishing Association, 1914), pp. 118–35; and R. Rocker, *Pioneers of American Freedom: Origin of Liberal and Radical Thought in America* (Los Angeles: Rocker Publications Committee, 1949). On anarchistic strains within abolitionism, see L. Perry, *Radical Abolitionism: Anarchy and the Government of God in Antislavery Thought* (Ithaca: Cornell University Press, 1973).

3 On Warren, see C. Sartwell (ed.), *The Practical Anarchist: Writings of Josiah Warren* (New York: Fordham University Press, 2018).

4 See Perry, *Radical Abolitionism*; J. J. Martin, *Men against the State: The Expositors of Individualist Anarchism in America, 1827–1908* (De Kalb, IL: Adrian Allen Associates, 1953); M. H. Blatt, *Free Love and Anarchism: The Biography of Ezra Heywood* (Urbana: University of Illinois Press, 1989); W. McElroy, *The Debates of Liberty: An Overview of Individualist Anarchism, 1881–1908* (Lanham, MD: Lexington Books, 2002).

the abolition of marriage), racial equality, pacifism, free speech, free-thought, and spiritualism.[5] The emergence of the United States' first national labour unions in the 1850s and 1860s found enthusiastic supporters, as well as critics, among the individualist anarchists. Some, such as *Liberty* editor Benjamin Tucker (1854–1939), supported strikes but opposed labour legislation and viewed unions as bureaucratic and coercive, while others took an active role in the labour movement, including Joseph A. Labadie (1850–1933), an organizer for the Knights of Labor, who in 1888 organized and became president of the Michigan Federation of Labor.[6] Even Tucker, however, considered himself a socialist, and a number of his close associates joined American branches of the International Working Men's Association (IWMA) between 1869 and the expulsion of its 'Yankee' branches by Marxists in 1871.[7]

Individualist anarchism was centred in north-eastern cities like Boston, with outposts of support throughout the midwest, dotted along the west coast, and in southern states like Texas and Tennessee. However, it was largely an intellectual rather than a social movement. Most of its adherents rejected not only electoral activity, but also violence and most forms of collective action, leaving rational argumentation and exemplary economic and communal experiments as their only instruments for change. These proved inadequate, and even as the individualists reached the height of their influence in the 1880s, they had already been eclipsed by a new current of anarchism with a mass working-class base. This first generation of American anarchists therefore had very little impact upon the movement's subsequent development.

---

5 In addition to the works cited above, see H. D. Sears, *The Sex Radicals: Free Love in High Victorian America* (Lawrence: Regents Press of Kansas, 1977); J. E. Passet, *Sex Radicals and the Quest for Women's Equality* (Urbana: University of Illinois Press, 2003). For circulation figures of these and other American anarchist periodicals, see K. Zimmer, A. Hermida, and J. Gregory, 'Anarchist Newspapers and Periodicals 1872–1940', *Mapping American Social Movements*, https://depts.washington.edu/moves/anarchist_map-newspapers.shtml.

6 C. R. Anderson, *All-American Anarchist: Joseph A. Labadie and the Labor Movement* (Detroit: Wayne State University Press, 1998).

7 On the American IWMA, see Blatt, *Free Love and Anarchism*; T. Messer-Kruse, *The Yankee International: Marxism and the American Reform Tradition, 1848–1876* (Chapel Hill: University of North Carolina Press, 1998); and M. Cordillot, 'Socialism v. Democracy? The IWMA in the USA, 1869–1876', in F. Bensimon, Q. Deluermoz, and J. Moisand (eds.), *'Arise Ye Wretched of the Earth': The First International in a Global Perspective* (Leiden and Boston: Brill, 2018), pp. 270–81.

The Haymarket Generation, 1870s–1890s

American anarchism's second generation consisted primarily of immigrants from western and central Europe (with Germans predominating), and a smaller number of native-born Americans.[8] It was also more firmly rooted in European and American socialist traditions, as well as in the labour movement, and it advocated mass collective action and the use of force in order to carry out 'the social revolution'. Its members also promoted variations of an economic system closer to conventional socialism, which they referred to – with much imprecision – as 'collectivism' or 'communism'.

Adherents of Proudhon's ideas could be found among the German and French socialists who emigrated following the failed Revolutions of 1848, and in the utopian settlements established in the United States by followers of Charles Fourier and Victor Considérant in the 1840s and 1850s. But it was rapid postbellum industrialization and urbanization, the economy's growing dependence upon cheap wage labour, and increasingly violent class conflict that allowed anarchism to attract a large following among the United States' growing number of working-class immigrants.

A number of these new anarchists came from the ranks of the Socialist Labor Party (SLP), following electoral and legislative disappointments. Initially calling themselves 'social revolutionaries', these defectors rejected electoral politics in favour of working-class direct action and armed revolution. The influence of the German agitator Johann Most (1846–1906), himself a former socialist who embraced anarchism around the time of his arrival in the United States in 1882, catalysed the transition of many social revolutionaries into full-fledged anarchists. In 1883 Most and other anarchists founded the International Working People's Association (IWPA), a loose-knit anarchist confederation which by 1886 counted around 5,000 members in some 100 branches across the United States, as well as at least fourteen affiliated newspapers in multiple languages.[9] At the movement's height there were more German and Czech anarchists in the United States than in Europe, and these years also mark the only period in American history when members of

---

8 The Irish, who overtook Germans as the largest immigrant group in the 1880s, were conspicuous by their absence among anarchist ranks. Irish-American radicalism instead consolidated into the Fenian movement for Irish independence, which in turn enjoyed widespread support – technical as well as moral – from anti-colonial anarchists.

9 For detailed studies of the IWPA, see P. Avrich, *The Haymarket Tragedy* (Princeton: Princeton University Press, 1984); F. Rosemont and D. Roediger (eds.), *Haymarket Scrapbook* (Chicago: Charles H. Kerr, 1986); B. C. Nelson, *Beyond the Martyrs: A Social History of Chicago's Anarchists, 1870–1900* (New Brunswick, NJ: Rutgers University Press, 1988).

anarchist organizations clearly outnumbered those of Marxist ones like the SLP.

The IWPA included three main factions: labour-oriented anarchists with strong connections to the Knights of Labor and other local unions; partisans of Most who dismissed union activity based on a belief in the 'iron law of wages' and instead advocated armed self-defence and 'propaganda by the deed' (including bombings and assassinations); and 'autonomists' who shared most of Most's beliefs but distrusted all formal organizations and viewed Most as a demagogue. There was, however, overlap between these standpoints. Union advocates such as Chicago's Albert Parsons (1848–87) believed the class struggle was inevitable and that labour unions would be the building blocks of a post-revolutionary society, but never embraced the general strike as a revolutionary tool, as syndicalists would later do, and instead looked to the Paris Commune – the people in arms, not the workers with their arms folded – as their model for revolution.[10]

The IWPA had a powerful influence on the American labour movement. In New York, IWPA co-founder Victor Drury (1825–1918), a French anarchist and former member of the First International, became a pivotal figure within the Knights of Labor and argued strongly against racial segregation and the organization's ban on Chinese members.[11] In Chicago, anarchists formed the Central Labor Union, a local federation that took the IWPA's platform as its own and included around 30,000 members. IWPA members also formed armed workers' militias to protect strikers from violence. The anarchists were ambivalent towards the movement for the eight-hour workday, but unionists like Parsons convinced most to back the campaign, which culminated in nationwide strikes on 1 May 1886.

Three days later, IWPA members held a meeting near Chicago's Haymarket Square to protest the police killing of striking workers. When police ordered the crowd to disperse, an unknown individual hurled a bomb towards the officers, and the explosion and police gunfire resulted in the deaths of seven policemen and at least four workers. Local authorities then charged eight IWPA members, including Parsons, with murder for having

---

10 On the factions and ideology of the IWPA, see Avrich, *Haymarket Tragedy*; T. Goyens, *Beer and Revolution: The German Anarchist Movement in New York City, 1880–1914* (Urbana: University of Illinois Press, 2007); J. Jones, *Goddess of Anarchy: The Life and Times of Lucy Parsons, American Radical* (New York: Basic Books, 2017); K. Zimmer, 'Haymarket and the Rise of Syndicalism', in C. Levy and M. S. Adams (eds.), *The Palgrave Handbook of Anarchism* (Cham: Palgrave Macmillan, 2019), pp. 353–69.
11 R. Weir, '"Here's to the men who lose!" The hidden career of Victor Drury', *Labor History* 36, 4 (1995), pp. 530–56.

allegedly conspired with the unidentified bomb-thrower. After a sensationalized and deeply flawed trial, the defendants were found guilty; one was sentenced to fifteen years, two more had their sentences commuted to life in prison, one committed suicide rather than face the gallows, and the remaining four were hanged on 11 November 1887.[12] Global outrage over the executions led to the international socialist movement's adoption of 1 May as International Workers' Day, or May Day, in honor of the Haymarket martyrs, and helped to radicalize a new generation of anarchist and syndicalist radicals.

'New Immigrants' and the Rise of Syndicalism, 1880s–1900s

By the time of the Haymarket Affair, immigration from southern and eastern Europe had begun to surge. Many Americans viewed these 'new immigrants', as alarmists dubbed them, as racially inferior to 'Nordic' or 'Anglo-Saxon' Europeans. The labour movement was also changing; the more inclusive Knights of Labor never recovered from its association with the Haymarket anarchists and internal feuds, and was quickly eclipsed by the new American Federation of Labor (AFL), which by the mid-1890s had dedicated itself to independence from all political movements and the exclusion of 'unskilled' workers from its craft unions. New immigrants therefore found themselves barred from most unions even as they laboured in some of the least desirable jobs within American industries.

In the 1890s, as Italians and east European Jews overtook Germans as the largest immigrant groups, they likewise came to comprise the largest segments of the anarchist movement. These immigrants, along with smaller numbers from Spain and Cuba, constituted American anarchism's third and largest generation of supporters. As with the Germans and Czechs of the second generation, the great majority were not anarchists when they arrived and were instead radicalized by the American environment. Their movement continued to focus on workers' struggles, but also devoted more attention to anti-imperialism, anti-racism, women's liberation, and transnational ties to anarchists outside the United States' borders.

---

12 On the trial, see Avrich, *Haymarket Tragedy*; J. R. Green, *Death in the Haymarket: A Story of Chicago, the First Labor Movement, and the Bombing That Divided Gilded Age America* (New York: Pantheon Books, 2006). For a controversial revisionist view, see T. Messer-Kruse, *The Trial of the Haymarket Anarchists: Terrorism and Justice in the Gilded Age* (New York: Palgrave Macmillan, 2011).

The first Yiddish-, Italian-, and Spanish-speaking anarchist groups appeared in the 1880s. Because of the similarity between the German and Yiddish languages, early Jewish anarchists were exposed to anarchism through German writings and speakers, especially Most. Italian and Spanish immigrants, by contrast, came from countries that had been major centres of the Bakuninist wing of the First International, and a small but influential number had been involved in anarchist activities prior to migrating. In many North American communities Italian- and Spanish-speaking anarchists, sometimes joined by French comrades, formed pan-ethnic 'Latin' anarchist groups, likewise facilitated by the similarities between their languages.[13] New English-language publications (many of them founded by multilingual immigrants) also appeared, assisting communication within the multi-ethnic movement and helping to attract a modest number of native-born Americans to the anarchist cause.

Enthusiasm for conspiratorial tactics and 'propaganda by the deed' ran high among the early Jewish anarchists, inspiring, for example, the 1892 attempt of Alexander Berkman (1870–1936) against the life of steel manager Henry Clay Frick in retaliation for the deaths of striking workers in Homestead, Pennsylvania. By the late 1890s, however, most Jewish anarchists had shifted to focus on gradual change via the development of labour unions, radical education, and producer and consumer co-operatives.[14] Factionalism was more endemic to the Italian-speaking movement, which remained split roughly in half between 'anti-organizationists' who, like the earlier autonomists, opposed all formal organizations (including anarchist federations) and advocated insurrectionary tactics; and 'organizationists' who advocated the creation of both large-scale anarchist organizations and militant labour unions. Spanish and Cuban anarchists, by contrast, shared a more unified stance, with most favouring militant unionism, leading to an eventual revolutionary outbreak. Nearly all members of every faction, however, were communist anarchists (though not all used that label) who envisioned

---

13 K. Zimmer, *Immigrants against the State: Yiddish and Italian Anarchism in America* (Urbana: University of Illinois Press, 2015); C. J. Castañeda and M. Feu (eds.), *Writing Revolution: Hispanic Anarchism in the United States* (Urbana: University of Illinois Press, 2019); G. R. Mormino and G. E. Pozzetta, *The Immigrant World of Ybor City: Italians and Their Latin Neighbors in Tampa, 1885–1985* (Urbana: University of Illinois Press, 1987).

14 See Berkman's own account in A. Berkman, *Prison Memoirs of an Anarchist* (Oakland, CA: AK Press, 2016). On the Jewish anarchist movement, see Zimmer, *Immigrants against the State*; J. J. Cohen, *Di yidish-anarkhistishe bavegung in Amerike. Historisher iberblik un perzenlekhe iberlebungen* [The Jewish Anarchist Movement in America: Historical Overview and Personal Reminiscences] (Philadelphia: Radical Library, Branch 273 Arbeter Ring, 1945).

a future economic system of workers' collective ownership of the means of production, with distribution organized in line with the principle 'from each according to ability, to each according to need'.[15]

Immigrant radicals also shaped working-class education and culture within their own communities. Anarchist study circles proliferated, as did educational lectures on a wide array of political, cultural, and scientific topics. Jewish anarchists were closely connected to the flourishing Yiddish theatre, and the Yiddish anarchist paper *Fraye Arbayter Shtime* (*Free Voice of Labour*, 1890–1977) became a major outlet for Yiddish poetry, literature, and cultural criticism. Italian and Hispanic anarchists, meanwhile, formed amateur theatre groups wherever they could, which proved an especially important venue for women's activism. Anarchist women and their male allies also promoted 'women's emancipation' and the abolition of patriarchy (while typically shunning the women's suffrage movement as inherently statist), and promoted and published information about birth control methods at a time when it was illegal to do so. Many faced arrest and prison for such activities, including famed Jewish anarchist Emma Goldman (1869–1940).[16] Goldman and several other anarchists were also among the few public defenders of homosexuals, and the anarchist movement provided a more tolerant space for non-traditional expressions of sexuality and gender than probably any other political movement of the day.[17]

Anti-imperialism and anti-racism also became major areas of concern. Among the causes anarchists supported were the Cuban struggle against Spain, the Irish and Indian independence movements, resistance to Italian imperialism in Africa, and opposition to the United States' territorial expansion into the Caribbean and Pacific. Anarchists were united in their opposition to imperialism, but divided over supporting nationalist anti-colonial

15 On these factions, see Zimmer, *Immigrants against the State*; P. Avrich, *Sacco and Vanzetti: The Anarchist Background* (Princeton: Princeton University Press, 1991); A. Senta, *Luigi Galleani: The Most Dangerous Anarchist in America*, trans. A. Asali and S. Sayers (Oakland, CA: AK Press, 2019); Castañeda and Feu, *Writing Revolution*.
16 On anarchist culture, see Zimmer, *Immigrants against the State*; M. Bencivenni, *Italian Immigrant Radical Culture: The Idealism of the* Sovversivi *in the United States, 1890–1940* (New York: New York University Press, 2011); J. Guglielmo, *Living the Revolution: Italian Women's Resistance and Radicalism in New York City, 1880–1945* (Chapel Hill: University of North Carolina Press, 2010). On Goldman, see K. E. Ferguson, *Emma Goldman: Political Thinking in the Streets* (Lanham, MD: Rowman & Littlefield, 2011); P. Avrich and K. Avrich, *Sasha and Emma: The Anarchist Odyssey of Alexander Berkman and Emma Goldman* (Cambridge, MA: Harvard University Press, 2012).
17 This topic deserves more research, but see T. Kissack, *Free Comrades: Anarchism and Homosexuality in the United States, 1895–1917* (Oakland, CA: AK Press, 2008); and M. Helquist, *Marie Equi: Radical Politics and Outlaw Passions* (Corvallis: Oregon State University Press, 2015).

movements that sought to establish new, independent nation-states.[18] They also consistently opposed Jim Crow segregation, the Asian exclusion movement, and anti-Mexican attitudes; however, because anarchism had little presence in the Deep South and Black Americans had not yet migrated to northern cities in large numbers, most inter-racial anarchist activity involved Japanese, Indian, Chinese, and Mexican immigrants.

By the first years of the twentieth century, anarchist groups could be found in every major American city, innumerable mining camps, and many small towns, as well as the recently acquired American territories of Puerto Rico, the Panama Canal Zone, and the Philippines. These groups were in turn linked to one another and to anarchist networks across the globe through the constant transnational circulation of anarchist periodicals and individual activists. Several American newspapers, including the *Fraye Arbayter Shtime* and the Italian *La Questione Sociale* (*The Social Question*; 1895–1908), served as global anarchist organs. US-based anarchists in turn helped to fund anarchist projects in countries such as Cuba, Italy, and Russia. Some intervened abroad more directly, by travelling to participate in the Cuban War of Independence (1895–8) and the 1905 Russian Revolution, and Italian immigrant anarchist Gaetano Bresci (1869–1901) returned to Italy in 1900 and assassinated King Umberto I (b. 1844) to avenge the military's massacre of protesters in Milan two years prior.[19]

Aside from Bresci, American proponents of 'propaganda by the deed' rarely put their beliefs into action before the First World War. The notable exception was the 1901 assassination of President William McKinley (b. 1843) at the hands of Leon Czolgosz (1873–1901), a son of Polish immigrants and recent convert to anarchism who appears to have been eager to prove his dedication to the cause.[20] By the time of Czolgosz's deed, however, most of

18 For an overview of these debates, see K. Zimmer, 'At War with Empire: The Anti-Colonial Roots of American Anarchist Debates during the First World War', in R. Kinna and M. S. Adams (eds.), *Anarchism, 1914–1918: Internationalism, Anti-Militarism and War* (Manchester: Manchester University Press, 2017), pp. 175–98.

19 The literature on American anarchist transnationalism includes K. R. Shaffer, *Black Flag Boricuas: Anarchism, Antiauthoritarianism, and the Left in Puerto Rico, 1897–1921* (Urbana: University of Illinois Press, 2013); K. R. Shaffer, *Anarchists of the Caribbean: Countercultural Politics and Transnational Networks in the Age of US Expansion* (Cambridge: Cambridge University Press, 2020); D. Turcato, *Making Sense of Anarchism: Errico Malatesta's Experiments with Revolution, 1889–1900* (New York: Palgrave Macmillan, 2012); T. Tomchuk, *Transnational Radicals: Italian Anarchists in Canada and the US, 1915–1940* (Winnipeg: University of Manitoba Press, 2015); Zimmer, *Immigrants against the State*; and Castañeda and Feu, *Writing Revolution*.

20 Two recent studies have done much to dispel the mythology of Czolgosz's alleged 'insanity'; see E. Rauchway, *Murdering McKinley: The Making of Theodore Roosevelt's America* (New York: Hill & Wang, 2003); S. Miller, *The President and the Assassin:*

the movement had rejected assassination as a viable tactic. Instead, anarchists in these decades focused on organizing workers into unions where none existed, and attempting to radicalize those unions that did.

Anarchist-led labour organizations were usually local – and often ethnically specific – efforts, focusing on the workplaces and industries where anarchists themselves worked, including garment and textile production, mining, cigar-making, and maritime labour. Anarchist minorities also enjoyed local influence within national organizations such as the Cigar Makers' International Union, the United Mine Workers of America, the International Ladies' Garment Workers' Union (ILGWU), and the Sailors' Union of the Pacific. Anarchism in these bodies functioned as an internal opposition to bureaucracy, centralized decision-making, and conciliatory approaches to labour conflicts. After 1905, several unions founded by anarchists, as well as anarchist-led locals of existing unions, affiliated with the IWW.[21]

Like the IWPA, most anarchists viewed unions as schools for raising workers' class consciousness, and strikes as vehicles to prepare them for the coming struggle against capitalism and the state. Unlike the IWPA, they no longer organized worker militias, although anarchist-led struggles – such as the 1902 silk strike in Paterson, New Jersey – still sometimes culminated in armed clashes between strikers and police. Over the course of the 1890s, however, anarchists increasingly discussed the general strike rather than insurrection as the means to initiate revolution. Some imagined the general strike as an essentially peaceful event, whereas others recognized that it would likely be met with force and require armed defence.

This embrace of the general strike illustrated the movement's strong, reciprocal ties to anarchism in Europe, where the doctrines of revolutionary syndicalism were developing at this time. Syndicalism found champions among anarchists of all backgrounds, including Emma Goldman and a reformed Johann Most, though Italian-American anarchists perhaps did the most to propagate the defining elements of syndicalist doctrine prior to the formation of the IWW: revolutionary unionism independent from political parties and electoral activity; working-class direct action (including strikes, boycotts, and sabotage); the revolutionary general strike; and the

McKinley, Terror, and Empire at the Dawn of the American Century (New York: Random House, 2011).

21 No reliable overview of anarchism's place in the American labour movement exists; for local case studies, see Zimmer, Immigrants against the State; Mormino and Pozzetta, Immigrant World of Ybor City; Castañeda and Feu, Writing Revolution.

democratic labour federation as the organizational basis of the future socialist society.

The Industrial Workers of the World and American Syndicalism, 1900s–1910s

Aside from anarchism, three other strains of radicalism contributed to the formation of the IWW: the shifting Marxism of the Socialist Labor Party, the left wing of the newer and larger Socialist Party of America, and the militant industrial unionism of the Western Federation of Miners (WFM). As a result, the IWW was itself a multi-faceted body that manifested different versions of syndicalism depending upon time, place, and ethnic group.

By the early 1900s SLP leader Daniel De Leon (1852–1914) had adopted syndicalist ideas via contact with European syndicalists and the French syndicalist press. De Leon, however, condemned syndicalists' rejection of party politics, and instead insisted that, although industrial unions were the primary sites and instruments of working-class power and electoral politics was a secondary 'reflex' of economic action, political campaigns were nevertheless valuable venues for socialist propaganda, and syndicalist unions would eventually aid the party in achieving an electoral majority. Only together, he argued, could the combination of a syndicalist general strike and a socialist government then successfully appropriate and socialize the means of production under workers' control. De Leon, however, insisted that these were all proper Marxist notions.[22]

Radical members of the Socialist Party also came to view workplace struggles as more important than electoral contests and to espouse European syndicalist ideas. Hard rock miners in the American West, meanwhile, formed the independent Western Federation of Miners in 1893, in the midst of a decade of virtual open warfare between workers and mine-owners. In 1898 the WFM established the Western Labor Union (renamed the American Labor Union in 1902) as a militant alternative to the AFL. In the early 1900s both the WFM and the American Labor Union adopted explicitly socialist platforms, but in practice they focused on workers' struggles rather than electoral campaigns.[23]

22 D. K. McKee, 'The influence of syndicalism upon Daniel De Leon', *The Historian* 20, 3 (1958), pp. 275–89.
23 On the IWW's many influences, see S. Salerno, *Red November, Black November: Culture and Community in the Industrial Workers of the World* (Albany: State University of New York Press, 1989).

Representatives of all three currents, as well as at least fourteen anarchists, participated in the founding of the IWW, as did Socialist Party leader Eugene V. Debs (1855–1926), himself the former president of the American Railway Union and a champion of industrial unionism. The new organization, which absorbed the American Labor Union and the SLP-affiliated Socialist Trade and Labor Alliance, began as an uneasy compromise between its constituent factions, only some of which identified as syndicalist. The original version of the famous preamble to the IWW constitution illustrated the tensions between its anarchist and revolutionary syndicalist wing, on the one hand, and its SLP and Socialist Party affiliates, on the other:

> The working class and the employing class have nothing in common. There can be no peace so long as hunger and want are found among millions of working people and the few, who make up the employing class, have all the good things of life.
>
> Between these two classes a struggle must go on until all the toilers come together on the political, as well as on the industrial field, and take and hold that which they produce by their labor through an economic organization of the working class, without affiliation with any political party.[24]

A series of factional struggles led to the exit of the WFM in 1907, and the expulsion of De Leon the following year. De Leon's supporters withdrew and formed their own version of the IWW, known as the 'Detroit IWW' before finally changing its name to the Workers' International Industrial Union in 1915, but this rival union never attracted more than a few thousand members and dissolved in 1924. Tensions with the Socialist Party, meanwhile, came to a head in 1912, when IWW members were ejected from the party for promoting 'direct action' over electoral politics.

In 1908, the union eliminated the political clause from its preamble, and added the more overtly syndicalist passage:

> The army of production must be organized, not only for the every-day struggle with the capitalists, but also to carry on production when capitalism shall have been overthrown. By organizing industrially we are forming the structure of the new society within the shell of the old.

In 1910, the IWW's English-language publications also began to endorse sabotage as practised by French syndicalists. Even then, many English-speaking IWW members, whose main influences were Marxist rather than

---

24 The preamble can be found in V. St John, *The IWW: Its History, Structure and Methods*, revised edn (Chicago: IWW Publishing Bureau, 1917). The revised version (referred to in the next paragraph) is also included in this source.

anarchist, resisted the syndicalist label and instead described the organiza-tion's ideology as 'revolutionary industrial unionism'. Members of the union's immigrant majority, however, were less averse to calling themselves syndicalists or anarcho-syndicalists.

Regardless, the IWW was a recognizably syndicalist organization. Like the Western Labor Union, it was intended to be a militant and inclusive alternative to the AFL. The IWW sought out and enrolled the 'unorgan-ized', including 'new immigrants', women, and Black, Asian, and Mexican workers. Its membership included disproportionately large num-bers of Finnish, Italian, Spanish, Mexican, Russian, and Scandinavian immigrants but, unlike anarchist groups at the time, it also enrolled large numbers of native-born Americans. After modest beginnings, the union grew rapidly in the 1910s, reaching more than 150,000 members in 1917. Many times that number of workers, however, belonged to the organization at some point.[25]

IWW members were concentrated among miners, lumbermen, and workers in the agricultural, maritime, oil, and textile industries. They led dozens of major strikes across these industries, and waged a number of 'free-speech fights' that saw them filling local jails for disobeying local bans on street speaking. The organization also developed a vibrant working-class counter-culture through its songs, poems, and mutual aid practices.[26] The IWW further spread overseas, establishing branches or locals in at least sixteen other countries between 1906 and 1925, and it influenced a number of additional syndicalist movements throughout the anglophone world.[27]

---

25 E. T. Chester, *The Wobblies in Their Heyday: The Rise and Destruction of the Industrial Workers of the World during the World War I Era* (Santa Barbara, CA: Praeger, 2014), p. 227. On the number of one-time IWW members, see J. S. Gambs, *The Decline of the IWW* (New York: Columbia University Press, 1932), p. 167; Salerno, *Red November, Black November*, pp. 24–5.

26 In addition to the works cited above, essential works on the IWW include M. Dubofsky, *We Shall Be All: A History of the Industrial Workers of the World*, 2nd edn (Urbana: University of Illinois Press, 1988); F. Rosemont, *Joe Hill: The IWW and the Making of a Revolutionary Workingclass Counterculture* (Chicago: Charles H. Kerr, 2003); P. Cole, *Wobblies on the Waterfront: Interracial Unionism in Progressive-Era Philadelphia* (Urbana: University of Illinois Press, 2007); and H. Mayer, *Beyond the Rebel Girl: Women and the Industrial Workers of the World in the Pacific Northwest, 1905–1924* (Corvallis: Oregon State University Press, 2018).

27 See A. Rosenthal, 'Radical border crossers: the Industrial Workers of the World and their press in Latin America', *Estudios Interdisciplinarios de América Latina y el Caribe* 22, 2 (2011), pp. 39–70; P. Cole, D. Struthers, and K. Zimmer (eds.), *Wobblies of the World: A Global History of the IWW* (London: Pluto Press, 2017).

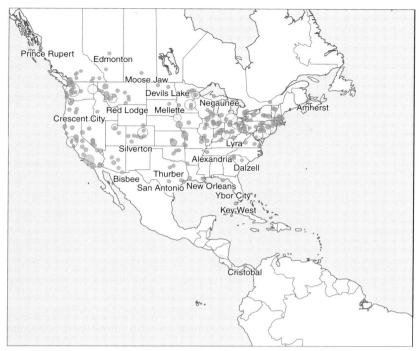

Map 19.1 Industrial Workers of the World, locals, 1905–1920. This map has been redrawn with permission from the IWW History Project, University of Washington (https://depts .washington.edu/iww/map_locals.shtml). The size of the circles indicates the number of locals, with the smallest circles representing one and the largest, for New York City, representing sixty-five.

Anarchist Apogee: Anarcho-Syndicalism and Modernism, 1900s–1910s

The years between the formation of the IWW and the First World War also marked the apex of US anarchism. The movement expanded its base of support into new immigrant communities, and American anarchist periodicals reached their peak circulation – well over 100,000 combined copies per issue – around 1910.[28] Anarchists of this era were deeply interested in libertarian education and cultural modernism, but even more so in syndicalism.

Following international outcry over the 1909 execution of anarchist educator Francisco Ferrer i Guardia by Spanish authorities, anarchists in the United States founded more than twenty 'Modern Schools' for children and

28 Zimmer, *Immigrants against the State*, pp. 5–6.

adults loosely based on Ferrer's libertarian pedagogy. Though only a few hundred pupils passed through these institutions, many schools became important radical community hubs for adults and children alike, and some were centres around which anarchist residential communities formed. Among those attracted to these endeavours were a number of prominent modernist artists and writers, many of whom identified as anarchists themselves. Through them, anarchist ideas and values were ingrained in much of the pre-war era's avant-garde and 'bohemian' art and culture.[29]

Even as the movement's Jewish, Italian, and Spanish segments continued to grow, other groups of immigrants began to form anarchist groups for the first time. Japanese and Chinese organizations appeared in California in 1906 and 1919, respectively, while the transnational Ghadar Party, founded in Oregon in 1913 by anti-colonial immigrants from British India, was deeply influenced by the anarchist and syndicalist ideas that its members encountered in the United States.[30] The most consequential new organizations, however, were the Partido Liberal Mexicano (Mexican Liberal Party, PLM), founded on US soil in 1905, and the Union of Russian Workers of the United States and Canada (URW), established in 1914.

The PLM began as a multi-tendency movement opposed to the Mexican president Porfirio Díaz, but within a few years most of its leaders and transnational membership had embraced anarchism and syndicalism, and the organization expanded its scope of action to include the labour struggles of Mexican workers on both sides of the US–Mexico border. Although the PLM was dominated by men and a masculine ethos, Mexican women also joined, and in some cases founded their own anarchist–feminist groups and publications. Thousands of Mexicans joined hundreds of local PLM groups throughout the American south-west, many of whom also belonged to the IWW, and the two organizations often supported one another's activities.[31]

29 P. Avrich, *The Modern School Movement: Anarchism and Education in the United States* (Princeton: Princeton University Press, 1980); A. Antliff, *Anarchist Modernism: Art, Politics, and the First American Avant-Garde* (Chicago: University of Chicago Press, 2001).

30 On these little-known groups, see F. G. Notehelfer, *Kōtoku Shūsui: Portrait of a Japanese Radical* (Cambridge: Cambridge University Press, 1971); Shuyao, 'History of Meizhou Gongyi Tongmeng Zonghui (Unionist Guild of America)', trans. Him Mark Lai, *Chinese America: History & Perspectives (Journal of the Chinese Historical Society of America)*, 2008, pp. 25–7; M. Ramnath, *Haj to Utopia: How the Ghadar Movement Charted Global Radicalism and Attempted to Overthrow the British Empire* (Berkeley: University of California Press, 2011).

31 For the PLM's rich history, see W. D. Raat, *Revoltosos: Mexico's Rebels in the United States, 1903–1923* (College Station: Texas A&M University Press, 1981); C. Lomnitz, *The Return of Comrade Ricardo Flores Magón* (New York: Zone Books, 2014); and Sonia Hernández, *For a Just and Better World: Engendering Anarchism in the Mexican Borderlands, 1900–1938* (Urbana: University of Illinois Press, 2021).

In 1911 the PLM organized the cross-border armed invasion of Mexicali and Tijuana as part of the opening phase of the Mexican Revolution, in hopes of establishing an autonomous anarchist territory from which the revolution could be spread throughout Mexico and the United States. This effort received aid from left-wing socialists, the IWW, and anarchists throughout the Atlantic world, and dozens of IWW members (including famed songwriter Joe Hill), and Italian-American anarchists fought within the PLM's forces before these were routed. In 1915, PLM members in Mexico also participated in cross-border raids into Texas inspired by a somewhat mysterious manifesto known as the 'Plan of San Diego', which the PLM faction helped to revise to include anarchist goals.[32] The PLM's leaders, meanwhile, faced frequent arrests (including attempts to illegally extradite them to Mexico), making co-ordination of such efforts difficult. Regardless, for more than a decade the PLM was the dominant manifestation of Mexican-American radicalism.

The Union of Russian Workers shared many features with the PLM, although it appeared nearly a decade later. Many of its leaders were refugees from the failed Russian Revolution of 1905, but its membership was largely composed of immigrant workers who emigrated following Russia's economic downturn of 1911 and were radicalized in the United States. Like the PLM, the URW focused both on supporting the revolutionary movement in its members' country of origin and on aiding the struggles of workers in the United States. The new organization was explicitly anarcho-syndicalist in orientation – in fact, its newspaper *Golos Truda* (*Voice of Labour*, 1911–17) was one of the first in the world to label itself an 'anarcho-syndicalist organ'. The URW's declaration of principles drew heavily on the IWW preamble, but added a clear commitment to communist anarchism and 'a forceful social revolution'. The URW was not itself a labour union, however (Russian anarchist groups commonly referred to themselves as 'unions'), so members were directed to join locals of the IWW wherever possible, and they took part in a number of major labour struggles within the ranks of the IWW and other unions during and after the First World War. The organization grew to

---

32 On these events, see L. L. Blaisdell, *The Desert Revolution: Baja California, 1911* (Madison: University of Wisconsin Press, 1962); David M. Struthers, *The World in a City: Multiethnic Radicalism in Early Twentieth-Century Los Angeles* (Urbana: University of Illinois Press, 2019), ch. 6; M. Presutto, 'The revolution just around the corner: Italian American radicals and the Mexican Revolution, 1910–1914', *Italian American Review* 7, 1 (2017), pp. 8–40; J. A. Sandos, *Rebellion in the Borderlands: Anarchism and the Plan of San Diego, 1904–1923* (Norman: University of Oklahoma Press, 1992); and B. Heber Johnson, *Revolution in Texas: How a Forgotten Rebellion and Its Bloody Suppression Turned Mexicans into Americans* (New Haven: Yale University Press, 2003).

as many as 12,000 members in 1918, distinguishing it as the largest anarchist federation in US history.[33]

Although most anarchists supported the IWW and many belonged to it, they also offered many critiques of the organization. The IWW's early entanglements with socialist parties were a failing in anarchists' eyes, as was the increasing centralization of its structure. Some questioned the wisdom of creating an organization separate from the mainstream unions of the AFL. In 1912 anarchist critics of this 'dual unionist' approach formed a short-lived Syndicalist Educational League with the goal of spreading syndicalist ideas and methods among workers regardless of union affiliation. The following year William Z. Foster (1881–1961), a syndicalist with anarchist sympathies, founded the more enduring Syndicalist League of North America with the goal of 'boring from within' the AFL, though this organization enrolled no more than a couple of thousand members. It would, however, form the basis of Foster's Trade Union Educational League, which in the 1920s became the Communist Party's foothold within the labour movement.[34]

War and Repression, 1910s–1920s

The First World War, the Russian Revolution, and the post-war 'Red Scare' completely reshaped American radicalism. The large majority of anarchists and IWW members stridently opposed the war and the United States' entry into it, although the overthrow of the Russian tsar caused some prominent Russian Jewish anarchists to belatedly support the Allied war effort. The Bolshevik seizure of power, meanwhile, pushed anti-radical paranoia to a fever pitch. Hundreds of radicals (including Emma Goldman and Alexander Berkman) were imprisoned for opposing military conscription or violating new wartime federal statutes limiting radical speech. Dozens of anarchist and IWW newspapers were suppressed, and in 1918 more than a hundred IWW leaders and organizers were sentenced to prison on flimsy charges of conspiring to interfere with the war effort. In retaliation, a small

---

33 Reliable works on the URW have only recently been published; see M. Grueter, 'Red Scare scholarship, class conflict, and the case of the anarchist Union of Russian Workers, 1919', *Journal for the Study of Radicalism* 11, 1 (Spring 2017), pp. 53–81; and L. Lipotkin, *The Russian Anarchist Movement in North America*, trans. M. Archibald (Edmonton, Ont.: Black Cat Press, 2019).

34 E. P. Johanningsmeier, 'William Z. Foster and the Syndicalist League of North America', *Labor History* 30, 3 (1989), pp. 329–53; J. R. Barrett, *William Z. Foster and the Tragedy of American Radicalism* (Urbana: University of Illinois Press, 1999).

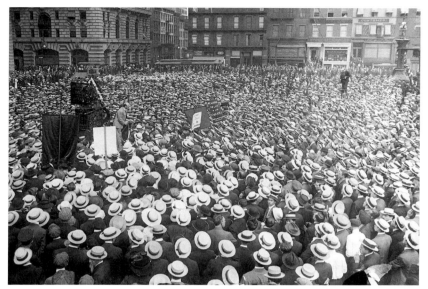

Fig. 19.1   Alexander Berkman speaking to an IWW rally, New York, 1914. (Bettmann/Getty Images.)

group of Italian anarchist insurrectionists co-ordinated a series of bombings targeting prominent anti-radical political and business figures. Although these attacks claimed only the lives of a night watchman and an unfortunate anarchist in the act of placing a device that exploded prematurely, they sparked a renewed wave of repression. Newly revised immigration statutes allowed for the deportation of any foreign-born anarchist (as well as members of the IWW or Communist Party), and thousands were arrested, though only around 1,000 were ultimately expelled.[35] Nevertheless, the damage dealt to the anarchist and syndicalist movements was considerable and permanent; the IWW was left a shadow of its former self, and both the PLM and the URW ceased to exist following the imprisonment and deportation of their leading figures. Furthermore, legislation passed in 1921 and 1924

35   D. Strang, *Keep the Wretches in Order: America's Biggest Mass Trial, the Rise of the Justice Department, and the Fall of the IWW* (Madison: University of Wisconsin Press, 2019); Avrich, *Sacco and Vanzetti*; B. Gage, *The Day Wall Street Exploded: A Story of America in Its First Age of Terror* (Oxford: Oxford University Press, 2009); K. Zimmer, 'The Voyage of the Buford: Political Deportations and the Making and Unmaking of America's First Red Scare', in K. Zimmer and C. Salinas (eds.), *Deportation in the Americas: Histories of Exclusion and Resistance* (College Station: Texas A&M University Press, 2018), pp. 132–63.

drastically reduced legal immigration from southern and eastern Europe, the main wellsprings of pre-war anarchist strength.

The new communist movement, meanwhile, attracted a substantial number of former anarchists and, especially, IWW members. For several years the communists endorsed the IWW and attempted to bring the union within their orbit, and dozens of IWW members participated in the Kuzbass Autonomous Industrial Colony in Siberia before its dissolution in 1926.[36] The IWW itself began to rebound in the early 1920s, but nearly collapsed entirely following a bitter 1924 split between an anarchist-backed 'decentralist' faction and a communist-supported 'centralist' faction. By the end of the decade its membership had plunged to between 3,000 and 8,000 and continued to decline thereafter.[37]

Anarchists in these years were perpetually on the defensive. They directed most of their energies to protesting the trial and 1927 executions of Italian anarchists Nicola Sacco (b. 1891) and Bartolomeo Vanzetti (b. 1888); to sending aid to imprisoned anarchists in Russia and Italy; to combating the growth of communist influence within the International Ladies' Garment Workers Union – which was led by Jewish anarchist Morris Sigman (1880–1931) from 1923 to 1928 – and other unions; and to combating the spread of fascism among Italian-Americans.[38] Embattled anarchists responded in two contradictory ways: on one hand, they formed several new, ethnic-based anarchist federations, including the Jewish Anarchist Federation of America and Canada (founded in 1921), the Federation of Spanish-Speaking Anarchist Groups in the United States (founded in 1929), and a succession of competing Russian anarchist federations. On the other hand, many created multi-ethnic, English-speaking 'international' groups to better reach the American public. Neither strategy, however, had its desired effect; the federations more often counted hundreds rather than thousands of members, and the international groups and their publications never reached a large audience.

Transformations, 1930s–1970s

Anarchists and syndicalists proved unable to effectively adapt to the changing demographic, political, and economic landscape of the interwar years. In the

36 On the Kuzbass Colony, see J. P. Morray, *Project Kuzbas: American Workers in Siberia (1921–1926)* (New York: International Publishers, 1983).
37 Gambs, *Decline of the IWW*; L. W. Robinson, 'Social Movement Organizations in Decline: A Case Study of the IWW', PhD dissertation, Northwestern University, USA, 1973.
38 Zimmer, *Immigrants against the State*, ch. 5; A. Cornell, *Unruly Equality: US Anarchism in the Twentieth Century* (Berkeley: University of California Press, 2016), ch. 3.

words of the foremost historian of anarchism in this era, 'the 1930s pitted an organizing anarchism without organizers against an insurrectionary anarchism without insurgents'.[39] The Great Depression, which proved a ripe opportunity for the Communist Party and the American labour movement, found anarchists and the IWW unprepared and increasingly isolated. Anarchists applauded the era's upsurge of worker militancy, but (correctly) viewed the new industrial unionist organization that it gave rise to, the Congress of Industrial Organizations (CIO), as a non-revolutionary body that became increasingly enmeshed in the politics of the Democratic Party. Most therefore continued to endorse the IWW, a union with a consequential presence in the 1930s only in the metal shops of Cleveland and among maritime workers. Jewish anarchist influence within the ILGWU was also on the decline, although individual officials and organizers, including future union vice-president Rose Pesotta (1896–1965), continued to play important roles in the organization.[40] Anarchists and syndicalists could also not embrace the welfare state created by the New Deal, even as many appreciated its new protections for workers and found employment in its federal jobs programmes.

Italian anarchists – both insurrectionists and anarcho-syndicalists – were fully engulfed in anti-fascist activities, both locally and transnationally. They produced anti-fascist literature, plays, and art, protested against Italy's invasion of Ethiopia, and battled Italian-American fascist supporters in the streets. They also funded underground anti-fascist efforts in Europe, and two Italian anarchists returned from the United States to carry out failed assassination attempts against Benito Mussolini.[41]

The Spanish Civil War (1936–9) sparked what proved to be the immigrant generations' final flurry of significant activity. The prominent role of Spain's anarchists in the struggle led to a spike in interest in anarchism and a temporary rise in the number and circulation of American anarchist periodicals. Anarchist groups also collected more than $100,000 to aid their comrades in Spain, and between 100 and 200 anarchists – mainly Italians and Spaniards – as well as dozens of IWW members left the United States to fight

39 Cornell, *Unruly Equality*, p. 143.
40 R. T. Wortman, *From Syndicalism to Trade Unionism: The IWW in Ohio, 1905–1950* (New York: Garland Publishing, 1985); F. Thompson and J. Bekken, *The Industrial Workers of the World: Its First One Hundred Years* (Cincinnati: Industrial Workers of the World, 2006); E. J. Leeder, *The Gentle General: Rose Pesotta, Anarchist and Labor Organizer* (Albany: State University of New York Press, 1993).
41 N. Pernicone, *Carlo Tresca: Portrait of a Rebel*, rev. edn (Oakland, CA: AK Press, 2010); R. Lenzi, *Facing toward the Dawn: The Italian Anarchists of New London* (Albany: State University of New York Press, 2019); Zimmer, *Immigrants against the State*; Tomchuk, *Transnational Radicals*.

in Spain, many never to return.[42] The defeat of Spain's Popular Front forces was a crushing blow to many American anarchists and syndicalists, who then found themselves divided on the question of whether or not to support the Allies against fascism in the Second World War.

Both wars were formative events for a younger generation of largely American-born anarchists (many of them the children of Jewish and Italian anarchist immigrants) who in the 1930s and 1940s created their own modest-sized groups and publications. Often disillusioned with syndicalism and insurrectionism alike, this generation was particularly receptive to outside influences, from Christian and Gandhian pacifism to radical psychology, Zen Buddhism, and Jewish mysticism. Many of these groups embraced pacifism and cultural radicalism as strategies for long-term, evolutionary change. A parallel, but autonomous Christian anarchist pacifist current emerged in 1933 in the form of the Catholic Worker Movement, which by the end of the decade had established twenty-five communal farms and 'houses of hospitality' to aid the poor and serve as models of mutual aid and non-hierarchical organization. A number of young anarchist men were imprisoned as conscientious objectors during the war, and formed lasting connections with other incarcerated radical pacifists. Individual anarchists subsequently played important roles in the anti-militarist War Resisters' League and in the early black civil rights-focused Congress of Racial Equality, and anarchism profoundly shaped the anti-authoritarian, and often explicitly anarchist, politics of the Beat Generation and many of its prominent writers.

By the 1950s, American anarchism had centred its attention on issues of anti-militarism, racial and gender equality, and sexual freedom, which it pursued through the tactics of non-violent direct action, cultural and artistic rebellion, and the creation of intentional communities. Its efforts increasingly focused on prefiguring ideal social relations, rather than mobilizing to overthrow existing institutions. Though anarchists numbered no more than several hundred nationwide in the early 1960s, the movements they had quietly helped to develop over the previous two decades strongly influenced the radical and counter-cultural politics of the era. In the absence of a large or formally organized anarchist movement, individual anarchists actively

---

42 K. Zimmer, 'The other volunteers: American anarchists and the Spanish Civil War, 1936–1939', *Journal for the Study of Radicalism* 10, 2 (2016), pp. 19–52; M. C. White, '"The Cause of the Workers Who Are Fighting in Spain Is Yours": The Marine Transport Workers and the Spanish Civil War', in Cole, Struthers, and Zimmer (eds.), *Wobblies of the World*, pp. 212–27; M. Brodie, *Transatlantic Anarchism during the Spanish Civil War and Revolution, 1936–1939: Fury over Spain* (New York: Routledge, 2020).

participated in the civil rights movement, the women's and gay liberation movements, and mobilizations against the Vietnam War. This New Left also looked to a number of anarchist and anarchist-influenced intellectuals for inspiration, such as Dorothy Day (1897–1980), David Dellinger (1915–2004), Paul Goodman (1911–72), and former Trotskyist Dwight Macdonald (1906–82), who delivered a talk on 'The Relevance of Anarchism' at the founding convention of Students for a Democratic Society (SDS). Groups such as the Diggers, the Yippies, and Black Mask/Up Against the Wall Motherfucker explicitly or implicitly embraced anarchist ideas, and an anarchist faction also grew within SDS, in which anarchist theorist and radical ecologist Murray Bookchin (1921–2006) was active.[43]

Contemporary Anarchism and Syndicalism, 1970s–Present

In the 1970s and 1980s, anarchism continued to be a formative influence on radical feminism and environmentalism, as well as the emerging punk counter-culture, which in turn introduced new generations of discontented youth to anarchist ideas. Anarchist organizing models based on horizontal power structures, consensus decision-making, autonomous affinity groups, and direct action proliferated among groups dedicated to environmental, anti-nuclear, anti-racist, animal rights, and HIV/AIDS activism, as well as the 'anti-globalization' movement of the 1990s and early 2000s, the Occupy movement, and the contemporary Antifa movement.[44]

In these same decades, American anarchist ideology branched into a number of new tendencies, such as anarcha-feminism, anarcho-primitivism, and 'post-left' anarchism, while older strains of anarcho-syndicalism and insurrectionary anarchism were also revived. The IWW, which in the 1960s had dropped to fewer than 200 members, likewise experienced a modest revival, launching several significant organizing drives among retail and service workers and counting a few thousand members by the second decade of the twenty-first century. However, since the mid-twentieth century, struggles for racial justice, feminism, anti-colonialism,

---

43 Anarchism in these decades is ably documented in Cornell, *Unruly Equality*, chs. 5–6.
44 Ibid., pp. 291–300; B. Epstein, *Political Protest and Cultural Revolution: Nonviolent Direct Action in the 1970s and 1980s* (Berkeley: University of California Press, 1993); G. Curran, *21st Century Dissent: Anarchism, Anti-Globalization and Environmentalism* (London: Palgrave Macmillan, 2006); M. Bray, *Translating Anarchy: The Anarchism of Occupy Wall Street* (Winchester, UK: Zero Books, 2013); M. Bray, *Antifa: The Anti-Fascist Handbook* (New York: Melville House, 2017).

environmentalism, immigrant rights, anti-fascism, and gender and sexual freedom have eclipsed class as the anarchist movement's central concerns. In this sense, contemporary anarchists incorporate many of the eclectic features of the first generation of individualist anarchists, but combine these with selected economic, tactical, and cultural elements of later generations. The result is a diverse and diffuse anarchism, but one that in the scope of its influence once again rivals Marxist varieties of American radicalism.

Further Reading

Avrich, Paul, *The Haymarket Tragedy* (Princeton: Princeton University Press, 1984).
  Sacco and Vanzetti: The Anarchist Background (Princeton: Princeton University Press, 1991).
Castañeda, Christopher J., and Montse Feu (eds.), *Writing Revolution: Hispanic Anarchism in the United States* (Urbana: University of Illinois Press, 2019).
Cole, Peter, David Struthers, and Kenyon Zimmer (eds.), *Wobblies of the World: A Global History of the IWW* (London: Pluto Press, 2017).
Cornell, Andrew, *Unruly Equality: US Anarchism in the Twentieth Century* (Berkeley: University of California Press, 2016).
Dubofsky, Melvyn, *We Shall Be All: A History of the Industrial Workers of the World*, 2nd edn (Urbana: University of Illinois Press, 1988).
Goyens, Tom, *Beer and Revolution: The German Anarchist Movement in New York City, 1880–1914* (Urbana: University of Illinois Press, 2007).
Martin, James J., *Men against the State: The Expositors of Individualist Anarchism in America, 1827–1908* (De Kalb, IL: Adrian Allen Associates, 1953).
Zimmer, Kenyon, *Immigrants against the State: Yiddish and Italian Anarchism in America* (Urbana: University of Illinois Press, 2015).

20

Mexican Socialism

JOHN MASON HART

The Origins of Ideas and Practices

The origins of Mexican syndicalism and socialism are rooted in the pre-Columbian, Spanish, and post-conquest working-class experiences that came together beginning in the sixteenth century and then evolved from that base during the era of the Industrial Revolution (1780–2000). The movement has emerged from its early beginnings within one of the world's most beleaguered working-class experiences into one that is now powerful enough to politically manage the nation and is capable of creating a more just social democratic society.

After the conquest, the very survival of the working-class communities and population was at stake, but over the next three centuries they reasserted themselves as co-operatives under the locally autonomous leadership of community artisans and utopian friars who defined an idealistic but eventually achievable agenda of worker self-directed *patio* industrial production, co-operative farming, and *pueblo* self-government.[1] The latter achievement had been acted out for centuries in Spain and Mesoamerica by way of what the Mexicans call Arenas de Comunidad where the locals, men and women, gathered to discuss the solutions to every type of challenge.

In contrast to the conquerors, many Spaniards, artisans and other workers, and missionaries came to New Spain imbued with beliefs that challenged state and elite political authority and monarchist cultural hegemony. Missionaries dedicated to St Francis of Assisi and St Ignatius of Loyola blanketed the countryside, establishing *pueblos* for the people and importing

---

1 A *patio* is a place of artisan production, usually outdoors and consisting of six to nine skilled and apprentice-level workers normally led by a *maestro*. A *pueblo* is a formally recognized incorporated settlement with a considerable degree of economic diversification within the populace.

Spanish laws for their protection. These laws recognized *pueblo* political autonomy and the rights to an agricultural regime of large *pueblo* co-operative properties (*ejidos*) and artisan *patio* workshops also often organized as co-operatives. The state allowed these concessions in return for the indigenous peoples' adoption of Christianity and loyalty to the crown. As a result the monarchy, perhaps because of oversight and neglect, actually fostered a form of workers' self-government, a forerunner of syndicalism and democracy.[2]

But the long-term survival of the communities depended on the active participation in the Arenas de Comunidad by a high percentage of the *vecinos* (citizens). Women played important roles in these community governance activities, which entailed union-like dialogues. Their eventual participation in the Independence Revolution of 1810 as suppliers to the besieged defenders of Mezcala island in Lake Chapala and their seizure of the Puente de Ixtla Hacienda in the 1910 revolution resulted from their longstanding active roles in *pueblo* defence in virtually every area of Mexico.[3]

In this manner the survivors of the imperialist conquest persevered against severe violence and great odds during the colonial age (1521–1821), emerging from the experience allied with sympathetic clergy and intellectuals and imbued with an enduring commitment to *pueblo* self-government that included social and cultural programmes together with rules of work and civic comportment. By the late eighteenth century, their experience with the friars' utopian socialism combined with *pueblo* autonomy and the growth of artisanry and markets to create workers' co-operatives based on democratic interactions such as public meetings run by local citizens. This adaptive ability on the part of the *pueblo* workers would carry over to the urban sector of society as the people continued to migrate to the cities in search of material wellbeing. Their experience in the *pueblos* would enable them to confront the hardships and the alien values imposed upon them by capitalist hegemony

2 G. Charles, *The Aztecs under Spanish Rule* (Stanford: Stanford University Press, 1954), provides a powerful overview of the process of compromise and assimilation that took place.
3 For Mezcala, see Mark Saad Saka, 'Clerical Insurrection and Agrarian Rebellion in Nineteenth-Century Mexico: The Siege of Mezcala, 1811–1815', Masters Thesis, University of Houston, USA, 1990. The Puente de Ixtle action is discussed in J. M. Hart, *Empire and Revolution: The Americans in Mexico since the Civil War* (Berkeley: University of California Press, 2003). The history of working-class women is treated in a number of outstanding books and articles including J. Tunon, *Women in Mexico: A Past Unveiled* (Austin: Institute of Latin American Studies and the University of Texas Press, 1999); and S. Schroeder, 'Women's Status and Occupation: Indian Women in New Spain', *Encyclopedia of Mexico*, vol. II (Chicago: Fitzroy and Dearborn, 1997), pp. 1615–18.

during the Industrial Revolution. They did so, often with the support of their clergy, by fighting for the essentials of their way of life – such as local ownership and administration of properties, protective tariffs for their artisans, gender relations that included women as artisans or even holding political roles, and the provision of services such as education – against what seemed like impossible odds. Those adjustments included forming legal committees that worked with the judiciary of the autocratic nation-state that co-operated openly with a national oligarchy that monopolized national wealth. These defence committees functioned throughout the era of land appropriations that began in the late eighteenth century and continued into the twentieth century. They protected their way of life by integrating their age-old practices of self-empowerment with the Spanish and Mexican court systems.

By the late nineteenth century, a handful of Mexican elites, joined by some of the most powerful capitalists in the United States, controlled both agriculture and industry on a national scale. Meanwhile, beginning in the late 1870s the government openly suppressed independent unions, as well as advocates of socialism and anarchism. The small elite of only 7,250 great estate owners, 45,000 small property holders, and some 150 American capitalists claimed well over 95 per cent of the nation's arable land. Less than one-tenth of 1 per cent of the national population owned virtually all forms of production, while the rural and industrial workers were strongly suppressed by a combination of military and police interventions that included forcible actions and imprisonments carried out against dissidents, students, and union organizers. The rural masses, numbering some 12,000,000, were essentially devoid of assets and faced the choice of working on the great estates or migrating to the cities or abroad. When they found work, it was usually offered at below subsistence wages in cotton, textile, and lumber mills, in mines, or on enormous ranches. Many were forced to accept debt peonage.

Before the nationalistic revolution of 1910, some 3,000,000 Mexicans lived in the urban sector and in the larger towns, but most of the factories were semi-rural. Many of the workers lived in company towns or in barracks near the factory sites and depended on company stores for rations. But beginning in the 1860s a growing number of rural and urban workers had gained penetrating interpretations of events from a growing number of libertarian socialist activists and Marxists. Some of them came from abroad carrying the ideas of Mikhail Bakunin, Pierre-Joseph Proudhon, and Joseph Fourier, but the Mexican working class already understood the issues from the standpoint of their long history of struggles and experience with libertarian co-operatives.

The Passage to Modernity

The strength of Mexican socialism derives from the enduring nature of its ancient *altepemeh* (s. *altepetl*, pre-Columbian village) and the *pueblos* that succeeded them during the colonial era between the sixteenth and nineteenth centuries. The original values which have come into the present from the ancient origins of that society are consistent with the Vietnamese co-op and the Russian *mir*. In the pre-Columbian era, the *altepemeh* and *cahob* (s. *cah*, small town) of the Nahuatl and Mayan cultures grew into a citizenry that numbered in the tens of millions and had developed remarkably self-contained and powerful cultures capable of developing one of the world's great hydraulic systems.

That know-how, originally based on locally invented ideas, then nurtured the origins and growth of civilization itself on a wider interactive basis starting between 3,500 and 7,000 years ago. After primitive beginnings, these creative working-class communities then reached out to each other, fostering the development of irrigated agriculture, hydraulic services, town planning, written language, civic architecture, geometry, and skilled artisan *patio* production that included tools and other service goods. Over the centuries, the community artisans and vendors interacted on a regular basis through trade, exploration, the exchange of ideas, and migration; for the purposes of armed defence, they often co-operated against city-states whose elites were bent on the expansion of their imperial power. During these thousands of years the Mesoamericans even demonstrated the capacity to survive catastrophes, such as asteroid impacts, floods, droughts, plagues, and famines; our knowledge of those experiences is only beginning to emerge.

These *altepemeh* and *cahob*, in addition to uniting in order to withstand the urban imperialists of their era, also co-operated in commerce and industry. The construction of roads was one such endeavour. They extended east and west across Mesoamerica and north and south from Central America to what is now the south-western United States. In the Maya areas these highways were known as Sac Be, and the *masewalob* or workers in each *cah* assumed responsibility for the maintenance of that portion of road or canal that pertained to them. Those rural communities that successfully resisted the inevitable arrival of outside intruders, however, were led by demonstrably highly skilled and intelligent workers capable of surmounting the challenges presented by their growing populations: urbanism, housing needs, tool-making, clothing, and mounting nutritional needs. Through their exchanges of products and ideas, they also created linguistic and other cultural linkages with their neighbours including similar beliefs and practices. Ethnic regions emerged during the prolonged era of pre-history by virtue of distinct local histories.

Indeed, the great initiatives of early Mesoamerican civilization derived from grassroots ideas and production. Over thousands of years, these workers designed, built, and maintained structures, canals, aqueducts, dams, and cities composed of stones cut by highly skilled masons to fit, and to serve mathematically designed cities and production complexes. Archaeologists now identify two key components in this evolution which became the cornerstones of socialism; one is the Arena de Comunidad, which served not only as the mechanism for the resolution of their immediate problems, but also as the communicative basis of dialogue in the *altepemeh* and *pueblos*. The other was a geometric design that charac-terized the towns and their buildings, altars, and temples, as they cele-brated their ancestors, deified them, and then identified themselves as the products of those histories.

For the people, those commemorations gave a deeper sense of meaning not only to their communities but also to their co-operative way of life. The *ejidos*, or co-operatives of individualized small holdings and communes, provided a social balance to the entire community that contributed to the sense of local importance. That sense of pride in co-operation and the physical presence of the Arena de Comunidad which facilitated their ability to arrive at collective and important decisions enabled the citizens of the *pueblos* to face the challenges of capitalism and urbanism when they arrived on the scene.

In order to maintain meeting clarity, through eye contact and hearing, the people formed circles while sitting on stone benches. These structures and forms of communications were then memorialized in the Hispanic era as '*círculos*' by the de facto socialist workers of the early nineteenth century. For countless centuries in the emergent regional centres of Mesoamerica, visitors had convened in the population centres and formed circles during discussions to reach co-operative or wider-ranging agreements. During these conclaves, visitors from neighbouring villages would stay in guest quarters or houses. Then, near the end of the nineteenth century, the combined residences and practices became memorialized in Spanish as '*casas*', places where important issues could be discussed by regionalized groups of workers. *Círculos* and *casas* would be fundamental elements in the development of the nineteenth- and twentieth-century Mexican working-class experience.

The directly active era in the creation of Mexican socialism began with the Independence Revolution of 1810. That uprising involved masses of miners, mill workers, plantation labourers and hacienda workers, and artisans who held *pueblo* meetings in their plazas, voting to overthrow the Spanish crown and establish Mexican nationhood. They did this in concert with *pueblo* clerics such as Miguel Hidalgo and José María Morelos who introduced the ideas of Abbé Raynal, Thomas Paine, and Thomas Jefferson through *pueblo* theatre presentations – originally written by Molière and Jean Racine and adapted by Padre Hidalgo – that questioned the validity of church and state claims to righteous power.

During the course of the nineteenth century, rural uprisings led by artisans, priests, mule-skinners, vendors, and other *pueblo* stalwarts challenged the state and the elites in the face of the land appropriations needed to continue the growth of Mexico's nascent capitalism. In the cases of the Chalco uprising of 1869 and the Huasteca Potosina uprising of 1879–84, libertarian socialists played central roles in helping mobilize the fighters. In each case the rebels fought to ensure the hegemony of *pueblo* authority, and in order to secure that objective they seized great estates and declared them communes and co-operatives. The degree of bloodshed was extreme in these uprisings, and the Mexican army liquidated entire villages in order to restore the authority of the elites or, as they put it, to maintain law and order. New workers were then brought in to repopulate the deserted areas, but this tactic failed in both cases. In Chalco and the Huasteca Potosina, the heirs of the late nineteenth-century rebels declared themselves Zapatistas and Villistas when the 1910 revolution began. In so doing, they once again posited the *pueblo* as the de jure basic unit of Mexican polity. They reasserted the lessons of the past.

Beginning in December 1861, the values and practices of Mexico's past came together with those of Europe. The date is marked by the arrival of Plotino Rhodakanaty in the port of Veracruz. Born in Greece, Rhodakanaty was a veteran rebel from the 1848 student uprisings in Germany and became a catalyst for the first overt manifestations of European socialism in Mexico. His father was a heroic casualty of the Greek independence movement against the Ottoman Empire and, as a small child, his Austrian mother had taken him to her family in Vienna, where he grew up. He then enrolled in the University of Frankfurt, where he took part in the 1840s anti-monarchist unrest before escaping the repression and ending up in Paris. He studied with

Proudhon for several years and heard about the crisis of appropriations from a Mexican student. He went to Barcelona, where he witnessed libertarian socialism in day-to-day practice and became a staunch adherent to that way of life. His arrival in Veracruz went unnoticed in the hullabaloo connected with the French invasion at that time. He then reached Mexico City without attracting the attention of the police, and secured a teaching position in the respectable and quite old Colegio de San Ildefonso, located immediately north of the National Cathedral in the centre of the downtown area. Virtually all of his male students were the sons of artisans who appreciated his anti-aristocratic and libertarian socialist teachings.

Within a few years a 'Bakuninist' student group became publicly visible at the school, and one of its most important efforts was to reach out to the workers in the growing complex of factories surrounding the city along the Camino al Ajusco to the south and on the road to Tepeji del Rio to the north. Strikes soon took place in both locales, and the French puppet, Emperor Maximilian, used his imperial gendarmes to repress them. Within the city a small nuclei of artisans, already active in guilds, dedicated to professional expertise and mutual aid, and advocating democratic political reform and workers' control of various economic sectors, became visible to the public. The first politically active groups in the working class emerged in the urban complex from among the typesetters, carriage and wagon drivers, textile workers, and tailors. They advocated independent workers' control of production through artisan *patios*, quality controls in each sector to be administered by the workers themselves, and support for the widows and orphans of the workers and the physically challenged.

A small group of Rhodakanaty's students continued their organizing efforts after leaving school. One of them, Francisco Zalacosta, ended up being executed by the Mexican army in 1880 after helping organize two rural insurrections over a ten-year period. In the first case President Benito Juarez issued a concession to a land developer to drain Lake Chalco located in the south-eastern corner of the Valley of Mexico. However, Chalco was an ancient city comprising fishermen, *chinampa* (paddy) farmers, and orchard operators (pecans and fruit) who could use the lake waters to flood their trees. The president's decision was linked to land development for a growing city. Zalacosta linked up with a local grower, Julio Chavez Lopez, and they called for the overthrow of the government and a social revolution in a manifesto addressed to all 'The Oppressed of the Universe'.

The rebellion quickly spread across the region into the state of Veracruz and was centred on a force numbering some 1,500 fighters. They had devised a seemingly intelligent strategy that called for the encirclement of Mexico City by marching north and then west, joining a number of *pueblos* that supported the revolt, until they reached Tepeji del Rio where additional recruits were waiting to receive arms and join them. However, the army surprised the rebels north-east of the city by using the Mexico City railroad to Veracruz to arrive at that point in a matter of hours, and destroyed them. Chavez Lopez was captured and marched back to Chalco, where the counter-insurgency forces executed him in the town plaza. His last words as he stood on the gallows were 'Viva el socialismo'. Zalacosta eluded capture and continued his work.

In 1871 the activists created the Círculo de Obreros (Circle of Workers) in Mexico City and added workers' participation in factory management to their artisan-influenced demand for workers' self-direction (*autogestión*). They also began to publish pamphlets and recruited textile workers from the urban periphery to join the cause. Their demands, in addition to relief from penury and abuse, included workers' education, self-management, and government support. Their successes led to an enlarged concentration of workers, which numbered some 50,000 workers by 1876. At that time they created the Congreso Nacional de Trabajadores (National Congress of Labourers; at times called the Congreso Nacional de Obreros, National Congress of Workers). Rhodakanaty and Zalacosta were joined at the time by a remarkable corpus of writers who wrote for a number of working-class weeklies. Two of them, *El Socialista* (*The Socialist*) and *El Hijo del Trabajo* (*Son of Labour*), garnered large followings, numbering in excess of 10,000 readers. One of the papers carried a red and black banner at the top of the front page. Restaurant workers and retail shop workers joined the union ranks, while branch groups took shape in the cities of Puebla, Guadalajara, and Morelia.

In late 1875, however, General Porfirio Diaz received endorsements from the leading financiers in New York to overthrow the democratically elected government of President Sebastián Lerdo de Tejada. In late 1875 President Lerdo had cancelled all of the railroad contracts made by the Mexican government with the US railroadmen. At that point Diaz gained the backing of a group of officers, including General Manuel Gonzalez, who dominated the area between Matamoros and Tampico on the Gulf coast. They favoured the creation of a US-owned railroad system which would enter the nation from the centre of the continent at El Paso and Laredo as well as on the Gulf coast at Matamoros and in the far west at San Luis, Sonora.

The army units favouring Diaz did not simply overthrow the government; they also dissolved the unions throughout the area around Mexico City, and those in Puebla, Morelia, and Guadalajara. In 1877 Diaz replaced the 50,000-member Congreso Nacional de Obreros with the 'TRUE Congreso Nacional de Obreros', and its newspapers took on a submissive demeanour, moving from radical doctrines to praise for the regime and calls for relief from various forms of hardship. Between 1879 and 1884 an insurrection of several thousand rural workers on the haciendas (whose owners were referred to as *hacendados*) in the Huasteca Potosina region north-east of Mexico City took over the region, declared communes and co-operatives on the great estates, and held their ground for almost five years, supported by 'communists' from Mexico City.

However, in 1883–4 the army carried out a scorched-earth campaign that virtually depopulated the region, which covered 20,000 square miles between Ciudad del Maiz in the north and Rio Verde in the south. Meanwhile, the army also crushed the radicals in Mexico City. By the mid-1880s, the socialist press in Mexico City had been silenced, and all news of union activity and the espousal of socialism had dropped from official view. However, several secret groups formed a few years later. One of the most important was a secret organization in the factory town of Rio Blanco, Veracruz, formed in 1892 for the declared 'defence of the workers against capitalism'.

At that point radical students in the National University began street protests against the police state. Led by the Flores Magón brothers, Ricardo, Jesús, and Enrique, students in the Law School, the protesters decried the dictatorship and held street marches replete with signs of protest. The regime used special police units, known by the students as '*cosacos* [Cossacks]', to disperse them and arrest the leaders. Crowds of sympathizers rallied to support them, and by 1900 civil protest groups had once again emerged in Mexico City and even held regional reunions. Ricardo Flores Magón attended one of these meetings and, when he was allowed to speak, he denounced Diaz and called for revolution. He, his brothers, and a small group of supporters escaped their impending arrest and retreated to Los Angeles, California, where they began a highly successful anti-government campaign advocating anarchist workers' democracy (*autogestión*), reformist socialism, liberal democracy, revolution, and *regeneración*, by which they meant the restoration of self-government and control of local resources (*tierra y libertad*, land and freedom) by the people, of whom more than 70 per cent were rural.

From 1900 until 1910, the Magonistas held rallies in East Los Angeles, where tens of thousands of Mexican exiles lived, and published two famous monthly newspapers with a circulation of 20,000, *La Revolución Social (The Social Revolution)* and *Regeneración (Regeneration)*. This activism would continue into the modern age. Over the next few years a network of supporters smuggled tens of thousands of copies into Mexico, where the authorities found them threadbare from repeated usage in the hands of strikers and rebels after hundreds of textile workers at Rio Blanco, Veracruz, rose up in 1907, took over the city, and killed policemen and soldiers during the fight.[4]

In that same year the workers at the mining site of Cananea, on the border just south of Bisbee, Arizona, assisted by US members of the Western Federation of Miners and future members of the Industrial Workers of the World rose up and took over the mines and the town. This mine was controlled by the boards of directors of the Phelps Dodge Corporation, the National City Bank, and the Southern Pacific Railroad. Only the combined intervention of the Arizona Rangers, ordered by the territorial governor of Arizona, and the Mexican army restored order. The authorities found anarchist and socialist workers from the United States among the strikers, along with the Magonista newspapers advocating anarchism and socialism.

By 1907 the carriage drivers and other workers were forming clandestine anarchist unions in Mexico City, by now a burgeoning metropolis. At that point strikes broke out in the factory towns of central Mexico, especially among the textile workers, who had been listening to readers in the factories reading aloud from Bakunin, Proudhon, Ricardo Flores Magón, and other anarchists. Between 1907 and the outbreak of the 1910 revolution, democratic socialism and *socialismo libertario* were the dominant working-class political doctrines, but the anarchists were by far the most active in organizing workers.

As Francisco Madero, a young and liberal member of the oligarchy, challenged Diaz in the presidential election, the workers continued to mobilize. In 1910 they formed the Gran Círculo de Obreros Libres (Grand Circle of Free Workers) and quickly claimed several thousand members, with many of them advocating outright workers' ownership, or at least shared control, of the means of production. Once again the centre of libertarian socialist strength rested with the teamsters, typesetters, stone-masons, and tailors, while the textile workers were divided between sympathies for anarcho-syndicalism and democratic socialism. Meanwhile, in November 1910, an amalgam of lumberjacks, miners, cowboys, and debt peons joined with local leaders, including Pancho Villa, mobilized. They soon marched north

---

4 For more on the Magonistas, see W. Albro, *Always a Rebel: Ricardo Flores Magón and the Mexican Revolution* (Fort Worth: Texas Christian University Press, 1992).

and attacked the army base at Ciudad Juarez, Chihuahua, because they perceived it as necessary for the procurement of arms.

After they captured the city in May 1911, President Diaz fled the country. Madero assumed the presidency later that year and quickly tried to forestall the *pueblo*-based demands for *tierra y libertad* and the union demands for workers' *autogestión*. Hoping for stability, he quickly endorsed a US type of trade and industrial union movement, and this latitude gave the anarchists and socialists the opportunity to organize with relatively little police interference. In February 1913 right-wing officers carried out his assassination with the US ambassador's approval, and an extreme right-wing general, Victoriano Huerta, seized the reins of government.

Huerta, distracted by the Zapatista revolution south of Mexico City, sent the army there because the Zapatistas were collectivizing the great estates. During 1913 the various factions of socialist workers, including some 2,000–3,000 anarcho-syndicalists, formed the Casa del Obrero Mundial (House of Global Labour) in Mexico City and claimed membership in the International Workingmen's Association in Amsterdam despite no record of their formal admission having been found there. Several less evident, but highly important groups belonged to the Casa. One comprised attorneys and another artists and intellectuals. They showered the Casa membership with ideas and supportive publicity. By the end of 1913 when the Huerta regime moved to repress the Casa, its membership numbered more than 50,000 and included the most highly skilled workers in central Mexico.

The wider Casa membership included professionals such as the electricians' union, teachers, lawyers, doctors, and typesetters, in addition to construction, textile, restaurant, and domestic workers. In 1914 some 2,000 of them had joined the Zapatista army. The *electricistas* kept the power plant at Nexcaca operative for years during the revolution. As the Huertista army lost battles and Villista and Zapatista forces closed in on the metropolitan areas of central Mexico, the socialist organizers spread across the region. By 1915 there were approximately 150,000 members in a nation of 15,000,000, where only 25 per cent of the people were urban.

The Casa gained considerable strength in several other important cities including Guadalajara, Morelia, Puebla, Veracruz, and Tampico. The oil, dock, and construction workers in Tampico were especially important. They were binational at the grassroots level with US socialists and anarchists from the Industrial Workers of the World taking part in the strike votes and meetings. The workers' principal demands involved participation in management, pay in gold-based currency rather than script monies, and better working conditions. The strikes led to violence when the US and British companies, along with the Huerta government (1913–14), the US Fleet in 1914, and the army of President Venustiano Carranza (1915–19) repeatedly broke up the work stoppages with strike-breakers and troops. The administration of President Woodrow Wilson chose its intervention at Veracruz rather than Tampico because that port afforded direct access to central Mexico and the potential of exercising authority over Mexico City.

In Mexico City the progressive intellectuals formed a group of orators and organizers headed by attorney Antonio Diaz Soto y Gama. They provided a powerful cadre of thinkers and influenced the outcome of the revolution by propagandizing various ideas, including revolutionary nationalism, anarchism, and democratic socialism. Even though the forces with working-class leadership (Villistas, Zapatistas, and the Casa del Obrero Mundial) lost on the battlefields to the *hacendado*-controlled Constitutionalists, their nationalist and socialist agenda of industrial nationalization and *pueblo* recuperation of appropriated properties eventually prevailed for most of the twentieth century.

In 1913 Diaz Soto y Gama left the Casa and joined with Otilio Montaño, a Zapatista intellectual who had attended the rural school in Ajusco in the 1880s when Plotino Rhodakanaty had taught there. Diaz Soto y Gama and Montaño enlarged on the Zapatistas' already strongly libertarian and democratic socialist thought. Their doctrine as explained in the Plan de Ayala and its follow-up addenda enlarged upon Rhodakanaty's and Proudhon's ideas by calling for autonomous *pueblos* to serve as the basic unit of government within a federal structure, workers' self-management, and working-class militias.

Emiliano Zapata, the leader of the rural insurrection in the south, was deeply socialistic. He and his adherents called for the re-creation of the communes and co-operatives that had survived for thousands of years before the Spanish crown and its capitalist allies began their campaign of resource appropriations in the 1780s. After independence in 1821 the Mexican elites continued that fateful effort until Diaz attempted to finalize the process after 1876. By bringing foreign capital into the economy, however, Diaz alienated not only the lower-status strata of the rural masses, but the small property owners as well. The Zapatistas were joined in their demands by their Villista allies in Durango and Chihuahua.

One example of Zapata's libertarian socialist agenda took place in 1913. As a young and aspiring painter, Diego Rivera was leaving the country to join Pablo Picasso as an apprentice in Paris, and he stopped in Morelos to visit

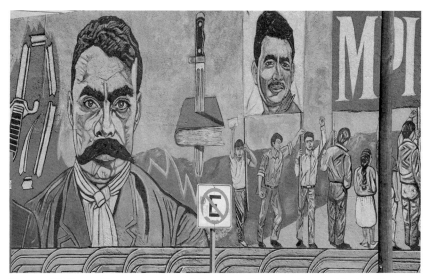

Fig. 20.1 Wall mural honouring the socialist general Emiliano Zapata, Mexico City, 2008. (Photo by Frédéric Soltan / Corbis via Getty Images.)

Zapata. At the plantation of Yautepec they discussed the works of Karl Marx for hours, and Zapata expressed his support for socialism and recommended that Rivera continue to study Marxism. Then, in 1915, Zapata offered Villista general Calixto Contreras, one of Pancho Villa's closest advisers, the presidency of Mexico because of his good character and because he supported the Magonista and Zapatista programmes. Contreras declined the offer because he thought he would be more effective on the battlefield continuing the fight for worker and peasant empowerment.

In 1914, civil war broke out between the largely rural revolutionaries with working-class leadership (the Villistas and Zapatistas) and the forces led by the oligarchic elites of the old-line colonial-era aristocratic Carranza, Elias, and Salido families of Coahuila and Sonora. That powerful combination, backed by US oil, railroad, mining, ranching, and agricultural interests, and the US government crushed the Villistas, the Zapatistas, and the Casa in 1915–16 and ended the chances for a full-blown socialist regime. In a series of fights beginning with the battle for the control of the oilfields at El Ebano, the great estate- and mine-owners in the north-west had already gained the support of the American capitalists in Mexico, led by the investors' syndicates of the Morgan and National City Banks, and their government.

Those anti-socialist activists included J. P. Morgan and J. P. Morgan Jnr, William and John D. Rockefeller, Collis Huntington, Anson Phelps, John Jacob Astor, James Bel Ali Haggin, James Stillman, and Andrew Carnegie. Colonel Edward Mandel House supported racial segregation in the United States and served as President Wilson's personal foreign policy adviser. He deeply disliked the democratic polity and collectivist economies advocated by the Zapatistas and Villistas. Wilson embargoed the Villista and Zapatista revolutionary forces while flooding their oligarchic opponents with the most up-to-date military supplies including Benz trucks, machine guns, and artillery. Despite the use of radical rhetoric by the revolutionaries to gain the support of 4,000–5,000 volunteers from the 'Red Brigades' of the Casa del Obrero Mundial in order to further 'the world-wide Proletarian Revolution', the elite-led forces followed up their victories over the Villistas and Zapatistas by crushing the Casa simultaneously in Tampico and Mexico City in 1916. The success of those efforts constituted a lasting defeat for the socialist cause that has endured for three generations.

Somewhat before the twentieth century and during the revolution, women workers undertook important organizing efforts in the state of Veracruz including Córdoba and Rio Blanco. The women at Rio Blanco, many of Mixtec ethnicity, advanced in an impressive manner, passing from rural backgrounds and illiteracy to positions of national leadership in their unions and as advocates of *autogestión*. In Córdoba the same advances took place, such as enrolments in socialist parties and the advocacy of community betterment including public education and health care services. In Mexico City, Morelos, and Guerrero they took part in public and clandestine party, union, and agrarian organizing throughout the twentieth century.[5] Beginning in the 1960s, women agrarian activists from the Centro Intercultural de Documentación in Cuernavaca worked closely with their counterparts in the *pueblos* between Iguala, Chilpanzingo, and Chilapa, actions that led the government to make some concessions to the *pueblos*, including the provision of electrical power and water purification services. The agrarian compromises, however, did not meet the needs of the growing populace, and from the 1960s into the early twenty-first century the unrest in Guerrero deepened,

5 For the development of the modern women's working-class movement in Mexico, see H. Fowler-Salamini, *Working Women, Entrepreneurs and the Mexican Revolution: The Coffee Industry of Córdoba, Veracruz* (Lincoln: University of Nebraska Press, 2013); and H. Fowler-Salamini and Mary K. Vaughn, *Women of the Mexican Countryside* (Tucson: University of Arizona Press, 1994).

until it erupted into student violence followed by a gross overreaction by the army.

During the period 1917 to 1919 the anarcho-syndicalist forces, who favoured workers' control of production and who had been a majority in the Casa, were finally able to reorganize, but they faced a powerful amalgam of unions that adopted the anarchist-derived name Confederación Regional de Obreros Mexicanos (Regional Confederation of Mexican Workers, CROM) and was supported by the Mexican government and recognized by American business interests and the American Federation of Labor (AFL). Union and government officials tied the CROM to the Mexican Department of Labour and maintained order and stability for the next decade, while marginalizing and using the army to suppress its anarchist and democratic socialist rival, the Confederación General de Trabajadores (General Confederation of Workers, CGT).

Meanwhile, in 1919, an amalgam of intellectuals and labour organizers created the Communist Party of Mexico. It joined the Communist International in 1919 with hopes of emulating the socialist successes underway in the Soviet Union. It carried that title as well as others until 1988, with various affiliates joining the party for special organizing projects. In 1977 it and three smaller socialist parties adopted the title 'Coalition of the Left' and followed a democratic strategy consistent with Eurocommunism, stressing social programmes that benefited workers. In 1981 the membership took the name Partido Socialista Unificado de México (Unified Socialist Party of Mexico) and later in the decade changed the name twice more, ending up as the Mexican Socialist Party. The name changed but the ideological content remained multi-tendency, meaning the membership supported a variety of pro-*campesino* (peasant farmer) and pro-worker programmes. The membership retained a strong Marxist core, however, and continued to be anti-imperialist, meaning that it opposed the economic and political hegemony imposed on Mexico by the combination of Mexican oligarchs and US corporations.

When the CROM collapsed in 1928 (due to a corruption scandal involving its leadership), many of its industrial and more specialized trade unions joined the anarcho-syndicalist CGT. But many of the former CROM leaders were openly opposed to socialism and continued collaborating with foreign capital, the AFL, and right-wing elements in the government. Their collaboration with the national leadership opposed not only socialism but also the efforts of the rank and file to maintain real wages and improve working conditions. CGT efforts to obtain better conditions, such as workers' housing, went ahead because of government support for the programmes under the presidency of Lazaro Cardenas (1934–40), who favoured a social democratic nation.

The effect of the merger followed by the short-term pro-labour stance of Cardenas resulted in the government finally assuming the deep control of the working class that it had sought since Francisco Madero's proposed alternative to the Casa in 1910–13. The Cardenas regime created the massive Confederation of Mexican Workers (Confederación de Trabajadores de México, CTM) under the Stalinist Vicente Lombardo Toledano, which satisfied many Mexican socialists for another decade. During the late 1930s and the early 1940s, the CTM reached a total membership of 1.5 million workers and blended socialism and nationalism into its official propaganda. Unfortunately for the socialists, Lombardo Toledano and Cardenas became estranged, and during the 1940s the CTM changed leadership and fell under regime supervision. By that time the anarcho-syndicalist labour movement and small Trotskyist parties had also been marginalized.

Meanwhile, the communists developed some strength among the public university faculties, in the petroleum workers' union, and in university student activist groups. But in the late 1940s the communist and socialist parties languished on the sidelines of Mexican polity. Pro-Soviet, Trotskyist, socialist, and labour parties had all been tolerated by the elite-controlled faction that emerged from the revolution, but during the Cardenas regime the government gained control over organized labour by helping the workers secure wage increases while granting sizeable concessions to the vast majority of the peasantry. By the late 1970s the land concessions totalled 120 million acres or 25 per cent of the nation's land surface via federal, state, and lower-level grants. During the decades that followed the Cardenas era, the ruling party of Mexico used the CTM and the agrarian reform programme as instruments of social control.

From the early 1940s through the late 1980s, the government changed its tactics and used repression to maintain order. The development of massive impoverished zones in the cities and the presence of starving peasants in the Sierra Madre mountains of Durango and Chihuahua, and in the states of Morelos, Guerrero, and Chiapas, led to localized socialist uprisings. Lucio Cabanas Barrientos and Genaro Vazquez Rojas led insurrections in the state of Guerrero that gained widespread peasant support. Between the mid-1960s and mid-1970s the Party of the Poor controlled large parts of rural Guerrero. In 1968 their units, armed with submachine guns, took positions on the high lands above Acapulco.

At this point, in the late 1960s and 1970s, the polarization of wealth, indescribable poverty, and the failure to provide adequate health and educational services caused the popular standing of the regime to diminish, despite the successes of the land reform programme. In the cities, a harsh labour law required the workers to obtain permission from the government before strikes could be called. When unauthorized strikes took place, the regime took punitive measures against miners, lumberjacks, and oil workers, and even imprisoned their leaders. In the larger cities the riot police, now known as *granaderos* rather than *cosacos*, raided socialist and communist party facilities and even bookstores.

The era of violent repression had begun in 1946 during the administration of the former chief of the nation's secret police, President Miguel Aleman (1946–52). Under the guise of protecting Mexico from the 'international communist conspiracy', Aleman, supported by the US government, shifted the regime to the extreme right. He created the Dirección Federal de Seguridad (Federal Security Directorate, DFS), a special secret police unit, and even granted refuge to escaped Nazis including the caretaker of Hermann Göring's art collection, part of which was then sold to wealthy Mexicans. The new state security strategy included the use of the DFS, the army, and the police to arrest strike leaders and the socialist left during the late 1940s through the 1970s. By the mid-1960s, the repression had become more extreme, shifting from mere prison sentences to thousands of 'disappearances' during the Mexican Dirty Wars that extended from 1968 to 1974. During that period, the army and government deployed the 'Falcons', a large unit of street thugs armed and trained by the Mexican government with its headquarters on the Calzada Tlalpan.

The Coming of Democratic Socialism in Modern Mexico

The crisis of 1968 resulted from the Mexican elites, economic and political, ignoring the basic needs of the people in a complex society and led to the eventual election of a democratic socialist president in 2018. The crisis began when *granaderos* attacked the students of Prep School Number One of the national university system. Sources close to President Gustavo Diaz Ordaz claimed that the students were having a gang fight and that the *granaderos* had entered the courtyard of the main building on campus to stop it, but that effort violated university autonomy. According to the authorities, no one was killed, but the incident gave agitators the pretext needed to mount a protest against the government's actions.

The students and their families offered a completely different picture of the pertinent events. They claimed that some of the students were protesting recent actions by the government in front of the National Palace, which was located only a few blocks from the school. Special army units in armoured vehicles with rubber tyres (which enabled their use on city streets) chased the students back into the courtyard of the school. The students shut and locked the ancient doors to the courtyard, but the troops blew the entry open with a rocket launcher, killing a number of the youngsters in the process. The students reported that thirty-two were killed, and the army cremated them at Army Base Number One in the Presidential Compound in Mexico City. For the next six months, demonstrators, sometimes numbering in their hundreds of thousands, regularly marched in protest from Chapultepec Park to the National Palace.

Led by a strike committee and a noted socialist economics professor, the students presented demands including the abolition of the *granaderos*, the initiation of an enormous workers' housing programme, the introduction of a socialized medicine programme serving the needs of the impoverished indigenous population and the workers, and a revitalized public education budget. In the meantime, the protesters set up barricades in the streets of Mexico City and confronted special riot troops. In July, the army commander, General Marcelino Garcia Barragan, announced a ban on demonstrations and marches. That was followed by a riot on 26 July in Alameda Park, when those in attendance to celebrate the Cuban Revolution were attacked by troops, who beat civilians with their truncheons.[6]

Finally, on 2 October 1968 the army committed a never-to-be-forgotten violation of human rights at the Tlaltelolco Plaza in Mexico City. Once again the students decided to challenge the government. What was actually at stake was a monopoly of power in the hands of a one-party state and a demand for a sharing of power by young idealistic socialists. At around 6 p.m. the army attacked about 15,000 students who had been gathering in the plaza for about two hours; after routing them by firing Browning automatic rifles into the crowd, the troops stormed the building on the east side of the plaza, attacking the thirteen to fifteen student leaders who had been offering the oratory on the third floor. As the soldiers charged into the building, they smashed into apartments and shot some residents while taking others into custody en route

---

6 The author witnessed many of these events personally.

to the third floor. The leader of the Chihuahua students and others fled down the back stairway and escaped towards the Paseo de la Reforma Norte. Several who did not flee were apprehended, and a few simply 'disappeared'. The others reported being held for days in interrogation and being beaten before gaining their release.

The army officers blamed the DFS officers for not identifying themselves and attributed the slaughter to that failure. However, the troops and special agents involved continued their attempts to shoot and beat bystanders for more than two hours after the initial exchange of gunfire.[7] These repressive measures were taken because radical and revolutionary socialism continued to exert a strong influence among workers, peasant activists, and academics, especially those in the state universities of Puebla and Michoacan and the National University, while rightists became increasingly powerful in the military and the official party.

In all three schools, the students and faculties worked together along with a minority of progressive and socialist government officials. In Puebla the Mexican Communist Party took an active role in developing what became the second-ranked public university in the nation. In reaction, the Mexican and US governments, business tycoons, and US universities and private foundations (NGOs) including the Rockefeller, Ford, and other academically prestigious programmes, joined with the US Central Intelligence Agency (CIA) in supporting labour movement and academic alternatives to socialist thought and syndicalism.

The most notable organization to emerge from this effort, the Inter-American Regional Organization of Workers (Organización Regional Interamericana de Trabajadores, ORIT) surfaced in the early 1950s as part of the anti-communist campaign launched by ultra-right-wing elements in the US government. For at least three decades, potential and actual union leaders were received as guests in the ORIT headquarters, a former nightclub in Cuernavaca. They received both ideological and tactical training in how to combat Marxism and 'communism'. At the same time, beginning in the aftermath of McCarthyism, US academics with anti-Marxist research projects and NGOs were subsidized by US foundations, while economic support for alternative schools in Mexico was provided through US and Monterrey elite economic interests and the NGOs. The funding provided support for the University of the Americas, the Colegio de México, and the Instituto Tecnologico de Monterrey.

---

7 The author personally witnessed bodies being thrown into trucks.

Many multi-national American corporations and NGOs joined in the effort to compete with socialist thought and unruly strike actions in the production facilities. Led by the American Metals Company of New York City and Phelps Dodge, among others, their efforts had moved into an attempt at cultural hegemony and now included the universities as well as the unions. American Metals had been an early participant in the creation of *charro* unions ('cowboy' or official unions), and now the company worked with prominent US academics not only to create *charro* unions in Mexico, Chile, and Peru, but also to use their influence to favour certain intellectuals over other, less pliable ones. One of the leading US historians of Mexico, Frank Tannenbaum of Columbia University, worked on an open basis with the chairman of American Metals not only to gain the selection of a co-operative union leader at the plant at Saltillo, Coahuila, and give the individual a comfortable residence, but also to wean young intellectuals away from Marxism and 'teach them our way of life'. The same transition took place in Chile as the indoctrination moved from the mining industry to the national university in Santiago. Meanwhile, in Mexico, socialist and union leaders were bribed and intimidated.

During the 1960s the government allowed university autonomy to flourish while the importance of Marxian socialist thought grew. By 1968 its strength had grown enormously among the students and intellectuals, while government authorities continued to repress the Communist Party and seemingly underestimated the power and nature of growing student unrest, largely because the students stressed the non-threatening terms 'democracy' and 'freedom'. But some of the students and faculty members had long worked alongside socialist rural workers and agrarian activists. As a result, notable altercations developed in rural agricultural areas, especially those in the states of Chiapas, Guerrero, Morelos, Durango, Chihuahua, and Veracruz, before the urban uprising of 1968. They continued into the 1990s Zapatista uprising of Mayan *campesinos* and *rancheros* (ranch-owners) in Chiapas. That movement eschewed patriarchal leadership, and within a decade virtually all of the more dynamic leaders were women.

By the early twenty-first century, after prolonged struggles with the more extreme reactionaries, who support imperialism and domestic capitalist dictatorship, a safer form of democratic or reformist socialism has been accepted by some members of the oligarchy. The idea of democratic socialism is now tolerated by a minority of the oligarchy, that 1 per cent of the population who hold 40 per cent of the nation's wealth. That minority, after centuries of struggle and oppressive treatment of those who created

Mesoamerican civilization and then fought on behalf of the poor and down-trodden, now believes that a greater commitment to the Mexican masses will uplift not just the working class but the overall situation for themselves as well.

Beginning in the 1980s, more than one-third of the urban working class has repeatedly voted for national political candidates who support socialism in its democratic form, and sizeable revolutionary resistance movements have arisen among rural workers across the nation. Now, with material conces-sions on their part, the elites can enjoy greater safety, cleaner air, greater longevity, a higher level of popular culture, a better quality of life, and socio-political stability. Let us see if under the leadership of President Manuel Andres Lopez Obrador there can be a peaceful social solution to the inequi-ties and injustice among a people who have created a distinct and exceptional civilization, dreamt of and fought for their ideals and independence, and survived for so long.[8]

Further Reading

Albro, Ward, *Always a Rebel: Ricardo Flores Magón and the Mexican Revolution* (Fort Worth: Texas Christian University Press, 1992).

Andrews, Gregg, *Shoulder to Shoulder? The American Federation of Labor, the United States and the Mexican Revolution, 1910–1924* (Berkeley: University of California Press, 1991).

Carr, Barry, *Marxism and Communism in Twentieth-Century Mexico* (Lincoln: University of Nebraska Press, 1992).

Caulfield, Norman, *Mexican Workers and the State: From the Porfiriato to NAFTA* (Fort Worth: Texas Christian University Press, 1998).

Hart, John Mason, *Anarchism and the Mexican Working Class, 1860–1931* (Austin: University of Texas Press, 1978).

 Revolutionary Mexico: The Coming and Process of the Mexican Revolution (Berkeley: University of California Press, 1987).

Hodges, Donald C., *Mexican Anarchism after the Revolution* (Austin: University of Texas Press, 1995).

LaBotz, Dan, *The Crisis of Mexican Labor* (New York: Praeger, 1988).

Padilla, Tanalis, *Rural Resistance in the Land of Zapata: The Jaramillista Movement and the Myth of the Pax Priísta* (Durham, NC: Duke University Press, 2008).

Poniatowska, Elena, *Massacre in Mexico* (Columbia: University of Missouri Press, 1991).

Saka, Mark Saad, *For God and Revolution: Priest, Peasant and Agrarian Socialism in the Mexican Huasteca* (Albuquerque: University of New Mexico Press, 2013).

8 See Dan LaBotz, *The Crisis of Mexican Labor* (New York: Praeger, 1988).

21

Anarchism and Syndicalism in Argentina

GEOFFROY DE LAFORCADE

In Argentina, militant newspapers and small circles of affinity groups, as well as craft-based societies of workers and artisans, and immigrant and artist groups, formed a vast and variegated constellation of anarchist tendencies before and after the turn of the twentieth century, some individualist, some insurrectionalist, and some favourable to organization and unification. Followers of Peter Kropotkin and Errico Malatesta advocated a loose federation of horizontally co-ordinated associations that would create new forms of anti-authoritarian participation and representation based on localities and regions, rather than unions or national governments. Much of the historiography in Argentina separates anarchist from syndicalist activism as idealized forms of ideology and organization, the former being opposed to authority, and the latter more grounded in class struggle. In fact, throughout the first half of the twentieth century, anarchist and syndicalist traditions converged, coalesced, and clashed in more complex and nuanced ways, each adopting aspects of the other and manifesting in ways that were more reflective of conditions and circumstances in Argentina itself than in the European societies where the movements were first theorized.

The 'Argentine exception' is that, unlike elsewhere in Latin America and even in Europe, 'anarcho-communists' were organized into a regional federation, the Federación Obrera Regional Argentina (Argentine Regional Workers' Federation, FORA) which not only engaged with, but also dominated, labour unions in the first decade of the century and remained active for decades thereafter. Until the Mexican Confederación General de Trabajadores (General Confederation of Workers, CGT) in 1921, it was the most influential organization in the hemisphere, with roots in anarchist and syndicalist movements. Many workers and activists in Argentina participated in the syndicalist movement without disavowing their allegiance to anarcho-communism. Both currents saw themselves as the embryo of a future non-capitalist society, both were opposed to parliaments and the state, and both drew their strength from interventions in labour processes, participation in strike movements, and economic sabotage, as well as in working-class education and cultural movements. The main difference was that one – revolutionary syndicalism – focused exclusively on forging class-based identities, and later gradually compromised with more centralized forms of organization and delegation, at the expense of craft or local-based voluntary associations. Conversely, while Argentine anarchists did not reject in wholesale fashion the Bakuninist and collectivist heritage of the International Working Men's Association (especially in the 1920s), the most prominent continuation of that tradition, the Industrial Workers of the World (IWW), had virtually no presence in the region (except in Chile). Distinctively Argentine expressions of both anarcho-communism and revolutionary syndicalism endured well into the 1930s and 1940s, often leaving lasting marks on modern Argentine labour movements.

Thus, while the term 'anarcho-syndicalist' is often ascribed in the beginning of the twentieth century to anarchists who participated in craft-based resistance societies and trade unions, a structured movement bearing that name did not emerge anywhere until after the First World War; the pre-war lineages of anarchism and syndicalism, while in many respects both indebted to the debates of the 1840s and later the First International, diverged. In Argentina, neither resembled, after the 1890s, anarchist individualism or socialism.[1] Both were solidly anchored in labour movements conceived as the main bedrock of revolutionary working-class politics. Unlike Hubert Lagardelle and Fernand Pelloutier in France, who saw revolutionary syndicalism as an extension of Marxism or a rupture with anarchism, Argentine affiliates of these rival movements eschewed, until the emergence of anarcho-bolshevism in the early 1920s, formal socialist doctrine, while remaining

---

1 General references for early Argentine anarchism and syndicalism are: D. Abad de Santillán and E. López Aango, *El anarquismo en el movimiento obrero* (Barcelona: Cosmos, 1925); D. Abad de Santillán, *La FORA. Ideología y trayectoria del movimiento obrero revolucionario en Argentina* (Buenos Aires: Proyección, 1971); E. Bilsky, *La FORA y el movimiento obrero (1900–1910)* (Buenos Aires: Centro Editor de América Latina, 1985); H. Del Campo, *Los anarquistas* (Buenos Aires: Centro Editor de América Latina, 1971); R. Falcón, *Los orígenes del movimiento obrero (1857–1899)* (Buenos Aires: Centro Editor de América Latina, 1984); S. Marotta, *El movimiento sindical argentino. Su génesis y desarrollo*, 2 vols. (Buenos Aires: Ediciones 'Lacio', 1960); J. Oddone, *Gremialismo proletario argentino* (Buenos Aires: Libera, 1949); I. Oved, *El anarquismo y el movimiento obrero en Argentina* (Mexico City: Siglo Veintiuno, 1978); J. Suriano, *Auge y caída del anarquismo. Argentina 1880–1930* (Buenos Aires: Capital Intelectual, 2005); H. Tarcus, *Diccionario biográfico de las izquierda argentina. De los anarquistas a la 'nueva izquierda' (1870–1976)* (Buenos Aires: Emecé, 2007); G. Zaragoza Rivera, *Anarquismo argentino (1876–1902)* (Madrid: Ediciones de la Torre, 1996).

anti-capitalist and avoiding in practice a wholesale break with the pre-war federalist and anarcho-communist tendencies of their originators. For the Italian activist Luigi Fabbri, who was active on both shores of the Río de la Plata region, syndicalism was 'anarchist socialism in action'.[2] The workers and intellectuals who first embraced revolutionary syndicalism in Argentina did so in a movement of dissidence within the Argentine Socialist Party, but riding a wave of powerful working-class insurgencies and against the backdrop of the embrace by the Argentine FORA of anarcho-communism, with which they intended to compete; it would take another decade for their organizations to become irremediably opposed. In the interim, fierce debates on the significance for social revolution of unions and labour struggles permeated the life of the anarchist FORA from 1901 to 1915, a period marked by the legally sanctioned deportation of activists in 1902, a full-scale crackdown on organized labour in 1910, and the promulgation of a male suffrage law in 1912. From 1906 onwards, revolutionary syndicalists sought to redirect its rank and file to their strategic goal of unification.

Thus, in Argentina, the experience of revolutionary syndicalism closely parallels that of anarchism, which fomented the culture of direct action, community activism, solidarity, and strikes from which it emerged. Malatesta, who was in the country from 1885 to 1889, was the driving force behind the critique of anarcho-individualist movements and existing mutualist associations, fuelling the debate between pro- and anti-organization tendencies in an incipient labour movement numerically dominated by European immigrants. The earliest French and Italian refugees arrived following the Paris Commune in the 1870s, and in 1879 El Descamisado (The Shirtless) was the first anarchist newspaper to publish, a year before Italian activist Ettore Mattei arrived bearing Malatesta's ideas, and five years before the latter founded an anarcho-communist circle with a group of Italian and Spanish workers. Malatesta, who wrote in Fortunato Serantoni's La Questione Sociale (The Social Question) and in Irish anarchist John O'Dwyer Craeghe's El Oprimido (The Oppressed), organized the Sociedad Cosmopólita de Obreros Panaderos (Cosmopolitan Society of Bakery Workers) in 1887, the first anarchist 'resistance society' in Argentina. A decade later, following a wave of strikes in Buenos Aires, Catalan cabinet-maker Gregorio Inglán Lafarga founded the newspaper La Protesta Humana (The Human Protest; renamed La Protesta in 1903), on the opposite side of a spectrum that included 'individualist' advocates of violent 'propaganda by the deed' behind the newspapers La

2 L. Fabbri, 'Il sindicalismo', Il Pensiero, 1 June 1905.

Liberté (*Liberty*) and *El Perseguido* (*The Hunted*). Finally, in 1898, Italian criminologist Pietro Gori began a four-year stay in Buenos Aires, during which he wrote a declaration of principles for a Federación Libertaria de Grupos Socialistas-Anarquistas (Libertarian Federation of Socialist–Anarchist Groups), created to combat anti-organization tendencies within the anarchist movement and to bring socialists under its umbrella.

Resistance Societies, Solidarity and Federalism, Anarchist Culture, and Critique

The concept of 'resistance societies' would become central to Argentine anarchism. They first emerged in the 1880s and 1890s from mutual aid societies and retained many of the latter's practices: the collection of contributions from workers to cover medical and disability benefits, support provided to spouses and families, the organization of social activities and of cultural events. They articulated short-term economic demands and maintained affiliations with local associations and bilingual newspapers. They also employed direct action tactics in which women and community members participated, such as boycotts and sabotage, solidarity strikes and slowdowns. One aspect of their activity that is rarely highlighted is their reliance on the control over hiring, which entailed alliances with overseers, such as foremen tasked with recruiting longshoremen and sailors, where the largest and most powerful resistance societies were based in the early years of the century.[3] Malatesta was a strong supporter of craft-based unionism and a believer in its integrative impact on workers of diverse ethnic origins, foreign and native, as well as its practice of direct democracy and capacity to co-ordinate solidarity between professions and localities, in the spirit of debate and deliberation. Antonio Pellicer Paraire, a Spanish anarchist who arrived in 1894, theorized resistance societies in a series of articles published by *La Protesta Humana* in 1900, describing them as organizations grounded in labour struggles but coordinated by anarchist principles through a loose alliance of local and regional federations.[4] Paraire and Pietro Gori influenced the creation of Argentina's first national labour confederation, the Federación Obrera Argentina (Argentine Workers' Federation, FOA) in 1901, originally in collaboration

---

3 G. de Laforcade, 'The Ghosts of Insurgencies Past: Waterfront Labor, Working-Class Memory, and the Contentious Emergence of the National-Popular State in Argentina', in B. Maxwell and R. Craib (eds.), *No Gods, No Masters, No Peripheries: Global Anarchisms* (Oakland, CA: Institute for Comparative Modernities/PM Press, 2015), pp. 180–214.
4 A. Pellicer Paraire, 'Organización obrera', *La Protesta Humana*, 1900–1.

with socialists, who left it in 1903 to form the Union General de Trabajadores (General Workers' Union, UGT), the kernel of the future revolutionary syndicalist movement. In 1904, on the heels of momentous strike movements driven mainly by transportation workers and their allies, the anarchist FOA became the Federación Obrera Regional Argentina, a structure inspired by Paraire's writings that rejected national borders and projected its influence throughout the Río de la Plata region. The FORA was officially declared 'anarcho-communist' at its fifth congress in 1905 (hence its denomination a decade later, when syndicalists took control of a sizeable portion of the organized labour movement, as the 'FORA-V').

The FORA envisaged two parallel arenas of struggle, economic and revolutionary, which it linked though 'solidarity pacts' between autonomous resistance societies and local federations based on community activism, the nuclei, in Paraire's words, of 'revolutionary communes' which were established throughout port cities and included 'affinity groups' other than workers. A unique aspect of this configuration was the checks on the power of the FORA itself; it was a type of anarchist organization which, Gori had warned, could turn authoritarian if it allowed its doctrinal principles or tactics to get in the way of direct democracy in the resistance societies.[5] Thus a leader such as Esteban Almada, who led the powerful longshoremen's society in 1904 and 1905, repeatedly overruled the federation when circumstances dictated tactical alliances with a rival social Catholic society, or when workers voted against FORA resolutions.[6] Finally, the 'solidarity pact' developed by the FORA in 1904 was directly inspired by the 1881 manifesto of the Workers' Federation of the Spanish Region, which advocated the 'reduction of existing political and juridical states to strictly economic functions, establishing in their place a free federation of free associations of free producers'.[7] Thus the economic, political, and moral emancipation of workers would be achieved through revolutionary association, not exclusively based in labour movements, and the complete independence of resistance societies from political groups. Revolutionary syndicalists, on the other hand, who focused on preparing workers for a post-capitalist society through unions, adopted

---

5 H. Finet, *Congrès d'Amsterdam, 1907. Le débat anarchie ou syndicalisme à la lumière de la réalité argentine, la FORA face aux tentatives d'union syndicale du mouvement ouvrier 1901–1915* (Orthez: Editions du Temps Perdu, 2007), p. 5.
6 G. de Laforcade, 'Straddling the Nation and the Working World: Anarchism and Syndicalism on the Docks and Rivers of Argentina, 1900–1930', in S. Hirsch and L. van der Walt (eds.), *Anarchism and Syndicalism in the Colonial and Post-Colonial World, 1880–1940* (Leiden and Boston: Brill, 2011), pp. 321–62.
7 Abad de Santillán, *La FORA*, pp. 119–20.

a form of neutrality that did not preclude the exercise by their constituents of political activities, especially after 1912, but barred ideological proselytization within the unions themselves. In practice, many 'syndicalist' unions included branches of their industrial organization that continued the traditions of anarchist resistance societies, alongside others that leaned towards socialism, and later communism; others were even in some cases favourable to the moderate Radical Civic Union.[8] What both currents shared was the principle of federalism, which guaranteed the autonomy of each society or union branch within a larger federation.

The anarcho-communism of the FORA-V was thus very different from that of the 1870s onwards in Europe, influenced by Kropotkin, which advocated spontaneity rather than organization, and viewed workers' economic demands as narrowly defined and unions as excessively bureaucratic. It bore closer resemblance to Malatesta's qualified definition of unions as a means but not an end, which translated into the exaltation of direct action as a strategy implemented in a co-ordinated fashion, with the ultimate goal of forging bonds of solidarity and community in opposition to authority, particularly that of the state and capitalist institutions. It represented a means of unifying a diverse prism of ethnicities and nationalities, communicating a message of emancipation at work and in society; of collective convergence around an idea of the 'proletariat' understood broadly to include workers and all the oppressed, regardless of race or gender.[9] It was a doctrine of integration and unification without the underlying homogenization of 'class' as an exclusive determination of identity, and saw the seeds of a future free society as sown through solidarity, not just unionization. The 'oppressed' were defined not only as salaried workers, but as the poor in general,[10] targets of criminalization and racialization on the part of government authorities which allied with incipient nationalist and nativist forces to 'other' anarchism's supporters and persecute or deport its leaders. The federalist networking undertaken by the FORA aimed to co-ordinate resistance societies and localities, and to forge regional and supra-national

8 L. Caruso, *Embarcados. Los trabajadores marítimos y la vida a bordo. Sindicato, empresas y Estado en el puerto de Buenos Aires, 1889–1921* (Buenos Aires: Imago Mundi, 2016).

9 J. Moya, 'Italians in Buenos Aires' Anarchist Movement: Gender Ideology and Women's Participation, 1890–1910', in D. R. Gabaccia and F. Iacovetta (eds.), *Women, Gender, and Transnational Lives: Italian Workers of the World* (Toronto: University of Toronto Press, 2002), pp. 189–216.

10 *El Perseguido. Voz de los Explotados*, 18 May 1890, cited by J. Moya, 'The positive side of sterotypes: Jewish anarchists in early twentieth-century Buenos Aires', *Jewish History* 18 (2004), p. 22.

solidarities cognizant of the autonomy of their component parts.[11] While many of its founders were of immigrant origin, mirroring the labouring classes themselves, the perception of the FORA's 'foreignness' is often exaggerated. Port workers, for example, mobilized the greatest numbers during strikes conducted during the high export season; many of them were provincial Argentines, and their leadership was predominantly 'native' following the mass deportations of immigrant agitators in 1902. Because voting was not an option for working-class men until after 1912 and genuine working-class citizenship remained elusive until the 1940s, they competed for the allegiance of both foreign and native-born workers against more atavistically inclined nationalist groups, particularly social Catholics and political supporters of the middle-class Radical Civic Union, which rose to prominence from the 1890s onwards.

The labels of 'dangerous' and 'foreign' ascribed to the FORA were derived from the revolutionary precepts of anarchism and the pathological representation by elites of the poor as unassimilable. Police forces, prisons, and immigration authorities kept records by nationality from 1882 onwards, as a means of documenting the sources of disorder. In 1889, following a period of massive strikes and protests, Miguel Cané proposed a legal path to the deportation of foreigners to rid the social fabric of 'European vagabonds and delinquents', targeting anarchists in particular as 'sources of perversion' representing a danger to the illiterate and impressionable masses. Conservative deputy Lucas Ayarragaray saw anarchists as degenerates and fanatics, and Argentine physicians associated them with mentally and biologically fragile crowds; even socialists, who opposed deportations, vilified anarchists as anti-social, questioning their patriotism and even their masculinity.[12] Ethnically, early anarchist activists reflected the composition of the urban working class, with Italians, Spaniards, and east European Jews featuring prominently in their ranks, until the over-representation of immigrants declined after the First World War. Legislative efforts to purge them used the language of contagion and vagrancy to criminalize and even medicalize their difference. Thus, the 1902 Residency Law and 1910 Social Defence Law, both of which resulted in extensive arrests and deportations, targeted

---

11 G. de Laforcade, 'Federative futures: waterways, resistance societies, and the subversion of nationalism in the early twentieth-century anarchism of the Rio de la Plata Region', *EIAL. Estudios Interdisciplinarios de América Latina y el Caribe* 22, 2 (July–December 2011), pp. 71–96.

12 J. Rodríguez, *Civilizing Argentina: Science, Medecine, and the Modern State* (Chapel Hill: University of North Carolina Press, 2006), p. 232.

anarchists in particular. Native anarchists and immigrants were equally subjected to coercive renewal, either to remote prisons in the far south or to neighbouring Uruguay, from which many often returned clandestinely. The purges did not succeed in stemming the tide of working-class insurgency, however. It is important to recognize that while revolutionary syndicalists gradually embraced nationalism, converging in the 1920s with conservative sectors in their defence of sovereignty and *argentinidad* (Argentine-ness), they never adopted the anti-immigrant principles of nativists, nor did they fully shed the cosmopolitan and federalist roots of their anarchist rivals within the labour movement.

Finally, women sometimes appeared in police records as anarchists, reflecting a gendered representation of social dangerousness as well as their participation in anarchist movements as community activists and their presence in riots, or places of urban working-class sociability such as brothels and taverns. Under-represented in resistance societies, women were nonetheless prominent leaders of the FORA (including Teresa Marchisio, Virginia Bolten, Pepita Guerra, María Collazo, Ramona Ferreyra, Teresa Caporaletti, Josefa Calvo, and Juana Ruoco Buela). They included well-respected orators and agitators, founders of anarchist schools and libraries, authors of articles and pamphlets, freethinking artists, and supporters of strikes. Many were militants not just of Argentine but also of trans-regional movements (particularly in Uruguay) and, like anarchist men, they maintained transnational connections with comrades in Europe.

Lucha Obrera (*Workers' Struggle*) in 1884 was considered by historian Max Nettlau to have been the first newspaper in Argentina to address women and their struggles directly, and *La Questione Sociale* broached the issue in 1885, before the first publication written entirely for women by women, *La Voz de la Mujer* (*Women's Voice*), appeared in 1896–7. It included articles covering all areas of anarchist criticism, from anti-clericalism and anti-militarism to direct action, in addition to topics such as free love, maternity, prostitution, domestic violence, and women's emancipation.[13] After *La Protesta* took up women's issues again in 1905, Bolten, Caporaletti, Collazo, Elisa Leotar, María Reyes, Violeta García, and Marta Newelstein founded the Centro Anarquista Femenino (Women's Anarchist Centre) in 1907, the year of an important tenement-dwellers' rent

13 L. Fernández Cordero, *Amor y anarquismo. Experiencias pioneras que pensaron y ejercieron la libertad sexual* (Buenos Aires: Siglo XXI, 2019); M. Molyneux, 'No God, no boss, no husband: anarchist feminism in nineteenth-century Argentina', *Latin American Perspectives* 13, 1 (Winter 1986), pp. 119–45; La Voz de la Mujer, *Periódico comunista anarquico* (Bogotá: Ediciones Gato Negro, 2011).

strike in Buenos Aires organized mostly by women affiliated with the FORA. Another important women's newspaper was the bi-weekly *Nuestra Tribuna* (*Our Tribune*) in 1922–4, headed by Ruoco Buela, Fidela Cuñado, Terencia Fernández, and María Fernández. While some men in the anarchist movement perceived their advocacy of free love and criticism of domesticity as a diversion, these women were precursors of anti-patriarchal advocacy in Argentina, and provoked fierce debates within the ranks of anarchism and socialism on sexuality, marriage, and the family. In the 1930s and 1940s, an anarchist medical discourse emerged on sexuality, procreative choice, and women's work among academics and professionals, which testifies to the far-reaching impact on Argentine society of working-class traditions of feminist activism. Prominent male anarchist authors such as Joaquín Falconnet (Pierre Quiroule) and Juan Lazarte also defended women's emancipation from an anarchist perspective.[14]

Fig. 21.1   Virginia Bolten, prominent labour organizer in Argentina and Uruguay, associated with the anarcha-feminist periodicals *La Voz de la Mujer* (1896–7) and *La Nueva Senda* (1909). (Imagoteca – Centro de Documentación e Investigación de la Cultura de Izquierdas (CeDInCI).)

14 J. J. Llaguno Thomas, 'Las mujeres anarquistas la historiografía latinoamericana. Entre la voz masculina y la organización propia (1890–1950)', *Revista Erosión* 7 (2017), pp. 51–9.

Argentine anarchists produced an impressive array of cultural works, through publications such as *El Sol* (*The Sun*) and *Martín Fierro* (edited by Alberto Ghiraldo) and *Tiempos Nuevos* (*New Times*, edited by Félix Basterra). They popularized now classical Argentine authors – Florencio Sánchez, Julio Molina y Vedia, Pascual Guaglianone, Arturo Montesano, and countless other prominent poets and playwrights – and developed themes such as vegetarianism and alternative therapies, as well as rationalist education. After the First World War, they intervened in discussions with Latin American radical intellectuals influenced by the Mexican Revolution, the University Reform Movement of 1918, and the Russian Revolution, published numerous serials reflecting a thriving anarchist arc of cultural influence, and established publishing houses such as La Protesta, the Editorial Argonauta, and Minerva. Acknowledging this cultural heritage is an antidote to accounts of anarchism as 'foreign' or exclusively drawn from European immigrant subcultures, which continued to thrive in the cosmopolitan city beyond the heyday of FORA influence. Anarchists continued and transformed the '*gauchesca*' literature and song that '*payadores*', or popular poet-songwriters of the interior, had developed well before the age of mass immigration. They transmitted their revolutionary messages not just through newspapers, pamphlets and books, but also through *habaneras*, *milongas*, and *tangos*, all dances which became popular cultural forms in the early stages of radio broadcasts, recording, and film.[15]

While some scholars have suggested that anarchists expressed disdain for working-class and popular cultural forms such as carnival, *saynètes*, or other expressions of street theatre, or with drinking and disorderly behaviour,[16] the reality is that artists from their ranks participated in them. It is important to remember that there were intellectuals, theorists, and educators within the FORA, but also resistance societies and community sympathizers immersed in the tumult and transgressions of work and everyday life, including forms of leisure, entertainment, and licentiousness, as well as settling of scores, not formally sanctioned by the 'Ideal'. The aesthetic avant-gardism of modernist authors such as Ghiraldo, or socially themed didacticism of theatre groups such as the Ernett Zacconi Philodramatic Academy in Buenos Aires and the travelling Caballeros del Ideal, achieved popularity not just by spreading

---

15 L. Domínguez, 'Un itinerario por los proyectos editoriales del anarquismo en Argentina. Cambios, maniobras y permanencies', *Izquierdas* 33 (May 2017), pp. 21–41.
16 J. Suriano, *Paradoxes of Utopia: Anarchist Culture and Politics in Buenos Aires, 1890–1910* (Chico, CA: AK Press, 2010).

propaganda but by telling stories that reflected social realities with which the labouring poor could identify.

Anarchist pamphlets, short stories, serial novels, and songs were anti-conformist and popular. All of this was part of a worldwide trend towards the democratization of reading and leisure, and the anarchist, socialist, and syndicalist movements all participated in the promotion of cultural literacy among working men and women. The creation of a working-class or popular culture and the translation and dissemination of classical works of literature and thought went hand in hand in the anarchist project, in the spirit of empowering the people with the tools to resist the education of church and state. In a heterogeneous society marked by the perpetual convergence of migrations from the hinterland to the city as well as from abroad, the exaltation of dissent and struggle often took the form of epic stories of labour insurgency and creative freedom at the margins. It was an apprenticeship of autonomy and a statement of artistic and social emancipation that may have been minoritarian, but forged an influential counter-culture in part because it emerged against the backdrop of a powerful and far-reaching organized labour movement that structured communities and connected localities across regions and borders, and an era of almost incessant strikes and solidarity movements.

From Socialism to Revolutionary Syndicalism and New Anarchist Directions

This perpetual staging of mass strikes, often led primarily by longshoremen, mariners, and other port workers with resistance societies that emphasized workers' control, gave rise to the emergence, early in the century, of revolutionary syndicalism as a rival to the anarchism of the FORA. We have already seen that resistance societies differed from trade unions in that workplace conflicts were but one aspect of their activity. As labour-based activism grew in scope and power, strikes became the primary focus of anarchist movements and generated syndicalist forms of action and organization. The importance of strikes in the revolutionary imagination of anarchists extended to broader sectors of the working class as their disruptive effect on the economy prompted efforts by employers and the state to regulate and domesticate them. Strikes were regarded as transformative acts of social warfare through direct action outside parliamentary and state-mediated authority, as generators of mass participation in a society that denied them collective rights of citizenship, as laboratories of solidarity and association, and as annunciatory statements of an imminent social revolution. They were virulently contested by mainstream socialist politicians such as Juan B. Justo, Nicholas Repetto, and Enrique Dickmann, who, since the party's foundation in 1896, preferred gradual parliamentary welfare reforms to the cathartic rituals and disorderly street violence of co-ordinated class conflict, and who fiercely opposed anarchism. Some, such as the first elected socialist deputy Alfredo Palacios (1904), recognized their expression of working-class aspirations and defended anarchists against persecution. Within the ranks of Argentine socialism, other leaders such as Gabriela de Coni, Julio Arraga, Luis Bernard, Aquiles Lorenzo, Emilio Troise, and Ernesto Piot theorized trade unions as the primary expression of class consciousness and introduced the revolutionary syndicalist doctrine to workers of the UGT, which split from the party in 1906. To mainstream socialists, revolutionary syndicalists were opponents of socialism and democracy, anarchists in disguise.[17]

Socialists had turned their backs on anarchist-inspired labour movements in 1903 when they left the FOA, the precursor of the FORA. The UGT originally embraced parliamentary welfare reformism but changed its position in 1905 following the establishment of a state of siege. Syndicalist leader Luis Barnard proposed a pact between socialist-led unions and the FORA, arguing that unity with anarchists, particularly in mobilizations during general strikes, should take precedence over ideological divisions, but the anarchists refused a formal alliance and instead proposed tactical co-operation at their fifth congress in 1905, which adopted 'anarcho-communism' as its platform. For anarchists, labour organization was a means to an end, the social revolution, whereas for revolutionary syndicalists it was both a means and an end, a 'revolutionary school' of working-class emancipation by the workers themselves, through which economic concessions would weaken the grip of capitalists on society. Consequently, syndicalists rejected the ideological precepts of anarchism and socialism as equally external interventions in the lives of workers and the pursuit of their class interests. Gori, Malatesta, Inglán Lafarga, and Pellicer Paraire had imposed labour-based activism on the Argentine anarchist movement, and laid the foundations for the domination of the FORA throughout the first decade of the twentieth century, arguing that everyday struggles over bread-and-butter

---

17 A. Belkin, *Sobre los orígenes del sindicalismo revolucionario en Argentina* (Buenos Aires: Ediciones CCC, 2007); A. Belkin, *Sindicalismo revolucionario y movimiento obrero en la Argentina. De la gestación en el Partido Socialista a la conquista de la FORA (1900–1915)* (Buenos Aires: Imago Mundi/Ediciones CEHTI, 2018).

issues did not conflict with the broader, cathartic objective of emancipation for all of society. Hence, from the onset, the FORA and the UGT found themselves aligned in their dedication to direct action, strikes, federalism, and organizational autonomy. Both believed the revolution imminent. However, under the leadership of Eduardo Gilimón, who took over the anarchist newspaper *La Protesta* from Ghiraldo in 1906, revolutionary syndicalism presented the danger of exalting unions and their economic demands at the expense of the doctrinal principles of anarchist communism. This gave syndicalists momentum to impose their authority over unions during strike movements in the years leading up to the state crackdown on organized labour in 1910. Later, syndicalist unions, especially among maritime and railway workers, occupied the space vacated by the FORA-V in the defence of working-class autonomy during Radical Civic Union-led efforts from 1916 onwards to implement government neutrality in strike movements and advance the economic agenda of a growing organized labour movement, without the revolution.

The separation of anarchist and syndicalist movements was a gradual process driven by the momentum of strike movements and protests. The key difference between them, reflected in the 1907 controversy opposing two prominent FORA leaders and collaborators of *La Protesta*, Gilimón and Fabbri, was that the former saw ideological proselytization as a necessity to avoid unions becoming corporatist structures instrumentalized by bureaucratic interests. Fabbri, once a close collaborator of Malatesta, feared that insisting on the doctrinal radicalization of workers threatened class solidarity on a larger scale. That same year, after a conflict in Rosario escalated into a general solidarity strike by workers in Buenos Aires and other major Argentine cities, the FORA and the UGT held a Congress of Unification on the initiative of the former. For the revolutionary syndicalists, this was the beginning of an effort to take control of the FORA. It would culminate, eight years later in 1915, in the division of the federation into the anarchist FORA-V, loyal to anarcho-communism and to the multi-tiered structure of the movement proposed by Paraire, and the syndicalist FORA-IX, which advocated for trade unionism by professional branch. Both surged in numbers following the split. Anarchists who found themselves reliant on alliances with syndicalists due to labour processes, production chains, or community networks sometimes nested within the federalist structure of syndicalist unions. This was the case, for example, of the sailors' and firemen's resistance society, created in 1903, which participated in the creation of the Federación Obrera Maritima (Maritime Labour Federation, FOM) led by former anarchist Francisco

García in 1910. As a section of what became the most powerful and influential syndicalist union, it continued to defend anarchist-inspired tactics well into the 1940s, producing prominent anarcho-bolshevik and revolutionary syndicalist leaders along the way. One famous labour leader of shipyard workers, Atilio Biondi, navigated all of these alignments over four decades and was still present when anarchists and syndicalists co-operated in an epic strike on the yards in the mid-1950s. Other anarchists worked to preserve their autonomy, even from the FORA, as the growth of political patronage and industrial unionism put pressure on the extra-parliamentary commitments of revolutionary movements rooted in the epic confrontations of the preceding decade.

Many historians have assumed anarchism to be a 'European' import with scant impact on the native workers, one which faded with the 'nationalization' of working-class allegiances and the growth of state–labour relations in the late 1930s and early 1940s. Syndicalism, while it is also traced to immigrant 'passers' or disseminators such as the Italian journalist Walter Mocchi and the French feminist Gabriela de Coni, is credited, on the other hand, with adjusting to the growing impact of national citizenship and the incorporation of native-born Argentines into unions.[18] This understanding fails to account for the cosmopolitan constituencies of both, their shared roots in mass mobilizations and working-class counter-cultures, and their multi-generational efforts to preserve labour movements from the centralization and limited reformism of trade union movements attached to political parties and the state.

Shifts in the ruling establishment's approach to workers' rights and class conflict began early, when Joaquín V. González, who authored the electoral law that allowed Alfredo Palacios to become the continent's first elected socialist deputy in 1904, developed the first national labour legislation in 1905. Anarchists, of course, opposed the law, and it was at the centre of the divorce between the Socialist Party and its revolutionary syndicalist faction in 1906. When Radical Civic Union leader Hipólito Yrigoyen became president in 1916, he adopted a position of state neutrality in strikes that increased the leverage of syndicalist unions committed to direct action against capitalists without interference from bureaucrats, parties, or legislators.

With this increasing willingness to accommodate social reform came an escalation of militarized repression of revolutionary labour movements.

18 D. Rock, *Politics in Argentina, 1890–1930: The Rise and Fall of Radicalism* (Cambridge: Cambridge University Press, 2009); E. Gilimón, *Un anarquista en Buenos Aires (1890–1910)* (Buenos Aires: Centro Editor de América Latina, 1971).

Subsequently, the rise of nationalist, nativist, and xenophobic organizations such as the Liga Patriótica Argentina (Argentine Patriotic League) led by the proto-fascist Manuel Carlés, and of employers' associations such as the Asociación Nacional del Trabajo (National Labour Association), presided over by shipping magnate Pedro Christopherson, became nemeses of both anarchist and syndicalist movements, which periodically united in labour mobilizations against them.[19] It was a replay of their showdowns with social Catholics and advocates of 'free labour' in the early 1900s, but in a more complex environment where the shifting and varied political allegiances of syndicalist unions' rank and file tempered, and sometimes rekindled, the revolutionary aspirations of their most radical constituencies. The leadership of the maritime workers' FOM, for example, drifted towards co-operation with the Yrigoyenist state and later reverted to revolutionary posturing in the early 1920s. The railway workers' Federación Obrera Ferrocarrilera (Railway Workers' Federation, FOF), the other pillar of the syndicalist FORA-IV, broke with syndicalism and gave way to the centralized, reformist Confederación Ferroviaria (Railway Confederation, CF), which leaned social-ist in subsequent years, spearheading the creation of the Confederación Obrera Argentina (Argentine Labour Confederation, COA) in 1924. Anarchists had little space within bureaucratic structures such as these. They retained a power of nuisance, however, in the case of the FOM, due to its federalist structure and connection to a range of anarchist-inspired autonomous unions in allied areas of riverine and maritime unionism and its far-reaching geographical network of organization in localities of the interior and Atlantic coast, where the original FORA remained influential into the 1940s. Throughout these years, both anarchists and syndicalists identified representative democracy as an elaborate system of political dom-ination in the defence of the interests of capital, and in the mid-1920s the FORA's anarchist leader Gilimón defended a quasi-Sorelian notion of the 'general strike' that was almost indistinguishable from the revolutionary syndicalist concept of preparing workers for a future free society.

Both currents also changed over the decades, in response to shifting circumstances in which opportunities for organization and class confronta-tion evolved. After taking over the UGT in 1906, forming the Confederación Obrera Regional Argentina (Argentine Regional Labour Confederation, CORA) in 1909 and dominating the FORA-IV in 1915, revolutionary

19 S. McGree Deutsch, *Counterrevolution in Argentina, 1900–1932: The Argentine Patriotic League* (Lincoln: University of Nebraska Press, 1986).

syndicalists founded the Unión Sindical Argentina (Union of Argentine Trade Unions, USA) in 1922 and revived it in 1936, once again under the hegemony of maritime workers. Leaders such as former anarchist Sebastián Marotta, former socialist Julio Arraga, and sailor Fortunato Marinelli played prominent roles in these organizations. Marotta, a construction worker, printer, and historian of the Argentine labour movement, participated in all of them. Arraga was an actor in the syndicalists' flirtations with the Yrigoyenist movement before joining, on the heels of the 1917 Bolshevik Revolution and the Italian *Biennio Rosso* of 1919–20, the Federación de Agrupaciones Sindicalistas Revolucionarias (Federation of Revolutionary Syndicalist Groups, FASR), rallying the International Federation of Trade Unions in Amsterdam and later the Profintern.[20] Marinelli unified the maritime workers' union in the late 1930s and 1940s and subsequently became one of the foremost advocates of labour's independence from the state under the Peronist regime, during (1950) and after (1956–7) which veteran anarchists and syndicalists in the port of Buenos Aires collaborated in momentous strike movements. In order to understand both the perenniality and the radicalization of anarchists and syndicalists in the 1920s, it is important to note the meteoric rise both movements enjoyed from 1917 and 1921, before and after the 1919 'Tragic Week' which is remembered as the fiercest state crackdown on workers in Argentina since 1910. The number of strikes in Buenos Aires increased by 70 per cent in the year after Yrigoyen's election in 1916, and the number of workers these strikes mobilized grew by 450 per cent. From 51 unions in December 1915, membership in the syndicalist FORA-IX grew to 70 a year later, 199 in December 1917, 232 by mid-1918, and 530 in 1920. What is often overlooked is that, during the same period (1915–20), the influence of the anarchist FORA-V extended from 21 resistance societies to well over 200.[21]

Much of this momentum rode on epic strikes in the nation's ports, which translated into an overwhelming force of maritime and railway workers in the syndicalist federation and of longshoremen and their allies in the anarchist one. Although the Yrigoyen administration would be remembered by later generations as the first Argentine political regime to open the floodgates of social reform, state repression continued and would escalate to

---

20 C. E. Aquino, 'Las disputas del sindicalismo revolucionario por los gremios ferroviarios durante la primera posguerra', *Archivos* 10 (March 2017), pp. 75–94.

21 G. de Laforcade, 'A Laboratory of Argentine Labor Movements: Dockworkers, Mariners, and the Contours of Class Identity in the Port of Buenos Aires, 1900–1950', PhD dissertation, Yale University, USA, 2001, p. 205.

unprecedented heights in the 1920s. The thriving FORA-IX had overseen the organization of unions of railroad, port, rural, packing-house, and petroleum workers in the territories of Santa Cruz, Chubut, and Tierra del Fuego, in a context of social polarization, economic uncertainty, and rising tensions with local land-owners and foreign capital. A revolt of Argentine and Chilean pastoral labourers in 1920–1 unleashed the bloodiest military crackdown in the history of the first half of the century when the government granted the Liga Patriótica and the Tenth Cavalry Regiment impunity to decimate the incipient labour movement in Patagonia at the cost of an estimated 1,500 lives. The subsequent defeat of a momentous strike in the port of Buenos Aires in 1921 opened a new era of militarization, as well as of radicalization in the ranks of syndicalist unions inspired by the Russian Revolution. They formed the FASR within the FORA-IX, and an anarcho-bolshevik faction emerged from the ranks of the FORA-V. In 1922 the FORA-IX merged with the anarcho-bolsheviks and autonomous unions to form the USA, which reclaimed the revolutionary fervour of the first decade of the century. The USA was led by seasoned revolutionary syndicalists Alejandro Silvetti and Luis Lotito; eight of its fourteen spokesmen represented waterfront unions – Eduardo Pereyra of the FOM, Manuel Gil of the cartmen's union, Juan Fernandez of the truckers' union, and four members of the shipyard workers' federation, Francisco Cruz, Juan Popovich, Hector Rebagliatti, and Domingo Marchesi, several of them long-time anarchists, as was the treasurer Atilio Biondi, a veteran of the early struggles of the century.

Throughout these decades, leaders of the FORA-V remained staunchly opposed to trade unionism for its own sake, and defended a model of anarchist organization that, while it co-existed, interacted, and sometimes even blended with revolutionary syndicalist movements in action, always retained its autonomy and originality. Emilio López Arango and Diego Abad de Santillán were among those who rejected the label 'anarcho-syndicalist'. In 1922 the FORA-V joined the revived International Workingmen's Association (IWA-AIT), which employed that vocabulary in its efforts to distinguish itself from the Red International of Trade Unions. Argentine anarchists aligned with *La Protesta* considered it ideologically ambiguous and foreign to their traditions, pointing out that the professed political neutrality of syndicalist trade unions did not prevent many of their members from engaging in electoral politics. What historian Hélène Finet calls the 'anarchist heterodoxy'[22] of the Argentine

---

22 H. Finet, 'Hétérodoxie anarchiste en Argentine. Analyse d'une déviance contre-démocratique', *Nuevo Mundo Mundos Nuevos*, CERMA, 2008, https://journals.openedition.org/nuevomundo/56503.

movement comprises not just the FORA-V and its deeply rooted traditions of local, trans-regional, and international federative networking among resistance societies and affinity groups, or its contributions to forging a working-class counter-culture of resistance to capitalism and the state, but also its diversity of expressions prior to 1905 and again in the wake of the First World War, particularly the emergence of insurrectionalist tendencies and anarcho-bolshevism in the 1920s. The use of violence had always been a matter of controversy in the movement, beginning in the heyday of anti-organization anarcho-individualism in the 1890s, when newspapers such as *La Voz de Ravachol* (*The Voice of Ravachol*), *El Perseguido*, and *El Rebelde* (*The Rebel*), and groups such as Los Dinamiteros (The Dynamiters) promoted propaganda by the deed and defended bombings and assassinations.[23] It emerged again in the 1920s with the division of the movement into a sector represented by the FORA-V (simply called the FORA after the dissolution of the FORA-IX into the USA) and *La Protesta,* and another driven by partisans of the Russian Revolution (Rodolfo González Pacheco, Teodor Antillí, Alfredo Bianchi) who supported, in the pages of their newspaper *La Antorcha* (*The Torch*), the social banditry of 'anarchist expropriators' led by the anti-fascist Italian Severino Di Giovanni, the Argentine-born Miguel Arcángel Roscigna, and the Spaniard Buenaventura Durruti.[24]

Confrontations, Mutations, Regional Expansion

By the second Yrigoyen presidency in 1928, reform-minded syndicalists had dislodged the revolutionary leadership and descended into all-out war with the anarchist FORA, finally merging the USA with the socialist COA after the 1930 military coup to form the Confederación General de Trabajo (General Confederation of Labour, CGT). The historically syndicalist FOM, meanwhile, led another major strike movement in 1928, in which all the rival tendencies within the national labour movement again converged. It even mobilized the South American secretariat of the Communist International, which issued a manifesto urging trade unions throughout the continent to form '*grupos de amigos* [friends' groups]' in support of the Argentine maritime workers. In addition to the syndicalist USA, the anarchist FORA-V, and the Argentine Communist Party, the strikers received the support of Yrigoyenist

---

23 R. E. Bittloch, *La théorie de la violence dans l'anarchisme argentin, 1890–1910* (Paris: Mémoire de Diplôme de l'EHESS, 1982).
24 F. López Trujillo, *Vidas en rojo y negro. Una historia del anarquismo en la Década Infame* (Buenos Aires: Letra Libre, 2005).

factions within a divided Radical Civic Union movement. Although the government made no attempt to revive the labour policies of the immediate post-war era, it did mediate in the conflict in the port, which ended in a resounding victory for the unions. Later, in 1937, the FOM spearheaded a revival of the syndicalist USA which would carry the syndicalist tradition into the 1940s, until they were shut down in 1950. Although syndicalists and anarchists by then represented a tiny fraction within the national industrial labour movement, they succeeded in continuing traditions of resistance and autonomy forged over a half-century in Buenos Aires and localities throughout the Argentine littoral and interior.

The Alianza Libertaria Argentina (Argentine Libertarian Alliance, ALA) formed in 1923, which federated a loose alliance of small craft societies, radical ethnic associations, and political groups associated with 'anarcho-bolshevism', among them a group of dissident FORA-V activists led by Rodolfo González Pacheco, was influential in the 1920s after its expulsion from the FORA in 1924. A prominent labour figure in the ALA was the aforementioned shipyard brazier Atilio Biondi, who led many of the alliance's members into the USA. The group around Pacheco and Antillí had edited its own newspapers and worked within *La Protesta* until 1915 before launching *La Obra* (*The Work*, 1915–19), *El Libertario* (*The Libertarian*, 1920), and finally *La Antorcha* in 1921. The Italian 'anarchist expropriator' Di Giovanni also published newspapers such as *Culmine* (*Culminate*, 1925–8) and *Anarchia* (*Anarchy*, 1930), two of many short-lived titles that reflected an effervescence of dissensions within anarchism throughout the period, culminating in the creation of the Comité Regional de Relaciones Anarquistas (Regional Anarchist Relations Committee, CRRA) two years after the 1930 military coup and the establishment of the Federación Anarco-Comunista Argentina (Argentine Anarcho-Communist Federation, FACA) in 1935, ancestor of the contemporary Federación Libertaria Argentina (Argentine Libertarian Federation, FLA, as it was renamed two decades later). The FACA participated actively in Argentine anti-fascist solidarity with the Spanish Civil War. It sent Jacobo Prince, Jacobo Maguid, Anita Piacenza, and José Grunfeld to Spain to collaborate with the Confederación Nacional del Trabajo (National Confederation of Labour–Iberian Anarchist Federation, CNT-FAI), which the prominent veteran of *La Protesta* and historian of the FORA Diego Abad de Santillán also joined, alongside former anarcho-bolsheviks González Pacheco and Horacio Badaraco. The FACA published *Acción Libertaria* (*Libertarian Action*) in the 1930s, *Solidaridad Obrera* (*Workers' Solidarity*) in the early 1950s, and later *Reconstruir* (*Reconstruction*); it considered itself a renewal of the early FORA and was a pioneer of what would later become the doctrine of 'especi-fismo' based on the 'social insertion' of anarchist organizers in autonomous and social movements as well as unions.[25]

The anarchist FORA, despite its struggles in the 1920s, retained a network of local and regional bastions rooted in the nation's port cities but which also expanded into the interior, where it had cast a wide network of solidarities during its 'second apogee' after the war. There were revolts of seasonal workers in the 'Pampa' of Buenos Aires province, and rural uprisings in Santa Fe, in Chaco, and in the southern province of Santa Cruz, all of which were actively supported by local workers' associations or Uniones de Obreros Locales (Local Workers' Unions, the local anarchist steering committees) that co-ordinated with anarchists from the capital. Convergences and tensions between the rival anarcho-communist, anarcho-bolshevik, and 'expropriator' tendencies played out in far-flung, remote localities where urban-based resistance societies fanned out as far south as Chubut and as far north as Salta. In northern Patagonia, for example, anarchists based in Bahía Blanca fomented resistance societies that joined the regional Federación Obrera Provincial de Buenos Aires (Provincial Labour Federation of Buenos Aires, FOPBA), created in 1922. They contributed to the emergence of libraries and affinity groups among bakers, brick-makers and masons, typographers, and loggers in cities such as General Roca, Allen, and Cipolletti, which in turn spread propaganda among rural workers occupied in the production of alfalfa, grapevines, fruit trees, and livestock, in the opening of canals and the clearing of fields, organizing strikes, boycotts, and protests and inviting fierce repression from the Patriotic League. Between 1922 and 1924, rivalries were common there between the FORA, which focused on organization and proselytization via La Protesta and the Agrupación Pensamiento Libre (Free Thought Group), and anarcho-bolsheviks who advocated an immediate revolution in the pages of La Antorcha and through a local group called Progreso y Cultura (Progress and Culture). The 'expropriator' faction, which prioritized violent insurrection, was also present. The aforementioned anarchist martyr Kurt Wilckens – a German immigrant who had been deported from the United States, who served as correspondent of Alarm in Hamburg and Der Syndikalist (The Syndicalist) in Berlin, and who killed Colonel Varela in 1923, before being himself murdered by a Patriotic League assassin in Villa Devoto prison – worked as a stevedore in

25 C. Penelas, Historia de la Federación Libertaria Argentina (Buenos Aires: Ediciones BP, 2006); Domínguez, 'Un itinerario por los proyectos editorials', p. 44.

Ingeniero White (Bahía Blanca) and as a farm worker in the Alto Valle of Río Negro.[26]

Anarchists were also present in the northern provinces, particularly Santa Fe and Salta, from which Argentine activists promoted solidarities throughout the Andean region. Antonio Fournakis, an organizer in Buenos Aires of the Unión Anarquista Balkánica Sud-Americana (South American Balkan Anarchist Union), which advocated abolishing national borders and federated anarchist groups throughout the continent, participated along with FORA activist Armando Triviño and printer Tomás Soria, an anarcho-bolshevik leader in Salta and Tucumán, in the organization of Bolivian anarchists in the 1920s; and one of the leaders of the Oruro section of the Bolivian Federación Obrera del Trabajo (Workers' Federation of Labour, FOT) was Luis Gallardo of the Argentine FORA.[27] In Peru, anarchist ideas circulated across the Andes from Buenos Aires, aided by the presence of activists from Argentina and Chile, many of whom passed through Salta on their way north. Pietro Gori had addressed a fledgling early anarchist movement in Salta in 1901, prior to its consolidation within the Federación Obrera de Salta (Labour Federation of Salta) in 1904. As in northern Patagonia, local resistance societies and anarcho-bolsheviks expanded their influence in the context of the Russian Revolution, the 'Tragic Week' of 1919 in Buenos Aires, and the ensuing surge in labour organization nationwide. The Agrupación Comunista Anarquista Despertar (Communist Anarchist Group 'Awakening') was a local branch first of the Unión Comunista Anarquista Argentina (Argentine Communist Anarchist Group, UCAA) and then of the ALA, which waged a fierce battle for hegemony in the region with the FORA though the pages of the newspaper El Coya (The Highlander). Correspondents of La Protesta and La Antorcha in Buenos Aires, Alberto Bianchi and Vicente Ferreito, organized conferences and cultural events in Salta, where the anarcha-feminist newspaper La Tribuna (The Tribune), edited by Juana Ruoco Buela, also circulated between 1922 and 1925, and where women were organized in the seamstresses' Sindicato de Obreras de la Aguja de Salta (Union of Needle Workers of Salta) led by Petrona Arias. The FORA

26 H. Scandizzo, 'Neuquén, el límite de la organización anarquista en la Patagonia Norte (1918–1923)', Revista de Historia 18 (November 2017), pp. 32–55; H. Scandizzo and J. Etchenique, 'Apuntes para una historia del anarquismo en el Alto Valle del Río Negro (1920–1930)', in Libro del IV Congreso de Historia Social y Política de la Patagonia Argentino-Chilena (Trevelín: Secretaría de Cultura de la Provincia de Chubut, 2001), pp. 1–14.

27 Z. Lehm Ardaya and S. Rivera Cusicanqui, Los artesanos libertarios y la ética del trabajo (La Paz: Editores del Taller de Historia Andina, 1988).

organized urban and domestic workers, artisans, street vendors, and other resistance societies into the Federación Obrera Local Salteña (Salta Local Labour Federation, FOLS).[28] Anarchist propagandists in the Argentine north-west often came from north-eastern towns along the Paraná River linking Buenos Aires to Asunción del Paraguay. They travelled via the vast network of syndicalist branches of mariners' unions co-ordinated by the FOM, spreading news of mobilizations and massacres such as those of farmers affiliated with the Federación Agraria Argentina (Argentine Agrarian Federation) in 1912 during the 'Grito de Alcorta' ('Cry of Alcorta', a massive rural protest in 1912), and the tannin workers of La Forestal (a British-owned quebracho tree company) in Santa Fe in 1921. They returned to the capital from the far northern reaches of Salta and Jujuy with dispatches regarding, for example, work conditions and class conflict on sugar plantations.

Anarchists also made inroads into the struggles of indigenous peoples from Chaco province to Patagonia. López Arango of the FORA advocated not only the inclusion of rural workers and peasants, representatives of the 'genuine physiognomy of American peoples', but also the 'elevation of the gaucho [mestizo trans-frontiersman] and the Indian' by anarchist movements.[29] In the same vein, the ALA's Badaraco wrote in 1932 that Argentines were a 'people nourished by many streams: Indians, Black people, gauchos, and immigrants endowed with knowledge in the noblest sense of the word, armed over the years with creativity from below, their own means of expression, democratic and combative memory'. Indigenous cultures, he continued, 'remain alive in so many parts of our land, and are present in the struggles and the dreams that we share as libertarians'.[30] Anarchists also developed, especially under the impulse of anarcho-bolsheviks, relations with revolutionary movements throughout Latin America, such as those of Augusto César Sandino in Nicaragua and Emiliano Zapata in Mexico, and even with the founders of Peruvian and Cuban communism, José Carlos Mariátegui and Julio Antonio Mella. French-born anarchist Joaquín Falconett, a historic leader of La Protesta, corresponded with Mexican anarchist Ricardo Flores Magón and related news

---

28 P. E. Cosso, 'Apuntes sobre el anarquismo salteño entre principios de siglo y el Golpe de Estado del Gral. Uriburu (1901–1930). La fructífera, abigarrada y represiva década del '20', in XVIII Jornadas de Investigación y Docencia de la Escuela de Historia (Salta: IEIH, 2018), pp. 1–24.

29 E. López Arango, 'La internationalización capitalista de la América Latina', Ideario (Buenos Aires: Ediciones de la ACAT, 1942), pp. 173–7.

30 J. Posales, Badaraco, el héroe prohibido. Anarquismo y lucha de clases en tiempos de infamia (Buenos Aires: Ediciones La Rosa Blindada, 2001), p. 221.

of the Mexican Revolution, as did Rodolfo González Pacheco and Teodoro Antillí, later the leading *transfuges* from the FORA to the ALA. After Flores Magon's death in 1922, Mexican and Argentine anarchists co-ordinated actions as transnationalism gained momentum throughout the decade. FORA stalwart Diego Abad de Santillán, who represented Latin America at the 1922 Berlin anarcho-syndicalist congress, defended their movements' independence and originality (particularly their insertion in rural and popular movements). Julio Díaz, then co-director of *La Protesta* with López Arango, participated in the organization of Central American anarchists in the mid-1920s in conjunction with the Mexican CGT, which helped co-ordinate the 1929 international anarchist conference in Buenos Aires of the Asociación Continental Americana de Trabajadores (American Continental Association of Workers, ACAT), affiliated with the IWA-AIT.[31]

Twilight and Legacy

Argentine anarchism declined in the 1930s, as bureaucratized mass trade unionism ushered in a new era of instrumentalization of labour by the state. Yet the rhizomes or subterranean roots of three decades of local, regional, and transnational organization and agitation, in constant tension and emulation with revolutionary syndicalism, averted its disappearance, in spite of the rivalries and dissensions that arose after the Russian Revolution and extended to competition with the anarcho-syndicalist IWW on a continental scale. The bedrock of anti-statist, federalist, urban / rural, feminist, anti-fascist, internationalist, and anti-Eurocentric orientations that permeated the movement in its heyday would continue to nourish anarchist-inspired cultural and social movements in later decades, after they had lost their firm imbrication in organized labour movements and mass-based counter-cultural movements. Syndicalism also lost its revolutionary edge with the apogee of the 'national popular' state in the 1940s and subsequent rise of Marxism-Leninism. There was ample evidence, however, by the turn of the following century, that traditions of anarchist and revolutionary syndicalist horizontalism and autonomy, as well as expressions of anarcha-feminism and anarcho-indigenism, remained relevant in a context of the slow dissolution of state-driven organizational forms and authoritarian socialist movements in the neoliberal era.

31 D. Téllez Anta, 'Redes anarquistas de apoyo mutuo en Latinoamérica. Relaciones entre México y Argentina en la década de 1920', Tesis de Licenciado, Universidad Nacional Autónoma de México, Mexico City, 2018, p. 15.

Further Reading

Baer, James, *Anarchist Immigrants in Spain and Argentina* (Urbana: University of Illinois Press, 2015).

Bayer, Osvaldo, *The Anarchist Expropriators: Buenaventura Durruti and Argentina's Working-Class Robin Hoods* (Chico, CA: AK Press, 2015).

de Laforcade, Geoffroy, and Kirwin Shaffer (eds.), *In Defiance of Boundaries: Anarchism in Latin American History* (Gainesville: University Press of Florida, 2015).

Hirsch, Steven, and Lucien van der Walt (eds.), *Anarchism and Syndicalism in the Colonial and Post-Colonial World, 1880–1940* (Leiden and Boston: Brill, 2011).

Munck, Ronaldo, with Ricardo Falcón and Bernardo Galitelli, *Argentina from Anarchism to Peronism: Workers, Unions, and Politics, 1855–1985* (Atlantic Highlands, NJ: Zed Books, 1987).

Suriano, Juan, *Paradoxes of Utopia: Anarchist Culture and Politics in Buenos Aires, 1890–1910* (Chico, CA: AK Press, 2010).

22

Anarchism and Syndicalism in Brazil

CLAUDIO BATALHA

Origins

Establishing precisely when socialism and anarchist socialism arrived in Brazil is far from an easy task. Throughout the nineteenth century, references to European socialist thinkers or social reformers were common in the Brazilian press. At least since the late 1840s, authors such as Claude-Henri de Saint-Simon, Charles Fourier, Pierre Leroux, Louis Blanc, and Pierre-Joseph Proudhon were frequently mentioned. Nevertheless, these references were often critical. In a way, anti-socialism preceded socialism as a structured social movement. This can be measured by the fearful reactions to the Paris Commune of 1871 and by favourable remarks on Otto von Bismarck's anti-socialist laws.[1] Unlike neighbouring Argentina, where early socialist groups of different tendencies were formed, until almost the end of the century references to socialism in Brazil were limited to newspaper articles, and no organized expression of that political philosophy blossomed. The rare exceptions include the short-lived Fourierist colonies established by French craftsmen in the early 1840s in southern Brazil, and the exiled Forty-Eighters, who mainly arrived in the 1850s and settled in Rio de Janeiro, then the nation's capital.[2] However, neither example had a significant impact on Brazilian society or recruited known followers among the local working classes.

---

1 F. Lourenço, '"Delito de lesa-humanidade". Os parlamentares do Império brasileiro frente à Comuna de Paris', in A. Boito Jnr (ed.), *A Comuna de Paris na história* (São Paulo: Xamã, 2001), pp. 171–81; A. de Oliveira, 'A questão socialista 1', *Gazeta de Notícias* 27 November 1878, p. 2.
2 On Fourierist colonies, see I. Gallo, 'A aurora do socialismo. Fourierismo e o falanstério do Saí (1839–1850)', PhD dissertation, Campinas, UNICAMP, Brazil, 2002; and I. Gallo, 'Une expérience de communauté fouriériste au Brésil. Le phalansthère de Saí (1841–1843)', in L. Vidal and T. Regina De Luca (eds.), *Les Français au Brésil xixe–xxe siècles* (Paris: Les Indes Savantes, 2011), pp. 165–80. On the *quarante-huitard* emigration, see L. Gregório Canelas, 'Franceses *quarante-huitards* no Império dos Trópicos (1848–1862)', MA dissertation, Campinas, UNICAMP, Brazil, 2007.

The first organized local socialist group was created in 1889 in the port city of Santos, São Paulo, followed in the next few years by other groups in Rio de Janeiro and São Paulo[3] and southern and north-eastern Brazil, especially in cities such as Rio Grande, Porto Alegre, Salvador, and Recife. In general, each of these groups published its own newspaper. Until 1930, a few short-lived regional workers' or socialist parties were formed but, unlike other cases in Latin America, no such party with national reach was created, which partly explains the absence of regular links with the Socialist International. Two main aspects shed light on the difficulty that socialist parties, which focused on electoral politics, faced in gaining strength and stability during the First Brazilian Republic (1889–1930): the electoral system and the extreme federalization of politics. Elections were marked by various types of fraud discouraging public participation, so few workers were enlisted as voters. Despite the existence of universal male suffrage, illiterate people, soldiers, members of religious orders, and foreigners (the last of whom represented an important part of the working class) were disenfranchised. Furthermore, the entire political system was state-based, and political parties were formed within the states, which made it nearly impossible to establish national parties.

The first manifestation of anarchism in Brazil was the Cecilia Colony, established in 1890 in the southern state of Parana. Under the leadership of Giovanni Rossi (1856–1943), a few Italian families and single individuals attempted to create a rural version of what Rossi termed 'experimental socialism'. This experiment was supposed to put into practice collective property and – with limited observance – Rossi's unique view of free love, which consisted of maintaining multiple and simultaneous romantic relationships. The Cecilia experiment was almost as short-lived as the Fourierist colonies that had been established some decades earlier: it ended after four years of activity. Following the breakup of the colony, Rossi stayed on in Brazil, working as an agronomist. There is no evidence that he influenced the spread of anarchism during those years, and he returned to Italy in 1907. Nevertheless, both Rossi and other members of the Cecilia Colony are part of a few mythical narratives claiming that they played a major role in the beginnings of anarchism in Brazil.[4]

---

3 Unless otherwise indicated, all mentions of Rio de Janeiro and São Paulo refer to the cities and not the states of the same name.
4 I. Felici, 'A verdadeira história da Colonia Cecília de Giovanni Rossi', *Cadernos AEL* 8–9 (1998), pp. 11–65; H. Isabel Mueller, *Flores aos rebeldes que falharam. Giovanni Rossi e a utopia anarquista* (Curitiba: Aos Quatro Ventos, 1999), pp. 180–220.

In a more urban and industrial setting, anarchist propaganda was an essential step towards gaining followers for the cause. In this sense, groups formed to disseminate this doctrine, and their periodicals, were the main means to achieve this. The first anarchist newspaper was *Primo Maggio* (*First of May*), published in 1892 in São Paulo. Written in Italian, it was a special issue celebrating May Day. A few weeks later, an Italian-language weekly *Gli Schiavi Bianchi* (*The White Slaves*) was launched in the same city. That was followed a year later by *L'Asino Umano* (*The Human Donkey*) and in 1894 by *L'Avvenire* (*The Future*), both Italian anarchist periodicals based in São Paulo.[5] One aspect that these newspapers shared was their target audience of Italians, the largest immigrant group in São Paulo state, and their lack of interest in addressing other groups, especially Brazilians, whom they considered 'unprepared'.[6] Therefore, these periodicals were unlikely to reach the Brazilian-born working class, of which freed black slaves and their descendants formed a major part. In a way, foreign workers echoed the prejudices of Brazil's dominant classes regarding the national workforce, part of which had been freed from bondage only a few years earlier, in 1888, by the abolition of slavery. In addition to the language spoken by its target audience, written propaganda had to cope with the high level of illiteracy: in 1900, 65 per cent of the population over the age of fifteen could not read or write.

Meanwhile, in Rio de Janeiro, anarchist papers such as *O Despertar* (*The Awakening*, 1898), *O Protesto* (*The Protest*, 1899–1900), and *O Golpe* (*The Blow*, 1900) were written in Portuguese. They were published in the national language of Brazil because the Italian immigrant population in Rio was not as large as it was in São Paulo, and most militants were Portuguese or Brazilian.

The vast majority of anarchist, socialist, and labour periodicals were short-lived, had trouble maintaining a regular publication schedule, and struggled with a lack of funding. Many of them were distributed free of charge, so their revenue depended on the financial contributions of their supporters and other forms of fund-raising. Very few managed to continue publication for several years, and still fewer were published daily for at least part of their existence.

---

5 I. Felici, 'Les italiens dans le mouvement anarchiste au Brésil, 1890–1920', Thèse de doctorat Université de la Sorbonne Nouvelle – Paris III, France, 1994, pp. 100–22 (note that the copy consulted was the the 2016 digital version, with page numbers that are different from the original 1994 printed copy); A. Trento, *Imprensa italiana no Brasil séculos XIX e XX* (São Carlos: EdUFSCar, 2013), p. 73.
6 Trento, *Imprensa italiana no Brasil*, p. 94.

The police kept a close eye on the political and social activism of foreign militants, and foreign governments and the Brazilian authorities frequently exchanged information about their activities. Since the very first years of the First Republic, foreign activists had faced deportation by governmental decree, whether or not a thorough investigation of their alleged crimes or proper judicial procedures had been conducted.

Anarchism and Labour: The Birth of Brazilian Syndicalism

The strikes of 1902–3 in the cities of São Paulo and Rio de Janeiro were a major milestone in the process of the anarchist approach to labour, reaching a wide range of trades and branches of industry. These strikes brought about the first labour unions, a major change compared to the previously dominant model of labour organizations in which mutual aid, trade union practice, and, occasionally, political action coexisted. In 1903, other branches of the labour movement in Rio accused *A Greve* (*The Strike*), an anarchist newspaper created during the textile workers' strike, of radicalizing the strikers.

However, the anarchist stance on labour was far from univocal. The main anarchist current in Brazil was anarcho-communism. Nevertheless, some proclaimed themselves anarcho-individualists – they were mostly middle-class intellectuals but also included some working-class militants, such as the Portuguese typographer Joaquim Mota Assunção (1879–?). The anarcho-communists themselves were divided between those who favoured partici-pation in labour organizations and their struggles, and those who completely rejected them. However, the same people could frequently shift from one position to the other for reasons dictated by circumstances or other motives. In São Paulo, more clearly than elsewhere, the main proponent of one of these opposing views was the Portuguese journalist Gregorio Nazianzeno de Vasconcelos (1878–1920), better known as Neno Vasco, who endorsed anarchist action in the labour movement. The group critical of this kind of action published the Italian-language weekly *La Battaglia* (*The Struggle*), launched in 1904 and produced without interruption until 1913 (changing its name in 1912 to *La Barricata* or *The Barricade*) – a rare feat for that type of publication.[7] According to this group, syndicalist action meant proposing short-term aims, such as wage increases or reduced working hours, losing

---

7 L. Biondi, 'Anarquistas italianos em São Paulo. O grupo do jornal anarquista *La Battaglia* e a sua da sociedade brasileira: o embate entre imaginários libertários e etnocêntricos', *Cadernos AEL* 8–9 (1998), p. 118.

sight of the ultimate goal of establishing a new society. The curious aspect of this internal debate is that both sides of the anarcho-communists usually referred to the same authors, such as Peter Kropotkin and Errico Malatesta, to endorse their views, but used writings produced in different periods. This conflict could be stronger or weaker at different times, but never ceased to be present in anarchist action.

Another aspect to be considered is that anarchist propaganda was not limited to newspapers and other publications, such as leaflets, brochures, and books, nor was their action restricted to trade union activity. Anarchists usually organized through affinity groups, and in most cases a newspaper resulted from the work of one such group. These affinity groups also worked through theatrical productions, staging amateur libertarian plays, in addition to organizing educational initiatives. Schools based on the model of Catalan anarchist Francisco Ferrer i Guardia were established, especially in São Paulo state, while a group mainly comprising anarcho-individualists founded a People's University in Rio in 1904.

Held in Rio de Janeiro in April 1906, the First Brazilian Workers' Congress marked a break with the previously dominant forms of labour organization and practices. To a major extent, this choice resulted less from a previously held theoretical standpoint and more from a pragmatic decision. Faced with the possible approval of a resolution proposing the creation of a workers' political party, the anarchist minority in the congress proposed an alternative solution: political neutrality based on a mild version of French revolutionary syndicalist principles for labour organizations. Although the inspiration doubtlessly arose from the French example, the word 'revolutionary', either as noun or adjective, was omitted from the congress's resolutions. As a result, the anarchist minority managed to win the votes of the majority of delegates. This Brazilian congress took place six months before the French Confédération Générale du Travail (General Confederation of Labour, CGT) adopted the Amiens Charter in October 1906 during its Ninth Congress, which consolidated revolutionary syndicalist principles.[8] The attendance at the Brazilian congress attested to the lack of effective nation-wide representation, as only five states were represented, including the Federal District, Rio de Janeiro (at the time, the Brazilian republic was divided into twenty states and the federal capital). The vast majority of the twenty-eight delegations came from Rio and São Paulo state.

8 Some authors suggest that the charter did not have the weight attributed to it by posterity. See D. Lindenberg, 'Le mythe de la charte d'Amiens', *Mil neuf cent* 24 (2006), pp. 41–55.

One of the main resolutions adopted by the 1906 congress was the establishment of the Brazilian Workers' Confederation (Confederação Operária Brasileira, COB), the first attempt to form a nationwide labour organization. The COB only became active two years later, in 1908, and depended entirely on the two local federations that attended the congress: the Rio de Janeiro Workers' Federation (Federação Operária do Rio de Janeiro, FORJ) and the São Paulo Workers' Federation (Federação Operária de São Paulo, FOSP). That same year saw the publication of the COB's official newspaper, *A Voz do Trabalhador* (*The Worker's Voice*), which became the main propaganda tool for syndicalism.

Since that first congress, revolutionary syndicalism, or at least syndicalism, formed part of the anarchist strategy in Brazilian trade unions. Many unions were organized on the basis of the principles established by that congress, adopting non-hierarchical collective boards and direct action as a method of struggle. This does not mean that revolutionary syndicalism as an autonomous movement did not already exist, especially in São Paulo, where Italian militants reproduced the same variant that originated in their homeland (there, it resulted from the Socialist Party's left-wing anti-parliamentarian dissidence). The main spokesperson for this form of revolutionary syndicalism was Alceste De Ambris (1874–1934), who was still a mainstream socialist when he first arrived in Brazil in 1898. In 1900, in São Paulo, he launched the newspaper *Avanti!* (*Forward!*), which adopted the same name and font on its masthead as its counterpart in Italy. Needless to say, it was published in Italian. However, when advocating the formation of different kinds of workers' organizations, including trade unions, the Brazilian *Avanti!* did not emphasize trade unionist action. In 1903, De Ambris returned to Italy to escape a prison sentence for defamation. Back in his homeland, he sided with the revolutionary syndicalists and followed them in 1907 when they broke with the Socialist Party. Two years later, De Ambris was back in São Paulo, this time to avoid arrest in Italy, and continued his political activity. It was a time of crisis in the Brazilian labour movement, when many of the organizations created in 1908 were forced to close. However, despite that difficult situation, in 1910 De Ambris founded the Italian-language weekly *La Scure* (*The Axe*), which attempted to set the standard for different movements and reorganize labour. Although anarchists occasionally published their views in that paper, positions closer to revolutionary socialism and syndicalism prevailed. The following year, De Ambris returned to Europe after the death of one of his brothers, who lived in Brazil.[9] He was not the only Italian revolutionary syndicalist to engage in militancy both in his homeland and in Brazil. If the form of syndicalism practised by many trade unions could be identified with this revolutionary syndicalism of Italian origin in many ways, it did not constitute a consistent ideological movement, unlike the latter, which aspired to a new society based on unions.

The years immediately following the First Workers' Congress, when numerous strikes occurred, brought the first important test for syndicalism. Between 1906 and 1908, major strikes broke out in several cities, some of them encompassing different trades demanding an eight-hour workday, as in Porto Alegre in 1906 and São Paulo a year later. Others involved strategic sectors for an economy focused on export commodities, such as ports and railroads. One of the last major strikes of that period, held in 1909, mobilized railroad workers in four north-eastern states that were part of the network of the British-owned Great Western of Brazil Railway Company. During that period, the number of labour unions organized along syndicalist lines increased in different parts of Brazil.

The growth of labour organizations was closely linked to a period of rising industrial wages and some success in labour conflicts. However, things began to change in 1907, as government taxation policies favoured imported manufactured goods. By 1909, this had led to a slowdown in industrial activity and unemployment. Under these circumstances, strikes tended to be defeated, and many labour organizations closed their doors.

Alongside increasing labour unrest, police and corporate repression became more intense, while legal means to restrain activism were reinforced. In 1907, the Brazilian congress approved the first expulsion law, known as the Adolfo Gordo Law, named after the representative who proposed it, although – as we have seen– the authorities had deported foreigners on political and other grounds before the expulsion laws came into effect.

Disagreements in the anarchist camp did not arise exclusively between partisans and critics of labour activism. In 1909, in Rio de Janeiro, anarcho-individualist militants broke with the anarcho-communist majority over the adoption of methods such as sabotage during strikes. By 1911, the anarcho-individualists had formed the Radical Socialist Party and published *A Vanguarda* (*The Vanguard*), a paper that criticized both anarchist and other socialist factions. Between 1913 and 1914, an acrimonious dispute involving

---

9 E. Toledo, *Travessias revolucionárias. Ideias e militantes sindicalistas em São Paulo e na Itália (1890–1945)* (Campinas: Editora da UNICAMP, 2004), ch. 2.

several newspaper articles, mainly published in *Voz do Trabalhador*, erupted between Neno Vasco and João Crispim. The main theorist and advocate of anarchist participation in syndicalism, Vasco had returned to Portugal by then, but still exerted a strong influence on the COB's policies. Crispim was a leader of the Local Workers' Federation of Santos (Federação Operária Local de Santos, FOLS), which adopted the same stance as the Argentine Regional Workers' Federation (Federación Obrera Regional Argentina, FORA) at its Fifth Congress of 1905, proposing that unions adopt anarchism in their programmes. Vasco believed that this position went against not only the organization of the proletariat as a class but also anarchism itself.[10] At that time, Crispim's influence was limited to Santos, while Vasco's was hegemonic among anarchists acting in trade unions. However, things would change in the following decade.

In 1911, the labour movement began to reorganize slowly as a certain resumption of industrial activity occurred, and some strikes took place. However, the COB, which had been inactive since 1909, was only re-established two years later. In response to the reformist labour unions that organized a labour congress in 1912, anarchists and syndicalists held another congress in 1913, once again in Rio de Janeiro. This time, the number of delegations had more than doubled compared to the 1906 congress, but the number of states represented, eight in total, was still modest. The resolutions adopted by this second congress reaffirmed the principles established in 1906, but the rhetoric was less contained, mentioning the possibility of a 'revolutionary general strike'. The main impact of this congress was a fresh surge of trade unions formed on the basis of syndicalist principles.

Shortly after that congress, the labour movement plunged into another period of crisis that grew more intense during the first years of the First World War. There were fewer strikes, the cost of living increased, and many labour associations ceased to exist. By 1915, both syndicalist unions and anarchists invested in the organization of an International Peace Congress, followed by the South American Anarchist Congress, both held in Rio de Janeiro in October. Since August 1914, the *Voz do Trabalhador* had reported on anti-war initiatives in Europe, and the following month syndicalists held anti-war rallies in several Brazilian cities. However, the COB, one of the main organizers of the Peace Congress, no longer existed by the time it took place. Despite the difficulties for travel as the First World War was raging, the Peace

---

10 Neno Vasco, 'O anarquismo no sindicato', *Voz do Trabalhador* 6, 38, 1 September 1913, p. 1.

Congress brought together delegates representing seven Brazilian states, as well as delegations from Argentina, Spain, and Portugal. In addition to Brazilian delegations, the foreign delegations that attended the anarchist congress mainly came from Argentina. Once more, this congress restated the anti-war position and discussed the anarchists' relationship with trade unions, warning against seeing syndicalism as the only means of anarchist action.[11]

Revolutionary syndicalism was mainly a phenomenon present in more industrialized southern Brazil. However, especially in the 1910s, some northern trade unions were converted to this conception. In Manaus, at least between 1910 and 1914, the printing workers' union had a syndicalist orientation, managing to put out a newspaper, *A Lucta Social* (*The Social Struggle*) in 1914, which published articles both by anarchists, such as Kropotkin, Saverio Merlino, and Anselmo Lorenzo, and by revolutionary syndicalists, such as Emile Pouget.[12] In 1914, in Salvador, the state capital of Bahia, the labour movement responded to the COB's appeal and staged anti-war demonstrations. In the north-eastern state of Pernambuco, the first attempts to organize a labour movement following these principles also dated from 1914, with the birth of the Federation of Working Classes, whose official outlet was the *Tribuna do Povo* (*People's Tribune*), replaced in 1919 by *A Hora Social* (*The Social Times*). Both newspapers frequently published articles on the Russian Revolution.[13]

Anarchism undoubtedly found more fertile soil in urban centres with a growing industrial proletariat, but isolated anarchist militants were also present in small towns in predominantly rural areas. Avelino Foscolo (1861–1944), a writer and chemist, became an anarchist in Taboleiro Grande (now Paraopeba), a small town in the state of Minas Gerais, where he published the bimonthly newspaper *A Nova Era* (*The New Era*, 1906–7), containing articles by Kropotkin, Jean Grave, Leo Tolstoy, and Elisée Reclus.

11 K. Willian dos Santos, 'Construindo o Congresso Internacional da Paz e o Congresso Anarquista Sul Americano. Cultura política e o trânsito de ideias e experiências anarquistas e sindicalistas entre o Brasil e a Argentina nas duas primeiras décadas do século XX', *Revista Espaço Acadêmico* 18, 201 (November 2018), p. 48.
12 M. L. Ugarte Pinheiro and L. Balkar Sá Peixoto Pinheiro (eds.), *Imprensa operária no Amazonas. Transcrições e fac-símiles* (Manaus: EDUA, 2004), pp. 74–112; M. L. Ugarte Pinheiro, *Folhas do Norte. Letramento e periodismo no Amazonas (1880–1920)* (Manaus: EDUA, 2015), pp. 196–214.
13 F. Duarte Bartz, 'Movimento operário e revolução social no Brasil. Ideias revolucionárias e projetos políticos dos trabalhadores organizados no Rio de Janeiro, São Paulo, Recife e Porto Alegre entre 1917 e 1922', PhD dissertation, Universidade Federal do Rio Grande do Sul (UFRGS), Brazil, 2014, p. 94.

An issue that helped throw anarchism into disarray during that period was the number of well-known European anarchists who adhered to interventionism, backing their national governments in the war. They included Kropotkin, Grave, and Charles Malato, who produced the Manifesto of the Sixteen in 1916. Brazil remained neutral until mid-1917, when the sinking of merchants ships by German U-boats led the government to declare war on Germany and its allies (its participation in the conflict was limited to sending a medical unit to the western front). Nevertheless, anti-war and anti-militarist feelings were firmly established among anarchists and other socialist groups. Even Italian revolutionary syndicalists based in São Paulo remained critical of Brazil's involvement in the war, although they usually tended to follow the policies of their movement in the old country, which endorsed interventionism.

General Strikes and the Russian Revolution

After 1917, anarchism faced two major challenges: dealing with changes introduced in the labour movement by the great strikes of 1917 and 1919, and interpreting the Russian Revolution. Both issues sparked controversy and division.

Until the various strike movements that erupted in some of Brazil's major cities, beginning in 1917, labour organization had mainly represented skilled male workers through craft unions. Although the strikes during those years involved both unskilled male workers and women, the latter played an important role in their organization and development. Thus, industrial unions were formed in certain branches that had previously been based

Fig. 22.1 Funeral procession for shoemaker José Martinez, São Paulo, July 1917. (História da Industrialização Collection, Edgard Leuenroth Archive, UNICAMP, Brazil.)

mainly on crafts, such as metal-workers and construction workers. Both the resolutions of the 1906 and 1913 congresses and the practice of labour leadership favoured craft unionism, albeit not discarding the possibility of forming industrial unions. In other words, some industrial unions were created before becoming an important issue in labour debate. In São Paulo, in particular, where the strike movement began in June 1917, becoming a general strike in the following month with common demands and a single leading committee, labour managed to show its power and obtain certain gains. Similar movements broke out in Rio de Janeiro and Porto Alegre. To some degree, they had to establish negotiations with the authorities, breaking one of the principles that guided direct action.

Some anarchist leaders who had previously denounced syndicalism during the demobilization of labour between 1914 and 1916 returned to trade union activism. This was not uncommon among anarchists, whose adherence to syndicalism increased when the labour movement was on the rise and tended to decrease in periods of crisis. In this sense, syndicalism was not an end but a tactical option to be explored under certain circumstances.

Despite their decisive role in the 1917 strikes, women were almost absent from leading positions in trade unions, even in sectors in which they played an important part or formed the majority of the workforce, such as the textile industry. There was just one woman among the frequent contributors to the COB's official newspaper, *Voz do Trabalhador*: Elvira Fernandes, who was also an occasional contributor to other working-class periodicals, writing articles backing anarchism. During the 1917 general strike in São Paulo, Maria Antonia Soares (1899–?) was an extremely active militant, despite her youth, and was known for her speeches at public meetings. She was the half-sister of Primitivo Raimundo Soares (1883–1947), with whom she collaborated on anarchist newspapers. Due to her activism during the strike, she was arrested along with her three sisters. Previously, in 1915, she had helped create the Centre for Women's Education and was a founding member of the Women's Centre of Young Idealists. She represented the latter organization at the International Anarchist Congress held in Rio that year.[14] The only situation in which women did play a leading role in the unions was when they represented exclusively female occupations, such as seamstresses. The anarchist Elvira Boni (1899–1990), who had been involved in the Anti-Clerical League and its amateur theatrical presentations when she was an

14 L. Biondi and E. Toledo, *Uma revolta urbana. A greve de 1917 em São Paulo* (São Paulo: Fundação Perseu Abramo, 2018), pp. 121–2.

apprentice seamstress in her early teens, organized a seamstresses' union in Rio in 1919. The following year, she represented that union at the Third Brazilian Workers' Congress. Maria Antonia Soares and Elvira Boni had much in common. They were born in the same year in São Paulo state, both were raised in working-class immigrant families – the former of Spanish and the latter of Italian origin – and both got involved in anarchism at an early age.

Precisely in this context, the Brazilian labour press showed a growing interest in the proposals of the Industrial Workers of the World (IWW). However, these references were more part of a theoretical debate on industrial unionism than effective proposals to reproduce the US organization's ideological stances. In fact, at this point, the Brazilian labour movement was striving for responses capable of dealing with the ongoing changes in the makeup of working-class activism. One of the main voices to express this interest was Astrojildo Pereira (1890–1965), an anarchist journalist and future secretary general of the Communist Party, particularly in a series of articles published in *A Plebe* (*The Plebs*), a São Paulo-based newspaper that became the most important and long-lived anarchist publication from 1917 onwards.[15]

Under the influence of the Russian Revolution, an unlikely alliance of anarchists, trade union leaders, and middle-class intellectuals staged a coup in Rio de Janeiro in November 1918. The movement planned for a military insurrection to be launched as strikes broke out among textile, metal, and construction workers. However, the military liaison for the conspiracy was an infiltrated agent, so there was no military backing for the movement initiated by trade unions. The leaders who did not manage to flee were soon arrested. The failed coup took place in a context in which the labour movement was considerably weakened by the Spanish flu epidemic, which infected 44 per cent of Rio's population and killed 1.5 per cent.

A few months later, in March 1919, some of the leaders of the failed uprising formed a short-lived Communist Party that was based on anarchist principles and far removed from the Bolshevik model. This party organized a communist conference in July, attended by twenty-two delegates. It was initially held in Rio, but after the first day police intervention forced it to move to the nearby city of Niteroi, where the conference's deliberations were concluded. Although the party intended to establish groups in different states, it did not survive the repression of labour organizations and anarchist

---

15 M. Zaidan Filho, 'As origens da política de unidade sindical no Brasil', *Revista de História* 119 (1988), pp. 142–3.

militants unleashed that year, when many foreign-born militants were deported. They included Luigi (Gigi) Damiani (1876–1953), one of the main representatives of the anti-syndicalist branch of anarcho-communism. Unlike 1917, when the strike movement that spread through the main Brazilian cities caught industrialists and authorities by surprise, the great 1919 strikes met with more organized industrial and state repression, and were mostly defeated in southern and south-eastern Brazil. However, a general strike in the north-eastern state of Bahia, where syndicalist influence was limited to some trades of construction workers – an unprecedented move in that part of the country – was victorious. Even so, the series of defeats continued in the main industrial cities the following year.

Under these troubling circumstances, another national labour congress took place in April 1920 in Rio de Janeiro. It was the Third Brazilian Workers' Congress, which, while maintaining much of the rhetoric of the previous congresses, approved resolutions more inclined towards pragmatism. They admitted mutualistic practices that had been condemned by previous congresses as incompatible with syndicalist principles. Furthermore, industrial unions of previously limited importance gained a place for themselves during this congress. In other words, the resolutions showed growing awareness of the new reality facing the working class. Mentions of syndicalism were still present, but the adjective 'revolutionary' was, once again, absent. However, despite the circumstances, the congress's attendees were more widely representative, both in the number of delegations (seventy-two representing nine different states) and in the diversity of the movements represented. For the first time since 1906, both syndicalist and reformist unions sent delegations, which helps us understand the nature of the resolutions reached.

During its early years, the Russian Revolution was well received in the Brazilian labour movement, even among anarchists, who tended to see it as the fulfilment of their goals. By 1920, however, the anarchist schoolteacher José Oiticica (1882–1957) began publishing a series of articles in *Voz do Povo* (*Voice of the People*), the newspaper of the Rio de Janeiro Workers' Federation, observing that, as with the French Revolution, the Russian Revolution was deviating from its aims. Around the same time, the printer known as Florentino de Carvalho, the pseudonym of Primitivo Raimundo Soares, published further criticism of the revolution in São Paulo's anarchist newspaper *A Plebe*. The Soviet repression of anarchists since 1918 and the critical evaluations of the new regime by Kropotkin and Emma Goldman began to raise doubts among their Brazilian brethren. However, for several months both Oiticica and Carvalho were isolated voices.

The prevailing attitude of anarchists regarding the Russian Revolution was to defend it, despite occasional critiques of Soviet policy. Many believed that the critics were basing their views on what might be called 'fake news' regarding events in Russia spread by the bourgeois press. It was only in March 1922 that a manifesto published by nine leading anarchists in *A Plebe* widened the irreversible rift between critics and defenders of that revolution. A few days later, the opposition concerning the interpretation of the Russian Revolution led to the formation of the Brazilian Communist Party, made up of former anarchists, a few socialists, and labour activists who seemed closer to syndicalism than to anarchism.

Changing Patterns

In the 1920s, revolutionary syndicalism lost influence, particularly in Rio, where the competition between anarchists and communists for the control of labour unions was more intense. In this context, the anarchists adopted the stance that trade unions should programmatically proclaim themselves anarchist (as proposed by the Argentinian entity FORA).[16] In a way, as trade unions under anarchist influence shifted to a more ideological stand-point, the revolutionary syndicalist tradition found more affinity with unions under communist influence, which advocated that unions should accept all workers, regardless of their creed. Furthermore, at least in its early years, the Red Trade Union International (Profintern) attracted IWW members and revolutionary syndicalists. At the same time, revolutionary syndicalism as an autonomous movement, represented by its Italian variant in São Paulo, disappeared from Brazil altogether.

By 1923, after losing control to the communists of the Workers' Federation of Rio de Janeiro (Federação dos Trabalhadores do Rio de Janeiro, FTRJ), which had been active since 1919, the anarchists re-established the FORJ – shut down by the police in 1917 – thus splitting union affiliations into two competing federations. Occasionally, rival unions with different doctrines were established in the same trade or branch of activity, but that situation rarely lasted. The division was so pronounced that, from 1924 onwards, even May Day, which supposedly expressed working-class unity, resulted in sep-arate celebrations held in different locations.

Among women, anarchism had been almost entirely a working-class phenomenon, but in the early 1920s the first examples of middle-class

---

16 For further information on the Argentine case, see Chapter 21 in this volume.

women endorsing libertarian ideas can be found. Among the most prominent was educator and writer Maria Lacerda de Moura (1887–1945), a pioneer of feminism in Brazil. In 1923, in São Paulo, she launched the women's magazine *Renascença (Rebirth)* and wrote several books on women's liberation.[17] Even among the working-class audience, a more feminist approach seemed to prevail by 1922. The seamstresses' union created in 1919 in Rio had been dissolved by then, but some of its members went on to establish the Women's Liberation Group. In 1923, they published a special May Day issue of *O Nosso Jornal (Our Newspaper)*, covering subjects such as women's education, feminism, and the organization of the working class. One article referred to *Renascença*, quoting Maria Lacerda de Moura at length on the need for social change and warning against the threat of fascism.[18]

During those years, labour activism and political activity in general were hampered by the state of siege decreed in response to the military uprisings of 1922 and 1924, as numerous trade unions were suspended and newspapers were shut down. Activists faced imprisonment or deportation, but could also be sent to the Colonial Settlement of Clevelândia (named for US president Grover Cleveland), a concentration camp established in the Oiapoque River region near the border with French Guiana in the Amazon, where anarchists, labour militants, mutinous soldiers, and common criminals were held. An official report produced in 1926 stated that 491 of the camp's 946 inmates died due to harsh conditions, tropical diseases, tuberculosis, and an outbreak of typhus fever.[19]

To some degree, the anarchists supported the military uprising of 1924, particularly in São Paulo, as that city was being devastated by legalist artillery bombardment. *A Plebe* expressed sympathy towards the movement on its front page and published a motion addressed to the Revolutionary Committee, which by then controlled the city. It contained six demands, including the establishment of an eight-hour workday, undersigned by twenty-eight anarchist labour leaders, among them Rodolpho Felippe, the newspaper's publisher.[20] Some memoirs indicate that, in Rio, José Oiticica

---

17 S. Schumacher and E. Vital Brazil (eds.), *Dicionário mulheres do Brasil. De 1500 até a atualidade* (Rio de Janeiro: Zahar, 2000), pp. 462–3.
18 *O Nosso Jornal* 1 May 1923.
19 P. S. Pinheiro, *Estratégias da ilusão. A revolução mundial e o Brasil* (São Paulo: Companhia das Letras, 1991), p. 104. For further information on this prison camp, see A. Samis, *Clevelândia. Anarquismo, sindicalismo e repressão política no Brasil* (São Paulo: Imaginário, 2002).
20 'Movimento Revolucionario', *A Plebe* 7, 244, 25 July 1924, pp. 1–2.

was the contact for the military conspiracy with anarchist unions.[21] This helps us understand why, more than other movements, anarchists were particularly targeted by repression once the revolt was defeated. Some of those who undersigned the motion published in *A Plebe* ended up in Clevelândia, and Oiticica was arrested at the school where he taught, serving time on three different prison islands.

The state of siege was lifted in December 1926 after being continually extended for more than four years, making it possible to reorganize labour and its ideological movements. Most of the political prisoners were also released. The leading anarchist newspaper, *A Plebe*, resumed publication in 1927 for the first time since 1924.

One of the main anarchist campaigns during that decade was part of the international movement in support of Nicola Sacco and Bartolomeo Vanzetti, anarchist immigrants to the United States who were accused of murder there. In 1921, a Pro-Sacco and Vanzetti Committee was created in Rio, followed by others in São Paulo and Porto Alegre. Although enthusiasm waned during the state of siege, the campaign resurfaced with a vengeance between 1926 and August 1927, when they were executed in the United States.

By 1927, the anarchist presence in Rio's labour movement was reduced to three unions affiliated with the newly rebuilt FORJ: construction workers, shoe workers, and foundrymen. This was partly due to government repression, but particularly to the ongoing competition with communists for union control. However, the anarchists still maintained control over numerous unions in São Paulo, where the Communist Party found it harder to establish its presence.

Another issue that increased the animosity between these movements was the Communist Party's decision to go into electoral politics. As the party did not legally exist, its candidates could not campaign under its own name. Instead, they ran for office through electoral fronts such as the Workers' Bloc (Bloco Operário, BO), created in early 1927 and renamed at the end of that year the Workers' and Peasants' Bloc (Bloco Operário e Camponês, BOC).

In Rio, the dispute between anarchists and communists continued, with sometimes tragic consequences. A meeting was held in February 1928 at the headquarters of the Printing Workers' Union, where the aim was to expose the textile workers' leader, who had recently defeated the communist

---

21 Everardo Dias, *História das lutas sociais no Brasil*, 2nd edn (São Paulo: Alfa-Omega, 1977), p. 134.

candidate in the union election, by accusing him of being a police agent. After Representative João Batista de Azevedo Lima (elected in 1927 to the Chamber of Deputies through the Workers' and Peasants' Bloc list) had levelled the charge and, just as the accused was about to speak in his own defence, the lights suddenly went out and shots were fired, wounding ten of those present and killing two. The men who died were a communist printing worker and a Spanish anarchist shoemaker, Antonino Dominguez, one of the signatories to the motion published in *A Plebe* in 1924. The anarchists blamed the communists for the shooting, while the communists claimed that it was a set-up by a police *agent provocateur*. The case of Dominguez, who had been active in São Paulo and later in Rio de Janeiro, illustrates the very common practice among working-class militants, particularly among skilled workers, of moving from one city to another in search of work or for political reasons.

By 1928, another industrial crisis began, sparked by the fall of coffee prices (Brazil's main export commodity) on the international markets and preceding and aggravated by the international crisis resulting from the Wall Street crash the following year. Consequently, both wages and working days were reduced, and unemployment rose. Nevertheless, strikes still broke out in different branches of industry in major cities.

The End of a Cycle

The First Brazilian Republic came to an end in October 1930, when Getúlio Vargas, the defeated opposition presidential candidate in that year's election, seized power in a military coup. The entire electoral campaign had been marked by the usual fraud and violence, but this time discontent led to a military revolt that changed the course of events. One of the first measures taken by the provisional government, which lasted until 1934 (when Vargas was appointed president by the Constituent Assembly chosen the previous year), was the creation of a Ministry of Labour in November 1930, demonstrating its intent to deal with issues that had long concerned the labour movement and reformist politicians.

In the early 1930s, anarchism had lost ground to the communists among Rio's trade unions, but it still maintained control of several important unions in São Paulo. Competition in the labour movement was not limited to communists and their Trotskyist dissenters, who gained a formal organization with the creation in São Paulo of the Internationalist Communist League (Liga Comunista Internacionalista, LCI) in 1931, but also included movements like the reformists and Catholics.

In 1931, the Vargas regime approved a law establishing official trade unions, which depended on state recognition. At first, the anarchists, communists, and Trotskyists rejected the law, preferring to continue with unions organized under the legislation regulating voluntary associations, as in the previous decades. However, by 1934, the communists and Trotskyists had changed their minds as the new corporatist-inspired constitution was approved that year, introducing representatives of official unions to be elected to parliament. This change of policy in both movements isolated the anarchists, as they were the sole group to reject official unions, weakening the anarchist presence in labour unions even further.

Despite their differences regarding labour policies, the anarchists, communists, Trotskyists, and socialists joined forces in October 1934, when the episode known as the Praça da Sé Battle took place: a confrontation pitting these groups against the integralists (a far-right militarized organization of fascist inspiration) in a square in downtown São Paulo, where the city's Catholic cathedral is located. The integralists had intended to hold a rally in the square, but were stopped by the anti-fascist response. The episode ended with seven dead from both sides and among police officers, and about thirty injured. Similar clashes on a smaller scale had been taking place since the previous year. While avoiding official participation in the different anti-fascist fronts created by the communists and the Trotskyists, the anarchists had engaged in anti-fascist activities since 1932, sometimes together with other movements.

In March 1935, following the creation of the National Liberation Alliance (Aliança Nacional Libertadora, ANL), a popular front movement in which the communists played a major role, the anarchists decided to take part. However, a few months later, the movement was banned after proposing the overthrow of the government. In November, an insurrectional attempt in the name of the ANL, but mainly orchestrated by the communists under the guidance of the Communist International and low-ranking military personnel, was followed by a wave of repression that made any open activity by labour and socialist groups impossible, forcing them underground. In 1937, the Vargas regime proclaimed itself the New State (Estado Novo – the same name adopted by the Salazar regime in Portugal), a dictatorship that lasted until 1945, during which imprisonment, torture, and even death were the fate reserved for any person involved in an attempt at organized resistance.

Anarchist groups and their news outlets reorganized in the post-war years, but they never regained their prior influence on the trade unions, and their labour activism waned.

Further Reading

Dulles, John W. F., *Anarchists and Communists in Brazil, 1900–1935* (Austin: University of Texas Press, 1973).

French, John D., *The Brazilian Workers' ABC: Class Conflict and Alliances in Modern São Paulo* (Chapel Hill: University of North Carolina Press, 1992).

Goés, Plínio de Jnr, Curry Stephenson Mallot, and Marc Pruyn (eds.), *The Luso-Anarchist Reader: The Origins of Anarchism in Portugal and Brazil* (Charlotte, NC: Information Age Publishing, 2016).

Hahner, June E., *Poverty and Politics: The Urban Poor in Brazil, 1870–1920* (Albuquerque: University of New Mexico Press, 1986).

Mattos, Marcelo Badaró, *Laborers and Enslaved Workers: Experiences in Common in the Making of Rio de Janeiro's Working Class, 1850–1920* (New York: Berghahn, 2017).

Meade, Teresa A., *'Civilizing' Rio: Reform and Resistance in a Brazilian City, 1889–1930* (University Park: Penn State University Press, 1997).

Toledo, Edilene, and Luigi Biondi, 'Constructing Syndicalism and Anarchism Globally: The Transnational Making of the Syndicalist Movement in São Paulo, Brazil, 1895–1935', in S. Hirsch and L. van der Walt (eds.), *Anarchism and Syndicalism in the Colonial and Postcolonial World, 1870–1940* (Leiden and Boston: Brill, 2010), pp. 363–93.

Wolfe, Joel, *Working Women, Working Men: São Paulo and the Rise of Brazil's Industrial Working Class, 1900–1955* (Durham, NC, and London: Duke University Press, 1993).

23

Anarchism and Syndicalism in Southern Africa

LUCIEN VAN DER WALT

Anarchism emerged in southern Africa from the 1880s, and revolutionary syndicalism became a significant factor from the early 1900s. These movements faced the challenges posed by colonial racism, rapacious capitalism, state violence, and a large but fragmented working class. Although the pioneers were white immigrant workers and exiles, the movement set down local roots and assumed a more cosmopolitan character, developing a significant influence on local black African and Coloured/*mestiço* populations, local Indians (south Asians), and some Afrikaners. The current's heyday was before the 1930s, but it revived from the 1990s, reappearing in several countries by 2010.

Southern Africa had significant local states, including modest empires, prior to the modern European presence. Portugal had a presence in what is now Angola on the south-west coast from 1483, and Mozambique on the south-east from 1507. The Dutch Vereenigde Oostindische Compagnie (VOC) had bases in Mauritius from 1638 and in what became South Africa from 1652. São Paulo da Assunção de Loanda (now Luanda) and Cape Town were established in 1598 and 1652. With the exception of the Cape Colony – first ruled by the VOC, and then Batavia, followed by Britain – European imperial power was largely confined to coastal areas as late as the 1860s. Southern Africa was a patchwork of black African ('native', Bantu-speaking) polities including kingdoms; Khoisan clans; Afrikaner and Coloured republics;[1] and European colonies ruled from abroad. Economies were largely agrarian and often semi-feudal; the exports were slaves, mainly

---

1 'Afrikaner' refers to a permanent local white Afrikaans-speaking population, and 'Coloured' (or 'brown') to a diverse, racially mixed, and typically Afrikaans-speaking and Christian population, here including Basters/Griquas, Cape Malay, and Oorlam, with substantial overlaps with Khoisan and ties to Afrikaners.

from Angola, and wine, wheat, and wool from Britain's Natal and Cape Colonies in the south.

Several factors converged to change the situation and lay the basis for anarchism to emerge as part of local working-class politics. Commercial diamond mining in the northern Cape from the 1860s was followed by large-scale underground gold mining on the Witwatersrand (the 'Rand') in the Zuid-Afrikaansche Republiek, or Transvaal, from the 1880s. Mining attracted vast European foreign direct investment, South Africa alone securing almost as much investment as the rest of the continent combined. By 1913 the Witwatersrand produced 40 per cent of the world's gold. Founded in the age of monopoly capitalism, mining was highly centralized: diamonds fell under the De Beers cartel, while gold was controlled by giant 'houses', co-ordinated through the Transvaal Chamber of Mines formed in 1887.

The mining boom drove railway construction from Cape Town, Durban (in Natal), and Lourenço Marques (now Maputo, in Mozambique), commercial farming, and early secondary industry. Older towns, like Cape Town, expanded; in two decades Lourenço Marques grew from a small outpost to a major harbour and rail complex. New towns sprang up overnight, like diamond-rich Kimberley, and the mining towns running east to west across the Rand, from Brakpan via Johannesburg to Randfontein. Johannesburg, to the south of the Transvaal's capital Pretoria, rose from a tent town in 1886 to a modern city of 250,000 in 1913, the economic hub of the whole region.

This was the era of the Scramble for Africa, and Britain expanded from the 1870s, independent polities either accepting protectorate status, as with Basutoland (now Lesotho), Bechuanaland (now Botswana), and Swaziland (Eswatini), or being conquered, as with the Zulu empire and Pedi kingdom in 1879, and the Transvaal and Orange Free State in 1899–1902. In 1909, Britain consolidated the non-protectorate territories into the Union of South Africa. The Cape, Free State, Natal, and Transvaal became provinces, with elected governments. The 'native reserves' were governed through indirect rule and customary laws. The new state was based overtly on white supremacy, with white men the overwhelming majority of voters in 1910. But as a self-governing Dominion, the new state had the same status in the British Empire as Australia and Canada. The population was around 6 million in 1911: 4 million black Africans, 1,276,000 whites, 525,000 Coloureds, and 150,000 Indians.

Portugal, faced with a British ultimatum, sought to secure its colonies' hinterlands in a process of (re)conquest lasting into the 1920s. The British South Africa Company (BSAC), sponsored by De Beers' Cecil John Rhodes, established Southern Rhodesia (now Zimbabwe) between Bechuanaland, South Africa, and Mozambique. Its economic hub, Bulawayo in the south, was linked to the Rand; its capital Salisbury (now Harare) was connected by rail to Bulawayo, and to Beira in Mozambique, a port 1,200 kilometres north of Lourenço Marques. North of the Zambezi, it established Northern Rhodesia, with Ndola as a trading post in the north, Broken Hill (now Kabwe) and Lusaka in the centre, and Livingstone in the far south as the capital until 1935. Nyasaland (now Malawi), a protectorate, was enclosed by Mozambique and Northern Rhodesia.

South Africa dominated the region. Basutoland and northern Mozambique served as labour reservoirs for its mines; members of the growing local white bourgeoisie were major investors; its population was larger; its white population was larger than that of even Algeria; its economy centred on manufacturing from the 1940s; alone on the continent, its independent peasantry was destroyed. It also made efforts to expand its territory: South West Africa was its colony from 1915, Southern Rhodesia was invited to join once BSAC rule ended in 1922: and repeated claims were made on the protectorates. Southern Rhodesia alone came close, a self-governing, white-ruled colony from 1923, with an increasingly developed capitalist economy.

1880s–1910s

It was within the working class generated by these upheavals that anarchism emerged. The urban working class expanded massively, including large-scale immigration into Africa. There were 195,000 black African and 22,000 white mine employees on the Rand in 1913; this leaves aside the numbers in, for example, other mines across the country and region, as well as workers in construction, the docks, railways, power, factories, and catering, domestic work, the civil service and military, and so on.

But the rapidly growing working class was fragmented on several axes. One was a basic divide between 'migrant workers' in the southern African sense – workers who work in town for wages, to support rural homesteads where their families reside, and to which they retire – and those residing with families and completely dependent on wages. This overlapped to some extent with race and skill, but not completely: most migrants were black men, often labourers, but some were skilled; wage-dependent workers included urbanized black people and farm labourers, most Coloureds and Indians, and immigrant and local whites including Afrikaners; not all these workers were skilled, as a large multi-racial factory proletariat and 'poor white' population attested. Coloureds and Indians faced racist laws and practices, but black workers and the black population generally were subject to both racist and coercive laws, including an internal passport system ('pass laws') for men, contracts criminalizing desertion, and (for migrants) housing in large closed barracks ('compounds').

The first active anarchist was apparently Henry Glasse, who from 1881 lived in Port Elizabeth, a small Cape port between Cape Town and Durban.[2] He imported Freedom Press materials from Britain, including texts by Peter Kropotkin and Errico Malatesta and papers such as *Freedom* and *Le Révolté* (*The Rebel*), and he translated Kropotkin texts into English. Italians working in Cape Town, Pretoria, and Florida (near Johannesburg) donated to Malatesta's *L'Agitazione* (*Agitation*), *La Rivoluzione Sociale* (*The Social Revolution*), and *Volontà* (*Will*) from the 1890s into the 1910s. The Portuguese had a system of criminal deportees (*degredados*), including politicals, like anarchists. Anarchist deportees sometimes escaped into South Africa when the ships docked, as did João Manuel Rodrígues in 1896.

The German-language magazine *Freiheit* (*Freedom*) had subscribers and correspondents in South Africa from the mid-1890s in East London – a small port near Port Elizabeth – and Johannesburg. The Afrikaner struggle in the Anglo-Boer War inspired anti-imperialists worldwide and attracted support from white immigrant workers on the Rand. German anarchist Fritz Brall helped found the Duitse Kommando (German Commando) in Johannesburg in 1899; *Freiheit* reported one reader killed, and another captured by British forces.

The Russian-langauge *Khleb i Volia* (*Bread and Will*), founded in 1903, had readers in Johannesburg. Yiddish-speaking Jews were the largest non-British white immigrant group, and Z. D. Fox was part of a group selling *Der Arbayter Fraynd* (*The Workers' Friend*) and *Fraye Arbayter Shtime* (*Free Voice of Labour*) in Johannesburg. In 1904, two alleged anarchists, John Sepoul and Henry

2 Useful material on South Africa into the 1930s may be found in F. A. Johnstone, 'The IWA on the Rand: Socialist Organising amongst Black Workers on the Rand 1917–1918', in B. Bozzoli (ed.), *Labour, Townships and Protest* (Johannesburg: Ravan Press, 1979), pp. 248–72; E. Mantzaris, *Labour Struggles in South Africa: The Forgotten Pages, 1903–1921* (Windhoek and Durban: Collective Resources Publications, 1995); L. van der Walt, 'Anarchism and Syndicalism in South Africa, 1904–1921: Rethinking the History of Labour and the Left', PhD, University of the Witwatersrand, South Africa, 2007; L. van der Walt, 'Anarchism and syndicalism in an African port city: the revolutionary traditions of Cape Town's multiracial working class, 1904–1924', *Labor History* 52, 2 (2011), pp. 137–71; G. Rey, *Afriques anarchistes. Introduction à l'histoire des anarchismes africains* (Paris: L'Harmattan, 2018).

Larsen, were arrested after making threats against Lord Alfred Milner, post-war governor of the Free State and Transvaal.

The early movement was based on circles of readers devoted to certain papers, or on involvement in broad left groups. Glasse, for example, helped found a Socialist Club in 1900 where he could expound his views. Jewish anarchists were involved in the local Bundist-inclined 'Friends of the Russian Freedom', founded in 1905. Wilfred Harrison, former British soldier turned anarchist, helped found a Social Democratic Federation (SDF) in Cape Town on May Day 1904. It was a broad group, but its lively anarchist section, of which another luminary was H. B. 'Barney' Levinson, set the pace. Soap-boxing and public events, including in the largely Coloured District Six, were the SDF's mainstay: Harrison was a famed orator; an SDF rally for the 1905 Russian Revolution at the City Hall attracted 1,500. The SDF ran a printing press and Socialist Choir, and published *Cape Socialist*, including Kropotkin extracts, courtesy of Glasse.

The SDF was active in unions, which started in southern Africa with the Amalgamated Society of Carpenters and Joiners in Cape Town in 1881. Unionism's pioneers were typically immigrants of British descent, inspired by a craft union model that restricted membership to qualified artisans in specific trades. More inclusive general and industrial unions emerged, such as a short-lived Knights of Labour active in Kimberley by 1890. Most unions had colour bars: those in the western Cape and Cape Town were exceptional in (sometimes) admitting Coloureds. Harrison was active in the Carpenters and the larger Cape Trades and Labour Council. The SDF formed a multi-racial General Workers Union in 1905, with Council backing – it was not, however, a syndicalist union. That year the SDF, the Council and the African Peoples Organisation – the APO, a Coloured group – organized large multi-racial unemployed demonstrations that ended in riots, with Levinson and others arrested.

In Johannesburg maverick militant Archie Crawford founded the weekly *Voice of Labour*, which became the first local socialist weekly. Crawford, the editor, and his partner, publisher Mary Fitzgerald, were not syndicalists (as often claimed) but opened the paper to a wide range of left opinion, including Glasse and Harrison. By 1910, the *Voice* had decidedly syndicalist and Industrial Workers of the World (IWW) leanings. A South African tour by Tom Mann early that year galvanized enthusiasts, with two rival bodies formed: an IWW branch, claiming affiliation to the Chicago IWW, and a Socialist Labour Party, following Daniel De Leon and the Detroit IWW.[3]

3 For background information, see Chapter 19 in this volume.

The IWW, led by the blacksmith Andrew Dunbar and tram-driver Tom Glynn, organized spectacular strikes in Johannesburg in 1911, and spread into Durban and Pretoria, where it drew members of the Amalgamated Society of Railway and Harbour Servants (later the National Union of Railway and Harbour Servants, NURHAS). The De Leonists, such as Yeshaya Israelstam, Phillip Roux, an Afrikaner chemist, and Scots such as John Campbell, focused on newspaper sales and soap-boxing.

Several efforts by Crawford to unite the socialist left – anarchists, syndicalists, orthodox socialists, reformers, and so on – fell apart. Differences were too deep, as responses to the union-backed push to form a South African Labour Party in 1909 showed. The IWW boycotted it, and Crawford, Harrison, and others tried to get it to adopt a radical platform but left when it adopted a mixture of segregation and socialism, 'White Labourism'; some De Leonists remained to bore-from-within.

Differences aside, Crawford, the anarchists, the IWW, and the De Leonists shared an antipathy to both the Labour Party's reformism *and* racism. 'Proletarian', the pseudonymous syndicalist editor of the *Voice* in 1910–11, declared the need for 'an organisation of wageworkers, black and white, male and female, young and old' to organize 'a universal general strike' for 'seizing and running . . . South Africa, for the benefit of workers to the exclusion of *parasites*'.[4] Despite their principles, neither IWWs nor De Leonists made inroads into the Coloured, Indian, or black populations. This was partly due to the segregated public sphere of towns such as Durban and Johannesburg – unlike the SDF's Cape Town – and a failure to directly organize around issues of racist and national oppression.

The IWW and the *Voice* collapsed in 1912, and the De Leonists were apparently deep inside the Labour Party, when a massive wave of strikes burst out from 1913 to 1914. Anarchists and syndicalists had very little influence on the events, which did not keep Jan Smuts, then minister of defence, from blaming it on a 'Syndicalist Conspiracy'.

But the big strikes did radicalize a new layer in the unions and the Labour Party, like George Mason of the carpenters' union, Bill Andrews, unionist and Labour member of parliament, David Ivon Jones, Labour's general secretary, and S. P. Bunting, an Oxford-trained lawyer. South Africa's entry into the First World War on Britain's side, and its subsequent invasion of South West Africa, helped provoke an armed Afrikaner rebellion; the war issues also led to splits in both the SDF and the Labour Party.

4 'Proletarian', 'The Problem of Coloured Labour', *Voice of Labour*, 27 October 1911.

The new radicals, many moving towards syndicalism, linked up with Dunbar, Roux, and other veterans, and sundry pacifists. to form a War-on-War League, also supported by Harrison. This held regular public events, and published an eclectic *War-on-War Gazette* in which Kropotkin, Karl Liebknecht, and Leo Tolstoy made appearances. Despairing of reforming the Labour Party, it reconstituted as the International Socialist League (ISL) in September 1915; the *Gazette* became the ISL's weekly *International*. It was not a loose group like the SDF, but had a significant degree of theoretical and tactical unity, the *International* representing official positions.

The ISL advocated 'the organisation of the workers on industrial or class lines, irrespective of race, colour or creed, as the most effective means of providing the necessary force for the emancipation of the workers'.[5] In a major advance on its predecessors, it regularly affirmed the need for the working class to fight racist and coercive laws; organize among the 'helot' races, win 'equal industrial and political status' for black, Coloured, and Indian people; oppose imperialism; and win poor white people away from the National Party, heart of a rising Afrikaner nationalism.[6] Rejecting craft and racially closed unions, the ISL favoured One Big Union to fight class exploitation and racial oppression, and take power; it dismissed nationalization as a pillar of an oppressive 'servile state' and aimed at a self-managed, union-based 'Industrial Republic'.[7]

The ISL spread countrywide, but never set up a section in Cape Town. Instead it had fraternal relations with the SDF, which still had real influence: in 1916, Harrison won 212 votes for a District Six municipal seat against an APO candidate's 543. It agitated within the orthodox unions, with limited success: the Building Workers Industrial Union, formed in 1916 and led by De Leonist Charlie Tyler, adopted a syndicalist platform. Andrews was appointed full-time ISL industrial organizer in 1918, the aim being to foster something on the lines of the Shop Stewards' and Workers' Committee Movement in Britain in the orthodox unions, and had some success among white workers in metals, mines, and rail.

But the ISL also took an unprecedented step: organizing unions among workers of colour. An Indian Workers Industrial Union was formed in Durban in 1917, then an Industrial Workers of Africa among black people in Johannesburg – the first black union – which spread to Cape Town, where it soon claimed 1,000 members, double the size of the largest affiliate of the

5 'The First Conference of the League', *The International*, 14 January 1916.   6 E.g., ibid.
7 'State Socialism', *The International*, 8 December 1916.

Cape Federation of Labour. From 1919, the ISL organized a Clothing Workers Industrial Union in Durban, Johannesburg, and Kimberley, and a small horse drivers' union. The ISL organized joint events with the APO and the South African Native Congress (SANNC, the African National Congress / ANC, from 1923), although it rejected all nationalism.

These unions were engaged in several notable strikes, among them an attempted general strike on the Witwatersrand by the ISL, Industrial Workers of Africa, and the SANNC left wing in 1918, and a joint strike by the Industrial Workers of Africa, representing mainly black workers, and the rival Industrial and Commercial Workers Union (ICU), then mainly representing Coloured workers, on the Cape Town docks in late 1919 (this action was backed by the Cape Federation of Labour and NURHAS).

Through such work, the ISL recruited a growing cadre of black, Coloured, and Indian members, among them Johnny Gomas, Bernard Sigamoney, and T. W. Thibedi. Syndicalism made an appearance in the SANNC in the person of ISL members such as Fred Cetiwe and Henry Kraai, who (SANNC moderate Sol Plaatje recalled) addressed that party's 1918 conference 'in short sentences, nearly every one of which began and ended with the word "strike"'.[8] Meanwhile, the ISL also had links to white ethnic minorities, with an important Yiddish-Speaking Branch and Greeks, such as Athonasis Pournaras, founder of a Greek Workers' Association among shop assistants in 1917.

In 1918, the SDF split, younger firebrands establishing a syndicalist Industrial Socialist League. Not to be confused with the ISL, it published the monthly *Bolshevik*: both leagues believed their syndicalist politics to be good Bolshevism, and the soviets just 'the Russian form of the Industrial Union'.[9] Like the ISL, the Cape group started among white workers, often immigrants – besides attracting support from the ageing Glasse, it also included men like Solomon Buirski – but it soon claimed 'coloured and Malay comrades'.[10] It worked with the Industrial Workers of Africa, but also formed a Sweets and Jam Workers Industrial Union, mostly Coloured but including black members such as Mpanpeni and Nodzandza. Key league members such as A. Z. Berman were in the leadership of the moderate Cape

8 Sol Plaatje, 'Letter to the General Secretary, De Beers, 3 August 1918', in B. Willan (ed.), *Sol Plaatje: Selected Writings* (Johannesburg and Athens, OH: Witwatersrand University Press and Ohio University Press, 1996), p. 237.
9 'Russian Workers Vindicate Marx', *The International*, 18 May 1917.
10 Letter from Manuel Lopes, *The Workers' Dreadnought*, 7 August 1920.

Fig. 23.1 Mass rally in Johannesburg, addressed by speakers from the Industrial Workers of Africa, the International Socialist League, and the Transvaal Native Congress, June 1918. (Used with permission, Patrick Pearson collection of photographs, Historical Papers Research Archive, University of the Witwatersrand, South Africa.)

Federation of Labour, which included some Coloured workers, and managed to get some radical resolutions passed – but not implemented.

Some ISL and Industrial Workers materials got into the mines, and some black migrants attended meetings on the Witwatersrand, but a black miners' union did not emerge despite a big strike in 1920. Some ISL materials entered Mozambique with returning migrants, and the ISL had contacts in Lourenço Marques, where the *International* was available.

Language, however, was a significant barrier, and the anarchist and syndicalist movement in Mozambique arose from separate sources, and developed separately, from that in South Africa. It centred on Lourenço Marques, the colonial capital from 1898 and the most populous urban centre. Most white workers lived in Beira or Lourenço Marques, with a large part of the urban workforce concentrated in crafts, commerce, light industry, and public works. Lourenço Marques had around 27,000 residents in 1912, with a black population of perhaps 10,000 in 1916; the railway and harbour complex was the largest employer, followed by the state bureaucracy.

Mozambique had by far the largest union movement in Portuguese Africa. The concentrated Lourenço Marques workforce aided labour organizing, an important site for anarchist/syndicalist activity. Portuguese workers started unions with the União Operária (Workers' Union) in 1901, but the most powerful was the Associação dos Ferroviários e Portuários (Association of Railway and Port Workers), formed in 1910, based in the railway and harbour complex. A Confederação Operária (Workers' Confederation) was formed in 1910, and a Sindicato Geral da Província de Moçambique (General Union of the Province of Mozambique) in 1921, with a headquarters for labour activity, the Casa dos Trabalhadores (House of Workers). Unions were small, if powerful, and generally reliant on expatriate militants. The Sindicato Geral represented just 2,000 workers in 1926: there were around 135,000 union members in South Africa in 1920, with 60,000 in the South African Industrial Federation (SAIF) in 1921. Few Mozambican unions organized black workers, and there were no black-based unions. The key exception was the Associação das Artes Gráficas de Lourenço Marques (Association of Graphic Arts of Lourenço Marques) formed around 1911, which included Goan Indians, *assimilados* – akin to *évolués* in Algeria – and *mestiços*, as well as white immigrants. Members of the Associação also had links to the Grêmio Africano (African Guild), a small *assimilado*- and *mestiço*-based advocacy group founded in 1906.[11]

Anarchism and syndicalism had a presence from the 1890s. Some activists were *degradados*: anarchists Cruz and Just, deported after an 1896 crackdown, served prison terms in Mozambique; Francisco Antunes Soares was killed in 1905 after escaping to Portugal; in 1910, anarchist deportee José Estêvam set up a Liga Revolucionária (Revolutionary League) in Lourenço Marques upon his release from prison.

Most free immigrants came from Lisbon, the hub of Portugal's powerful anarchist/syndicalist movement, centred on the União Operária Nacional (National Workers' Union, formed in 1914) and Confederação Geral do Trabalho (General Confederation of Labour (CGT), formed in 1919), publisher of the daily *A Batalha* (*The Battle*). In 1909, Lourenço Marques anarchists published *Pró-Mártir* (*Pro-Martyr*), a pamphlet about the anarchist educator Francisco Ferrer i Guardia, executed by the Spanish state in that same year. Ferrer had admirers in the local unions and labour press, which commemorated his death for years. A Grupo Libertário Francisco Ferrer (Francisco Ferrer Libertarian Group) operated in 1911. In 1915, an anarchist group called Ressurgir emerged.

Anarchists were part of the editorial board of the republican paper *O Incondicional* (*The Unconditional*), founded in 1910; *Os Simples* (*The Simple*), published from 1911, showed anarchist influences; the anarchist Eduardo Carlos Pereira was on the board of *O Germinal* (*Germinal*), a left-wing paper

---

11 Key sources include J. Capela, *O Movimento Operário em Lourenço Marques, 1898–1927* (Porto: Centro de Estudos Africanos da Universidade do Porto, 2009 [1981]); H. Dousemetzis and G. Loughran, *The Man Who Killed Apartheid: The Life of Dimitri Tsafendas* (Johannesburg: Jacana Media, 2018); J. M. Penvenne, 'João dos Santos Albasini (1876–1922): the contradictions of politics and identity in colonial Mozambique', *Journal of African History* 37, 3 (1996), pp. 419–64.

in 1914; anarchists and syndicalists formed part of the editorial group of *O Emancipador* (*The Emancipator*), a weekly founded in 1919, closely associated with the Associação dos Ferroviários e Portuários, and widely distributed across the colony. *A Batalha* was also readily available. It carried articles from Lourenço Marques, while *O Emancipador* reprinted *A Batalha* articles, supplied it with reports, sold subscriptions, and raised funds towards its costs. *A Batalha* had, notably, some subscribers among Indians at the port. Some anarchists were prominent in the unions, such as Pereira, João Maria Borges, Manuel Alves Cardiga, Eduardo Franco Martins, and João Vás. Willy Waddington, an anarcho-syndicalist and journalist, worked with the printers and railway workers. CGT members such as Raúl Neves Dias and José António de Almeida, who came to Lourenço Marques to work at the Imprensa Nacional, would have associated with the Associação das Artes Gráficas.

Greek anarchists also played a role. Michalis Tsafandakis became a prosperous partner in a Lourenço Marques ship repair firm. He was friends with anarchist Dimitrios Spanos, who arrived via South Africa and ran the city's leading bookshop. Spanos was in contact with the ISL and sold the *International*.

While the colonial system was profoundly racist, there was still something of a cosmopolitan culture in Lourenço Marques, drawing in *assimilados* and other literate black people, Goans, *mestiços*, and white people – but not the black population employed in low-wage, casual, or coerced (*chibalo*) labour. These were the core readership of the local press, patrons of Spanos' shop, the heart of an intense café culture, the participants in which ranged from white trade unionists to the famed João dos Santos Albasini, leader of Grêmio Africano; anarchist, Masonic, republican, and orthodox socialist ideas circulated.

Anarchists and syndicalists were not the leading left force, and the unions do not seem to have adopted their positions. The Sindicato Geral, for example, voted to affiliate to the CGT in Portugal, but on condition it was not obliged to adopt 'anarchist tactics'. The Associação das Artes Gráficas affiliated to its syndicalist counterpart in Portugal, but also set up close links with the moderate craft-based South African Typographers' Union (SATU). The local Partido Socialista Português (Portuguese Socialist Party), which ran the Centro Socialista de Lourenço Marques (Socialist Centre of Lourenço Marques), was the key force, including in *O Emancipador* and *O Germinal*. Anarchists were also affected by the repressive environment that existed even before the onset of dictatorship in 1926. Pereira was deported in 1916; Cardiga and Martins were arrested in 1917 after a strike and expelled from Lourenço

Marques; Borges and Cardiga were arrested during a 1920 strike; Cardiga was one of twenty-seven workers deported in 1921, although he managed to return.

There was a small anarchist and syndicalist presence in Angola, but nothing like Mozambique's. Angola's population, around 4.5 million in 1900, was second only to South Africa, but it was barely affected by the mining revolution and attracted few immigrants before the 1940s. There was little urban or industrial development outside rail and mining, and the latter employed just 8,697 in 1939, including 160 white workers. Urban *assimilados* and *mestiços* were important in Luanda; white numbers were too small to largely displace them in the government or trades, as in Mozambique: the colony's white population was 20,000 in 1920, plus 2,500 Afrikaners in the south.

Before the 1940s, anarchists in Angola tended to be *degredados*, some imprisoned, others exiled to remote areas. Deportees formed the Grupo Juventude Rebelde (Rebel Youth Group) in Luanda in 1906. António Caldiera escaped from penal servitude, but was recaptured in Lisbon in 1905, and sent to Guinea Bissau. More arrived in the deportations following the November 1918 general strike in Portugal. But unionism, syndicalist or otherwise, struggled to take root in the colony. The local labour movement was tiny, with small workplaces and unremitting repression. The civil servants' union Associação dos Funcionários Públicos da Província de Angola (Association of Civil Servants of the Province of Angola) was dissolved by the governor in 1921; another union was refused legal status for admitting black members; a big railway strike by white workers in 1923 was crushed by the military.

1920S–1940S

The anarchist and syndicalist movement in South Africa was, then, the oldest and the largest in the region at the start of the 1920s. Its key influences were those of the English-speaking world, like the IWW, De Leonism, and Freedom Press. In the Portuguese colonies, it was the Latin traditions that counted.

The ISL was also the largest, most important radical left group in southern Africa before the Communist Party of South Africa (CPSA). Its project was impressive, but not without weaknesses. For example, the various syndicalist unions, and other small union initiatives, were not linked to one another in a federation, nor were they linked to the workers' committees.

The old IWW/De Leonist divide, centring on running in state elections, also came to a head. Dunbar and other IWW veterans in the ISL, along with most of the Yiddish-Speaking Branch, opposed the De Leonism of Andrews, Bunting, and Jones, and eventually moved over to the Industrial Socialist League, which renamed itself the Communist Party in October 1920. The first communist party in Africa, it adopted an anti-parliamentary One Big Union position, and linked up with Sylvia Pankhurst's 'council communists'. This party and the ISL sent rival applications to the Comintern, which replied by demanding unity. The two groups merged with the SDF and others to form the official CPSA, whose leadership included Andrews, Bunting, and Harrison.

While the CPSA accepted the Comintern's 'Twenty-One Conditions', the party history admits 'syndicalist concepts remained ... for many years after its foundation'. Dunbar's circle remained in the CPSA, working with Pankhurst's newspaper *Workers' Dreadnought*. In 1922, white mine-workers went on strike; the showdown snowballed into a general strike by the SAIF. Workers' militias ('commandos') proliferated; control passed to a Council of Action. Founded in 1921, this emerged from the workers' committees, led by syndicalists including Percy Fisher, Ernie Shaw, and Harry Spendiff. Expanded into a Committee of Action, including Andrews, it pushed the strike into armed insurrection. This was crushed by Smuts with martial law, with thousands arrested, including CPSA leaders, the *International* briefly suppressed, and four executed; Fisher and Spendiff committed suicide.

Few from the syndicalist unions joined the early CPSA, which initially focused on white labour. In mid-1920, the ICU, Industrial Workers of Africa, and other small black and Coloured unions merged into an expanded ICU banner. The ICU was a home for Kraai, Gomas, and others. ICU leaders, notably Clements Kadalie, a charismatic Nyasa immigrant, often showed syndicalist influences: they spoke of One Big Union 'abolishing the Capitalist Class' with 'industrial organisation', and an emancipatory strike. In 1925, it adopted a version of the IWW preamble. In 1927, the ICU was approaching 100,000 members in South Africa, mostly black farm labourers and tenant farmers. Rumours swept the country that the union would return white farms to black workers and tenants on Christmas Day.

It is, above all, by reference to the ICU that we can speak of syndicalist elements in other British southern African territories.[12] The 1920 unity congress resolved to organize beyond the borders of South Africa. The ICU

12 For a partial overview, see L. van der Walt, '"One Great Union of Skilled and Unskilled Workers, South of the Zambezi": Garveyism, Liberalism and Revolutionary Syndicalism in the Industrial and Commercial Workers Union of Africa, 1919–1949',

attracted interest in Mozambique, championed by journalist Dick Khosa, but no branches were formed. However, the ICU soon spread into southern South West Africa. The colony had 14,000 white residents in 1914, and 200,000 others.[13] The arid south had a large Coloured population that blurred into Khoisan and some white farms, but copper and diamond mining dominated from 1907. Small mining towns spread across the southern desert, like Elizabeth Bay, Kolmanskop, and Pomona, and were connected to the Atlantic (and supplies) by Lüderitz, which also had a large fishing industry. The mines and railways were worked by a small white working class, South African black and Coloured workers recruited in Cape Town, and black migrant workers from the northern region. Lüderitz itself also had a small population of Afro-Caribbean people and Liberians. German workers pioneered unions in 1913, and a small federation was formed by 1920. German socialist papers were available, and the ISL and International had a presence.

South Africa's occupation was followed by a strike wave. Jimmy La Guma, a young Coloured worker from Cape Town, initiated a strike at Pomona in 1918. Arrested and blacklisted, he found work in Lüderitz, contacted Kadalie, and set up an ICU section in December 1920. When he returned to South Africa in 1921 to work for the ICU (and then the CPSA), he was succeeded by John de Clue and William Adriaanse. Lüderitz was represented at the 1921 and 1923 ICU congresses in South Africa. Branches were also established in Keetmanshoop, an administrative and railway hub in the farming region, in 1922, and in Elizabeth Bay in 1926. Two black South Africans, Timothy and Naphtali, were deported for ICU agitation in Walvis Bay that year. South West African delegates were apparently present at the December 1927 ICU congress.

There were two delegates from Basutoland, a small landlocked protectorate with a population of around 600,000, enclosed by South Africa, at the 1920 unity congress. ICU branches were established on the border in 1926. The union's April 1927 congress resolved to send an organizer, and two

European Social Science History Conference, Vienna, Austria, 23–26 April. The definitive study of Kadalie is H. Dee, 'Clements Kadalie: Trade Unionism, Migration and Race in Southern Africa, 1918–1930', PhD dissertation, University of Edinburgh, UK, 2020. P. Wickens, 'The Industrial and Commercial Workers' Union of Africa', PhD dissertation, University of Cape Town, South Africa, 1973, remains outstanding.

13 See T. Emmett, 'Popular Resistance in Namibia, 1920–1925', in T. Lodge (ed.), *Resistance and Ideology in Settler Societies* (Johannesburg: Ravan Press, 1986), pp. 6–48; L. van der Walt, 'The Industrial and Commercial Workers Union in South West Africa: Syndicalism, Garveyism and Resistance in South African-ruled Namibia, 1920–1925', paper presented at the 27th Biennial Conference of the Southern African Historical Society, Rhodes University, Makhanda, South Africa, 24–6 June 2019.

Basutoland delegates attended the December 1927 congress. Finally, in 1928, the ICU's Keable 'Mote established seven branches.[14]

Anarchist and syndicalist influences entered a serious decline in the second half of the 1920s. There is little sign of the ICU in South West Africa after 1927. There was a small group of German-speaking anarchists in Windhoek in the 1920s, but details are scarce. The ICU's Basutoland branches were short-lived.

Portugal came under a series of dictatorships from mid-1926. The CGT was driven underground, *A Batalha* was banned, and the crackdown spread to the colonies. The Associação dos Ferroviários e Portuários held big strikes in 1925 and 1926. The latter lasted eight days in the face of intense repression, the railways were militarized, strikers were evicted from their homes and fired, leaders were deported, *O Emancipador* was suppressed, the Casa dos Trabalhadores was seized: the gains won by the unions over decades were, in short, dismantled. Local anarcho-syndicalists were among the workers' leaders deported. Those who remained active in the labour movement, like Borges and Cardiga, had their hands full trying to rebuild the battered unions. The repression effectively ended labour action into the 1930s.

There were more deportations from Portugal to Angola.[15] Mário Castelhano, editor of *A Batalha*, was deported in November 1927. He and other anarchists were sent to Novo Redondo (now Sumbe), some 300 kilometres south of Luanda, then inland to the villages Amboiva, Conda, and Vila Nova de Seles (now Seles). Castelhano and fellow anarchist Manuel Henrique Rijo found clerical work at a local plantation. Castelhano's memoirs of this time were harshly critical of colonialism, arguing for class-based unity across race.

Francisco Quintal, Arnaldo Simões Janário, and Alvaro Ramos formed an anarchist organization in Sá da Bandeira (now Lubango) in the interior around 1928. Antonio Inacio Martins, deported on the same ship as Quintal and Janário, served his term as forced labour on the railway from Luanda to Malange in the north, and was in contact with the Sá da Bandeira group. Sustained work was difficult. Quintal escaped Angola in 1929, joining the Portuguese underground. Castelhano and Rijo were deported to the Azores in 1930. Castelhano was then shipped to Cape Verde, but escaped to Madeira *en route*. Castelhano and Janário (back in Portugal from 1933) were involved in

14 S. Neame, *The Congress Movement: The Unfolding of the Congress Alliance 1912–1961*, vol. II, *April 1926–1928* (Cape Town: HSRC Press, 2015), pp. 244 n. 454, 357, 384–5, 486.
15 There is no study of anarchism in Angola. Useful sources include M. Castelhano, *Quatro anos de deportação* (Lisbon: Seara Nova, 1975); E. Rodrigues, *Uma visão da história do movimento libertário em Portugal*, www.agrorede.org.br/ceca/edgar/AnarPort.html (n.d.).

an unsuccessful CGT–Partido Comunista Português (Portuguese Communist Party) uprising, following which they were sent to the notorious Tarrafal concentration camp in Cape Verde.

In South Africa, an independent syndicalist presence in the orthodox unions ended in the 1920s with the destruction of the Council of Action. Men like Fisher and Spendiff had tried to steer into revolution a strike that had been provoked by replacement of white workers by cheap black labour, and opposed the racial clashes that broke out, but the racist tide flowed against them. In 1924 the Labour Party and National Party replaced Smuts with the coalition Pact government. The Pact government sought to break the country's reliance on the gold mines and economic dependence on Britain through a programme of economic nationalism, with new state industries and import-substitution industrialization. It also introduced state welfare for Coloureds and whites, mechanisms for setting minimum wages, and the first national collective bargaining system. This system was open to Coloureds, Indians, and whites, but specifically excluded pass-bearing black people. Discrimination in wages and welfare remained, and job colour bars were legally entrenched. These measures did, however, help bureaucratize the union movement, reeling from 1922, and dampen militancy.

The Comintern's Third Period helped uproot syndicalist traces in the CPSA. The CPSA cut ties to bodies considered reformist, including the ANC and ICU, and set about Bolshevizing itself. By the early 1930s, membership had fallen by 80 per cent, and most of the old guard was gone. Some on the left, like Harrison, gave up or, like Dunbar, drifted away; others, like Thibedi, moved towards Trotskyism; some, like Andrews, were later reinstated; others, like Gomas and La Guma, remained in the CPSA throughout.

There were a few anarchists in the 1930s, like Sarah Neppe, an elderly Jew who attended CPSA events, and English anarchist Leonard Motler, who was in South Africa in the early 1920s, returned in the late 1930s or early 1940s, and had connections to SATU and the party. Sholem Schwarzbard, the anarchist who assassinated Ukrainian nationalist leader Symon Petliura in 1926, moved in 1937 or 1938 to Cape Town, where he is buried.

The ICU in South Africa did not deliver on the millenarian hopes it inspired. Instead it entered into a dramatic decline. Repression played a role, but the ICU also had serious problems, including over-reliance on charismatic leaders, corruption, in-fighting, and a lack of a coherent strategy. It also lost experienced militants when it purged CPSA members like Gomas and Thibedi. Membership collapsed and the union splintered.

But the ICU had a new lease of life to the north. Northern Rhodesia initially developed via white-owned farms in the south, mining and railways at Broken Hill, peasant farming, and exporting migrant labour. With the expiry of the BSAC charter, the colony reverted to the crown; a small, limited white legislature was established. Migrant workers and others returning from South Africa and Southern Rhodesia came back with subversive ideas, Kadalie had local correspondents, and the ICU's *Workers' Herald* reached Livingstone and Lusaka.[16] Kadalie also had connections in Nyasaland, where, for example, Isa Macdonald Lawrence was prosecuted for receiving the *Workers' Herald* and Marcus Garvey's *Negro World*.

Southern Rhodesia developed on the basis of coal, chrome, large-scale white commercial farms, and peasant cash-cropping – there was significant land expropriation. The white population rose from 12,596 in 1904 to 49,910 in 1931; the black population was around 2 million. A self-governing colony from 1923, it adopted racial laws and policies similar to South Africa's, including a 1930 Land Apportionment Act formally allocating 51 per cent of land to white people. A significant white working class emerged, mainly English-speaking and of British descent. Unions were formed from 1913, like the Rhodesia Railway Workers' Union (RRWU), founded in 1917 – active in Mozambique and both Rhodesias – and the Rhodesia Mine and General Workers' Association, founded in 1919. A Rhodesia Labour Party was established in 1923, and a Southern Rhodesia Trades and Labour Council in 1939, with a White Labourite outlook.

The ideas of the ICU were circulating by the mid-1920s, and a formal request for aid was sent to the ICU in South Africa in 1926.[17] Robert Sambo was dispatched to Bulawayo in 1927, and worked with John Mphamba to set up a branch. Sambo was deported and replaced by Masotsha 'Sergeant' Ndlovu, who rebuilt the ICU in Rhodesia. Charles Mzingeli established a Salisbury branch, and others followed, especially in rural areas hit by the Land Act. Its ideas, like those of the ICU in South Africa, were a mishmash, but did include some class politics: 'The ICU is for proletarian people', its enemies the 'capitalist class'.

---

16 For Malawi, see Dee, 'Clements Kadalie'; for Zambia, see H. Meebelo, *African Proletarians and Colonial Capitalism: The Origins, Growth and Struggles of the Zambian Labour Movement to 1964* (Lusaka: Kenneth Kaunda Foundation, 1986).

17 See P. Nyathi, *Masotsha Ndlovu* (Ardbennie and Harare: Longman Zimbabwe, 1998); B. Raftopoulous and I. Phimister, *Keep on Knocking: A History of the Labour Movement in Zimbabwe, 1900–1997* (Harare: Baobab Books, 1997), pp. 1–54; T. Ranger, *The African Voice in Southern Rhodesia, 1898–1930* (London: Heinemann, 1970).

The ICU was the largest black mass movement in Southern Rhodesia between the wars, lasting into the late 1930s, also making an organized appearance in Northern Rhodesia. The latter had been transformed by the opening up of the Copperbelt around Ndola, the colony soon becoming the world's second-largest copper supplier. New mining towns were formed along with a large working class. In 1939, the mines employed 24,900, including 2,700 whites; the total population was 1.5 million black people, 15,000 whites, and 1,000 Asians. In 1931, Joseph Kazembe – deported from South Africa – made an effort to found the ICU in Livingstone. In 1932 black mineworkers, mainly migrants, went on strike: Kazembe made a fiery speech at Ndola and was arrested. There is no evidence of the ICU starting the strike, and it was marginalized by new unions in the 1940s, like the Rhodesia Railways African Employees Association (RRAEA) founded in Bulawayo in 1944 and the Northern Rhodesian African Mineworkers' Union in 1947. Most white mine workers were expatriates, founding strong but economistic unions; some workers came from radical backgrounds. Tommy Graves, who arrived in 1930, had been an IWW organizer in the United States, where he was jailed and then deported. He was dismissed from Roan Antelope Mine on the Copperbelt in 1939, partly due to this background.

1940s–1990s

Anarchism and syndicalism were in the doldrums until the 1990s, overtaken by communists and nationalists.[18] Kadalie ran a remnant of the ICU from East London into the 1940s. Réshard Gool's semi-fictional account of Cape Town on the eve of apartheid, *Cape Town Coolie*, features several anarchists, including the narrator. Motler wrote a very mild introduction to SATU's official history in 1952 – perhaps understandable given the wide scope of the 1950 Suppression of Communism Act; the CPSA was dissolved and reconstituted as the underground South African Communist Party (SACP) in 1953. After the ANC was banned in 1961, it joined the SACP in armed struggle through uMkhonto weSizwe (MK). At least one self-described anarchist tried to join MK. The New Left arrived belatedly: it had some libertarian elements, which left an imprint on the rising unions of the 1970s, notably the Federation of

---

18 See L. van der Walt, 'From Below: An Overview of South African Politics at a Distance from the State, 1917–2015, with Dossier of Texts', in K. Helliker and L. van der Walt (eds.), *Politics at a Distance from the State: Radical and African Perspectives* (London and New York: Routledge, 2018), pp. 111–63.

South African Trade Unions (FOSATU, founded in 1979). FOSATU's radical 'workerism' had some parallels with syndicalism, but was distinct from it.

Augusto José Godinho, veteran of the 1934 Portuguese uprising, moved to Luanda, Angola, after 1945. He stayed in contact with comrades abroad, returning to Portugal in the late 1950s. Manual Firmo, who fought in the Spanish Revolution and survived Tarrafal, also immigrated, later joined by his brothers, also anarchists. He worked in forestry and then the Benguela railways, before returning to Portugal. They were part of massive post-war migration to Portugal's African colonies: in 1975, the white population was 500,000, 10 per cent of the total.

Luis Laranjeira taught in Luanda before independence, and for some years afterwards. The Partido Comunista Português had a small presence from the 1940s, fostering a Partido Communista de Angola (Communist Party of Angola) in 1955, which then helped found the Movimento Popular de Libertação de Angola (Popular Movement for the Liberation of Angola, MPLA). The MPLA came to adopt Marxism-Leninism and armed struggle; it was a non-racial formation, including *mestiço*, Asian, and white members. Inocêncio da Câmara Pires, an anarchist and *mestiço* from a prominent Luanda family, joined the MPLA in France in the 1950s. An accredited representative of the MPLA's foreign department, he died in 1966. The MPLA established a one-party state in 1975, replacing the Estado Novo state-run unions with its own state-run União Nacional de Trabalhadores (National Union of Workers).

World-renowned botanist and anarchist Aurélio Quintanilha worked in Mozambique from 1943, blocked from university jobs in Portugal. He became a supporter of the Frente de Libertação de Moçambique (Liberation Front of Mozambique, FRELIMO), a non-racial national liberation movement allied to the MPLA, and close to the ANC and SACP. It established large 'liberated zones' in northern Mozambique and set up a one-party state in 1975, complete with state-run Organização dos Trabalhadores de Moçambique (Workers' Organization of Mozambique). Quintanilha became an honoured citizen. In 1981, he stated that he retained anarcho-syndicalist sympathies, but accepted the need for a revolutionary state. Waddington, meanwhile, edited the FRELIMO-controlled newspaper *Notícias* (*News*) after independence.

Both Marxist-Leninist regimes faced armed counter-revolutionary movements, backed by South Africa; in addition, Angola became a Cold War hotspot with Chinese, Cuban, Soviet, and United States involvement. By the time peace arrived in the 1990s, FRELIMO and MPLA had dropped Marxism-Leninism, and millions had died.

In Southern Rhodesia, a Reformed Industrial and Commercial Workers Union (RICU) was established in Salisbury by Mzingeli.[19] Mzingeli, who later recalled following Kadalie 'like Jesus', was a popular speaker and tireless tribune who also had contacts among white liberals and radicals. The RICU was really a community-based protest group; it had a Women's Club and won elections to the township Advisory Board. It lost influence as new unions emerged, and was driven from the public sphere by a new generation of intolerant nationalists, later crystallized around the leftist, non-racial Zimbabwe African People's Union (ZAPU), linked to the ANC/SACP and the blood-and-soil nationalist Zimbabwe African National Union (ZANU) of Robert Mugabe. Mzingeli died a few months after ZANU won the first non-racial elections in 1980, while Ndlovu ended up in ZAPU, which was markedly less militarized than Mugabe's ZANU. Small Marxist groups emerged after 1980, and, although Dambudzo Marechera's 1980 novel *Black Sunlight* provided a sympathetic engagement with anarchism, there was no local anarchist current until the 2000s.

1990s–Present

A second wave of anarchism and syndicalism started in South Africa in the 1990s, spreading to Zambia, Swaziland (Eswatini), and Zimbabwe.[20] It had no direct connection to the older tradition, was smaller and drew heavily on Platformism and Latin American *especifismo*, emphasizing anarchist political organizations with theoretical and tactical unity, and working within and with existing movements and struggles. In southern Africa, this included efforts to reform existing unions into syndicalist ones, rather than forming new unions. There were also some short-lived efforts to form 'workers' assemblies' and an IWW branch among the unorganized.

Strong anarchist support for engaging existing unions also reflected their impressive role in anti-apartheid and post-independence struggles and ongoing power. South Africa's economy grew 450 per cent from 1948 to 1994. Union membership reached 2.7 million in 1991, concentrated in the Congress of South African Trade Unions (COSATU). COSATU was formally allied to the ANC

---

19 Raftopoulous and Phimister, *Keep on Knocking*, pp. 55–90; T. Scarnecchia, *The Urban Roots of Democracy and Political Violence in Zimbabwe: Harare and Highfield, 1940–1964* (Rochester, NY: Rochester University Press, 2008).

20 Rey, *Afriques anarchistes*; L. Maisiri, P. Nyalungu, and L. van der Walt, 'Anarchist/syndicalist and independent Marxist intersections in post-apartheid struggles, South Africa: the WSF/ZACF current in Gauteng, 1990s–2010s', *Globalizations* 17, 5 (2020), pp. 797–819.

and SACP in the Tripartite Alliance in 1990, but was willing to confront the ANC government elected in 1994 with general strikes. The Zambia Congress of Trade Unions and the Zimbabwe Congress of Trade Unions shook off state control, the former sponsoring the Movement for Multi-Party Democracy (MMD) that installed its former chairman as state president in 1991, the latter confronting but defeated by Mugabe. The Swaziland Federation of Trade Unions (SFTU) worked with the illegal People's United Democratic Movement (PUDEMO) and its Swaziland Youth Congress (SWAYOCO) against the absolute monarchy of King Mswati III. A small land-locked kingdom between Mozambique and South Africa, Eswatini had an economy based on migrant labour, commercial farms, forestry, and mining, closely linked to South Africa.

Anarchist circles emerged in South Africa in the early 1990s, the first public one being the Azanian Anarchist Alliance in Johannesburg in 1991. Others included the Anarchist Awareness League, the Durban Anarchist Federation, the Anarchist Revolutionary Movement (ARM), and Zabalaza (Struggle) Books. In 1995, ARM's 'class struggle' wing became the Workers Solidarity Federation (WSF), which embraced Platformism and published *Workers Solidarity*. The WSF recruited students and workers, especially from COSATU, and helped establish a 'workers' assembly' in 1996. It expanded into Durban and Cape Town, and helped form the Anarchist and Workers' Solidarity Movement in Lusaka in 1998. The latter's Wilstar Choongo opposed the corrupt, neo-liberal MMD government. He died of meningitis in 1999, aged thirty-five.

In 1999, the WSF dissolved, its projects reorganized as Bikisha Media Collective in Johannesburg and Zabalaza Action Group (ZAG) in Durban. Bikisha members became deeply involved in the Workers' Library and Museum, a workers' centre, and campaigns against neo-liberalism. They helped found, and were deeply involved in, the Anti-Privatisation Forum (APF) coalition formed on the Rand in 2000. ZAG was involved in the Concerned Citizens Forum and another 'workers' assembly', and tried to foster an IWW branch. The groups published *Zabalaza*, established an Anarchist Black Cross (ABC), and ran workshops called Red and Black Forums (RBFs). Other anarchist groups emerged among unemployed youth in the Soweto APF: the Black Action Group in Motsoaledi shack settlement, and Shesha Action Group in Dlamini.

On May Day 2003, all these groups plus Zabalaza Books joined the Zabalaza Anarchist Communist Federation (ZACF). The ZACF, like Bikisha before it, formally adopted the WSF's positions, but the focus shifted steadily to township-based struggles and the APF, based among the black unemployed, pensioners, and poor. The ZACF focused on work with the APF and its own Phambili Motsoaledi Community Project. This had a 'people's library', shack, and food garden, and published *Vuka Motsoaledi* (*Awake Motsoaledi*). In 2005, the ZACF initiated the Motsoaledi Concerned Residents association, which joined the APF. That year Phillip Nyalungu, a founder member of the Phambili project and the ZACF, was arrested for anti-election protests. Through the ABC, it won over Abel Ramarope, a jailed former guerrilla, who set up an anarchist study group in Pretoria Central Prison.

The ZACF always had Swazi members. Mandla Dlamini and Mandla 'MK' Khosa had come to South Africa for work, and helped found the Motsolaedi project and the ZACF; they also established a small ZACF presence in Swaziland, into which materials were smuggled and where MK ran a study circle with SWAYOCO activists. In 2005, he was among those jailed after police attacked a SWAYOCO demonstration in Manzini. In 2006, the ZACF was falsely accused of involvement in a bombing campaign, and MK fled to South Africa. He died in Swaziland in 2019.

By 2007, the ZACF was under strain, with burnouts, resignations, and faltering projects. The December congress restructured the organization into the Zabalaza Anarchist Communist Front, the name signalling the adoption of a new, tighter structure and focus. The ABC was hived off, the Swaziland section became a separate, allied group, and all the remaining collectives in the ZACF became branches. The rebooted ZACF published *Zabalaza News*, and ran RBFs with APF affiliates in Orange Farm, Sebokeng (near Sharpeville), and Soweto; set up a reading group with the Landless People's Movement (LPM) and APF members in Protea South, Soweto; co-founded the Coalition Against Xenophobia in 2008; and participated in the 'Nope!' anti-election campaign. There was some return to union work, including with outsourced workers, and joining the Solidarity Committee for a union-led factory occupation near Krugersdorp on the Witwatersrand in 2010.

WSF materials were sent to Harare in the 1990s, but anarchism emerged in the 2000s. Unions fought the regime and helped launch the Movement for Democratic Change (MDC), but Mugabe's increasingly predatory state cracked down and eventually collapsed the economy. The ZACF made contact with anarchists at the 2004 Zimbabwe Social Forum in Harare, recruiting at least one. The Zimbabweans were involved in the MDC left, and in the political hip-hop scene through Toyitoyi Artz Kollektive and the Uhuru Network. The Kollektive described itself as 'an anti-capitalist, anti-authoritarian, affinity group', the Uhuru Network as 'a class conscious movement . . . against the capitalist slave masters'.[21] These activities inspired the founding of the Cape Town-based, anarchist-influenced Soundz of the South hip-hop group in 2008.

The APF collapsed in 2010, but its affiliates survived. The ZACF continued to work with them, and was also a co-founder of the countrywide Democratic Left Front in 2012. In 2013, ZACF militants from Benoni, Khutsong, Sebokeng, and Soweto attended the National Assembly of the Unemployed, in Makhanda (Grahamstown), a small Eastern Cape town where the ZACF had established a presence. RBFs were complemented by ongoing Anarchist Political Schools from 2010. The schools fostered the ZACF-linked Inkululeko Anarchist Collective and Tokologo Anarchist Collective, the latter publishing *Tokologo*.

The whole radical left struggled to gain ground especially from the 2010s, a period marked by ANC and COSATU schisms, economic crisis, rising populism, and sectarianism. The ZACF's influence can still, however, be seen today in various spaces for popular, worker and union education and engagement.

Further Reading

Capela, José, *O movimento operário em Lourenço Marques, 1898–1927* (Porto: Centro de Estudos Africanos da Universidade do Porto, 2009 [1981]).

Emmett, Tony, 'Popular Resistance in Namibia, 1920–1925', in T. Lodge (ed.), *Resistance and Ideology in Settler Societies* (Johannesburg: Ravan Press, 1986), pp. 6–48.

Maisiri, Leroy, Phillip Nyalungu, and Lucien van der Walt, 'Anarchist/syndicalist and independent Marxist intersections in post-apartheid struggles, South Africa: the WSF/ZACF current in Gauteng, 1990s–2010s', *Globalizations* 17, 5 (2020), pp. 797–819.

Mantzaris, Evangelos, *Labour Struggles in South Africa: The Forgotten Pages, 1903–1921* (Windhoek and Durban: Collective Resources Publications, 1995).

Penvenne, Jeanne Marie, 'João dos Santos Albasini (1876–1922): the contradictions of politics and identity in colonial Mozambique', *Journal of African History* 37, 3 (1996), pp. 419–64.

Raftopoulous, Brian, and Ian Phimister, *Keep on Knocking: A History of the Labour Movement in Zimbabwe, 1900–1997* (Harare: Baobab Books, 1997).

Rey, Guillaume, *Afriques anarchistes. Introduction à l'histoire des anarchismes africains* (Paris: L'Harmattan, 2018).

van der Walt, Lucien, 'Anarchism and syndicalism in an African port city: the revolutionary traditions of Cape Town's multiracial working class, 1904–1924', *Labor History* 52, 2 (2011), pp. 137–71.

21 Toyitoyi Artz Kollektive, 'We Are Toyitoyi', 22 October 2013, http://toyitoyi .blogspot.com/2013/10/we-are-toyitoyi.html.

'Bakunin's heirs in South Africa: race, class and revolutionary syndicalism from the IWW to the International Socialist League', *Politikon: South African Journal of Political Studies* 30, 1 (2004), pp. 67–89.

'The first globalisation and transnational labour activism in southern Africa: white labourism, the IWW and the ICU, 1904–1934', *African Studies* 66, 2–3 (2007), pp. 223–51.

24

Anarchism and Syndicalism in China

GOTELIND MÜLLER

Introduction

The study of anarchism and syndicalism in China and their historical role has to confront several problems. Politically, neither in the PRC (People's Republic of China) nor in Taiwan during its GMD (Guomindang, 'KMT', or National Party) period (1945–90s) were these topics welcome, and in consequence sources were hidden away or censored, and, in any case, were not easy to access, while former activists were wary of talking openly about a past they had been discouraged from remembering. It is only since the 1980s that a limited easing has set in on both sides of the Taiwan Strait. The CCP (Chinese Communist Party) as well as the GMD, both Leninist parties in structure, viewed anarchism as an enemy. Still, several of their members had had contact with anarchism or had even been declared anarchists at some point.[1] Syndicalism, in turn, is theoretically obsolete in a socialist state like the PRC, founded in 1949, where independent (non-CCP) trade unions are not supposed to exist any longer,[2] let alone revolutionary labour unions; in martial law-era Taiwan (1949–87) the mainland-derived GMD considered any independent labour activism dubious at best, dangerous at worst, fearing not only communist infiltration but also an intersection of labour and ethnicity

---

1 For an overview on the history of anarchism in China, see P. Zarrow, *Anarchism and Chinese Political Culture* (New York: Columbia University Press, 1990); A. Dirlik, *Anarchism in the Chinese Revolution* (Berkeley: University of California Press, 1991); and G. Müller, *China, Kropotkin und der Anarchismus. Eine Kulturbewegung im China des frühen 20. Jahrhunderts unter dem Einfluß des Westens und japanischer Vorbilder* (Wiesbaden: Harrassowitz, 2001).
2 See J. Chan, 'Assessing Working-Class Power in Postsocialist China', in K. H. Roth (ed.), *On the Road to Global Labour History* (Leiden and Boston: Brill, 2018), pp. 164–83. More generally, an overview on the state of the art regarding work and labour relations in China through history is provided by C. Moll-Murata, 'China', in K. Hofmeester and M. van der Linden (eds.), *Handbook Global History of Work* (Berlin and Boston: De Gruyter Oldenbourg, 2018), pp. 15–31.

issues with local Taiwanese workers.[3] Nevertheless, both the GMD and the CCP had been active earlier in the twentieth century in the Chinese labour movement, each tending to wrest influence from the anarchists in their struggle for gaining power and support from various societal forces and strata.

The topic of anarchism and syndicalism in China will be dealt with here roughly for the period 1907–37, that is, taking the founding of the first self-declared Chinese anarchist groups in 1907 in Tokyo and Paris as a starting point, and the beginning of the full-scale Sino-Japanese War in 1937 as the end. The issues to address are manifold: they include the various ways of reception and adaptation of anarchism v. Marxism and the entangled motivations from the Chinese point of view; and industrialization and the rise of the labour question, paying heed also to the traditional 'guild system' in China and its relation to the nascent syndicalist movement. Additionally, gender relations, their redefinition, and alternative life practices which included experiments with the creation of communes and the rejection of marriage and of the Chinese concept of family all need to be covered to do justice to the concerns of the actors themselves.

Internationalism v. nationalism is a further line of inquiry,[4] with major milestones represented by the Chinese Revolution of 1911–12, ending the monarchy and empire by creating a Chinese republican state for the first time; the First World War and its effects on China, not the least in the realm of the economy and labour; the Versailles Peace Treaty negotiations which spurred the May Fourth Protest Movement in 1919, feeding into the larger ongoing New Culture Movement; the rivalry between the two political parties, the GMD and the newly established CCP, over the course of the 1920s, from co-operation in the First United Front (1924–7) to the 1927 purges of the CCP; and finally the Japanese threat intensifying over the course of the 1930s and leading to full-scale war. On the other hand, international integration – not only within Asia (above all with Japan and Korea, to which South-East Asia with its many Chinese migrants and labourers was added), but also with the larger world (namely with France, but to a lesser extent also with the UK, the United States, and Russia) – is a distinct feature to be considered.

---

3 See M. Ho, 'The rise and fall of Leninist control in Taiwan's industry', *China Quarterly* 189 (2007), pp. 162–79.
4 See G. Müller, 'Thinking Globally, Acting Locally: Chinese Anarchists between National and International Concerns (1900–1930s)', in W. Kirby, M. Leutner, and K. Mühlhahn (eds.), *Global Conjectures: China in Transnational Perspective* (Münster: LIT, 2006), pp. 103–20.

To establish and maintain all these ties and networks, beyond the individual dimension of travelling people and personal connections, a decisive means for keeping up international involvement was language, namely Esperanto, which had a significant influence on anarchist activists in East Asia, much more so than in the West.[5] It offered an 'internationalist' means to break out of the 'cultural sphere of (Chinese) character writing' – as has been advocated again by some East Asian 'cultural conservatives' in recent decades – without the need to adopt a hegemonic discursive means 'belonging' to some other nation(s) such as, for example, English. Esperanto 'belonged' to no one and was valued as a 'scientific' trans-cultural creation, promising equality to its users.

Journals formed a central means and medium of organization and agitation, especially since anarchists were wary of organizational discipline smacking of authority. Thus, to some degree, journals and publication ventures stood in for organizations as forums for a free exchange of ideas and for a free association of activists.

The issue of anarchism and education, sustained not least by the towering figure in world anarchism of the time, Peter Kropotkin, who elaborated – for example, in his *Fields, Factories and Workshops* (1899) – on the necessity of combining head and hand, agriculture and industry, work and study, inspired the Chinese anarchists to engage themselves in this regard. They did so from both sides of the scale: on the one hand offering education to Chinese labourers, including those migrating to Europe, or even designing programmes to help them migrate, covering basic education and literacy in Chinese, which also spurred language reform attempts; but on the other hand also motivating intellectuals to do manual work, earning their living and having unmediated contact with labour. Thus, the anarchist-designed work-and-study programmes for the Chinese in France (and China) during and after the First World War, as well as the Labour University in Shanghai of the late 1920s, were further products of such endeavours.

---

5 On the role of Esperanto in Chinese anarchism, see G. Müller with G. Benton, 'Esperanto and Chinese anarchism, 1907–1920: the translation from diaspora to homeland', *Language Problems and Language Planning* 30, 1 (2006), pp. 45–73; and G. Müller with G. Benton, 'Esperanto and Chinese anarchism in the 1920s and 1930s', *Language Problems and Language Planning* 30, 2 (2006), pp. 173–92. See also Benedict Anderson's assertion that anarchist internationalism was possible only 'if linguistic communication was successful' (p. xvi): B. Anderson, 'Preface', in S. Hirsch and L. van der Walt (eds.), *Anarchism and Syndicalism in the Colonial and Postcolonial World, 1870–1940* (Leiden: Brill, 2010), pp. xiii–xxix.

Syndicalism, on the other hand, was something the anarchists engaged in early on, trying (increasingly unsuccessfully) to keep their position in the labour movement between the ever stronger competitors of the GMD and the CCP. Although there was some tension worldwide between syndicalism and anarchism, it is noteworthy that most Chinese anarchists, in spite of the split between 'right-wing' and 'left-wing'/'pure' anarchists in the late 1920s, were positive towards syndicalism. In fact, in contrast to the self-declared pure anarchists elsewhere, the pure anarchists in China remained committed to syndicalism. Thus, the basic thrust in the long run was a combination of the main current of Kropotkinian anarcho-communism with anarcho-syndicalism.

The Beginnings: The Tokyo and Paris Groups between Diaspora and Homeland (1907–1912)

Though anarchist ideas in a broader sense were present in Chinese discourse earlier, the first distinct groups of Chinese anarchists appeared outside China and, furthermore, roughly at the same time: in 1907 in Tokyo and Paris. In China itself, the ruling Qing dynasty's repressive policies precluded the free formation of such groups. The groups used journals as their main medium: in Tokyo, *Tianyi* (*Natural Justice*) (1907–8) and later *Hengbao* (*The Chinese Anarchist News: Equity*) (1908) represented the anarchist group there around the couple Liu Shipei, a prodigious young scholar trained in the Chinese classics, and his wife He Zhen; in Paris the journal *Xin shiji* (*New Century*) (1907–10) styled itself after the French model *Les Temps Nouveaux*, edited by the French anarchist Jean Grave, with which it officially shared a postal address. In fact, both the Tokyo and the Paris groups had more or less close contacts with anarchist circles in Japan and France respectively.[6] Nevertheless, it is obvious that they still followed their own agendas, not just transferring foreign models into Chinese. In Tokyo, a notable distinct feature was the strong anarcha-feminism mainly driven by He Zhen (a female author),[7] which was unparalleled in the Japanese anarchist–socialist discourse of the time, in which gender issues played a role, but in a much less radical and prominent way than with He Zhen. While the Japanese were more inclined to advocate 'free love' and a rejection of state intervention via family

---

6 While the contacts in Tokyo were very close, those in Paris were more one-sided: the Chinese were well informed about the French while the opposite was less true.

7 See P. Zarrow, 'He Zhen and anarcho-feminism in China', *Journal of Asian Studies* 47, 4 (1988), pp. 796–813.

law in the vein of Emma Goldman, He Zhen focused on gender and exploitation. She demanded radical equality between partners (for example, widowers were only to partner with widows), but also addressed the exploitation between women, namely in the Chinese family system, with the subjugation of young women under their mothers-in-law, or of concubines under official wives. On the other hand, although the Tokyo group proclaimed a strong affinity to peasants and rural life – given the tiny Chinese industrial proletariat at the time – and introduced not only Kropotkin, but also Leo Tolstoy along with Laozi, the latter as a 'Chinese ancestor' of anarchism,[8] in its second publication *Hengbao*, dominated by Liu Shipei, it took up labour issues more directly. In the latter journal, strikes in China were reported, but also radical activities and strikes worldwide, and the journal was very strongly concerned with internationalism via language – that is, Esperanto – thus offering something to foreign readers, too. A key term for the Tokyo group was *pingdeng* (equality), which also had some Buddhist connotations and overtones;[9] it was employed to stand for a rejection of any asymmetrical relationship, be it social, linguistic, or gendered.

The Paris group surrounding the biologist Li Shizeng and the materialist-oriented scholar Wu Zhihui, in turn, made its own mark by a strong scientific orientation compared to the more classical–humanist thrust of the Tokyo group. Here, Esperanto was also pointedly discussed, if rather on a theoretical basis; in the Paris case, this was even connected to a radical attack on the Chinese script as an emblem of Chineseness and a sign of backwardness.

This interest in language issues distinguished the Chinese anarchists from their respective host countries to some degree at least, though in terms of Esperanto the Japanese anarchists were very much involved in the matter themselves. In fact, it was Ōsugi Sakae who would become the most prominent among the Japanese anarchists teaching the Chinese the language. However, the Japanese anarchists did not link it to attempts to reform the Japanese language, while the French anarchists' interest in Esperanto, as far as they had any, was limited to internationalism and the practical side of communication. In a sense, one could argue that the more a 'language

---

8 One should note that this view on Laozi had been voiced already in the West, too, and most notably was picked up (and thus supported) by Kropotkin himself.
9 Buddhist connections on both an intellectual and a personal level were ample with the Tokyo group, in marked contrast to the Japanese 'comrades'.

disadvantage' was perceived, the more Esperanto was considered a possible remedy.

Gender, on the other hand, was an issue central to He Zhen, but did figure also in the (male) Paris group. The latter typically linked it to their attack on Chinese tradition and its social, economic, and ritual subjugation of women.[10] In terms of practised new lifestyles, the 'connecting member' between the two groups, Zhang Ji, who moved from Tokyo to Paris, was the only one to experiment with communal life: he put ideas into practice, joining an international agrarian commune in France for some time. The experiment ended in economic failure, but in its quest to move beyond theorizing it foreshadowed the lifestyle experiments in China of some years later.

Furthermore, both the Tokyo and the Paris groups, located in two industrializing countries, discussed labour issues and closely followed international trends in syndicalism in their journals, the longer-lasting Paris group more thoroughly than the Tokyo group. The Paris group was also involved in labour issues in practical terms via a bean curd factory that biologist Li Shizeng had set up in France. For this factory, he recruited young Chinese from home and experimented there with labour education and the formation of a 'new Chinese worker' in a European setting: literate, educated, 'civilized', and self-conscious, to prepare for future developments in China.

In sum, the anarchists in Tokyo and mainly in Paris were the ones to introduce Western ideas on syndicalism and information on workers' movements to a Chinese readership. While the circulation of *Hengbao* is hard to establish beyond the Chinese community in Japan, *Xin shiji* was obviously successfully smuggled into China and distributed, as illustrated by the example of Shifu, who was to become *the* Chinese anarchist and reference for syndicalism in China.

The Early Years of the Republic: The Paris Group, Shifu, Anarcho-Communism and Anarcho-Syndicalism

After the demise of the Qing dynasty in 1911–12, anarchism and syndicalism could take root in China itself. While the Tokyo group left only a rather

---

10 This theoretical stance did not necessarily translate into changed personal lifestyles among the Paris group members. See also G. Müller, 'Knowledge Is Easy – Action Is Difficult: The Case of Chinese Anarchist Discourse on Women and Gender Relations and Its Practical Limitations', in M. Leutner and N. Spakowski (eds.), *Women in China: The Republican Period in Historical Perspective* (Münster: LIT, 2005), pp. 86–106.

indirect legacy,[11] the members of the Paris group – who at the same time had been active members in Sun Yat-sen's anti-Qing Revolutionary Alliance, the forerunner of the GMD – moved back to China. The political choice of the key figures of the Paris group to support the nationalist GMD was driven by the evolutionary argument that it was the 'first step in the right direction', namely, to eradicate the monarchy and establish a republic. In this, they applied the idea of 'revolution' as an accelerated 'evolution', taken from Elisée Reclus, the French anarchist geographer who had been presented and translated in *Xin shiji* together with his close friend Kropotkin.

Once the republic was in place, the question arose as to how much further anarchists should involve themselves in politics, which created tensions among them. The options chosen by former members of the Paris group ranged from taking on political roles at the highest level (Cai Yuanpei, the Humboldtian 'educator of China', who had been connected to the Paris group while studying in Germany, briefly became minister of education), to minor political roles, to pure abstention. To allow for such 'graded' behaviour, the group designed associations where one could pledge more or fewer 'rules of abstention' which included not only politics, but also habits and lifestyles, for example, not taking concubines or not consuming opium, but also abstention from meat. In fact, although Li Shizeng, the most active vegetarian, argued for vegetarianism also from a biologist–scientist view and thus had worked on experiments on possible uses of soy beans in France to offer an alternative to the meat-loving Europeans,[12] a strong moral basis to these abstention associations is apparent.[13] The more explicitly anarchist one was consequently literally called the 'Society for the Advancement of Virtue [Jindehui]'.

Still, the more radically minded, who found the 'graded' approach of the Paris group unsatisfying, opted for grouping around Liu Sifu, *the* Chinese anarchist who called himself 'Shifu' (with not only an incidental homophone

11 There are few personal continuities, largely because of the political volte-face of the key couple, Liu Shipei and He Zhen, who suddenly left the revolutionary camp; the circumstances remain murky. The most important continuity was Jing Meijiu, who later published various anarchism-related journals in China and continued their very peculiar combination of classical scholarship and anarchism.
12 Here one may note a longstanding East Asian trope of perceiving Westerners as aggressive meat-devouring people. For all his scientism, Li Shizeng linked vegetarianism also to the anarchist rejection of dominance and to Kropotkin's biology-based 'mutual aid' idea.
13 This moral impetus in anarchism is something often overlooked, but not exclusive to the Chinese anarchists. The 'graded' taking over of commitments calls to mind Buddhist practices among lay followers to take on single vows, though in content the Paris group was explicitly anti-religious.

Fig. 24.1 [Liu] Shifu (1884–1915). (Svintage Archive/Alamy Stock Photo.)

reference to Buddhism where the term stands for a 'Buddhist master').[14] In hindsight, he stated that he had become 'converted' to anarchism by reading *Xin shiji* in prison while serving his sentence for a failed assassination attempt on a Manchu official. However, after his release, he first resumed his nationalist-driven anti-Manchu assassination attempts, still believing that the elimination of key political figures would bring about the solution. But when the republic was finally established, he became quickly disillusioned and frustrated, and thus finally and fully embraced Kropotkin's anarchist approach to aim at a fundamentally new societal order about which he had read in *Xin shiji*.

Shifu insisted on obligatory abstinence from any political commitment and pleaded for a thorough rejection of authority in all forms, including the patriarchal family (and thus declined to use his family name 'Liu' any longer).

14 On Shifu, see E. S. Krebs, *Shifu, Soul of Chinese Anarchism* (Lanham, MD: Rowman & Littlefield, 1998).

He practised the rejection of marriage via a 'free love' relationship with his companion, and wanted to set an example by living in a commune-like fashion with friends and relatives. When the founding of an agrarian commune did not work out, he turned to his urban surroundings, first in Guangzhou, then in Shanghai. To counter the Paris group's 'abstention societies', which he deemed not 'thorough enough', he had set up his own more radical 'Conscience Society [*xinshe*]' in 1912 – again a name with a strong moral implication. His active propagation of Esperanto, vegetarianism (a feature not generally typical of anarchists worldwide and with some Buddhist overtones in his case, clearly distinct from Li Shizeng's scientific perspective), and an increasing interest in labour issues were further trademarks of his anarchist style, all referring to the basic Kropotkinian notion of anarchism being directed against any type of 'authority'. Although the Paris group had already started to actively involve itself with Chinese workers in France, it was only with Shifu and – above all – his followers that anarcho-syndicalism established itself in China.

The First World War influenced this development insofar as on the one hand mainly France and the UK (but also Russia) recruited Chinese labourers to fill in for the men who had left for the front in the home industries there, or for helping on the battlefield in non-combatant roles.[15] The Paris group reacted to this development and quickly designed educational programmes for Chinese workers in Europe, mainly in France, typically concentrating not only on literacy – a precondition for effective propaganda work – or basic knowledge conveyed in evening classes, but also on habits (such as those regarding hygiene or social customs) and 'ideological' education to bring forth a 'new' and 'aware' Chinese labourer. In their eyes, a stay in Europe was a precious chance and befitting every Chinese person to become more 'civilized'. Thus, Li Shizeng of the Paris group also spearheaded a recruitment programme of his own in China, hoping to counter the exploitation of Chinese workers that had formerly been rampant with the contracts offered by private recruiting companies, guaranteeing the workers, for example, equal pay with French workers. In this context, the first Chinese-language workers' journal was designed in France with easily readable texts for education: *Huagong zazhi (Chinese Labour Journal)* (1917–18).

---

15 The most recent book-length English-language study on the Western recruitment of Chinese workers, G. James, *The Chinese Labour Corps (1916–1920)* (Hong Kong: Bayview Educational, 2013), though otherwise very detailed, largely ignores the anarchist side. Most workers were employed in France, even if contracted by the UK.

At the same time, the Paris group – which had already set up preparatory co-education schools in China before the First World War for students willing to go to France to study (challenging educational and social customs doubly since co-education in itself was as unconventional in a country where girls' schools were still fairly recent, as were their curricula, which integrated practical working skills, following European models) – sent some graduates in groups to French colleges. The outbreak of war, though, jeopardized the transfer of more students and therefore their opportunities to study in France. The Paris group therefore tried to use the wartime European labour shortage also in creative ways as an opportunity to send more Chinese students (and not just workers) over to France (and occasionally Britain) via 'work-and-study' programmes that also included some women.[16] These programmes were designed to help them finance their studies through work, while at the same time they would become more 'holistic' personalities through their working experience. Furthermore, they would also become economically independent from their families. Still, the Paris group's main interest lay in opening up ways for young Chinese students to come to Europe, mainly to France, while work and workers as such were purely secondary to them. Thus, their final and most long-lasting endeavour was the provincially financed university-level programme of the Institut Franco-Chinois in Lyon which started after the First World War and was supposed to generate a French-educated elite which would then build up a new university system back in China. In a way, the Paris group, themselves intellectuals, cared mainly about the intellectuals after all.

On the other hand, in China itself, the First World War opened up a great chance for Chinese (and Japanese) industrialists to develop their enterprises with less competition from the West. Thus, the war meant a boom for China's economy. As a consequence, the labour question came to the fore, too, and it was the anarchists, who were now strongly involved in syndicalist issues under the initial lead of Shifu, who tried to convince the workers that the traditional guild system – with its integration of employers and workers in one association – was detrimental to their interests. Furthermore, he criticized the organizational pattern of groupings according to regional provenance (the so-called native place

16 See G. Barman and N. Dulioust, 'Un groupe oublié. Les étudiantes-ouvrières chinoises en France', *Études chinoises* 7, 2 (1987), pp. 9–46, and G. Müller, 'Chinese Women between Education and Money: Ideal and Realities of the Female Worker-Students in the First Years of the Republic' (University of Heidelberg, 2013), DOI: https://doi.org/10.11588/heidok.00015416.

organizations)[17] typical among migrants in the industrializing metrop-
olises, which made it easy for employers to play off one group of
workers against another, thus undermining the common interest of the
working class and rendering the weapon of strikes ineffective. In short,
he tried to convince them that they needed a common working-class
consciousness beyond their regional identities based on common dialect
and habits. Shifu mainly used his journal *Minsheng* (*People's Voice*;
Esperanto title: *Voĉo de la Popolo*) (1913–21) and leaflets as the medium
for agitation, though one may note that the language he used was still of
the elitist classical variety.

Shifu himself died in 1915, that is, early in the First World War and in the
midst of the crisis in world anarchism caused by the split between the
supporters of the Allies as the 'lesser evil', around grand master Kropotkin,
and those anarchists who remained strictly neutral in the conflict – to whom
Shifu pledged allegiance. His followers, however, were to be the main core in
the future development of anarchism and syndicalism in China. In fact, they
would turn him into a symbol by the introduction of the term 'Shifuism',
denoting a pure uncompromising attitude among anarchists.[18]

May Fourth: Anarchism, Marxism, Labour, Gender, and Communes

The peak of anarchist and syndicalist activities was around the time of the so-
called May Fourth movement: more strictly speaking, this movement was
connected to the peace treaty negotiations in Versailles after the First World
War, where the Japanese were (successfully) trying to hold on to their rights
in Shandong in China, which they had wrested from the Germans early in the
war. When this news leaked in May 1919, protests in China exploded. From
a wider perspective, this protest movement, however, was only the epicentre
of a larger movement of renewal and questioning of received customs,
lifestyles, language forms, values, and so on, which may be roughly dated
from 1915 to 1923 and is conventionally termed the 'New Culture Movement'.
A key experience triggering this development was the quick usurpation of
power in the newly established republic by strongman Yuan Shikai, who
turned the freshly installed parliamentary democratic system into a farce,

17 On this, see B. Goodman, *Native Place, City and Nation: Regional Networks and Identities
in Shanghai, 1853–1937* (Berkeley: University of California Press, 1995).
18 The common anarchist forum *Jinhua/La Evolucio* (*Evolution*) titled its issue commemorating Shifu in 1919 'Shifuism [Shifu zhuyi]'.

leading the country straight into a new kind of dictatorship (even including an attempt to recreate a monarchy), halted only by Yuan's sudden death in 1916. As with Shifu, this experience of failure of the early republic generated a wave of questions. In the transition from empire to nation, and under divided rule following Yuan's short-lived dictatorship with competing power centres in north and south China, societal forces looked for an opportunity to express themselves.

Subsequently, labour issues came to the forefront, and the anarchists spearheaded the genre of labour journals inside China with *Laodong/La Laboristo* (*Labour/er*) in 1918, issued by Wu Zhihui of the Paris group together with former followers of Shifu, who were by now experienced in syndicalist work in South-East Asia among the Chinese migrants there. Thus, the two strands of the anarchist movement merged via syndicalist issues. While this journal – in contrast to *Huagong zazhi* in France for Chinese workers there – was still fairly elitist in language use (as Shifu's *Minsheng* had been as well), writing instead 'on labour', and survived only for some months, the subsequent *Laodongzhe* (*Labourer*) of 1920–1 was directed towards a less educated readership. In terms of content, though, both journals frequently referred to Shifu.

In the intellectual climate of the May Fourth era, new journals and groups sprang up everywhere, translations and reports about alternative lifestyles elsewhere in the world circulated, and ideologies of all kinds competed. Certainties of old became obsolete in the rush for 'the new'. In this context, various kinds of socialisms were discussed as well. Although there had been translations of and reports about worldwide socialist trends, ideas, and movements in Chinese-language publications for roughly two decades by then, the developments in Russia since 1917 and the establishment of an alternative system by the Soviets seemed to prove that in this case ideas were not only printed, but also put into practice, and not only in small areas like invididual communes, but also on a larger scale. Therefore, the societal discussions, typically in journals, led to the formation of political groups, and for the anarchists journals were the main and most congenial forums around which they coalesced. It is from now on that one may speak of an 'anarchist movement' in China in a meaningful way.

Marxist Bolshevism, too, became a potent factor in the course of May Fourth, though it certainly did not represent the whole movement, as PRC historiography – deliberately ignoring the liberal and anarchist sides of May Fourth – would have it. The main argument for Bolshevism was simply its having 'succeeded' in the Russian Revolution, though it is an irony of history that it was the anarchists in the journal *Laodong* who first introduced the October Revolution in China, initially misinterpreting it as quasi-anarchist. Knowledge of Marxism in a strict sense was, in turn, more the domain of GMD scholars at the time, who were mainly interested in the economic side of things. But now economic theories were of lesser interest than the outlook of potentially successful revolutionary action. Thus, with the help of the Comintern, Chinese radicals both inside China and outside (mainly in France, but also in Japan) shifted towards the Soviet model during the critical time of late 1919 to early 1921 and eventually founded the CCP (officially in July 1921). And since the Chinese (bolshevist) Communists perceived the labour movement to be an integral part of their *raison d'être*, they quickly tried to gain a foothold there.

Given that at the time the main industrialized parts of China were the southern and coastal areas, namely Shanghai and Guangzhou, the main labour struggles were concentrated there. Guangzhou specifically was a stronghold of anarchists as well as the GMD, and thus the still tiny CCP which, in a sense, 'came from the north', had a hard time taking over the leadership of the labour movement there. In 1921, with the common May Day demonstration in Guangzhou under the banners of Marx and Kropotkin side by side, the peak of co-operation was reached; thereafter the GMD, the anarchists, and the Marxists in the labour movement parted ways. Subsequently, they fought each other over influence on the labour movement, and each tried to claim strikes and 'martyrs', even if not explicitly political ones, for themselves.[19] After the 1923 accord between Sun Yat-sen, the leader of the GMD, and the Soviets – who agreed to help Sun if he allowed CCP members to enter his GMD on an individual basis – the star of the Marxist communists was rising, while the role of the anarchists in general, and in the labour movement in Guangzhou in particular, started to decline.

Beyond the labour activities, which included, in good anarchist tradition, evening schools for workers and other educational endeavours, the anarchists at the time very strongly advocated new lifestyles, not the least new gender relations, since the family was perceived as the major site of power

---

19 A good example is two early 'martyrs' of the labour movement in Hunan, Pang Renquan and Huang Ai, killed by the local warlord in 1922; they had never expressed any ideological preferences but were subsequently claimed by all sides. See G. Müller, 'Anarchism, Marxism, and Nationalism in China: Between Conflict, Cooperation, and Continuities', in S. Hirsch and L. van der Walt (eds.), *Radical Encounters in the Colonial and Postcolonial World, 1870–1940: Anarchist, Marxist, and Nationalist Struggles* (London and New York: Routledge, forthcoming).

production where the individual suffered from 'authority', be it between the generations or between the sexes. This was also attractive for many young Chinese other than those who were inclined towards anarchism. Furthermore, work and study were to be combined, as Kropotkin and other anarchists had advocated. But non-anarchist models like the 'Atarashiki mura [new village]' movement of Japanese author Mushakōji Saneatsu were also widely discussed, thus leading to a mushrooming of communes, often short-lived, but aiming at allowing the usually young students of both sexes to sustain themselves by working on their own; in China, though, this was mostly in urban settings, close to their universities.[20] Beyond the idealist concept of a holistic personality, this was also supposed to free the students from economic dependence on their families, and women from dependence on men. Societal and economic realities quickly ended the idealistic attempts, but the ideal of communal life was established, and it was a test case to 'organize' oneself freely from the bottom up in a society more used to top-down procedures.

The broader uniting bond among anarchists remained, however, largely the common publishing endeavours with several journals. Many such journals were short-lived for internal but also for external reasons such as censorship; others were longer-lived, but almost always consciously connected to worldwide anarchism via publication exchanges and with the integration of Esperanto for facilitating international communication to reach beyond the language barrier. Chinese anarchists of the time were self-consciously part of world anarchism and strongly internationalist, and they were largely modernist since only very few ever advocated a home-grown 'Chinese-style anarchism' à la Laozi.[21] They also kept close contacts with anarchists not only from Europe (beyond France, especially the UK, but also Germany) and the United States (for example, Alexander Berkman and Emma Goldman), but also from Japan and Korea. While Shifu, who had received help from Japanese anarchist Ōsugi Sakae for the publication of Minsheng, had been mourned by Ōsugi and others in Japan after his early death, the Chinese anarchists, in turn, used the murder by the Japanese police of Ōsugi, his partner Itō Noe, and a young nephew in 1923 during the Great

20 See G. Müller, 'Atarashiki mura versus Xincun: The Chinese Reception of a Japanese Model of Alternative Ways of Living' (Heidelberg: University of Heidelberg, 2013), DOI: https://doi.org/10.11588/heidok.00015393.
21 This strand, which partly reflected the Tokyo group's legacy, appeared again in the early 1920s, but was rejected by most of the Chinese anarchists, who instead wanted to be linked with modernity and scientism à la Kropotkin.

Kantō Earthquake chaos as a further opportunity to show anarchist inter-nationalist solidarity, commemorating the 'East Asian anarchist martyr'. Ōsugi had visited China twice and combined anarchism and syndicalism in Japan.[22] He and his followers had remained deeply involved with their Chinese comrades. Furthermore, Ōsugi had also been in the forefront of the split between the anarchists and the bolshevists, who had begun to be seen as ideologically incompatible.[23] Several Chinese anarchists who had been invited to the fledgling Soviet Russia in early Comintern attempts to make 'converts' added to the split by reporting negatively on what they experienced.

The debates over the 'failed experiment' of the Soviet system raged not only in China but also among the Chinese students in France, where the anarchists – due to the Paris group's work-and-study programmes – were at first still in a strong position. The translations of international anarchists and their critical reports added substantially to the Chinese ones. The fate of Kropotkin, who had returned to Russia after the February Revolution and had become disillusioned and marginalized after the October Revolution, as well as that of other famous Russian anarchists such as Berkman and Goldman, who had been expelled from the United States as 'radicals' to go 'back' to Soviet Russia, and who made the difficulties of the anarchists in the Soviet state known to the West, were frequently discussed topics. After the funeral of Kropotkin in 1921, the last occasion at which anarchists in Soviet Russia were able to appear in public, repression set in. Thus, the attempts of co-operation between bolshevist Communists and the anarchists (who went on to claim the term 'communism' for anarcho-communism in the vein of Kropotkin against the Marxist Bolsheviks) among the Chinese came to an end, too: inside China, but also in France and elsewhere.

The Mid-1920s: Between the GMD and the CCP, and the Fight to Represent the Workers

In the mid-1920s, conflicts between the anarchists, the GMD, and the CCP came to a head. While the CCP and the GMD worked on their First United Front (1924–7), however problematic that was in practice, the anarchists

22 His most important contribution in this regard was the journal *Rōdō undō* (*Labour Movement*).
23 Ōsugi had initially tested possible co-operation with the Soviets during his Shanghai visit, but came away disillusioned. In Japan, the so-called *ana–boru* (anarchist–bolshevist) dispute subsequently escalated.

found themselves squeezed out. Although members of the Paris group, most outspokenly Wu Zhihui, strongly argued for the necessity of an 'anarchist wing' *inside* the GMD to counter the CCP influence in that party so as not to 'lose' it to them, most Chinese anarchists abhorred such an idea as treasonous to anarchist principles and 'Shifuism'.

During the 'May Thirtieth Movement' of 1925, triggered by the shooting of a Chinese labour agitator in a foreign-owned factory in Shanghai, leading to anti-imperialist demonstrations with further bloodshed, labour issues strongly linked up with anti-imperialism. Here, the CCP could capitalize on its (by then well established) standing in the labour movement, boosting its numbers over the following months, while the anarchists, who had mixed feelings about the strong nationalist overtones in this anti-imperialist upsurge in the labour movement and beyond, stood apart.

The subsequent military 'Northern Expedition' (1926–8), starting from Guangzhou in the south, to unite China under the military command of Chiang Kai-shek, who had managed to establish himself as successor to Sun Yat-sen in the GMD after the latter's death in 1925, was the other big historical event the anarchists merely watched from the sidelines. The CCP, in turn, also profited in this case by quickly installing mass organizations behind the northward-moving military front (which in turn embittered many in the GMD).

Therefore, the mid-1920s were a critical period for the Chinese anarchists: many questioned the stance on organization prevalent in anarchism, that is, an aversion to it, and the non-interventionism. While the strictly organized CCP scored victory after victory, the anarchists were divided on these issues,[24] which also cost them their influence in the labour movement. The discussion was not only a Chinese one, certainly; international debates in anarchism worldwide on the issue of organizational principles – not least those triggered by the controversial proposal by the émigré Ukrainian anarchists Nestor Makhno and Peter Arshinov to 'learn the lesson' of Bolshevik success and organize more effectively – as well as the debates on the relationship between means and ends raging at the time, came to the forefront for the Chinese as well. Furthermore, the ongoing 'national revolution', GMD-style, provoked the question of whether the option of standing aside to keep one's 'purity', rather than dirtying oneself in helping the 'better'

24 A decisive contribution came from young Chinese anarchists by then in France, including the well-known writer Ba Jin, who pleaded for less abstention in societal affairs, though at the same time declaring themselves 'pure anarchists' with no connections to politics.

side, was not a form of treason, de facto helping the worst and leaving the Chinese people alone, besides making oneself superfluous – a discussion that recalled the one between Kropotkin and his critics at the outbreak of the First World War. This issue deeply divided the Chinese anarchists, led to acrimonious debates in anarchist publications, which often faltered in consequence, and left behind scars that would still be visible in future years.[25]

The Late 1920s to 1930s: Anarchism, Syndicalism, and the Debate Concerning 'Pure' Anarchism

The conflicts peaked when the United Front between the GMD and the CCP, which had never run smoothly, was forcefully crushed in 1927, first by Chiang Kai-shek, by then acting as head of the GMD 'right wing', and then terminated only months later by the rival GMD 'leftists', in order to establish a GMD national government. The CCP was outlawed and persecuted and thus went underground, and radicals of all stripes were hunted down. The year 1927 thus marked a decisive point in Chinese history.

The anarchists had, as mentioned, links to the GMD (and its predecessor) from the times of the Paris group's establishment, while the CCP had been an arch-enemy almost from the start. Nevertheless, whether to use this as an argument to side with the 'lesser evil', as the 'GMD anarchists' (themselves under pressure from other wings of the GMD) advocated, who were now regrouped around the journal Geming zhoubao (Revolution Weekly), or whether to stay true to their principles but thus aloof from all others, as the 'pure anarchists' advocated, became the centre of the debate. Especially problematic was the fact that Geming zhoubao now sided with the GMD 'right wing', driven by its deep animosity towards the CCP, but thus appearing to sustain those who were responsible for the large-scale bloody purges of all kinds of 'leftists' (even if they were only suspected as such) and thus as bedfellows of 'reactionaries'. In fact, when the GMD Nanjing government became more settled, any further explicit anarchist propaganda became dangerous as well. Geming zhoubao thus had to close in 1929, and in the early 1930s open anarchist agitation largely disappeared.

Beyond publications, anarchist initiatives of these years also included ventures in education in an urban setting. One anarchist, a key figure of the May Fourth events and former 'New Village' activist, ran a small college

---

25 For example, the 'anarchist left' surrounding Lu Jianbo in Shanghai would attack perceived 'middle-of-the-roaders' such as Ba Jin as well as the 'rightists' of the GMD's 'anarchist wing'.

in the suburbs of Shanghai with an anarchist curriculum and integration of classroom study with agricultural practice. The larger enterprise in the area was, however, the Labour University, which was set up in 1927 in Shanghai in a renewed attempt to combine head and hand in education, thus continuing the ideal that Kropotkin and others had voiced, and taking the Labour University of Charleroi in Belgium as a model.[26] However, the Labour University in Shanghai was 'national' and supposed to educate GMD cadres for the labour movement. From the side of the anarchists, it was de facto an attempt to inherit the co-operation model that the CCP and the GMD had established with Shanghai University earlier, during the years of the United Front (and closed due to its end), but now as a co-operative anarchist–GMD venture. In sum, even in this case the Chinese anarchists involved tried to take the place the CCP had had to vacate, assuming erroneously that the GMD would be more tolerant in the long run towards anarchists than towards the CCP. Li Shizeng, for one, now reinterpreted anarchism more in a Proudhonian way and advocated federalism. He thus limited himself instead to arguing against too much centralization. But even this seemed 'too radical' in the perspective of many in the GMD, while Wu Zhihui now spoke very inclusively of a 'revolution of all' – to counter the class struggle idea – with anarchism as the goal in a distant future. Although the Labour University invited some foreign anarchists, like former collaborators of Ōsugi from Japan and Paul Reclus, nephew of Elisée, from France, as well as offering Esperanto classes, the anarchist identity became ever more spurious, and when the Japanese bombardment of Shanghai destroyed the campus in 1932 it was inconceivable to reopen it thereafter.

Anarchist educational enterprises were also installed in less industrialized settings, namely in Fujian, where one existed until the mid-1930s. Here, anarchist internationalism was played out again by recruiting foreign, especially Japanese, anarchists as staff, some of whom came over from the (by that time) disappointing Labour University. This local educational enterprise also, notably, served as a military training ground, since the anarchists there pointed out the futility of mere discourse in a highly militarized age. However, this endeavour was also not free from GMD connections.[27] The military aspect was a far cry from the declared anti-militarism that had earlier

---

26 The classic study on the Labour University is M. K. Chan and A. Dirlik, *Schools into Fields and Factories: Anarchists, the Guomindang, and the Labor University in Shanghai, 1927–1932* (Durham, NC: Duke University Press, 1991).

27 See M. Yamaguchi and H. Sakai, *Ba Jin de shijie* [Ba Jin's World] (Beijing: Dongfang chubanshe, 1995), pp. 252–315.

been integral to Chinese anarchism, but it implicitly acknowledged the GMD experience of the Whampoa Military Academy from the United Front era. The goal of the academy had been to train an ideologically 'aware' military, with Soviet advisers but Sun Yat-sen's ideas as the 'ideology'; without such a military the Northern Expedition would not have been possible. The Fujian endeavours of the anarchists, too, had to be stopped soon, but they became memorialized by well-known author Ba Jin, who visited and wrote about them in fictionalized form.

Other anarchists, however, opted rather for a purely discursive and literary–cultural way of expressing anarchist ideals in the increasingly stifling atmosphere, arguing that the end never justifies dubious means. And if the ideal could not be realized now, it should at least be kept pure for potential future enactment when the time would be ripe. Literature – which also became a substitute arena for the Marxists, especially after their *annus horribilis* of 1927, as Proletarian Literature – thus became a further field for anarchists in which, not least, the author Ba Jin was very active; he wrote and translated much revolutionary literature, and also made known to Chinese readers international anarchist 'cases' like the Sacco and Vanzetti executions.[28] Furthermore, Ba Jin at that time was still an active Esperantist, and via Esperanto he also made known to the world the events in Chinese anarchism. But his 'purist'/'leftist' critics, namely Lu Jianbo and Mao Yibo, were also interested in literature and Esperanto. While Mao Yibo, trained at the GMD–CCP-run Shanghai University during the United Front era, was the anarchist who, most of all, tried to introduce the idea of class consciousness and class conflict into Chinese anarchism while attacking the Marxists from the 'left', Lu Jianbo particularly stressed Esperanto and gender issues as intrinsic to anarchism,[29] and he was also active as an anarcho-syndicalist in Shanghai before he was forced to leave for the countryside of his native Sichuan.

The debate on 'pure' anarchism also had close parallels, for example in Japan, although in China the purists did not reject syndicalism but all the

---

28 On this case, see P. Avrich, *Sacco and Vanzetti: The Anarchist Background* (Princeton: Princeton University Press, 1991). Nicola Sacco and Bartolomeo Vanzetti were anarchist immigrants who were executed, perhaps wrongfully, in the United States in 1927 for murder.

29 Lu often used Esperanto to send his views on the Chinese situation to Western anarchist publications. He also corresponded with Emma Goldman on issues of gender and was active in the anarchist movement together with his wife. This was rare, since many other young anarchists perceived love relationships as a potential danger to activism. Some advocated remaining single so as to dedicate themselves fully to 'the cause'. Ba Jin depicted such discussions in his works.

same definitely understood themselves as anarcho-syndicalist. Here, the issue of 'purity' was rather a political one of siding with the GMD or not. It may also be noted that in tendency the more pragmatic anarchists, including the 'GMD anarchists', were older, while the advocates of pure anarchism were usually of a younger generation. Still, even among the younger advocates, evaluations of the best course to take were diverging, and once the full-blown war between China and Japan started, in 1937, the case of purity v. organizational compromises became critical again, against the background of national crisis. At that point, the developments in the Spanish Civil War and the anarchist role therein, which had previously nurtured some hope, gave way to widespread frustration, and the Chinese anarchists were back on local ground, working in education, publications, or cultural endeavours, but largely separated from the workers. By then, anarchist syndicalism had become a thing of the past.

Final Remarks

The history of anarchism and syndicalism in China was partly coextensive, but in a late industrializing nation, with almost continually repressive political systems, the role of syndicalism was rather circumscribed. Chinese anarchism, though mainly staying in the Kropotkinian mainstream of the time, stood out in its strong commitment to gender, new lifestyles, and language issues. Communication with the outer world was preferably conducted via Esperanto as a means not favouring native speakers, and as a modern, rational, and scientific tool, while internally – and not least with regard to simple workers – the complicated Chinese script and literary language were perceived as obstacles to be levelled. Therefore, such issues of language, including reform of Chinese, were connected to the education of Chinese workers, be it in China or in France, while from the other side the educated elites were supposed not to live from the labour of others but instead work themselves and sustain themselves by their own hands. This ideal of a 'holistic' person was in the background of various endeavours the anarchists undertook, while their aversion towards organization beyond a loose grouping made them less effective at putting this into practice than were their ideological rivals. Although their practical limitations became obvious over time, their questioning of the legitimacy of subjecting people to some authority's will from above by a strict bottom-up approach left some legacy nevertheless, even if it was underground.

In sum: the case of Chinese anarchism and syndicalism, in China itself or beyond, throws into relief the historical *and* methodological inadequacy of conceptualizing such movements in purely 'national' categories, as their international embeddedness in larger networks as well as discourses, and the role of labour migration, for example, show clearly. Furthermore, they also demonstrate that issues less prominent in supposedly 'standard' European cases, such as language or the family system, may very well be perceived as crucial in settings and by actors elsewhere in the world.[30] They thus provide a strong case to argue for approaches transcending 'methodological nationalism' and 'European monadology', as Marcel van der Linden put it years ago in the context of devising a more global understanding of labour history,[31] pointing to the need for a transnational perspective.[32] Chinese anarchism, being not merely a social and political, but also a *cultural* movement, as I have argued in detail elsewhere,[33] adds to this the suggestion that (trans-)*cultural* aspects be given their due as well.

Further Reading

Chan, Ming K., and Arif Dirlik, *Schools into Fields and Factories: Anarchists, the Guomindang, and the Labor University in Shanghai, 1927–1932* (Durham, NC: Duke University Press, 1991).

Dirlik, Arif, *Anarchism in the Chinese Revolution* (Berkeley: University of California Press, 1991).

'Workers, Class, and the Socialist Revolution in Modern China', in J. Lucassen (ed.), *Global Labour History: A State of the Art* (Berlin: Peter Lang, 2006), pp. 373–95.

Krebs, Edward S., *Shifu, Soul of Chinese Anarchism* (Lanham, MD: Rowman & Littlefield, 1998).

Moll-Murata, Christine, 'China', in K. Hofmeester and M. van der Linden (eds.), *Handbook Global History of Work* (Berlin and Boston: Walter de Gruyter, 2018), pp. 15–31.

Müller, Gotelind, 'Anarchism, Marxism, and Nationalism in China: Between Conflict, Cooperation, and Continuities', in S. Hirsch and L. van der Walt (eds.), *Radical Encounters in the Colonial and Postcolonial World, 1870–1940: Anarchist, Marxist, and Nationalist Struggles* (London and New York: Routledge, forthcoming).

---

30 See more generally on the 'input' of non-European cases L. van der Walt and S. Hirsch, 'Rethinking Anarchism and Syndicalism: The Colonial and Postcolonial Experience, 1870–1940', in S. Hirsch and L. van der Walt (eds.), *Anarchism and Syndicalism in the Colonial and Postcolonial World, 1870–1940* (Leiden: Brill, 2010), pp. xxxi–lxxiii.

31 M. van der Linden, *Workers of the World* (Leiden: Brill, 2008), pp. 3–5.

32 For a recent discussion of the transnational approach to anarchism and syndicalism, see C. Bantman and B. Altena (eds.), *Reassessing the Transnational Turn: Scales of Analysis in Anarchist and Syndicalist Studies* (New York and London: Routledge, 2015).

33 See Müller, *China, Kropotkin und der Anarchismus*.

China, Kropotkin und der Anarchismus. Eine Kulturbewegung im China des frühen 20. Jahrhunderts unter dem Einfluß des Westens und japanischer Vorbilder (Wiesbaden: Harrassowitz, 2001).

Xu, Guoqi, *Strangers on the Western Front: Chinese Workers in the Great War* (Cambridge, MA: Harvard University Press, 2011).

25

Anarchist Transnationalism

CONSTANCE BANTMAN

Introduction: The Transnational Turn in the Historiography of Anarchism

Research into the history of anarchism as a transnational movement has been remarkably dynamic since the mid-2000s, uncovering or revisiting rich individual and collective histories of mobilities and exchange, and making a significant theoretical contribution to the transnational turn in the humanities and social sciences. In return, the study of anarchism has been reinvigorated by the new perspectives afforded by transnational approaches, which have opened up new territories for empirical study and allowed a much finer understanding of the movement's political, social, and cultural history, and the nature and scope of anarchist internationalism and national attachments, as well as of anarchism's relationship with labour organizations – to name just a few key areas. The umbrella term 'anarchist transnationalism' has become a shorthand to capture the (forced, voluntary, hindered) intense circulation of anarchists, individually or in groups, as well as of printed material, money, and, as a result, ideas, with this mobility being a defining feature of the movement and a transformative force, as well as a pressing concern for authorities. This chapter charts these circulations, with a focus on chronology, geography, and types of mobilities and interactions, before considering language barriers, policing, and border hardening, as well as national sentiment, as key determinants hindering and shaping circulations and exchanges. The heuristic value of the transnational perspective is then assessed across several theoretical contexts. The last section investigates the hegemonic and exclusionary implications which constitute an important strand of the research into anarchist transnationalism.

Situating Anarchist Transnationalism

The history of anarchist transnationalism is often regarded as heir to the history-from-below approaches developed in E. P. Thompson's *The Making of the English Working Class* and informing biographical labour dictionaries such as France's *Le Maitron. Dictionnaire biographique du mouvement ouvrier* (*Le Maitron: Biographical Dictionary of the Workers' Movement*).[1] The publication of Davide Turcato's 2007 article 'Italian anarchism as a transnational movement, 1885–1915' may be used here as a formal starting point for the scholarly subfield of research into anarchist transnationalism, through its cogent formulation of a methodology focused on re-examining the Italian anarchist movement by incorporating its international outposts as key activist centres, and the publications, groups, and individuals binding international locales and levels of organization, with major revisionist implications: 'A transnational analysis reveals new forms of integration, continuity, and organization, based on the mobility of militants, resources, and ideas across the Atlantic Ocean and Mediterranean Sea.'[2] As exemplified in this seminal example, the term 'anarchist transnationalism' captures two defining characteristics of the movement and its functioning: first, the central importance of multi-scalar flows of people, propaganda material, money, and ideas, as well as the predominantly – but not exclusively – informal nature of these exchanges. These were also the premises of another influential and contemporaneous study of global mobilities and ideological cross-fertilizations in the pre-1940 heyday of anarchist transnationalism: Benedict Anderson's *Under Three Flags* (2005), which explored the complex intellectual interactions of anarchism with national independence mobilizations on a truly global scale, through the itineraries of Filipino writers José Rizal and Isabelo de los Reyes.[3]

The bulk of studies on anarchist transnationalism focus on the last decades of the long nineteenth century, starting in the 1870s, in response to the internationalist and revolutionary impulsion of the French Commune, 'an unabashedly cosmopolitan event which renounced the centralised French state and identified itself as part of a broader federated cosmopolitan order',[4]

---

[1] *Le Maitron. Dictionnaire biographique du mouvement ouvrier*, https://maitron.fr/, last accessed 14 September 2020.

[2] D. Turcato, 'Italian anarchism as a transnational movement, 1885–1915', *International Review of Social History* 52, 3 (2007), p. 407.

[3] B. Anderson, *Under Three Flags: Anarchism and the Anti-Colonial Imagination* (London and New York: Verso, 2005).

[4] C. Levy, 'Anarchism and Cosmopolitanism', in C. Levy and M. Adams (eds.), *The Palgrave Handbook of Anarchism* (Cham: Palgrave, 2019), p. 128.

the reformulation of anarchism in the anti-authoritarian International, the Jura Federation, and its international diffusion. The intense, multi-faceted cross-border activism of anarchists in this period is one aspect of the 'great acceleration' of the years 1870–1914: it was propelled by breakthroughs in transport and communication which, combined with imperial circulations, labour migration, students' and intellectuals' travels, and the forced displacements caused by repression, resulted in intensive and extensive cross-border print and personal mobilities, in an increasingly global world. As illustrated by Jose Moya's vivid rendition of the dizzying multi-directional mobilities of the period: 'French, Italian and Spanish migrants took [anarchism] to Algeria and other areas of European settlement in North Africa. German and Bohemian immigrants played a leading role in its introduction to the United States in the 1870s but by the early twentieth century they were outnumbered by Italian and Jewish newcomers. Spanish and Italian militants disseminated it throughout Latin America. Upper-class students returning from European sojourns introduced it to China.'[5]

The ever-expanding map of transnational anarchism indicates the movement's global presence and connectedness, but also its strong local anchorage in many areas. The Italian anarchist diaspora was as far-reaching as it was active, in France and Britain, northern Africa, the United States, and Latin America;[6] it existed transnationally through the mobility of exiles, economic migrants, and high-profile globe-trotting activists such as Errico Malatesta and Pietro Gori, as well as the print networks created by widely disseminated publications such as *La Questione Sociale* (*The Social Question*, Paterson, New Jersey) and *Cronaca Sovversiva* (*Subversive Chronicle*, Barre, Vermont). The transnational personal and print networks of Hispanic anarchism also stretched across western Europe, the United States, and Latin America as

---

[5] J. Moya, 'Anarchism', in A. Iriye and P.-Y. Saunier (eds.), *The Palgrave Dictionary of Transnational History* (New York: Palgrave, 2009), pp. 39–40.

[6] P. Di Paola, *The Knights Errant of Anarchy: London and the Italian Anarchist Diaspora (1880–1917)* (Liverpool: Liverpool University Press, 2013); K. Zimmer, *Immigrants against the State: Yiddish and Italian Anarchism in America* (Urbana: University of Illinois Press, 2015); L. Galián Hernández and C. Paonessa, 'Caught between internationalism, transnationalism and immigration: a brief account of the history of anarchism in Egypt until 1945', *Anarchist Studies* 26, 1 (2018), pp. 29–54; J. Guglielmo, *Living the Revolution: Italian Women's Resistance and Radicalism in New York City, 1880–1945* (Chapel Hill: University of North Carolina Press, 2012); T. Tomchuk, *Transnational Radicals: Italian Anarchists in Canada and the US 1915–1940* (Winnipeg: University of Manitoba Press, 2015); K. R. Shaffer, 'Latin Lines and Dots: Transnational Anarchism, Regional Networks, and Italian Libertarians in Latin America', https://zapruderworld.org/journal/past-vols/volume-1/latin-lines-and-dots-transnational-anarchism-regional-networks-and-italian-libertarians-in-latin-america/, last accessed 18 September 2020.

well as Australia; a distinctive feature of Hispanic anarchism was the recurrence of brutal repressive episodes which mobilized global anarchist communities in protest and gave the Hispanic and international movement powerful symbols, in particular through the martyr figure of the Catalan pedagogue, anarchist, and syndicalist Francisco Ferrer i Guardia, executed in 1909.[7] Jewish anarchism formed another important global nexus, arising in the context of exile due to the persecutions of Jews in eastern Europe and the Russian Empire.[8]

The remarkably diverse geographical scales and types of interactions examined in transnational studies reflect the complexities of these circulations, their economic and political impact on the host areas, and overlap with other transnational movements and ideologies. A brief survey of a few well-known examples of transnational anarchist activism is illustrative of this diversity. In many cases, the term 'transnational' refers to the migration of a linguistic or national group to a foreign country or city, for instance, the thousands of first- and second-generation Yiddish-speaking and Italian immigrants in the United States who became anarchists, the French anthracite miners of New Jersey who also turned to anarchism, or Italian workers in Argentina.[9] As anarchists found themselves increasingly targeted by repression, exile became another major push factor, alongside economic migration: before the First World War, London hosted very active groups of Italian, French, German, and east European Jewish anarchists, alongside British anarchist circles.[10] Other major anarchist urban 'hubs' included Paris, Chicago, New York, San Francisco, Los Angeles, and Buenos Aires.[11]

[7] C. J. Castañeda and M. Feu (eds.), *Writing Revolution: Hispanic Anarchism in the United States* (Urbana: University of Illinois Press, 2019); R. Mason, *The Spanish Anarchists of Northern Australia: Revolution in the Sugar Cane Fields* (Cardiff: University of Wales Press, 2018).

[8] Zimmer, *Immigrants against the State*; J. C. Moya, 'The positive side of stereotypes: Jewish anarchists in early-twentieth-century Buenos Aires', *Jewish History* 18, 1 (2004), pp. 19–48; William Fishman, *East End Jewish Radicals 1875–1914* (London: Duckworth, 1975).

[9] M. Cordillot, *Révolutionnaires du Nouveau Monde. Une brève histoire du mouvement socialiste francophone aux Etats-Unis (1885–1922)* (Montreal: Lux, 2010), pp. 30–44.

[10] Di Paola, *The Knights Errant of Anarchy*; C. Bantman, *The French Anarchists in London, 1880–1914: Exile and Transnationalism in the First Globalisation* (Liverpool: Liverpool University Press, 2013); E. Lichtenstein, 'A Transatlantic Revolutionary Moment? The Dynamics of Cross-Border Activism in Europe and the United States, 1900–1923', PhD dissertation, University of Glasgow, UK, ongoing.

[11] D. Struthers, *The World in a City: Multiethnic Radicalism in Early Twentieth-Century Los Angeles* (Urbana: University of Illinois Press, 2019); T. Goyens (ed.), *Radical Gotham: Anarchism in New York City from Schwab's Saloon to Occupy Wall Street* (Urbana: University of Illinois Press, 2017); Moya, 'The positive side of stereotypes'.

Regional exchanges were often remarkably dense, for instance, in the Caribbean around Havana (extending to the south of the United States and to Mexico), in the Mediterranean basin (from Morocco to Palestine, including Algeria, Tunisia, Egypt, Lebanon, Syria, and Jordan),[12] and across the anarchist Atlantic.[13] These geographies challenge established narratives of anarchism and radicalism, redrawing local maps by highlighting unheeded connections.[14]

The density of the demographic flows within which anarchist transnationalism was embedded also varied greatly, from thousands of migrants to a single individual. Neither was it strictly correlated with their impact within their communities, the anarchist movement, and host societies: the role of individual activists, highly mobile or not, should not be underestimated, be it in bridging remote geographical areas through their writings or travels, as periodical editors, as prominent public speakers and agitators – or all of the above, such as Errico Malatesta, Emma Goldman, Louise Michel, and the less well-known but extremely well-connected Indian nationalist activist and globetrotter M. P. T. Acharya.[15] Nor should transnationalism be equated solely with personal mobility, as the assumed and often verified link between transnationalism and personal mobility has been refined in recent years in favour of a more complex repertoire of circulations, in which print networks and visual culture have been increasingly foregrounded. Thus, the many ways in which anarchist publications connected groups and individuals across different areas, often with an impressive geographical reach, make anarchist print culture an important research theme, for scholars of the movement as well as of periodical history.[16] Texts – theoretical essays, periodicals, pamphlets, and placards, both in their original language(s) and in translated versions – were of

[12] I. Khuri-Makdisi, *The Eastern Mediterranean and the Making of Global Radicalism 1860–1914* (Berkeley: University of California Press, 2013).
[13] M. Migueláñez Martínez, 'Atlantic Circulation of Italian Anarchist Exiles: Militants and Propaganda between Europe and Río de la Plata (1922–1939)', 2014, https://zapruder world.org/journal/past-vols/volume-1/atlantic-circulation-of-italian-anarchist-exiles-militants-and-propaganda-between-europe-and-rio-de-la-plata-1922-1939/, last accessed 19 September 2020; K. Shaffer, 'Tropical Libertarians: Anarchist Movements and Networks in the Caribbean', in S. Hirsch and L. Van der Walt (eds.), *Anarchism and Syndicalism in the Colonial and Postcolonial World, 1870–1940* (Leiden and Boston: Brill, 2010), pp. 273–320.
[14] L. Carminati, 'Alexandria, 1898: nodes, networks, and scales in nineteenth-century Egypt and the Mediterranean', *Comparative Studies in Society and History* 59, 1 (2017), pp. 127–53.
[15] O. Birk Laursen, '"Anarchism, pure and simple": M. P. T. Acharya, "Anti-colonialism and the international anarchist movement"', *Postcolonial Studies* 23, 2 (2020), pp. 241–55.
[16] J. Yeoman, *Print Culture and the Formation of the Anarchist Movement in Spain, 1890–1915* (New York and Abingdon: Routledge, 2020), pp. 16–20; C. Bantman, 'Jean Grave and

prime importance to anarchist identity and movement formation, and they circulated globally: Malatesta's *Fra Contadini* (*Between Peasants*) initiated a dialogue with Japanese anarchism, while the prominent Japanese anarchist Kōtoku Shūsui read Peter Kropotkin's writings while in prison and later translated them, contributing to the diffusion of anarchism in Japan and beyond.[17] Korean anarchists read Chinese and Japanese anarchist works and local anarchist writings, but also translations of Bakunin, Kropotkin, Malatesta, and Elisée Reclus.[18] Those same authors were equally influential among Brazilian anarchists, with a considerable reach, from the larger port cities, where this literature entered the country, down to small towns. Even far less well-known French theorists such as Sébastien Faure and Jean Grave were read in Brazil and internationally.[19] These flows were not limited to theoretical writings: the plays and novels of the French writer Octave Mirbeau were also read by anarchists all over the world, along with Henrik Ibsen and Emile Zola.

The transnational circulation of ideas was facilitated by the many periodicals, however transient, and pamphlets printed by anarchists in their host countries. The study conducted by Tom Goyens on the diffusion of the important German-language periodical *Freiheit* (*Freedom*), printed in London and then New York, provides a good example of the deep international and local penetration of this material, extending to fifteen destinations in the UK and Ireland, comprehensive European coverage, and hundreds of towns and cities across thirty-eight US states, leaving no continent untouched, despite having far fewer entry points in South America, Australia, Asia, and Africa.[20] A similarly impressive picture of lively periodical culture, multi-lingualism, and extensive geographical coverage emerges from the map of anarchist newspapers and periodicals in the United States between 1872 and 1940, which features 274 publications across 18 different languages, from Chinese

French anarchism: a relational approach (1870s–1914)', *International Review of Social History* 62, 3 (2017), pp. 451–77; D. Laqua, 'Political Contestation and Internal Strife: Socialist and Anarchist German Newspapers in London, 1878–1910', in C. Bantman and A. C. Suriani da Silva (eds.), *The Foreign Political Press in Nineteenth-Century London: Politics from a Distance* (London: Bloomsbury, 2018), pp. 135–54.

[17] F. Dornetti, '*Fra Contadini* di Errico Malatesta, da Firenze a Tokyo', *Annali di Ca' Foscari. Serie orientale* 56 (2020), pp. 593–624; C. Tsuzuki, 'Anarchism in Japan', *Government and Opposition* 5, 4 (1970), pp. 501–22.

[18] D. Hwang, 'Korean Anarchism before 1945: A Regional and Transnational Approach', in Hirsch and van der Walt (eds.), *Anarchism and Syndicalism*, pp. 101–2.

[19] E. Toledo and L. Biondi, 'Constructing Syndicalism and Anarchism Globally: The Transnational Making of the Syndicalist Movement in São Paulo, Brazil, 1895–1935', in Hirsch and van der Walt (eds.), *Anarchism and Syndicalism*, p. 375.

[20] T. Goyens, '*Freiheit*: Geographical Reach of an Anarchist Newspaper (1879–1910)', https://txgoyens.wixsite.com/tomgoyens/mapping-anarchism, last accessed 18 September 2020.

to Yiddish and Czech to Ukrainian, including several multi-lingual endeavours. This, Kenyon Zimmer notes, 'reflected the immigrant majority and transnational nature of the American movement'.[21] As suggested by these examples and pointed out by James Michael Yeoman, the term 'translocalism' is another worthy contender to capture the functioning of anarchism, 'for [which] the local arena was a site of action for international goals. By establishing connections within and beyond nations, anarchists could build networks that spanned the borders of the local, regional and national without the need for formal structures, such as political party.'[22]

This far-reaching and sophisticated print culture fulfilled multiple roles: from theoretical debate and dissemination to community-building on multiple scales, as well as practical organization, advertising meetings and new groups, individual and group correspondence, and even sharing information to thwart police surveillance. It also had a strong multiplying function, as anarchist periodicals advertised and resold one another, and included bibliographies of key books and pamphlets as well as practical instructions on how to acquire them. These exchanges fostered a global anarchist (counter-) culture, which existed through multiple formal and informal, physical and immaterial spaces: labour organizations, local clubs, restaurants or indeed drinking places, musical groups, and schools served as meeting points for international activists,[23] as did political, social, and recreational activities (demonstrations, funerals, picnics, bicycle rides, conferences, dramatic and musical soirees, and so on). These transnational identities were reinforced by shared symbols and references, such as the key dates of the anarchist commemorative calendar, celebrating the beginning of the Paris Commune (18 March), the execution of the 'Chicago martyrs' in 1887 (11 November), and May Day. All of these were amplified by the press, which reported on meetings, commemorations, and agitations across multiple locales.

After 1914, the political divisions triggered by the First World War over the question of participation in the war effort versus faithfulness to the movement's internationalist principles caused a lasting split in the movement, while competition from both Bolshevism and state-led socialism further weakened the internationalist ideals that had underpinned this first wave of

---

[21] K. Zimmer, 'Anarchist Papers and Periodicals, 1872–1940', https://depts.washington.edu/moves/anarchist_map-newspapers.shtml, last accessed 15 September 2020.

[22] J. M. Yeoman, 'Salud y Anarquía desde Dowlais: the translocal experience of Spanish anarchists in South Wales, 1900–1915', *International Journal of Iberian Studies* 29, 3 (2016), p. 275.

[23] T. Goyens, *Beer and Revolution: The German Anarchist Movement in New York City, 1880–1914* (Urbana: University of Illinois Press, 2007).

transnational activism. Nonetheless, while it disrupted the European movement organizationally and ideologically, the war did not put an end to cross-
border activism. The Spanish Civil War was another essential moment of
transnational solidarity and organizing, when, as summarized by Morris
Brodie, 'activists from across the globe flocked to Spain to fight against
fascism and build the revolution behind the front lines. Those that stayed
at home set up groups and newspapers to send money, weapons and
solidarity to their Spanish comrades.'[24] The intense repression that followed
General Francisco Franco's victory triggered waves of exile which, in turn,
created new sites of transnational activism, from neighbouring France,
looking at the inspiration of Cuba, or, far further afield, in Venezuela.[25]

In most studies, 1940 is the cut-off date, due to a combination of factors:
generational ones, as the anarchism that had flourished in migratory settings
waned with ageing and assimilation.[26] Ideology, too, with the insurmountable material and ideological challenges of the Second World War and then
the Cold War, when, as summarized by Kenyon Zimmer, 'Anarchists'
antinational cosmopolitanism appeared completely irrelevant as the world
was consumed in yet another global conflict between patriots fighting on
behalf of competing fatherlands, empires, and "races".'[27] Chronologies differed across locales and circumstances: Kirwin R. Shaffer notes that 'by the
1920s and early 1930s Caribbean anarchists were on the ropes in political and
labour struggles' – the twilight of a site of remarkable regional and global
activism, with the exception of Cuba.[28] In Egypt, 1914 signalled the end of the
first wave of anarchist transnationalism, largely owing to the presence of
European (Italian) exiles at a time of international opening of the economy;
however, the second wave which followed, in the interwar period, came
about as a result of the rise of fascism and a disillusionment with parliamentary politics. This extended chronology, Laura Galián Hernández and
Costantino Paonessa argue, is essential in highlighting the importance of

---

[24] M. Brodie, *Transatlantic Anarchism during the Spanish Civil War and Revolution, 1936–1939: Fury over Spain* (Abingdon and New York: Routledge, 2020), p. i.
[25] J. Thorne, 'Laboratories of Dissent: A Cartography of Anarchist Resistance to Franco in Prison and in Exile, 1960–1975', PhD dissertation, Royal Holloway, University of London, UK, ongoing; D. Evans, 'Uprooted cosmopolitans? The post-war exile of Spanish anarchists in Venezuela, 1945–1965', *Journal of Iberian and Latin American Studies* 2, 2 (2019), pp. 321–42.
[26] Tomchuk, *Transnational Radicals*, p. 186.
[27] Zimmer, *Immigrants against the State*, p. 207.
[28] K. R. Shaffer, *Anarchists of the Caribbean: Countercultural Politics and Transnational Networks in the Age of US Expansion* (Cambridge: Cambridge University Press, 2020), p. 273.

the Egyptian anarchist tradition, and 'understanding the developments of non-party politics in the history of modern Egypt'[29] – thereby avoiding diffusionist narratives implied in the focus on the long nineteenth century, which revolve around notions of influences and ideological imports from European anarchism via exiles and migrants.

The intense mobility of anarchists and their printed material resulted in political and cultural transfers, making the movement transnational in its ideological makeup and functioning. Many key doctrines were elaborated through circulation, as illustrated by the theories of political violence referred to as 'propaganda by the deed'. The March 1881 assassination of the Russian tsar, Alexander II, proved extremely influential internationally, accelerating ongoing debates over political violence: Russian nihilism was channelled into the anarchist concepts of propaganda by the deed and illegalism, formally adopted at the July 1881 London Social Revolutionary Congress, which advocated physical violence and all possible means to bring about the revolution, soon crossing physical and ideological boundaries, into anti-colonial activism, for instance.[30]

The diffusion of propaganda by the deed was a major catalyst for the wave of anarchist-inspired terrorism that unfolded globally from the 1880s and lasted until the 1930s. It is notable that both successful and attempted assassinations reflected the international anarchist milieu: the French president Sadi Carnot was killed in 1894, by the Italian anarchist Sante Geronimo Caserio, as was Elizabeth of Austria, who died at the hand of Luigi Luccheni in 1898 – while the rumoured 1892 bomb plot of Walsall, UK, had allegedly been concocted in a local anarchist club, between British, French, and Italian comrades – and at least one Franco-Irish spy, Auguste Coulon.[31] Nunzio Pernicone and Fraser M. Ottanelli's study shows how deeply embedded in transnational connections Italian anarchist violence was, from inception to reception. A similar conclusion arises from Mark Bray's study on 'the Anarchist Inquisition' centring on Spain between 1890 and 1910, which emphasizes the striking global echo of repression and mobilization attempts among anarchists.[32] The executions of perpetrators which followed most of

---

[29] Galián Hernández and Paonessa, 'Caught between internationalism, transnationalism and immigration', p. 29.
[30] Maia Ramnath, *Decolonizing Anarchism* (Oakland, CA: AK Press, 2011).
[31] Bantman, *French Anarchists*, pp. 104–6.
[32] N. Pernicone and F. M. Ottanelli, *Assassins against the Old Order: Italian Anarchist Violence in Fin-de-Siècle Europe* (Urbana: University of Illinois Press, 2018); M. Bray, *The Anarchist Inquisition: Terrorism and Human Rights in Spain and France, 1890–1910* (Ithaca: Cornell University Press, 2022).

these attacks created tales of martyrdom that became central to the movement's global culture, for instance, with the cult and commemoration of Ravachol and Michele Angiolillo as well as Ferrer. The critique of political violence also contributed to the transnational development of anarchist educationalism, spurring another important area of transnational theoretical reflection and activism. Similar examples of transnational theoretical discussion, implementation, and reaction can be provided for other pillars of anarchist ideology; thus with revolutionary syndicalism and industrial unionism, which developed partly in response to propaganda by the deed.[33]

A number of grey areas pertaining to both 'transnational' and 'anarchism' must be flagged in conclusion to this introductory overview, to avoid any implication of rigidity. These uncertainties reflect in a large part the movement's blurred ideological and organizational boundaries, its evolving nature, and the specificities of local contexts and movements. These ambiguities arise from primary sources: as with any studies on anarchism, the label might have been erroneously ascribed or be disputed, and individuals and groups evolved into or out of anarchism at various stages. These ambiguities were exacerbated in exilic and migratory contexts, where a host of other displaced and marginalized groups and individuals rubbed shoulders with anarchists. Another challenge is posed by the ideological fluidity of anarchism and its local variations, for instance, through local coalitions with other revolutionary movements. Lastly, it is notable from the examples developed here that some sectors of the anarchist movement were more transnational than others: even bearing in mind the above remarks about ideological fluidity, the field is dominated by studies on anarchist communism and related movements, and little has been written on the transnational dimensions of individualist anarchism in its various incarnations, although several examples suggest that this was another area of multi-faceted exchanges. There were important intellectual filiations, such as the international reception of Max Stirner.[34] The anti-organizationalist current of the 1880s–90s partly emerged within the Franco-Italian circles of Greater Paris and then London. Early twentieth-century Indian anti-colonialists had links with the major French individualist publication *L'Anarchie* (*Anarchy*); Virendranath 'Chatto' Chattopadhyaya had several friends in the French

[33] Bantman, *French Anarchists*; P. Cole, D. Struthers, and K. Zimmer (eds.), *Wobblies of the World: A Global History of the IWW* (London: Pluto Press, 2013).
[34] Andrea Dimitri, 'Radical Individualities: Max Stirner and French individualism' [working title], PhD dissertation, University College London, ongoing.

anarchist illegalist Bonnot Gang.[35] Prominent individualist publications such as Boston's *Liberty*, Madrid's *La Revista Blanca* (*The White Review*), and Paris's *L'Anarchie* were clearly transnational in their makeup, focus, and diffusion. Nonetheless, these are glimpses of far broader ideological traditions and webs of connections, whose histories still need to be written.

Obstacles to Transnationalism

While the circulations of anarchists and their ideas are impressive in their scope, intensity, resilience, and inventiveness, the many hurdles to unfettered transnational mobilities and exchanges, and the steps taken to overcome them, form an integral part of these histories. These hurdles fall under three major categories.

The most constraining limitation imposed on cross-border anarchist activism was police surveillance and censorship, soon formalized into transnational anti-anarchist campaigns and supra-state co-ordination. Even more than 'national' anarchists, exiles and immigrants as well as publications intended for cross-border circulation were vulnerable to repression, since they were exposed to laws targeting anarchists and political radicals, as well as measures aimed specifically at foreign anarchists. This legislation often focused on border control against the circulation of anarchists and their publications, as with the 1903 Alien Immigration Act in the United States, or Britain's 1905 Aliens Act, which redefined the concept of asylum in a far more restricted way. Argentina's 1902 Residency Law and Brazil's 1907 'Adolfo Gordo' law made provisions for the deportation of foreigners suspected of being anarchists. However, these laws could have unwanted consequences: the persecutions which, in most countries, were put in place in response to the progress of anarchism and its terrorist associations from the 1880s onwards triggered successive waves of exiles which spurred transnational activism. German anarchism developed in the various exile milieux created by the 'anti-socialist laws' passed from 1878 onwards. Similarly, anti-anarchist repression in France led to the expulsion in 1894 of many Italian anarchists who then relocated to London, thus creating more complex transnational activist configurations. Overall, however, policing was a major constraint: local studies have stressed how anarchist activism was

[35] O. Birk Laursen, 'Anti-colonialism, terrorism and the "politics of friendship": Virendranath Chattopadhyaya and the European anarchist movement, 1910–1927', *Anarchist Studies* 27, 1 (2019), p. 50.

Fig. 25.1 Circulations of anarchists and print material, and the international surveillance imposed on them: the police identification portrait of Emile Pouget, a French exile in London in 1894–5 and the editor of the highly influential *Père Peinard*. (Photo by Sepia Times/Universal Images Group via Getty Images.)

hampered by policing in all its forms. From 1894, Italy's exceptionally harsh *domicilio coatto* sanction threatened with confinement anyone suspected of the slightest brush with anarchism, as did France's 'Wicked Laws' that same year.[36] The 'micro' dimensions of policing, largely focused on intelligence gathering, could also prove very effective in hampering any activism:[37] in most areas of

[36] Pernicone and Ottanelli, *Assassins against the Old Order*, pp. 77–87. 'First promulgated on August 15, 1863, *domicilio coatto* had been initially designed for the suppression of criminal acts, such as brigandage ... This meant confinement in a wretched prison ... or [on] small, desolate islands off the coast of ... Sicily and southern Italy' (ibid., p. 33).

[37] R. Bach Jensen 'The pre-1914 anarchist "lone wolf" terrorist and governmental responses', *Terrorism and Political Violence* 26, 1 (2014), pp. 86–94.

intense anarchist activism, daily surveillance, infiltrated agents, and even *agents provocateurs* were a daily reality whose presence exacerbated discord and disruption, as well as self-censorship, alongside the routine seizure of printed material and police raids on anarchist haunts and printing rooms.

From the late nineteenth century onwards, national police and diplomatic services sought to work collaboratively in order to control anarchist movements transnationally.[38] This resulted in formal international agreements to share information about anarchists and strengthen repressive measures. The International Anti-Anarchist Rome Conference (1898) was convened to 'suggest the best means of repressing anarchist work and propaganda'; twenty of the delegates from twenty-one countries signed its concluding protocol. In 1904, the St Petersburg Protocol was endorsed by delegates predominantly from eastern and northern Europe. Its dispositions focused on centralizing information about anarchists and disseminating scientific surveillance techniques such as the French identification method *portrait parlé*, which had been circulating globally in response to anarchism;[39] extended repressive powers were also suggested.[40] These protocols did not bring about clear changes in practices, as information-sharing at the local and diplomatic levels usually resulted in tense negotiations, and mutual distrust remained marked. Nonetheless, they were an important step towards international intelligence co-operation, famously heralding the creation of Interpol. Supra-national co-operation progressed apace in Latin America, with international conferences in Buenos Aires (1905 and 1920) and São Paulo (1912). This expansion of supra-national policing as a result of the perceived threat of a largely imaginary 'Black International' shows the tight interplay of anarchist and police/state transnationalism – a reminder that, historically, anarchism has played a key role in the development of national and supra-state policing and the implementation of strict border regimes,[41] and

---

[38] P. Di Paola, 'The spies who came in from the heat: the international surveillance of the anarchists in London', *European History Quarterly* 37, 2 (2007), pp. 189–215.

[39] D. Galeano and M. García Ferrari, 'The *bertillonage* in the South American Atlantic World', *Criminocorpus*, http://journals.openedition.org/criminocorpus/402, last accessed 19 September 2020; I. Yilmaz, 'Anti-Anarchism and Security Perceptions during the Hamidian Era', https://zapruderworld.org/journal/past-vols/volume-1/anti-anarchism-and-security-perceptions-during-the-hamidian-era/, last accessed 19 September 2020. *Portrait parlé* was a standardized method of criminal identification developed by the French criminologist Alphonse Bertillon, consisting of a detailed description of an individual's physical characteristics, using measurements.

[40] P. Knepper, *The Invention of International Crime: A Global Issue in the Making, 1880–1914* (Basingstoke: Palgrave, 2010), pp. 68–97.

[41] R. Bach Jensen, *The Battle against Anarchist Terrorism* (Cambridge: Cambridge University Press, 2013).

also that anarchist transnationalism must be understood alongside competing forms of transnational organization: states and corporations.

There were also internal obstacles to transnational circulation and activism. Among them, language barriers have been a significant – albeit far from insurmountable – impediment to practical solidarity and the exchange of ideas, often leading to the de facto segregation of anarchist groups along linguistic lines, and making language and cultural isolation a recurring theme in studies highlighting limitations on transfers and co-operation. Conversely, the structuring constraint of language is demonstrated by the greater level of personal and militant interaction between anarchists who shared a language – for instance, within and between the global Hispanic and Italian anarchist diasporas, or between French and Italian activists, with French operating as a *lingua franca*. Anarchists tried to overcome this obstacle through various strategies. Language lessons were a staple in the weekly schedule of anarchist clubs and schools, especially in international 'hubs'. Multi-lingual comrades acted as translators and interpreters, and also reported on international events in the press: Voltairine de Cleyre, Charles Malato, Max Nettlau, Aristide Pratelle, and Kōtoku Shūsui may all be cited as important linguistic mediators. Hopes were pinned on Esperanto to overcome language barriers, but this very real interest remained largely theoretical, despite some forays in China and Japan, and some interesting links created by Spain's Internacional Juvenil Anarquista in the late 1940s as part of a wider organizational push.[42] A few multi-lingual periodicals were also printed; these initiatives were both practical and a symbolical display of internationalism. The importance of visual elements in anarchist print culture also represented another form of mitigation for these difficulties, functioning as a trans-cultural medium.

While linguistic obstacles may be described as practical hurdles, national sentiment and patriotism were far more powerful ideological barriers. This was not necessarily the case, however: for many exiles and migrants, displacement provided opportunities to enact cosmopolitan ideals, forge new ties, and gain new insights, beyond yearnings for the homeland. Theory-focused scholarship has shown the reductive nature of the dichotomy between internationalism and national attachment. Turcato has demonstrated that anarchists recognized some forms of national attachment, while Ruth Kinna and Matthew Adams have argued that Kropotkin's widely followed and commented-upon support for the war in 1914 was fully

[42] G. Müller-Saini and G. Benton, 'Esperanto and Chinese anarchism in the 1920s and 1930s', *Language Problems and Language Planning* 30 (2006), pp. 173–92; Evans, 'Uprooted cosmopolitans', p. 326.

consistent with his earlier positions and should not be interpreted as all-out anti-Germanic nationalism.[43] At a more grassroots level, the focus on transnational activism across various contexts also has the considerable merit of putting to the test the internationalist credentials of anarchism, a central questioning for a movement advocating and enacting cosmopolitanism and internationalism as a pillar of its political philosophy. Labour militancy in local, primarily revolutionary organizations was an important internationalist terrain for anarchists in almost every area where significant exile or migrant groups were present, although it did not often materialize into large-scale, community-wide involvement.[44] Several studies have reversed the alleged tension between local, national, and internationalist ties: Raymond Craib has examined Chilean activist Casimiro Barrios as a 'sedentary' anarchist, emphasizing that the local is shaped by the transnational, and that scales of activism are intertwined, not separated.[45] The social movement concept of '(up)rooted cosmopolitanism' has also found some historical echoes showing the interplay rather than competition of levels of belonging or, to use Danny Evans' phrase, the productive 'antinomies' inherent in the concept.[46] Nonetheless, many studies converge in identifying a lively if clearly delineated cosmopolitanism, hinging on individual (often elite) sociabilities and shared international gatherings, in particular around commemorative and festive events (before 1914), but bounded by linguistic limitations, ideological dissensions, and a focus on home politics. Lucia Carminati also notes that despite the anarchists' significant contribution to 'the development of working-class political radicalism and the militant labor movement in Egypt . . . Italian anarchists in Alexandria were not immune to nationalism', and, much as they endeavoured to emancipate themselves from the nation-state and empire, anarchists remained subjected to their 'organising force'.[47] This was even truer in the post-1914, and indeed post-1940 periods, when communist parties monopolized working-class internationalism, the Second World War

---

[43] D. Turcato, 'Nations without Borders: Anarchists and National Identity', in C. Bantman and B. Altena (eds.), *Reassessing the Transnational Turn: Scales of Analysis in Anarchist and Syndicalist Studies* (New York and Abingdon: Routledge, 2015), pp. 25–42; R. Kinna, 'Kropotkin's Theory of the State: A Transnational Approach', ibid., pp. 43–61; M. Adams, 'Anarchism and the First World War', in Levy and Adams (eds.), *Palgrave Handbook of Anarchism*, pp. 389–407.

[44] Cole, Struthers, and Zimmer (eds.), *Wobblies of the World*; G. de Laforcade and K. Shaffer (eds.), *In Defiance of Boundaries: Anarchism in Latin American History* (Gainesville: University Press of Florida, 2015).

[45] R. Craib, 'Sedentary Anarchists', in Bantman and Altena (eds.), *Reassessing the Transnational Turn*, pp. 139–56.

[46] Evans, 'Uprooted cosmopolitans', p. 337.   [47] Carminati, 'Alexandria, 1898', p. 150.

made even more acute the dilemma of supporting the state in a global conflict, and the Cold War hardened borders – with anarchists at the mercy of ever more elaborate repressive apparatuses.[48]

Broader Interpretations and Frameworks

Transnationalism is often described as 'a perspective' lending itself to a variety of interpretative frameworks, methodologies, and themes. The considerable empirical and methodological findings of the collective work into transnational anarchism account for Bert Altena's remark that '[i]t has almost become a cliché to regard this transnational anarchism as a model for a transnational movement' – a claim which is qualified in the conclusion of this chapter, but nevertheless underlines the relevance of anarchism to a wide range of other fields.[49] This section highlights and critiques the key theoretical findings associated with transnational approaches.

Beyond the recovery of fascinating histories of mobilities and exchanges, a recurring impact of the shift to a transnational perspective has been a comprehensive revision of existing historiography and the re-characterization of national histories of anarchism. As discussed above, Turcato's methodological proposition had considerable revisionist implications for the history of Italian anarchism, as he advocated looking at the Italian anarchist presence in the United States and worldwide in order to correct dominant historiographic narratives, in which 'cyclical patterns of advances and retreats inadequately explain how anarchism sustained itself over time'.[50] This shift in perspective also contributes to debunking narratives emphasizing the irrationality of the anarchist movement and its exponents.[51] Similarly, Dongyoun Hwang's account of anarchism in Korea from 1919 to 1980 concludes with the terse remark that 'the study of Korean anarchism must consider its origins in foreign soils, that is, China and Japan', uncovering 'some kind of transnational radical networks of discourse and practice that connected regional anarchists and radicals' among East Asian anarchists.[52] Other studies

---

[48] Evans, 'Uprooted cosmopolitans', p. 322.
[49] B. Altena, 'A Networking Historian: The Transnational, the National, and the Patriotic in and around Max Nettlau's *Geschichte der Anarchie*', in Bantman and Altena (eds.), *Reassessing the Transnational Turn*, p. 62.
[50] Turcato, 'Italian anarchism', p. 407.
[51] D. Turcato, *Making Sense of Anarchism: Errico Malatesta's Experiments with Revolution, 1889–1900* (New York: Palgrave Macmillan, 2012).
[52] D. Hwang, *Anarchism in Korea: Independence, Transnationalism, and the Question of National Development, 1919–1984* (Albany: State University of New York Press, 2016), p. 210.

have shown the transnational origins of ideas and practices hitherto errone-ously interpreted in strictly national contexts, for instance, revolutionary syndicalism.

Exploring the intersection between anarchism and movements of national emancipation has been an important area of investigation. (Post-)colonial studies have therefore emerged as a fruitful research site, showing the complex entanglements between anarchist and national liberation move-ments, exploring the seemingly antinomic notion of anarchist emancipatory nationalism, and adaptations of anarchism to local activist realities and needs, as well as their limitations. This has been the focus of several important edited volumes arguing that transnational approaches have converged with other 'de-centring' revisionist approaches,[53] yielding an important reassess-ment of the centrality and specificities of anarchism and syndicalism in anti-imperial struggles in the late nineteenth to mid-twentieth centuries, which in fact exceeded the Marxist contribution to these movements.[54] Geoffroy de Laforcade and Kirwin Shaffer have highlighted how, in Latin America, anarchists have contributed to 'the creation of modern "national" identities', allowing new forms of working-class organization, transnational relation-ships with émigré communities in the United States, and 'class ties among people of diverse race, political sympathy, and origin'.[55] This involved adapt-ing the anarchist message to 'ethnic realities', but the emphasis on ethnic or national cohesion might also translate into 'ethnic violence' or expressions of downright racial prejudice, providing a stern reminder of the practical limitations of theoretical anti-racism.[56] This anti-colonial militancy was sig-nificant in post-war independence movements, for instance, with the French anarchists' contribution to Algeria's anti-colonial movement – despite the Spanish anarchist exiles' non-interventionist positions.[57] In other colonial contexts, such as Venezuela, anarchists joined politically heterogeneous transnational emancipatory movements focused on overthrowing right-wing dictatorships, but were again faced with material obstacles (for instance,

[53] Hirsch and Van der Walt (eds.), *Anarchism and Syndicalism*; B. Maxwell and R. Craib (eds.), *No Gods, No Masters, No Peripheries: Global Anarchisms* (Oakland, CA: PM Press, 2015); de Laforcade and Shaffer (eds.), *In Defiance of Boundaries*.
[54] Hirsch and Van der Walt (eds.), *Anarchism and Syndicalism*, p. xxxii.
[55] De Laforcade and Shaffer (eds.), *In Defiance of Boundaries*, pp. 8–9.
[56] Ibid., p. 12; M. Baxmeyer, '"Mother Spain, We Love You!" Nationalism and Racism in Anarchist Literature during the Spanish Civil War (1936–1939)', in Bantman and Altena (eds.), *Reassessing the Transnational Turn*, pp. 193–209.
[57] L. Galián, *Colonialism, Transnationalism, and Anarchism in the South of the Mediterranean* (Cham: Palgrave, 2020), pp. 3, 73.

securing visas) and ideological divisions over the very principle of such interventions.[58]

Trying to compare waves of terrorism has been another major focus, accounting for much of the attention which the movement has received in recent years in academia and the media, with transnational anarchist networks being examined as an early example of the post-2001 wave of terrorism – a problematic comparison. This search for historical parallels has several facets. The transnational functioning of nineteenth-century anarchism was discussed in the protracted academic debate which followed James Gelvin's 2008 article comparing al-Qaeda's terrorism and the 1890s wave of propaganda by the deed, presenting extremist jihadism as a form of Islamic anarchism. Among the similarities that underpinned Gelvin's argument featured both movements' reliance on a highly decentralized structure built upon semi-autonomous cells. Richard Bach Jensen, a leading specialist on nineteenth-century anarchism and its policing and one of Gelvin's detractors, acknowledged that the global scale and radical, anti-system targets and ambitions, the emphasis on direct action, and the use of suicide attacks were indeed shared – albeit extremely reductive – features between the two terrorist waves.[59] A number of studies have also centred on the themes of immigration and asylum in conjunction with terrorism, pointing out that the main parallels between the two waves of terrorism are to be found in the reception and instrumentalization of these events, with a view to stigmatizing foreigners and restricting civil liberties.

Hegemonic Discourses and Exclusionary Implications

While they have made visible many important communities and histories of activism, transnational narratives are not without problematic limitations, which are the result of archival silences as well as historiographic assumptions.

First, as exemplified above by examples of the global dissemination of the anarchist canon, pointing out the global influence and presence of European writings, groups, and individuals, as well as their role as triggers for local

---

[58] Evans, 'Uprooted cosmopolitans', pp. 331–3.
[59] J. Gelvin, 'Al Qaeda and anarchism: a historian's reply to terrorology', *Terrorism and Political Violence* 20, 4 (2008), pp. 563–81; R. Bach Jensen, 'Nineteenth-century anarchist terrorism: how comparable to the terrorism of al-Qaeda?', *Terrorism and Political Violence* 20, 4 (2008), pp. 589–96.

movements, can easily lead to Western-centric and diffusionist narratives. In some cases, the focus on transnational flows and interactions has led to a tendency to lessen or misinterpret the significance of 'native' movements by over-emphasizing circulations and the role of exiles and immigrants. Laura Galián's study of colonialism, transnationalism, and anarchism in the south of the Mediterranean points out the various levels at which such diffusionism and Eurocentrism operate, both historically and in the historiography, by underlining 'the persisting power relations among activists', as well as the lack of literature on anarchism and the anti-authoritarian experiences of Arab Mediterranean societies. The academic endeavour to decolonize anarchism thus requires recognizing 'non-Western anti-authoritarian and anarchist narratives, which are not always and not only enunciated as a self-declared ideology', as is the case in many non-Western areas.[60] These remarks can be extrapolated to many areas, especially in colonial and imperial contexts. It can be argued that one of the strengths of the research into anarchist transnationalism has been the rapidity with which such biases have been identified and begun to be addressed. This has been achieved primarily by restating the multi-directional cross-influences and the changing meaning and modalities of anarchism through mobility. Thus, Nadine Willems' study of Japanese anarchism challenges 'a simplistic centre–periphery framework of understanding ... Instead, anarchism is re-evaluated as a dynamic set of concepts and practices that drew from a wide range of inspirations, both foreign and indigenous.'[61] Moreover, the complexities of dissemination should not be overlooked, as Arif Dirlik has pointed out in reference to the Chinese and broader East Asian context: local interpretations of literature, for instance, were remarkably sophisticated and adapted to local needs and contexts, and diffusionist and universalist critiques should not always be taken at face value.[62]

Along the same exclusionary lines, women's experiences and the circulation of feminist ideas constitute another – rather momentous – blind spot. The role and experience of women in exile and in transnational configurations have been examined, in particular in Jennifer Guglielmo's research on Italian workers in the United States.[63] There is a degree of uncertainty

---

[60] Galián, *Colonialism, Transnationalism, and Anarchism*, p. 4.
[61] N. Willems, 'Transnational anarchism, Japanese revolutionary connections, and the personal politics of exile', *Historical Journal* 61, 3 (2018), p. 721.
[62] A. Dirlik, 'Anarchism and the Question of Place: Thoughts from the Chinese Experience', in Hirsch and van der Walt (eds.), *Anarchism and Syndicalism*, pp. 131–2.
[63] J. Guglielmo, *Living the Revolution: Italian Women's Resistance and Radicalism in New York City, 1880–1945* (Urbana: University of Illinois Press, 2010).

regarding the actual presence and involvement of women in anarchist activism in migratory and exilic settings: several factors account for 'the lack of participation of women', starting with the de facto male-dominated composition of these mobile groups.[64] Processes of archival and masculinist invisibilization must also be stressed, leading to under-representation in the historiography, even when women are known to have been an important component of exile groups and significantly involved in their activism and sociabilities. This absence replicates at least partly archival gaps – a characteristic of nationally focused studies on anarchism which is amplified in transnational contexts. The ultimate factor for the lack of feminine voices is ultimately the masculinist outlook of contemporary witnesses of the movement, be they internal or external to it, which also informs the historian's gaze. This reflects women's relegation to the domestic sphere, but also the gendered distribution of activist roles, which devalues their specific forms of political involvement, 'through strategies of mutual aid [and] collective direct action, [within] the multi-ethnic, radical subculture that took shape within their urban working-class communities'.[65] Women's voices were also marginalized and under-recognized in more visible forms of activism, such as newspaper and pamphlet writing and decision-making in groups.[66]

The revision of this erasure is ongoing: Brodie has highlighted the militancy of international women in the Durruti Column during the Spanish Civil War, such as Simone Weil, Georgette Kokoczinski (a.k.a. La Mimosa), and Clara Thalmann.[67] Famous anarchist women's experiences of transnationalism have been researched, for instance, Emma Goldman and Louise Michel, gendering exile and transnationalism, albeit in the context of exceptionalist narratives.[68] This scarcity is correlated with a lack of studies on the transnational circulation of anarchafeminism, which compounds the patriarchal stance of many anarchist theorists vis-à-vis women and feminism – although again, this reflects

[64] Tomchuk, *Transnational Radicals*, p. 113.
[65] J. Guglielmo, 'Transnational feminism's radical past: lessons from Italian immigrant women anarchists in industrializing America', *Journal of Women's History* 22, 1 (2010), p. 12.
[66] Tomchuk, *Transnational Radicals*, pp. 113–26; C. Bantman, 'Louise Michel's London years: a political reassessment (1890–1905)', *Women's History Review* 26, 6 (2017), pp. 994–1012.
[67] M. Brodie, 'Volunteers for anarchy: the International Group of the Durruti Column in the Spanish Civil War', *Journal of Contemporary History* 56, 1(2021), pp. 28–54.
[68] Bantman, 'Louise Michel's London years'; F. Jacob, *Emma Goldman and the Russian Revolution: From Admiration to Frustration* (Berlin: De Gruyter Oldenbourg, 2021).

processes of silencing and invisibilization rather than the absence of such discussions. The shortage of studies on these themes is also linked to the predominance of transnational anarchist communism, which has partly sidelined examinations of transnational anarchist individualism and 'life-style' experiments, in which gender emancipation and problematics surrounding the body and reproductive rights were foregrounded. The global dimensions of anarchist co-operativism, however, are starting to be explored.[69]

Conclusion

As an academic subgenre, anarchist transnationalism can be described as a success: the historian of transnationalism Pierre-Yves Saunier has high-lighted the exemplary 'recasting of the history of anarchism' from this perspective since the early 2000s, whereby this historiography 'has incorporated many other streams' documenting a wide range of interactions and mobilities, in order 'to uncover the salient and not-so-salient tributaries that constitute circulatory regimes'.[70] While claiming to assess institutional success is an uneasy exercise in the context of a radical egalitarian movement like anarchism, some indicators cannot be ignored, from landmark publications giving pride of place to transnational entanglements, to a strong presence at important conferences, as well as sustained interest on the part of doctoral students. It can be argued that this 'transnational turn' has been a factor allowing anarchist studies to be well represented in academia and inspire new generations of scholars, at a time when entry into academia has become ever more challenging. Nonetheless, much remains to be done to enhance the relevance of anarchist transnationalism to cognate research fields, but also to contemporary experiences of activism, especially in relation to global justice and refugee solidarity movements.[71]

Further Reading

Bantman, Constance, and Bert Altena (eds.), *Reassessing the Transnational Turn: Scales of Analysis in Anarchist and Syndicalist Studies* (New York and Abingdon: Routledge, 2015).

---

[69] R. Kramm, 'Trans-imperial anarchism: cooperatist communalist theory and practice in imperial Japan', *Modern Asian Studies* 55, 2 (2020), pp. 552–86.
[70] P.-Y. Saunier, *Transnational History* (Basingstoke: Palgrave McMillan, 2013), p. 73.
[71] Levy, 'Anarchism and Cosmopolitanism'.

de Laforcade, Geoffroy, and Kirwin R. Shaffer (eds.), *In Defiance of Boundaries: Anarchism in Latin American History* (Gainesville: University Press of Florida, 2015).

Hirsch, Steven, and Lucien van der Walt (eds.), *Anarchism and Syndicalism in the Colonial and Postcolonial World, 1870–1940* (Leiden and Boston: Brill, 2010).

Turcato, Davide, 'Italian anarchism as a transnational movement, 1885–1915', *International Review of Social History* 52, 3 (2007), pp. 407–44.

26

The Global Revival of Anarchism and Syndicalism

FELIPE CORRÊA

This chapter critically discusses the anarchist, anarcho-syndicalist, and revolutionary syndicalist revival taking place in much of the globe over the past three decades. It is based on an extensive literature review (books, texts, documents, and websites) in various languages and dozens of interviews with anarchists and syndicalists from all over the world. I hope that it may serve as a starting point for further research, being rectified, improved, and developed in the process.

Anarchism and syndicalism within the period discussed here (1990–2019) can be best understood as part of a broad global movement contesting neoliberalism amidst a context of crisis of the left. As prominent members of the anti-authoritarian/libertarian segment of this movement – holding at once a revolutionary, anti-capitalist, and anti-statist position – the anarchists and syndicalists became a relevant force, better known, better respected, and better able to (sometimes strongly) influence the course taken by popular movements in various countries.

After raising some theoretical–methodological and contextual issues, I will consider important questions for this period: what were the most relevant currents, expressions, and debates among the anarchists and syndicalists? What were their biggest international efforts? What were their achievements? What were some of their historical and theoretical interests?

This research would not have been possible without the studies and the militancy of more than two decades, but also without the support offered by several comrades. I want to thank in particular the members of the Institute for Anarchist Theory and History (IATH) and the volunteers from the group 'Contemporary Global Anarchism/ Syndicalism', who helped to collect data, as well as numerous people who helped with interviews and information. To all of them, I offer my deepest gratitude. I also want to thank Jonathan Payn, for helping with various issues throughout the research and writing; José Antonio Gutiérrez Danton, for translating this chapter and commenting on previous versions; and Marcel van der Linden, for the discussions and suggestions throughout the editing and revision of the text.

Contemporary Anarchism and Syndicalism:
Methodological Issues

Various studies on contemporary anarchism suffer from a rather narrow perspective. This is, for instance, the case with research influenced by the rise of the Global Justice Movement (the 'Anti-Globalization' Movement) and related works which claim that around the year 2000 a 'new anarchism' emerged. Despite some strengths, these studies have several weaknesses.[1] Generally speaking, they use an extremely broad and ahistorical definition of anarchism, to the point that any person or movement living within or acting upon certain principles – depending on the author, these range from opposition to domination to the defence of certain principles (anti-capitalism, anti-statism, direct action, prefigurative politics)[2] – is considered an anarchist. Therefore, anarchists would be all who broadly hold anti-authoritarian or libertarian positions. Thus, these authors abandon historical criteria and do not contextualize anarchism as a phenomenon whose diffusion, presence, and influence can and has to be mapped and understood in time and space. We know, for instance, that other political and philosophical traditions (libertarian Marxists, autonomists, some indigenous movements and religious currents) sometimes reflect some of these principles, but can only be considered as anarchists arbitrarily.

Now, if the definition of anarchism in these studies is too broad, they also resort to generalizations based on a very restricted number of cases; mostly they are Eurocentric and focus in particular on the North Atlantic (despite presenting themselves as studies on anarchism in general). Geographically speaking, they tend to ignore the majority of the world, where we find very significant experiences. But that is not all. Their separation of 'old' and 'new' anarchism is based on superficial and ahistorical criticisms of the former – typically

---

[1] D. Graeber, 'The new anarchists', *New Left Review* 2, 13 (January–February 2002), pp. 61–73; A. Grubacic, 'Towards Another Anarchism' (2003), https://zcomm.org/znetarticle/toward s-another-anarchism-by-andrej-grubacic, last accessed 3 May 2020; A. Grubacic and D. Graeber, 'Anarchism, or the Revolutionary Movement of the Twenty-First Century' (2004), https://theanarchistlibrary.org/library/andrej-grubacic-david-graeber-anarchism-or-the-revolutionary-movement-of-the-twenty-first-centu, last accessed 3 May 2020; U. Gordon, 'Anarchism reloaded', *Journal of Political Ideologies* 12, 1 (February 2007), pp. 29–48; U. Gordon, *Anarchy Alive! Anti-Authoritarian Politics from Practice to Theory* (London: Pluto Press, 2008); T. Ibáñez, *Anarquismo en movimiento. Anarquismo, neoanarquismo y postanarquismo* (Buenos Aires: Anarres, 2014).

[2] Consensus is not, as David Graeber has argued, an anarchist principle. In both the past and the present, all over the world, it has been but one of the decision-making mechanisms of anarchists and syndicalists; voting procedures (majority or two-thirds, for example) were and are still widespread.

described as sectarian and class-reductionist – and an over-rating of the latter, typically exaggerating its dimensions and often reducing contemporary anarchism to it. Such studies simply dismiss hundreds or perhaps thousands of anarchist collectives and initiatives, dozens of anarchist organizations and federations, and various anarcho-syndicalist and revolutionary syndicalist organizations (often with thousands of members), which, without a doubt, have had an impact on millions of people around the world.

A Historical and Global Approach and Some Precise Definitions

To overcome these shortcomings, the present study is based on three theoretical–methodological notions. First, I try to develop a historical and global approach, which rejects ahistorical and Eurocentric studies, thus broadening considerably the geographical scope of analysis.[3] Secondly, I apply a precise definition of anarchism, based on a global analysis of its 150 years of history, which I have referred to in more detail elsewhere.[4] According to this definition, anarchism is a libertarian and anti-authoritarian form of revolutionary socialism, a form of socialism that is simultaneously anti-capitalist and anti-statist and that strives to replace the present system of domination with a new system based on self-management. Anarchism's content is expressed in three main notions:

(i) Rational critique (from a plural epistemological–philosophical and theoretical–methodological perspective) of the capitalist and statist society and of all forms of domination: class (labour exploitation, political–bureaucratic domination, physical coercion, and cultural alienation), gender, race, or nationality.

(ii) Defence of a new society, self-managed and federalist, which includes: property socialization (reconciled with family property in the country-side), democratic self-government (political socialization, management of workers' associations, federalist delegation), self-managed culture (new ethics, education, communication, recreation), and an end to social classes and domination in general.

(iii) A key strategy to promote that structural social transformation through the strengthening of the bulk of the oppressed classes (wage labourers in

---

[3] L. van der Walt, 'Global anarchism and syndicalism: theory, history, resistance', *Anarchist Studies* 24, 1 (2016), pp. 85–106.
[4] F. Corrêa, *Bandeira negra. Rediscutindo o anarquismo* (Curitiba: Prismas, 2015).

the cities and countryside, peasants, the precarious, and the marginalized) and their victory in a social revolution that requires some level of violence and which will last some time. In this process, the struggle has to be self-managed (prefigurative politics), the means have to be subordinated to the ends, and the seizure of positions of power in the capitalist economy and state has to be rejected.

Anarchism in this sense is a political ideology/doctrine, created through the thought and action of intellectuals, militants, and social movements in different continents between 1868 and 1886. Its major expressions in these years were to be found in western Europe (Spain, France, Italy, Portugal, and Switzerland); in North America (USA); in Latin America (Cuba, Mexico, and Uruguay); and in the north of Africa (Egypt). In this period, the main strategy of the anarchists was revolutionary syndicalism and anarcho-syndicalism; thus, these forms of struggle became historically part of the anarchist tradition. After 1886, and especially at the beginning of the twentieth century, anarchism spread globally and, with progress and setbacks, secured a significant position among the working class and the revolutionary left all over the world.

Political expressions which do not have a historical relationship with this current (persons, groups, communities, movements against domination, anti-statists, and so forth that never had contact with or referred to historical anarchism) can be labelled anti-authoritarian or libertarian.

Progressive Statism, Neoliberalism, and Anarchist/Syndicalist Political Culture

The third theoretical–methodological element consists of situating our object in its historical context so that it can be discussed adequately. Anarchism experienced a revival in the years 1960–80, gradually reversing the ebb-tide since the Second World War. Throughout these two decades, older initiatives still had influence, notably in Spain, where a significant clandestine and exile movement remained active, and in Uruguay, where the Uruguayan Anarchist Federation (FAU) played a crucial role in the armed and mass struggles from 1963 until the 1973 coup. There was also a significant presence in the international New Left in countries such as Canada, France, and Japan, and less impressively in the United States, Italy, and the Netherlands.

Anarcho-syndicalism and revolutionary syndicalism regained momentum in various regions around the world in the late 1970s. Important was the revival of the influential National Confederation of Labour (CNT) in Spain which, with the end of Francisco Franco's dictatorship, became public again and managed to organize tens of thousands of members. Anarchist groups mushroomed all over the world in the period 1970–80, including parts of Africa, Asia, Latin America, the Middle East, and, from the end of the 1980s, in the former Soviet bloc. International efforts were made in this direction: the International of Anarchist Federations (IFA) was founded in 1968; the syndicalist International Workers Association (IWA-AIT) has been growing since the late 1970s; and the Industrial Workers of the World (IWW), originally US-based only, has expanded to various countries.[5] However, it was only in the 1990s that, in terms of growth, there was a break with the preceding years, for both anarchism and syndicalism entered into a new phase of development, in which they progressively strengthened until the 2010s. Certain global structural factors were determinant in this break.

One of them dealt with the crisis of the three main political-economic expressions of what one could call 'progressive statism', including the social democratic welfare (Keynesian) state, the 'socialist' state of the Marxist-Leninists, and the industrializing state of the anti-imperialist nationalists.[6] In the developed world, the Keynesian welfare states weakened in a context of decreasing labour productivity, reduced growth, and declining profit rates, in combination with the United States' declining global leadership. In the former 'socialist' bloc, the end of the USSR and the fall of the Berlin Wall led, in a short period of time, to a massive decline of state-led economies and central planning. In the so-called Third World, the import-substitution-industrialization projects failed; most of these countries would adhere to the structural adjustment programmes promoted by the International Monetary Fund (IMF).[7]

Different responses to this crisis emerged over the years. The most important one came from the right wing in the form of economic neo-liberalism, which was imposed on most of the world during the 1980s and 1990s; the IMF and the World Bank (WB) were crucial in this global

---

[5] S. Hirsch and L. van der Walt, 'Final Reflections: The Vicissitudes of Anarchist and Syndicalist Trajectories, 1940 to the Present', in S. Hirsch and L. van der Walt (eds.), *Anarchism and Syndicalism in the Colonial and Postcolonial World, 1870–1940* (Leiden and Boston: Brill, 2010), pp. 395–412.

[6] P. J. Taylor, 'The crisis of the movements: the enabling state as quisling', *Antipode* 23, 2 (April 1991), pp. 214–28.

[7] Ibid.; L. van der Walt, 'Back to the future: revival, relevance and route of an anarchist/syndicalist approach for twenty-first-century left, labour and national liberation movements', *Journal of Contemporary African Studies* 34, 3 (2016), pp. 348–67.

expansion.[8] The globalization of neoliberal capitalism and the concurrent financialization of the economy brought about a massive increase in social inequality, income concentration, environmental destruction, and an erosion of social welfare wherever it existed. States contributed to this, deregulating economies and frequently resorting to repression against dissent. Mass media spread the neoliberal ideology globally.[9] During these years, there was also a considerable growth of neo-fascism (more or less supportive of the neo-liberal premises, depending on the region) which, although far from hege-monic, strengthened a rather active far right that festered on perennial issues such as xenophobia, racism, chauvinism, and discrimination against minorities.[10]

In this context, countless social conflicts surfaced, the internet providing an ever more important technological ally for the communications of move-ments in their struggle. Among the growing left-wing resistance, progressive statist expressions persisted (mainly social democratic and, to a lesser degree, Marxist or nationalist), but these would increasingly lose legitimacy – as managers of the state they proved incapable of countering neoliberalism.[11] Therefore, radical left alternatives emerged or re-emerged, particularly those critical of statism. Among them, we find some with a global appeal, such as the Zapatistas in Mexico, who were deeply influential in anarchism, and the Anti-Globalization Movement, in which anarchists were at the forefront.[12] The revival of anarchism, anarcho-syndicalism, and revolutionary syndical-ism, from 1990, is a part of those libertarian expressions claiming that, in order to defeat neoliberalism, the very foundations of capitalism and the state need to be questioned, placing rural and urban workers at the heart of a liberating project, which should be based on economic self-management and federalist politics.

The crises of progressive statism and of the left wing, together with neo-liberal globalization, had a deep impact on the continued revival of

---

[8] N. Chomsky, *Profit over People: Neoliberalism and Global Order* (New York: Seven Stories, 1999).

[9] M. Chossudovsky, *Globalization of Poverty and the New World Order* (Montreal and Quebec: Global Research, 2003); D. Harvey, *A Brief History of Neoliberalism* (Oxford: Oxford University Press, 2005); L. Dowbor, *The Age of Unproductive Capital: New Architectures of Power* (Newcastle upon Tyne: Cambridge Scholars Publishing, 2019).

[10] M. Bray, *ANTIFA: The Anti-Fascist Handbook* (New York and London: Melville House, 2017).

[11] C. Tilly and L. Wood, *Social Movements, 1768–2008* (Boulder and London: Routledge, 2009); Harvey, *Brief History of Neoliberalism*; I. Ness (ed.), *New Forms of Worker Organization: The Syndicalist and Autonomist Restoration of Class-Struggle Unionism* (Oakland, CA: PM Press, 2014).

[12] Tilly and Wood, *Social Movements*; Chomsky, *Profit over People*.

anarchism/syndicalism. Most of the struggles and movements in which the anarchists/syndicalists were involved should be seen in this context. Nonetheless, there were also important regional factors. The development of anarchism and syndicalism in Latin America and southern Africa is directly linked to the end of the dictatorships and apartheid. In Russia, its development is related to the mobilizations that resulted in the demise of the Soviet Union. In North Africa and parts of the Middle East, the Arab Spring was essential.[13]

This development, however, cannot be properly explained merely contextually or structurally. The groups, networks, organizations, and movements of anarchists and syndicalists were important. Many of them were deeply devoted to the cause and went to prison, were wounded, or were even killed because of their convictions. Their personal and collective efforts contributed enormously to the advances made. The political culture was determinant – it is impossible to explain the differential presence and impact of anarchism/syndicalism in distinct countries without taking it into account. Save for a few exceptions, one can say that the bigger anarchism's historical impact in a region, and the more this historical tradition had been kept alive in the preceding decades (by old militants, organizations, political culture, mobilizations, and actions) – allowing a bridge with new actors – the easier it was to involve new actors and the larger the impact of contemporary anarchists and syndicalists.

Geographical Presence, Significant Currents, Expressions, and Debates

Geographically speaking – and taking into account criteria such as size, persistence, political and social influence, national reach, theoretical contributions, and practical achievements – it can be said that both anarchists and syndicalists had a clear presence and influence around the globe after 1990.

In well-researched regions with an important anarchist tradition, such as Europe and North America, the most relevant movements developed in France, Italy, Spain, Germany, and the United States. In eastern Europe, Greece was important. Other regions with a significant tradition, but less researched, given scholarship's dominant Eurocentrism, include Latin America (Mexico, Brazil, Argentina, Uruguay, Chile), the western Pacific (Australia), and East Asia. In regions with a weaker historical tradition,

---

[13] Van der Walt, 'Back to the future'.

Fig. 26.1 Protesters attending a demonstration called by the Catalan CGT (workers' union) at Passeig de Gracia during a general strike in Catalonia, Barcelona, 3 October 2017. (Lluis Gene/AFP via Getty Images.)

such as sub-Saharan Africa, there was a considerable presence in South Africa, Nigeria, and Sierra Leone. In North Africa, there was a small-scale movement in Egypt and Tunisia during the 2010s. In southern and South-East Asia, as well as in the Middle East and Central Asia, the most relevant movements developed in Turkey and Syria (Kurdistan), and to a lesser degree in Bangladesh, Indonesia, Israel, and Palestine.

Taking into account all the regions where anarchism and/or syndicalism had some impact, it is possible to speak of the existence of six major anarchist and syndicalist currents and expressions.

(i) First, we have the *syndicalist organizations*, that is anarcho-syndicalist and revolutionary syndicalist organizations which attempted to become mass organizations. Their historical references go back to the International Workers Association (IWA-AIT) of 1922–39. 'They are syndicalist organizations that are involved principally, but not exclusively, in the realm of [labour], with an ultimate revolutionary goal.'[14]

---

[14] ICL-CIT, 'Statutes of the International Confederation of Labour' (2018), www.icl-cit.org/statutes, last accessed 3 May 2020.

They are based 'on the class struggle, [and aim] to unite all workers in combative economic organizations', with a dual objective: 'to carry on the day-to-day revolutionary struggle for the economic, social and intellectual advancement of the working class within the limits of present-day society' and educating the masses towards a revolution that allows them 'to take possession of all the elements of social life'.[15] The workers affiliated to those organizations are not necessarily anarchists, but identify with the libertarian and anti-authoritarian principles of those unions. Depending on the circumstances, organizations may more or less promote anarchism; their decisions can be made consensually or by voting. These organizations may be constituted as multi-trade unions, as industrial unions, or as factions within bigger unions.

(ii) Secondly, we have *heterogeneous specific organizations ('synthesists')*, which gather anarchists for multiple works, on a heterogeneous basis. Their historical references are, other than the classics (Mikhail Bakunin, Peter Kropotkin, Pierre-Joseph Proudhon), the Anti-Authoritarian International of 1872, the Bologna Conference of 1920, and the contributions of Errico Malatesta, Sébastien Faure, and Volin (Vsevolod Eikhenbaum).

These organizations assert the 'need to have a specific organization' of anarchists to promote anarchism. Their members identify with anarchism and its principles, although they allow 'ideological and practical pluralism as long as it is compatible with these principles', or 'tendencies' pluralism', and a diversity of strategies. They recognize the 'autonomy of each group' in broader federations, so they can gravitate towards 'anarcho-syndicalism, anarchist communism, neo-Malthusianism, anarchist pacifism, etc.', or even all or none of these tendencies.[16] Therefore, they use 'synthesis as a method': that is, each group 'regulates its internal constitution and activities in complete autonomy, establishes its programme of action, its operation mode, its denomination', and so forth.[17]

They make many propaganda efforts, although they recognize that 'ideological propaganda alone is insufficient, and participation in daily struggles is necessary'; therefore, they promote syndicalism and social

[15] IWA-AIT, 'The Statutes of Revolutionary Unionism (IWA)' (2020), https://iwa-ait.org/content/statutes, last accessed 3 May 2020.
[16] FAF, 'Principes de Base/Pacte Associatif de la Fédération Anarchiste' (2016), https://federation-anarchiste.org/?g=FA_Principes_de_Base, last accessed 3 May 2020.
[17] FAI, 'Patto Associativo della Federazione Anarchica Italiana – FAI' (n.d.), http://federazioneanarchica.org/archivio/patto.html, last accessed 3 May 2020.

struggles. Their notion of responsibility is 'personal and not collective', thus the decisions of their congresses and other instances, like their actions, may or may not be shared and implemented by all members.[18]

(iii) Thirdly, there are *homogeneous specific organizations ('platformists'/'especi-fistas')*; they are built by anarchists, on a homogeneous basis, and focus on propaganda and the development of mass movements – of workers, people in a neighbourhood, students, and others. Their historical references are Bakunin and his alliance,[19] and the Delo Truda (Workers' Cause) group and its 'Organizational Platform' of 1926, together with classical authors such as Malatesta, Luigi Fabbri, and Kropotkin, among others.

These groupings defend the need for 'specific anarchist organizations', but they operate on the basis of organizational dualism, recommending the organization of anarchists on the one hand, and the involvement in popular movements on the other.[20] In unions and social movements they promote a programme which, in general, resembles revolutionary syndicalism.

They do not advocate a plurality of trends and positions, but favour 'theoretical unity' – that is, 'collective responsibility' – and strategic, programmatic, and 'tactical unity'.[21] Applying federalist and self-managed decision-making processes, the organizations have common political lines which are mandatory for their groups, nuclei, and members. They seek consensus but, if this is impossible, they work with different forms of voting.[22]

(iv) Fourthly, there are *insurrectionary groups and individuals*. These include individuals, affinity groups, and informal associations that reclaim anarchism's insurrectionary tradition. They are critical of the structured mass and anarchist organizations, which they denounce as bureaucratic, and they consider violence to be the potential trigger for insurrections and revolutionary movements. Their historical references are more fluid, including classical anarchists such as Luigi Galleani, Ravachol (François Königstein), Severino Di Giovanni, and others – generally associated with 'propaganda by the deed', anarchist illegalism, and the Black International of 1881 – and more recent authors such as Alfredo Bonanno. Often they are close to individualist, anti-civilizational, anti-technology, primitivist, nihilist, and post-modern conceptions.

[18] FAF, 'Principes de Base'. [19] See Chapter 13 in this volume.
[20] FAU, 'Declaración de Principios de FAU' (1993), http://federacionanarquistauruguaya.uy/declaracion-de-principios-de-fau, last accessed 3 May 2020.
[21] ZACF, 'Constitution of the ZACF' (2013), https://zabalaza.net/organise/constitution-of-the-zacf/, last accessed 3 May 2020.
[22] FdCA, 'The Political Organization' (1985), www.fdca.it/fdcaen/organization/sdf/sdf_po.htm, last accessed 3 May 2020.

Their understanding of insurrectionalism is that of a practice, a method, based on the idea of 'informal organization', 'without plenaries, representatives, delegates, or committees, without any of those bodies that lead to the emergence of leaders, charismatic figures, and to the imposition of discourse specialists'. They often discuss anonymously and, whenever they organize informally, the affinity groups and individuals do not know each other; their dialogue is through action, without decision-making procedures.[23] They eschew a programme, they establish general objectives for action, and everybody can freely decide how to achieve them. The radicalism of militancy is more important to them than the number of participants.[24]

Their actions – backed by the notion of permanent attack and their rejection of waiting, mediation, and compromise – are mostly violent. For the insurrectionists, violence is at the heart of their strategy, and it is not linked to the prior or concomitant organization of mass movements. Though they sometimes accept the fight for immediate demands, they promote their maximum programme constantly, independently of the historical conditions: the time for insurrection is always now. 'We are for the immediate, destructive attack against the structures, individuals, and organizations of capital, state, and all forms of oppression' (Bonanno).[25]

(v) Fifthly, there are *diverse collectives*, comprising only anarchists or also other anti-authoritarians. They have diverse historical references, ranging from classical and contemporary anarchism, to the practical and theoretical contributions of other libertarian currents. They are mostly political collectives, propaganda groups, urban squatters, social centres, info-shops, libraries, publishing and research groups, co-operatives, communities, and so forth. These collectives are present in all regions with an anarchist presence: depending on the area, they can be organized locally, regionally, or even nationally.

(vi) Sixth, we find *anti-authoritarians and libertarians in general*; these include movements, groups, and individuals who may be labelled anti-authoritarian or libertarian in the broad sense given here. Just like the collectives, they can be more or less close to anarchism,

---

[23] FAInformale, 'Premier Communiqué de la FAI' (2004), http://apa.online.free.fr/imprimer sans.php3?id_article=237&nom_site=Agence%20Presse%20Associative%20(APA)&url_si te=http://apa.online.free.fr, last accessed 3 May 2020.
[24] Killing King Abacus, *Some Notes on Insurrectionary Anarchism* (Santa Cruz, CA: KKA, 2006).
[25] Do or Die, 'Insurrectionary Anarchy!', *Do or Die* 10 (2003).

have anarchist members or be aligned with libertarian Marxism, autonomism, indigenous movements, religious currents, and so on.

These currents and expressions are based on the different responses to various questions at the core of anarchist/syndicalist debates. The main controversies of the period under review involved six primary issues. The first concerns the need for organization, with positions that go from its firm defence to the rejection of formal structures, allowing us to identify organizationalist and anti-organizationalist positions. The second is the nature of organization and grouping. Some defend the need for mass organizations and others for specific organizations. Some defend both types (mass and specific), and others prefer informal and non-structured groups and associations. On this issue, the discussions also address how decisions are made, if voting and delegation are accepted or not, if the militants know each other or not, and the level of autonomy and unity allowed or expected from them. They also address the form of specific organization, allowing us to identify heterogeneous and homogeneous models, and its main area of activity: building and participating in mass movements and/or propaganda and education and/or armed attacks, and so forth.

The third controversial issue is the understanding of the struggle, with some opting for permanent attack and others for advancing or falling back, as determined by historical conditions. This has to do with how the militancy gravitates towards principlism (complete political rigidity, because 'reality is imperfect') or pragmatism ('anything goes' in order to intervene in reality, even betraying principles). The fourth is the nature of movements to be constructed and/or reinforced. Different positions exist regarding coalitions with non-anarchists, and alliances with and/or participation in reformist or non-anarchist unions or social movements. The same is true of positions referring to: the acceptance or not of struggles for short-term reforms; the articulation or not of a minimum programme or a maximum programme; the acceptance or not of negotiations, conciliation, or mediation in struggles; and the level of concern about public opinion. The fifth controversy is the relationship with the state, and involves participating or not in election of union committees or representatives, and receiving or not, directly or indirectly, resources from the state. Finally, the sixth is the relationship between revolutionary violence and mass movements and struggles, with some defending concomitant initiatives and others believing that violence can create mass and revolutionary mobilizations.

Transnational Efforts

Depending on the case, more or less linked to these currents and expressions, over the past three decades anarchists and syndicalists have conducted remarkable transnational efforts.

Among the most important syndicalist mass organizations is the International Workers Association. This international brought together anarcho-syndicalist and revolutionary unions throughout these years, but it experienced huge crises, which peaked in 2016. That year, the three largest organizations were expelled – the National Confederation of Labour (CNT, Spain), the Italian Labour Union (USI), and the Free Workers Union (Freie Arbeiterinnen- und Arbeiter-Union, FAU, Germany) – representing between 80 and 90 per cent of the workers' base of the IWA-AIT. The remaining organizations today (2020) have fewer than 1,000 members, mostly in Europe. The expelled organizations joined forces with others in 2018 to create the International Confederation of Labour (ICL-CIT). They have about 10,000 members, mostly in Europe and the Americas, where we find the Industrial Workers of the World (IWW, USA and Canada)[26] and Argentina's Regional Workers' Federation (FORA).[27]

International syndicalist gatherings bring together a considerable number of these organizations to discuss the international context and promote internationalism: in the United States in 1999 (i99), in Germany in 2002 (i02), and in France in 2007 (i07). This last gathering, organized by CNT-France (Vignoles), assembled dozens of unions from all over the world; most participants came from African unions.[28]

The biggest representative of the heterogeneous specific organizations is the International of Anarchist Federations (IAF), founded in 1968, based mostly in Europe, although trying to expand to Latin America. They have possibly

---

[26] Between 1990 and 2019, the IWW attempted to become an international network. In addition to the United States and Canada, it had small confederates in the United Kingdom, Germany, Finland, Iceland, Russia, Poland, Sierra Leone, Uganda, Australia, and New Zealand. See F. Thompson and J. Bekken, *The Industrial Workers of the World: Its First 100 Years* (Cincinnati: IWW, 2006).

[27] L. Akai, 'Why Do We Need a Third International?' (2016), https://theanarchistlibrary .org/library/laure-akai-why-do-we-need-a-third-international, last accessed 3 May 2020; V. Damier, *Anarcho-Syndicalism in the 20th Century* (Edmonton, Ont.: Black Cat, 2009), pp. 199–202; CNT, 'Más Allá de la AIT (2016)', Part 1: https://noticiasayr.blogspot.com /2016/12/mas-alla-de-la-ait-1-parte.html, Part 2: https://noticiasayr.blogspot.com/201 6/12/mas-alla-de-la-ait-2-parte.html, last accessed 3 May 2020; Rabioso, 'La Crisis de la AIT desde la Perspectiva de la CNT (2016)', Part 1: https://noticiasayr.blogspot.com /2016/11/la-crisis-de-la-ait-desde-la.html, Part 2: https://noticiasayr.blogspot.com/201 6/11/la-crisis-de-la-ait-desde-la_2.html, last accessed 3 May 2020.

[28] CNT-F, 'Conférences Internationales Syndicales – i07' (2007), www.anarkismo.net/art icle/5434, last accessed 3 May 2020.

around 2,000 members, in a dozen organizations. Among the most important organizations in this current, given its historical relevance, we find the Iberian Anarchist Federation (FAI) and, because of their contemporary relevance, the Argentine Libertarian Federation (FLA), the Italian Anarchist Federation (FAI), and the French-speaking Anarchist Federation (FAF).[29]

The biggest representative of the homogeneous specific organizations is the Anarkismo.net network, a multi-lingual website created in 2005 with organizations based mostly in Europe and South America. They have possibly around 1,000 members, in a dozen organizations. Among the most important organizations in this current we find, for its historical relevance, the Uruguayan Anarchist Federation (FAU) and, because of their contemporary relevance, the Alternative Libertaire (AL)/Libertarian Communist Union (UCL, France), the Federation of Anarchist Communists (FdCA)/Alternativa Libertaria (AL, Italy), the Workers Solidarity Movement (WSM, Ireland), the Brazilian Anarchist Coordination (CAB), and Revolutionary Anarchist Action (DAF, Turkey).[30]

The most important representatives of the insurrectionary groups and individuals are to be found in the Mediterranean, specifically in Italy and Greece. Among them, there is an Informal Anarchist Federation, established in 2002–3. This InformalAF has carried out some forty attacks (mostly bombings) against political, police, military, prison, and business targets as part of a dozen campaigns. With time, they paved the way for the International Revolutionary Front, which in 2011 brought together important Greek groups, such as the Conspiracy of Cells of Fire and Revolutionary Struggle, which had expanded to other European and Latin American countries.[31] I should also mention Elephant Books, a London-based publishing house with international reach. Since these groups are clandestine, it is difficult to know their dimensions; however, their numbers are possibly lower than those of the homogeneous and heterogeneous specific organizations.

Other than the meetings and conferences of the organizations mentioned, there have been other international gatherings, more or less global in nature, for theoretical and practical purposes. For instance, there was an

---

[29] See https://i-f-a.org/members, last accessed 3 May 2020.

[30] See http://anarkismo.net/about_us, last accessed 3 May 2020.

[31] FAInformale, 'Quattro Anni . . . Documento Incontro FAI a 4 Anni dalla Nascita' (2006), www.sebbenchesiamodonne.it/quattro-anni-dicembre-2006-documento-incontro-federazione-anarchica-informale-a-4-anni-dalla-nascita, last accessed 3 May 2020; FAInformale/FRI, 'Non Dite che Siamo Pochi' (2011), www.sebbenchesiamodonne.it/non-dite-che-siamo-pochi/, last accessed 3 May 2020.

International Libertarian Gathering in Spain (1995), the gathering of the Anti-Authoritarian Insurrectionary International (Italy, 2000), the Anarchists Encounters (Brazil, 2002), the International Anarcha-Feminist Conference (England, 2014), and the Mediterranean Anarchist Gathering (Tunis, 2015). In 2012 the International Anarchist Gathering in Switzerland, which took place in Saint-Imier, brought together thousands of people from all over the world for five days of activities.

New anti-authoritarian and libertarian movements also emerged. The biggest and most influential of these was the Mexican indigenous armed movement led by the Zapatista National Liberation Army (Ejército Zapatista de Liberación Nacional, EZLN). The Zapatistas, who went public in 1994 in the struggle against neoliberalism, managed 55 municipalities with 300,000 people in Chiapas and became a global referent, even for anarchists/syndicalists.[32] There were, on the margins, contributions of anarchists and syndicalists in Mexico (Self-Managing Libertarian Unity and the Love and Rage Revolutionary Anarchist Federation) and other countries (Spain's General Confederation of Labour, for instance) to their experience.

Zapatistas were among the signatories who founded in 1998 Peoples' Global Action (PGA), a network of social movements that spearheaded the global resistance movement and co-ordinated the Global Action Days against neoliberalism. It aims at becoming 'a *global instrument for communication and coordination* for all those fighting against the destruction of humanity and the planet by the global market, building up local alternatives and peoples' power'.[33] Massive global mobilizations took place from 1999 onwards; the one in Seattle (the 'Battle of Seattle'), in November that year, gave global visibility to the movement, which kept its momentum until 2002. Most mobilizations took place in the United States and Europe, but there was also considerable involvement in other continents; anarchists were influential in these.[34]

---

[32] EZLN, *Ya Basta! Ten Years of the Zapatista Uprising* (Oakland, CA: AK Press, 2004); J. Vidal, 'Mexico's Zapatista Rebels, 24 Years on and Defiant in Mountain Strongholds', *The Guardian*, 17 February 2018.
[33] PGA, 'PGA Bulletin, num. 0' (1997), www.nadir.org/nadir/initiativ/agp/en/pgainfos/bulletino.htm, last accessed 3 May 2020.
[34] N. Ludd, *Urgência das ruas. Black Bloc, Reclaim the Streets e os Dias de Ação Global* (São Paulo: Conrad, 2002); B. Epstein, 'Anarchism and the anti-globalization movement', *Monthly Review* 53, 4 (September 2001), pp. 1–14; Gordon, *Anarchy Alive!*

In 1999 the Independent Media Center (Indymedia) was created as a global communication network with an important contribution from anarchists. It managed sites all over the world (90 in 2002; 150 in 2006); its open access policy – readers could publish their own articles and comments – and the various technological tools developed before the most known social networks, broke with the hegemonic discourse of the mainstream media and gave voice to people's movements, but was also innovative, leading the way for the technological developments in later years.[35]

It is also important to mention the hundreds or thousands of collectives, which often had transnational contacts, as part of networks, influencing and staying in touch with each other. Among the most representative of this trend, we find the various Antifa (anti-fascist) collectives all over the world, some of them explicitly anarchist, some of them with a broader political profile. The internationalization of the Antifa militant model during those years was crucial, and the anarchists played a decisive role.[36] Likewise, there were countless Anarchist Black Cross (ABC) groups, dedicated to supporting political prisoners. Espousing an abolitionist perspective, they maintained communication with the prisoners, visited them, sent them political literature, raised funds, and organized solidarity demonstrations.[37] In the academic and research fields, there are initiatives such as networks and institutes like the North American Anarchist Studies Network (NAASN), the Anarchist Studies Network (ASN), and the Institute for Anarchist Theory and History (ITHA-IATH).

The so-called Black Bloc also deserves a mention, as an action tactic used in street demonstrations, based on a common visual identity (black masks and clothes) and combative forms of protest, including the destruction of property and confrontation with the police. Its origins are in Europe in the 1980s, spreading internationally in the wake of the Global Justice Movement during the 1990s and 2000s, and appearing in different places such as Brazil and Egypt in 2013. Though anarchists were not the only ones to participate in it, they were central in this process.[38] There were also subcultural experiences, linked

---

[35] E. Giraud, 'Has radical participatory online media really "failed"? Indymedia and its legacies', *Convergence: The International Journal of Research into New Media Technologies* 20, 4 (2014), pp. 419–37.

[36] Bray, *ANTIFA*.

[37] ABC, 'Starting an Anarchist Black Cross Group: A Guide' (2018), https://theanarchistli brary.org/library/anarchist-black-cross-starting-an-anarchist-black-cross-group-a-guide, last accessed 3 May 2020.

[38] F. Dupuis-Déri, *Who's Afraid of the Black Blocs? Anarchy in Action around the World* (Oakland, CA: PM Press, 2014).

to punk (anarcho-punk mostly)[39] that, in different countries, were critical to anarchism's growth and, to a lesser degree, others linked to alternative rock, hardcore, straight edge, skinhead, hip-hop, organized ultras/hooligans, and similar groups.

Successes and Setbacks

The period under consideration was marked by anarchist, anarcho-syndicalist, and revolutionary syndicalist successes and setbacks.[40]

Mass and Specific Organizations

Syndicalism's widest experience occurred in Spain, with the General Confederation of Labour (CGT), the fourth most important labour union in the country. It grew from 50,000 members in the 1990s to 100,000 in 2020, covering almost 3.5 per cent of all Spanish trade union members. Additionally, the CGT went from 5,000 elected union delegates to 7,000, representing several million workers in various industries.[41]

Also relevant was the IWW initiative. Although a much smaller union (with a few thousand members), it became notorious for the focus on workers of little interest to big unions, such as retail and services, in which campaigns in fast-food chains were notable. Wobblies (IWW members) also stood out for organizing strikes within the US prison-industrial complex.[42]

In Nigeria, the syndicalist Awareness League (AL) reached 1,000 members in fifteen states in the 1990s, anti-militarism being their main struggle.[43] In Sierra Leone, between 1988 and the early 1990s, a section of the IWW was created, the first syndicalist experience in the country; in 1997, despite the civil war, it organized more than 3,000 diamond miners.[44]

---

[39] J. Donaghey, 'Bakunin brand vodka: an exploration into anarchist-punk and punk-anarchism', *Anarchist Developments in Cultural Studies* 1 (2013), pp. 138–70.
[40] For a more complete and in-depth picture of these achievements and events, apart from other bibliographic references, see a dossier with more complete references to sources in various languages available at https://ithanarquista.wordpress.com/contemporary-anarchism. See also 'Further Reading'.
[41] José Maria Olaizola (former CGT general secretary), interview, Felipe Corrêa, Madrid, June 2020; Sandra Iriarte Massoulard (current CGT international relations secretary), interview, Felipe Corrêa, Madrid, August 2020.
[42] Thompson and Bekken, *The Industrial Workers of the World*, pp. 209–37.
[43] S. Mbah and I. E. Igariwey, *African Anarchism: An Exploration of the Theory and Practice of Anarchism in the African Continent* (Cape Town: Bolo'bolo, 2014), pp. 64–6.
[44] IWW Sierra Leone, 'Letters' (1997), www.struggle.ws/africa/west.html, last accessed 3 May 2020.

FELIPE CORRÊA

Fig. 26.2 XIII Latin American Gathering of Autonomous People's Organizations (ELAOPA), in the city of Viamão, Brazil, March 2019. (Photo courtesy of Luís Gustavo Ruwer da Silva.)

In Latin America, the Uruguayan Anarchist Federation had a pivotal role in the promotion and networking of so-called *especifismo*, whose continental presence started in the 1990s; the Brazilian Anarchist Co-ordination was its most important result. Since 2003 the *especifistas* worked on the Latin American Gathering of Autonomous People's Organizations (ELAOPA), which created a transnational network of a combative and independent current of unions and social movements in thirteen gatherings in different countries.[45]

Journals, Books, and Other Media

In the United States, anarchists created CrimethInc, a collective with thorough propaganda work (books, journals, posters, videos, podcasts, and social networks). It made countless resources available for reproduction and achieved international influence. Also in the United States, editorial houses such as AK Press and PM Press published hundreds of books between 1990 and 2019; during these years the journal *Fifth Estate*, founded in the 1960s,

---

[45] FAG, *FAG 20 anos. A enraizar anarquismo com luta e organização* (Porto Alegre: Deriva, 2015).

published 62 issues and the Institute of Anarchist Studies (IAS) funded more than 100 research projects all over the world; the Riseup collective developed safe technological tools to store data and for communication among militants.[46]

In France, the Anarchist Federation stood out for its propaganda work; during these years it published more than a thousand issues of its paper *Le Monde Libertaire* (*The Libertarian World*), founded in the 1950s. It also had daily programmes on Radio Libertaire (Libertarian Radio, FM and online), along with the Publico bookshop, which served as a collective space for activities in Paris, and the editorial house Les Editions du Monde Libertaire.[47]

Mass Demonstrations

In Greece, the anarchists demonstrated much strength between 1989 and 1995, even establishing an 'anarchist neighbourhood' in Athens (Exarcheia), which was crucial to the demonstrations against austerity. During the 2008 riots, for a month they stood out for their intense protests, the destruction of property, and the occupation of schools and universities, paving the way for the radical riots of 2010–12.[48] In the United States, anarchists and libertarians were the main organizers of Occupy Wall Street in New York, which mobilized thousands of people with the slogan 'We are the 99%', questioning social inequality and the financialization of capitalism; this movement expanded nationally and internationally.[49]

In Argentina, anarchists participated in the massive 2001 protests (*Argentinazo*) and were the soul of various unemployed workers' movements (*piqueteros*) in Greater Buenos Aires.[50] In Chile, they stood out in the students' movement, with the Libertarian Students' Network (FEL), and their contribution to the 'Penguins' (school students) Revolution' (2006), and some other important mobilizations, including those of 2019.[51] In Mexico, they participated in the Oaxaca Commune in 2006, which for five months occupied and

---

[46] See https://pt.crimethinc.com/about, last accessed 3 May 2020; www.akpress.org/about.html, last accessed 3 May 2020; https://blog.pmpress.org/about/, last accessed 3 May 2020; www.fifthestate.org, last accessed 3 May 2020; https://anarchiststudies.org/about-2/, last accessed 3 May 2020; https://riseup.net/pl/about-us, last accessed 3 May 2020.

[47] See https://federation-anarchiste.org, last accessed 3 May 2020.

[48] R. Vasilaki, '"We are an image from the future": reading back the Athens 2008 riots', *Acta Scientiarum, Education* 39, 2 (April–June 2017), pp. 153–61.

[49] M. Bray, *Translating Anarchy: The Anarchism of Occupy Wall Street* (Winchester, UK, and Washington, DC: Zero Books, 2013), p. 4.

[50] N. Diaz, *Anarquismo en el Movimiento Piquetero* (Neuquén: Kuruf, 2019).

[51] Scott Nappalos, 'Entrevista con Felipe Ramírez, del FEL de Chile' (2012), www.anarkismo.net/article/24145, last accessed 3 May 2020; Pablo Abufom, 'Los Seis

controlled part of the city.[52] And, in Brazil, they were relevant to the June 2013 transport protests that drew millions and the Black Bloc to the streets.[53]

North Africa, the Middle East, and Asia

Another success was the development in regions with a smaller presence. In North Africa, the Arab Spring marked the return of anarchism to the region, with a feminist emphasis. In Egypt, the Libertarian Socialist Movement was created in 2011; in 2013 the Black Bloc was noticeable in Cairo protests. In Tunis, the group Libertarian Commons organized a Mediterranean Anarchists Meeting in 2015.[54]

In Israel, between 2003 and 2008, Anarchists Against the Wall (AAW) participated in hundreds of demonstrations in favour of the Palestinian cause, opposing the wars against Lebanon (2006) and Gaza (2008).[55] In Turkey, Revolutionary Anarchist Action was created in 2007 and developed an important presence through the federation of five collectives.[56] In Lebanon, there were organizations such as Libertarian Communist Alternative and the more recent Kafeh movement. More recently, the Anarchist Union of Afghanistan and Iran was created.[57]

In Asia, two important experiences consolidated in the 2010s. The Bangladesh Anarcho-Syndicalist Federation (BASF) had 60 federated groups and 1,500 members in 2014; of these almost half were women.[58] In Indonesia, there were the Regional Workers' Fraternity (Persaudaraan Pekerja

Meses que Transformaron Chile' (2020), www.anarkismo.net/article/31771, last accessed 3 May 2020.

[52] Sérgio Sánchez, 'Anarquía y Corrientes Libertarias en el Movimiento Insurreccional Oaxaqueño' (2007), https://kaosenlared.net/anarqu-a-y-corrientes-libertarias-en-el-movimiento-insurreccional-oaxaque-o/, last accessed 3 May 2020.

[53] W. de Moraes, 2013. *Revolta dos governados* (Rio de Janeiro: WSM, 2018).

[54] L. Galián, 'Squares, Occupy Movements and Arab Revolutions', in C. Levy and M. Adams (eds.), *The Palgrave Handbook of Anarchism* (London: Palgrave Macmillan, 2019), pp. 715–32.

[55] U. Gordon and O. Grietzer (eds.), *Anarchists Against the Wall: Direct Action and Solidarity with the Palestinian Popular Struggle* (Oakland, CA: AK Press, 2013), pp. 5–38.

[56] CW, 'Building Autonomy in Turkey and Kurdistan: an interview with Revolutionary Anarchist Action' (2015), www.opendemocracy.net/en/north-africa-west-asia/build ing-autonomy-in-turkey-and-kurdistan-interview-with-revolutionar/, last accessed 3 May 2020.

[57] Enough Is Enough 14, 'Interview with #Kafeh, Anarchist Movement in Lebanon' (2020), https://enoughisenough14.org/2020/02/07/interview-with-kafeh-anarchist-movement-i n-lebanon/, last accessed 3 May 2020; A Las Barricadas, 'Interview with the Anarchist Union of Afghanistan & Iran' (n.d.), https://enoughisenough14.org/2018/06/15/a-las-barri cadas-interview-with-the-anarchist-union-of-afghanistan-iran, last accessed 3 May 2020.

[58] BASF, 'Question & Answers with BASF' (2018), https://bangladeshasf.com/question-answers-with-basf/, last accessed 3 May 2020.

Regional, PPR), a network with a presence in seven regions, and the more recent Anarcho-Syndicalist Workers' Fraternity (Persaudaraan Pekerja Anarko Sindikalis, PPAS).[59]

Rojava Revolution

In northern Syria, in 2012, the Rojava Revolution appeared, the biggest anti-authoritarian revolutionary movement of this period, which started as a fruit of the Arab Spring. This is an attempt to build an ecological and multi-ethnic society, with a self-managed economy, grassroots democracy (without the state, based on communes and councils), and women's liberation, against capitalism, the state, and patriarchy. It offers libertarian solutions to issues such as health, education, conflict resolution, and defence. Anarchists have a minor influence, through the theory of democratic confederalism (through the work of Murray Bookchin), and through anarchist groups such as the International Revolutionary People's Guerrilla Forces (IRPGF, 2017–18) and their LGBT unit, The Queer Insurrection and Liberation Army (TQILA).[60]

Beyond Class Struggle

Most anarchist/syndicalist organizations have engaged in class-based struggles, mobilizing formal and informal workers, wage earners, and precarious workers. Many of those organizations also work on issues related to ecology, anti-racism, anti-imperialism, feminism, and so on. At the same time, other organizations, collectives, and affinity groups have devoted themselves exclusively to these questions.

For instance, in the United States there have been initiatives such as Earth First, the Earth Liberation Front, and animal defence groups engaged in environmental struggles and the promotion of veganism; movements such as Anarchist People of Color (APOC), whose members include former Black Panthers, have been devoted to anti-racist struggles. In Colombia the collective Alas de Xue, and in Mexico the collective Popular Indigenous Council of Oaxaca–Ricardo Flores Magón (CIPO–RFM) and the Magonista Zapatista

[59] V. Damier and K. Limanov, 'Anarchism in Indonesia' (2017), https://libcom.org/library/short-essay-about-history-anarchism-indonesia, last accessed 3 May 2020; V. Damier and K. Limanov, 'History of Anarchism in Malaya/Singapore/Malaysia' (2017), https://libcom.org/library/history-anarchism-malaya-singapore-malaysia, last accessed 3 May 2020.
[60] Editorial Descontrol (ed.), *La Revolución Ignorada. Liberación de la mujer, democracia directa, y pluralismo radical en oriente medio* (Barcelona: Descontrol, 2016).

Alliance (AMZ), emphasized the struggle against the oppression of native and indigenous peoples.[61]

In many countries, anarchists/syndicalists mobilized against US imperialism during the Gulf, Afghan, and Iraq Wars. In Israel, the AAW contributed to the Palestinian national liberation struggle. In the Middle East and North Africa, there was a clear engagement with feminist struggles, as in other cases such as those of BAWU (Bangladesh Anarcho-Syndicalist Women's Union), Mujeres Creando in Bolivia, and the Revolutionary Anarcha-Feminist Group (RAG) in Ireland. The last two – and others, such as the Fag Army in Sweden – also promoted struggles against homophobia and transphobia.[62]

Permanence, Regularity, and Organization

Turning to the setbacks, in general, anarchists had difficulties in ensuring the permanence of their organizational efforts. The most evident examples are the Nigerian AL and Sierra Leonean IWW, which – despite their relevant activities and numerous members in the late 1980s and the 1990s – disappeared without leaving descendants. But this has also occurred with countless other syndicalist and anarchist organizations. This fact was complemented by the difficulties related to efforts undertaken. Possibly the most notorious example is the Global Justice Movement which, by focusing its intervention on mass days of global action, demonstrated a very low capacity to carry out daily and regular grassroots work. Another setback was the difficulty with organizational issues. It seems to me that anti-organization efforts, as well as the *modus operandi* of various organizations, have hindered not only the continuity of efforts and accumulation, but also an adequate impact on reality. Exemplary cases in this regard are the United States and Greece, which, despite the large number of anarchists, could not articulate really massive and influential organizations.

---

[61] See http://www.earthfirst.org, last accessed 3 May 2020; www.originalelf.com/earthlib.htm, last accessed 3 May 2020; www.coloursofresistance.org/tag/anarchist-people-of-color, last accessed 3 May 2020; https://ithanarquista.files.wordpress.com/2020/08/alasdexue.pdf, last accessed 3 May 2020; www.nodo50.org/cipo, last accessed 3 May 2020; https://zapateando2.wordpress.com/2006/12/14/la-alianza-magonista-zapatista-se-deslinda-del-cipo-rfm/, last accessed 3 May 2020.

[62] Gordon and Grietzer (eds.), *Anarchists Against the Wall*, pp. 5–38; BASF, 'Question & Answers'; http://mujerescreando.org, last accessed 3 May 2020; http://ragdublin.blogspot.com, last accessed 3 May 2020; https://blog.shops-net.com/26729461/1/queer-anarchism.html, last accessed 3 May 2020.

Capacity, Social Force, and Influence

It also seems to me that the period in question showed an important transformation of the (potential) capacity for realization of anarchists and syndicalists into a real social force, with the ability, on different occasions, to engage in the real dispute of the forces that shape power relations in society. However, the influence of this force was, in general, quite limited. With few exceptions, this has happened to mass and specific organizations of all countries that, despite participating in countless episodes and movements, were the most relevant political forces in only a few cases. Despite their growth, anarchists and syndicalists had difficulties in their attempts to grow widely and develop more significantly in less traditional regions.

Unresolved Dilemmas

Finally, there are some unresolved practical and theoretical issues that, as I understand them, contributed to the setbacks mentioned. Anarchists and syndicalists, even with their criticisms of liberal and other socialist currents, had difficulties finding a solid path between certain positions.[63]

To mention some of them: *principlism/sectarianism v. pragmatism*, with the principlist/sectarian positions prevailing on different occasions, complicating growth and impact on reality; *class v. other forms of domination*, in that, if class reductionism was not so common, the social liberal forms of identitarianism penetrated strongly among certain sectors; *discipline/commitment v. uncommitted autonomism*, in that, trying to avoid authoritarian positions, discarding commitment to decisions and effectiveness in revolutionary struggle was not uncommon; *democratism v. federalist self-management*, with people often rejecting grassroots delegation, which is essential to articulating collective decisions, and insisting on the notion that everyone must decide on everything ('democratism') and that all participants represent only themselves; *theory v. practice*, the positions holding that only practice is important and all the answers are to be found in the practice, disavowing important theoretical reflections; *tactics v. strategy*, both with lack of strategic discussions and substitution of strategies for tactics or even the elevating of strategic/tactical issues to the status of principles; and *destruction v. construction*, showing the capacity to mobilize against capitalist or statist measures, in protests and other actions, but with

---

[63] J. A. G. Danton, *Problemas e possibilidades do anarquismo* (São Paulo: Faísca, 2011); F. Corrêa, 'Balanço crítico acerca da Ação Global dos Povos', in H. Parra et al. (eds.), *Movimentos em marcha* (São Paulo: Independente, 2013), pp. 215–19, 227–31, 247–55, 257–67, 269–75, 289–302.

little ability to boost their own agenda and constructive alternatives to capitalism and the state.

History and Theory

All over the world there has been a renewed interest in the history of anarchism, anarcho-syndicalism, and revolutionary syndicalism, as well as in the translation of classical and recent writings, together with theoretical discussion on various issues.

It is important to mention physical archives like the Kate Sharpley Library, originally in the UK and later in the United States; the International Centre for Anarchist Research (CIRA) in Switzerland; the International Institute of Social History (IISH) in the Netherlands; the Bibliothek der Freien in Germany; the Anarchistische Bibliothek in Austria; and online databases such as Libcom, the Anarchist Library, and Zabalaza Books. There are numerous institutes and research networks, journals and papers, academic groups and meetings, such as the international conferences of the ASN and the journal *Anarchist Studies*. There is much physical and online propaganda through Anarchist Bookfairs (in the United States, Brazil, the UK, Ireland, Hong Kong, and so on); through publishing houses, such as Jura Books (Australia), Freedom Press (the UK), and Anarres (Argentina); magazines such as *Rivista Anarchica* (*Anarchist Magazine*, Italy) and *Ekintza Zuzena* (*Direct Action*, Spain); papers such as *El Libertario* (*The Libertario*, Venezuela) and *Class War* (the UK); and online news outlets such as A-Infos.

Generally speaking, there has been an attempt to rescue the often neglected historical role and the contributions of anarchists and syndicalists. In this process, particular attention has been given to the colonial and postcolonial world (not just to the North Atlantic axis), to the grassroots (not just to the 'big men'), and also to people of colour, indigenous people, women, and LGBTQ+ people. Subjects such as class, ecology, race/ethnicity, nationality, gender, and sexuality are increasingly discussed, often with the contributions of classical anarchists/syndicalists as a starting point. Below are some interesting examples, which of course are far from representing the entire output of the period.

Various works have developed a concept of class deeply intertwined with the notion of power, beyond the purely economic sphere, linking property of the means of production (exploitation) with the ownership of the means of management, control, and coercion (political–bureaucratic domination and physical coercion), and with the property of the means of production and dissemination of knowledge (cultural–ideological domination). Thus, they explore not only the very phenomenon of power, but also the relationship between various forms of domination between social classes in the statist–capitalist system.[64]

Others have worked on ecological questions, providing a critical explanation of the global environmental crisis, and contributing to the development of solutions. In the case of deep ecology, there is a break with anthropocentrism, understanding the right of all animals and plants to coexist with humanity, in a practically untouched natural setting. In the case of social ecology, it is understood that the majority of environmental problems have their roots in this society, and that the environmental crisis will not be solved without a massive transformation of contemporary capitalism and the establishment of ethical limits to human intervention in nature.[65]

Various authors have worked on subjects related to race, ethnicity, and nationality. Some have even advocated the notion of 'black anarchism'[66] or an 'anarcho-indigenous alliance';[67] others have proposed ways to decolonize anarchism.[68] Beyond recovering the contributions of anarchists / syndicalists in that field, it has been pointed out that racism is connected with the emergence of capitalism and the modern state, and how it has been used historically to divide the working class. Also, imperialism has been conceptualized as the means to subdue all classes of the oppressed countries used by the dominant classes of oppressing countries. In this sense, writers have argued that the struggle against racism, imperialism, and neo-colonialism can be fought only on class-based, anti-statist, and anti-capitalist grounds, that is, in opposition to nationalism.[69]

Emphasizing the contributions of women and LGBTQ+ people, anarchist writings on gender and sexuality have engaged in a critical dialogue with

---

[64] A. Errandonea, *Sociologia de la dominación* (Montevideo and Buenos Aires: Nordan and Tupac, 1989); CAB, 'Nossa concepção de poder popular', *Socialismo Libertário* 1, 2012; CAB, 'Capitalismo, estado, luta de classes e violência', *Socialismo Libertário* 4, 2020.

[65] M. Bookchin et al., *Deep Ecology and Anarchism: A Polemic* (London: Freedom Press, 1997); M. Bookchin, 'What Is Social Ecology?' (1993), https://theanarchistlibrary.org/library/murray-bookchin-what-is-social-ecology-1, last accessed 3 May 2020.

[66] L. K. Ervin, 'Anarchism and Black Revolution' (1993), https://theanarchistlibrary.org/library/lorenzo-kom-boa-ervin-anarchism-and-the-black-revolution, last accessed 3 May 2020.

[67] Alas de Xue, 'Aliança Anarco-Indígena', *Protesta!* 3, 2006.

[68] M. Ramnath, *Decolonizing Anarchism* (Oakland, CA: AK Press, 2011).

[69] ZACF, 'Fighting and Defeating Racism' (2010), https://zabalaza.net/2010/11/28/fighting-and-defeating-racism-zacf/, last accessed 3 May 2020; ZACF, 'Anti-Imperialism and National Liberation' (2010), https://zabalaza.net/2010/11/28/anti-imperialism-and-national-liberation-zacf/, last accessed 3 May 2020.

other intellectual contributions (intersectionality, class-based and radical feminism, queer theory, and so on). They criticize not only anarchism/ syndicalism – which, despite its opposition to all forms of domination, was often unable to overcome its own oppressive practices – but also transformative projects centred on gender and sexuality. They explore the relationship between these issues and the capitalist and statist system, and also their relationship to classes and identities.[70]

Balance and Concluding Remarks

Anarchism and syndicalism have, since the 1990s, grown consistently and can by now be considered as a relevant radical force. They revived a political culture that, no matter how humble, was capable of responding to the demands of new social movements, offering alternatives to social democracy and authoritarian socialism/communism. This revival was spurred by the anti-authoritarian resistance that was emerging, and in some places being facilitated by the prior existence of active groups and people who kept the 'flame lit' and became a referent for the new generations.

Depending on the context, of moments of advances and of withdrawals, of bigger or lesser influence, the anarchist/syndicalist organizations networked internationally, nationally, regionally, and locally. They had a global presence, although each macro-region had its own dynamics. Save for some exceptions, anarchism and syndicalism tended to prosper more in urban and developed countries and regions rather than in rural and developing ones. A certain degree of democracy, literacy, and access to modern means of communication (the internet, for instance) were important too. Wars, communicational isolation, extreme poverty, and authoritarian regimes (whether left or right) hampered their development.

Overall, we should definitely not under- or overestimate the role of anarchists/syndicalists in this period. Compared to other progressive forces (social democrats, Marxists, nationalists, autonomists), anarchists and syndicalists after 1990 remained a minority force. They had a minor but important influence on struggles, movements, and organizations. And in a few cases they even became a strong or majority influence. But, in general, they did not become a dominant force.

---

[70] Dark Star (ed.), *Quiet Rumors: An Anarcha-Feminist Reader* (Oakland, CA: AK Press, 2002); C. B. Darring et al., *Queering Anarchism: Addressing and Undressing Power and Desire* (Oakland, CA: AK Press, 2012).

There have been setbacks, defeats, and countless problems. But there have been remarkable gains and advances too. Among the most significant are the massive diffusion of notions of direct democracy and horizontalism, and the concurrent criticism of vanguard parties; the strengthening of feminist struggles embedded in broader mobilizations; the unionization of sectors historically neglected by traditional unions (immigrants, precarious workers, and prison workers, for a few examples); and, especially, the direct contribution to immediate improvements in terms of work, housing, education, health, and rights in general.

Further Reading

Graham, Robert, *Anarchism: A Documentary History of Libertarian Ideas*, vol. III, *The New Anarchism, 1974–2012* (Montreal and New York: Black Rose, 2013).

Hirsch, Steven, and Lucien van der Walt, 'Final Reflections: The Vicissitudes of Anarchist and Syndicalist Trajectories, 1940 to the Present', in S. Hirsch and L. van der Walt (eds.), *Anarchism and Syndicalism in the Colonial and Postcolonial World, 1870–1940* (Leiden and Boston: Brill, 2010), pp. 395–412.

Jun, Nathan (ed.), *Brill's Companion to Anarchism and Philosophy* (Leiden and Boston: Brill, 2018).

Kinna, Ruth (ed.), *The Continuum Companion to Anarchism* (London and New York: Continuum, 2012).

van der Walt, Lucien, 'Back to the future: revival, relevance and route of an anarchist/syndicalist approach for the twenty-first century left, labour and national liberation movements', *Journal of Contemporary African Studies* 34, 3 (2016), pp. 348–67.

Index

Page numbers in *italics* refer to content in figures and maps;
page numbers in **bold** refer to content in tables.

Index

utopian socialism, 8, 126–7, 136–9
  See also Fourier, Charles; Owen, Robert;
    Saint-Simon
utraquism, 82

Vaillant, Auguste, 368
Valpreda, Pietro, 440–1
Vanzetti, Bartolomeo, 484
Varlin, Eugène, 242, 250, 254, 255–6
Vasco, Neno, 537, 541
vegetarianism, 583, 585
Venezuela, 615
vigilantism, 395
violence. *See* terrorist attacks
Voice of Labour, 557–8
von Stein, Lorenz, 9, 196, 225
von Wesendonk, Otto G., 52
Voyage en Icarie, 188, 191, 192–5, 200,
  208–209
Voz de la Mujer, La, 517
Voz do Povo, 546
Vrai Christianisme, 191, 204
Vuilleumier, Marc, 256

Wagner, Adolph, 15
Wallace, Alfred Russel, 164
Walter, Nicolas, 464
War Commentary, 462–3
war, theories on, 298, 304
Ward, Colin, 462–4
Warren, Josiah, 467
Washington, George, 127
Watts, John, 159
Weill, Georges, 144–5
Weitling, Wilhelm, 215, *223*
  concepts of socialism and communism,
    224–5
  German communism in diaspora, 230–1
  German workers in Paris, 215–20
  marginalization of artisan communism,
    226–9
  praise and persecution, 222–4
  proletarianism and religious discourse,
    220–2
Western Federation of Miners (WFM),
  476, 477
Westminster Review, 159
What Is Property?, 291
What Is the Third Estate?, 134
What the ILP Is Driving At, 450
Wheeler, Anna, 154
White Revolution (1963–79), 54
Wilckens, Kurt, 529

Willems, Nadine, 617
Williams, George, 87
Wilson, Charlotte, 448
Winstanley, Gerrard, 97–8
women
  Anabaptists, 89, 91
  anarchist transnationalism, 617–19
  Argentina, 517–18, *518*, 530
  Bakunin's philosophy, 318
  Brazil, 544–5, 547–8
  Britain, 451, 456
  China, 119, 580, 582
  contemporary anarchism, 645–6
  Fourierism, 174–5, 180
  France, 364
  Hussites, 82–4, 86
  Icarian movement, 209–10
  International Working Men's Association,
    250–3
  Islamic thought, 68, 72–6
  Italy, 431–5
  Kropotkin's philosophy, 341
  Marxism, 281–2
  Mexico, 480, 490, 502–3
  Owenism, 154
  Proudhon's anti-feminism, 300–5
  Saint-Simonism, 136, 142
  Sasanian Empire (224–651), 48–9
  Spain, 396–9
  United States, 473
Woodhull, Victoria, 252
working day (eight-hour day), 177–8, 240, 274,
  540, 548
Working Men's Association (WMA),
  11
World Bank (WB), 625
Wright, Fanny, 153
Wu Zhihui, 581, 592

Xiao Zhaogui, 107, 115
Xin shiji, 580, 582, 584

Yang Xiuqing, 107, 111
Yeoman, James Michael, 605
Young, Brigham, 207
Yrigoyen, Hipólito, 523, 525
Yuan Shikai, 587

Zabalaza Anarchist Communist Federation
  (ZACF), 573–5
zakāt, 66
Zalacosta, Francisco, 495–6
Zambia, 573